W9-BFN-390

Great news!
MyEconLab can help you improve your grades!

With your purchase of a new copy of this textbook, you received a Student Access Kit for **MyEconLab** for Bade/Parkin. Your Student Access Kit looks like this:

DON'T THROW IT AWAY!

What is **MyEconLab** and how will it help you? **MyEconLab** is an extensive online learning environment with a variety of tools to help raise your test scores and increase your understanding of economics. **MyEconLab** includes the following resources:

- ***Foundations eText:*** Your textbook in an online interactive format, with animated graphs and audio narrations
- ***Foundations eStudy Guide:*** The Study Guide online, integrated with the eText
- ***Foundations Interactive:*** An online tutorial that allows you to manipulate variables, draw graphs, review concepts, and self-test
- ***Diagnostic Quizzes:*** Four levels of quizzes with instant grading and feedback
- ***Office Hours:*** A link that allows you to ask the textbook authors economics-related questions
- ***MathXL for Economics:*** A basic math skills tutorial with help on creating and interpreting graphs, solving applied problems using graphs, calculating ratios and percentages, and calculating average, median and mode
- Many other text-specific Web resources!

If you did not purchase a new textbook or cannot locate the Student Access Kit and would like to access the resources in **MyEconLab** for Bade/Parkin, you may purchase a subscription online with a major credit card at www.myeconlab.com/bade.

To activate your prepaid subscription:

1. Locate the **MyEconLab** Student Access Kit that came bundled with your textbook.
2. Ask your instructor for your **MyEconLab** course ID.*
3. Go to www.myeconlab.com/bade. Follow the instructions on the screen and use the access code in your **MyEconLab** Student Access Kit to register as a new user.

* If your instructor does not provide you with a Course ID, you can still access most of the online resources listed above. Go to www.myeconlab.com/bade to register.

FOUNDATIONS *of* MACROECONOMICS

Second Edition

Robin Bade

Michael Parkin

University of Western Ontario

Boston San Francisco New York
London Toronto Sydney Tokyo Singapore Madrid
Mexico City Munich Paris Cape Town Hong Kong Montreal

Editor-in-Chief	Denise Clinton
Senior Editor	Victoria Warneck
Editorial Assistant	Catherine Bernstock
Executive Development Manager	Sylvia Mallory
Senior Project Manager	Mary Clare McEwing
Supplements Editor	Jason Miranda
Senior Administrative Assistant	Dottie Dennis
Senior Media Producer	Melissa Honig
Senior Marketing Manager	Stephen Frail
Online Marketing Specialist	Katherine Kwack
Managing Editor	James Rigney
Senior Production Supervisor	Nancy Fenton
Senior Design Manager	Regina Kolenda
Technical Illustrator	Richard Parkin
Electronic Publisher	Sally Simpson
Senior Manufacturing Buyer	Hugh Crawford
Copy Editor	Barbara Willette
Indexer	Robin Bade

Library of Congress Cataloging-in-Publication Data

Bade, Robin.
Foundations of macroeconomics / Robin Bade, Michael Parkin.--2nd ed.
p. cm.
Includes bibliographical references and index.
ISBN 0-321-17858-0 (pbk.)
1. Macroeconomics. I. Parkin, Michael, 1939– II. Title
HB172.5 .B334 2003
339—dc21 2002038301

Copyright © 2004 by Pearson Education, Inc., publishing as Pearson Addison Wesley.

All rights reserved. No part of this publication may be reproduced, stored in a retrieval system, or transmitted, in any form or by any means, electronic, mechanical, photocopying, recording, or otherwise, without the prior written permission of the publisher.

For information on obtaining permission for the use of material from this work, please submit a written request to Pearson Education, Inc., Rights and Contracts Department, 75 Arlington Street, Suite 300, Boston, MA 02116 or fax your request to (617) 848-7047.

Printed in the United States of America.

1 2 3 4 5 6 7 8 9 10—WCT—07 06 05 04 03

Text and photo credits appear on page C–1, which constitutes a continuation of the copyright page.

To Erin, Tessa, Jack, and Abby

About the Authors

Robin Bade was an undergraduate at the University of Queensland, Australia, where she earned degrees in mathematics and economics. After a spell teaching high school math and physics, she enrolled in the Ph.D. program at the Australian National University, from which she graduated in 1970. She has held faculty appointments at the University of Edinburgh in Scotland, at Bond University in Australia, and at the Universities of Manitoba, Toronto, and Western Ontario in Canada. Her research on international capital flows appears in the *International Economic Review* and the *Economic Record*.

Robin first taught the principles of economics course in 1970 and has taught it (alongside intermediate macroeconomics and international trade and finance) most years since then. She developed many of the ideas found in this text while conducting tutorials with her students at the University of Western Ontario.

Michael Parkin studied economics in England and began his university teaching career immediately after graduating with a B.A. from the University of Leicester. He learned the subject on the job at the University of Essex, England's most exciting new university of the 1960s, and at the age of 30 became one of the youngest full professors. He is a past president of the Canadian Economics Association and has served on the editorial boards of the *American Economic Review* and the *Journal of Monetary Economics*. His research on macroeconomics, monetary economics, and international economics has resulted in more than 160 publications in journals and edited volumes, including the *American Economic Review*, the *Journal of Political Economy*, the *Review of Economic Studies*, the *Journal of Monetary Economics*, and the *Journal of Money, Credit, and Banking*. He is author of the best-selling textbook, *Economics* (Addison-Wesley), now entering its Sixth Edition.

Robin and Michael are a wife-and-husband duo. Their most notable joint research created the Bade-Parkin Index of central bank independence and spawned a vast amount of research on that topic. They don't claim credit for the independence of the new European Central Bank, but its constitution and the movement toward greater independence of central banks around the world were aided by their pioneering work. Their joint textbooks include *Macroeconomics* (Prentice-Hall), *Modern Macroeconomics* (Pearson Education Canada), and *Economics: Canada in the Global Environment*, the Canadian adaptation of Parkin, *Economics* (Addison-Wesley). They are dedicated to the challenge of explaining economics ever more clearly to an ever-growing body of students.

Music, the theater, art, walking on the beach, and four fast-growing grandchildren provide their relaxation and fun.

Macroeconomics

Brief Contents

Contents

PART 2 MONITORING THE MACROECONOMY 111

Preface

We began the preface to our first edition of *Foundations of Macroeconomics* by attempting to answer a question that we thought would be on many people's minds: *Why*? With Michael's book, *Economics*, Sixth Edition, an established, best-selling text, why on earth would we write a new book?

In retrospect, as we publish the Second Edition of *Foundations of Macroeconomics*, we find ourselves wondering more and more why we didn't write *Foundations* sooner. The response from the economics community has been tremendous. Clearly, many of you agree with our view that

- Most introductory economics textbooks try to do too much;
- Students too frequently get lost in a sea of detail; and
- Economics is a subject that can be learned only by doing it.

We have encountered this view from our own students, and we have heard it echoed by literally hundreds of colleagues across the United States and throughout the world. But creating a teaching and learning system that takes this view seriously is no easy task. *Foundations of Macroeconomics* is the result of our best effort to do so and to help students and teachers meet the challenges we all face.

LOWERING THE BARRIERS TO ENTRY

Most economics professors want to teach a serious, analytical course that explains the core principles of our subject and helps students apply these principles in their lives and jobs. We are not content to teach "dumbed-down" economics. But most students drown rather than learn to swim when thrown into the deep end of the pool. In this book and its accompanying learning tools, we make painstaking efforts to lower the barriers to learning and to reach out to the beginning student.

We focus on core concepts. We steer a steady path between an overload of detail that swamps the students and a minimalist approach that leaves the student dangling with too much unsaid. We explain tough concepts with the simplest, most straightforward language possible, and we reinforce them with clear, fully explained graphs. And we offer students a rich array of active learning tools that provide alternative ways of accessing and mastering the material.

Focus on Core Concepts

Each chapter of *Foundations* concentrates on a manageable number of main ideas (most commonly three or four) and reinforces each idea several times throughout the chapter. This patient, confidence-building approach guides students through unfamiliar terrain and helps them to focus their efforts on the most important tools and concepts of our discipline.

Diagrams That Tell the Whole Story

We developed the style of our diagrams with extensive feedback from faculty focus group participants and student reviewers. All figures make consistent use of color to show the direction of shifts and contain detailed, numbered captions designed to direct students' attention step by step through the action. Because beginning students of economics are often apprehensive about working with graphs, we have made a special effort to present material in as many as three ways—with graphs, words, and tables—in the same figure. And in an innovation that seems necessary but is to our knowledge unmatched, nearly all of the information supporting a figure appears on the same page as the figure itself. No more flipping pages back and forth!

Many Learning Tools for Many Learning Styles

Our text and its integrated print and electronic learning package recognize that students have a variety of learning styles. Some learn easily by reading the textbook; others benefit from audio and visual reinforcement. All students can profit from an active learning approach. Your students' textbooks come with access to a suite of innovative learning tools, including tutorial software, an eText featuring animated graphs with audio voiceovers, interactive quizzes, and more.

PRACTICE MAKES PERFECT

Everyone agrees that the only way to learn economics is to do it! Reading and remembering doesn't work. Active involvement, working problems, repeated self-testing: These are the ingredients to success in this subject. We have structured this text and its accompanying electronic and print tools to encourage learning by doing. The central device that accomplishes this goal is a tightly knit learning system based on our innovative *Checklist-Checkpoints* structure.

Checklists

Each chapter opens with a *Chapter Checklist*—a list of (usually) three or four tasks the student will be able to perform after completing the chapter. Each

Checklist item corresponds to a section of the chapter that engages the student with a conversational writing style, well-chosen examples, and carefully designed illustrations.

Checkpoints

A full-page *Checkpoint*—containing a Practice Problem with Solution and a parallel Exercise—immediately follows each chapter section. The Checkpoints serve as stopping points and encourage students to review the concept and to practice using it before moving on to new ideas. Diagrams and tables bring added clarity to the Checkpoint problems and solutions.

Each Checkpoint also contains a page reference to the corresponding material in the Study Guide as well as a reference to the corresponding section of our online learning environment. We describe these learning tools more fully below.

Chapter Checkpoints

At the end of each chapter, a *Chapter Checkpoint* summarizes what the student has just learned with a set of key points and a list of key terms. It also contains a further set of questions divided into three groups: Exercises, Critical Thinking, and Web Exercises.

Conveying the Excitement

Students learn best when they can see the point of what they are studying. We show the point in a series of *Eye On…* features. Current and recent events appear in *Eye on the U.S. Economy* boxes. We place our present experience in global and historical perspectives with *Eye on the Global Economy* and *Eye on the Past* boxes. All of our *Eye On…* boxes connect theory with reality.

WHAT'S NEW IN THE SECOND EDITION

Much has happened in the world since the first edition of *Foundations of Macroeconomics* was written. The Bush administration took office and spurred Congress to pass a large and controversial tax cut package. For the first time in a decade, the U.S. economy slipped into recession in early 2001; many Americans saw their personal wealth decline as the stock market fell. The tragic events of September 11, 2001, left an indelible mark on our memories and brought far-reaching consequences for our economy.

Foundations of Macroeconomics, Second Edition, seeks to make sense of these and other major events of the early 2000s. Examples and data have been thoroughly updated to provide students with a compelling and current text that reflects the world that they live in.

In addition, we have made a number of improvements in coverage, organization, and structure, the most important of which we explain here.

Hardcover Economics Edition

By popular demand, *Foundations* is now offered as a single, hardcover volume, *Foundations of Economics*. We retain, however, our much-liked innovation of distinct front ends for the micro and macro splits: The first four chapters of micro introduce the big ideas of microeconomics, and the first four chapters of macro introduce the big ideas of macroeconomics. The hardcover economics edition is a synthesis of the two.

One-Semester Split

We were told by many that *Foundations*, with its focus on core concepts, would be well-suited to a one-semester principles course that covers both micro and macro. A one-semester split, *Essential Foundations of Economics*, will be available in summer 2003.

Extensive Updating

Every chapter has been revised to ensure that the data used are the latest available. In most cases, our data run through 2002 and in some cases reflect events at the beginning of 2003.

More prominent placement of *AS-AD*

We provide an initial overview of the *AS-AD* model at the beginning of Chapter 8—our first macro theory chapter—to serve as the over-arching model for understanding macroeconomic performance in both the long term and the short term. The model is developed in detail and used to explain the business cycle in Chapter 14 and then used extensively to discuss stabilization policy issues in Chapters 16–18. Chapter 8 continues to provide a clear explanation of the forces that determine potential GDP and the natural unemployment rate.

Simplified Coverage of Money and Inflation

Chapter 13, "Money, Interest, and Inflation," has been carefully revised to simplify and strengthen our explanation of the relationship between money growth and inflation in the long run and the distinction between short-run equilibrium and long-run equilibrium in the money market.

The Business Cycle and Current State of the U.S. Economy

We have switched the order of our chapters on the Keynesian cross model and multiplier (now Chapter 15) and the *AS-AD* model and the business cycle (now Chapter 14). The *AS-AD* business cycle chapter includes a new "Eye on the U.S. Economy" that describes the anatomy of the 2001 recession and slow recovery of 2002 and also looks at the factors to which the NBER paid special attention in dating the onset of the 2001 recession.

Thorough Yet Self-Contained and Optional Coverage of Keynesian Cross

Our coverage of the Keynesian cross is now located entirely within Chapter 15. We offer a thorough treatment of this topic for those who wish to teach it. But the material is optional. It gives the student a look behind the *AD* curve, an explanation of the multiplier, and a discussion of the role of business inventories in the adjustment process that follows a change in autonomous expenditure at a business cycle turning point. The chapter also explains the relationship between the *AD* curve and the *AE* curve.

Expanded Explanation of Supply Side Effects of Fiscal Policy

Chapter 16, which explains the effects of monetary policy and fiscal policy, contains an expanded explanation of the supply side effects of fiscal policy. This chapter also includes a discussion of the Bush 2003 tax cut proposals and an account of the 2001–2002 interest rate cuts.

New Coverage of the Stabilization Policy Debate

Chapter 18, which reviews the debate on how best to use monetary policy and fiscal policy, contains a new discussion of the idea that price level targeting might result in greater stability of real GDP and so provide a "free lunch." It also explains the Taylor rule and the McCallum rule for monetary policy and compares the operation of each of these rules with the Fed's actual policy during the 1990s and 2000s.

Expanded End-of-Chapter Exercises

Because of the Checklist-Checkpoint organization of our text, we devote much more space to review and problem solving than other texts. Nonetheless, in this new edition we have expanded our end-of-chapter exercises to three full pages. Two pages offer a series of analytical exercises that parallel those in the Checkpoints, and one page provides a rich array of Critical Thinking and Web Exercises.

Expanded Web Resources

The Foundations Web site now delivers the e-Text—*the entire textbook*—in PDF format with hyperlinks to all the other components of our Web resources. We have prepared a Flash animation accompanied by an audio explanation of every figure in the textbook. We have created a set of new diagnostic quizzes for every Checkpoint with feedback that includes hyperlinks to the e-Text and other Web-based review materials. And we have provided a comprehensive set of Web exercises with external links for every chapter.

Course Management with MyEconLab

Every student who buys a new textbook receives a prepaid subscription to MyEconLab. New to the Second Edition of *Foundations,* MyEconLab delivers all of the resources available on the Foundations Web site in a comprehensive online course. Instructors who use MyEconLab gain access to powerful course management tools, and their students gain access to additional learning resources that we describe below.

ORGANIZATION

Our text focuses on core topics with maximum flexibility. We cover all the standard topics of the principles of macroeconomics curriculum. And we do so in the order that is increasingly finding favor in the principles course. We believe that a powerful case can be made for teaching the subject in the order in which we present it here. The organizing device is the idea that at full employment, the real economy is influenced by only real variables and the price level is proportional to the quantity of money. This idea has been incredibly productive in advancing our understanding of both the full employment economy and the business cycle. By having a firm understanding of the forces that determine potential GDP, the student better appreciates the more complex interactions of real and monetary factors that bring economic fluctuations. Further, the student sees that the long-term trends in our economy play a larger role in determining our standard of living and cost of living than do the fluctuations around those trends.

Deciding the order in which to teach the components of macroeconomics involves a balancing act that trades off the cumulative nature of the material against the desire to cover topics that are in the news early in the course. There is little disagreement that the place to begin is with production possibilities and demand and supply, followed by the definitions and measurement of the key macroeconomic variables. We provide a carefully paced and thoroughly modern treatment of these topics.

The course then divides naturally into three parts. The first explains the real economy at full employment (potential GDP, investment, saving, the real interest rate, and economic growth, including policies for achieving faster growth). The second explains the money economy (determining the interest rate in the short run and price level and inflation rate in the long run). The third explains economic fluctuations (interactions between the real and monetary sectors and stabilization policy issues).

Extensive reviewing suggests that most teachers agree with our view on how to organize the course. But we recognize that there is a range of opinion about sequencing, and we have structured our text so that it works equally well if other sequences are preferred. Some teachers want to follow the measurement material with the aggregate expenditure (fixed price level) model and aggregate demand and aggregate supply. Money and economic fluctuations come next. And the influences on potential GDP and economic growth either come last or are omitted. Our text supports this sequence. After Chapter 7, it is possible to jump to either Chapter 14 (*AS-AD* and the Business Cycle) or Chapter 15 (Aggregate Expenditure). The money chapters (11, 12, and 13) can be covered next followed by stabilization policy (Chapters 16, 17, and 18).

The flexibility chart on p. xxxvi provides detailed information that enables you to rearrange the chapters in a variety of ways. And the alternative course chart on p. xxxvii offers some suggestions of other possible paths through the book.

A RICH ARRAY OF SUPPORT MATERIALS FOR THE STUDENT

Foundations of Macroeconomics is accompanied by the most comprehensive set of learning tools ever assembled. All the components of our package are organized by Checkpoint topic so that the student may move easily between the textbook, the Study Guide, eText, interactive tutorial, and online diagnostic quizzes, while mastering a single core concept.

The variety of tools that we provide enables students to select the path through the material that best suits their individual learning styles. The package is technology-enabled, not technology-dependent. Active learners will make extensive use of the *Foundations Interactive* tutorial and the animated graphics of eText, our online version of the textbook. Reflective learners may follow a print-only path if they prefer.

Study Guide

Neil Garston (California State University–Los Angeles), Tom Larson (California State University–Los Angeles), and Mark Rush (University of Florida) have prepared a Study Guide that is available in both print and electronic formats. The Study Guide provides an expanded Chapter Checklist that enables the student to break the learning tasks down into smaller, bite-sized pieces; self-test materials; expanded explanations of the solutions to the practice problems in the text; and additional practice problems. To ensure consistency across the entire package, the authors who wrote the questions for the Test Banks also wrote the self-test questions for the Study Guide.

Foundations Interactive

A Java and JavaScript tutorial software program that runs in a Web browser, *Foundations Interactive* contains electronic interactive versions of most of the textbook figures. The student manipulates the figures by changing the conditions that lie behind them and observes how the economy responds to events. Quizzes that use five question types (fill-in-the-blank, true-or-false, multiple-choice, complete-the-graph, and numeric) can be worked with, or optionally without, detailed feedback. *Foundations Interactive* is available through the Foundations Web site and within the MyEconLab course.

Foundations Web Site

The Foundations Web site is a powerful and tightly integrated online learning environment. For students, the site includes

- eText—the entire textbook in PDF format with hyperlinks to all the other components of the Web site and with animated figures accompanied by audio explanations prepared by us
- eStudy Guide—the entire Study Guide online
- *Foundations Interactive*—tutorials, quizzes, and graph tools that make curves shift and graphs come to life with a click of the mouse
- Diagnostic quizzes for every Checkpoint with feedback that includes hyperlinks to the e-text, e-Study Guide, and *Foundations Interactive*
- Economics in the News updated daily during the school year
- Online "Office Hours"—ask a question via e-mail, and one of us will respond within 24 hours!
- Economic links—links to sites that keep students up to date with what's going on in the economy and that enable them to work end-of-chapter Web Exercises

MyEconLab course

MyEconLab delivers the entire content of the Foundations Web site in a course management system. Students whose instructors use MyEconLab gain access not only to the resources of the Foundations Web site, but also to

- MathXL for Economics—a powerful tutorial to refresh students on the basics of creating and interpreting graphs; solving applied problems using graphs; calculating ratios and percentages; performing calculations; calculating average, median and mode; and finding areas
- Research Navigator™—a one-stop research tool, with extensive help on the entire research process, including evaluating sources, drafting, and documentation, as well as access to a variety of scholarly journals and publications, a complete year of search for full-text articles from the *New York Times*, and a "Best of the Web" Link Library of peer-reviewed Web sites
- eThemes of the Times—thematically related articles from the *New York Times* accompanied by critical thinking questions

The Student Access Kit that arrives bundled with all new books walks students step-by-step through the registration process.

The Econ Tutor Center

Staffed by qualified, experienced college economics instructors, the Econ Tutor Center is open five days a week, seven hours a day. Tutors can be reached by phone, fax, and e-mail. The Econ Tutor Center hours are designed to meet your students' study schedules, with evening hours Sunday through Thursday. Students receive one-on-one tutoring on examples, related exercises, and problems. Please contact your Addison-Wesley representative for information on how to make this service available to your students.

Economist.com Edition

The premier online source of economic news analysis, economist.com provides your students with insight and opinion on current economic events. Through an agreement between Addison-Wesley and *The Economist*, your students can receive a low-cost subscription to this premium Web site for three months, including the complete text of the current issue of *The Economist* and access to *The Economist's* searchable archives. Other features include Web-only weekly articles, news feeds with current world and business news, and stock market and currency data. Professors who adopt this special edition will receive a complimentary one-year subscription to economist.com.

The Wall Street Journal Edition

Addison-Wesley is also pleased to provide your students with access to *The Wall Street Journal*, the most respected and trusted daily source for information on business and economics. For a small additional charge, Addison-Wesley offers your students a 10-week subscription to *The Wall Street Journal* print edition and *The Wall Street Journal Interactive Edition*. Adopting professors will receive a complimentary one-year subscription to both the print and interactive versions.

Financial Times Edition

Featuring international news and analysis from journalists in more than 50 countries, the *Financial Times* will provide your students with insights and perspectives on economic developments around the world. The *Financial Times Edition* provides your students with a 15-week subscription to one of the world's leading business publications. Adopting professors will receive a complimentary one-year subscription to the *Financial Times* as well as access to the Online Edition at FT.com.

A QUALITY-ASSURED SUPPORT SYSTEM FOR THE INSTRUCTOR

Our instructor resource tools are the most comprehensive, carefully developed, and accurate materials ever made available. *Foundations Interactive*, the Study Guide, the diagnostic quizzes on the Foundations Web site, the PowerPoint lecture notes, the Instructor's Manual, and the Test Banks all key off the Checkpoints in the textbook. The entire package has a tight integrity. We are the authors of *Foundations Interactive*, the diagnostic quizzes, and PowerPoint notes. We have paid close attention to the design, structure, and organization of the Web site. And we have helped in the reviewing and revising of the Study Guide, Instructor's Manual, and Test Banks to ensure that every element of the package achieves the consistency that students and teachers need.

Instructor's Manual

Prepared by Richard Gosselin (Houston Community College) and Mark Rush, the Instructor's Manual contains chapter outlines and road maps, answers to in-text exercises, additional exercises with solutions, and a virtual encyclopedia of suggestions on how to enrich class presentation and use class time efficiently.

Three Test Banks

Three separate Test Banks are available for *Foundations of Macroeconomics*, with more than 5,000 multiple-choice, true-false, numerical, fill-in-the-blank, short-answer, and essay questions. New to this edition, integrative questions build on material from more than one Checkpoint or more than one chapter. Mark Rush reviewed and edited questions from six dedicated principles instructors to form one of the most comprehensive testing systems on the market. Our questions authors are Ali Ataiifar (Delaware County Community College), Diego Mendez–Carbajo (Illinois Wesleyan University), William Mosher (Assumption College), Terry Sutton (Southeast Missouri State University), Cindy Tori (Valdosta State University), and Nora Underwood (University of California–Davis). These Test Bank authors also wrote questions for the Study Guide to ensure consistency.

PowerPoint Resources

We have created the PowerPoint resources on the basis of our 10 years of experience using this tool in our own classrooms. Every figure and table—every single one, even those used in Checkpoint questions and solutions—is included in the PowerPoint lecture notes. Many of the figures and tables are animated so that you can build them gradually in the classroom. Key figures can be expanded to full-screen size or shrunk to make space for text explanations at a single mouse click during a lecture. We have determined the optimal build sequence for the animated figures and have produced them with the same degree of clarity and precision as the figures in the text.

The speaking notes sections of the PowerPoint files provide material from the Instructor's Manual on teaching tips and suggestions.

MyEconLab

New to the Second Edition of *Foundations*, MyEconLab delivers all of the interactive resources available on the Foundations Web site in a comprehensive online course. With MyEconLab, instructors can customize existing content and add their own. They can manage, create, and assign tests to students, choosing from our over 5,000-question test bank, or upload tests they've written themselves. MyEconLab also includes advanced tracking features that record students' usage and performance and a Gradebook feature to see students' test results. Please refer to the Instructor Quick Start Guide or contact your Addison-Wesley sales representative to set up MyEconLab for your course.

Videos

A comprehensive series of lecture videos accompanies the text. The videos follow the same Checklist-Checkpoint format as the book itself and feature presentations by Robin Bade, Michael Parkin, Kaya Ford (Northern Virginia Community College), Gary Latanich (Arkansas State University), Kirk Gifford (Brigham Young University, Idaho), and Carol Dole (State University of West Georgia). The videos are available on VHS tapes and on CD-ROM.

Overhead Transparencies

Full-color overhead transparencies of *all* figures from the text will improve the clarity of your lectures. They are available to qualified adopters of the text (contact your Addison-Wesley sales representative).

Instructor's Resource Disk with Computerized Test Banks

This CD-ROM contains Computerized Test Bank files, Test Bank and Instructor's Manual files in Microsoft Word, and PowerPoint files. All three Test Banks are available in Test Generator Software (TestGen-EQ with QuizMaster-EQ). Fully networkable, the CD-ROM is available for Windows and Macintosh. TestGen-EQ's graphical interface enables instructors to view, edit, and add questions; transfer questions to tests; and print different forms of tests. Tests can be formatted by varying fonts and styles, margins, and headers and footers, as in any word-processing document. Search and sort features let the instructor quickly locate questions and arrange them in a preferred order. QuizMaster-EQ, working with your school's computer network, automatically grades the exams, stores the results on disk, and allows the instructor to view and print a variety of reports.

FastFax Testing

FastFax Testing is designed for instructors who do not have access to a computer or an assistant who can help prepare tests for students. Simply choose from a large pool of questions in the print test banks and include custom headers if you like. Fill out the test information sheet that lists instructor-selected questions and test preferences that describe how the test should be generated. You may even request multiple forms of a test and receive answer keys for each one.

Turnaround time is usually 48 hours or less and test pages can be mailed or faxed back to you by the date the test is needed. FastFax Testing is fast, reliable, and free to qualified adopters of this text.

ACKNOWLEDGMENTS

Working on a project such as this generates many debts that can never be repaid. But they can be acknowledged, and it is a special pleasure to be able to do so here and to express our heartfelt thanks to each and every one of the following long list, without whose contributions we could not have produced *Foundations*.

Mark Rush is our Study Guide, Instructor's Manual, and Test Bank coordinator and manager. He assembled, polished, wrote, and rewrote these materials to ensure their close consistency with the text. He and we were in constant contact as all the elements of our text and package came together. Mark also made many valuable suggestions for improving the text and the Checkpoints. His contribution went well beyond that of a reviewer. And his effervescent sense of humor kept us all in good spirits along the way. Working closely with Mark, Neil Garston and Tom Larson wrote content for the Study Guide and Richard Gosselin wrote content for the Instructor's Manual. Ali Ataiifar, Diego Mendez-Carbajo, William Mosher, Terry Sutton, Cindy Tori, and Nora Underwood provided questions for the Study Guide and Test Banks.

The ideas that ultimately became *Foundations* began to form over dinner at the Andover Inn in Andover, Massachusetts, with Denise Clinton and Sylvia Mallory. We gratefully acknowledge Sylvia's role not only at the birth of this project but also in managing the entire development team. Denise has been our ongoing inspiration for almost 10 years. She is the most knowledgeable economics editor in the business, and we are privileged to have the benefit of her enormous experience.

The success of *Foundations* owes much to Victoria Richardson Warneck, our outstanding sponsoring editor. We are in awe of Victoria's extraordinary editorial craft. It has been, and we hope it will for many future editions remain, a joy to work with her.

Mary Clare McEwing has been our indomitable development editor, ably assisted by Dottie Dennis. We said in the preface to the first edition that Mary Clare had rounded up the best group of reviewers we'd ever worked with. We are astounded to report that for this edition, she has surpassed even the high standards she previously achieved. Mary Clare has steered the revision along through several redrafts and polishes. And she began the design process with focus groups that told us what teachers and students look for in the design of a textbook.

Gina Kolenda converted the raw ideas into this outstandingly designed text. Meredith Nightingale provided the detailed figure designs.

Jason Miranda did an incredible job as editor of our print supplements and coordinated the work of our large team of coauthors.

Michelle Neil, Executive Media Producer, and Melissa Honig, our technology gurus, have brought much to this project. Michelle spearheaded the effort to set up MyEconLab, worked creatively to improve our technology systems, and worked with our editors and us to develop our media strategy. Melissa built our Web site and worked tirelessly to help develop the engine that drives *Foundations Interactive*. They have both been sources of high energy, good sense, and level-headed advice and have quickly found creative solutions to all our technology problems.

Nancy Fenton, our ever cheerful, never stressed production supervisor, ensured that all the elements eventually came together to bring our text out on schedule. Sally Simpson, our electronic production administrator, performed her magic to make our pages look beautiful. And Hugh Crawford oversaw the manufacturing process and worked with the printers and binders to produce beautiful, on-time books.

Our marketing manager, Adrienne D'Ambrosio, added enormous value, not only by being acutely intelligent and having a sensitive understanding of the market, but also by sharpening our vision of our text and package. As this revision was in progress, Adrienne moved on to become an economics acquisitions editor, and Stephen Frail joined us as marketing manager. Jit Teo and Catherine Bernstock stayed late many nights fielding requests from the sales force, and Kathy Kwack managed our online marketing efforts.

Our copy editor, Barbara Willette, and supplements copy editor, Sheryl Nelson, gave our work a thorough review and helpful polish.

Richard Parkin, our technical illustrator, created the figures in the text, the dynamic figures in the online version of the text, the illustrations in *Foundations Interactive*, and the animated versions of the figures in the PowerPoint presentations and contributed many ideas to improve the clarity of our illustrations. Laurel Davies created and edited the *Foundations Interactive* database and acted as its accuracy checker and reviewer.

Jeannie Gillmore, our personal assistant, worked closely with us in creating *Foundations Interactive* and the diagnostic Web quizzes and served as a meticulous accuracy checker on the text, Study Guide, and Instructor's Manual. Harry Ellis of the University of North Texas, John Graham of Rutgers University, Kate Krause of the University of New Mexico, Stephen McCafferty of Ohio State University, and Paul Poast of Ohio State University also provided careful accuracy reviews.

Jane McAndrew, economics librarian at the University of Western Ontario, went the extra mile on many occasions to help us track down the data and references we needed.

Finally, our reviewers, whose names appear on the following pages, have made an enormous contribution to this text. In the many texts that we've now written, we've never seen reviewing of the quality that we enjoyed on this project. It has been a pleasure (if at times a challenge) to respond constructively to their many excellent suggestions.

Robin Bade
Michael Parkin
London, Ontario, Canada
robin@econ100.com
michael.parkin@uwo.ca

Reviewers

Charles Aguilar, El Paso Community College
Seemi Ahmad, Dutchess Community College
William Aldridge, Shelton State Community College
Ali Ataiifar, Delaware County Community College
John Baffoe-Bonnie, Pennsylvania State University, Delaware County Campus
A. Paul Ballantyne, University of Colorado
Sue Bartlett, University of South Florida
Klaus Becker, Texas Tech University
John Bethune, Barton College
David Bivin, Indiana University–Purdue University at Indianapolis
Geoffrey Black, Boise State University
Barbara Brogan, Northern Virginia Community College
Christopher Brown, Arkansas State University
Nancy Burnett, University of Wisconsin at Oshkosh
Barbara Caldwell, University of South Florida
Bruce Caldwell, University of North Carolina, Greensboro
Robert Carlsson, University of South Carolina
Shawn Carter, Jacksonville State University
Jack Chambless, Valencia Community College
Joni Charles, Southwest Texas State University
Robert Cherry, Brooklyn College
Paul Cichello, Xavier University
Quentin Ciolfi, Brevard Community College
Jim Cobbe, Florida State University
John Cochran, Metropolitan State College
Ludovic Comeau, De Paul University
Carol Conrad, Cerro Coso Community College
Christopher Cornell, Fordham University
Richard Cornwall, University of California, Davis
Kevin Cotter, Wayne State University
Tom Creahan, Morehead State University
Elizabeth Crowell, University of Michigan at Dearborn
Susan Dadres, Southern Methodist University
Jeffrey Davis, ITT Technical Institute (Utah)
Dennis Debrecht, Carroll College
Al DeCooke, Broward Community College
Vince DiMartino, University of Texas at San Antonio
Carol Dole, State University of West Georgia
John Dorsey, University of Maryland, College Park
Marie Duggan, Keene State College
David Eaton, Murray State University
Harry Ellis, University of North Texas
Stephen Ellis, North Central Texas College
Carl Enomoto, New Mexico State University
Gary Ferrier, University of Arkansas
Rudy Fichtenbaum, Wright State University
Kaya Ford, Northern Virginia Community College

Robert Francis, Shoreline Community College
Roger Frantz, San Diego State University
Arthur Friedberg, Mohawk Valley Community College
Julie Gallaway, Southwest Missouri State University
Neil Garston, California State University at Los Angeles
Lisa Geib-Gunderson, University of Maryland
Linda Ghent, Eastern Illinois University
Kirk Gifford, Ricks College
Maria Giuili, Diablo Valley Community College
Mark Gius, Quinnipiac College
Randall Glover, Brevard Community College
Stephan Gohmann, University of Louisville
Richard Gosselin, Houston Community College
John Graham, Rutgers University
Warren Graham, Tulsa Community College
Jang-Ting Guo, University of California, Riverside
Dennis Hammett, University of Texas at El Paso
Leo Hardwick, Macomb Community College
Mehdi Haririan, Bloomsburg University
Paul Harris, Camden County Community College
Gus Herring, Brookhaven College
Michael Heslop, Northern Virginia Community College
Steven Hickerson, Mankato State University
Andy Howard, Rio Hondo College
Yu Hsing, Southeastern Louisiana University
Matthew Hyle, Winona State University
Harvey James, University of Hartford
Russell Janis, University of Massachusetts at Amherst
Ted Joyce, City University of New York, Baruch College
Arthur Kartman, San Diego State University
Chris Kauffman, University of Tennessee
Diane Keenan, Cerritos College
Brian Kench, University of Tampa
John Keith, Utah State University
Douglas Kinnear, Colorado State University
Morris Knapp, Miami-Dade Community College
Steven Koch, Georgia Southern University
Kate Krause, University of New Mexico
Joyce Lapping, University of Southern Maine
Tom Larson, California State University, Los Angeles
Robert Lemke, Florida International University
Tony Lima, California State University at Hayward
Kenneth Long, New River Community College
Marty Ludlum, Oklahoma City Community College
Roger Mack, De Anza College
Michael Magura, University of Toledo
Mark Maier, Glendale College
Paula Manns, Atlantic Cape Community College
Kathryn Marshall, Ohio State University
Drew E. Mattson, Anoka-Ramsey Community College
Stephen McCafferty, Ohio State University
Thomas McCaleb, Florida State University

Diego Mendez-Carbajo, Illinois Wesleyan University
Thomas Meyer, Patrick Henry Community College
Meghan Millea, Mississippi State University
Michael Milligan, Front Range Community College
Jenny Minier, University of Miami
David Mitchell, Valdosta State University
William Mosher, Assumption College
Ronald Nate, Brigham Young University, Idaho
Michael Nelson, Texas A&M University
Charles Newton, Houston Community College Southwest
Melinda Nish, Salt Lake Community College
Lee Nordgren, Indiana University at Bloomington
William C. O'Connor, Western Montana College–University of Montana
Charles Okeke, College of Southern Nevada
Sanjay Paul, Elizabethtown College
Ken Peterson, Furman University
Tim Petry, North Dakota State University
Charles Pflanz, Scottsdale Community College
Paul Poast, Ohio State University
Greg Pratt, Mesa Community College
Fernando Quijano, Dickinson State University
Karen Reid, University of Wisconsin, Parkside
Mary Rigdon, University of Texas, Austin
Helen Roberts, University of Illinois, Chicago
Barbara Ross-Pfeiffer, Kapiolani Community College
Jeffrey Rous, University of North Texas
Udayan Roy, Long Island University
Mark Rush, University of Florida
Joseph Santos, South Dakota State University
Roland Santos, Lakeland Community College
Ted Scheinman, Mount Hood Community College
Jerry Schwartz, Broward Community College
Gautam Sethi, Bard College
Martin Spechler, Indiana University
John Stiver, University of Connecticut
Terry Sutton, Southeast Missouri State University
Donna Thompson, Brookdale Community College
James Thorson, Southern Connecticut State University
Marc Tomljanovich, Colgate University
Cynthia Royal Tori, Valdosta State University
Ngoc-Bich Tran, San Jacinto College South
Nora Underwood, University of California, Davis
Christian Weber, Seattle University
Jack Wegman, Santa Rosa Junior College
Jason White, Northwest Missouri State University
Benjamin Widner, Colorado State University
Barbara Wiens-Tuers, Pennsylvania State University, Altoona
William Wood, James Madison University
Ben Young, University of Missouri, Kansas City
Michael Youngblood, Rock Valley College
Joachim Zietz, Middle Tennessee State University
Armand Zottola, Central Connecticut State University

Foundations of Macroeconomics: Flexibility Chart

Core Principles

1. **Getting Started**
2. **The U.S. and Global Economy**
   Not just a descriptive chapter. Defines the factors of production and introduces the circular flow model.
3. **The Economic Problem**
   Carefully paced and complete first look at the fundamental economic problem. Includes explanation of efficiency and comparative advantage.
4. **Demand and Supply**
   Carefully paced and complete explanation of this core topic.

These chapters are similar to the corresponding chapters in *Foundations of Economics* and *Foundations of Microeconomics*, but are not identical and are an introduction specifically to macroeconomics.

5. **GDP and the Standard of Living**
   Explains expenditure and income approaches and chain type index method of measuring real GDP
6. **Jobs and Unemployment**
   Describes labor market measures and sources of unemployment.
7. **The CPI and the Cost of Living**
   Emphasizes the interpretation and use of CPI.
8. ***AS-AD* and Potential GDP**
   A quick first look at the AS-AD model—the workhorse of macro—followed by a careful account of the determination of potential GDP.
9. **Investment and Saving**
10. **Economic Growth**

These chapters explain the real economy in the long run—classical macro—but placed in the broad context of the *AS-AD* framework. They may be studied after Chapters 11–18, but we think they work better at this point in the course. Even if you defer 9 and 10, it is a good plan to cover 8 at this point.

11. **Money and the Monetary System**
13. **Money, Interest, and Inflation**

These chapters explain the money economy in the long run and the short run. They may be studied after Chapters 14 and 15.

14. ***AS-AD* and the Business Cycle**
    A carefully paced but comprehensive account of the AS-AD model and its use in understanding the business cycle.

Chapter 14 may be studied before Chapter 8, in which case it will replace the first part of that chapter.

Policy Applications

16. **Fiscal and Monetary Policy Effects**
    A straightforward account of how fiscal and monetary actions influence aggregate demand, aggregate supply, real GDP, and the price level.
17. **The Short-Run Policy Tradeoff**
    An explanation of the sources of the short-run tradeoff and the forces that keep shifting it.
18. **Fiscal and Monetary Policy Debates**
    A balanced coverage of all the main ideas about how fiscal and monetary policy should be used to stabilize the economy, stimulate growth, and maintain price stability.

Optional

1. **Appendix: Making and Using Graphs**
   Good for students with a fear of graphs.

12. **Money Creation and Control**
    If you don't want to explain in detail how open market operations work, you may omit this chapter.
15. **Aggregate Expenditure**
    The Keynesian cross model. If you don't want to explain how unplanned inventory changes set off a multiplier process, you may omit this chapter.
19. **International Trade**
    Extensive discussion of gains from trade and costs of protection. Can be covered any time after Chapter 3 (with care).
20. **International Finance**
    Application of demand and supply to foreign exchange market. Can be covered any time after Chapter 4 (with care).

Four Alternative Macro Sequences

Early Long-Run Fundamentals	Early Short-Run Fluctuations	Keynesian Perspective	Monetarist Perspective
1. Getting Started	1. Getting Started	1. Getting Started	1. Getting Started
2. The U.S. Economy	2. The U.S. Economy	2. The U.S. Economy	2. The U.S. Economy
3. The Economic Problem	3. The Economic Problem	3. The Economic Problem	3. The Economic Problem
4. Demand and Supply	4. Demand and Supply	4. Demand and Supply	4. Demand and Supply
5. GDP and the Standard of Living	5. GDP and the Standard of Living	5. GDP and the Standard of Living	5. GDP and the Standard of Living
6. Jobs and Unemployment	6. Jobs and Unemployment	6. Jobs and Unemployment	6. Jobs and Unemployment
7. The CPI and the Cost of Living	7. The CPI and the Cost of Living	7. The CPI and the Cost of Living	7. The CPI and the Cost of Living
8. *AS-AD* and Potential GDP	14. *AS-AD* and the Business Cycle	15. Aggregate Expenditure	8. *AS-AD* and Potential GDP
9. Investment and Saving	15. Aggregate Expenditure	14. *AS-AD* and the Business Cycle	14. *AS-AD* and the Business Cycle
10. Economic Growth	11. Money and the Monetary System	17. The Short-Run Policy Tradeoff	11. Money and the Monetary System
11. Money and the Monetary System	12. Money Creation and Control	11. Money and the Monetary System	12. Money Creation and Control
12. Money Creation and Control	13. Money, Interest, and Inflation	13. Money, Interest, and Inflation	13. Money, Interest, and Inflation
13. Money, Interest, and Inflation	16. Fiscal and Monetary Policy Effects	16. Fiscal and Monetary Policy Effects	16. Fiscal and Monetary Policy Effects
14. *AS-AD* and the Business Cycle	17. The Short-Run Policy Tradeoff	18. Fiscal and Monetary Policy Debates	17. The Short-Run Policy Tradeoff
15. Aggregate Expenditure	18. Fiscal and Monetary Policy Debates	10. Economic Growth	18. Fiscal and Monetary Policy Debates
16. Fiscal and Monetary Policy Effects	8. *AS-AD* and Potential GDP	19. International Trade	10. Economic Growth
17. The Short-Run Policy Tradeoff	9. Investment and Saving	20. International Finance	19. International Trade
18. Fiscal and Monetary Policy Debates	10. Economic Growth		20. International Finance
19. International Trade	19. International Trade		
20. International Finance	20. International Finance		

CHAPTER 1

Getting Started

CHAPTER CHECKLIST

When you have completed your study of this chapter, you will be able to

1. **Define economics, distinguish between microeconomics and macroeconomics, and explain the questions of macroeconomics.**
2. **Describe what economists do and some of the problems they encounter.**
3. **Explain four core ideas that define the way economists think about macroeconomic questions.**
4. **Explain why economics is worth studying.**

You are studying macroeconomics at a time of enormous change. MP3 music, DVD movies, cell phones, palm pilots, and a host of other gadgets, tools, and toys have transformed the way we work and play. But the terrorist attacks of September 11, 2001 and the ensuing war against terrorism have sent shockwaves through our economy and created huge uncertainty about the future.

Outside the United States, more than 1 billion of the world's 6.3 billion people survive on $1 a day or less. Disturbed by the combination of increasing wealth and persistent poverty, some people are pointing to globalization as the source of growing economic inequality.

Your course in macroeconomics will help you to understand the powerful forces that are shaping this world and help you to interpret the macroeconomic events that affect your life and work.

1.1 DEFINITIONS AND QUESTIONS

All economic questions and problems arise because human wants exceed the resources available to satisfy them. We want good health and long lives. We want good schools, colleges, and universities. We want well-run day-care facilities. We want a peaceful and secure world. We want spacious and comfortable homes. We want a huge range of sports and recreational equipment from running shoes to jet skis. We want the time to enjoy our favorite sports, video games, novels, music, and movies; to travel to exotic places; and just to hang out with friends.

In the world of politics, it is easy to get carried away with the idea that we can have it all. Politicians tell us they will provide all the extra public services that we want, and at the same time, they will cut our taxes so that we can spend more on the things that we enjoy.

Despite the promises of politicians, we cannot have it all. The ability of each of us to satisfy our wants is limited by time and by the incomes we earn and the prices we pay for the things we buy. These limits mean that everyone has unsatisfied wants. Our ability as a society to satisfy our wants is limited by the productive resources that exist. These resources include the gifts of nature, our own labor and ingenuity, and tools and equipment that we have produced.

Scarcity
The condition that arises because the available resources are insufficient to satisfy wants.

Our inability to satisfy all our wants is called **scarcity**. The poor and the rich alike face scarcity. A child wants a $1.00 can of soda and two 50¢ packs of gum but has only $1.00 in his pocket. He faces scarcity. A millionaire wants to spend the weekend playing golf *and* spend the same weekend at the office attending a business strategy meeting. She faces scarcity. A society wants to provide vastly improved health care, install an Internet connection in every classroom, explore space, clean polluted lakes and rivers, and so on. Society also faces scarcity.

Faced with scarcity, we must make choices. We must *choose* among the available alternatives. The child must *choose* the soda *or* the gum. The millionaire must choose the golf game *or* the meeting. As a society, we must *choose* among health care, computers, space exploration, the environment, and so on.

Incentive
A reward or a penalty—a "carrot" or a "stick"—that encourages or discourages an action.

The choices we make depend on the incentives we face. An **incentive** is a reward or a penalty—a "carrot" or a "stick"—that encourages or discourages an

Even parrots face scarcity!

Not only do I want a cracker—we all want a cracker!

©The New Yorker Collection 1985
Frank Modell from cartoonbank.com. All Rights Reserved.

action. If the price of gum rises and the price of soda falls, the child has an *incentive* to choose less gum and more soda. If a profit of $10 million is at stake, the millionaire has an *incentive* to attend the meeting and skip the golf game. As computer prices tumble, school boards have a stronger *incentive* to connect more classrooms to the Internet.

Economics is the social science that studies the choices that we make as we cope with *scarcity* and the *incentives* that influence and reconcile our choices. The subject divides into two main parts:

- Microeconomics
- Macroeconomics

Economics
The social science that studies the choices that we make as we cope with *scarcity* and the *incentives* that influence and reconcile our choices.

Microeconomics

Microeconomics is the study of the choices that individuals and businesses make and the way these choices respond to incentives, interact, and are influenced by governments. Some examples of microeconomic questions are: Why are more people buying SUVs and fewer people buying minivans? How will a cut in the price of the Sony PlayStation and Microsoft Xbox affect the quantities of these items that people buy?

Microeconomics
The study of the choices that individuals and businesses make and the way these choices respond to incentives, interact, and are influenced by governments.

Macroeconomics

Macroeconomics is the study of the aggregate (or total) effects on the national economy and the global economy of the choices that individuals, businesses, and governments make. Some examples of macroeconomic questions are: Why did production and jobs expand so rapidly in the United States during the 1990s? Why has Japan had a long period of economic stagnation? Why does the Federal Reserve sometimes raise interest rates and sometimes lower them?

Macroeconomics
The study of the aggregate (or total) effects on the national economy and the global economy of the choices that individuals, businesses, and governments make.

The distinction between microeconomics and macroeconomics is similar to the distinction between two views of a display of national flags in an Olympic stadium. The micro view (left) is of a single participant and the actions he or she is taking. The macro view (right) is the patterns formed by the joint actions of all the people participating in the entire display.

Macroeconomic Questions

The three big issues that macroeconomics tries to understand are

- The standard of living
- The cost of living
- Economic fluctuations—recessions and expansions

The Standard of Living

Standard of living
The level of consumption of goods and services that people enjoy, on the average; it is measured by average income per person.

Goods and services
The objects that people value and produce to satisfy human wants. Goods are physical objects, and services are tasks performed for people.

The **standard of living** is the level of consumption of goods and services that people enjoy, on the average, and is measured by average income per person. **Goods and services** are the objects that people value and produce to satisfy human wants. Goods are physical objects such as golf balls. Services are tasks performed for people such as haircuts. The nation's farms, factories, construction sites, shops, and offices produce a dazzling array of goods and services that range from necessities such as food, houses and apartments, and health-care services to leisure items such as ocean cruises, SUVs, and DVD players.

In 2003, the quantity of goods and services produced by the nation's farms, factories, shops, and offices, measured by their value in today's prices, was 20 times greater than that in 1903. But over that same 100 years, the population of the United States increased to not quite four times its 1903 level. Because we now produce more goods and services per person, we have a much higher standard of living than our grandparents had.

Unemployment
The state of being available and willing to work but unable to find an acceptable job.

For most of us, achieving a high standard of living means finding a good job. And if we lose our job, it means spending some time being unemployed while we search for the right new job. **Unemployment** is the state of being available and willing to work but unable to find an acceptable job. In the United States in 2003, employment was high and unemployment was low. In January 2003, 63 percent of adults had jobs and only 6 percent of people who thought of themselves as being in the labor force were looking for jobs but unable to find them. Some other countries—for example, Canada, France, and Germany—experience higher unemployment rates than does the United States.

Will the standard of living continue to rise? Will your world and the world of your children be more prosperous than today's? What kind of job will you find when you graduate? Will you have a lot of choice, or will you face a labor market with a high level of unemployment in which jobs are hard to find?

Your study of macroeconomics will help you to understand the progress that economists have made in seeking answers to questions like these.

Rising living standards have transformed working in the home from drudgery to a form of leisure.

The Cost of Living

The **cost of living** is the number of dollars it takes to buy the goods and services that achieve a given standard of living. A rising cost of living, which is called **inflation**, means a shrinking value of the dollar. A falling cost of living, which is called **deflation**, means a rising value of the dollar.

Cost of living
The number of dollars it takes to buy the goods and services that achieve a given standard of living.

Inflation
A situation in which the cost of living is rising and the value of money is shrinking.

Deflation
A situation in which the cost of living is falling and the value of money is rising.

Has the cost of living increased or decreased? If we look back over the past 100 years, we see that it has increased and the value of the dollar has shrunk. In your great-grandparents' youth, when the electric light bulb was the latest big thing, the average American earned a wage of $1 a day. But your great-grandparents' dime would buy what you need a dollar to buy today. So the dollar of 2003 is worth only one tenth of the dollar of 1903. If the value of the dollar continues to shrink at its average rate of loss since 1903, by the time you retire (sure, that's a long time in the future), you'll need $3.30 to buy what $1 buys today. The dollar of 2053 will be worth about one third of the value of the dollar of 2003.

You've seen that over the years, our standard of living has increased. Why doesn't a rising *cost* of living mean that people must constantly cut back on their spending and endure a *falling* standard of living? The answer is that incomes have increased faster than the cost of living.

During the past few years, the cost of living has increased slowly and some people have even begun to talk about the possibility of a return to deflation, something we have not experienced for more than 60 years. Can we avoid the extremes of deflation and rapid inflation and keep our cost of living stable?

In your study of macroeconomics, you will learn what economists have discovered about the answers to questions like these.

Economic Fluctuations: Recessions and Expansions

Over long periods, both the standard of living and the cost of living have increased. But these increases have not been smooth and continuous. Our economy fluctuates in a **business cycle**, a periodic but irregular up-and-down movement in production and jobs.

Business cycle
A periodic but irregular up-and-down movement in production and jobs.

"Three hundred dollars' of regular."

©The New Yorker Collection 2000
David Sipress from cartoonbank.com. All Rights Reserved.

An inflation rate of 20 percent a year maintained for 25 years would make a $300 tank of gas look like a bargain.

FIGURE 1.1
Business Cycle Phases and Turning Points

Practice Online

In a business cycle expansion, production and jobs increase. In a recession, production and jobs shrink. An expansion ends at a peak, and a recession ends at a trough.

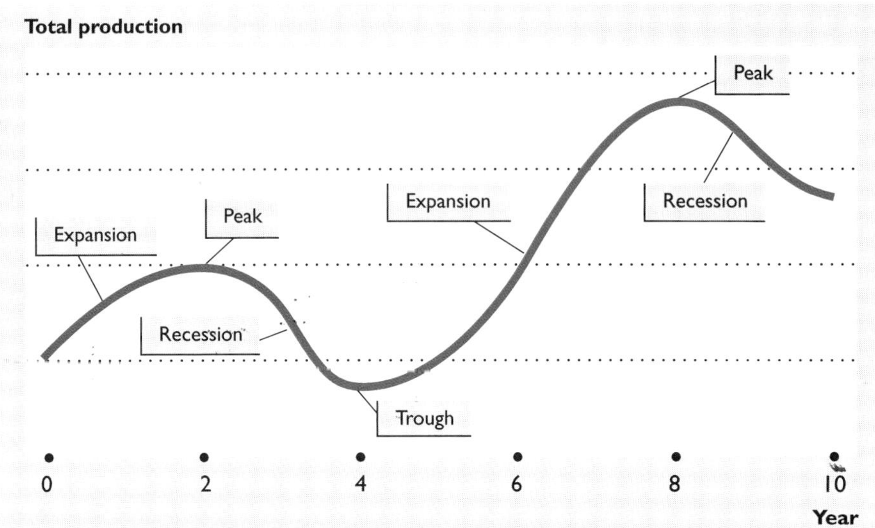

When production and jobs increase, the economy is in a business cycle *expansion*. When production and jobs shrink, the economy is in a *recession*.

Figure 1.1 illustrates the phases and turning points of a business cycle. The economy in this figure has a recession from year 2 to year 4, then an expansion through year 8, followed by another recession through year 10. An expansion ends at a peak, and a recession ends at a trough.

The last recession in the United States occurred in 2001. The U.S. economy had an unusually long expansion that ran from the trough of the 1991 recession until early 2001.

Great Depression
A period during the 1930s in which the economy experienced its worst-ever recession.

The worst recession ever experienced occurred during the 1930s in an episode called the **Great Depression**. During this period, production in the United States shrank by more than 20 percent.

When a recession occurs, unemployment increases. During the Great Depression, a quarter of the U.S. labor force was unable to find jobs. During the early 1980s, a recession saw the U.S. unemployment rate climb to 10 percent of the labor force.

During an expansion, construction booms and jobs are plentiful, but in a recession, unemployment lines lengthen.

CHECKPOINT 1.1

1 **Define economics, distinguish between microeconomics and macroeconomics, and explain the questions of macroeconomics.**

Study Guide pp. 2–5

Practice Online 1.1

Practice Problems 1.1

1. Economics studies choices that arise from one fact. What is that fact?
2. Sort the following headlines into those that deal with (i) the standard of living, (ii) the cost of living, and (iii) unemployment and the business cycle:
   a. Production per person has grown for the tenth straight year.
   b. Another price hike for consumers?
   c. Firms lay off more workers as orders decline.
   d. States pay out more unemployment compensation.
   e. New robots boost production across a wide range of industries.
   f. Money doesn't buy what it used to.

Exercises 1.1

1. Every day, we make many choices. Why can't we avoid having to make choices?
2. Check your local news media for headlines that examine each of the three questions of macroeconomics.
3. Which of the following media headlines anticipate a recession and which anticipate an expansion?
   a. U.S. jobless claims increase.
   b. Wall Street forecasts rising production.
   c. Housing starts rise.
   d. Firms recall workers.
   e. Automakers worried as car sales plummet.

Solutions to Practice Problems 1.1

1. Choices arise because our wants exceed the resources available to satisfy them. In deciding which wants will be satisfied, we must make choices. We cannot have everything we want.

2a. Deals with the standard of living because when production per person increases, income per person, which measures the standard of living, increases—consumption per person increases.

2b. Deals with the cost of living because as the prices that consumers have to pay for goods and services increases, the cost of living increases.

2c. Deals with unemployment and the business cycle because as orders decline, production decreases and more workers become unemployed.

2d. Deals with unemployment and the business cycle because states pay out more unemployment compensation only when the economy goes into a recession.

2e. Deals with the standard of living because robots that increase production across a wide range of industries increase income per worker—consumption per person increases.

2f. Deals with the cost of living because the value of money has fallen. The value of money falls when the prices of goods and services increase, which increases the cost of living.

1.2 ECONOMICS: A SOCIAL SCIENCE

We've defined economics as the *social science* that studies the choices that individuals and societies make as they cope with scarcity. We're now going to look at the way economists go about their work as social scientists and at some of the problems they encounter.

The major goal of economists is to discover how the economic world works. In pursuit of this goal, economists (like all scientists) distinguish between two types of statements:

- What *is*
- What *ought to be*

Statements about what *is* are called *positive* statements. They say what is currently understood about the way the world operates. A positive statement might be right or wrong. And we can test a positive statement by checking it against the data. When a chemist does an experiment in her laboratory, she is attempting to check a positive statement against the facts.

Statements about what *ought to be* are called *normative* statements. These statements depend on opinions and cannot be tested. When Congress debates a motion, it is ultimately trying to decide what ought to be. It is making a normative statement.

To see the distinction between positive and normative statements, consider the controversy about global warming. Some scientists believe that 200 years of industrial activity and the large quantities of coal and oil that we burn are increasing the carbon dioxide content of the earth's atmosphere with devastating consequences for life on this planet. Other scientists disagree. The statement "Our planet is warming because of an increased carbon dioxide buildup in the atmosphere" is a positive statement. It can (in principle and with sufficient data) be tested. In contrast, the statement "We should cut back on our use of carbon-based fuels such as coal and oil" is a normative statement. You may agree with or disagree with this statement, but you can't test it. It is based on values. Health-care reform provides an economic example of the distinction. "Universal health care will cut the amount of work time lost to illness" is a positive statement. "Every American should have equal access to health care" is a normative statement.

The task of economic science is to discover and catalog positive statements that are consistent with what we observe in the world and that enable us to understand how the economic world works. This task is a large one that can be broken into three steps:

- Observing and measuring
- Model building
- Testing

Observing and Measuring

The first step toward understanding how the economic world works is to observe and measure it. Economists keep track of huge amounts of economic data. Some examples are the amounts and locations of natural and human resources; wages and work hours; the prices and quantities of the different things produced; taxes and government spending; and the volume of international trade.

Model Building

The second step is to build models. An **economic model** is a description of some aspect of the economic world that includes only those features of the world that are needed for the purpose at hand. A model is simpler than the reality it describes. What a model includes and what it leaves out result from *assumptions* about what are essential and what are inessential details.

Economic model
A description of some aspect of the economic world that includes only those features that are needed for the purpose at hand.

You can see how ignoring details is useful—even essential—to our understanding by thinking about a model that you see every day: the TV weather map. The weather map is a model that helps to predict the temperature, wind speed and direction, and precipitation over a future period. The weather map shows lines called isobars—lines of equal barometric pressure. It doesn't show the interstate highways. The reason is that we think the location of the highways has no influence on the weather but the air pressure patterns do have an influence.

An economic model is similar to a weather map. It tells us how a number of variables are determined by a number of other variables. For example, an economic model of Boston's "Big Dig"—a $15 billion project to place the city's major highways underground—might tell us the impact of the project on house prices, apartment rents, jobs, and commuting times.

Economists use a variety of methods to describe their economic models. Most commonly, the method is mathematical. And if you plan on a career in economics, you will study a good deal of math. But the basic ideas of all economic models can be described using words and pictures or diagrams. That is how economic models are described in this text.

A rare exception is a model called the Phillips Economic Hydraulic Computer, shown here. Bill Phillips, a New Zealand-born engineer-turned-economist, created this model using plastic tubes and Plexiglas tanks at the London School of Economics in 1949. The model still works today in a London museum.

The Phillips Economic Hydraulic Computer: Colored water in plastic tubes and Plexiglas tanks illustrates the effects of government actions on incomes and expenditures. This model economy is in a London museum.

Testing

The third step is testing models. A model's predictions might correspond to or conflict with the data. If there is a conflict, the model needs to be modified or rejected. A model that has repeatedly passed the test of corresponding well with real-world data is the basis of an economic theory. An **economic theory** is a generalization that summarizes what we understand about the economic choices that people make and the economic performance of industries and nations.

Economic theory
A generalization that summarizes what we understand about the economic choices that people make and the economic performance of industries and nations based on models that have repeatedly passed the test of corresponding well with real-world data.

The process of building and testing models creates theories. For example, meteorologists have a theory that if the isobars form a particular pattern at a particular time of the year (a model), then it will snow (reality). They have developed this theory by repeated observation and by carefully recording the weather that follows specific pressure patterns.

Economics is a young science. Although philosophers have written about economic issues since the time of the ancient Greeks, it is generally agreed that as a modern social science, economics was born in 1776 with the publication of Adam Smith's *The Wealth of Nations*. Over the years since then, economists have discovered many useful theories. But in many areas, economists are still looking for answers. The gradual accumulation of economic knowledge gives most economists some faith that their methods will eventually provide usable answers.

But progress in economics comes slowly. A major reason is that it is difficult in economics to unscramble cause and effect.

Eye on the Past

Adam Smith and the Birth of Economics as a Modern Social Science

Many people had written about economics before Adam Smith, but he made economics a social science.

Born in 1723 in Kirkcaldy, a small fishing town near Edinburgh, Scotland, Smith was the only child of the town's customs officer. Lured from his professorship (he was a full professor at 28) by a wealthy Scottish duke who gave him a pension of £300 a year—ten times the average income at that time—he devoted ten years to writing his masterpiece, *An Inquiry into the Nature and Causes of the Wealth of Nations*, published in 1776.

Why, Adam Smith asked in that book, are some nations wealthy while others are poor? He was pondering these questions at the height of the Industrial Revolution. During these years, new technologies were applied to the manufacture of textiles, iron, transportation, and agriculture.

Adam Smith answered his questions by emphasizing the role of the division of labor and free markets. To illustrate his argument, he used the example of a pin factory. He guessed that one person, using the hand tools available in the 1770s, might make 20 pins a day. Yet, he observed, by using those same hand tools but breaking the process into a number of individually small operations in which people specialize—by the division of labor—ten people could make a staggering 48,000 pins a day. One draws out the wire, another straightens it, a third cuts it, a fourth points it, a fifth grinds it. Three specialists make the head, and a fourth attaches it. Finally, the pin is polished and packaged.

But a large market is needed to support the division of labor: One factory employing ten workers would need to sell more than 15 million pins a year to stay in business!

Unscrambling Cause and Effect

Are computers getting cheaper because people are buying them in greater quantities? Or are people buying computers in greater quantities because they are getting cheaper? Or is some third factor causing both the price of a computer to fall and the quantity of computers to increase? Economists want to answer questions like these, but doing so is often difficult. The central idea that economists (and all scientists) use to unscramble cause and effect is *ceteris paribus*.

Ceteris Paribus

Ceteris paribus
Other things remaining the same (often abbreviated as *cet. par.*).

Ceteris paribus is a Latin term (often abbreviated as *cet. par.*) that means "other things being equal" or "if all other relevant things remain the same." Ensuring that other things are equal is crucial in many activities, and all successful attempts to make scientific progress use this device. By changing one factor at a time and holding all the other relevant factors constant, we isolate the factor of interest and are able to investigate its effects in the clearest possible way.

Economic models, like the models in all other sciences, enable the influence of one factor at a time to be isolated in the imaginary world of the model. When we use a model, we are able to imagine what would happen if only one factor changed. But *ceteris paribus* can be a problem in economics when we try to test a model.

Laboratory scientists, such as chemists and physicists, perform controlled experiments by actually holding all the relevant factors constant except for the one under investigation. In economics (and astronomy), we usually observe the outcomes of the *simultaneous* operation of many factors. Consequently, it is hard to sort out the effects of each individual factor and to compare the effects with what a model predicts. To cope with this problem, economists take three complementary approaches:

- Natural experiments
- Econometric investigations
- Economic experiments

Natural Experiments

A natural experiment is a situation that arises in the ordinary course of economic life in which the one factor of interest is different and other things are equal (or similar). For example, Canada has higher unemployment benefits than the United States, but the people in the two nations are similar. So to study the effects of unemployment benefits on the unemployment rate, economists might compare the United States with Canada.

Econometric Investigations

Econometric investigations use statistical tools, the most common of which is correlation. **Correlation** is the tendency for the values of two variables to move in a predictable and related way. For example, there is a correlation between the amount of cigarette smoking and the incidence of lung cancer. There is also a correlation between the size of a city's police force and the city's crime rate. Two economic examples are the correlation between household income and spending and the correlation between the price of a telephone call and the number of calls made. We must be careful to interpret a correlation correctly. Sometimes a correlation shows the strength of a *causal* influence of one variable on the other. For example, smoking causes lung cancer and higher incomes cause higher spending. Sometimes the direction of causation is hard to determine. For example, does a larger police force *detect* more crimes or does a higher crime rate cause a larger police force to be hired? And sometimes a third factor causes both of the correlated variables. For example, advances in communication technology have caused both a fall in the price of phone calls and an increase in the quantity of calls. So the correlation between the price and quantity of phone calls has a deeper cause.

Correlation
The tendency for the values of two variables to move in a predictable and related way.

Sometimes, the direction of cause and effect can be determined by looking at the timing of events. But this method must be handled with care because of a problem known as the *post hoc* fallacy.

Post Hoc *Fallacy* Another Latin phrase—*post hoc ergo propter hoc*—means "after this, therefore because of this." The ***post hoc* fallacy** is the error of reasoning that a first event *causes* a second event because the first occurred before the second. Suppose you are a visitor from a far-off world. You observe lots of people shopping in early December, and then you see them opening gifts and celebrating on Christmas Day. Does the shopping cause Christmas, you wonder? After a deeper study, you discover that Christmas causes the shopping. A later event causes an earlier event.

***Post hoc* fallacy**
The error of reasoning that a first event *causes* a second event because the first occurred *before* the second.

Just looking at the timing of events often doesn't help to unravel cause and effect in economics. For example, the stock market booms, and some months later

the economy expands—jobs and incomes grow. Did the stock market boom cause the economy to expand? Possibly, but perhaps businesses started to plan the expansion of production because a new technology that lowered costs had become available. As knowledge of the plans spread, the stock market reacted to *anticipate* the economic expansion.

To disentangle cause and effect, economists use economic models to interpret correlations in the data. And when they can do so, they perform experiments.

Economic Experiments

Economic experiments are a relatively new approach. These experiments put real subjects in a decision-making situation and vary the influence of interest to discover how the subjects respond to one factor at a time. Most economic experiments are done using students as the subjects. But a few are done using the actual people whose behavior economists want to understand and predict. An example of an economic experiment on actual subjects is one that was designed to discover the effects of changing the way welfare benefits are paid in New Jersey. Another experiment was conducted to discover how telecommunications companies would bid in different types of auctions for the airwave frequencies they use to transmit cellular telephone messages. Governments have made billions of dollars using the results of this experiment.

CHECKPOINT 1.2

Study Guide pp. 5–7

Practice Online 1.2

2 **Describe what economists do and some of the problems they encounter.**

Practice Problems 1.2

1. Classify the following statements as positive or normative:
   a. Unemployed workers have to wait too long before being rehired.
   b. Doctors earn, on the average, more than the governor of Florida.
2. Provide two examples of the *post hoc* fallacy.

Exercise 1.2

Classify each statement as positive or normative and suggest how economists might test each positive statement:

a. The government surplus should be spent on national defense.
b. Free trade will harm developing countries.
c. Cuts to public education in the United States have been too high.

Solutions to Practice Problems 1.2

1a. The statement is a normative one because it cannot be tested.
1b. The statement is a positive one because it can be checked against the data.

2. Examples are: New Year celebrations cause January sales. A booming stock market causes a Republican president to be elected.

1.3 MACROECONOMIC IDEAS

To understand what brings changes in the standard of living and the cost of living and what generates economic fluctuations, economists build and test economic models based on four core ideas:

- Macroeconomic performance results from rational choices that respond to the incentives people face.
- The standard of living improves when production per person increases.
- The cost of living rises when the quantity of money increases faster than production.
- Economic fluctuations result from expenditure and productivity fluctuations.

Rational Choice and Incentives

The most basic idea of economics is that in making choices, people act rationally. A **rational choice** is one that uses the available resources to most effectively satisfy the wants of the person making the choice. Only the wants and preferences of the person making the choice are relevant to determine its rationality.

Rational choice
A choice that uses the available resources to most effectively satisfy the wants of the person making the choice.

But how do people choose rationally? How does a person decide how much to save and how much to spend? How does America Online decide how many servers and high-speed Internet connections to install? How did governments decide to build the interstate highway system?

We make rational choices by comparing *costs* and *benefits*. Economists think about costs and benefits in a special and revealing way.

Cost: What You Must Give Up

Whatever you choose to do, you could have done something else instead. One of these other things is the *best* alternative given up. The best thing that you *must* give up to get something is the **opportunity cost** of the thing that you get. The thing that you could have chosen—the highest-valued alternative forgone—is the cost of the thing that you did choose.

Opportunity cost
The opportunity cost of something is the best thing that you *must* give up to get it.

"There's no such thing as a free lunch" is not a clever but empty saying. It expresses the central idea of economics: that every choice involves a cost.

We use the term *opportunity cost* to emphasize that when we make a choice in the face of scarcity, we give up an opportunity to do something else. You can quit school right now, or you can remain in school. Suppose that if you quit school, the best job you can get is at McDonald's, where you can earn $5,000 during the year. The opportunity cost of remaining in school includes the things that you could have bought with this $5,000. The opportunity cost also includes the value of the leisure time that you must forgo to study.

Benefit: Gain Measured by What You Are Willing to Give Up

The **benefit** of something is the gain or pleasure that it brings. Benefit is how a person *feels* about something. You might be very anxious to get the latest version of a video game. It will bring you a large benefit. And you might have almost no interest in the latest Yo-Yo Ma cello concerto CD. It will bring you a small benefit.

Benefit
The benefit of something is the gain or pleasure that it brings.

Economists measure the benefit of something by what a person *is willing to* give up to get it. You can buy CDs, sodas, or magazines. The sodas or magazines that you *are willing to* give up to get a CD measure the benefit you get from a CD.

On the Margin

Margin
A choice on the margin is a choice that is made by comparing *all* the relevant alternatives systematically and incrementally.

A choice on the **margin** is a choice that is made by comparing *all* the relevant alternatives systematically and incrementally. For example, you must choose how to divide the next hour between studying and e-mailing your friends. To make this choice, you must evaluate the costs and benefits of the alternative possible allocations of your next hour. You choose on the margin by considering whether you will be better off or worse off if you spend an extra few minutes studying or an extra few minutes e-mailing.

Marginal cost
The opportunity cost that arises from a one-unit increase in an activity. The marginal cost of something is what you *must* give up to get one more unit of it.

Marginal benefit
The benefit that arises from a one-unit increase in an activity. The marginal benefit of something is *measured by* what you *are willing to* give up to get *one more* unit of it.

The opportunity cost of a one-unit increase in an activity is called marginal cost. **Marginal cost** is what you *must give up* to get one more unit of something. For example, the marginal cost of another year in school is a year's forgone income and leisure time. The benefit of a one-unit increase in an activity is called marginal benefit. **Marginal benefit** is what you gain when you get one more unit of something. Marginal benefit is *measured by* what you *are willing to* give up to get *one more* unit of something. For example, your marginal benefit of another year in school is measured by the income and leisure time that you are willing to forgo.

If the marginal cost of another year in school is less than the marginal benefit, your rational choice is to remain in school. If the marginal cost exceeds the marginal benefit, your rational choice is to drop out of school. We make a rational choice and use our resources in the way that makes us as well off as possible when we take those actions for which marginal benefit exceeds or equals marginal cost.

Responding to Incentives

A change in marginal cost or a change in marginal benefit brings a change in the incentives that we face and leads us to change our actions. For example, suppose that job opportunities improve. Instead of being able to earn $5,000 at McDonald's, you can now get a job that pays $30,000 a year. The marginal cost of remaining in school has increased, and it might now be rational to quit school and take this newly available job. In the choice that we've just described, you are responding to a change in incentives. A central idea of economics is that because people make rational choices, by looking for changes in marginal cost and marginal benefit, we can predict the way people respond to changes in incentives.

For these students, the opportunity cost of being in school is worth bearing.

For the fast-food worker, the opportunity cost of remaining in school is too high.

The Standard of Living and Productivity

The dollar value of a nation's production can increase for any of three reasons: prices and wage rates rise, the number of people employed increases, or production per person increases. Total production per person employed is called **productivity**. Only an increase in productivity brings a higher standard of living.

Productivity
Total production per person employed.

A rise in prices and wage rates brings higher incomes, but only in terms of dollars, not in terms of the quantity of goods and services that the income can buy. The extra income is just enough to pay the higher prices, not enough to buy more goods and services.

An increase in the number of people employed brings an increase in *total* production but not an increase in production per person. Living standards increase when people, on the average, consume more goods and services. And on the average, people can consume more only if production per person increases. So only an increase in production per person—an increase in productivity—brings an increase in the standard of living.

For example, by automating a car production line, each autoworker can produce more output. If each worker can produce more cars, then there will be more cars for more people to enjoy owning.

Often, automation means that jobs are lost. Automation on farms and in coal mines, steel mills, and car factories has led to a large decrease in the number of jobs in these industries. If automation leads to job loss, how can automation at the same time lead to an increase in the standard of living? The standard of living increases because the people who lose their jobs to automation eventually find new ones that pay an even greater wage, on the average, than the old job did. So by increasing output per person, total production increases, we are able to buy more goods and services, and we enjoy a higher standard of living.

The Cost of Living and the Quantity of Money

You've seen that the *cost of living* is the number of dollars it takes to buy the goods and services that achieve a given standard of living. So a rising cost of living, called *inflation*, means that more dollars are needed to buy the same fixed quantity of goods and services.

Inflation is caused by an increase in the quantity of money that is not matched by an increase in the quantity of goods and services. The Federal Reserve determines the quantity of money in the U.S. economy by methods that you will learn about in Chapter 12. But to see the *effect* of an increase in the quantity of money, suppose that the U.S. government mails $1,000 in new $20 bills to every person in the United States. Nothing else has changed. People are doing the same jobs as before and producing the same quantities of goods and services as before.

What do you think happens when people open their mail and find their $1,000? Most people will go out and spend it. But there are no more goods and services to buy. There is too much money chasing too few goods. As people bring more money to market, sellers see that they can raise their prices. But when sellers go to buy their supplies, they find that the prices they must pay have also increased. With too much money around, prices rise and money loses value.

In some countries, inflation has been rapid. One such country is Russia. During the 1990s, prices in Russia increased at an average rate of 156 percent per year. In the United States during the 1990s, prices increased at an average rate of 2 percent a year.

Expenditure and Productivity Fluctuations

The economic fluctuations that we call the business cycle are the least well-understood phenomena of macroeconomics. Despite this lack of understanding, economists know a lot about the anatomy of the business cycle. That is, economists have accumulated a great deal of data that describe the ups and downs of economic activity. The sources of economic fluctuations can be placed in two broad groups:

- Expenditure fluctuations
- Productivity fluctuations

Expenditure Fluctuations

Expenditure fluctuations bring fluctuations in jobs and production and are one of the sources of the business cycle. For example, high interest rates killed business expenditure on new buildings and equipment during the early 1980s. Business expenditure also shrank during the early 1990s. But through the rest of the 1990s, the growing information economy brought a surge in expenditures. Expenditure plans of governments, foreigners, and individuals also fluctuate.

Productivity Fluctuations

Productivity fluctuations also bring economic fluctuations. For example, during the 1970s, a disruption of oil supplies and a series of large oil-price increases decreased productivity and brought recession. During the 1990s, the spread of information-age technologies brought an increase in productivity that created a rapid and unusually prolonged expansion.

Smoothing the Business Cycle

It is generally agreed that economic fluctuations are undesirable. Recessions bring unemployment, and deep and long recessions such as the Great Depression bring enormous economic hardship and even social unrest. An overly strong expansion is undesirable because it brings an increase in prices that outpaces the increases in some people's incomes.

Macroeconomics has made a great deal of progress in smoothing the business cycle but not in eliminating it. We cannot predict when a recession or a recovery will occur, and we cannot prevent recession. But we do know how to limit the damage from recession and keep an expansion from becoming too strong. You will learn about these aspects of macroeconomics in Chapters 14 through 18.

Economists do not know how to prevent recession and maintain a continuous expansion.

CHECKPOINT 1.3

3 **Explain four core ideas that define the way economists think about macroeconomic questions.**

Study Guide pp. 7–9

Practice Online 1.3

Practice Problems 1.3

1. Kate usually plays tennis for two hours a week, and her grade on math tests is usually 70 percent. Last week, after playing two hours of tennis, Kate thought long and hard about playing for another hour. She decided to play another hour of tennis and cut her study time by one additional hour. But the grade on last week's math test was 60 percent.
   a. What was Kate's opportunity cost of the third hour of tennis?
   b. Was Kate's decision to play the third hour of tennis rational?
   c. Did Kate make her decision on the margin?

2. Classify each of the following events as (i) an influence on the standard of living or the cost of living and (ii) an expenditure or a productivity source of economic fluctuations:
   a. A new computer chip doubles the speed of a PC.
   b. A new process lowers the cost of producing fiber-optic cable.
   c. Telephone companies increase their spending on cellular networks.
   d. Expenditure is increasing, prices are rising, but production is stagnant.

Exercises 1.3

1. Steve Fossett spent a lot of money trying to be the first person to circumnavigate the world in a hot-air balloon. Anheuser-Busch offered a prize of $1 million for the first balloonist to do so in 15 days nonstop. What was the opportunity cost of Steve Fossett's adventure? But Steve Fossett was not the first person to circumnavigate the world in a balloon, so did he get any benefits? Why did Anheuser-Busch offer the prize?

2. Classify each of the following events as an influence on the standard of living or the cost of living and as an expenditure or productivity source of economic fluctuations:
   a. DVD technology arrives.
   b. Prices that consumers pay rise, and so do wages.
   c. New technology increases the average productivity in the nation.
   d. The nation's output increases faster than the inflation rate.

Solutions to Practice Problems 1.3

1a. Kate's opportunity cost of the third hour of tennis was the ten percentage point drop in her grade. If Kate had not played tennis for the third hour, she would have studied and her grade would not have dropped. The best alternative forgone is her opportunity cost of the third hour of tennis.
1b. Kate's decision was rational if her marginal benefit exceeded her marginal cost.
1c. Kate's decision was made on the margin because she considered the benefit and cost of *one additional hour* of tennis.

2a. Standard of living; productivity.
2b. Standard of living and cost of living; productivity.
2c. Standard of living; expenditure.
2d. Cost of living; expenditure.

1.4 WHY ECONOMICS IS WORTH STUDYING

In 1961, Mick Jagger, then the 19-year-old lead singer with a group that would become the Rolling Stones, enrolled in an economics degree program at the London School of Economics. During the day, he was learning about opportunity cost, and each night, his rock group was earning today's equivalent of $120. Mick soon realized that his opportunity cost of remaining in school was too high, and so he dropped out. (A faculty advisor is reputed to have told Mick that he would not make much money in a rock band. But within a few months, the Rolling Stones, along with the Beatles, shot to international stardom and multimillion-dollar recording contracts!)

Mick Jagger used one of the big ideas of economics to make his own rational decision. And you can do the same. Let's look at the benefits and costs of studying economics and check that the benefits outweigh the costs.

Two main benefits from studying economics are

- Understanding
- Expanded career opportunities

Understanding

George Bernard Shaw, the great Irish dramatist and thinker, wrote, "Economy is the art of making the most of life." Life is certainly full of economic problems, some global or national in scope and some personal.

Every day, on television, on the Internet, and in newspapers and magazines, we hear and read about global or national economic issues: Should Nike pay higher wages to its workers in Asia? Is there too much economic inequality in the world today? How can we improve health care, welfare, and education? Are taxes too high or too low? Will the Federal Reserve increase interest rates next week?

And every day in your own life, you're confronted with personal economic choices: Will you buy pizza or pasta? Will you skip class today? Will you put your summer earnings in the bank or the stock market?

Studying economics equips you with tools and insights that help you to understand the world's problems, to participate in the political debate that surrounds them, and to understand and solve your personal economic problems.

John Maynard Keynes, a famous British economist of the twentieth century, wrote, "The ideas of economists . . . , both when they are right and when they are wrong, are more powerful than is commonly understood. Indeed the world is ruled by little else. Practical men [and women, he would have written today], who believe themselves to be quite exempt from any intellectual influences, are usually the slaves of some defunct economist."

Keynes was correct. You can't ignore economic ideas. They are all around you. You use them every day in your personal life and in your work. You use them when you vote and when you argue with your friends. But you don't need to be the slave of some defunct economist. By studying economics, you will learn how to develop your own ideas and to test them against the ideas of others. As you progress with your study of economics, you will start to listen to the news and read your newspaper with a deeper understanding of what's going on. You will also find yourself increasingly using the economics that you are learning when you make your own economic choices.

Expanded Career Opportunities

Robert Reich, a former U.S. Secretary of Labor, predicts that the three big jobs of the 21st century will be what he calls *problem identifying*, *problem solving*, and *strategic brokering*. The people who are good at these tasks command soaring incomes. And there is no better way to train yourself in these skills than to study economics. You can think of economics as a workout regimen for your brain. Almost everything that you study in economics is practice at thinking abstractly and rigorously about concrete things. You will constantly be asking, "What if?" Although students of economics learn many useful economic concepts, it is the training and practice in abstract thinking that really pays off.

Most students of economics don't go on to major in the subject. And even those who do major in economics don't usually go on to become economists. Rather, they work in fields such as banking, business, management, finance, insurance, real estate, marketing, law, government, journalism, health care, and the arts. A course in economics is a very good choice for a pre-med, pre-law, or pre-MBA student.

Economics graduates are not the highest-paid professionals. But they are close to the top, as you can see in Figure 1.2. Engineers and computer scientists, for example, earn up to 20 percent more than economics graduates. Economics graduates earn more than most others, and significantly, they earn more than business graduates.

FIGURE 1.2
Average Incomes

Practice Online

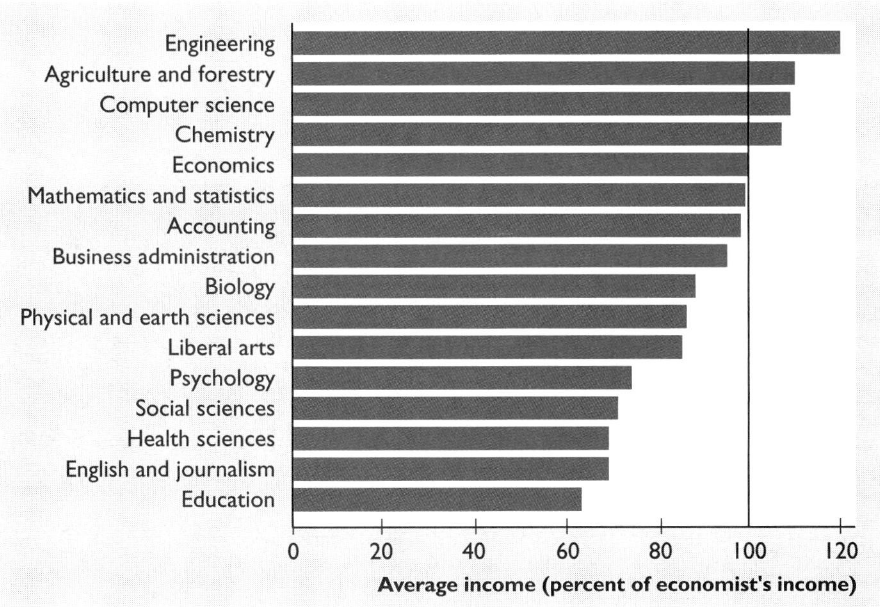

Graduates in disciplines that teach *problem identifying*, *problem solving*, and *strategic brokering* (engineering, computer science, and economics) are at the top of the earnings distribution.

SOURCES: U.S. Department of Commerce, Bureau of the Census, *Educational Background and Economic Status: Spring 1990*, Current Population Reports, Series P-70, No. 32, and *Statistical Abstract of the United States*, 1994, Table 246, and authors' calculations.

The Costs of Studying Economics

Regardless of what you study, you must buy textbooks and supplies and pay tuition. So these expenses are *not* part of the opportunity cost of studying economics.

One cost of studying economics is forgone knowledge of some other subject. If you work hard at studying economics, you must forgo learning some other subject. You can't study everything.

Another cost, the main cost of studying economics, is forgone leisure time. Economics is a demanding subject, and it takes time to master. Most students say that they find it difficult. They often complain that they understand the subject when they read the textbook or listen to their instructor but then, when they take an exam, they just can't figure out the correct answers.

The trick is practice, or learning-by-doing. Economics is not a subject that you learn by memorizing things. You must memorize definitions and technical terms. But beyond that, memory is not your main mental tool. Working problems and learning how to analyze and solve problems are the key. And this activity is time consuming.

Benefits Versus Costs

So which is larger: the benefit or the cost? Economics says that only you can decide. You are the judge of value or benefit to yourself. So you must weigh the benefits and the costs that we've identified (and consider any others that are important to *you*).

If you're clear that the benefits outweigh the costs, you're well on your way to having a good time in your economics course. If the costs outweigh the benefits, don't waste your time. Life is too short.

If you're on the fence, try to get more information. But if you remain on the fence, complete this one course in economics and then decide.

CHECKPOINT 1.4

Study Guide pp. 9–10

Practice Online 1.4

4 **Explain why economics is worth studying.**

Practice Problem 1.4

A student is choosing between an economics course and a popular music course. List two opportunity costs and two benefits from taking a course in economics.

Exercise 1.4

Why did Mick Jagger quit his economics course? What are some of the benefits that Mick Jagger might have given up?

Solution to Practice Problem 1.4

Opportunity costs include forgone leisure and forgone appreciation of popular music. Benefits include expanded career opportunities, better understanding of the world, and better problem-solving skills.

CHAPTER CHECKPOINT

Key Points

1 Define economics, distinguish between microeconomics and macroeconomics, and explain the questions of macroeconomics.

- Economics is the social science that studies the choices that we make as we cope with scarcity and the incentives that influence and reconcile our choices.
- Microeconomics is the study of the choices that individuals and businesses make and the way these choices respond to incentives, interact, and are influenced by governments.
- Macroeconomics studies trends in the standard of living and the cost of living and economic fluctuations—recessions and expansions.

2 Describe what economists do and some of the problems they encounter.

- Positive statements are about what is, and they can be tested. Normative statements are about what ought to be, and they cannot be tested.
- To explain the economic world, economists build and test economic models.
- Economists use the *ceteris paribus* assumption to try to disentangle cause and effect, and they use natural experiments, econometric investigations, and economic experiments.

3 Explain four core ideas that define the way economists think about macroeconomic questions.

- Macroeconomic performance results from rational choices.
- The standard of living improves when production per person increases.
- The cost of living rises when the quantity of money increases faster than production.
- Economic fluctuations occur when expenditure or productivity fluctuate.

4 Explain why economics is worth studying.

- The benefits of studying economics are understanding of the economic world and expanded career opportunities.
- The costs of studying economics are forgone knowledge of some other subject and leisure time.

Key Terms

Benefit, 13
Business cycle, 5
Ceteris paribus, 10
Correlation, 11
Cost of living, 5
Deflation, 5
Economic model, 9
Economic theory, 9
Economics, 3
Goods and services, 4
Great Depression, 6
Incentive, 2
Inflation, 5
Macroeconomics, 3
Margin, 14
Marginal benefit, 14
Marginal cost, 14
Microeconomics, 3
Opportunity cost, 13
Post hoc fallacy, 11
Productivity, 15
Rational choice, 13
Scarcity, 2
Standard of living, 4
Unemployment, 4

Exercises

1. Provide three examples of scarcity that illustrate why even the wealthiest people who live in the most lavish luxury still face scarcity.

2. Provide two examples of incentives, one a carrot and the other a stick, that have influenced major government decisions during the past few years.

3. Think about the following news items and label each one as involving a microeconomic or a macroeconomic issue:
   a. An increase in the tax on cigarettes will decrease teenage smoking.
   b. It would be better if the United States spent more on cleaning up the environment and less on space exploration.
   c. A government scheme called "work for welfare" will reduce the number of people who are unemployed.
   d. An increase in the number of police on inner-city streets will reduce the crime rate.

4. Assign each of the following news items to one of the three macroeconomic issues: (i) the standard of living, (ii) the cost of living, or (iii) economic fluctuations.
   a. The government should cut taxes to encourage greater work effort.
   b. An interest rate cut will stimulate job creation.
   c. Gas prices are too high.
   d. Lower gas prices will stimulate the production of many goods and services.
   e. Expect a big increase in layoffs.
   f. Mechanization and automation bring rising unemployment.
   g. Work for welfare will reduce the number of part-time workers.

5. Think about the following news items and label each one as a positive or a normative statement. In the United States,
   a. The poor pay too much for housing.
   b. The number of farms has decreased over the last 50 years.
   c. The population in rural areas has remained constant over the past decade.

6. Explain how economists try to unscramble cause and effect. Explain why economists use the *ceteris paribus* assumption.

7. What is correlation? What approaches do economists use to try to sort out the cause-and-effect relationship that a correlation might indicate? Describe each of these approaches.

8. What is the *post hoc* fallacy? Which of the following statements are examples of the *post hoc* fallacy? Which statements confuse cause and effect?
   a. After a devastating hurricane, the government allocates millions of dollars to cleaning up the mess. Economic activity increases. So a hurricane causes an expansion.
   b. During a strong expansion, production increases, employment increases, and prices rise faster than normal. The cause of the strong expansion is the increase in employment.
   c. Automation eliminates some jobs and brings a recession.
   d. When the stock market plunges, a recession follows.

9. Pam, Pru, and Pat are deciding how they will celebrate the New Year. Pam prefers to go on a cruise, is happy to go to Hawaii, but does not want to go skiing. Pru prefers to go skiing, is happy to go to Hawaii, but does not want to go on a cruise. Pat prefers to go to Hawaii or to take a cruise but does not

want to go skiing. Their decision is to go to Hawaii. Is this decision rational? What is the opportunity cost of the trip to Hawaii for each of them? What is the benefit each gets?

10. Your school has decided to increase the intake of new students next year. What economic concepts would your school consider in reaching its decision? Would the school make its decision at the margin?

11. Describe how the standard of living, the cost of living, and unemployment vary over the business cycle.

12. Devastating rain brings extensive flooding to a nation's agricultural regions. Describe the effects of this event on the nation's standard of living.

Critical Thinking

13. Think about each of the following situations and explain how they affect incentives and might change the choices that people make.
    - **a.** Drought hits the Midwest.
    - **b.** The World Series begins tonight, and there is a thunderstorm warning in effect for the stadium.
    - **c.** The price of a personal computer falls to $50.
    - **d.** Political instability in the Middle East cuts world oil production and sends the price of gasoline to $2 a gallon.
    - **e.** Your school builds a new parking garage that increases the number of parking places available but doubles the price of parking on campus.
    - **f.** A math professor awards grades based on the percentage of questions answered correctly and an economics professor awards grades based on rank in class—the top 10 percent get As, the bottom 10 percent get Cs, and the rest of the class get Bs regardless of the percentage of questions answered correctly.

14. It is 1931, and close to one in five people is unable to find a job. Describe the effects of such a situation on the standard of living of a family. Compare and contrast this situation with that of today.

15. "Spider-Man" was the most successful movie of 2002, with box office receipts of more than $400 million. Creating a successful movie brings pleasure to millions, generates work for thousands, and makes a few people rich.
    - **a.** What contribution does a movie like "Spider-Man" make to coping with scarcity?
    - **b.** Does the decision to make a blockbuster movie mean that some other, more desirable activities get fewer resources than they deserve?
    - **c.** Was your answer to part **b** a positive or a normative answer? Explain.
    - **d.** Who decides whether a movie is going to be a blockbuster?
    - **e.** How do you think the creation of a blockbuster movie influences what, how, and for whom goods and services are produced?
    - **f.** What do you think are some of the marginal costs and marginal benefits that the producer of a movie faces?
    - **g.** Suppose that Tobey Maguire had been offered a bigger and better part in another movie and that to hire him for "Spider-Man," the producer had to double Tobey's pay. What incentives were changed? How might the changed incentives have changed the choices that people made?
    - **h.** How do you think the creation of a blockbuster movie influences the standard of living and the cost of living (i) in the nation as a whole and (ii) in the area in which the movie is shot?

Practice Online

Web Exercises

If you haven't already done so, take a few minutes to visit your Foundations Web site, sign in, and obtain your username and password. Browse the site and become familiar with its structure and content. You'll soon appreciate that this Web site is a very useful and powerful learning tool. For each chapter, you will find quizzes, e-text, e-study guide, interactive tutorials and graphics, and animations of your textbook figures. You will also find the links you need to work the Web exercises.

Use the links on your Foundations Web site to work the following exercises.

16. Visit some news Web sites and review today's economic news. Summarize a news article that deals with an economic issue that interests you. Say whether the story deals with a microeconomic or a macroeconomic issue.
17. Visit the Campaign for Tobacco-Free Kids. Obtain data on changes in state tobacco taxes and changes in state tobacco consumption.
    - **a.** Calculate the percentage change in tobacco taxes in each of the states for which you have data.
    - **b.** Make a graph that plots the percentage change in the tobacco tax on the x-axis and the percentage change in state tobacco consumption on the y-axis.
    - **c.** Describe the relationship between these two variables. (Look at pages 25, 26, and 27 if you need help with making and interpreting your graph.)
    - **d.** How would you expect a rise in the tobacco tax to influence the incentive for a young person to smoke cigarettes?
    - **e.** Do the data that you've obtained confirm what you expected or were you surprised by the data? Explain your answer.
    - **f.** What can you infer about cause and effect in the data on tobacco taxes and tobacco consumption?
    - **g.** What is the main obstacle to drawing a strong conclusion about the effect of tobacco taxes on tobacco consumption?
18. Visit the *Statistical Abstract of the United States* and obtain data on the levels of average annual pay and the percentage of persons with a bachelor's degree in each of the states.
    - **a.** Which state has the highest average pay, and which has the lowest?
    - **b.** Where in the ranking of average pay does your state stand?
    - **c.** Which state has the highest percentage of people with a bachelor's degree and which has the lowest?
    - **d.** Where in the ranking of people with a bachelor's degree does your state stand?
    - **e.** What do you think these numbers tell us about what, how, or for whom goods and services are produced?
    - **f.** What is the difficulty in using these numbers to determine whether education levels influence pay levels?
19. Visit the Inflation Calculator. Then make this choice: You can have $11 and pay the prices of 1800, or you can have $100 and pay the prices of 2000. Which do you prefer and why?
20. Visit the Federal Reserve and view the latest edition of the Beige Book. What are the recent changes in the standard of living and the cost of living in the United States and in your region?

APPENDIX: MAKING AND USING GRAPHS

When you have completed your study of this appendix, you will be able to

1. **Interpret a scatter diagram, a time-series graph, and a cross-section graph.**
2. **Interpret the graphs used in economic models.**
3. **Define and calculate slope.**
4. **Graph relationships among more than two variables.**

Basic Idea

A graph represents a quantity as a distance and enables us to visualize the relationship between two variables. To make a graph, we set two lines called *axes* perpendicular to each other, like those in Figure A1.1. The vertical line is called the y-axis, and the horizontal line is called the x-axis. The common zero point is called the *origin*. In Figure A1.1, the x-axis measures income in thousands of dollars per year. A movement to the right shows an increase in income, and a movement to the left shows a decrease in income. The y-axis represents expenditure, measured in thousands of dollars per year. To make a graph, we need a value of the variable measured on the x-axis and a corresponding value of the variable measured on the y-axis. For example, if income is $10,000 a year, expenditure is also $10,000 a year at point *A* in the graph. If income is $30,000 a year, expenditure is $25,000 a year at point *B* in the graph. Graphs like that in Figure A1.1 can be used to show any type of quantitative data on two variables.

FIGURE A1.1
Making a Graph

Practice Online

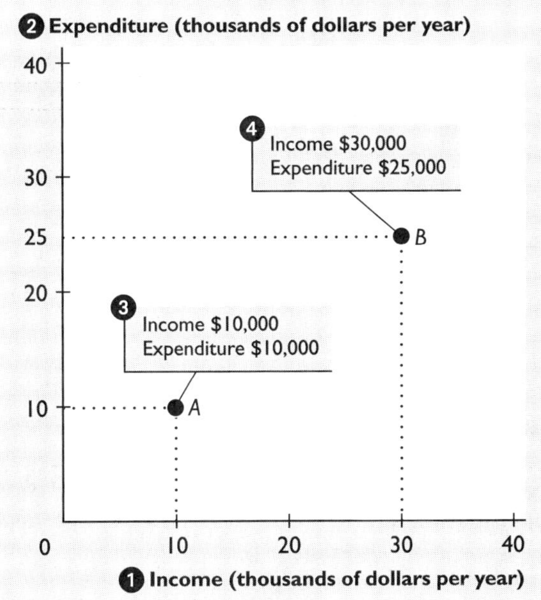

All graphs have axes that measure quantities as distances.

1. The horizontal axis (x-axis) measures income. A movement to the right shows an increase in income.
2. The vertical axis (y-axis) measures expenditure. A movement upward shows an increase in expenditure.
3. Point *A* shows that when income is $10,000 a year, expenditure is $10,000 a year.
4. Point *B* shows that when income is $30,000 a year, expenditure is $25,000 a year.

Interpreting Data Graphs

Scatter diagram
A graph of the value of one variable against the value of another variable.

A **scatter diagram** is a graph of the value of one variable against the value of another variable. It is used to reveal whether a relationship exists between two variables and to describe the relationship. Figure A1.2 shows two examples.

Figure A1.2(a) shows the relationship between expenditure and income. Each point shows expenditure per person and income per person in the United States in a given year from 1992 to 2002. The points are "scattered" within the graph. The label on each point shows its year. The point marked 96 shows that in 1996, income per person was $21,100 and expenditure per person was $20,100. This scatter diagram reveals that as income increases, expenditure also increases.

Figure A1.2(b) shows the relationship between the number of minutes of international phone calls made from the United States and the average price per minute. This scatter diagram reveals that as the price per minute falls, the number of minutes called increases.

Time-series graph
A graph that measures time on the *x*-axis and the variable or variables in which we are interested on the *y*-axis.

A **time-series graph** measures time (for example, months or years) on the *x*-axis and the variable or variables in which we are interested on the *y*-axis. Figure A1.2(c) shows an example. In this graph, time (on the *x*-axis) is measured in years, which run from 1972 to 2002. The variable that we are interested in is the U.S. unemployment rate, and it is measured on the *y*-axis.

A time-series graph conveys an enormous amount of information quickly and easily, as this example illustrates. It shows when the value is

1. High or low. When the line is a long way from the *x*-axis, the unemployment rate is high. When the line is close to the *x*-axis, the unemployment rate is low.
2. Rising or falling. When the line slopes upward, as in 1980, the unemployment rate is rising. When the line slopes downward, as in 1997, the unemployment rate is falling.
3. Rising or falling quickly and slowly. If the line is steep, then the unemployment rate is rising or falling quickly. If the line is not steep, the unemployment rate is rising or falling slowly. The unemployment rate rose quickly in 1982 and slowly in 1991. The unemployment rate fell quickly in 1984 and slowly in 1985.

Trend
A general tendency for the value of a variable to rise or fall.

A time-series graph also reveals whether the variable has a trend. A **trend** is a general tendency for the value of a variable to rise or fall. You can see that the unemployment rate had a general tendency to fall through the 1980s and 1990s. That is, although the unemployment rate fluctuated, it fell more than it rose.

With a time-series graph, we can compare different periods quickly. Figure A1.2(c) shows that the 1990s were different from the 1970s and 1980s. The unemployment rate fluctuated more violently during the 1970s and 1980s than it did in the 1990s. This graph conveys a wealth of information, and it does so in much less space than we have used to describe only some of its features.

Cross-section graph
A graph that shows the values of an economic variable for different groups in a population at a point in time.

A **cross-section graph** shows the values of an economic variable for different groups in a population at a point in time. Figure A1.2(d) is an example of a cross-section graph. It shows unemployment rates in seven major countries in 2002. This graph uses bars rather than dots and lines, and the length of each bar indicates a nation's unemployment rate. Figure A1.2(d) enables you to compare the unemployment rates in these seven countries. And you can do so much more quickly and clearly than by looking at a list of numbers.

FIGURE A1.2
Data Graphs

Practice Online

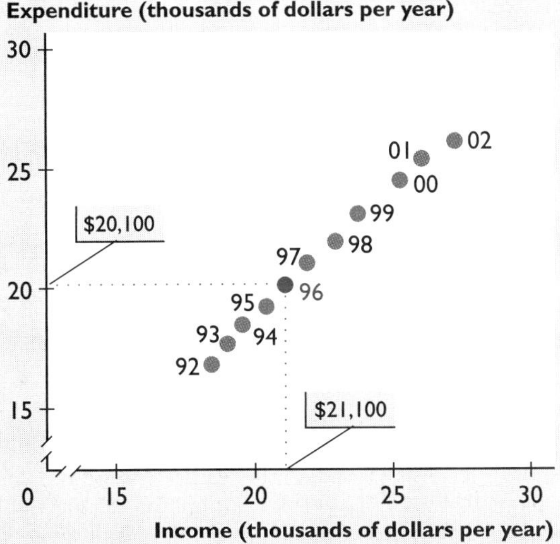

(a) Scatter Diagram: Expenditure and income

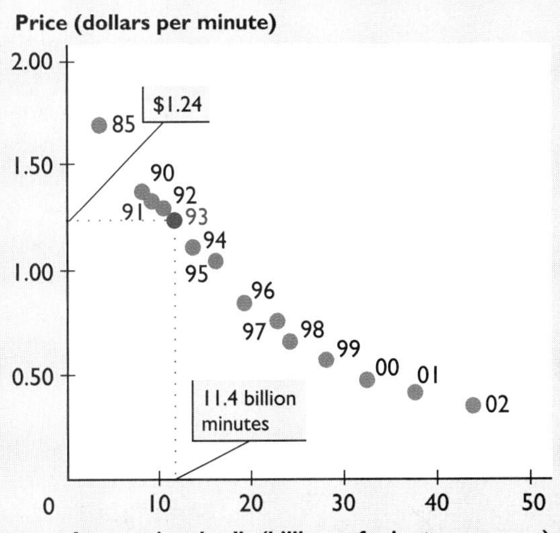

(b) Scatter Diagram: Price and quantity of calls

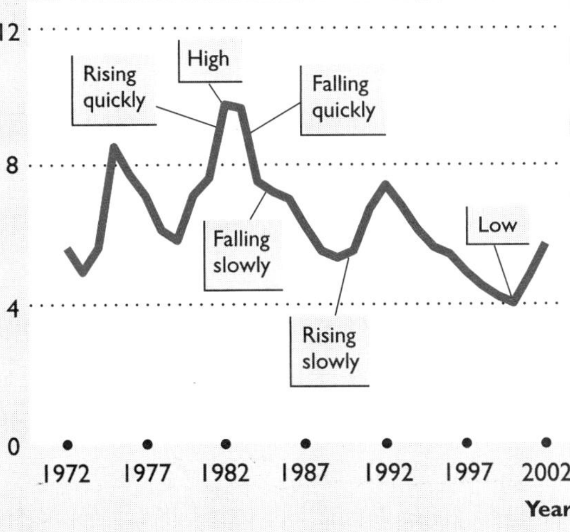

(c) Time Series: The U.S. unemployment rate

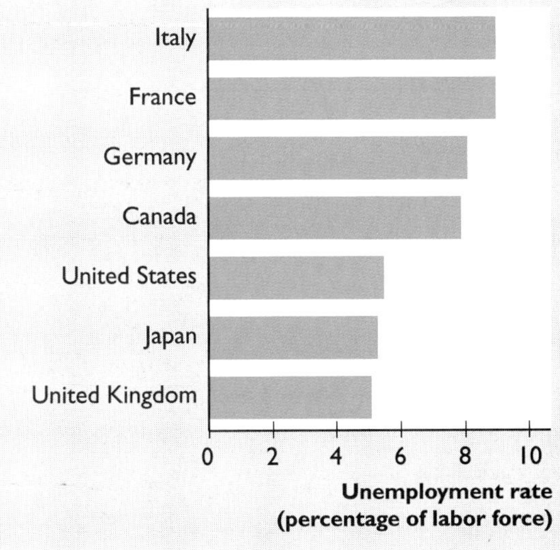

(d) Cross Section: Unemployment in seven countries

A scatter diagram reveals the relationship between two variables. In part (a), as income increases, expenditure increases. In part (b), as the price per minute falls, the number of minutes called increases.

A time-series graph plots the value of a variable on the *y*-axis against time on the *x*-axis. Part (c) plots the U.S. unemployment rate each year from 1972 to 2002. The graph shows when unemployment was high and low, when it increased and decreased, and when it changed quickly and slowly.

A cross-section graph shows the value of a variable across the members of a population. Part (d) shows the unemployment rate in each of seven major countries in 2002.

Interpreting Graphs Used in Economic Models

We use graphs to show the relationships among the variables in an economic model. An *economic model* is a simplified description of the economy or of a component of the economy such as a business or a household. An economic model consists of statements about economic behavior that can be expressed as equations or as curves in a graph. Economists use models to explore the effects of different policies or other influences on the economy in ways similar to those used to test model airplanes in wind tunnels and models of the climate.

Positive relationship or direct relationship
A relationship between two variables that move in the same direction.

Linear relationship
A relationship that graphs as a straight line.

Figure A1.3 shows graphs of the relationships between two variables that move in the same direction. Such a relationship is called a **positive relationship** or a **direct relationship**.

Part (a) shows a straight-line relationship, which is called a **linear relationship**. The distance traveled in 5 hours increases as the speed increases. For example, point *A* shows that 200 miles is traveled in 5 hours at a speed of 40 miles an hour. And point *B* shows that the distance traveled increases to 300 miles if the speed increases to 60 miles an hour.

Part (b) shows the relationship between distance sprinted and recovery time (the time it takes the heart rate to return to its normal resting rate). An upward-sloping curved line that starts out quite flat but then becomes steeper as we move along the curve away from the origin describes this relationship. The curve slopes upward and becomes steeper because the extra recovery time needed from sprinting another 100 yards increases. It takes less than 5 minutes to recover from sprinting 100 yards but more than 10 minutes to recover from sprinting 200 yards.

Part (c) shows the relationship between the number of problems worked by a student and the amount of study time per day. An upward-sloping curved line that starts out quite steep and becomes flatter as we move away from the origin

FIGURE A1.3
Positive (Direct) Relationships

Practice Online

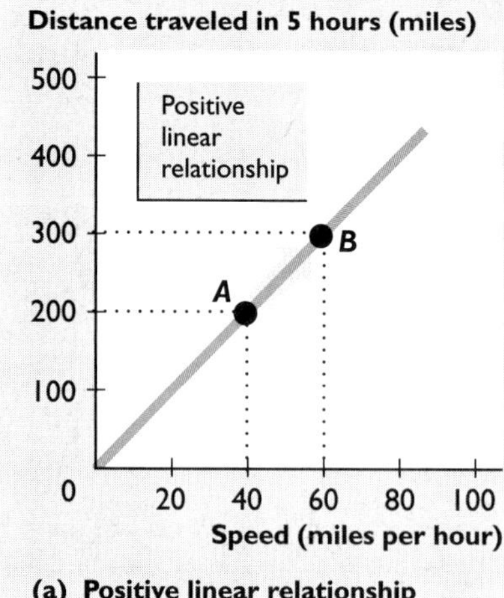

(a) Positive linear relationship

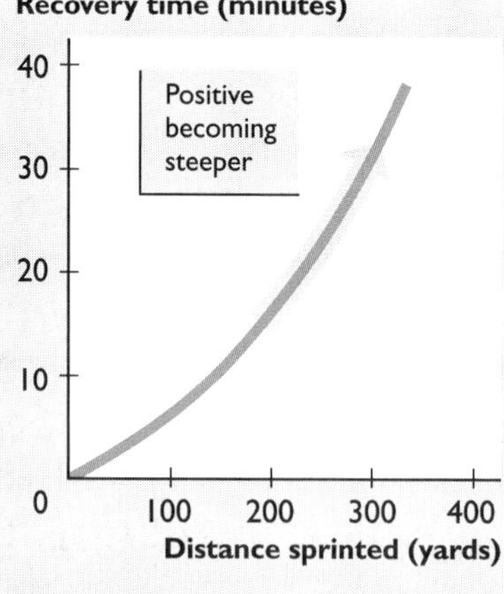

(b) Positive becoming steeper

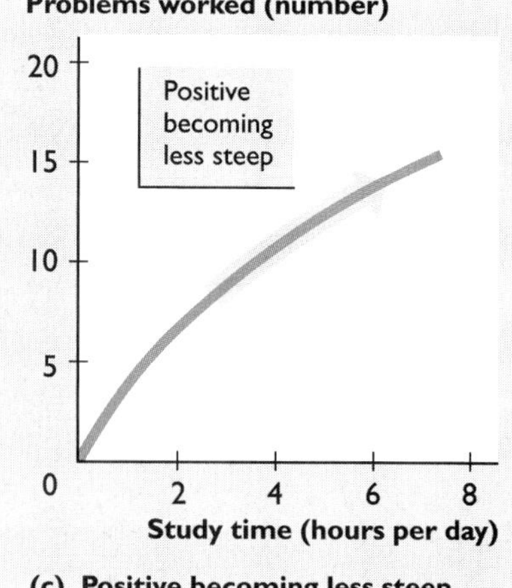

(c) Positive becoming less steep

Part (a) shows that as speed increases, the distance traveled increases along a straight line.

Part (b) shows that as the distance sprinted increases, recovery time increases along a curve that becomes steeper.

Part (c) shows that as study time increases, the number of problems worked increases along a curve that becomes less steep.

shows this relationship. Study time becomes less effective as you increase the hours worked per day and become more tired.

Figure A1.4 shows relationships between two variables that move in opposite directions. Such a relationship is called a **negative relationship** or an **inverse relationship**.

Negative relationship or inverse relationship
A relationship between two variables that move in opposite directions.

Part (a) shows the relationship between the number of hours for playing squash and the number of hours for playing tennis when the total number of hours available is five. One extra hour spent playing tennis means one hour less playing squash and vice versa. This relationship is negative and linear.

Part (b) shows the relationship between the cost per mile traveled and the length of a journey. The longer the journey, the lower is the cost per mile. But as the journey length increases, the cost per mile decreases, and the fall in the cost gets smaller. This feature of the relationship is shown by the fact that the curve slopes downward, starting out steep at a short journey length and then becoming flatter as the journey length increases. This relationship arises because some of the costs are fixed, such as auto insurance, and the fixed costs are spread over a longer journey.

Part (c) shows the relationship between the amount of leisure time and the number of problems worked by a student. Increasing leisure time produces an increasingly large reduction in the number of problems worked. This relationship is a negative one that starts out with a gentle slope at a small number of leisure hours and becomes steeper as the number of leisure hours increases. This relationship is a different view of the idea shown in Figure A1.3(c).

Many relationships in economic models have a maximum or a minimum. For example, firms try to make the largest possible profit and to produce at the lowest possible cost. Figure A1.5 shows relationships that have a maximum or a minimum.

FIGURE A1.4
Negative (Inverse) Relationships

Practice Online

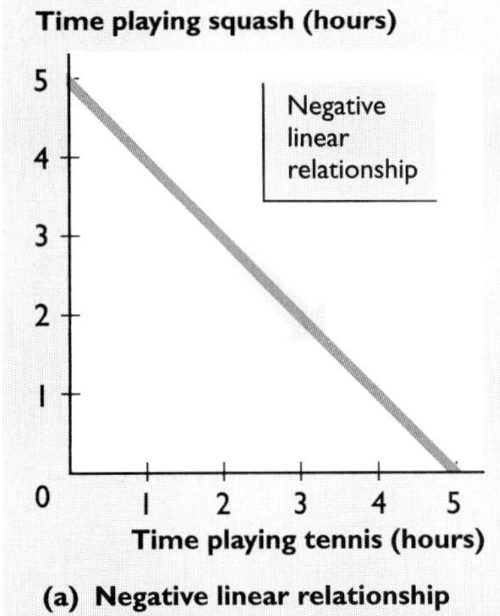

(a) Negative linear relationship

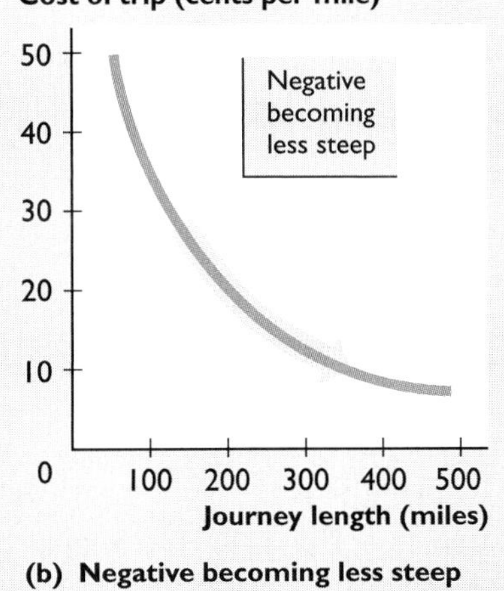

(b) Negative becoming less steep

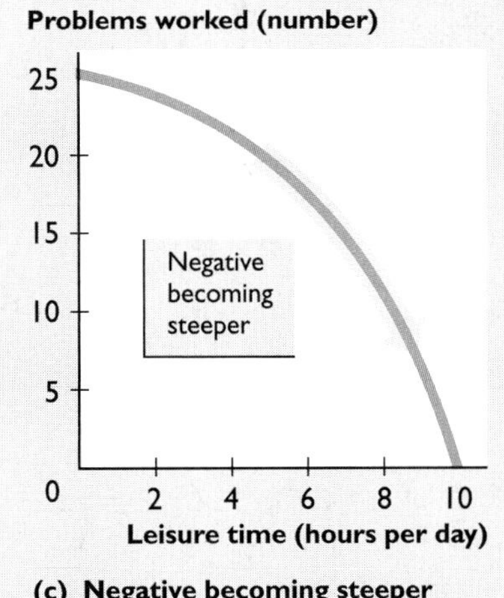

(c) Negative becoming steeper

Part (a) shows that as the time playing tennis increases, the time playing squash decreases along a straight line.

Part (b) shows that as the journey length increases, the cost of the trip falls along a curve that becomes less steep.

Part (c) shows that as leisure time increases, the number of problems worked decreases along a curve that becomes steeper.

FIGURE A1.5
Maximum and Minimum Points

Practice Online

In part (a), as the rainfall increases, the curve ❶ slopes upward as the yield per acre rises, ❷ is flat at point *A*, the maximum yield, and then ❸ slopes downward as the yield per acre falls.

In part (b), as the speed increases, the curve ❶ slopes downward as the cost per mile falls, ❷ is flat at the minimum point *B*, and then ❸ slopes upward as the cost per mile rises.

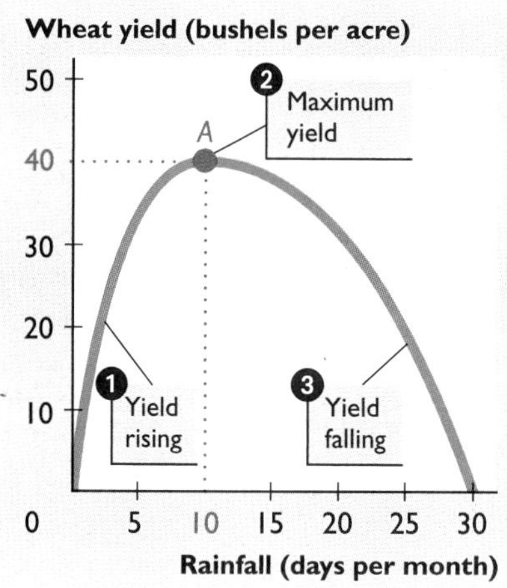

(a) Relationship with a maximum

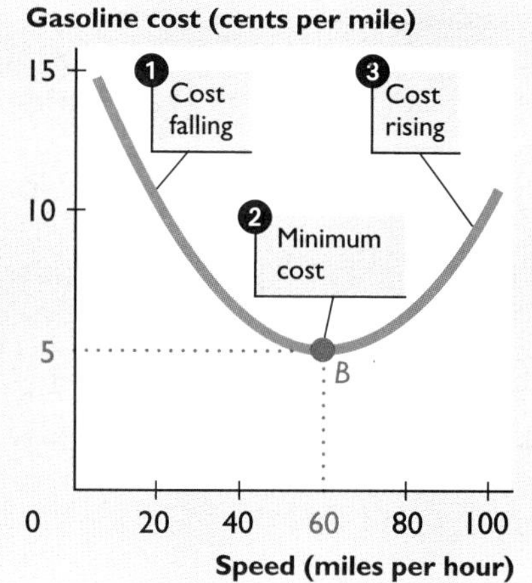

(b) Relationship with a minimum

Part (a) shows the relationship that starts out sloping upward, reaches a maximum, and then slopes downward. Part (b) shows a relationship that begins sloping downward, falls to a minimum, and then slopes upward.

Finally, there are many situations in which, no matter what happens to the value of one variable, the other variable remains constant. Sometimes we want to show two variables that are unrelated in a graph; Figure A1.6 shows two graphs in which the variables are independent.

FIGURE A1.6
Variables That Are Unrelated

Practice Online

In part (a), as the price of bananas increases, the student's grade in economics remains at 75 percent. These variables are unrelated, and the curve is horizontal.

In part (b), the vineyards of France produce 3 billion gallons of wine no matter what the rainfall in California is. These variables are unrelated, and the curve is vertical.

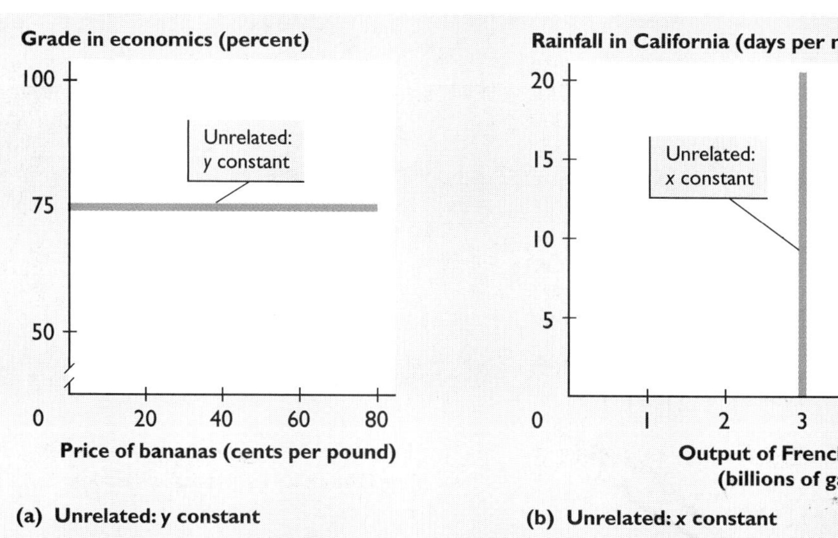

(a) Unrelated: y constant

(b) Unrelated: x constant

The Slope of a Relationship

We can measure the influence of one variable on another by the slope of the relationship. The **slope** of a relationship is the change in the value of the variable measured on the y-axis divided by the change in the value of the variable measured on the x-axis. We use the Greek letter Δ (delta) to represent "change in." So Δy means the change in the value of y, and Δx means the change in the value of x, and the slope of the relationship is

$$\Delta y \div \Delta x.$$

Slope
The change in the value of the variable measured on the y-axis divided by the change in the value of the variable measured on the x-axis.

If a large change in y is associated with a small change in x, the slope is large and the curve is steep. If a small change in y is associated with a large change in x, the slope is small and the curve is flat.

Figure A1.7 shows you how to calculate slope. The slope of a straight line is the same regardless of where on the line you calculate it—the slope is constant. In part (a), when x increases from 2 to 6, y increases from 3 to 6. The change in x is +4—that is, Δx is 4. The change in y is +3—that is, Δy is 3. The slope of that line is 3/4. In part (b), when x increases from 2 to 6, y *decreases* from 6 to 3. The change in y is *minus* 3—that is, Δy is –3. The change in x is plus 4—that is, Δx is 4. The slope of the curve is –3/4 . In part (c), we calculate the slope at a point on a curve. To do so, place a ruler on the graph so that it touches point A and no other point on the curve, then draw a straight line along the edge of the ruler. The slope of this straight line is the slope of the curve at point A. This slope is 3/4.

FIGURE A1.7
Calculating Slope

Practice Online

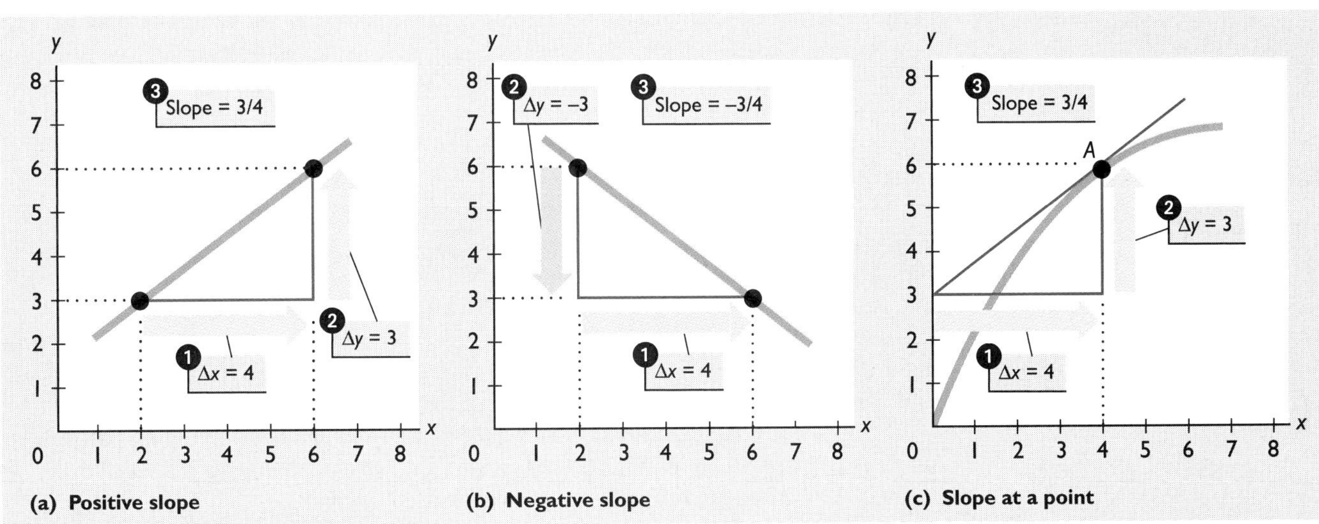

In part (a), ❶ when Δx is 4, ❷ Δy is 3, so ❸ the slope ($\Delta y/\Delta x$) is 3/4.

In part (b), ❶ when Δx is 4, ❷ Δy is –3, so ❸ the slope ($\Delta y/\Delta x$) is –3/4.

In part (c), the slope of the curve at point A equals the slope of the red line. ❶ When Δx is 4, ❷ Δy is 3, so ❸ the slope ($\Delta y/\Delta x$) is 3/4.

Relationships Among More Than Two Variables

We have seen that we can graph the relationship between two variables as a point formed by the x and y values. But most of the relationships in economics involve relationships among many variables, not just two. For example, the amount of ice cream consumed depends on the price of ice cream and the temperature. If ice cream is expensive and the temperature is low, people eat much less ice cream than when ice cream is inexpensive and the temperature is high. For any given price of ice cream, the quantity consumed varies with the temperature; for any given temperature, the quantity of ice cream consumed varies with its price.

Figure A1.8 shows a relationship among three variables. The table shows the number of gallons of ice cream consumed per day at various temperatures and ice cream prices. How can we graph these numbers?

To graph a relationship that involves more than two variables, we use the *ceteris paribus* assumption.

Ceteris Paribus

The Latin phrase *ceteris paribus* means "other things remaining the same." Every laboratory experiment is an attempt to create *ceteris paribus* and isolate the relationship of interest. We use the same method to make a graph.

Figure A1.8(a) shows an example. This graph shows what happens to the quantity of ice cream consumed when the price of ice cream varies while the temperature remains the same. The curve labeled 70°F shows the relationship between ice cream consumption and the price of ice cream if the temperature is 70°F. The numbers used to plot that curve are those in the first and fourth columns of the table in Figure A1.8. For example, if the temperature is 70°F, 10 gallons are consumed when the price is 60¢ a scoop and 18 gallons are consumed when the price is 30¢ a scoop. The curve labeled 90°F shows consumption as the price varies if the temperature is 90°F.

We can also show the relationship between ice cream consumption and temperature while the price of ice cream remains constant, as shown in Figure A1.8(b). The curve labeled 60¢ shows how the consumption of ice cream varies with the temperature when the price of ice cream is 60¢ a scoop, and a second curve shows the relationship when the price of ice cream is 15¢ a scoop. For example, at 60¢ a scoop, 10 gallons are consumed when the temperature is 70°F and 20 gallons when the temperature is 90°F.

Figure A1.8(c) shows the combinations of temperature and price that result in a constant consumption of ice cream. One curve shows the combination that results in 10 gallons a day being consumed, and the other shows the combination that results in 7 gallons a day being consumed. A high price and a high temperature lead to the same consumption as a lower price and a lower temperature. For example, 10 gallons of ice cream are consumed at 90°F and 90¢ a scoop, at 70°F and 60¢ a scoop, and at 50°F and 45¢ a scoop.

With what you've learned about graphs in this Appendix, you can move forward with your study of economics. There are no graphs in this textbook that are more complicated than the ones you've studied here.

FIGURE A1.8
Graphing a Relationship Among Three Variables

Practice Online

Price (cents per scoop)	Ice cream consumption (gallons per day)			
	30°F	50°F	70°F	90°F
15	12	18	25	50
30	10	12	18	37
45	7	10	13	27
60	5	7	10	20
75	3	5	7	14
90	2	3	5	10
105	1	2	3	6

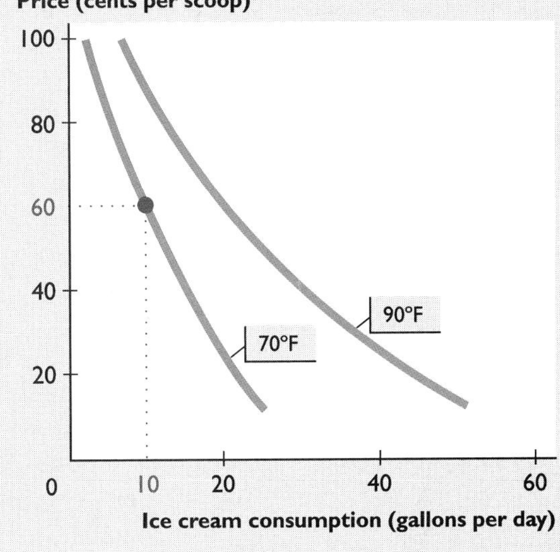

(a) Price and consumption at a given temperature

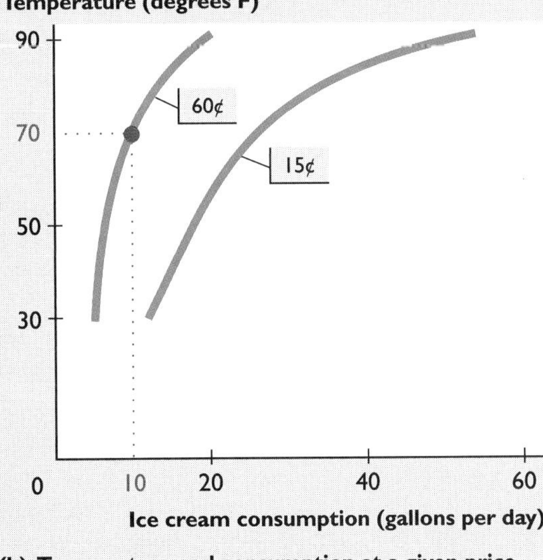

(b) Temperature and consumption at a given price

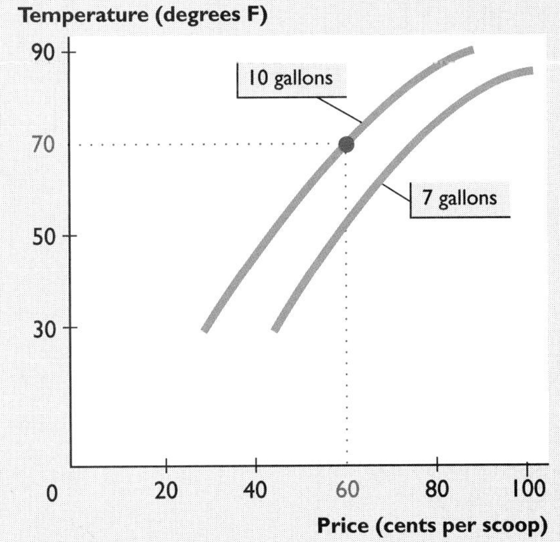

(c) Temperature and price at a given consumption

The table tells us how many gallons of ice cream are consumed each day at different prices and different temperatures. For example, if the price is 60¢ a scoop and the temperature is 70°F, 10 gallons of ice cream are consumed. This set of values is highlighted in the table and each part of the figure.

Part (a) shows the relationship between price and consumption when temperature is held constant. One curve holds temperature at 90°F, and the other at 70°F.

Part (b) shows the relationship between temperature and consumption when price is held constant. One curve holds the price at 60¢ a scoop, and the other at 15¢ a scoop.

Part (c) shows the relationship between temperature and price when consumption is held constant. One curve holds consumption at 10 gallons, and the other at 7 gallons.

APPENDIX CHECKPOINT

Study Guide **pp. 14–19**

Practice Online A1.1

	A	B	C	D
1	1992	43	4	23
2	1993	47	5	24
3	1994	56	6	25
4	1995	57	11	25
5	1996	57	17	27
6	1997	55	26	29
7	1998	56	32	30
8	1999	58	37	31
9	2000	62	43	32
10	2001	66	48	33
11	2002	69	53	34

Exercises

The spreadsheet provides data on the U.S. economy: Column A is the year; the other columns are actual and projected expenditures per person in dollars per year on recorded music (column B), Internet services (column C), and movies in theaters (column D). Use this spreadsheet to answer exercises 1, 2, 3, 4, and 5.

1. Draw a scatter diagram to show the relationship between expenditure on recorded music and expenditure on Internet services. Describe the relationship.
2. Draw a scatter diagram to show the relationship between expenditure on Internet services and expenditure on movies in theaters. Describe the relationship.
3. Draw a scatter diagram to show the relationship between expenditure on recorded music and expenditure on movies in theaters. Describe the relationship.
4. Draw a time-series graph of expenditure on Internet services. Say in which year or years (a) expenditure was highest, (b) expenditure was lowest, (c) expenditure increased the most, and (d) expenditure increased the least. Also, say whether the data show a trend and describe its direction.
5. Draw a time-series graph of expenditure on recorded music. Say in which year or years (a) expenditure was highest, (b) expenditure was lowest, (c) expenditure increased the most, and (d) expenditure increased the least. Also, say whether the data show a trend and describe its direction.
6. Draw a graph to show the relationship between the two variables x and y:

x	0	1	2	3	4	5	6	7	8
y	0	1	4	9	16	25	36	49	64

   a. Is the relationship positive or negative?
   b. Calculate the slope of the relationship between x and y when x equals 2 and when x equals 4.
   c. How does the slope of the relationship change as the value of x increases?
   d. Think of some economic relationships that might be similar to this one.

7. Draw a graph to show the relationship between the two variables x and y:

x	0	1	2	3	4	5	6	7	8
y	60	49	39	30	22	15	9	4	0

   a. Is the relationship positive or negative?
   b. Calculate the slope of the relationship between x and y when x equals 2 and when x equals 4.
   c. How does the slope of the relationship change as the value of x increases?
   d. Think of some economic relationships that might be similar to this one.

8. The table gives the price of an umbrella, rainfall, and the number of umbrellas purchased. Draw graphs to show the relationship between:
   a. The price and the number of umbrellas purchased, holding rainfall constant.
   b. The number of umbrellas purchased and rainfall, holding the price constant.
   c. Rainfall and the price, holding the number of umbrellas purchased constant.

Price (dollars per umbrella)	Umbrellas (number per day)		
	0	1	2
	(inches per day)		
10	7	8	12
20	4	7	8
30	2	4	7
40	1	2	4

The U.S. and Global Economies

CHAPTER 2

CHAPTER CHECKLIST

When you have completed your study of this chapter, you will be able to

1. **Describe what, how, and for whom goods and services are produced in the United States.**
2. **Use the circular flow model to provide a picture of how households, firms, and governments interact.**
3. **Describe the macroeconomic performance—standard of living, cost of living, and economic fluctuations—of the United States and other economies.**

Economic activity arises from scarcity—the available resources are insufficient to meet all our wants. Macroeconomics studies the aggregate (or total) effects on the national economy and the global economy of the choices that individuals, businesses, and governments make. The three big issues that macroeconomics tries to understand are what determines the standard of living, the cost of living, and economic fluctuations—recessions and expansions.

Most of your macroeconomics course is about theories that *explain* and in some cases enable economists to make *predictions* about macroeconomic performance. But in this chapter, we are going to *describe* the main features of the U.S. and global economies. You will learn about the resources available and how they are used, the current levels and changes in the standard of living and the cost of living, and economic fluctuations in the United States and the world as a whole.

2.1 WHAT, HOW, AND FOR WHOM?

Walk around a shopping mall and pay close attention to the range of goods and services that are being offered for sale. Go inside some of the shops and look at the labels to see where various items are manufactured. The next time you travel on an interstate highway, look at the large trucks and pay attention to the names and products printed on their sides and the places in which the trucks are registered. Open the Yellow Pages and flip through a few sections. Notice the huge range of goods and services that businesses are offering.

You've just done a sampling of *what* goods and services are produced and consumed in the United States today.

What Do We Produce?

In macroeconomics, we divide the vast array of goods and services produced into four large groups:

- Consumption goods and services
- Investment goods
- Government goods and services
- Export goods and services

Consumption Goods and Services

Consumption goods and services
Goods and services that are bought by individuals and used to provide personal enjoyment and contribute to a person's standard of living.

Consumption goods and services are items that are bought by individuals and used to provide personal enjoyment and contribute to a person's standard of living. They include items such as housing, SUVs, popcorn and soda, movies and chocolate bars, microwave ovens and inline skates, and dental and dry cleaning services.

Investment Goods

Investment goods
Goods that are bought by businesses to increase their productive resources.

Investment goods are goods that are bought by businesses to increase their productive resources. They include items such as auto assembly lines and shopping malls, airplanes, and oil tankers.

Government Goods and Services

Government goods and services
Goods and services that are bought by governments.

Government goods and services are items that are bought by governments. Governments purchase missiles and weapons systems, travel services, Internet services, police protection, roads, and paper and paper clips.

Export Goods and Services

Export goods and services
Goods and services produced in one country and sold in other countries.

Export goods and services are items produced in one country and sold in other countries. U.S. export goods include the airplanes produced by Boeing that Singapore Airlines buys and the computers produced by Dell that Europeans buy.

Figure 2.1 provides a snapshot of the division of total production in the United States in 2002 into these four groups. You can see that consumption goods and services have the largest share at 61 percent of the total. Investment goods accounts for 13 percent of total production. Goods and services bought by governments take 17 percent of the total, and 9 percent is exported.

FIGURE 2.1
What We Produce

Practice Online

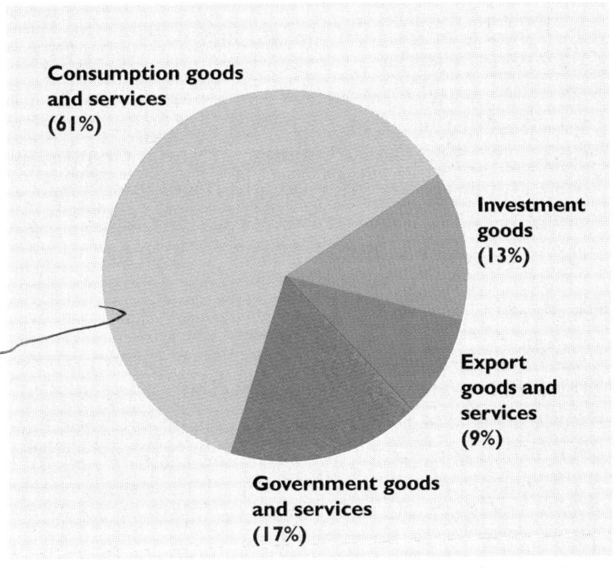

SOURCE: Bureau of Economic Analysis.

In 2002, consumption goods and services accounted for 61 percent of total production. Investment goods accounted for 13 percent, government goods and services accounted for 17 percent, and exports accounted for 9 percent of total production.

How Do We Produce?

Goods and services are produced by using productive resources. Economists call the productive resources **factors of production**. Factors of production are grouped into four categories:

- Land
- Labor
- Capital
- Entrepreneurship

Factors of production
The productive resources used to produce goods and services—land, labor, capital, and entrepreneurship.

Land

In economics, **land** includes all the "gifts of nature" that we use to produce goods and services. Land is what, in everyday language, we call *natural resources*. It includes land in the everyday sense, minerals, energy, water, and air, and wild plants, animals, birds, and fish. Some of these resources are renewable, and some are nonrenewable. The U.S. Geological Survey maintains a national inventory of the quantity and quality of natural resources and monitors changes to that inventory.

Land
The "gifts of nature," or *natural resources*, that we use to produce goods and services.

Labor

Labor is the work time and work effort that people devote to producing goods and services. It includes the physical and mental efforts of all the people who work on farms and construction sites and in factories, shops, and offices. The Census Bureau and Bureau of Labor Statistics measure the nation's labor force every month. In the United States today, 144 million people have jobs or are available for work and they provide about 234 billion hours of labor a year.

Labor
The work time and work effort that people devote to producing goods and services.

The quantity of labor increases as the adult population increases. The quantity of labor also increases if a larger percentage of the population takes jobs. During the past 50 years, a larger proportion of women have taken paid work and this trend has increased the quantity of labor.

Human capital
The knowledge and skill that people obtain from education, on-the-job training, and work experience.

The quality of labor depends on how skilled people are. Economists use a special name for human skill: human capital. **Human capital** is the knowledge and skill that people obtain from education, on-the-job training, and work experience. You are building your own human capital right now as you work on your economics course and other subjects. And your human capital will continue to grow when you get a full-time job and become better at it. Human capital improves the *quality* of labor. Today, more than 80 percent of the U.S. population has completed high school and 25 percent has a college or university degree.

Capital

In everyday language, we talk about money, stocks, and bonds as being capital. These items are *financial capital*, and they are not productive resources. They enable people to provide businesses with financial resources, but they are *not* used to produce goods and services. They are not capital.

Capital
Tools, instruments, machines, buildings, and other constructions that have been produced in the past and that businesses now use to produce goods and services.

Capital consists of the tools, instruments, machines, buildings, and other constructions that have been produced in the past and that businesses now use to produce goods and services. Capital includes hammers and screwdrivers, computers, auto assembly lines, office towers and warehouses, dams and power plants, airports and airplanes, shirt factories, and cookie shops. The Bureau of Economic Analysis in the U.S. Department of Commerce keeps track of the total value of capital, which grows over time. In the United States today, it is around $20 trillion.

Eye on the Past

Changes in Human Capital

Human capital in the United States has expanded during the past 90 years. The number of years of schooling is one measure of human capital. The figure shows the growth of human capital in the United States over the past century using this measure. In 1910, some 25 percent of the population had less than five years of elementary school and fewer than 3 percent had a college or university degree. The number of high school and college graduates has increased steadily over the past 90 years.

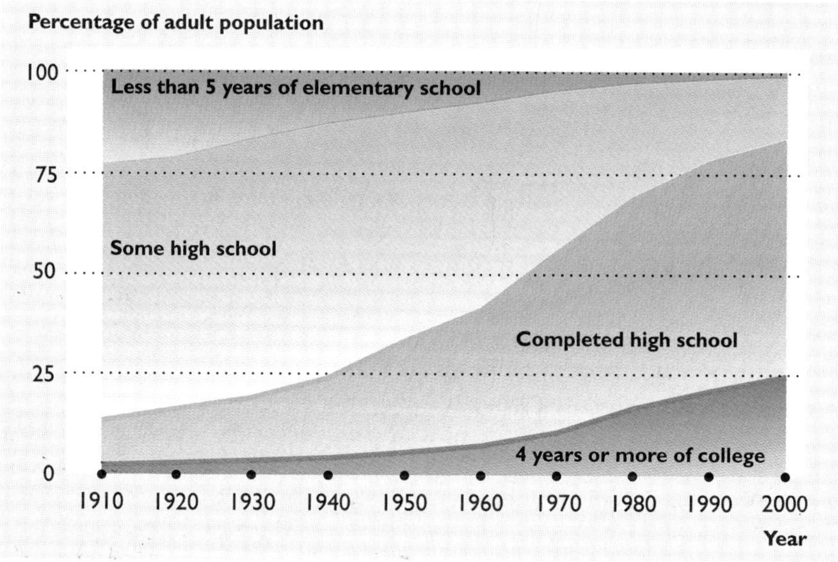

SOURCE: U.S. Census Bureau, *Statistical Abstract of the United States*, 2002.

Entrepreneurship

Entrepreneurship is the human resource that organizes labor, land, and capital. Entrepreneurs come up with new ideas about what and how to produce, make business decisions, and bear the risks that arise from these decisions.

The quantity of entrepreneurship is hard to describe or measure. At some periods, there appears to be a great deal of imaginative entrepreneurship around. People such as Sam Walton, who created Wal-Mart, one of the world's largest retailers; Bill Gates, who founded the Microsoft empire; and Michael Dell, who established Dell Computers, are examples of extraordinary entrepreneurial talent. But these highly visible entrepreneurs are just the tip of an iceberg that consists of hundreds of thousands of people who run businesses, large and small.

Entrepreneurship
The human resource that organizes labor, land, and capital.

For Whom Do We Produce?

Who gets the goods and services that are produced depends on the incomes that people earn and the goods and services that they choose to buy. A large income enables a person to buy large quantities of goods and services. A small income leaves a person with few options and small quantities of goods and services.

People earn their incomes by selling the services of the factors of production they own. **Rent** is paid for the use of land, **wages** are paid for the services of labor, **interest** is paid for the use of capital, and entrepreneurs receive a **profit** (or incur a **loss**) for running their businesses.

Which factor of production in the United States earns more income: labor or capital? Figure 2.2 provides the answer. The figure shows the **functional distribution of income**, which is the distribution of income among the factors of production. Labor earns most of the income: 72 percent of total income in 2002. Capital income—corporate income and net interest income—was 17 percent in 2002. The proprietors of businesses, whose earnings are a mixture of labor and capital income, earned 9 percent of total income in 2002. Personal rental income was 2 percent in 2002. These percentages remain remarkably constant over time.

Rent
Income paid for the use of land.

Wages
Income paid for the services of labor.

Interest
Income paid for the use of capital.

Profit (or loss)
Income earned by an entrepreneur for running a business.

Functional distribution of income
The distribution of income among the factors of production.

FIGURE 2.2
The Functional Distribution of Income in the United States

Practice Online

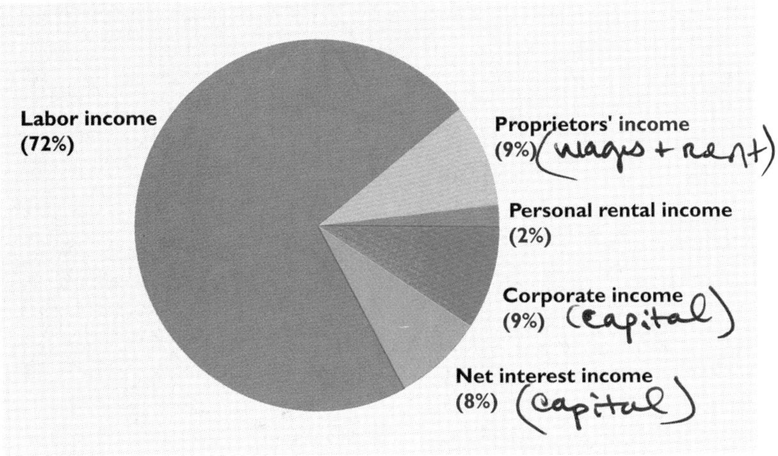

SOURCE: Bureau of Economic Analysis.

Incomes determine who consumes the goods and services produced. In 2002, labor income was 72 percent of total income, capital income (corporate income and net interest income) was 17 percent, and proprietors' income, which includes both wages and rent, was 9 percent. Personal rental income was 2 percent of the total.

Personal distribution of income
The distribution of income among households.

Figure 2.3 shows the **personal distribution of income**, which is the distribution of income among households. Incomes are shown in five groups, each of which represents 20 percent of the population. If incomes were equal, each 20 percent group would earn 20 percent of total income. You know that incomes are unequal, and the figure provides a measure of just how unequal they are.

The poorest 20 percent of households receive only 5 percent of total income. Servers at McDonald's, who average around $6.50 an hour; checkout clerks, gas station attendants, and textile and leather workers all of whom earn less than $10 an hour are in this group. The average income of this group in 2001 was about $10,000.

The second poorest 20 percent receives about 10 percent of total income. The income of this group in 2001 was about $25,000.

The middle 20 percent receive 16 percent of total income. The income of this group in 2001 was about $43,000. All three of these groups—the poorest 60 percent of households receive only 31 percent of total income.

The second richest 20 percent receives 23 percent of total income. The average income in this group in 2001 was about $67,000, and the highest income of this group was $83,500. So 80 percent of households receive less than $83,500 a year.

The richest 20 percent of households receive 50 percent of total income. The average income of this group in 2001 was $146,000. But the group includes people who receive very high incomes like Tiger Woods, who won several million dollars in prize money and received substantially more than this amount in endorsements, and Alex Rodriguez who received a salary of $22 million in 2002.

So the 20 percent of the population with the highest incomes get half of the goods and services produced. The other 80 percent share the remaining half.

FIGURE 2.3
The Personal Distribution of Income in the United States

Practice Online

In 2001, the richest 20 percent of the population received 47 percent of total income. The poorest 20 percent received only 5 percent of total income.

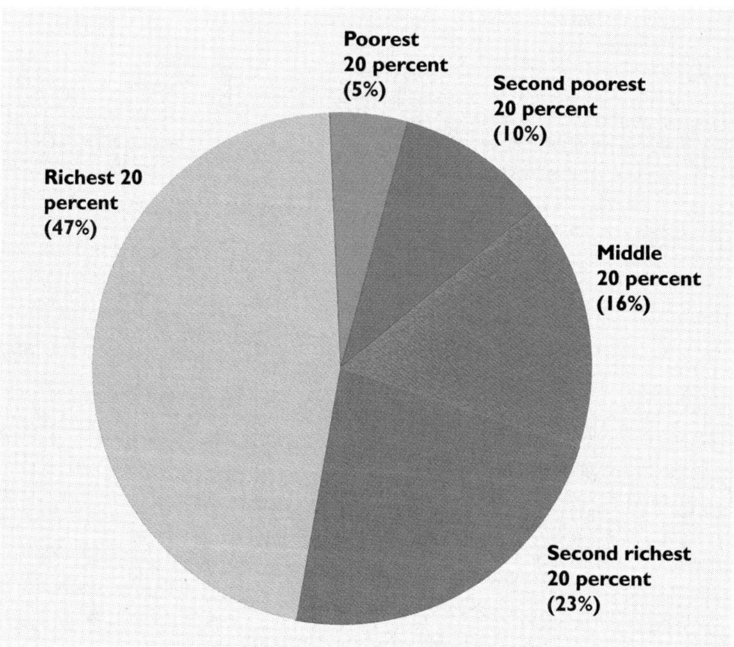

SOURCE: U.S. Census Bureau, *Money Income in the United States: 2001*, Current Population Reports P60-218, 2002.

CHECKPOINT 2.1

1 Describe what, how, and for whom goods and services are produced in the United States.

Study Guide pp. 24–26

Practice Online 2.1

Practice Problems 2.1

1. Name the four broad categories of goods and services that we use in macroeconomics, provide an example of each (different from those in the chapter), and say what percentage of total production each accounted for in 2002.
2. Name the four factors of production and the incomes they earn.
3. Distinguish between the functional distribution of income and the personal distribution of income.
4. In the United States, which factor of production earns the largest share of income and what percentage does it earn?

Exercises 2.1

1. What is the distinction between consumption goods and services and investment goods? Which of them brings an increase in productive resources?
2. Describe the changes that have occurred in the education levels of the U.S. labor force during the last few decades.
3. If everyone were to consume an equal quantity of goods and services, what percentage of total income would the poorest 20 percent of individuals have to receive from higher-income groups? What percentage would the second poorest 20 percent have to receive?
4. Compare the percentage of total U.S. income that labor earns with the percentage earned by all the other factors of production combined.

Solutions to Practice Problems 2.1

1. The four categories are consumption goods and services, investment goods, government goods and services, and export goods and services. An example of a consumption service is a haircut, of an investment good is an oil rig, of a government service is police protection, and of an export good is a computer chip sold to Ireland. Of total production, consumption goods and services are 61 percent; investment goods are 13 percent; government goods and services are 17 percent; and export goods and services are 9 percent.
2. The factors of production are land, labor, capital, and entrepreneurship. Land earns rent; labor earns wages; capital earns interest; and entrepreneurship earns profit or incurs a loss.
3. The functional distribution of income shows the percentage of total income received by each factor of production. The personal distribution of income shows the percentage of total income received by households.
4. Labor is the factor of production that earns the largest share of income in the United States. In 2002, labor earned 72 percent of total income.

2.2 CIRCULAR FLOWS

Circular flow model
A model of the economy that shows the circular flow of expenditures and incomes that result from decision makers' choices, and the way those choices interact to determine what, how, and for whom goods and services are produced.

We can organize the data you've just studied using the **circular flow model**—a model of the economy that shows the circular flow of expenditures and incomes that result from decision makers' choices and the way those choices interact to determine what, how, and for whom goods and services are produced. Figure 2.4 shows the circular flow model.

Households and Firms

Households
Individuals or groups of people living together.

Firms
The institutions that organize the production of goods and services.

Households are individuals or groups of people living together. The 109 million households in the United States own the factors of production—land, labor, capital, and entrepreneurship—and choose the quantities of these resources to provide to firms. Households also choose the quantities of goods and services to buy.

Firms are the institutions that organize the production of goods and services. The 20 million firms in the United States choose the quantities of the factors of production to hire and the quantities of goods and services to produce.

Markets

Households choose the quantities of the factors of production to provide to firms, and firms choose the quantities of the services of the factors of production to hire. Households choose the quantities of goods and services to buy, and firms choose the quantities of goods and services to produce. How are these choices coordinated and made compatible? The answer is: by markets.

Market
Any arrangement that brings buyers and sellers together and enables them to get information and do business with each other.

A **market** is any arrangement that brings buyers and sellers together and enables them to get information and do business with each other. An example is the market in which oil is bought and sold—the world oil market. The world oil market is not a place. It is the network of oil producers, oil users, wholesalers, and brokers who buy and sell oil. In the world oil market, decision makers do not meet physically. They make deals by telephone, fax, and the Internet.

Goods markets
Markets in which goods and services are bought and sold.

Factor markets
Markets in which factors of production are bought and sold.

Figure 2.4 identifies two types of markets: goods markets and factor markets. **Goods markets** are markets in which goods and services are bought and sold. **Factor markets** are markets in which factors of production are bought and sold.

Real Flows and Money Flows

When households choose the quantities of land, labor, capital, and entrepreneurship to offer in factor markets, they respond to the incomes they receive—rent for land, wages for labor, interest for capital, and profit for entrepreneurship. When firms choose the quantities of factors to hire, they respond to the rent, wages, interest, and profits they must pay to households.

Similarly, when firms choose the quantities of goods and services to produce and offer for sale in goods markets, they respond to the amounts that they receive from the expenditures that households make. And when households choose the quantities of goods and services to buy, they respond to the amounts they must pay to firms.

Figure 2.4 shows the flows that result from these choices made by households and firms. The real flows are shown in orange. These are the flows of the factors of production that go from households through factor markets to firms and the goods and services that go from firms through goods markets to households. The money flows go in the opposite direction. These flows are the payments made in exchange for factors of production (blue flow) and expenditures on goods and services (red flow).

Lying behind these real flows and money flows are millions of individual choices about what to consume, what to produce, and how to produce. These choices result in buying plans by households and selling plans by firms in goods markets. And the choices result in selling plans by households and buying plans by firms in factor markets. When these buying plans and selling plans are carried out, they determine the prices that people pay and the incomes they earn and so determine for whom goods and services are produced. You'll learn in Chapter 4 how markets coordinate the buying plans and selling plans of households and firms and make them compatible.

Firms produce most of the goods and services that we consume. But governments provide some of the services that we enjoy. And governments play a big role in modifying for whom goods and services are produced by changing the distribution of income. So we're now going to look at the role of governments in the U.S. economy and add them to the circular flow model.

FIGURE 2.4
The Circular Flow Model

Practice Online

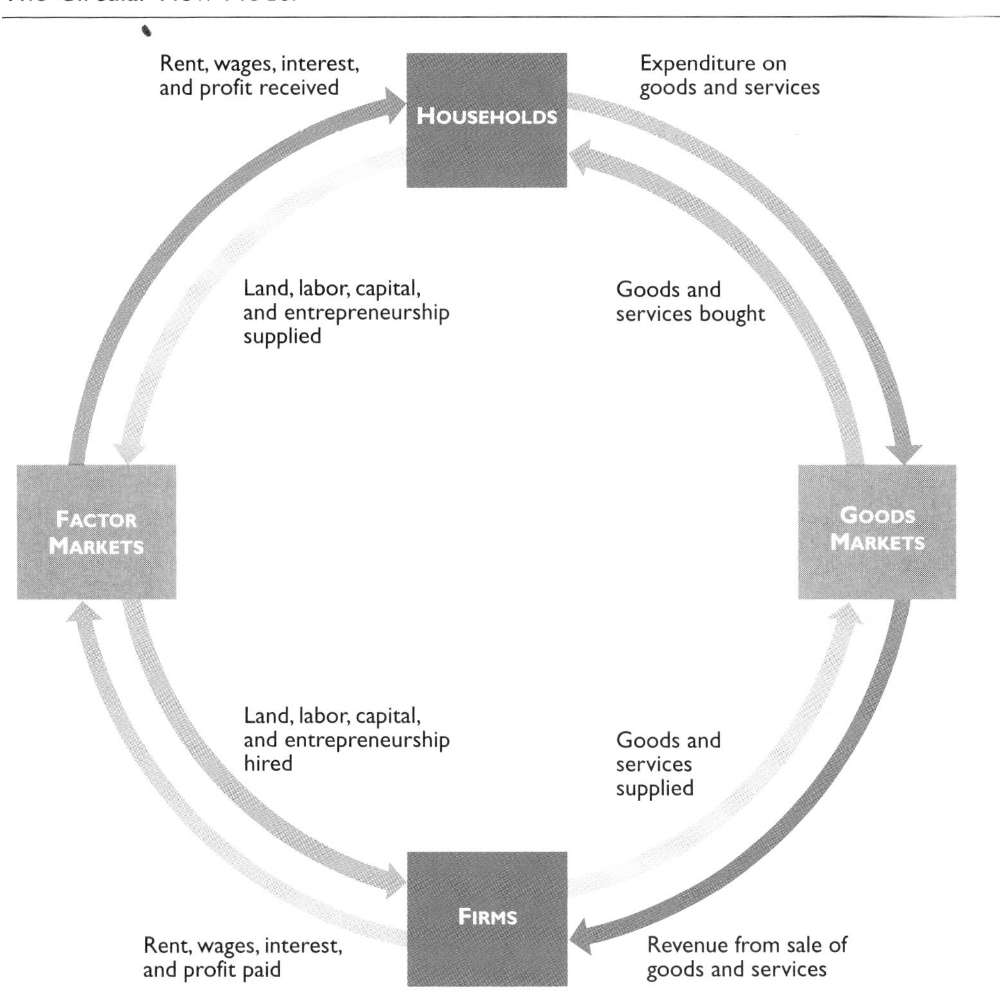

The orange flows are the factors of production that go from households through factor markets to firms and the goods and services that go from firms through goods markets to households.

The blue flow is the incomes earned by the factors of production and the red flow is the expenditures on goods and services.

The choices that generate these flows determine what, how, and for whom goods and services are produced.

Governments

More than 86,000 organizations operate as governments in the United States. Some are tiny like the Yuma, Arizona, school district and some are enormous like the U.S. federal government. We divide governments into two levels:

- Federal government
- State and local government

Federal Government

The federal government's major expenditures are to provide

1. Public goods and services
2. Social security and welfare payments
3. Transfers to state and local governments

The goods and services provided by the federal government include the legal system, which defines property rights and enforces contracts, and national defense. Social security and welfare benefits, which include income for retired seniors and programs such as Medicare and Medicaid, are transfers from the federal government to households. Transfers to state and local governments are payments designed to provide more equality across the states and regions.

The federal government finances its expenditures by collecting a variety of taxes. The main taxes paid to the federal government are

1. Personal income taxes
2. Corporate (business) income taxes
3. Social security taxes

In 2002, the federal government spent and raised in taxes more than $2 trillion—about 20 percent of the total value of all the goods and services produced in the United States in that year.

State and Local Government

The state and local governments' major expenditures are to provide

1. Goods and services
2. Welfare benefits

The goods and services provided by state and local governments include the state courts and law enforcement authorities, schools, garbage collection and disposal, water supplies, roads, and sewage management. Welfare benefits provided by state governments include unemployment benefits and other aid to low-income families.

State and local governments finance these expenditures by collecting taxes and receiving transfers from the federal government. The main taxes paid to state and local governments are

1. Sales taxes
2. Property taxes
3. State income taxes

In 2002, state and local governments spent more than $1.3 trillion—about 13 percent of the total value of all the goods and services produced in the United States in that year.

Governments in the Circular Flow

Figure 2.5 adds governments to the circular flow model. As you study this figure, first notice that the outer circle is the same as Figure 2.4. In addition to these flows, governments buy goods and services from firms. The red arrows that run from the governments through the goods markets to firms show this expenditure.

Households and firms pay taxes to governments. The green arrows running directly from households and firms to governments show these flows. Also, governments make money payments to households and firms. The green arrows running directly from governments to households and firms show these flows. Taxes and transfers are direct transactions with governments and do not go through the goods markets and factor markets.

Not part of the circular flow and not visible in Figure 2.5, governments provide the legal framework within which all transactions occur. For example, they operate the courts and legal system that enable contracts to be written and enforced.

FIGURE 2.5

Governments in the Circular Flow

Practice Online

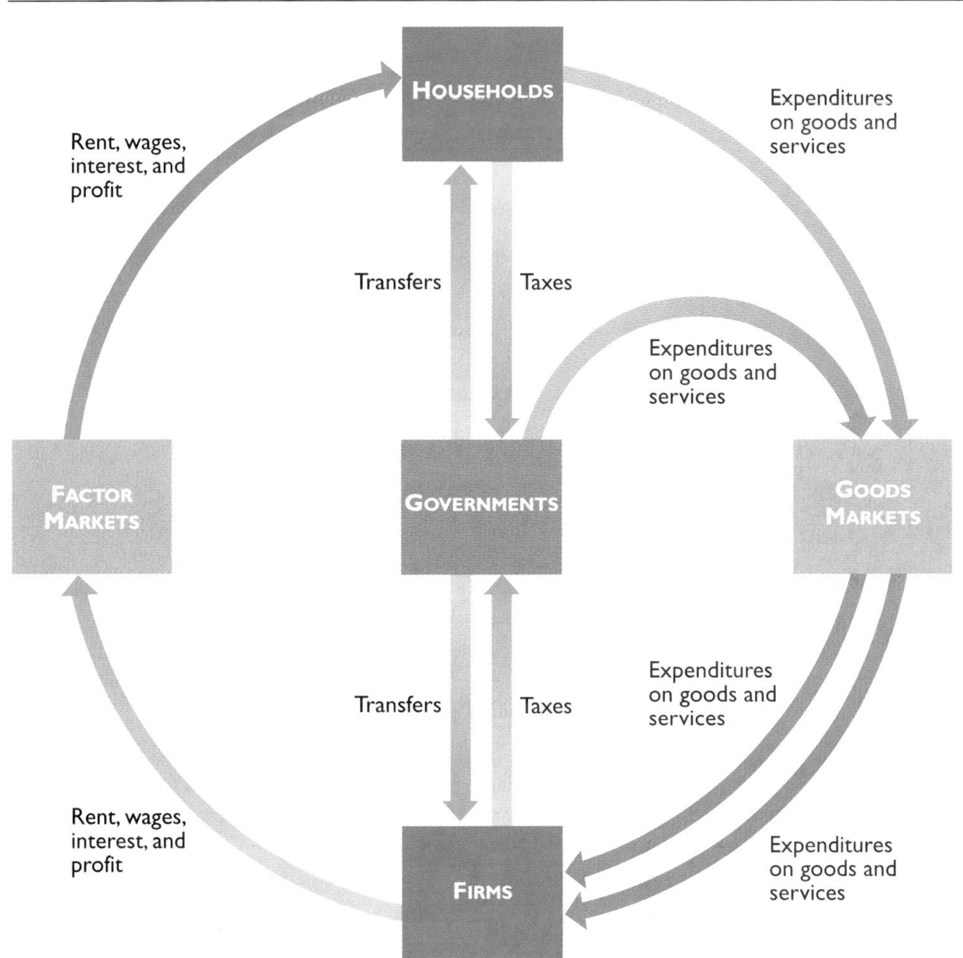

The green flows from households and firms to governments are taxes, and the green flows from governments to households and firms are money transfers.

The red flow from governments through goods markets to firms is the expenditures on goods and services by governments.

Federal Government Expenditures and Revenue

What are the main items of expenditures by the federal government on goods and services and transfers? And what are its main sources of tax revenue? Figure 2.6 answers these questions.

You can see that by far the largest part of what the federal government spends is on social security benefits and other transfers to persons. National defense also takes a big slice of the federal government's expenditures. The interest payment on the national debt is another large item. The **national debt** is the total amount that the federal government has borrowed to make expenditures that exceed tax revenue—to run a government budget deficit. The national debt is a bit like a large credit card balance. And paying the interest on the national debt is like paying the minimum required monthly payment.

National debt
The total amount that the federal government has borrowed to make expenditures that exceed tax revenue—to run a government budget deficit.

Transfers to other levels of government also use up a large part of the federal government's expenditures. Purchases of goods and services (other than national defense) are relatively small, and subsidies and aid to other countries take a tiny slice of expenditures.

Most of the tax revenue of the federal government—almost a half of it—comes from personal income taxes. And two thirds of the rest comes from social security taxes. Corporate income taxes are a small part of the federal government's revenue.

FIGURE 2.6
Federal Government Expenditures and Revenue

Practice Online

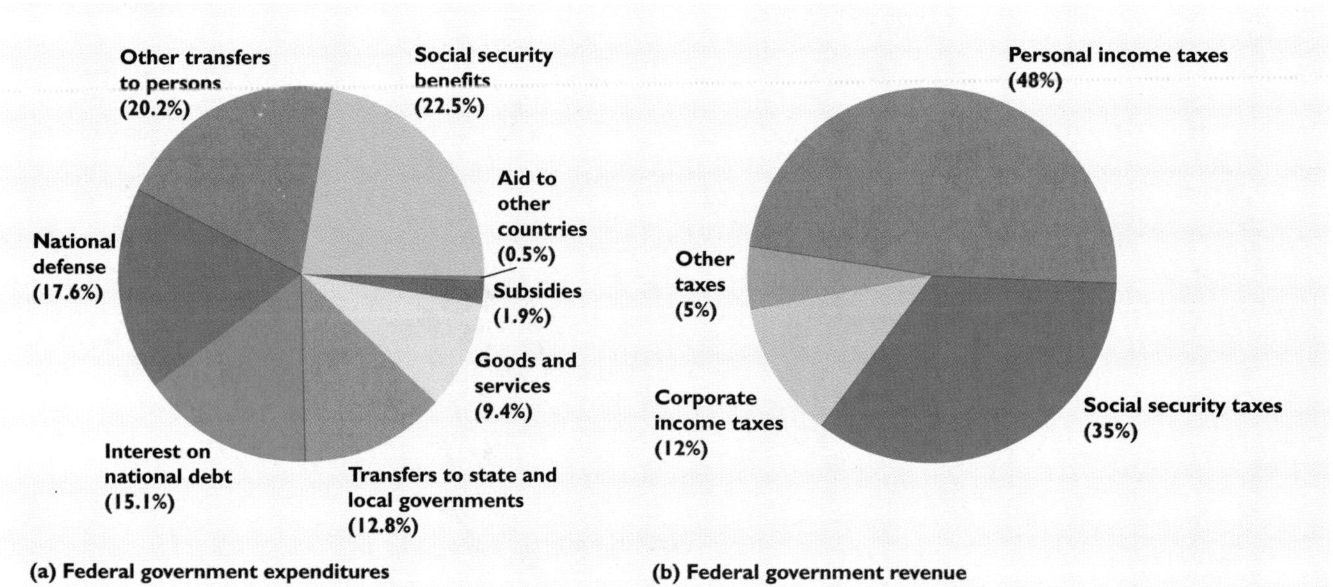

SOURCE: Bureau of Economic Analysis.

Social security benefits and other transfers to persons are the largest slice of federal government expenditures. National defense, interest on the national debt, and transfers to state and local governments also are a large share.

Most of the federal government's revenue comes from personal income taxes and social security taxes. Corporate income taxes are only a small part of total revenue.

State and Local Government Expenditures and Revenue

What are the main items of expenditures by the state and local governments on goods and services and transfers? And what are their main sources of revenue? Figure 2.7 answers these questions.

You can see that education is by far the largest part of the expenditures of state and local governments. This item covers the cost of public schools, colleges, and universities. It absorbs 40 percent of total expenditures—approximately $520 billion, or $1,870 per person.

Welfare benefits are the second largest item, and it takes 20 percent of total expenditures. Highways are the next largest item, and they account for 8 percent of total expenditures. The remaining 32 percent is spent on other local public goods and services such as police services, garbage collection and disposal, sewage management, and water supplies.

Sales taxes and transfers from the federal government bring in similar amounts—about 25 percent of total revenue. Property taxes account for 21 percent of total revenue. Individual income taxes account for 15 percent, and corporate income taxes account for 3 percent. The remaining 13 percent comes from other taxes such as estate taxes.

FIGURE 2.7
State and Local Government Expenditures and Revenue

Practice Online

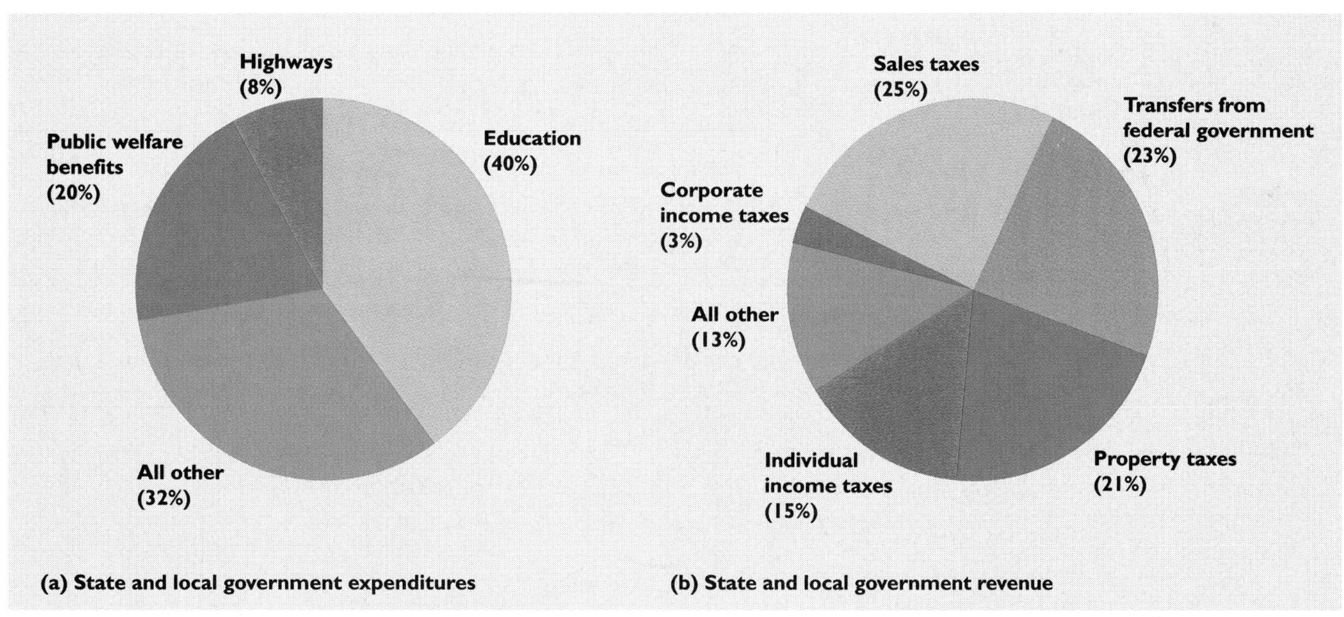

SOURCE: Bureau of Economic Analysis.

Education, highways, and public welfare benefits are the largest slice of state and local government expenditures.

Most of the state and local government revenue comes from sales taxes, property taxes, and transfers from the federal government.

Eye on the Global Economy

Production and People in the World Today

In the United States, 5 percent of the world's people produce 22 percent of the value of the world's output. The figure shows the percentages of population and production for other nations and regions.

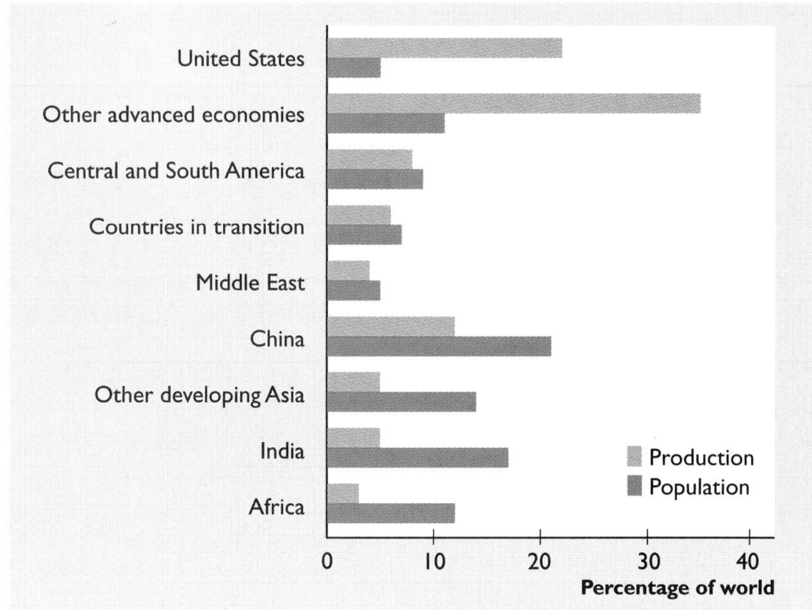

SOURCE: International Monetary Fund, *World Economic Outlook* database.

CHECKPOINT 2.2

Study Guide **pp. 27–29**

Practice Online 2.2

2 **Use the circular flow model to provide a picture of how households, firms, and governments interact.**

Practice Problem 2.2

What are the real flows and money flows that run between households, firms, and governments in the circular flow model?

Exercises 2.2

1. What are the choices made by households and firms that determine what, how, and for whom goods and services are produced? Where, in the circular flow model, do those choices appear?
2. How do the actions of governments modify what, how, and for whom goods and services are produced? Where, in the circular flow model, do those choices appear?

Solution to Practice Problem 2.2

The real flows are the services of factors of production from households to firms and the goods and services from firms to households and from firms to governments. The money flows are factor incomes, household and government expenditures on goods and services, taxes, and transfers.

2.3 MACROECONOMIC PERFORMANCE

Macroeconomic performance has three dimensions:

- Standard of living
- Cost of living
- Economic fluctuations

Standard of Living

The standard of living depends on the quantities of goods and services produced and the number of people among whom those goods and services are shared. The greater the value of production per person, the higher is the standard of living, other things remaining the same. For the world as a whole, the average value of goods and services produced is $21 per person per day. But there is an enormous range around that average. Let's begin our exploration of global living standards by looking at the size and distribution of the population.

World Population

Visit the Web site of the U.S. Census Bureau and find the population clocks. On September 8, 2002, the U.S. clock recorded a population of 287,991,639. The world clock recorded a global population of 6,248,847,500. The U.S. clock ticks along showing a population increase of one person every 14 seconds. The world clock spins much faster, adding 34 people in the same 14 seconds.

Classification of Countries

The world's 6.25 billion (and rising) population lives in 184 economies classified by the International Monetary Fund into three broad groups:

- Advanced economies
- Developing economies
- Transition economies

Advanced Economies Advanced economies are the 28 countries (or areas) that have the highest standards of living. The United States, Japan, Italy, Germany, France, the United Kingdom, and Canada belong to this group. So do four new industrial Asian economies: Hong Kong, South Korea, Singapore, and Taiwan. The other advanced economies include Australia, New Zealand, and most of the rest of Western Europe. Almost 1 billion people live in the advanced economies.

Developing Economies Developing economies are the 128 countries in Africa, Asia, the Middle East, Europe, and Central and South America that have not yet achieved a high standard of living for their people. The standard of living in these economies varies a great deal, but in all cases, it is much lower than that in the advanced economies, and in some cases, it is extremely low. Almost 5 billion people live in the developing economies.

Transition Economies Transition economies are the 28 countries in Europe and Asia that were, until the early 1990s, part of the Soviet Union or its satellites. These countries include Russia, Hungary, Poland, and the Czech Republic.

The economies in this group are small—only 200 million people in total—but are important because they are in transition (hence the name) from a system of state-owned production, central economic planning, and heavily regulated markets to a system of free enterprise and unregulated markets.

Living Standards Around the World

Figure 2.8 shows the distribution of living standards around the world in 2002, measured in dollars per day. You can see that in the United States, the average income is $100 a day. This number tells you that an average person in the United States can buy goods and services that cost $100, which is close to five times the world average. Canada has an average income close to 90 percent of that in the United States. Japan, Germany, France, Italy, the United Kingdom, and the other advanced economies have average incomes around two thirds that of the United States. Living standards fall off quickly as we move farther down the table, with India and the African continent achieving average incomes of only $5 a day.

Most people live in the countries that have incomes below the world average. You can see this fact by looking at the population numbers shown in the figure. The poorest five countries or regions—China, Central Asia, Other Asia, India, and Africa—have a total population of 4 billion.

FIGURE 2.8
The Standard of Living Around the World

Practice Online

Average income per person ranges from $5 a day in Africa to $100 a day in the United States. The world average is $21 a day. Russia and Central and South America have incomes that are close to the world average.

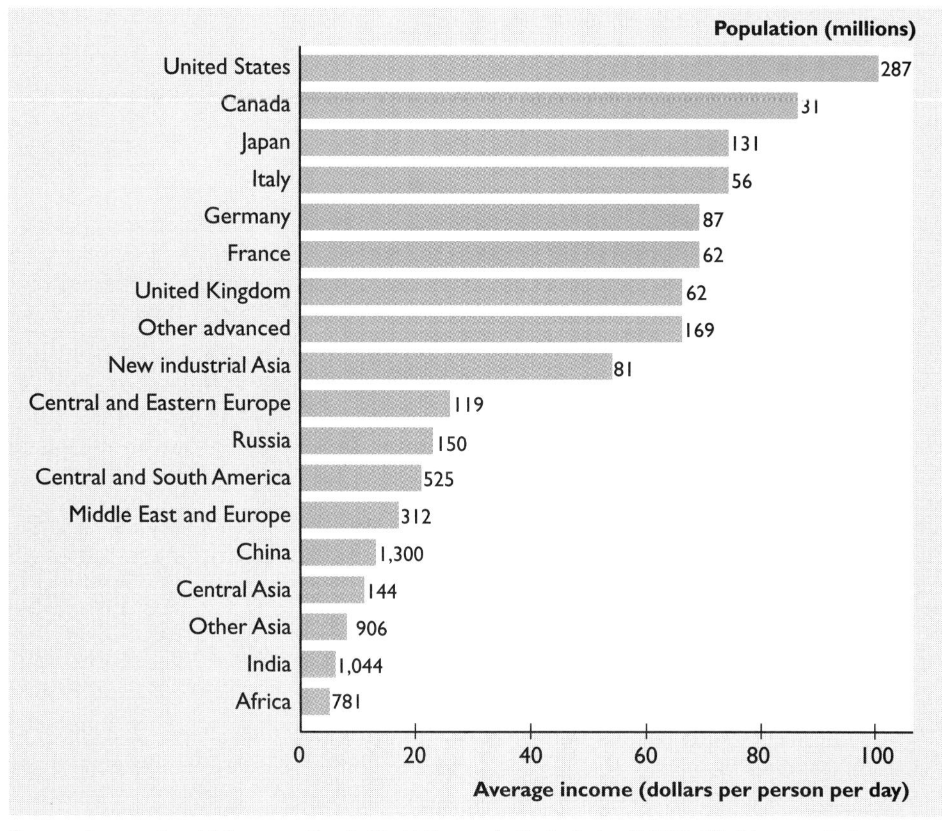

SOURCE: International Monetary Fund, *World Economic Outlook*, April 2002, Washington, D.C.

Unemployment and Living Standards

Unemployment is another factor that influences the standard of living. If jobs are easy to find, then when people lose their jobs they will find new ones after only a short period of unemployment. But if jobs are hard to find, then when people lose their jobs they will find new ones only after a long period of unemployment.

Unemployment rates vary enormously around the world. In the United States, the average unemployment rate during the past 20 years has been 6 percent. That is, for every 100 people in the labor force, 94 have jobs and 6 are looking for jobs but can't find them. At this average unemployment rate, it takes an unemployed person an average of about 15 weeks to find an acceptable job.

Figure 2.9 shows the distribution of unemployment rates among developed countries, on the average for the 1980s and 1990s. (Note that the European Union average includes some of the other countries shown separately.)

The United States has one of the world's lowest unemployment rates. Only Japan and the new industrial economies of Asia (Hong Kong, Korea, Singapore, and Taiwan) have lower rates. Canada, the European Union, and other advanced economies have higher rates. And two members of the European Union—Spain and Ireland—have extremely high unemployment rates.

Figure 2.9 does *not* show the unemployment rates of the developing and transition economies. Why not? No one knows what they are. Data on unemployment is expensive to collect, and only the rich advanced economies devote resources to its measurement. Even though developing and transition economies do not measure unemployment rates, they are likely to be substantially higher than those in the advanced economies and might even exceed the high rate of Spain.

Why unemployment rates differ across economies is a difficult question to answer and is one of the challenges of macroeconomics.

FIGURE 2.9
Unemployment Rates Around the World

Practice Online

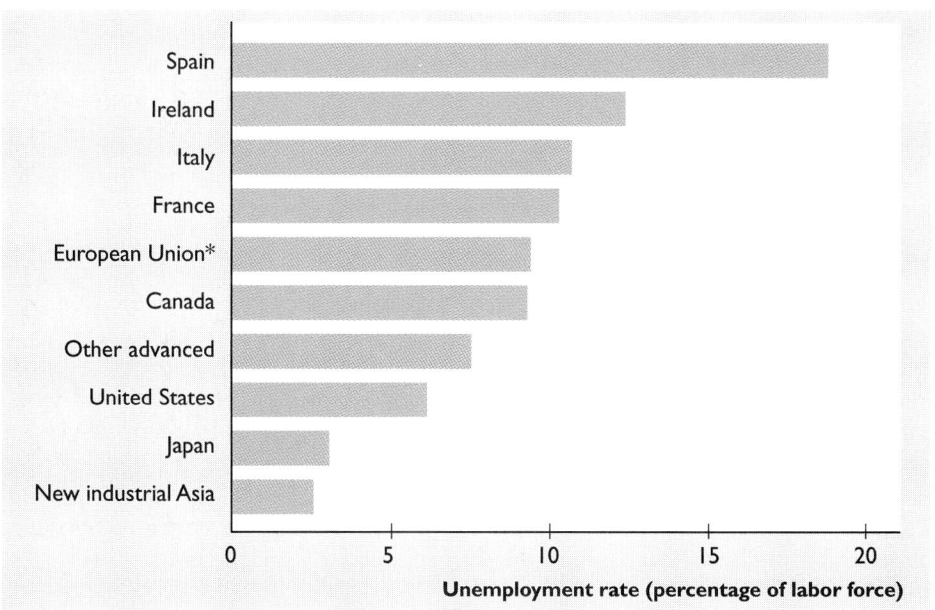

SOURCE: International Monetary Fund, *World Economic Outlook*, April 2002, Washington, D.C.

During the 1980s and 1990s, the average unemployment rate in Spain was much higher than in most advanced economies. The unemployment rate in the United States is among the lowest, but it is not as low as in Japan and in the new industrial Asian economies.

* The European Union average is the average for all 15 member countries, including Spain, Ireland, Italy, and France.

Cost of Living

The cost of living is the amount of money it takes to buy the goods and services that achieve a given standard of living. In the United States, we measure money in dollars. So the cost of living in the United States is the number of dollars it takes to buy the goods and services that achieve a given standard of living. In the United Kingdom, it is the number of pounds; in Japan, the number of yen; in Russia, the number of rubles; and in Indonesia, the number of rupiahs.

Prices in Different Currencies

TABLE 2.1 THE PRICE OF A BIG MAC IN TEN CURRENCIES

Country or Region	Name of currency	Price of a Big Mac
United Kingdom	Pound	2.00
United States	Dollar	2.50
Euro area	Euro	2.67
Brazil	Real	3.60
South Africa	Rand	9.70
Israel	Shekel	13.90
Russia	Ruble	35.00
Japan	Yen	294
South Korea	Won	3,000
Indonesia	Rupiah	14,700

To make this idea concrete, think about the price of a Big Mac. Table 2.1 shows some prices in 10 currencies. The average price of a Big Mac in the United States is \$2.50. In the United Kingdom, it is £2.00, and in Japan, it is ¥294. So in the United Kingdom, it costs a smaller number of money units to buy a Big Mac than it does in United States, and in Japan, it costs a larger number of money units. But the price of a Big Mac is actually *more* in the United Kingdom than in either the United States or Japan. The reason is that a pound is worth \$1.55, so £2.00 is equivalent to \$3.10. And a pound is worth 182 yen, so £2.00 is equivalent to ¥364.

Inflation

The number of money units that something costs is not very important, but the rate at which the number of money units is changing is important. A rising cost of living, called inflation (see p. 5), is measured by the percentage change in the cost of living. Most countries experience inflation, but its rate varies enormously. In the United States, the inflation rate during the 1980s and 1990s was 3 percent a year. To put this number into perspective, a Big Mac that cost \$2.50 in 2002 cost \$1.80 in 1992 and \$1.30 in 1982. Inflation at this rate is not generally regarded as a big problem. But it is a problem that we need to understand.

Most of the advanced economies have low inflation rates, as you can see in Figure 2.10. But the developing economies have higher inflation rates, some of them spectacularly so. In Central and South America, the average inflation rate during the 1980s and 1990s was 107 percent a year. A 100 percent change means a doubling. At this inflation rate, prices are rising by 6 percent a *month*. Inflation this rapid poses huge problems as people try to avoid holding onto money and struggle to cope with an ever-falling value of money.

Economic Fluctuations

Economies expand at an uneven pace and sometimes shrink for a while. These ebbs and flows of economic activity are the business cycle (see p. 5). The most recent recessions in the United States occurred in 1991 when production fell by 1.3 percent and in 2001 when production fell by 0.6 percent.

The most serious recent recessions occurred in Asia. Japan's production shrank by 1 percent and production in the new industrial Asian economies shrank by 2.4 percent in 1998 amidst a crisis of confidence in their currencies and financial systems. Many firms failed during this so-called Asia crisis. The deepest and lengthiest recession of the 1990s was in the transition economies. Production in Russia and its neighbors decreased by 33 percent between 1990 and 1994.

Figure 2.11 shows the recessions and expansions that we've just described.

FIGURE 2.10
Inflation Rates Around the World

Practice Online

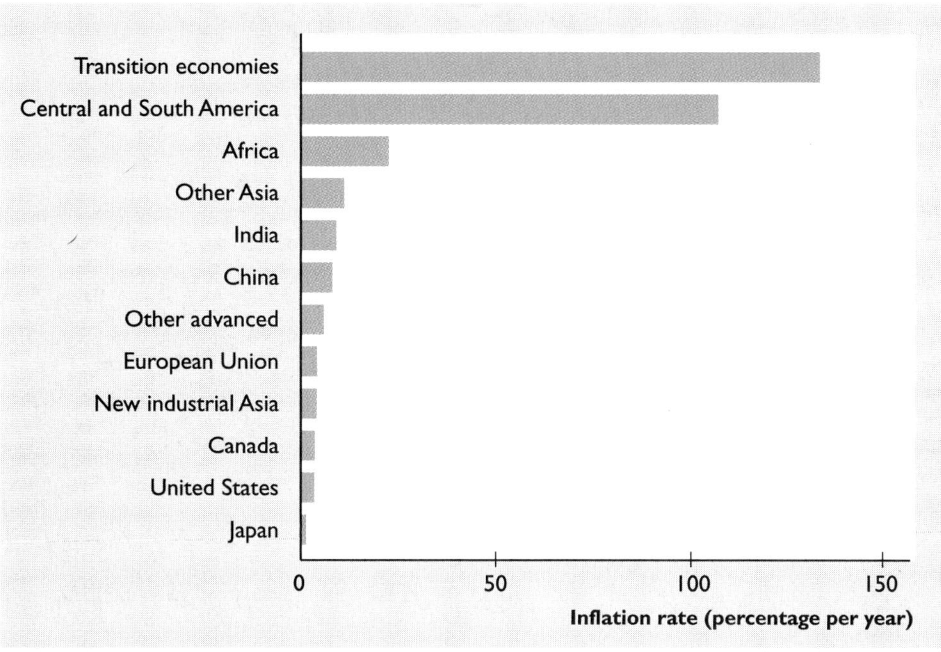

SOURCE: International Monetary Fund, *World Economic Outlook*, April 2002, Washington, D.C.

The most severe inflation has occurred in the transition economies (Russia and its neighbors) and Central and South America. In the United States and the other advanced economies, inflation rates were very low during the 1990s.

FIGURE 2.11
Business Cycles in the Global Economy

Practice Online

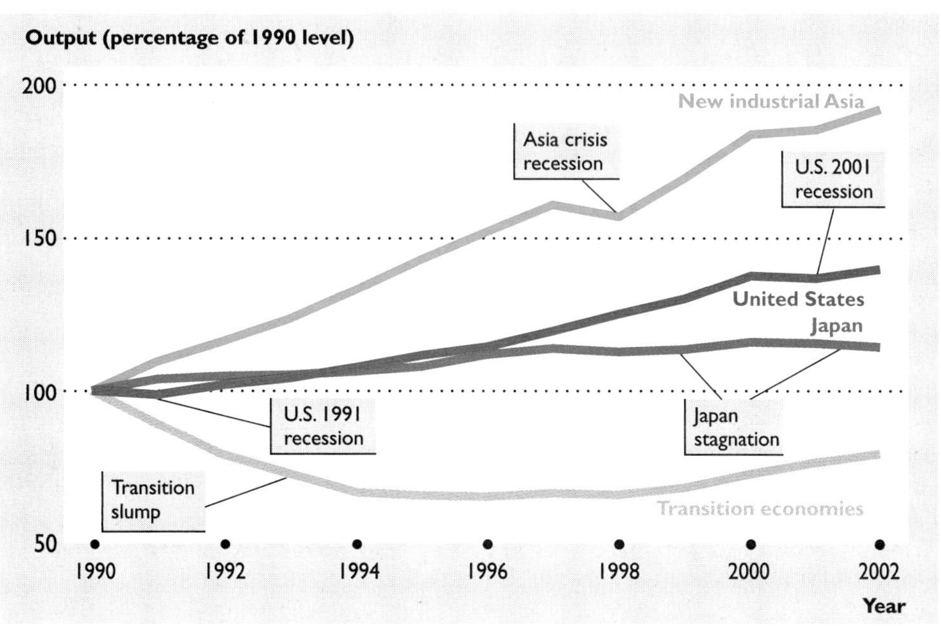

SOURCE: International Monetary Fund, *World Economic Outlook*, April 2002, Washington, D.C.

The United States had recessions in 1991 and 2001. Japan and the new industrial countries of Asia had a sharp recession in 1998. The transition economies had a long and deep recession for most of the 1990s.

CHECKPOINT 2.3

Study Guide pp. 29–31

Practice Online 2.3

3 **Describe the macroeconomic performance—standard of living, cost of living, and economic fluctuations—of the United States and other economies.**

Practice Problems 2.3

1. What percentage of the world's population live in developing economies and what was the range of incomes that these people earned in 2002?
2. What percentage of the world's population live in advanced economies and what was the range of incomes that these people earned in 2002?
3. What percentage of the world's population live in the United States and what was the average income that Americans earned in 2002?
4. Which countries or regions experienced high inflation during the 1990s?
5. Which countries or regions experienced recession during the 1990s and the early 2000s?

Exercises 2.3

1. What is the current world population and how rapidly is it growing? What is the current U.S. population and how rapidly is it growing? Is the U.S. population becoming larger or smaller relative to the world population?
2. Classify the following countries as (a) advanced, (b) developing, or (c) transition: Canada, Bolivia, Brazil, China, Colombia, Germany, Ghana, India, Japan, Korea, New Zealand, Russia, Singapore, the United States, Vietnam.
3. What was the average income in the world as a whole in 2002? Which regions or nations were closest to that world average, which were the farthest above it, and which were the farthest below it?
4. What was the average U.S. inflation rate during the 1990s? Is inflation at this rate considered to be a serious problem? Why or why not?
5. Compare and contrast the most recent U.S. recession with the most recent recessions in Asia and the transition economies. Which was the deepest? Which lasted the longest?

Solutions to Practice Problems 2.3

1. Approximately 80 percent of the world's population lives in developing economies. In 2002, their average daily incomes ranged from $5 in Africa to $21 in Central and South America.
2. Approximately 16 percent of the world's population lives in advanced economies. In 2002, their average daily incomes ranged from about $55 in the new industrial economies of Asia to $100 in the United States.
3. In 2002, the population of the United States was 287 million—about 5 percent of the world's 6.25 billion population. The average income in the United States was $100 a day.
4. The transition economies and parts of Central and South America experienced high inflation during the 1990s.
5. The transition economies, Japan, and the new industrial economies of Asia experienced recession during the 1990s. The United States was in recession in 1991 and 2001, but for the rest of the 1990s it experienced expansion.

Key Points

1 Describe what, how, and for whom goods and services are produced in the United States.

- Consumption goods and services represent 61 percent of total production; investment goods represent 13 percent.
- Goods and services are produced by using the four factors of production: land, labor, capital, and entrepreneurship.
- The incomes people earn—rent for land, wages for labor, interest for capital, and profit for entrepreneurship—determine who gets what is produced.

2 Use the circular flow model to provide a picture of how households, firms, and governments interact.

- The circular flow model shows the real flows of factors and goods and the corresponding money flows of incomes and expenditures.
- Governments in the circular flow receive taxes, make transfers, and buy goods and services.
- Social security and other transfers to persons, national defense, interest on the national debt, and transfers to other levels of government make up most of the federal government's expenditures, and personal income taxes pay the largest share of these expenditures.
- Education, welfare benefits, and highways account for most of the expenditures of the state and local governments, and sales taxes, transfers from the federal government, and property taxes pay for these expenditures.

3 Describe the macroeconomic performance—standard of living, cost of living, and economic fluctuations—of the United States and other economies.

- The standard of living, measured by income per person per day, ranges from an average of $5 in Africa to $100 in the United States.
- Inflation is low in most of the world but has been rapid in the transition economies (Russia and others) and in Central and South America.
- The United States had recessions in 1991 and 2001. Japan, the new industrial economies of Asia, and the transition economies had recessions during the 1990s.

Key Terms

Capital, 38
Circular flow model, 42
Consumption goods and services, 36
Entrepreneurship, 39
Export goods and services, 36
Factor markets, 42
Factors of production, 37
Firms, 42
Functional distribution of income, 39
Goods markets, 42
Government goods and services, 36
Households, 42
Human capital, 38
Interest, 39
Investment goods, 36
Labor, 37
Land, 37
Market, 42
National debt, 46
Personal distribution of income, 40
Profit (or loss), 39
Rent, 39
Wages, 39

Exercises

1. Which of the following items are not consumption goods and services and why?
   - **a.** A chocolate bar
   - **b.** A ski lift
   - **c.** A golf ball
   - **d.** An interstate highway
   - **e.** An airplane
   - **f.** A stealth bomber
2. Which of the following items are not investment goods and why?
   - **a.** An auto assembly line
   - **b.** A shopping mall
   - **c.** A golf ball
   - **d.** An interstate highway
   - **e.** An oil tanker
   - **f.** A construction worker
3. Which of the following items are not factors of production and why?
   - **a.** Vans used by a baker to deliver bread
   - **b.** 1,000 shares of Amazon.com stock
   - **c.** Undiscovered oil
   - **d.** A garbage truck
   - **e.** A pack of bubble gum
   - **f.** The President of the United States
   - **g.** Disneyland
4. List the factors of production and the types of incomes that each factor earns. Use the information provided in Figure 2.2 to describe the functional distribution of income and to determine which factor of production earns the largest percentage of total income.
5. You've seen that the distribution of income is unequal. Why do you think it is unequal?
6. On a graph of the circular flow model, label the flows in which the following items occur.
   - **a.** Capital owned by households and used by firms
   - **b.** Computers sold by firms to governments and households
   - **c.** Labor hired by firms
   - **d.** Land rented to businesses
   - **e.** Taxes paid by households and firms
   - **f.** Unemployment benefits
   - **g.** Wages paid by firms
   - **h.** Dividends paid by businesses
   - **i.** Profit paid to entrepreneurs
7. Review the sources of government revenue and determine who pays most of the taxes: workers, businesses, or consumers. Do the same groups that pay most of the federal taxes also pay most of the state and local taxes?
8. Review the information provided in Figure 2.8 about the standard of living around the world. Which regions of the world have the highest standard of living and which regions have the lowest standard of living?

Critical Thinking

9. "If the trends in schooling continue, at some point in the future, everyone will have a college degree and no one will be available to work as a janitor or garbage collector." Critically evaluate this statement.

10. "Income is unequally distributed, but because wages account for more than 70 percent of total income, any redistribution from the rich to the poor means taking from wage earners to give to others." What is wrong with the reasoning in this statement?

11. You've seen in Figure 2.6(a) that the federal government spends almost as much on debt interest as it spends on national defense. Why do you think the federal government has such a big interest bill? Wouldn't it be better if the government paid off its debts and stopped paying interest? How could the government pay off its debts?

12. You've seen in Figure 2.6(b) that all levels of government get only a small part of their revenues from taxing businesses. Why do you think businesses pay a small share of taxes? Wouldn't it be better if businesses paid more taxes and individuals paid less? Explain your answer.

13. The world population is increasing by 34 persons every 14 seconds, and people in Africa and much of Asia live on an average of only $5 a day. At the same time, the population of the United States is growing by only *one* person every 14 seconds, and our average income is $100 a day. Should we be concerned by these facts about the global economy? Organize your answer around the following four points:
    - **a.** Why do you think average income is much larger in the United States than in most of the rest of the world?
    - **b.** Why do you think world population growth is so rapid?
    - **c.** Do you think Americans should make larger donations to the people in poorer developing nations?
    - **d.** Do you think the United States should buy more cheap foreign-produced food, clothing, electronic goods, and other manufactured goods from the people of the poor developing nations?

14. Think about unemployment in the United States and around the world.
    - **a.** Do you think that unemployment is a problem? Why or why not?
    - **b.** Why do you think the unemployment rate is lower in the industrial economies of Asia than anywhere else?
    - **c.** Why do you think the unemployment rate is higher in Europe than anywhere else?
    - **d.** Do you think that Americans should be concerned that the U.S. unemployment rate is higher than that in Japan?
    - **e.** Can you think of any policies that might lower the unemployment rate?

15. Think about inflation in the United States and around the world.
    - **a.** Do you think that a rising cost of living is a problem? Why or why not?
    - **b.** Do you think that a *falling* cost of living would be a problem? Why or why not?
    - **c.** Why do you think the inflation rate in Central and South America is higher than that in the United States?

Practice Online

Web Exercises

Use the links on your Foundations Web site to work the following exercises.

16. Visit the Bureau of Economic Analysis at the U.S. Department of Commerce.
    a. Find the data for the most recent quarter on expenditure on consumption goods and services, investment goods, government goods and services, and export goods and services.
    b. Calculate the percentages of the total that each accounts for.
    c. Compare the numbers that you have calculated with those in Figure 2.1 on page 37. Which items, if any, have increased and which have decreased? Can you think of any reasons that might make these percentages change?
17. Visit the Bureau of Economic Analysis at the U.S. Department of Commerce.
    a. Find the data for the most recent quarter on the incomes of the factors of production.
    b. Calculate the percentages of the total income that each factor of production receives.
    c. Compare the numbers that you have calculated with those in Figure 2.2 on page 39. Which items, if any, have increased and which have decreased?
    d. Can you think of any reasons that might make these percentages change?
    e. Can you think of any reasons that might keep these percentages roughly constant?
18. Draw a graph to show the circular flow model. Use the data from exercises 16(a) and 17(a) and, against each arrow, place the values that represent the U.S. economy in the most recent quarter.
19. Visit the Bureau of Economic Analysis at the U.S. Department of Commerce.
    a. Find the data for the most recent quarter on government expenditures on goods and services and taxes.
    b. Calculate the percentages of the total that each item accounts for.
    c. Compare the numbers that you have calculated with those in Figure 2.6(a) on page 46 and Figure 2.7(a) on page 47. Which items, if any, have increased and which have decreased?
    d. Can you think of any reasons that might make these percentages change?
20. Draw a graph to show governments in the circular flow model. Use the data from exercises 16(a), 17(a), and 19(a) and, against each arrow, place the values that represent the U.S. economy in the most recent quarter.
21. Visit the Web site of the U.S. Census Bureau and look at the population clocks for the United States and the world. By how much have the populations of the United States and the world changed since September 8, 2002 (the numbers on page 49)? Which is growing at the faster rate, the United States or the world?
22. Visit the Web site of the International Monetary Fund's *World Economic Outlook*.
    a. Find some data on production and incomes, and compare the growth in living standards in the United States with those in other countries and regions and with the world average.
    b. Find some data on inflation, and compare the United States with other countries and regions and with the world average.

CHAPTER 3

The Economic Problem

CHAPTER CHECKLIST

When you have completed your study of this chapter, you will be able to

1. **Use the production possibilities frontier to illustrate the economic problem.**
2. **Calculate opportunity cost.**
3. **Explain how people gain from specialization and trade.**
4. **Explain how technological change and increases in capital and human capital expand production possibilities.**

You learned in Chapter 1 that all economic problems arise from scarcity, that scarcity forces us to make choices, and that in making choices, we try to get the most value out of our scarce resources by comparing marginal costs and marginal benefits. You learned in Chapter 2 what, how, and for whom goods and services are produced in the U.S. and global economies. And you used your first economic model, the circular flow model, to illustrate the choices and interactions that determine what, how, and for whom goods and services are produced.

In this chapter, you will study another economic model, one that illustrates scarcity, choice, and cost and that helps us to understand the choices that people and societies actually make. You will also discover how we gain by specializing and trading with each other and how economic growth expands our production possibilities.

3.1 PRODUCTION POSSIBILITIES

Every working day in the mines, factories, shops, and offices and on the farms and construction sites across the United States, we produce a vast array of goods and services. In the United States in 2002, 234 billion hours of labor equipped with $20 trillion worth of capital produced $10 trillion worth of goods and services. Globally, 6 trillion hours of labor and $100 trillion of capital produced $47 trillion worth of goods and services.

Although our production capability is enormous, it is limited by our available resources and by technology. At any given time, we have fixed quantities of the factors of production, and these factors embody a fixed state of technology. Because our wants exceed our resources, we must make choices. We must rank our wants and decide which wants to satisfy and which to leave unsatisfied.

To illustrate the limits to production, we focus our attention on two goods only and hold the quantities produced of all the other goods and services constant. That is, we use the *ceteris paribus* assumption. We look at a *model* of the economy in which everything remains the same except for the production of the two goods we are currently considering.

Production Possibilities Frontier

Production possibilities frontier
The boundary between combinations of goods and services that can be produced and combinations that cannot be produced, given the available factors of production and the state of technology.

The **production possibilities frontier** is the boundary between the combinations of goods and services that can be produced and the combinations that cannot be produced with a fixed quantity of available factors of production—land, labor, capital, and entrepreneurship—that embody a given state of technology. Let's look at the production possibilities frontier for bottled water and CDs.

Land can be used for either water-bottling plants or CD factories. Labor can be trained to work as water bottlers or as CD makers. Capital can be devoted to tapping springs and making water filtration plants or to the computers and lasers that make CDs. And entrepreneurs can devote their creative talents to managing water resources and bottling factories or to running electronics businesses that make CDs. In every case, the more resources that get used to produce bottled water, the fewer are left for producing CDs.

We can illustrate the production possibilities frontier by using either a table or a graph. The table in Figure 3.1 describes six production possibilities for bottled water and CDs—alternative combinations of quantities of these two goods that we can produce.

One possibility, in column *A*, is to devote no factors of production to making bottled water, so bottled-water production is zero. In this case, we can devote all the factors of production to making CDs and produce 15 million a year. Another possibility, in column *B*, is to devote resources to bottled-water production that are sufficient to produce 1 million bottles a year. But the resources that are being used in water-bottling plants must be taken from CD factories. So we can now produce only 14 million CDs a year. Columns *C*, *D*, *E*, and *F* show other possible combinations of the quantities of these two goods that we can produce. In column *F*, we use all our resources to produce 5 million bottles of water a year and have no resources for producing CDs.

The graph in Figure 3.1 illustrates the production possibilities frontier, *PPF*, for bottled water and CDs. It is a graph of the production possibilities in the table. The *x*-axis shows the production of bottled water, and the *y*-axis shows the production of CDs. Each point on the graph labeled *A* through *F* represents the corresponding column in the table. For example, point *B* represents the production of 1 million bottles of water and 14 million CDs. These quantities also appear in column *B* of the table.

The *PPF* is a valuable tool for illustrating the effects of scarcity and its consequences. It puts three features of production possibilities in sharp focus. They are the distinctions between

- Attainable and unattainable combinations
- Full employment and unemployment
- Tradeoffs and free lunches

FIGURE 3.1

The Production Possibilities Frontier

Practice Online

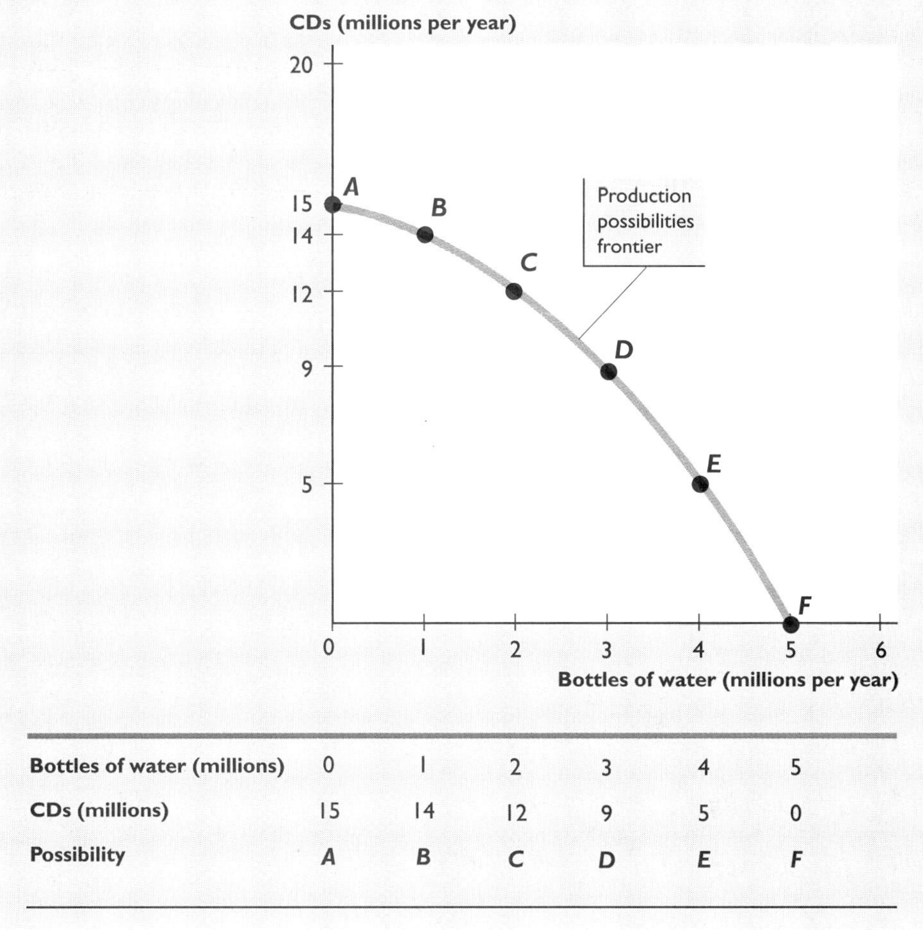

Bottles of water (millions)	0	1	2	3	4	5
CDs (millions)	15	14	12	9	5	0
Possibility	*A*	*B*	*C*	*D*	*E*	*F*

The table and the graph show the production possibilities frontier for bottled water and CDs. Point *A* tells us that if we produce no bottled water, the maximum quantity of CDs we can produce is 15 million a year. Points *A, B, C, D, E,* and *F* in the figure represent the columns of the table. The line passing through these points is the production possibilities frontier.

Attainable and Unattainable Combinations

Because the *PPF* shows the *limits* to production, it separates attainable combinations from unattainable ones. We can produce combinations of bottled water and CDs that are smaller than those on the *PPF*, and we can produce any of the combinations *on* the *PPF*. These combinations of bottled water and CDs are attainable. But we cannot produce combinations that are larger than those on the *PPF*. These combinations are unattainable.

Figure 3.2 emphasizes the attainable and unattainable combinations. Only the points on the *PPF* and inside it (in the orange area) are attainable. The combinations of bottled water and CDs beyond the *PPF* (in the white area), such as the combination at point *G*, are unattainable. These points illustrate combinations that cannot be produced with our current resources and technology. The *PPF* tells us that we can produce 4 million bottles of water and 5 million CDs at point *E* or 2 million bottles of water and 12 million CDs at point *C*. But we cannot produce 4 million bottles of water and 12 million CDs at point *G*.

Full Employment and Unemployment

Full employment occurs when all the available factors of production are being used. Unemployment occurs when some factors of production are not used.

The most noticed unemployment affects labor. There is always some unemployed labor, and in a recession, the amount of unemployment can be large. But land and capital can also be unemployed. Land is often unemployed while its owner is trying to work out the land's most valuable use. Look around where you live and you'll probably be able to find at least one or two city blocks that are

FIGURE 3.2
Attainable and Unattainable Combinations

Practice Online

The production possibilities frontier, *PPF*, separates attainable combinations from unattainable ones. We can produce at any point inside the *PPF* (the orange area) or *on* the frontier. Points outside the production possibilities frontier such as point *G* are unattainable.

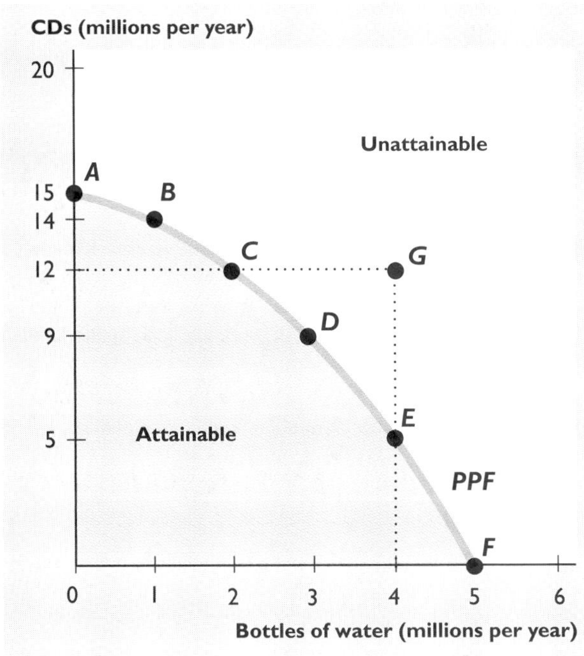

currently unemployed. Capital often lies idle. For example, thousands of automobiles are unemployed in parking lots; and restaurant tables and kitchens are often unemployed.

Figure 3.3 illustrates the effects of unemployment. With unemployed resources, the economy might produce at point *H*. Here, with some resources *employed*, it is possible to produce 3 million bottles of water and 5 million CDs. But with full employment, it is possible to move to points such as *D* or *E*. At point *D*, there are more CDs and the same quantity of bottled water as at point *H*. And at point *E*, there are more bottles of water and the same quantity of CDs as at point *H*.

Tradeoffs and Free Lunches

A **tradeoff** is a constraint or limit to what is possible that forces an exchange or a substitution of one thing for something else.

Tradeoff
A constraint or limit to what is possible that forces an exchange or a substitution of one thing for something else.

If the federal government devotes more resources to finding a cure for AIDS and cuts its transfers to state and local governments, a move that forces state and local governments to increase class sizes and cut back on school libraries and computer facilities, we face a tradeoff between health care and education. If the federal government devotes more resources to national defense and fewer resources to NASA's space exploration program, we face a tradeoff between defense and the space program.

If lumber producers cut down fewer trees to conserve spotted owls, we face a tradeoff between paper products and wildlife. If Ford Motor Company decreases the production of trucks to produce more SUVs, we face a tradeoff between two types of vehicle. If a student decides to take an extra course and cut back on her weekend job, she faces a tradeoff between course credits and income.

FIGURE 3.3
Full Employment and Unemployment

Practice Online

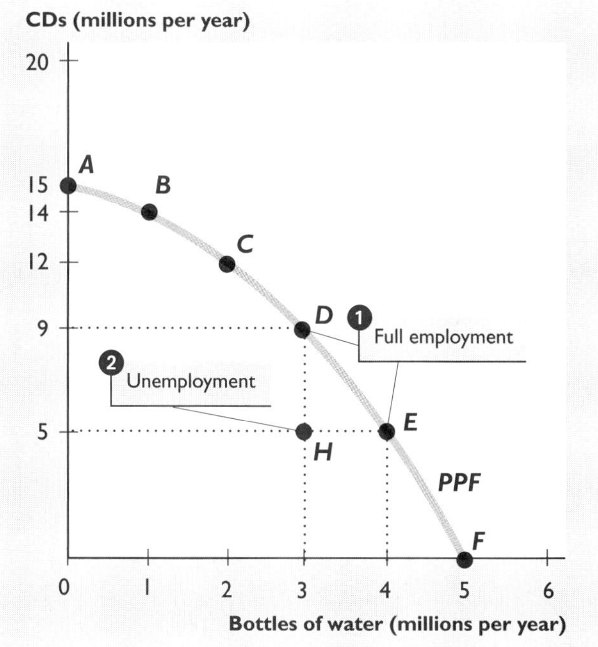

1. When resources are fully employed, production occurs at points on the *PPF* such as *D* and *E*.
2. When resources are unemployed, production occurs at a point inside the frontier such as point *H*.

The *PPF* in Figure 3.4 illustrates the idea of a tradeoff. If we produce at point *E* and would like to produce more CDs, we must forgo some bottled water. For example, we might move from point *E* to point *D*. We exchange some bottles of water for some CDs.

Economists often express the central idea of economics—that every choice involves an opportunity cost—with the saying "There is no such thing as a free lunch." (see Chapter 1, p. 13). But suppose some resources are not being used or are not being used in their most productive way. Isn't it then possible to avoid opportunity cost and get a free lunch?

The answer is yes. You can see this answer in Figure 3.4. If production is taking place *inside* the *PPF* at point *H*, then it is possible to move to point *D* and increase the production of CDs by using currently unused resources or by using resources in their most productive way. There is a free lunch.

So when production takes place at a point on the *PPF*, we face a tradeoff. But we don't face a tradeoff if we produce inside the *PPF*. More of some goods and services can be produced without producing less of some others.

Because of scarcity and the attempt to get the most out of our scarce resources, we do not leave factors of production idle or use them unproductively if we can avoid it. And if such a situation arises, people seek ways of putting their resources to productive employment. It is for these reasons that economists emphasize the tradeoff idea and deny the existence of free lunches. We might *occasionally* get a free lunch, but we *persistently* face tradeoffs.

FIGURE 3.4
Tradeoffs and Free Lunches

Practice Online

1. When resources are fully employed, we face a tradeoff. If we are producing 5 million CDs a year at point *E*, to produce 9 million CDs at point *D*, we must trade some bottled water for CDs and move along the *PPF*.

2. When resources are unemployed, there is a free lunch. If we are producing 5 million CDs a year at point *H*, to produce 9 million CDs at point *D*, we move to the *PPF* and get a free lunch.

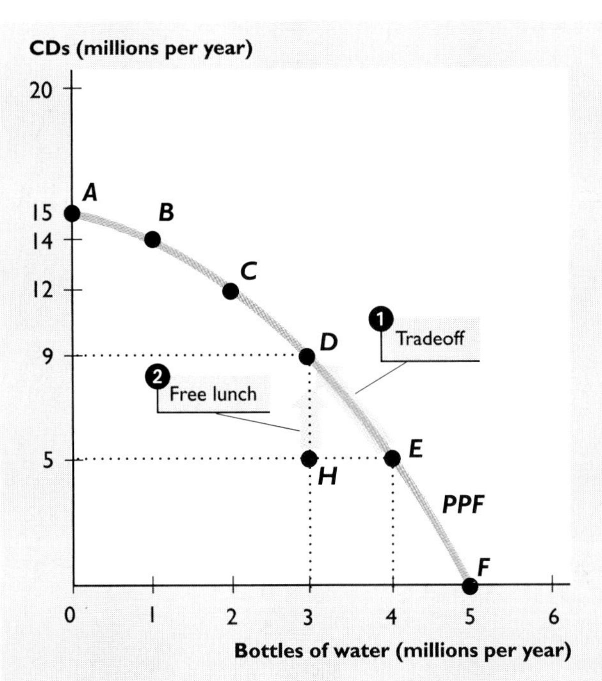

CHECKPOINT 3.1

1 Use the production possibilities frontier to illustrate the economic problem.

Study Guide **pp. 36–39**

Practice Online 3.1

Practice Problems 3.1

1. Robinson Crusoe, the forerunner of the television program *Survivor*, lived alone on a deserted island. He spent his day fishing and picking fruit. He varied the time spent on these two activities and kept a record of his production. Table 1 shows the numbers that Crusoe wrote in the sand. Use these numbers to make Crusoe's *PPF* if he can work only 8 hours a day.
2. Which combinations (pounds of each) are attainable and which are unattainable: (i) 10 fish and 30 fruit, (ii) 13 fish and 26 fruit, (iii) 20 fish and 21 fruit?
3. Which combinations (pounds of each) use all of Crusoe's available 8 hours a day: (i) 15 fish and 21 fruit, (ii) 7 fish and 30 fruit, (iii) 18 fish and 0 fruit?
4. Which combinations (pounds of each) provide Crusoe with a free lunch and which confront him with a tradeoff when he increases fruit by 1 pound: (i) 0 fish and 36 fruit, (ii) 15 fish and 15 fruit, (iii) 13 fish and 26 fruit?

TABLE 1

Hours	Fish (pounds)		Fruit (pounds)
0	0		0
1	4.0	or	8
2	7.5	or	15
3	10.5	or	21
4	13.0	or	26
5	15.0	or	30
6	16.5	or	33
7	17.5	or	35
8	18.0	or	36

Exercises 3.1

1. In the winter, both fish and fruit are harder to find and Robinson Crusoe can work only 5 hours a day. Table 2 shows the quantities that Crusoe can produce in winter. Use these numbers to make Crusoe's *PPF* in winter.
2. Which combinations (pounds of each) are attainable and which are unattainable: (i) 7.5 fish and 11 fruit, (ii) 9 fish and 11 fruit, (iii) 5.5 fish and 14 fruit?
3. Which combinations (pounds of each) use all Crusoe's available 5 hours a day, which provide Crusoe with a free lunch, and which confront him with a tradeoff: (i) 10 fish and 0 fruit, (ii) 9 fish and 6 fruit, (iii) 3 fish and 16 fruit?

TABLE 2

Hours	Fish (pounds)		Fruit (pounds)
0	0		0
1	3.0	or	6
2	5.5	or	11
3	7.5	or	15
4	9.0	or	18
5	10.0	or	20

Solutions to Practice Problems 3.1

1. Table 3 sets out Crusoe's *PPF*. He has 8 hours a day for fishing and fruit picking. He can produce the combinations of fish and fruit that lie on his *PPF* if he uses a total of 8 hours a day. If he picks fruit for 8 hours, he picks 36 pounds and catches no fish—row *A*. If he picks fruit for 7 hours, he picks 35 pounds and has 1 hour for fishing in which he catches 4 pounds—row *B*. Check that you can construct the other rows of Table 3.
2. (i) 10 fish and 30 fruit is attainable because row *D* tells us that Crusoe can produce 10.5 fish and 30 fruit. (ii) 13 fish and 26 fruit is attainable—row *E*. (iii) 20 fish and 21 fruit is unattainable because when Crusoe picks 21 pounds of fruit, he can catch only 15 pounds of fish (row *F*).
3. (i) 15 fish and 21 fruit uses all 8 hours—it is on his *PPF* (row *F*). (ii) 7 fish and 30 fruit does not use all 8 hours—it is inside his *PPF* (row *C*). (iii) 18 fish and 0 fruit uses all 8 hours—it is on his *PPF* (row *I*).
4. (i) 0 fish and 36 fruit involves a tradeoff—it is on his *PPF*. (ii) 15 fish and 15 fruit provides a free lunch—it is inside his *PPF*. (iii) 13 fish and 26 fruit involves a tradeoff—it is on his *PPF*.

TABLE 3

Possibility	Fish (pounds)		Fruit (pounds)
A	0	and	36
B	4.0	and	35
C	7.5	and	33
D	10.5	and	30
E	13.0	and	26
F	15.0	and	21
G	16.5	and	15
H	17.5	and	8
I	18.0	and	0

3.2 OPPORTUNITY COST

You've just seen that along the *PPF*, all choices involve a tradeoff. But what are the terms of the tradeoff? How much of one item must be forgone to obtain an additional unit of another item—a large amount or a small amount? The answer is given by opportunity cost—the best thing you must give up to get something (see p. 13). The *PPF* enables us to calculate opportunity cost.

The Opportunity Cost of a Bottle of Water

The opportunity cost of a bottle of water is the decrease in the quantity of CDs divided by the increase in the number of bottles of water as we move down along the *PPF* in Figure 3.5.

At point *A*, we produce no bottles of water and 15 million CDs. At point *B*, we produce 1 million bottles of water and 14 million CDs. If we move from point *A* to point *B*, the quantity of water increases by 1 million bottles and the quantity of CDs decreases by 1 million. So the opportunity cost of 1 bottle of water is 1 CD.

At point *C*, we produce 2 million bottles of water and 12 million CDs. If we move from point *B* to point *C*, the quantity of water increases by 1 million bottles and the quantity of CDs decreases by 2 million. So the opportunity cost of 1 bottle of water is now 2 CDs.

Repeat these calculations, moving from *C* to *D*, from *D* to *E*, and from *E* to *F*, and check that you can obtain the opportunity costs shown in the table and graph.

FIGURE 3.5
Calculating the Opportunity Cost of a Bottle of Water

Practice Online

Movement along *PPF*	Decrease in quantity of CDs	Increase in quantity of bottled water	Decrease in CDs divided by increase in bottled water
A to *B*	1 million	1 million	1 CD per bottle
B to *C*	2 million	1 million	2 CDs per bottle
C to *D*	3 million	1 million	3 CDs per bottle
D to *E*	4 million	1 million	4 CDs per bottle
E to *F*	5 million	1 million	5 CDs per bottle

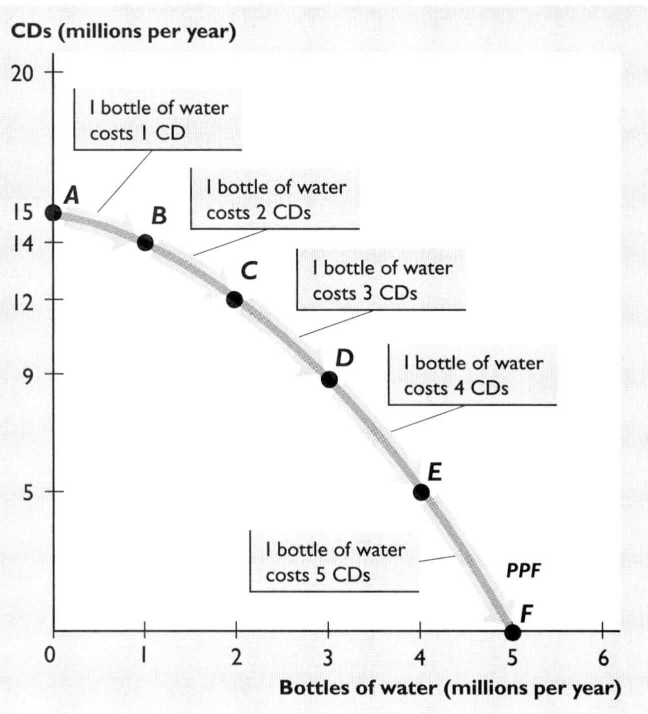

Moving down the *PPF* from *A* to *F*, the opportunity cost of a bottle of water increases as the quantity of bottled water produced increases.

The Opportunity Cost of a CD

The opportunity cost of a CD is the decrease in the quantity of water divided by the increase in the quantity of CDs as we move up along the *PPF* in Figure 3.6.

At point *F*, we produce no CDs and 5 million bottles of water. At point *E*, we produce 5 million CDs and 4 million bottles of water. If we move from point *F* to point *E*, the quantity of CDs increases by 5 million and the quantity of water decreases by 1 million bottles. So the opportunity cost of 1 CD is 1/5 of a bottle of water.

At point *D*, we produce 9 million CDs and 3 million bottles of water. If we move from point *E* to point *D*, the quantity of CDs increases by 4 million and the quantity of water decreases by 1 million bottles. So the opportunity cost of a CD is now 1/4 of a bottle of water.

At point *C*, we produce 12 million CDs and 2 million bottles of water. If we move from point *D* to point *C*, the quantity of CDs increases by 3 million and the quantity of water decreases by 1 million bottles. So the opportunity cost of a CD is now 1/3 of a bottle of water.

Again, repeat these calculations moving from *C* to *B* and from *B* to *A* and check that you can obtain the opportunity costs shown in the figure.

Opportunity Cost Is a Ratio

You've seen that to calculate the opportunity cost of a bottle of water, we divide the quantity of CDs forgone by the increase in the quantity of water. And to calculate the opportunity cost of a CD, we divide the quantity of bottled water for-

FIGURE 3.6

Calculating the Opportunity Cost of a CD

Practice Online

Movement along *PPF*	Decrease in quantity of bottled water	Increase in quantity of CDs	Decrease in bottled water divided by increase in CDs
B to *A*	1 million	1 million	1 bottle per CD
C to *B*	1 million	2 million	1/2 bottle per CD
D to *C*	1 million	3 million	1/3 bottle per CD
E to *D*	1 million	4 million	1/4 bottle per CD
F to *E*	1 million	5 million	1/5 bottle per CD

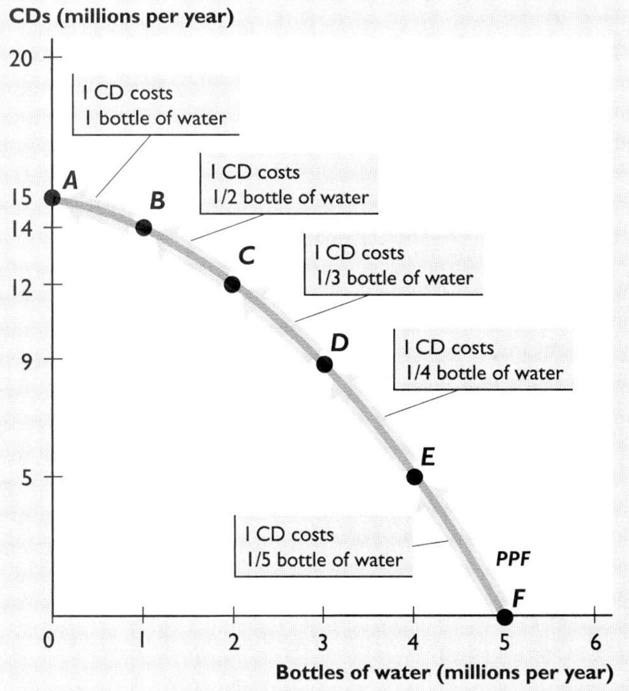

Moving up the *PPF* from *F* to *A*, the opportunity cost of a CD increases as the quantity of CDs produced increases.

gone by the increase in the quantity of CDs. So opportunity cost is a ratio—the change in the quantity of one good divided by the change in the quantity of the other good. The opportunity cost of producing water is equal to the inverse of the opportunity cost of producing CDs. Check this proposition by returning to the calculations we've just worked through. When we move along the *PPF* from point *C* to point *D*, the opportunity cost of a bottle of water is 3 CDs. The inverse of 3 is ⅓, so if we increase the production of CDs and decrease the production of water by moving from point *D* to point *C*, the opportunity cost of a CD must be ⅓ of a bottle of water. This number is correct—it is the number we've just calculated.

Increasing Opportunity Cost

The opportunity cost of a bottle of water increases as the quantity of bottled water produced increases. And the opportunity cost of a CD increases as the quantity of CDs produced increases. The phenomenon of increasing opportunity cost is reflected in the shape of the *PPF*. It is bowed outward. When a large quantity of CDs and a small quantity of water are produced—between points *A* and *B* in Figure 3.5—the frontier has a gentle slope. A given increase in the quantity of bottled water costs a small decrease in the quantity of CDs, so the opportunity cost of a bottle of water is a small quantity of CDs.

When a large quantity of bottled water and a small quantity of CDs are produced—between points *E* and *F* in Figure 3.5—the frontier is steep. A given increase in the quantity of bottled water costs a large decrease in the quantity of CDs, so the opportunity cost of a bottle of water is a large quantity of CDs.

The production possibilities frontier is bowed outward because resources are not equally productive in all activities. Production workers with many years of experience working for Aqua Springs are very good at bottling water but not very good at making CDs. So if we move some of these people from Aqua Springs to Sony, we get a small increase in the quantity of CDs but a large decrease in the quantity of bottled water.

Similarly, engineers and production workers who work at Sony are good at making CDs but not very good at bottling water. So if we move some of these people from Sony to Aqua Springs, we get a small increase in the quantity of bottled water but a large decrease in the quantity of CDs. The more we try to produce of either good, the less productive are the additional resources we use to produce that good and the larger is the opportunity cost of a unit of that good.

Increasing Opportunity Costs Are Everywhere

Just about every activity that you can think of is one with an increasing opportunity cost. We allocate the most skillful farmers and the most fertile land to the production of food. And we allocate the best doctors and least fertile land to the production of health-care services. If we shift fertile land and tractors away from farming to hospitals and ambulances and ask farmers to become hospital porters, the production of food drops drastically and the increase in the production of health-care services is small. The opportunity cost of a unit of health-care services rises. Similarly, if we shift our resources away from health care toward farming, we must use more doctors and nurses as farmers and more hospitals as hydroponic tomato factories. The decrease in the production of health-care services is large, but the increase in food production is small. The opportunity cost of a unit of food rises.

CHECKPOINT 3.2

2 **Calculate opportunity cost.**

Study Guide **pp. 39–41**

Practice Online 3.2

Practice Problems 3.2

1. Use Robinson Crusoe's production possibilities shown in Table 1 to calculate his opportunity cost of a pound of fish. Make a table that shows Crusoe's opportunity cost of a pound of fish as he increases the time he spends fishing and decreases the time that he spends picking fruit.
2. If Crusoe increases his production of fruit from 21 pounds to 26 pounds and decreases his production of fish from 15 pounds to 13 pounds, what is his opportunity cost of a pound of fruit? Explain your answer.
3. If Crusoe is producing 10 pounds of fish and 20 pounds of fruit, what is his opportunity cost of a pound of fruit and a pound of fish? Explain your answer.

TABLE 1

Possibility	Fish (pounds)	Fruit (pounds)
A	0	36
B	4.0	35
C	7.5	33
D	10.5	30
E	13.0	26
F	15.0	21
G	16.5	15
H	17.5	8
I	18.0	0

Exercises 3.2

1. Use Robinson Crusoe's production possibilities in winter shown in Table 2 to calculate his opportunity cost of a pound of fruit. Make a table that shows Crusoe's opportunity cost of a pound of fruit as he increases the time he spends picking fruit and decreases the time he spends fishing.
2. If Crusoe currently catches 5.5 pounds of fish and picks 11 pounds of fruit a day, calculate his opportunity cost of a pound of fruit and of a pound of fish. Explain your answer.
3. If Crusoe increases the amount of fish caught from 5.5 to 7.5 pounds and decreases the amount of fruit picked from 15 to 11 pounds, what is his opportunity cost of a pound of fish? Explain your answer.
4. Does Crusoe's opportunity cost of a pound of fruit increase as he spends more time picking fruit? Explain why or why not.

TABLE 2

Possibility	Fish (pounds)	Fruit (pounds)
A	0	20
B	3.0	18
C	5.5	15
D	7.5	11
E	9.0	6
F	10.0	0

Solutions to Practice Problems 3.2

1. Crusoe's opportunity cost of a pound of fish is the decrease in fruit divided by the increase in fish as he moves along his *PPF*, increasing the time he spends fishing and decreasing the time he spends picking fruit. For example, when Crusoe spends no time fishing, he produces the quantities in row *A* in Table 1. When he spends more time fishing and moves to row *B* in Table 1, the increase in fish is 4 pounds and the decrease in fruit picked is 1 pound. So the opportunity cost of a pound of fish is ¼ pound of fruit. Check that you can derive the other rows of Table 3.
2. The opportunity cost of a pound of fruit is ⅖ pound of fish. When fruit increases by 5 pounds, fish decreases by 2 pounds. The opportunity cost of a pound of fruit is 2 pounds of fish divided by 5 pounds of fruit. This opportunity cost is the inverse of the opportunity cost of fish (move from *E* to *F* in Table 3).
3. If Crusoe is producing 10 pounds of fish and 20 pounds of fruit, his opportunity cost of fruit and of fish is zero because he can increase the production of both without decreasing the production of either. He is producing a combination inside his *PPF*.

TABLE 3

Move from	Increase in fish (pounds)	Decrease in fruit (pounds)	Opportunity cost of fish (pounds of fruit)
A to *B*	4.0	1	0.25
B to *C*	3.5	2	0.57
C to *D*	3.0	3	1.00
D to *E*	2.5	4	1.60
E to *F*	2.0	5	2.50
F to *G*	1.5	6	4.00
G to *H*	1.0	7	7.00
H to *I*	0.5	8	16.00

3.3 SPECIALIZATION AND TRADE

People can produce several goods, or they can concentrate on producing one good and then trading some of their own goods for those produced by others. Concentrating on the production of only one good is called *specialization*. We are going to discover how people gain by specializing in the production of the good in which they have a *comparative advantage*.

Comparative Advantage

Comparative advantage
The ability of a person to perform an activity or produce a good or service at a lower opportunity cost than someone else.

A person has a **comparative advantage** in an activity if that person can perform the activity at a lower opportunity cost than someone else. Let's explore the idea of comparative advantage by looking at two water-bottling plants, one operated by Tom and the other operated by Nancy.

Tom produces both water and bottles, and Figure 3.7 shows his production possibilities frontier. It tells us that if Tom uses all his resources to produce water, he can produce 1,333 gallons an hour. The *PPF* in Figure 3.7 also tells us that if Tom uses all his resources to make bottles, he can produce 4,000 bottles an hour. To produce more water, Tom must decrease his production of bottles. For each additional 1,000 gallons of water produced, Tom must decrease his production of bottles by 3,000.

Tom's opportunity cost of producing 1 gallon of water is 3 bottles.

Similarly, if Tom wants to increase his production of bottles, he must decrease his production of water. For each 1,000 bottles produced, he must decrease his production of water by 333 gallons. So

Tom's opportunity cost of producing 1 bottle is 0.333 gallon of water.

FIGURE 3.7
Production Possibilities at Tom's Water-Bottling Plant

Practice Online

Tom can produce bottles and water along the production possibilities frontier *PPF*. For Tom, the opportunity cost of 1 gallon of water is 3 bottles and the opportunity cost of 1 bottle is ⅓ of a gallon of water. If Tom produces at point *A*, he can produce 1,000 gallons of water and 1,000 bottles an hour.

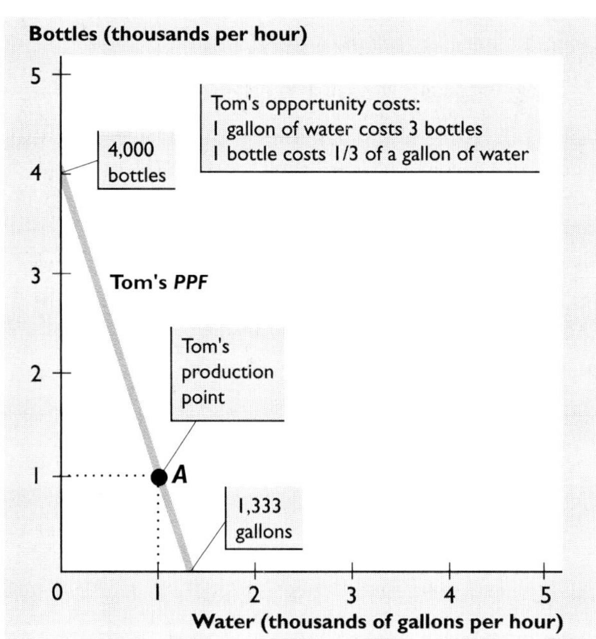

Tom's *PPF* is linear because his workers have similar skills. So if he reallocates them from one activity to another, he faces a constant opportunity cost.

Nancy also produces water and bottles. But Nancy owns a much better spring than Tom. At the same time, her bottle-making equipment is less productive than is Tom's. These differences between the two plants mean that Nancy's production possibilities frontier—shown along with Tom's *PPF* in Figure 3.8—is different from Tom's. If Nancy uses all her resources to produce water, she can produce 4,000 gallons an hour. If she uses all her resources to make bottles, she can produce 1,333 an hour. Nancy's *PPF* is linear, like Tom's, so she faces a constant opportunity cost. For each 1,000 additional bottles produced, she must decrease her production of water by 3,000 gallons.

Nancy's opportunity cost of producing 1 bottle is 3 gallons of water.

Similarly, if Nancy wants to increase her production of water, she must decrease her production of bottles. For each additional 1,000 gallons of water produced, she must decrease her production of bottles by 333. So

Nancy's opportunity cost of producing 1 gallon of water is 0.333 bottle.

Suppose that Tom and Nancy produce both bottles and water and that each produces 1,000 bottles and 1,000 gallons of water—1,000 gallons of bottled water—an hour. That is, each produces at point *A* on their production possibilities frontiers. Total production is 2,000 gallons of bottled water an hour.

In which of the two activities does Nancy have a comparative advantage? Nancy has a comparative advantage in producing a good if her opportunity cost is lower than Tom's opportunity cost of producing that same good. Nancy has a

FIGURE 3.8
The Gains from Specialization

Practice Online

1. Tom and Nancy each produce at point *A* on their respective *PPFs*. Tom has a comparative advantage in bottles, and Nancy has a comparative advantage in water.
2. If Tom specializes in bottles, he produces at point *B* on his *PPF*.
3. If Nancy specializes in water, she produces at point *B'* on her *PPF*.

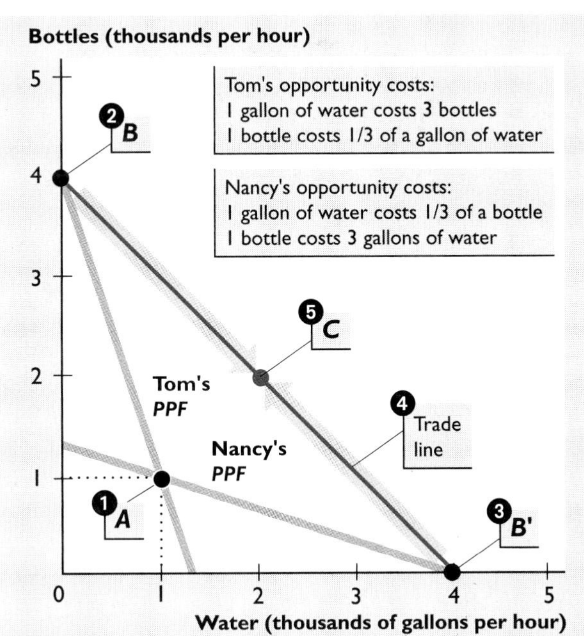

4. They exchange water and bottles along the red "Trade line." Nancy buys bottles from Tom for less than her opportunity cost of producing them, and Tom buys water from Nancy for less than his opportunity cost of producing it.
5. Each goes to point *C*—a point outside his or her individual *PPF*—where each has 2,000 bottles of water an hour. Tom and Nancy increase production with no change in resources.

comparative advantage in producing water. Nancy's opportunity cost of a gallon is 0.333 bottle, whereas Tom's opportunity cost of a gallon is 3 bottles.

Tom's comparative advantage is in producing bottles. Tom's opportunity cost of a bottle is 0.333 gallon of water, which is less than Nancy's opportunity cost of 3 gallons of water. So Tom has a comparative advantage in producing bottles.

Because Nancy has a comparative advantage in water and Tom has a comparative advantage in bottles, they can both gain from specialization and exchange.

Achieving the Gains from Trade

If Tom specializes in bottles, he can produce 4,000 bottles an hour—point *B* on his *PPF*. If Nancy specializes in water, she can produce 4,000 gallons an hour—point *B*' on her *PPF*. By specializing, Tom and Nancy together can produce 4,000 gallons of water and 4,000 bottles an hour—double their total production without specialization. By specialization and trade, Tom and Nancy can get *outside* their individual production possibilities frontiers.

To achieve the gains from specialization, Tom and Nancy must trade with each other. Suppose that each hour, Nancy produces 4,000 gallons of water, Tom produces 4,000 bottles, and Nancy supplies Tom with 2,000 gallons of water in exchange for 2,000 bottles. Tom and Nancy move along the red "Trade line" to point *C*. At this point, each produces 2,000 gallons of bottled water an hour.

By specializing and trading with each other, both Tom and Nancy can double their production from 1,000 to 2,000 bottles of water an hour. The increases in production that each achieves are the gains from specialization and trade.

Both Nancy and Tom share in the gains. Nancy gets bottles for 1 gallon of water per bottle instead of 3 gallons per bottle. Tom gets water for 1 bottle per gallon instead of 3 bottles per gallon. Nancy gets her bottles more cheaply and Tom gets his water more cheaply than when they produced both water and bottles.

Absolute Advantage

Absolute advantage
When one person is more productive than another person in several or even all activities.

Suppose that Nancy invents a production process that makes her four times as productive as she was before in the production of both water and bottles. With her new technology, Nancy now has an **absolute advantage**—she is more productive than Tom in both activities.

But Nancy does not have a *comparative* advantage in both goods. She can produce four times as much of *both* goods as before, but her *opportunity cost* of 1 bottle is still 3 gallons of water. Her opportunity cost is higher than Tom's. So Nancy can still get bottles at a lower cost by trading water for bottles with Tom.

The key point to recognize is that it is *not* possible for *anyone* to have a comparative advantage in everything, even though they might have an absolute advantage in everything. So gains from specialization and trade are always available when opportunity costs diverge.

The principle of comparative advantage and the gains from specialization and trade explain why each individual specializes in a small range of economic activities. It is also the driving force behind international trade. Mexico and the United States, like Tom and Nancy, can *both* gain by specializing in the activities in which they have a comparative advantage and trading with each other. The absolute advantage of the United States is no obstacle to reaping mutual gains from trade.

CHECKPOINT 3.3

3 **Explain how people gain from specialization and trade.**

Study Guide pp. 41–44

Practice Online 3.3

Practice Problem 3.3

Tony and Patty produce scooters and snowboards. Figure 1 shows their production possibilities per day.

a. Calculate Tony's opportunity cost of a snowboard.
b. Calculate Patty's opportunity cost of a snowboard.
c. Who has a comparative advantage in producing snowboards?
d. Who has a comparative advantage in producing scooters?
e. If they specialize and trade, how many snowboards and scooters will they produce?

FIGURE 1

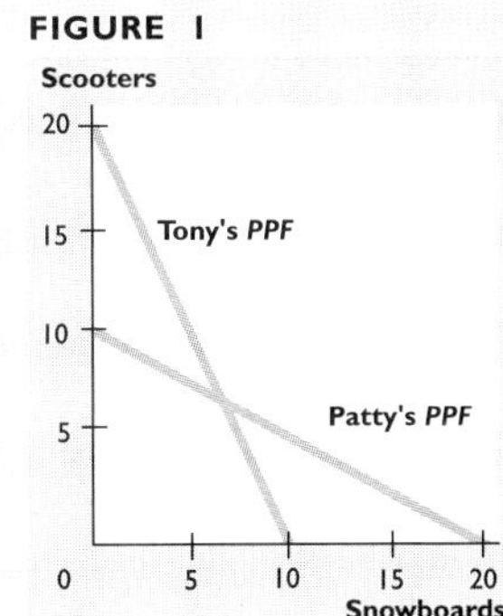

Exercises 3.3

1. Sara and Sid produce boards and sails for windsurfing. Figure 2 shows their production possibilities per day.
   a. Calculate Sara's opportunity cost of a board.
   b. Calculate Sid's opportunity cost of a board.
   c. Who has a comparative advantage in producing boards?
   d. Who has a comparative advantage in producing sails?
   e. If they specialize and trade, how many boards and sails will they produce?
2. If Sid in exercise 1 installs a new machine that doubles his production possibilities:
   a. Who now has a comparative advantage in producing boards?
   b. Are there any gains for Sara and Sid if they specialize and trade? Explain why or why not.

FIGURE 2

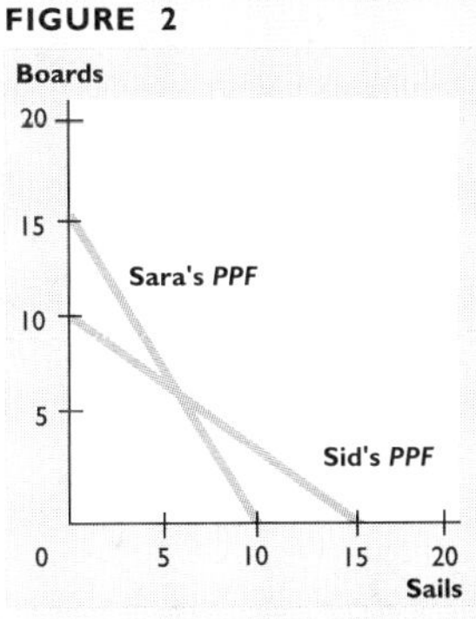

Solution to Practice Problem 3.3

a. Tony's opportunity cost of a snowboard is 2 scooters. If Tony uses all his resources to make scooters, he can make 20 a day. If he uses all his resources to make snowboards, he can make 10 a day. For each snowboard Tony makes, he forgoes making 2 scooters.
b. Patty's opportunity cost of a snowboard is ½ of a scooter. If Patty uses all her resources to make scooters, she can make 10 a day. If she uses all her resources to make snowboards, she can make 20 a day. For each snowboard Patty makes, she forgoes making ½ of a scooter.
c. Patty has a comparative advantage in producing snowboards because her opportunity cost of a snowboard is less than Tony's.
d. Tony has a comparative advantage in producing scooters. For each scooter made, Tony forgoes making ½ of a snowboard. His opportunity cost of a scooter is ½ of a snowboard. For each scooter made, Patty forgoes making 2 snowboards. Her opportunity cost of a scooter is 2 snowboards. Tony's opportunity cost is lower than Patty's.
e. Patty specializes in snowboards, and Tony specializes in scooters. Together, they produce 20 snowboards and 20 scooters.

3.4 EXPANDING PRODUCTION POSSIBILITIES

Economic growth
The sustained expansion of production possibilities.

During the past 30 years, production possibilities per person in the United States have doubled. Such a sustained expansion of production possibilities is called **economic growth**. Can economic growth enable us to overcome scarcity and avoid opportunity cost? It cannot. The faster we make production possibilities grow, the greater is the opportunity cost of economic growth.

Three key factors influence economic growth: technological change, the expansion of human capital, and capital accumulation. Technological change is the development of new goods and services and of better ways of producing existing goods and services. The expansion of human capital is the improvement in the quality of labor that comes from education, on-the-job training, and work experience. Capital accumulation is the growth of capital resources.

As a consequence of technological change, the expansion of human capital, and capital accumulation, we have cars that enable us to produce more transportation than when we had only horses and carriages; we have satellites that make communications possible on a global scale, far beyond what we could produce using the earlier cable technology. We have water-bottling plants that enable us to produce billions of gallons of bottled water each year.

But when we use resources to develop new technologies, educate and train people, and produce new capital equipment, we must decrease our current production of consumption goods and services. This decrease in the current production of consumption goods and services is the opportunity cost of economic growth. Let's look at this opportunity cost.

Economic Growth in an Industry

Instead of studying the *PPF* of bottled water and CDs, we'll hold the quantity of CDs produced constant and study the *PPF* for bottled water and water-bottling plants. Figure 3.9 shows this *PPF* as the curve *JKL*. Along this *PPF*, if we use all our resources to produce water-bottling plants, we can produce 3 plants a year at point *J*. In this case, we produce no bottled water. We can produce 2 water-bottling plants and 3 million bottles of water a year at point *K*, or we can produce no water-bottling plants and 5 million bottles of water at point *L*.

The amount by which our production possibilities expands depends on the resources we devote to building new bottling plants and training people to operate them. If we devote no resources to this activity (point *L*), the *PPF* remains at *JKL*—the light orange curve in Figure 3.9. If we decrease the current production of bottled water and build 2 new bottling plants (point *K*), then in the future, we'll have more bottled-water production possibilities and our *PPF* rotates outward to the position shown by the orange curve. Next period if we produce 2 new bottling plants, we produce at point *K'*. The more resources we devote to producing bottling plants now, the greater is the expansion of our production possibilities in the future.

Economic growth brings a benefit—expanded production possibilities in the future. But economic growth is not free. To make it happen, we must decrease the production of goods for consumption now. In Figure 3.9, we move from *L* to *K* and forgo 2 million bottles of water for consumption now. The opportunity cost of more bottling plants in the future is fewer bottles of water today. Also, economic growth is no magic formula for abolishing scarcity. Economic growth rotates the *PPF* outward, but on the new *PPF*, we continue to face opportunity costs. The ideas about economic growth that we have explored in the setting of the water-bottling industry also apply to nations, as you can see in Eye on the Global Economy.

FIGURE 3.9
Expanding Production Possibilities

Practice Online

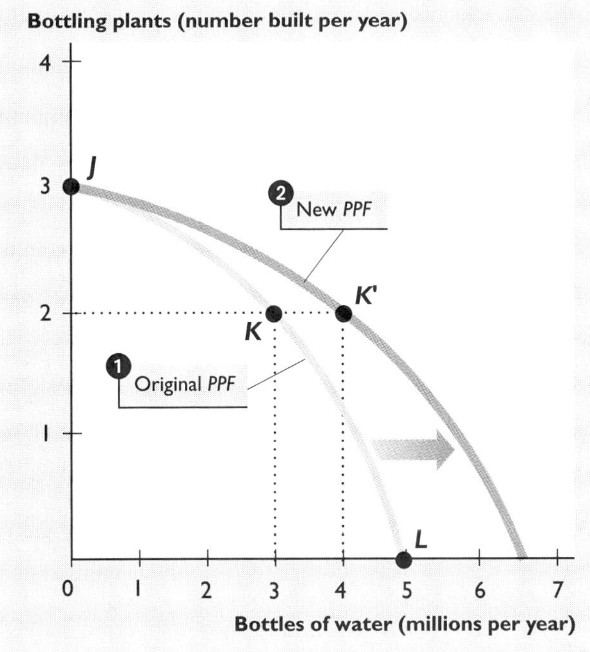

1. The original *PPF* shows the limits to the production of bottled water and water-bottling plants, with the production of all other goods and services remaining the same. If we devote no resources to producing water-bottling plants and produce 5 million bottles of water a month, we remain stuck at point *L*. But if we decrease water production to 3 million bottles a year and produce 2 water-bottling plants, at point *K*, our production possibilities will expand.

2. After a year, the production possibilities frontier shifts outward to the new *PPF* and we can produce at point *K'*, a point outside the original *PPF*. We can shift the *PPF* outward, but we cannot avoid opportunity cost. The opportunity cost of producing more bottled water in the future is less bottled water in the present.

CHECKPOINT 3.4

4 Explain how technological change and increases in capital and human capital expand production possibilities.

Study Guide pp. 44–45

Practice Online 3.4

Practice Problem 3.4

The table shows a nation that produces education services and consumption goods. If the nation currently produces 500 graduates a year and 2,000 units of consumption goods, what is the opportunity cost of growth?

Possibility	Education services (graduates)	Consumption goods (units)
A	1,000	0
B	750	1,000
C	500	2,000
D	0	3,000

Exercise 3.4

If the nation in the table uses all its resources to produce consumption goods, at what rate will the economy grow? If the nation increases the graduates from 0 to 750, will the nation experience economic growth? Explain your answer.

Solution to Practice Problem 3.4

The opportunity cost is 1,000 units (3,000 minus 2,000) of consumption goods forgone.

Eye on the Global Economy

Economic Growth in the United States and Hong Kong

The United States and Hong Kong provide a striking example of the effects of choices on the expansion of production possibilities. In 1960, production possibilities per person in the United States were more than four times those in Hong Kong (see the figure). Over the past 40 years, the United States has devoted one fifth of its resources to accumulating capital and the other four fifths to consumption. In 1960, the United States chose point *A* on its *PPF*. Hong Kong has devoted one third of its resources to accumulating capital and two thirds to consumption. In 1960, Hong Kong chose point *A* on its *PPF*.

Since 1960, both countries have experienced economic growth, but growth in Hong Kong has been more rapid than in the United States. Because Hong Kong devoted a bigger fraction of its resources to accumulating capital, its production possibilities expanded more quickly than those in the United States.

By 2000, the production possibilities per person in Hong Kong had reached 80 percent of those in the United States. If Hong Kong continues to devote more resources to accumulating capital than does the United States (at point *B* on its 2000 *PPF*), Hong Kong will continue to grow more rapidly than the United States and its *PPF* will eventually move out beyond our own. But if Hong Kong increases consumption and decreases capital accumulation (moving to point *D* on its 2000 *PPF*), its rate of economic growth will slow.

The United States is typical of the rich industrial countries, which include Western Europe and Japan. Hong Kong is typical of the fast-growing Asian economies, which include Taiwan, Thailand, South Korea, and China. Growth in these Asian countries slowed during the Asia crisis of 1998, but quickly rebounded. Production in these countries expands by between 5 percent and almost 10 percent a year. If these high growth rates are maintained, these countries will eventually close the gap on the United States.

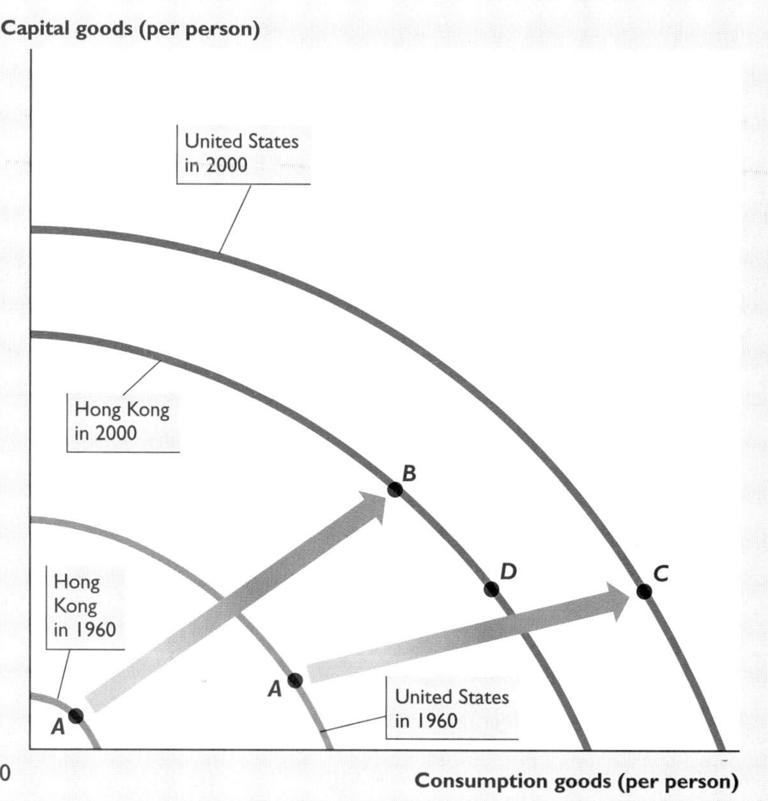

CHAPTER CHECKPOINT

Key Points

1 Use the production possibilities frontier to illustrate the economic problem.

- The production possibilities frontier, *PPF*, describes the limits to what we can produce by fully and efficiently using all our available resources.
- Points inside and on the *PPF* are attainable. Points outside the *PPF* are unattainable.
- If production is at a point on the *PPF*, resources are fully employed. If production is at a point inside the *PPF*, resources are unemployed.
- If production is at a point on the *PPF*, we face a tradeoff—to produce more of one good, we must produce less of another good. If production is at a point inside the *PPF*, there is a free lunch—we can produce more of both goods.

2 Calculate opportunity cost.

- Along the *PPF*, the opportunity cost of X (the item on the x-axis) is the decrease in Y (the item on the y-axis) divided by the increase in X.
- The opportunity cost of Y is the inverse of the opportunity cost of X.
- The opportunity cost of producing a good increases as the quantity produced increases.
- Opportunity cost increases because resources are not equally productive in all activities.

3 Explain how people gain from specialization and trade.

- A person has a comparative advantage in an activity if he or she can perform that activity at a lower opportunity cost than someone else.
- We gain by specializing in the activity in which we have a comparative advantage and trading.

4 Explain how technological change and increases in capital and human capital expand production possibilities.

- Technological change and increases in capital and human capital expand production possibilities.
- The greater the quantity of resources that are devoted to advancing technology and accumulating capital, the greater is the expansion of our production possibilities.
- The opportunity cost of economic growth is the decrease in current consumption.

Key Terms

TABLE 1

Corn (bushels per year)		Beef (pounds per year)
1,000	and	0
800	and	900
600	and	1,200
400	and	1,400
200	and	1,450
0	and	1,500

TABLE 2

Entertainment (units)		Good food (units)
100	and	0
80	and	30
60	and	50
40	and	60
20	and	65
0	and	67

Exercises

1. Table 1 shows the quantities of corn and beef that a farm can produce.
   a. Draw a graph of the farm's production possibilities frontier.
   b. Can the farm produce 500 bushels of corn and 500 pounds of beef?
   c. Can the farm produce 800 bushels of corn and 1,200 pounds of beef?
   d. What is the opportunity cost of the farm expanding beef production from 900 pounds to 1,200 pounds per year?
   e. What is the opportunity cost of the farm expanding corn production from 400 bushels to 600 bushels per year?
   f. If the farm produces 400 bushels of corn and 1,400 pounds of beef a year, is the farm using its resources efficiently? Explain your answer.

2. On Survivor Island, the only resources are 5 units of capital and 10 hours of labor a day. Table 2 shows the maximum quantities of entertainment and good food that Survivor Island can produce.
   a. Draw Survivor Island's production possibilities frontier.
   b. The people on Survivor Island want to produce 50 units of entertainment and 50 units of good food. Is this output attainable? If they do, does this output fully employ all the resources? What would be the opportunity cost of producing an additional unit of entertainment?
   c. The people on Survivor Island want to produce 40 units of entertainment and 60 units of good food. Is this output attainable? If they do, do they face a tradeoff? What would be the opportunity cost of producing an additional unit of entertainment?
   d. What can you say about the opportunity cost of a unit of good food as the people on Survivor Island allocate more resources to producing good food?

3. In 8 hours, Willy can produce either 50 sundaes or 20 pizzas. In 8 hours, Wendy can produce either 20 sundaes or 50 pizzas.
   a. Calculate Willy's opportunity cost of a sundae.
   b. Calculate Wendy's opportunity cost of a sundae.
   c. Who has a comparative advantage in producing pizzas?
   d. If Willy and Wendy specialize, how many sundaes and how many pizzas will they produce?

4. Tom can produce either 5 kites and 3 jigsaw puzzles an hour or 3 kites and 4 jigsaw puzzles an hour. Tessa can produce either 6 kites and 2 jigsaw puzzles an hour or 2 kites and 5 jigsaw puzzles an hour.
   a. Calculate Tom's opportunity cost of a kite.
   b. Calculate Tessa's opportunity cost of a kite.
   c. Who has a comparative advantage in producing kites?
   d. Who has a comparative advantage in jigsaw puzzles?

5. Tom and Tessa in exercise 4 specialize in producing the good in which they have a comparative advantage.
   a. Who specializes in producing kites?
   b. Who specializes in producing puzzles?
   c. What are the quantities of jigsaw puzzles and kites produced?
   d. Would Tom and Tessa get any gains from specializing production and trading with each other?

6. Table 3 shows the quantities of robots and consumption goods that the country Alpha can produce along its production possibilities frontier.
   a. If, in a year, Alpha produces 2,000 units of consumption goods, will Alpha experience economic growth? Explain.
   b. If, in a year, Alpha produces 1,100 units of consumption goods, will Alpha experience economic growth? Explain.
   c. If Alpha currently produces no robots and now decides to produce 1 robot, what is the cost of its economic growth?

TABLE 3

Robot services (units)		Consumption goods (units)
0	and	2,000
1	and	1,900
2	and	1,700
3	and	1,400
4	and	1,000
5	and	500

7. People can now obtain music from Web sites such as emusic and MP3.com.
   a. Have these Web sites changed the *PPF* for recorded music and other goods and services? If so, how has it changed?
   b. Is there still a tradeoff between recorded music and other goods and services, or is the opportunity cost of recorded music now zero?

8. AIDS has become an acute problem in Africa.
   a. How has the spread of AIDS influenced the *PPF* of the economies of Africa?
   b. Has the spread of AIDS increased the opportunity cost of some goods and services? Has it decreased the opportunity cost of anything?

9. A farm grows wheat and produces pigs. The opportunity cost of producing each of these products increases as more of it is produced.
   a. Make a graph that illustrates the farm's *PPF*.
   b. The farm adopts a new technology, which allows the farm to use fewer resources to fatten pigs. Use your graph to illustrate the impact of the new technology on the farm's *PPF*.
   c. With the farm using the new technology in part **b**, has the opportunity cost of producing a ton of wheat changed? If so, how? If not, why not?

10. Explain how each of the following items might change the U.S. production possibilities frontier. In each case, is an opportunity cost incurred? If so, what is it? If not, why not?
    a. A larger percentage of the government budget spent on education.
    b. The government spends more on Medicare and less on building the space station.
    c. Wild brush fires sweep through large parts of California and Arizona.

11. Each worker in Canada can produce 10 cars per year, while each worker in Mexico can produce 3 cars per year. But each worker in Mexico can produce 3 tons of steel per year, while each worker in Canada can produce 6 tons of steel per year. Mexico has 100 million workers, and Canada has 25 million workers. Suppose that each country produces only cars and steel.
    a. Draw a graph of Canada's production possibilities frontier.
    b. Draw a graph of Mexico's production possibilities frontier.
    c. Calculate the opportunity cost of producing 1 ton of steel in each country.
    d. Calculate the opportunity cost of producing 1 car in each country.
    e. Does either country have an absolute advantage? Which one?
    f. In which country is the marginal cost of producing a car lower?

Critical Thinking

12. After the terrorist attacks on the United States on September 11, 2001, Congress allocated increased resources to national defense, homeland security, and intelligence gathering. At the same time, Congress voted for lower taxes. Think about the effects of these choices in terms of the production possibilities frontier for two groups of goods and services: "national security" and "other goods and services."
    a. Show on a graph of the *PPF* the changes that have occurred since September 11, 2001.
    b. Do you think that the opportunity cost of a unit of national security has increased or decreased? Explain your answer.
    c. Do you think that the opportunity cost of a unit of other goods and services has increased or decreased? Explain your answer.
13. The Kyoto agreement requires countries to achieve greenhouse gas reduction targets over the next ten years. The Canadian government has signed the Kyoto agreement but the U.S. government will not sign it.
    a. As the Canadian government allocates more resources to reducing pollution, how do you think the Canadian *PPF* will change?
    b. Do you think that Canadian economic growth will change by more than U.S. economic growth changes? Or will growth in neither country be affected?
    c. Do you think that Canada's opportunity cost of producing goods and services will change?
    d. Do you think that Canada will gain or lose some of its comparative advantage relative to the United States? Explain your answer.

Practice Online

Web Exercises

Use the links on your Foundations Web site to work the following exercises.

14. Visit the U.S. Census Bureau population clocks.
    a. What is the estimated population of the United States?
    b. What is the estimated population of the world?
    c. How fast is the U. S. population increasing? (Use the second timer on your computer clock to determine the pace of increase.)
    d. How fast is the world population increasing?
    e. What do the population increases that you've found imply about the U.S. *PPF* and the world *PPF*? Which is moving faster?
15. Review the article *What's an MBA Really Worth*?
    a. Is it rational for a person to enroll in an MBA program?
    b. Why don't more people or fewer people enroll in MBA programs?
    c. If an MBA can be done part time and online, does that lower the cost of obtaining an MBA or does it increase the cost?
    d. Would you expect more people to do an MBA part time or more full time? Explain why. Is there any conflict between your answers to parts **c** and **d**? Explain why not.
16. Visit the Bureau of Economic Analysis and find data on the things that the United States exports and imports.
    a. What are the three largest exports (by value)?
    b. What are the three largest imports (by value)?
    c. In which items do you think the United States has a comparative advantage?
    d. In which items do you think other countries have a comparative advantage?
    e. Can you tell just by knowing the items that we export and import whether the United States has an absolute advantage in any of these items?

CHAPTER 4

Demand and Supply

CHAPTER CHECKLIST

When you have completed your study of this chapter, you will be able to

1 **Distinguish between quantity demanded and demand and explain what determines demand.**

2 **Distinguish between quantity supplied and supply and explain what determines supply.**

3 **Explain how demand and supply determine price and quantity in a market and explain the effects of changes in demand and supply.**

4 **Explain how price ceilings, price floors, and sticky prices cause shortages, surpluses, and unemployment.**

Faced with scarcity, we specialize in the activity at which we have a comparative advantage. We sell the services of our factors of production in factor markets, and we buy the goods and services that we consume in goods markets.

In this chapter, you study the tools of demand and supply that explain how markets work. You will learn how the choices people make about what to buy and sell determine the quantities and prices of the goods and services produced and consumed and the quantities of the factors of production employed.

Through the rest of your course in macroeconomics, you will use these demand and supply tools to understand the forces that influence the standard of living and the overall level of economic activity. Soon, you will find yourself using the tools of demand and supply every time you think about a price or a quantity in your everyday life.

MARKETS

When you need a new pair of running shoes, want a bagel and a latte, plan to upgrade your entertainment system, or need to fly home for Thanksgiving, you must find a place where people sell those items or offer those services. The place in which you find them is a *market*. You learned in Chapter 2 that a market is any arrangement that brings buyers and sellers together. A market has two sides: buyers (demanders) and sellers (suppliers). There are markets for *goods* such as apples and hiking boots, for *services* such as haircuts and tennis lessons, for *resources* such as computer programmers and earthmovers, and for other manufactured *inputs* such as memory chips and auto parts. There are also markets for money such as Japanese yen and for financial securities such as Yahoo! stock. Only imagination limits what can be traded in markets.

Some markets are physical places where the buyers and sellers meet and where an auctioneer or a broker helps to determine the prices. Examples of this type of market are the New York Stock Exchange and wholesale fish, meat, and produce markets.

Some markets are groups of people spread around the world who never meet and know little about each other but are connected through the Internet or by telephone. Examples of this type of market are the e-commerce markets and currency markets.

But most markets are unorganized collections of buyers and sellers. You do most of your trading in this type of market. An example is the market for basketball shoes. The buyers in this \$3 billion-a-year market are the 45 million Americans who play basketball (or those who want to make a fashion statement) and are looking for a new pair of shoes. The sellers are the tens of thousands of retail sports equipment and footwear stores. Each buyer can visit several different stores, and each seller knows that the buyer has a choice of stores.

For most of this chapter, we'll study a market that has so many buyers and sellers that no one can influence the price. In the final section we'll study markets in which the government tries to influence the price or a seller sets the price or in which buyers and sellers together agree on a price.

Markets for stocks...

currency...

and running shoes.

4.1 DEMAND

First, we'll study the behavior of the buyers in a market. The **quantity demanded** of any good, service, or resource is the amount that people are willing and able to buy during a specified period at a specified price. For example, when spring water costs $1 a bottle, you decide to buy 2 bottles a day, so this is your quantity demanded of spring water.

Quantity demanded
The amount of any good, service, or resource that people are willing and able to buy during a specified period at a specified price.

The quantity demanded is measured as an amount *per unit of time*. For example, your quantity demanded of water is 2 bottles *per day*. We could express this quantity as 14 bottles per week or some other number per month or per year. But without a time dimension, a particular number of bottles has no meaning.

Many things influence buying plans, and one of them is price. We look first at the relationship between quantity demanded and price. To study this relationship, we keep all other influences on buying plans the same and we ask: How, other things remaining the same, does the quantity demanded of a good change as its price varies? The law of demand provides the answer.

The Law of Demand

The **law of demand** states

> **Other things remaining the same, if the price of a good rises, the quantity demanded of that good decreases; and if the price of a good falls, the quantity demanded of that good increases.**

So the law of demand states that when all else remains the same, if the price of a Palm Pilot falls, people will buy more Palm Pilots; or if the price of a baseball ticket rises, people will buy fewer tickets.

Why does the quantity demanded increase if the price falls, all other things remaining the same?

The answer is that faced with a limited budget, people always have an incentive to find the best deals they can. If the price of one item falls and the prices of all other items remain the same, the item with the lower price is a better deal than it was before. So people buy more of this item. Suppose, for example, that the price of bottled water fell from $1 a bottle to 25 cents a bottle while the price of Gatorade remained at $1 a bottle. Wouldn't some people switch from Gatorade to water? By doing so, they save 75 cents a bottle, which they can spend on other things that they previously couldn't afford.

Think about the things that you buy and ask yourself: Which of these items does *not* obey the law of demand? If the price of a new textbook were lower, other things remaining the same (including the price of a used textbook), would you buy more new textbooks? Then think about all the things that you do not now buy but would if you could afford them. How cheap would a PC have to be for you to buy *both* a desktop and a laptop? There is a price that is low enough to entice you!

Demand Schedule and Demand Curve

Demand is the relationship between the *quantity demanded* and the *price* of a good when all other influences on buying plans remain the same. The quantity demanded is *one* quantity at *one* price. *Demand* is a *list of quantities at different prices* illustrated by a demand schedule and a demand curve.

Demand
The relationship between the quantity demanded and the price of a good when all other influences on buying plans remain the same.

Demand schedule
A list of the quantities demanded at each different price when all the other influences on buying plans remain the same.

Demand curve
A graph of the relationship between the quantity demanded of a good and its price when all the other influences on buying plans remain the same.

A **demand schedule** is a list of the quantities demanded at each different price when *all the other influences on buying plans remain the same*. The table in Figure 4.1 is a demand schedule for bottled water. It tells us that if the price of water is $2.00 a bottle, the quantity demanded is 8.5 million bottles a day. If the price of water is $1.50 a bottle, the quantity demanded is 9 million bottles a day. The quantity demanded increases to 10 million bottles a day at a price of $1.00 a bottle and to 12 million bottles a day at a price of 50 cents a bottle.

A **demand curve** is a graph of the relationship between the quantity demanded of a good and its price when all the other influences on buying plans remain the same. The points on the demand curve labeled *A* through *D* represent the rows *A* through *D* of the demand schedule. For example, point *B* on the graph represents row *B* of the demand schedule and shows that the quantity demanded is 9 million bottles a day when the price is $1.50 a bottle. Point *C* on the demand curve represents row *C* of the demand schedule and shows that the quantity demanded is 10 million bottles a day when the price is $1.00 a bottle.

The downward slope of the demand curve illustrates the law of demand. Along the demand curve, when the price of the good *falls*, the quantity demanded *increases*. When the price of a bottle of water falls from $1.00 to $0.50, the quantity demanded increases from 10 million bottles a day to 12 million bottles a day. And when the price *rises*, the quantity demanded *decreases*. When the price rises from $1.00 to $1.50 a bottle, the quantity demanded decreases from 10 million bottles a day to 9 million bottles a day.

FIGURE 4.1
Demand Schedule and Demand Curve

Practice Online

The table shows a demand schedule, which lists the quantity of water demanded at each price if all other influences on buying plans remain the same. At a price of $1.50 a bottle, the quantity demanded is 9 million bottles a day.

The demand curve shows the relationship between the quantity demanded and price, everything else remaining the same. The downward-sloping demand curve illustrates the law of demand. When the price falls, the quantity demanded increases; and when the price rises, the quantity demanded decreases.

	Price (dollars per bottle)	Quantity demanded (millions of bottles per day)
A	2.00	8.5
B	1.50	9.0
C	1.00	10.0
D	0.50	12.0

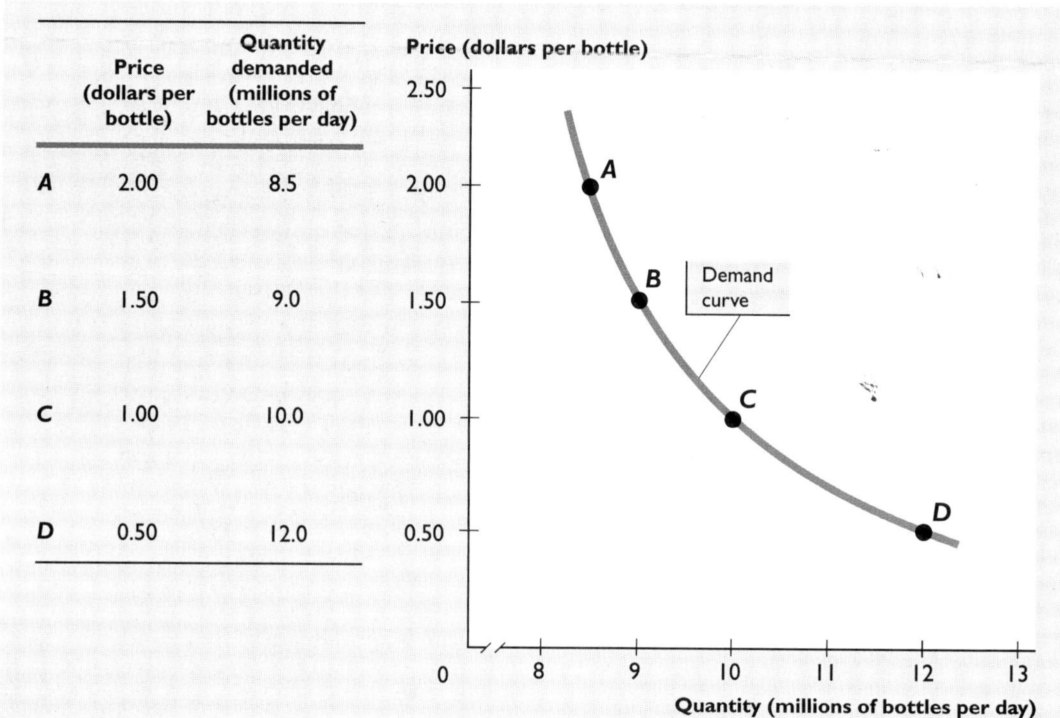

Changes in Demand

The demand curve shows how the quantity demanded changes when the price changes but *all other influences on buying plans remain the same.* When the price changes, we call the resulting change in buying plans a **change in the quantity demanded**. When any influence on buying plans other than the price of the good changes, there is a **change in demand**.

Change in the quantity demanded
A change in the quantity of a good that people plan to buy that results from a change in the price of the good.

Change in demand
A change in the quantity that people plan to buy when any influence on buying plans, other than the price of the good, changes.

The main influences on buying plans that change demand are

- Prices of related goods
- Income
- Expectations
- Number of buyers
- Preferences

Prices of Related Goods

A change in the price of one good can bring a change in the demand for a related good. Related goods are either substitutes or complements. A **substitute** for a good is another good that can be consumed in its place. Chocolate cake is a substitute for cheesecake, a taxi ride is a substitute for a subway ride, and bottled water is a substitute for Gatorade.

Substitute
A good that can be consumed in place of another good.

The demand for a good *increases* if the price of one of its substitutes *rises*; and the demand for a good *decreases* if the price of one of its substitutes *falls*. That is, the demand for a good and the price of one of its substitutes move in the *same direction*. For example, the demand for cheesecake increases when the price of chocolate cake rises.

A **complement** of a good is another good that is consumed with it. Salsa is a complement of tortilla chips, wrist guards are a complement of in-line skates, and bottled water is a complement of fitness center services.

Complement
A good that is consumed with another good.

The demand for a good *decreases* if the price of one of its complements *rises*; and the demand for a good *increases* if the price of one of its complements *falls*. That is, the demand for a good and the price of one of its complements move in *opposite directions*. For example, the demand for salsa decreases when the price of tortilla chips rises.

Income

A good is a **normal good** if a rise in income brings an increase in demand and a fall in income brings a decrease in demand. For example, if you buy more bottled water when your income increases, then bottled water is a normal good. Most goods are normal goods (hence the name).

Normal good
A good for which demand increases when income increases.

A good is an **inferior good** if a rise in income brings a *decrease* in demand and a fall in income brings an *increase* in demand. For example, if you buy fewer plastic milk crates and more bookcases when your income increases, then a plastic milk crate is an inferior good.

Inferior good
A good for which demand decreases when income increases.

Expectations

Expected future income and prices influence demand. For example, you're offered a well-paid job that starts next summer, so you go to Cancun during spring break. Your demand for vacation travel has increased. Or if you expect the price of ramen noodles to rise next week, you buy enough to get you through the rest of the school year. Your demand for ramen noodles has increased.

Number of Buyers

The greater the number of buyers in a market, the larger is demand. For example, the demand for parking spaces, movies, bottled water, or just about anything is greater in New York City than it is in Boise, Idaho.

Preferences

When *preferences* change, the demand for one item decreases and the demand for another item (or items) increases. Better information about the health hazards of tobacco has changed preferences. This change in preferences has decreased the demand for cigarettes and increased the demand for nicotine patches.

Preferences also change when new goods become available. For example, the development of MP3 has decreased the demand for CDs and increased the demand for Internet services and personal computers.

Illustrating a Change in Demand

Figure 4.2 illustrates a change in demand and distinguishes it from a change in the quantity demanded. When the price of the good changes, there is *change in the quantity demanded*, shown by a *movement along the demand curve*. When demand changes, *the demand curve shifts*. Figure 4.2 illustrates two changes in demand. Initially, the demand curve is D_0. When the demand for bottled water decreases, the demand curve shifts leftward to D_1. On demand curve D_1, the quantity demanded is smaller at each price. And when the demand for bottled water increases, the demand curve shifts rightward to D_2. On demand curve D_2, the quantity demanded is greater at each price.

FIGURE 4.2

Change in Quantity Demanded Versus Change in Demand

Practice Online

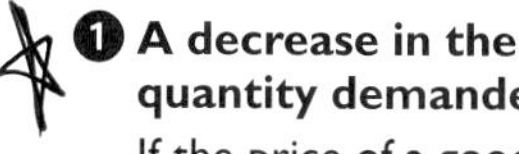

1 A decrease in the quantity demanded

If the price of a good rises, *cet. par.*, the quantity demanded decreases. There is a movement up along the demand curve D_0.

2 A decrease in demand

Demand decreases and the demand curve shifts leftward (from D_0 to D_1) if

- The price of a substitute falls.
- The price of a complement rises.
- The price of the good is expected to fall or income is expected to fall in the future.
- Income decreases.*
- The number of buyers decreases.

* Bottled water is a normal good

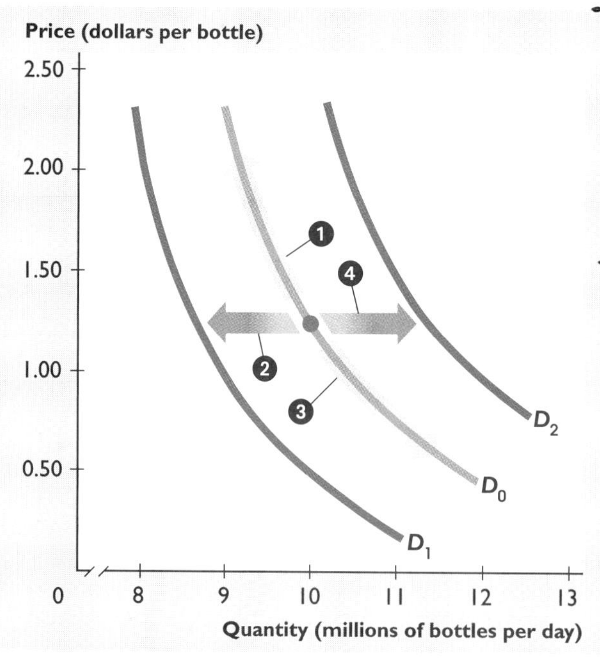

3 An increase in the quantity demanded

If the price of a good falls, *cet. par.*, the quantity demanded increases. There is a movement down along the demand curve D_0.

4 An increase in demand

Demand increases and the demand curve shifts rightward (from D_0 to D_2) if

- The price of a substitute rises.
- The price of a complement falls.
- The price of the good is expected to rise or income is expected to rise in the future.
- Income increases.*
- The number of buyers increases.

CHECKPOINT 4.1

1 Distinguish between quantity demanded and demand and explain what determines demand.

Study Guide **pp. 53–55**

Practice Online 4.1

Practice Problem 4.1

In the market for scooters, several events occur, one at a time. Explain the influence of each event on the quantity demanded of scooters and on the demand for scooters. Illustrate the effects of each event by either a movement along the demand curve or a shift in the demand curve for scooters and say which event (or events) illustrates the law of demand in action. These events are

a. The price of a scooter falls.
b. The price of a bicycle falls.
c. Citing rising injury rates, cities and towns ban scooters from sidewalks.
d. Income increases.
e. Rumor has it that the price of a scooter will rise next month.
f. Scooters become unfashionable and the number of buyers decreases.

Exercise 4.1

The cell phone was invented in 1973, and during the first 20 years of its life, few people used one, except as a car phone. But during the 1990s, the use of cell phones increased dramatically and the price of cell phone service fell.

a. Are there any substitutes for cell phones? If so, provide an example.
b. Do cell phones have any complements? If so, provide an example.
c. What are the main developments that brought about the dramatic increase in cell phone use during the 1990s?
d. Which of the developments that you have identified increased the demand for cell phones? Illustrate these effects by using the demand curve for cell phones.
e. Which of the developments that you have identified increased the quantity demanded of cell phones? Illustrate these effects by using the demand curve for cell phones.

FIGURE 1

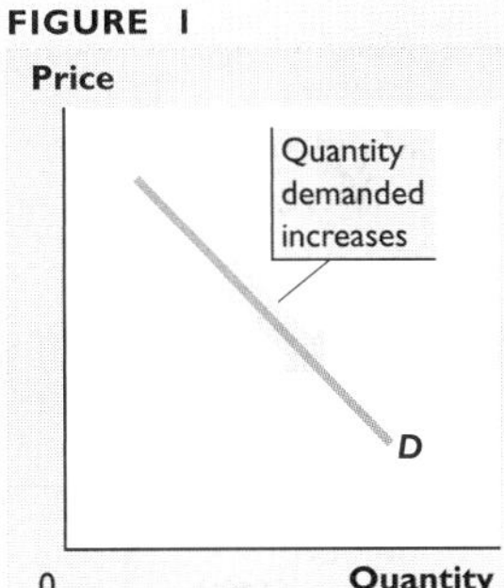

Solution to Practice Problem 4.1

a. A fall in the price of a scooter increases the quantity demanded of scooters, shown by a movement down along the demand curve for scooters (Figure 1). It is an example of the law of demand in action.
b. A bicycle is a substitute for a scooter. So when the price of a bicycle falls, the demand for scooters decreases. The demand curve shifts leftward (Figure 2).
c. The ban on scooters changes preferences and decreases the demand for scooters. The demand curve shifts leftward (Figure 2).
d. A scooter is (likely) a normal good. So when income increases, the demand for scooters increases. The demand curve shifts rightward (Figure 2).
e. A rise in the expected price of a scooter increases the demand for scooters now. The demand curve shifts rightward (Figure 2).
f. A decrease in the number of buyers decreases the demand for scooters. The demand curve shifts leftward (Figure 2).

FIGURE 2

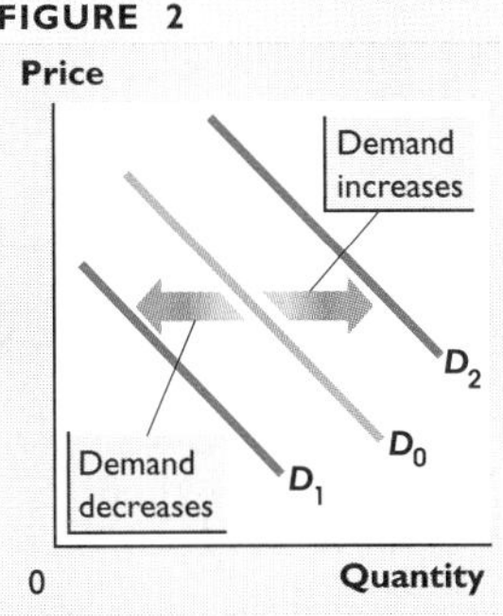

4.2 SUPPLY

A market has two sides. On one side are the buyers, or demanders, that we've just studied. On the other side of the market are the sellers, or suppliers. We now study the forces that determine suppliers' plans.

Quantity supplied
The amount of any good, service, or resource that people are willing and able to sell during a specified period at a specified price.

The **quantity supplied** of a good, service, or resource is the amount that people are willing and able to sell during a specified period at a specified price. For example, when the price of spring water is $1.50 a bottle, a spring owner decides to sell 2,000 bottles a day, so this is the quantity supplied of spring water by this individual producer. (As in the case of demand, the quantity supplied is measured as an amount *per unit of time*.)

Many things influence selling plans, and one of them is the price. We look first at the relationship between quantity supplied of a good and its price. To study this relationship, we keep all other influences on selling plans the same. And we ask: How, other things remaining the same, does the quantity supplied of a good change as its price varies? The law of supply provides the answer.

The Law of Supply

The **law of supply** states

> **Other things remaining the same, if the price of a good rises, the quantity supplied of that good increases; and if the price of a good falls, the quantity supplied of that good decreases.**

So the law of supply states that when all else remains the same, if the price of bottled water rises, spring owners will offer more water for sale; if the price of a CD falls, Sony Corp. will offer fewer CDs for sale.

Why, other things remaining the same, does the quantity supplied increase if the price rises? The basic answer is that when the production of a good or service increases, the opportunity cost of producing it increases (Chapter 3, p. 68). But if the price exceeds the opportunity cost of production, then it is profitable to increase the quantity supplied. So a higher price makes it profitable to produce a larger quantity and incur a higher opportunity cost.

For example, to increase the quantity of bottled water produced per day, a spring owner must hire more labor and run the bottling plant at a faster rate. The opportunity cost per bottle produced increases. If the price of a bottle of water rises from $1 a bottle to $2 a bottle, while the prices of everything else, including wage rates and the prices of other inputs, remain the same, the spring owner will increase production and incur the higher opportunity cost. By doing so, the spring owner will earn a larger profit.

The law of supply also applies to the things that you own and can offer for sale. If, for example, the used book dealer offered a higher price for last year's textbooks, wouldn't you think about selling that handy math text?

Supply Schedule and Supply Curve

Supply
The relationship between the quantity supplied and the price of a good when all other influences on selling plans remain the same.

Supply is the relationship between the quantity supplied and the price of a good when all other influences on selling plans remain the same. The quantity supplied is *one* quantity at *one* price. *Supply* is a *list of quantities at different prices* illustrated by a supply schedule and a supply curve.

A **supply schedule** lists the quantities supplied at each different price when all the other influences on selling plans remain the same. The table in Figure 4.3 is a supply schedule for bottled water. It tells us that if the price of water is 50 cents a bottle, the quantity supplied is 8 million bottles a day. If the price of water is $1.00 a bottle, the quantity supplied is 10 million bottles a day. The quantity supplied increases to 11 million bottles a day at a price of $1.50 a bottle and to 11.5 million bottles a day at a price of $2.00 a bottle.

Supply schedule
A list of the quantities supplied at each different price when all the other influences on selling plans remain the same.

A **supply curve** is a graph of the relationship between the quantity supplied of a good and its price when all the other influences on selling plans remain the same. The points on the supply curve labeled *A* through *D* represent the rows *A* through *D* of the supply schedule. For example, point *C* on the graph represents row *C* of the supply schedule and shows that the quantity supplied is 10 million bottles a day when the price is $1.00 a bottle. Point *B* on the supply curve represents row *B* of the supply schedule and shows that the quantity supplied is 11 million bottles a day when the price is $1.50 a bottle.

Supply curve
A graph of the relationship between the quantity supplied of a good and its price when all the other influences on selling plans remain the same.

The upward slope of the supply curve illustrates the law of supply. Along the supply curve, when the price of the good *rises*, the quantity supplied *increases*. When the price of a bottle of water rises from $1.50 to $2.00, the quantity supplied increases from 11 million bottles a day to 11.5 million bottles a day. And when the price *falls*, the quantity supplied *decreases*. When the price falls from $1.50 to $1.00 a bottle, the quantity supplied decreases from 11 million bottles a day to 10 million bottles a day.

FIGURE 4.3
Supply Schedule and Supply Curve

Practice Online

	Price (dollars per bottle)	Quantity supplied (millions of bottles per day)
A	2.00	11.5
B	1.50	11.0
C	1.00	10.0
D	0.50	8.0

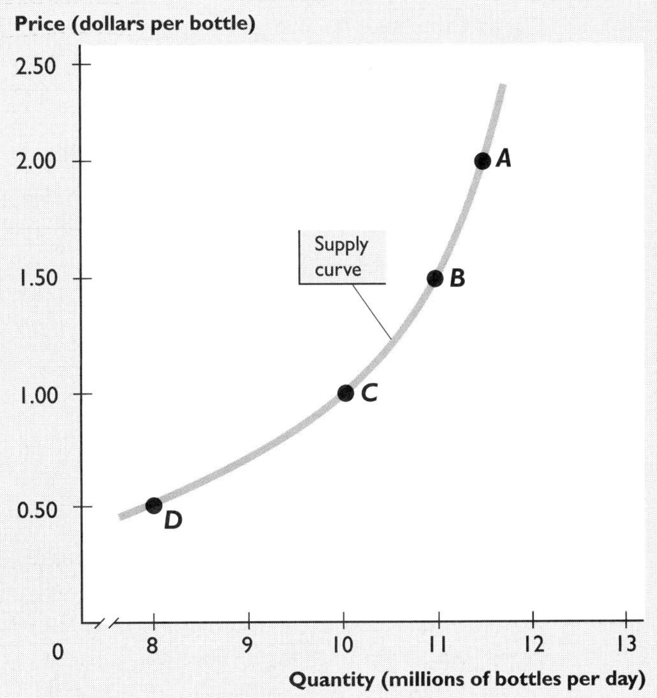

Price (dollars per bottle)
2.50
2.00
1.50
1.00
0.50
0
8 9 10 11 12 13
Quantity (millions of bottles per day)
Supply curve
A B C D

The table shows a supply schedule, which lists the quantity of water supplied at each price if all other influences on selling plans remain the same. At a price of $1.50 a bottle, the quantity supplied is 11 million bottles a day.

The supply curve shows the relationship between the quantity supplied and price, everything else remaining the same. The upward-sloping supply curve illustrates the law of supply. When the price rises, the quantity supplied increases; and when the price falls, the quantity supplied decreases.

Changes in Supply

Change in the quantity supplied
A change in the quantity of a good that suppliers plan to sell that results from a change in the price of the good.

Change in supply
A change in the quantity that suppliers plan to sell when any influence on selling plans, other than the price of the good, changes.

The supply curve shows how the quantity supplied changes when the price changes but *all other influences on selling plans remain the same*. When the price changes, we call the resulting influence on selling plans the **change in the quantity supplied**. When any influence on selling plans other than the price of the good changes, there is a **change in supply**.

The main influences on selling plans that change supply are

- Prices of related goods
- Prices of resources and other inputs
- Expectations
- Number of sellers
- Productivity

Prices of Related Goods

Substitute in production
A good that can be produced in place of another good.

A change in the price of one good can bring a change in the supply of a related good. Related goods are substitutes in production or complements in production. A **substitute in production** for a good is another good that can be produced in its place. Button-fly jeans are substitutes in production for cargo pants in a clothing factory. The supply of a good *decreases* if the price of one of its substitutes in production *rises*; and the supply of a good *increases* if the price of one of its substitutes in production *falls*. That is, the supply of a good and the price of one of its substitutes in production move in *opposite directions*. For example, the supply of cargo pants decreases when the price of button-fly jeans rises.

Complement in production
A good that is produced along with another good.

A **complement in production** of a good is another good that is produced along with it. Cowhide is a complement in production of beef. The supply of a good *increases* if the price of one of its complements in production *rises*; and the supply of a good *decreases* if the price of one of its complements in production *falls*. That is, the supply of a good and the price of one of its complements in production move in the *same direction*. For example, the supply of cowhide increases when the price of beef rises.

Prices of Resources and Other Inputs

Supply changes when the price of a resource or other input used to produce the good changes. The reason is that resource and input prices influence the cost of production. And the more it costs to produce a good, the smaller is the quantity supplied of that good (other things remaining the same). For example, if the wage rate of bottling-plant workers rises, it costs more to produce a bottle of water. So the supply of bottled water decreases.

Expectations

Expectations about future prices have a big influence on supply. For example, Boston's Big Dig is placing its freeways underground. A real estate developer expects the price of office space to rise when the Big Dig is completed. So instead of building new office space now, she plans to build it later when the price is higher. This action makes the supply of office space today less than it otherwise would have been. Expectations of future input prices also influence supply. If the developer expects builders' wages to rise next year, she might build new office space now before the wage rise occurs. This action increases the supply of office space today.

Number of Sellers

The greater the number of sellers in a market, the larger is supply. For example, many new sellers have developed springs and water-bottling plants in the United States and the supply of bottled water has increased.

Productivity

Productivity is output per unit of input. An increase in productivity lowers costs and increases supply. A decrease in productivity has the opposite effect and decreases supply. Technological change is the main influence on productivity. For example, advances in electronic technology have lowered the cost of computers and increased their supply. Natural events such as weather patterns change farm productivity and change the supply of agricultural products.

Illustrating a Change in Supply

Figure 4.4 illustrates a change in supply and distinguishes it from a change in the quantity supplied. When the price of the good changes, there is *change in the quantity supplied,* shown by a *movement along the supply curve*. When supply changes, *the supply curve shifts*. Figure 4.4 illustrates two changes in supply. Initially, the supply curve is S_0. When the supply of bottled water decreases, the supply curve shifts leftward to S_1. On supply curve S_1, the quantity supplied is smaller at each price. And when the supply of bottled water increases, the supply curve shifts rightward to S_2. On supply curve S_2, the quantity supplied is greater at each price.

FIGURE 4.4

Change in Quantity Supplied Versus Change in Supply

Practice Online

1 A decrease in the quantity supplied

If the price of a good falls, *cet. par.*, the quantity supplied decreases. There is a movement down along the demand curve S_0.

2 A decrease in supply

Supply decreases and the supply curve shifts leftward (from S_0 to S_1) if

- The price of a substitute in production rises.
- The price of a complement in production falls.
- A resource price or other input price rises.
- The price of the good is expected to rise.
- The number of sellers decreases.
- Productivity decreases.

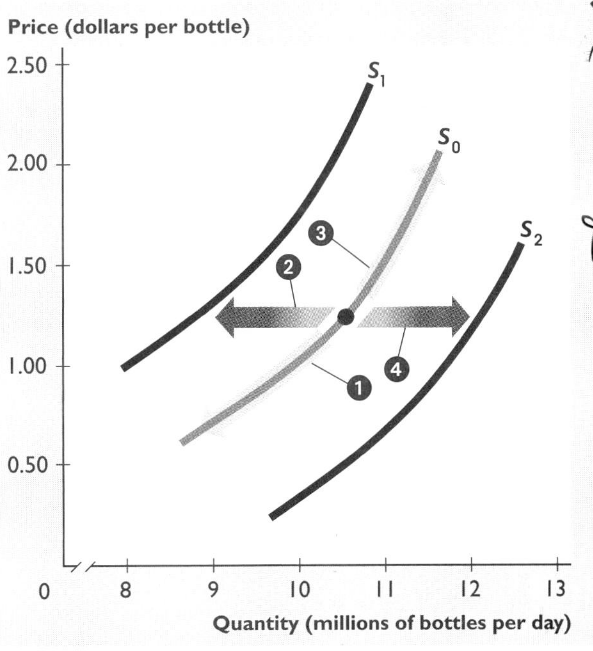

3 An increase in the quantity supplied

If the price of a good rises, *cet. par.*, the quantity supplied increases. There is a movement up along the supply curve S_0.

4 An increase in supply

Supply increases and the supply curve shifts rightward (from S_0 to S_2) if

- The price of a substitute in production falls.
- The price of a complement in production rises.
- A resource price or other input price falls.
- The price of the good is expected to fall.
- The number of sellers increases.
- Productivity increases.

CHECKPOINT 4.2

Study Guide **pp. 55–58**

Practice Online 4.2

2 **Distinguish between quantity supplied and supply and explain what determines supply.**

Practice Problem 4.2

In the market for timber beams, several events occur one at a time. Explain the influence of each event on the quantity supplied of timber beams and the supply of timber beams. Illustrate the effects of each event by either a movement along the supply curve or a shift in the supply curve of timber beams and say which event (or events) illustrates the law of supply in action. These events are

a. The wage rate of sawmill workers rises.
b. The price of sawdust rises.
c. The price of a timber beam rises.
d. The price of a timber beam is expected to rise next year.
e. Environmentalists convince Congress to pass a new law that reduces the amount of forest that can be cut for timber products.
f. A new technology lowers the cost of producing timber beams.

Exercise 4.2

In the market for DVDs, several events occur one at a time. Explain the influence of each event on the quantity supplied of DVDs and the supply of DVDs. Illustrate the effects of each event by either a movement along the supply curve or a shift of the supply curve of DVDs, and say which event (or events) illustrates the law of supply in action. These events are

a. The price of a CD falls.
b. The price of a DVD falls.
c. The price of a DVD is expected to fall next year.
d. The number of producers of DVDs increases.
e. The wage rate paid to DVD factory workers increases.
f. A new robot technology lowers the cost of producing DVDs.

FIGURE 1

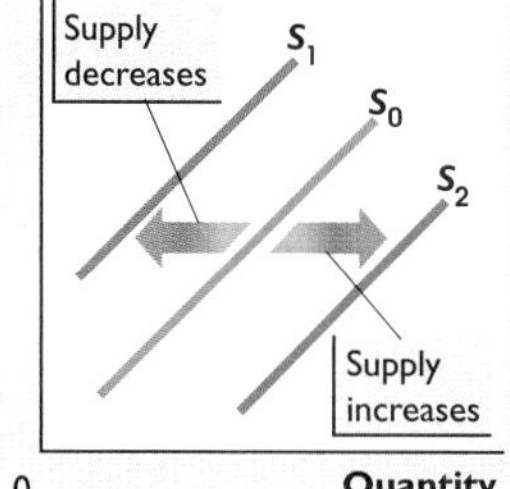

FIGURE 2

Price

Quantity supplied increases

S

0

Quantity

Solution to Practice Problem 4.2

a. A rise in the wage rate of sawmill workers decreases the supply of timber beams. The supply curve of timber beams shifts leftward (Figure 1).
b. Sawdust and timber beams are complements in production. A rise in the price of sawdust increases the supply of timber beams. The supply curve of timber beams shifts rightward (Figure 1).
c. A rise in the price of a timber beam increases the quantity supplied of timber beams, which is shown as a movement up along the supply curve of timber beams (Figure 2). It is an example of the law of supply in action.
d. The expected rise in the price of a timber beam decreases the supply of timber beams now. The supply curve of timber beams shifts leftward (Figure 1).
e. The new law decreases the supply of timber beams. The supply curve of timber beams shifts leftward (Figure 1).
f. The new technology increases the supply of timber beams and shifts the supply curve rightward (Figure 1).

4.3 MARKET EQUILIBRIUM

In everyday language, "equilibrium" means "opposing forces are in balance." In a market, the opposing forces are those of demand and supply. Buyers want the lowest possible price, and the lower the price, the greater is the quantity that they plan to buy. Sellers want the highest possible price, and the higher the price, the greater is the quantity that they plan to sell.

Market equilibrium occurs when the quantity demanded equals the quantity supplied—when buyers' and sellers' plans are consistent. The **equilibrium price** is the price at which the quantity demanded equals the quantity supplied. The **equilibrium quantity** is the quantity that is bought and sold at the equilibrium price.

Market equilibrium
When the quantity demanded equals the quantity supplied—when buyers' and sellers' plans are consistent.

Equilibrium price
The price at which the quantity demanded equals the quantity supplied.

Equilibrium quantity
The quantity that is bought and sold at the equilibrium price.

Figure 4.5 shows the market for bottled water. The market equilibrium occurs where the demand curve and the supply curve intersect. The equilibrium price is $1 a bottle, and the equilibrium quantity is 10 million bottles a day.

At the equilibrium price, buying plans and selling plans are balanced. People would buy more water at a lower price, and bottlers would sell more water at a higher price. But at a price of $1 a bottle, the quantity that people plan to buy equals the quantity that bottlers plan to sell. The opposing forces of buying plans and selling plans are exactly balanced at a price of $1 a bottle.

An equilibrium might be stable or unstable. Balance an egg on its pointed end (if you can!) and then give it a nudge. The egg rolls over onto its side. The equilibrium was unstable. Now balance an egg on its side and give it a nudge. The egg rocks for a moment but soon settles down in its equilibrium again. Market equilibrium is like an egg balanced on its side. The market is constantly pulled toward a stable equilibrium in which neither buyers nor sellers can improve their positions by changing either the price or the quantity.

FIGURE 4.5
Equilibrium Price and Quantity

Practice Online

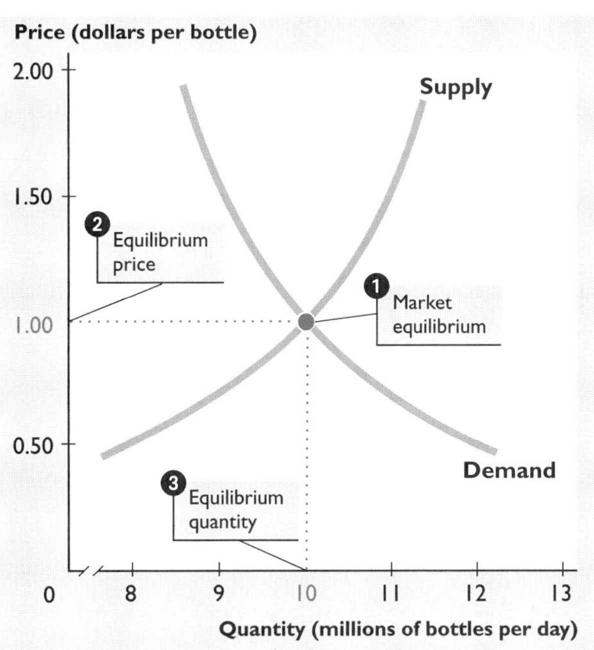

1. Market equilibrium occurs at the intersection of the demand curve and the supply curve.
2. The equilibrium price is $1.00 a bottle.
3. At the equilibrium price, the quantity demanded and the quantity supplied are 10 million bottles a day, which is the equilibrium quantity.

Price: A Market's Automatic Regulator

When equilibrium is disturbed, the market forces restore it. The **law of market forces** states

> **When there is a shortage, the price rises; when there is a surplus, the price falls.**

Surplus or excess supply
A situation in which the quantity supplied exceeds the quantity demanded.

Shortage or excess demand
A situation in which the quantity demanded exceeds the quantity supplied.

Price is the regulator that pulls the market toward its equilibrium. If the price is above the equilibrium price, there is a **surplus** or **excess supply**—the quantity supplied exceeds the quantity demanded—and the price falls. If the price is below the equilibrium price, there is a **shortage** or **excess demand**—the quantity demanded exceeds the quantity supplied—and the price rises.

In Figure 4.6(a), when the price is $1.50 a bottle, suppliers would like to sell 11 million bottles but demanders buy only 9 million bottles. There is a surplus of 2 million bottles, and the price begins to fall. As the price falls, the quantity demanded increases, the quantity supplied decreases, and the surplus decreases. The price falls until there is no surplus and comes to rest at $1 a bottle.

In Figure 4.6(b), at 75 cents a bottle, demanders would like to buy 11 million bottles but suppliers sell only 9 million bottles. There is a shortage of 2 million bottles, and the price begins to rise. As the price rises, the quantity supplied increases, the quantity demanded decreases, and the shortage decreases. The price rises until there is no shortage and comes to rest at $1 a bottle.

FIGURE 4.6
The Forces That Achieve Equilibrium

Practice Online

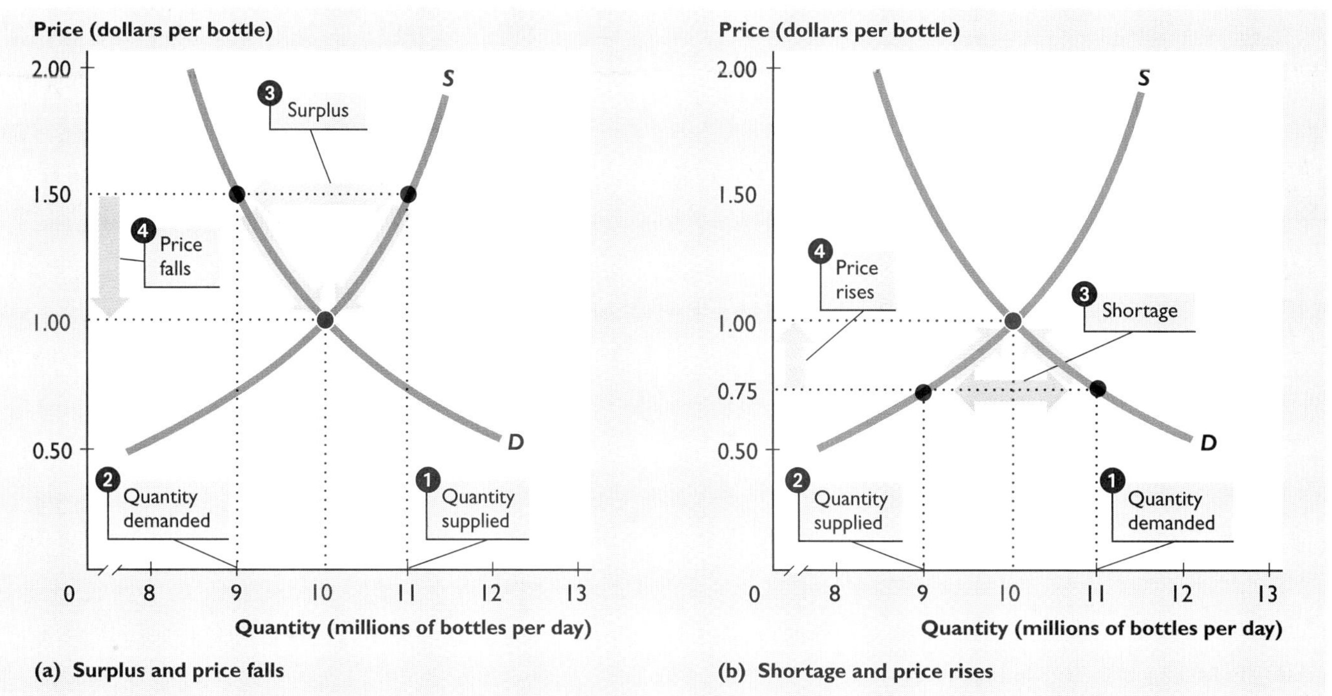

At $1.50 a bottle, ❶ the quantity supplied is 11 million bottles, ❷ the quantity demanded is 9 million bottles, ❸ the surplus is 2 million bottles, and ❹ the price falls.

At 75 cents a bottle, ❶ the quantity demanded is 11 million bottles, ❷ the quantity supplied is 9 million bottles, ❸ the shortage is 2 million bottles, and ❹ the price rises.

Effects of Changes in Demand

Markets are constantly hit by events that change demand and supply and bring changes in price and quantity. Some events change demand, and some events change supply. And sometimes these events occur together. We'll look at all the possible cases. But we'll look first at the effects of changes in demand.

In Figure 4.7, the supply curve is *S* and initially, the demand curve is D_0. The equilibrium price is $1 a bottle, and the equilibrium quantity is 10 million bottles.

Suppose that a new study is published that raises concerns about the safety of the public water supply. The demand for bottled water increases. In Figure 4.7(a), the demand curve *shifts rightward* to D_1. At $1 a bottle, there is now a shortage, so the price rises and the quantity supplied increases. The price rises to $1.50 a bottle, and the quantity increases to 11 million bottles a day.

When demand changes, there is *no change in supply*. But there is a *change in the quantity supplied*—a movement along the supply curve.

Next, suppose that a new zero-calorie sports drink is invented and the demand for bottled water decreases. In Figure 4.7(b), the demand curve *shifts leftward* to D_2. At the initial price of $1.00 a bottle, there is now a surplus, so the price falls and the quantity supplied decreases. The price falls to 75 cents a bottle, and the quantity decreases to 9 million bottles a day.

FIGURE 4.7
The Effects of a Change in Demand

Practice Online

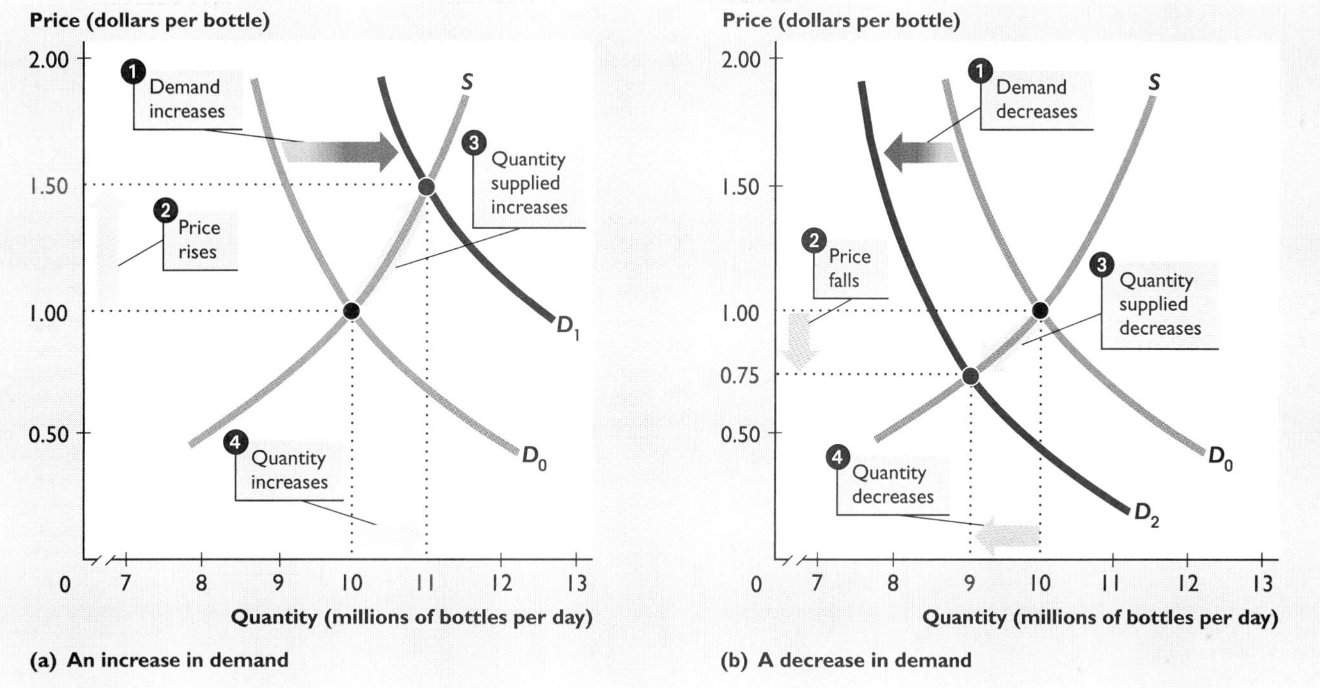

An increase in demand ❶ shifts the demand curve rightward to D_1, ❷ raises the price, ❸ increases the quantity supplied, and ❹ increases the equilibrium quantity.

A decrease in demand ❶ shifts the demand curve leftward to D_2, ❷ lowers the price, ❸ decreases the quantity supplied, and ❹ decreases the equilibrium quantity.

Effects of Changes in Supply

Let's now work out what happens when supply changes.

In Figure 4.8, the demand curve is D and initially, the supply curve is S_0. The equilibrium price is $1 a bottle, and the equilibrium quantity is 10 million bottles.

Suppose that European water bottlers buy springs and open up bottling plants in the United States. The supply of bottled water increases. In Figure 4.8(a), the supply curve shifts rightward to S_1. At the initial price of $1.00 a bottle, there is now a surplus, so the price falls and the quantity demanded increases. The price falls to 75 cents a bottle, and the quantity increases to 11 million bottles a day.

When supply changes, there is *no change in demand*. But there is a *change in the quantity demanded*—a movement along the demand curve.

Next, suppose that a drought dries up some springs and the supply of bottled water decreases. In Figure 4.8(b), the supply curve shifts leftward to S_2. At the initial price of $1 a bottle, there is now a shortage, so the price rises and the quantity demanded decreases. The price rises to $1.50 a bottle, and the quantity decreases to 9 million bottles a day.

The new equilibrium price is $1.50 a bottle. Again, there is *no change in demand*. There is a *decrease in the quantity demanded*—a movement along the demand curve. The equilibrium quantity decreases to 9 million bottles a day.

FIGURE 4.8

The Effects of a Change in Supply

Practice Online

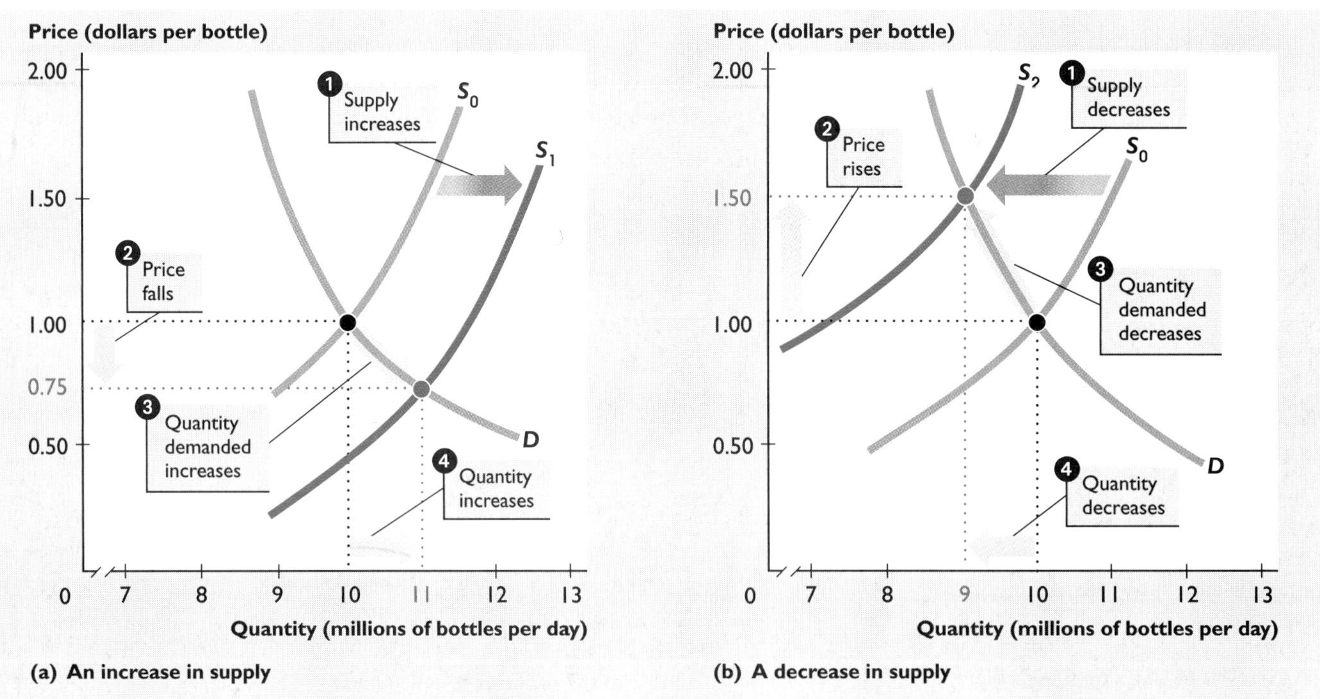

An increase in supply (1) shifts the supply curve rightward to S_1, (2) lowers the price, (3) increases the quantity demanded, and (4) increases the equilibrium quantity.

A decrease in supply (1) shifts the supply curve leftward to S_2, (2) raises the price, (3) decreases the quantity demanded, and (4) decreases the equilibrium quantity.

Eye on the Global Economy

A Change in the Demand for Roses

Colombia and Ecuador grow most of the world's roses. On the average, the quantity of roses sold worldwide is around 6 million bunches a month. And the average price that consumers pay is around $40 a bunch.

But one month, February, is not a normal month. Each year in February, the quantity of roses bought increases to four times that of any other month. The reason: Valentine's Day. And on Valentine's Day, the price of a bunch of roses doubles.

The demand-supply model explains these facts. The figure shows the supply curve of roses and two demand curves. The blue demand curve is the demand for roses in a normal month. This demand curve intersects the supply curve at an equilibrium price of $40 a bunch and an equilibrium quantity of 6 million bunches.

In February, the demand curve shifts rightward to the red curve. The February demand curve for roses intersects the supply curve at an equilibrium price of $80 a bunch and an equilibrium quantity of 24 million bunches.

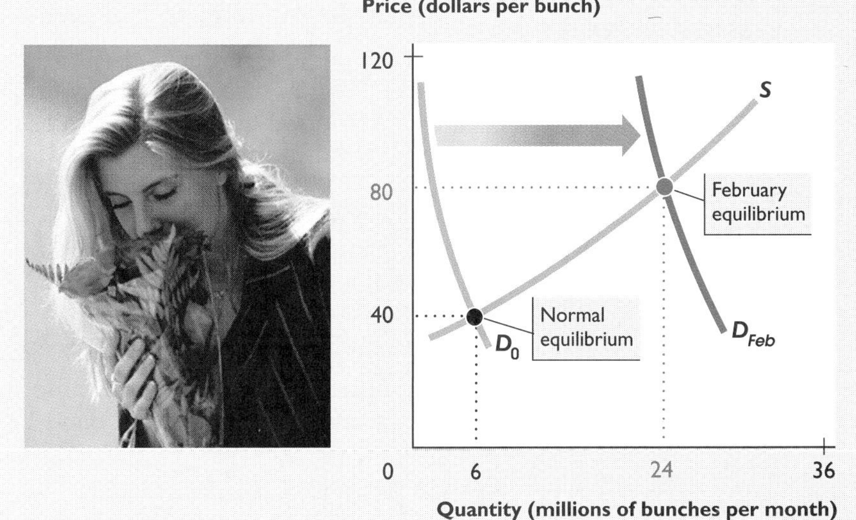

A Change in the Supply of Wheat

During 2002, the price of wheat soared from around $130 per metric ton to $190. The price increase was the consequence of a widespread global drought that decreased production and decreased the supply of wheat.

According to USDA estimates, wheat production fell from about 107 million metric tons in 2001 to about 100 million in 2002. Production was worst hit in the United States, Canada, Argentina, Australia, and the EU—the five largest wheat exporters. Production was up in Russia, Ukraine, and Kazakstan, allowing these countries to gain market share.

The figure shows the effect of the decrease in production. The supply of wheat decreased and the supply curve shifted leftward. The price of wheat increased and the quantity of wheat demanded decreased. (The figure assumes there was no change in the demand for wheat in 2002.)

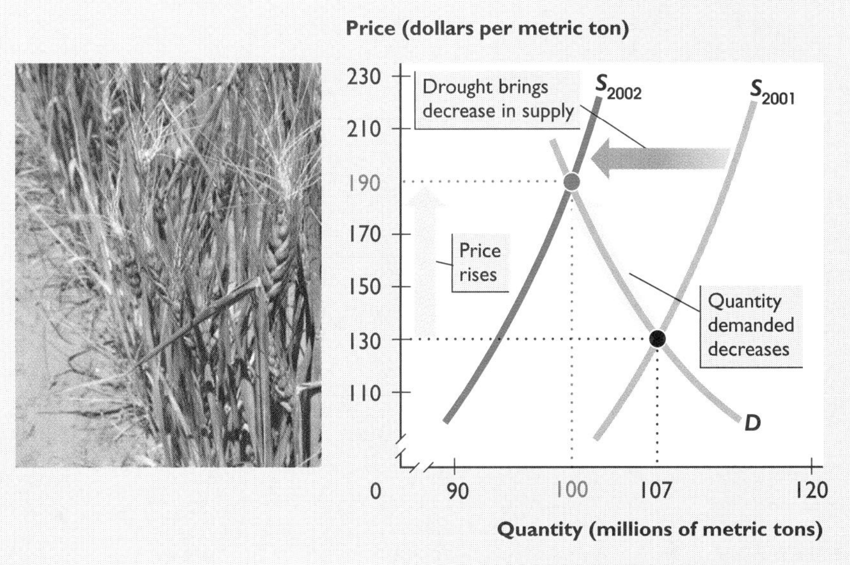

SOURCES: www.fas.usda.gov/grain/circular/2002/06-02/wht_txt.htm and www.uswheat.org/

Changes in Both Demand and Supply

What happens to the price and quantity in the market for bottled water when an event that changes demand occurs at the same time as an event that changes supply? Let's find out by studying the four possible combinations of simultaneous changes in demand and supply.

Increase in Demand and Increase in Supply

Either an increase in demand or an increase in supply increases the equilibrium quantity. But an increase in demand raises the price, and an increase in supply lowers the price. So when demand and supply increase together, the quantity increases and the price might rise, fall, or stay the same. Figure 4.9(a) shows what happens in the market for bottled water when concern about the safety of tap water increases demand and the opening of new bottling plants increases supply. The quantity increases and, because the increase in demand is greater than the increase in supply, the price rises.

Decrease in Demand and Decrease in Supply

Either a decrease in demand or a decrease in supply decreases the equilibrium quantity. But a decrease in demand lowers the price, and a decrease in supply raises the price. So when demand and supply decrease together, the quantity decreases and the price might rise, fall, or stay the same. Figure 4.9(b) shows what happens in the market for bottled water when the invention of a new sports drink

FIGURE 4.9
Demand and Supply Change in the Same Direction

Practice Online

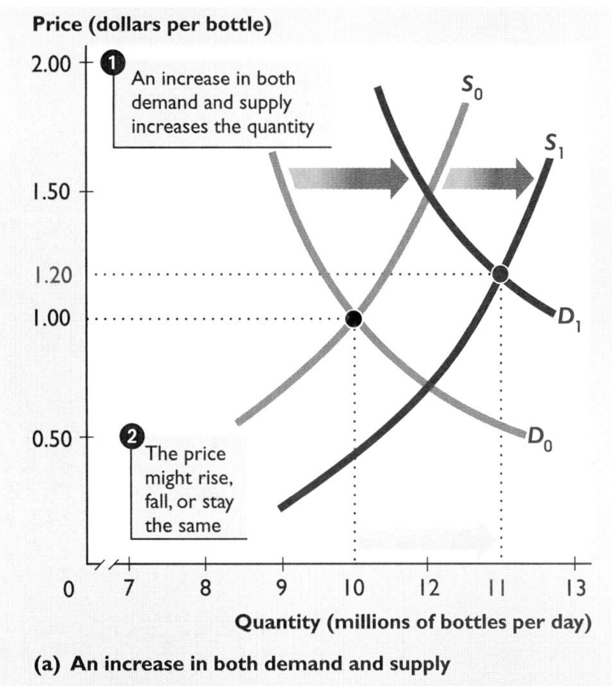

(a) An increase in both demand and supply

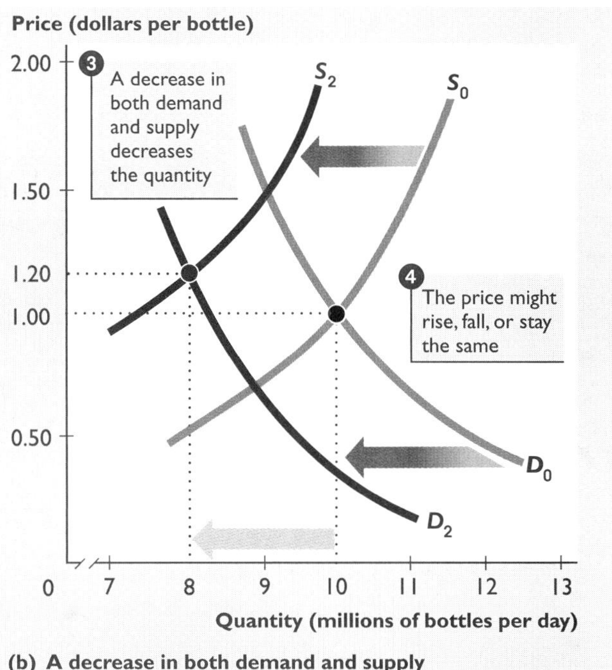

(b) A decrease in both demand and supply

decreases demand and a drought decreases supply. The quantity decreases and, because the decrease in supply is greater than the decrease in demand, the price rises.

Increase in Demand and Decrease in Supply

Either an increase in demand or a decrease in supply raises the equilibrium price. But an increase in demand increases the quantity, and a decrease in supply decreases the quantity. So when an increase in demand and a decrease in supply occur together, the price rises and the quantity might increase, decrease, or stay the same. Figure 4.10(a) shows what happens in the market for bottled water when concern about the safety of tap water increases demand and a drought decreases supply. The price rises and, because the increase in demand equals the decrease in supply, the quantity remains constant.

Decrease in Demand and Increase in Supply

Either a decrease in demand or an increase in supply lowers the price. But a decrease in demand decreases the quantity, and an increase in supply increases the quantity. So when a decrease in demand and an increase in supply occur together, the price falls and the quantity might increase, decrease, or stay the same. Figure 4.10(b) shows what happens in the market for bottled water when the invention of a new sports drink decreases demand and the opening of new bottling plants increases supply. The price falls and, because the decrease in demand equals the increase in supply, the quantity remains constant.

FIGURE 4.10

Demand and Supply Change in Opposite Directions

Practice Online

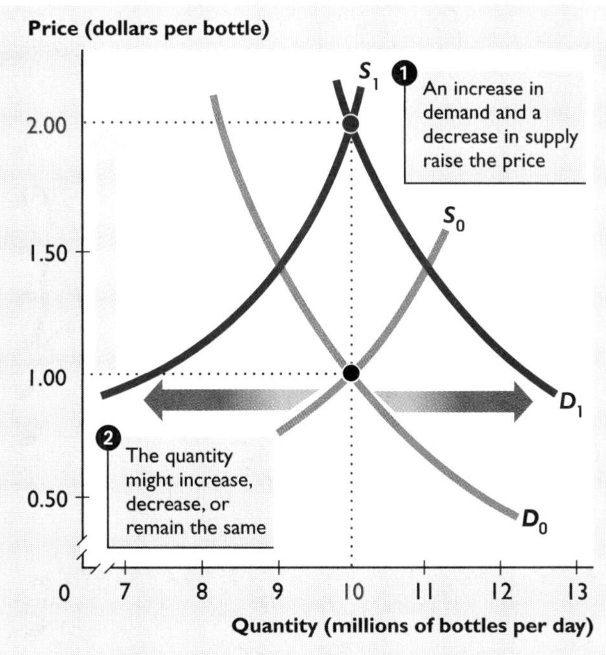

(a) An increase in demand and a decrease in supply

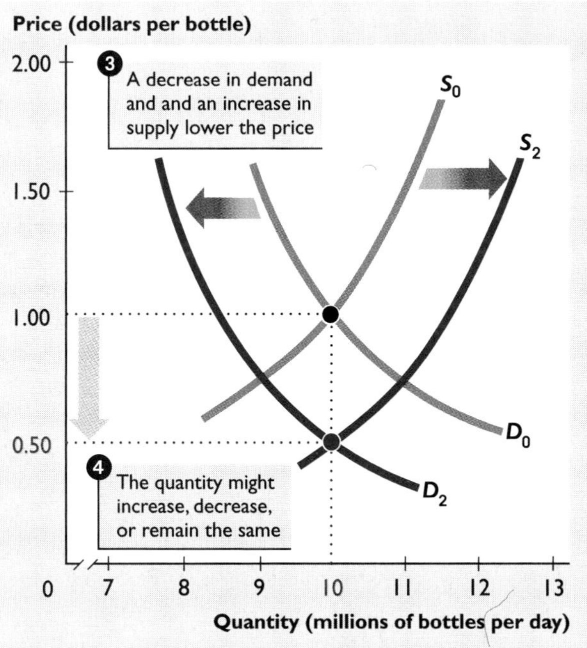

(b) A decrease in demand and an increase in supply

CHECKPOINT 4.3

Study Guide pp. 59–61

Practice Online 4.3

3 Explain how demand and supply determine price and quantity in a market and explain the effects of changes in demand and supply.

Practice Problem 4.3

Price (dollars per carton)	Quantity demanded (cartons per day)	Quantity supplied (cartons per day)
1.00	200	110
1.25	175	130
1.50	150	150
1.75	125	170
2.00	100	190

The table shows the demand and supply schedules for milk.

a. What is the market equilibrium in the milk market?

b. Describe the situation in the milk market if the price is $1.75 a carton.

c. If the price is $1.75 a carton, explain how the market reaches equilibrium.

d. A drought decreases the quantity supplied by 45 cartons a day at each price. What is the new equilibrium and how does the market adjust to it?

e. Milk becomes more popular, and the quantity demanded increases by 5 cartons a day at each price. Improved feeds for dairy cows increase the quantity of milk supplied by 50 cartons a day at each price. If there is no drought, what is the new equilibrium and how does the market adjust to it?

Exercise 4.3

Price (dollars per roll)	Quantity demanded (rolls per week)	Quantity supplied (rolls per week)
2.00	3,000	1,000
3.00	2,500	1,500
4.00	2,000	2,000
5.00	1,500	2,500
6.00	1,000	3,000

The table shows the demand and supply schedules for rolls of film.

a. What is the market equilibrium?

b. If the price of film is $3 a roll, describe the situation in the film market. Explain how market equilibrium is restored.

c. A rise in income increases the quantity demanded of film by 1,000 rolls a week at each price. Explain how the film market adjusts to its new equilibrium.

d. The number of film production lines increases the quantity supplied of film by 750 rolls a week at each price. People switch to digital cameras and the quantity demanded of film decreases by 250 rolls a week at each price. With no rise in income, explain how the film market adjusts to its new equilibrium.

FIGURE 1

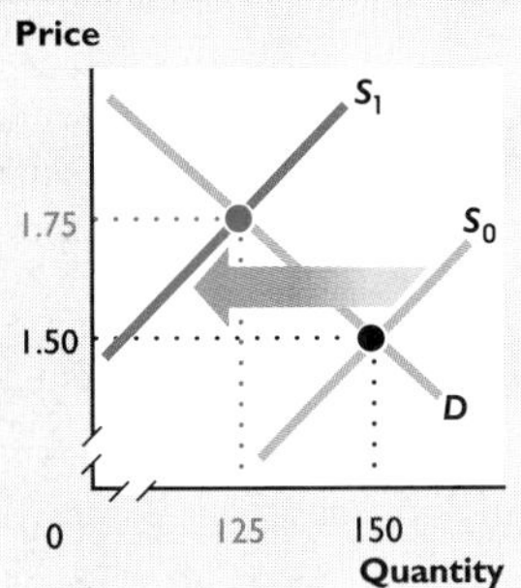

FIGURE 2

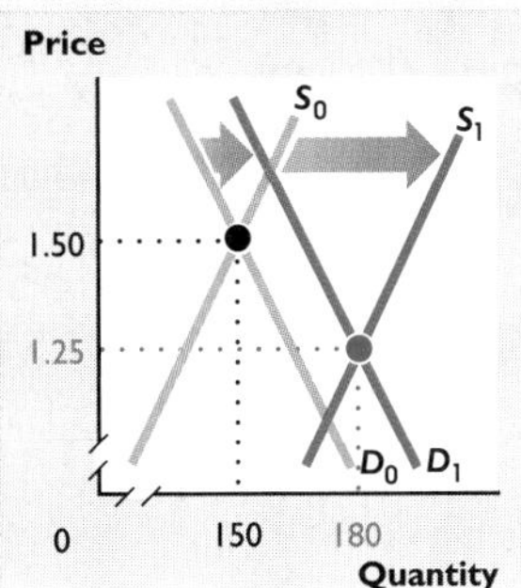

Solution to Practice Problem 4.3

a. Figure 1 shows the market equilibrium at $1.50 a carton and 150 cartons a day.

b. At $1.75 a carton, the quantity demanded (125 cartons) is less than the quantity supplied (170 cartons), so there is a surplus of 45 cartons a day.

c. At $1.75 a carton, there is a surplus of milk. As suppliers lower the price, the quantity demanded increases, the quantity supplied decreases, and the surplus decreases. The price falls until the surplus disappears at $1.50 a carton.

d. The supply curve *shifts leftward* by 45 cartons a day at each price. At $1.50, the quantity demanded (150 cartons) exceeds the quantity supplied (105 cartons) and there is a shortage of milk and the price begins to rise. As the price rises, the quantity demanded decreases, the quantity supplied increases, and the shortage decreases. The price rises to $1.75 a carton, and the quantity decreases to 125 cartons a day (Figure 1).

e. The demand curve *shifts rightward* by 5 cartons a day at each price. The supply curve *shifts rightward* by 50 cartons a day at each price. At $1.50 a carton, the quantity demanded (155 cartons) is less than the quantity supplied (200 cartons). There is surplus and the price begins to fall. As the price falls to $1.25 a carton, the quantity increases to 180 cartons a day (Figure 2).

4.4 PRICE RIGIDITIES

You've seen that price adjustments bring market equilibrium. But suppose that for some reason, the price in a market does not adjust. What happens then? The answer depends on why the price doesn't adjust. There are three broad reasons:

- Price ceiling
- Price floor
- Sticky price

Price Ceiling

A **price ceiling** is the highest price at which it is legal to trade a particular good, service, or factor of production. An example of a price ceiling is a **rent ceiling** on houses and apartments—a law that makes it illegal for landlords to charge a rent that exceeds a set limit. How does a rent ceiling affect the rental market for apartments?

Landlords decide the quantity of apartments to supply, and the higher the rent, the greater is the quantity of apartments supplied. Families decide the quantity of apartments to demand, and the lower the rent, the greater is the quantity of apartments demanded. The rent adjusts to make the quantity of apartments demanded equal to the quantity supplied.

Figure 4.11 illustrates a housing market. In this market, the demand for housing curve is *D* and the supply of housing curve is *S*. Market equilibrium occurs at a rent of $550 a month with 4,000 apartments rented.

Suppose the government thinks that no one should have to pay a rent as high as $550 a month and decides it wants to lower the rents. Can the government help families by passing a rent ceiling law?

Price ceiling
The highest price at which it is legal to trade a particular good, service, or factor of production.

Rent ceiling
A law that makes it illegal for landlords to charge a rent that exceeds a set limit—an example of a price ceiling.

FIGURE 4.11
A Rental Apartment Market

Practice Online

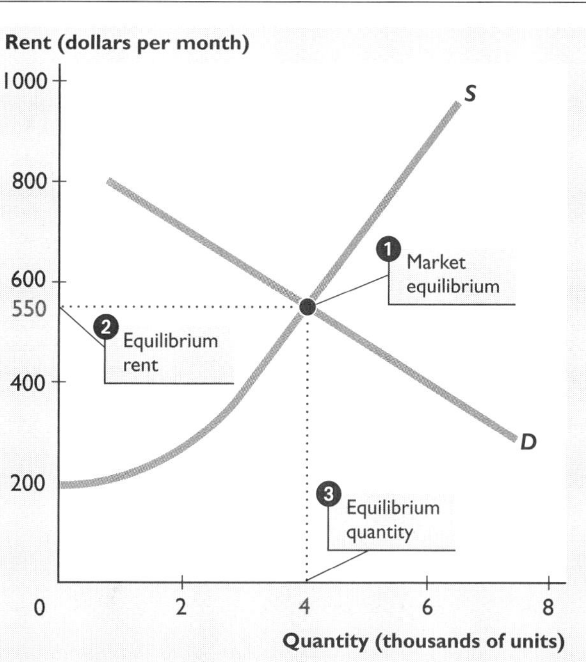

1. Market equilibrium is determined by the demand for apartments and the supply of apartments for rent.
2. The equilibrium rent is $550 a month.
3. At the equilibrium rent, the equilibrium quantity of apartments rented is 4,000.

The effect of a rent ceiling depends on whether it is imposed at a level above or below the equilibrium rent. In Figure 4.11, the equilibrium rent is $550 a month. With a rent ceiling above $550 a month, nothing would change. The reason is that people are already paying $550 a month, and because this rent is below the rent ceiling, the rent paid doesn't change.

But a rent ceiling set *below* the equilibrium rent has powerful effects on the market. The reason is that it attempts to prevent the rent rising high enough to regulate the quantities demanded and supplied. The law and the market are in conflict, and one (or both) of them must yield.

Figure 4.12 shows one effect of a rent ceiling that is set below the equilibrium rent. The rent ceiling is $400 a month. We've shaded the area above the rent ceiling because a rent in this region is illegal. At a rent of $400 a month, the quantity of housing supplied is 3,000 units and the quantity demanded is 6,000 units. So there is a shortage of 3,000 units of housing.

The first effect, then, of a rent ceiling is a housing shortage. People are seeking a larger amount of housing than builders and owners of existing buildings have an incentive to make available.

But the story does not end here. Somehow the 3,000 units of housing that owners are willing to make available must be allocated among people who are seeking 6,000 units. Blocking rent adjustments that bring the quantity of apartments demanded into equality with the quantity supplied doesn't end scarcity. When the law prevents the rent from rising to allocate housing resources, some other allocation mechanism must be used. Of the many possibilities, one is first-come-first-served. Another is imposing restrictions such as "no pets." But most people would regard the use of these mechanisms for allocating scarce housing resources as clearly worse than allowing the rent rise.

FIGURE 4.12
A Rent Ceiling Creates a Shortage of Apartments

Practice Online

A rent ceiling is imposed below the equilibrium rent. In this example, the rent ceiling is $400 a month.

1. The quantity of apartments supplied decreases to 3,000.
2. The quantity of apartments demanded increases to 6,000.
3. A housing shortage of 3,000 apartments arises.

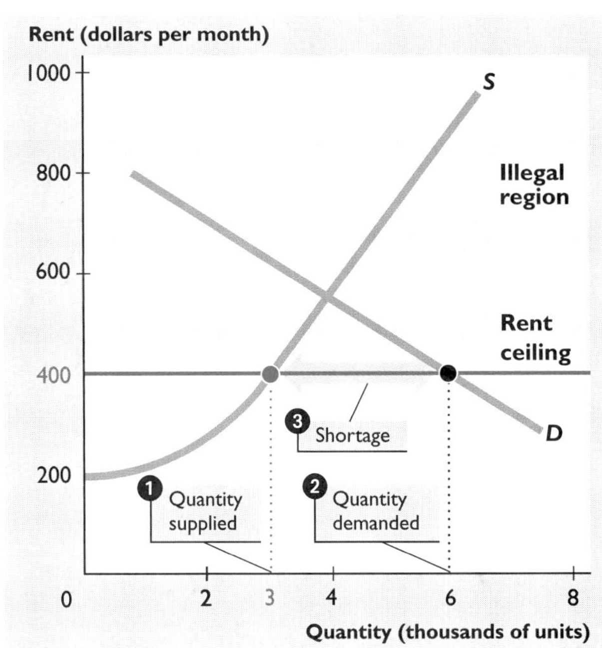

Price Floor

A **price floor** is the lowest price at which it is legal to trade a particular good, service, or factor of production. An example of a price floor is the **minimum wage law**, which is a government regulation that makes hiring labor for less than a specified wage illegal. Firms are free to pay a wage rate that exceeds the minimum wage but may not pay less than the minimum. How does the minimum wage affect the labor market?

Price floor
The lowest price at which it is legal to trade a particular good, service, or factor of production.

Minimum wage law
A government regulation that makes hiring labor for less than a specified wage illegal—an example of a price floor.

Firms hire labor, so they decide how much labor to demand. The lower the wage rate, the greater is the quantity of labor that firms demand. Households decide how much labor to supply. The higher the wage rate, the greater is the quantity of labor households are willing to supply. The wage rate adjusts to make the quantity of labor demanded equal to the quantity supplied.

Figure 4.13 shows the market for fast-food servers in Yuma, Arizona. In this market, the demand for labor curve is *D* and the supply of labor curve is *S*. Equilibrium occurs at a wage rate of $5 an hour with 5,000 people employed as servers.

Suppose that the government thinks that no one should have to work for a wage rate as low as $5 an hour and decides that it wants to increase the wage rate. Can the government improve conditions for these workers by passing a minimum wage law?

The effect of a price floor depends on whether it is set below or above the equilibrium price. In Figure 4.13, the equilibrium wage rate is $5 an hour, and at this wage rate, firms hire 5,000 workers. If the government introduced a minimum wage below $5 an hour, nothing would change. The reason is that firms are already paying $5 an hour, and because this wage exceeds the minimum wage, the wage rate paid doesn't change. And firms continue to hire 5,000 workers.

The aim of a minimum wage is to boost the incomes of low-wage earners, so the minimum wage will exceed the equilibrium wage of the lowest-paid labor.

FIGURE 4.13
A Market for Fast-Food Servers

Practice Online

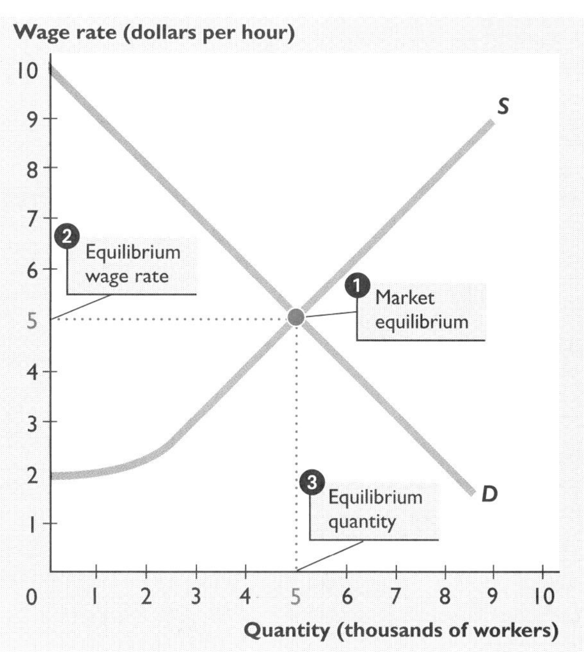

1. Market equilibrium is determined by the demand for and the supply of fast-food servers.
2. The equilibrium wage rate is $5 an hour.
3. At the equilibrium wage rate, the equilibrium quantity of fast-food servers is 5,000.

Suppose that the government introduces a minimum wage of $7 an hour. Figure 4.14 shows the effects of this law. Wage rates below $7 an hour are illegal, so we've shaded the illegal region below the minimum wage. Firms and workers are no longer permitted to operate at the equilibrium point in this market because it is in the illegal region. Market forces and the law are in conflict.

The government can set a minimum wage. But it can't tell employers how many workers to hire. If firms must pay $7 an hour for labor, they will hire only 3,000 workers. At the equilibrium wage rate of $5 an hour, they hired 5,000 workers. So when the minimum wage is introduced, firms fire 2,000 workers.

But at a wage rate of $7 an hour, another 2,000 people who didn't want to work for $5 an hour now try to find work as servers, so at $7 an hour, the quantity supplied is 7,000 workers. With 2,000 workers fired and another 2,000 looking for work at the higher wage rate, 4,000 people who would like to work as servers are unemployed.

Somehow, the 3,000 jobs available must be allocated among the 7,000 people who are available for and willing to work. How is this allocation achieved? The answer is the same as in the housing market: first-come-first-served and discrimination replace price as the means of allocating resources.

Sticky Price

In most markets, a law does not restrict the price. But in some markets, the buyer and seller agree on a price for a fixed period, and in others, the seller sets a price that changes infrequently. For example, in some labor markets, firms enter into

FIGURE 4.14
A Minimum Wage Creates Unemployment

Practice Online

A minimum wage is introduced above the equilibrium wage rate. In this example, the minimum wage is $7 an hour.

1. The quantity of labor demanded decreases to 3,000 workers.
2. The quantity of labor supplied increases to 7,000 workers.
3. 4,000 people are unemployed.

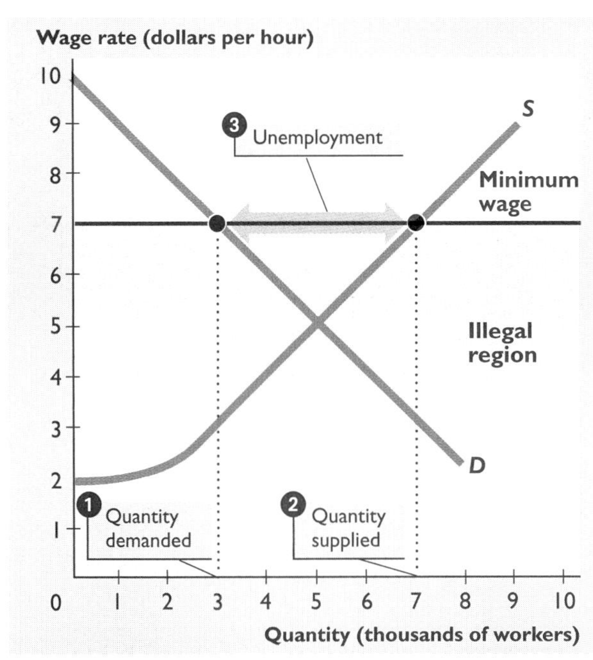

long-term contracts with labor unions that fix wage rates for at least one year and often for as many as three years. Borrowers and lenders often agree on an interest rate that is fixed for the term of a loan, which could be for as long as 20 years. And many commodities such as sugar, oil, and coal are traded on long-term contracts.

In these markets, the price adjustment process that is described in Figure 4.6 on p. 94 is slowed down. Prices do adjust, but not quickly enough to avoid shortages or surpluses.

If demand increases or if supply decreases after a price (or wage) contract is struck, there is a shortage. The quantity supplied is less than the quantity demanded. So the quantity supplied determines the quantity that is actually traded, and buyers' plans are frustrated. The price gradually rises as contracts come up for renewal, but in the intervening period, a shortage persists.

Similarly, if demand decreases or if supply increases after a price (or wage) contract is struck, there is a surplus. The quantity demanded is less than the quantity supplied. So the quantity demanded determines the quantity that is actually traded, and sellers' plans are frustrated. In the labor market, the sellers are workers, and some of them become unemployed. The price (or wage rate) gradually falls as contracts come up for renewal, but in the intervening period, a surplus and above-normal unemployment persist.

Eye on the U.S. Economy

The Federal Minimum Wage

The federal government's *Fair Labor Standards Act* sets the minimum wage, which was last changed in 1997, when it was raised to $5.15 an hour.

The minimum wage creates unemployment. But how much unemployment does it create?

Until recently, most economists believed that a 10 percent increase in the minimum wage decreased teenage *employment* by between 1 and 3 percent.

David Card of the University of California at Berkeley and Alan Krueger of Princeton University have challenged this view. They claim that following a rise in the minimum wage in California, New Jersey, and Texas, the *employment* rate of low-income workers *increased*. They suggest three reasons why a rise in the minimum wage rate might increase employment:

(1) Workers become more conscientious and productive.

(2) Workers are less likely to quit, so costly labor turnover is reduced.

(3) Managers make a firm's operations more efficient.

Most economists are skeptical about these ideas. They say that if higher wages make workers more productive and reduce labor turnover, firms will freely pay workers a higher wage. And they argue that there are other explanations for the employment increase that Card and Krueger found.

Daniel Hamermesh of the University of Texas at Austin says that they got the timing wrong. Firms *anticipated* the minimum wage rise and so cut employment *before* it occurred. Looking at employment changes *after* the minimum wage increased missed its main effect. Finis Welch of Texas A&M University and Kevin Murphy of the University of Chicago say the employment effects that Card and Krueger found are caused by regional differences in economic growth, not changes in the minimum wage.

Also, looking only at employment misses the effect of the minimum wage on the supply of labor. The minimum wage brings an increase in the number of people who drop out of high school to look for work.

CHECKPOINT 4.4

Study Guide pp. 62–64

Practice Online 4.4

4 **Explain how price ceilings, price floors, and sticky prices cause shortages, surpluses, and unemployment.**

FIGURE 1

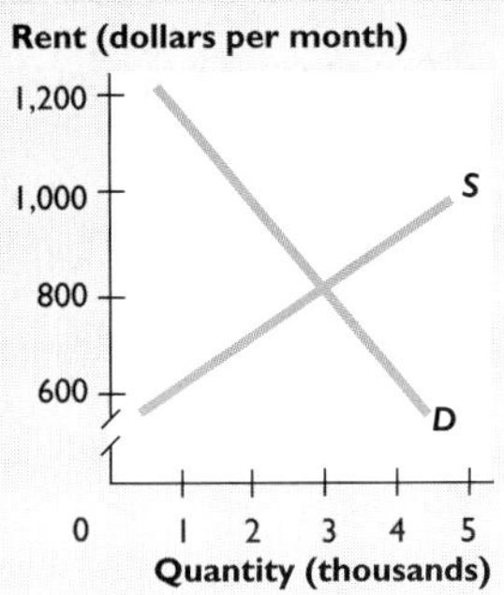

FIGURE 2

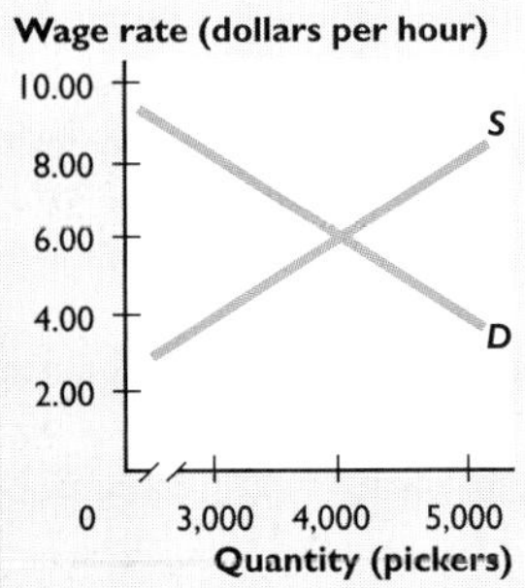

FIGURE 3

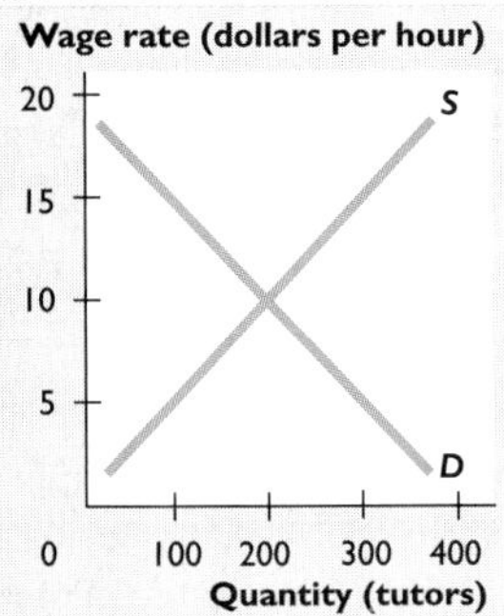

Practice Problems 4.4

1. Figure 1 shows the rental market for apartments in Corsicana, Texas.
   a. What is the rent and how many apartments are rented?
   b. If the city government imposes a rent ceiling of $900 a month, what is the rent and how many apartments are rented?
   c. If the city government imposes a rent ceiling of $600 a month, what is the rent and how many apartments are rented?
2. Figure 2 shows the market for tomato pickers in southern California.
   a. What is the equilibrium wage rate of tomato pickers and what is the equilibrium quantity of tomato pickers employed?
   b. If California introduces a minimum wage for tomato pickers of $4 an hour, how many tomato pickers are employed and how many are unemployed?
   c. If California introduces a minimum wage for tomato pickers of $8 an hour, how many tomato pickers are employed and how many are unemployed?

Exercise 4.4

Figure 3 shows a market for private math tutors in Madison organized by the Students' Union.

a. What is the wage rate that math tutors earn and how many are employed?
b. If the Students' Union sets the minimum wage for private math tutors at $8 an hour, how many tutors are employed and what wage rate do they earn?
c. If the Students' Union sets the minimum wage for private tutors at $15 an hour, how many tutors are employed and what wage rate do they earn?
d. At which minimum wage ($8 an hour or $15 an hour) will some math tutors be unemployed? How many will be unemployed?

Solutions to Practice Problems 4.4

1a. Equilibrium rent is $800 a month, and 3,000 apartments are rented (Figure 4).
1b. A rent ceiling of $900 a month is above the equilibrium rent, so the outcome is the market equilibrium rent of $800 a month with 3,000 apartments rented.
1c. With a rent ceiling of $600 a month, 1,000 apartments are rented (on the supply curve) and the rent is $600 a month (the rent ceiling) (Figure 4).

FIGURE 4

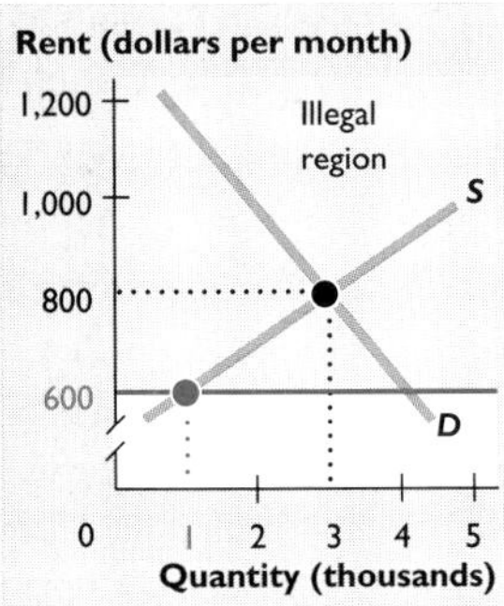

2a. Equilibrium wage is $6 an hour, and 4,000 pickers are employed (Figure 5).
2b. The minimum wage of $4 an hour is below the equilibrium wage rate, so 4,000 tomato pickers are employed and none are unemployed.
2c. The minimum wage of $8 an hour is above the equilibrium wage rate, so 3,000 tomato pickers are employed (on the demand curve), and 5,000 people would like to work as tomato pickers for $8 an hour (on the supply curve), so 2,000 are unemployed (Figure 5).

FIGURE 5

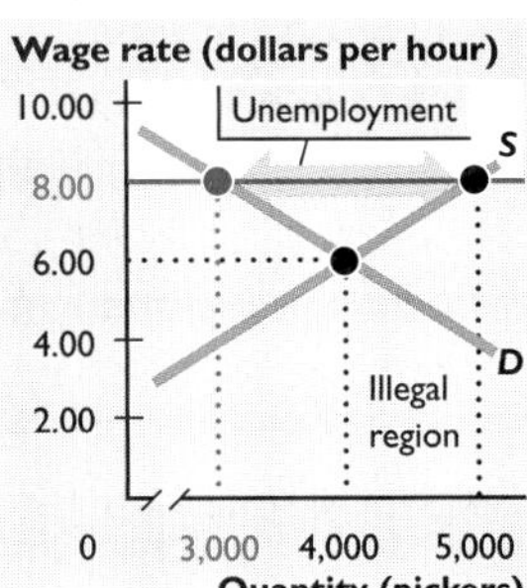

CHAPTER CHECKPOINT

Key Points

1 Distinguish between quantity demanded and demand and explain what determines demand.

- Other things remaining the same, the quantity demanded increases as the price falls and decreases as the price rises—the law of demand.
- Changes in the prices of related goods, income, expectations about future prices and income, the number of buyers, and preferences change demand.

2 Distinguish between quantity supplied and supply and explain what determines supply.

- Other things remaining the same, the quantity supplied increases as the price rises and decreases as the price falls—the law of supply.
- Changes in the prices of related goods, prices of resources and other inputs, expectations about future prices and input prices, number of sellers, and productivity change supply.

3 Explain how demand and supply determine price and quantity in a market and explain the effects of changes in demand and supply.

- The price adjusts to maintain market equilibrium—to keep the quantity demanded equal to the quantity supplied. A surplus brings a fall in the price; a shortage brings a rise in the price.
- An increase in demand increases both the price and the quantity; a decrease in demand decreases both the price and the quantity. An increase in supply increases the quantity but decreases the price; a decrease in supply decreases the quantity but increases the price.

4 Explain how price ceilings, price floors, and sticky prices cause shortages, surpluses, and unemployment.

- A price ceiling below the equilibrium price creates a shortage.
- A price floor above the equilibrium price creates a surplus (unemployment in the labor market).
- Sticky prices create temporary shortages and surpluses (unemployment in the labor market).

Key Terms

Exercises

1. Explain how each of the following situations changes the demand or supply of air travel.
   a. Airfares tumble, while long-distance bus fares don't change.
   b. The price of jet fuel rises.
   c. Airlines reduce the number of flights each day.
   d. People expect airfares to increase next summer.
   e. As the winter in the Northeast turns very cold, many people decide to take a mid-winter break in Florida.
   f. With deep snow in the Rockies, many people flock to the ski slopes.
   g. The price of train travel falls.
   h. The price of a pound of air cargo increases.

2. Explain how each of the following items influences the demand for and supply of jeans.
   a. A new technology becomes available that cuts the time it takes to manufacture a pair of jeans by 50 percent.
   b. The price of the cloth (denim) used to make jeans falls.
   c. Jeans go out of fashion.
   d. The price of a pair of jeans falls.
   e. The wage rate paid to garment workers increases.
   f. Disney, CNN, and most baseball clubs start to produce jeans.
   g. The price of a denim skirt doubles.
   h. People's incomes increase.

3. Use the laws of demand and supply to explain whether the following statements are true or false. In your explanation, distinguish between a change in demand and a change in the quantity demanded and between a change in supply and a change in the quantity supplied.
   a. The United States does not allow oranges from Brazil (the world's largest producer of oranges) to be sold in the United States. If Brazilian oranges were sold in the United States, oranges and orange juice would be cheaper.
   b. If soccer becomes more popular in the United States and basketball becomes less popular, the price of a pair of basketball shoes will rise.
   c. It is more expensive to ski in Aspen in the winter than in the spring.
   d. If the price of frozen yogurt falls, the quantity of ice cream consumed will decrease and the price of ice cream will rise.

4. What is the effect on the equilibrium price and quantity of orange juice of the following events if they occur one at a time?
   a. The price of apple juice decreases.
   b. The price of apple juice decreases and the wage rate paid to orange grove workers increases.
   c. Orange juice becomes more popular and a cheaper machine for picking oranges is used.
   d. Joggers switch from bottled water to orange juice.

5. Gasoline producers invent a new fuel that is cheaper and cleaner than gasoline. All new cars use the new fuel. Use a demand-supply graph to explain the effect of this new fuel on
   a. The price of gasoline and the quantity of gasoline bought.
   b. The price of a used car.

6. The table shows the demand and supply schedules for mouse pads.
   a. What is the market equilibrium?
   b. If the price of a mouse pad is $7.00, describe the situation in the market. Explain how market equilibrium is restored.
   c. Explain what happens to the market equilibrium and how the market adjusts to its new equilibrium if a fall in the price of a computer changes the quantity demanded of mouse pads by 20 a week at each price.
   d. Explain what happens to the market equilibrium in part **a** and how the market adjusts if new voice-recognition software changes the quantity demanded by 10 mouse pads a week at each price and at the same time the cost of producing a mouse pad falls and changes the quantity supplied by 30 a week at each price.

Price (dollars per pad)	Quantity demanded	Quantity supplied
	(mouse pads per week)	
3.00	160	120
4.00	150	130
5.00	140	140
6.00	130	150
7.00	120	160
8.00	110	170

7. "As more people buy computers, the demand for Internet service will increase and the price of an Internet service will decrease. The decrease in the price of an Internet service will decrease the supply of Internet services." Is this statement true or false? Explain your answer.

8. "With oil $30 a barrel, war drums beating, and world economic recovery hanging in the balance, expectations are that the Organization of the Petroleum Exporting Countries (OPEC) will increase production at their 21 September meeting," according to a news item on September 15, 2002.
   a. Draw a demand-supply graph to illustrate the situation in the world oil market on September 15, 2002. The price is $30 a barrel, and output is 76.7 million barrels a day.
   b. OPEC was expected to increase its production in October by 1 million barrels a day. Show the effect of this expected increase on your graph. How will the price of oil change? Explain your answer.
   c. If war breaks out in the Middle East, what changes will occur in the world oil market? Use a demand-supply graph to illustrate your answer.

9. During 2002, wheat growers in Canada and Australia experienced drought. As a result, the amount of wheat harvested in Canada and Australia was expected to be smaller than usual.
   a. Draw a demand-supply graph to show the equilibrium in the world wheat market in a normal year.
   b. Use your graph to illustrate the effect of the smaller harvests in Canada and Australia, assuming that other wheat-growing countries have experienced normal growing conditions.
   c. What do you predict will happen to the price of wheat and the quantity sold in 2002?
   d. What do you predict will happen to the price of bread in 2002?
   e. If the government freezes the price of bread at its 2001 price, will there be a shortage of bread or a surplus of bread? Use a demand-supply graph to illustrate your answer.

10. Bakers earn $10 an hour, gas pump attendants earn $6 an hour, and copy shop workers earn $7 an hour. If the government introduces a minimum wage of $7 an hour, explain how the markets for bakers, gas pump attendants, and copy shop workers will respond initially to the minimum wage.

Critical Thinking

11. In 1995, 90 salmon farms operated in British Columbia. In 1995, the Canadian government banned the creation of any new salmon farms because the farms create pollution and might introduce disease into the wild salmon population. In September 2002, the Canadian government lifted this ban. The Heart and Stroke Foundation tells us that "salmon is one of the healthiest foods we can eat. There's no shortage of it. We're eating three times as much of it as we did just a few years ago."
    - **a.** What do you predict happened to the price of farm-raised salmon and the quantity of farm-raised salmon grown from 1996 through 2001?
    - **b.** What effect do you think the lifting of the ban will have on the price of farm-raised salmon and the quantity of farm-raised salmon bought?
    - **c.** If disease breaks out in the salmon farms of British Columbia, describe what effects it will have on the market for wild Pacific salmon.

12. The Andean Trade Preferences Act, signed in 1988, was designed to encourage South American farmers to switch from growing drug crops such as coca to growing flowers. U.S. restrictions on flower imports from these South American countries were removed.
    - **a.** What incentives do you think were needed to encourage Andean farmers to switch from growing drug crops to growing roses?
    - **b.** As Andean farmers started to grow roses, what happened to the world price of roses?
    - **c.** How did U.S. rose growers respond as Andean roses entered the U.S. rose market?

Practice Online

Web Exercises

Use the links on your Foundations Web site to work the following exercises.

13. Obtain information about the history of the price of crude oil.
    - **a.** What are the major changes that have occurred in the market for crude oil?
    - **b.** On what two occasions did the price of oil rise by the largest amount?
    - **c.** What events occurred to trigger the price hikes that you've just described?
    - **d.** Did the events that you've just described change the demand for crude oil, the supply, both, or neither? Explain your answer.
    - **e.** Use the law of market forces and demand-supply graphs to explain the changes in the price and quantity of crude oil on the two occasions you identified in part **b**.
    - **f.** How do you think the price of crude oil influences the markets for coal and natural gas?
    - **g.** How do you think the advances in technology that increased fuel efficiency in automobiles, airplanes, and home heating furnaces have influenced the world market for crude oil?

14. Visit eBay.
    - **a.** What is eBay? Describe how eBay works.
    - **b.** Do you think the prices of the items traded on eBay are determined by demand and supply or in some other way? Explain your answer.

CHAPTER 5

GDP and the Standard of Living

CHAPTER CHECKLIST

When you have completed your study of this chapter, you will be able to

1. **Define GDP and explain why the value of production, income, and expenditure are the same for an economy.**
2. **Describe how economic statisticians measure GDP in the United States.**
3. **Distinguish between nominal GDP and real GDP and define the GDP deflator.**
4. **Explain and describe the limitations of real GDP as a measure of the standard of living.**

You've seen that equilibrium quantities and prices in the markets for goods, services, and factors of production determine *what, how,* and *for whom* goods and services are produced. What and for whom goods and services are produced influence the standard of living, a central concern of macroeconomics.

A focus on the standard of living directs our attention to the value of *total* production rather than the production of each individual good or service. You will discover that several different factors contribute to the standard of living, but one indicator dominates the others. It is called gross domestic product, or GDP. In this chapter, you will find out how economic statisticians measure GDP. You will also learn about other indicators of the standard of living as well as the scope and limitations of GDP as a measure of the standard of living.

5.1 GDP, INCOME, AND EXPENDITURE

How does your standard of living compare with that of your parents when they were your age? Who is better off: you or a college student in Beijing, China?

We defined the *standard of living* in Chapter 1 (p. 4) as the level of consumption of goods and services that people enjoy, *on the average*, measured by average income per person. So to answer the questions we've just posed, you might try to discover who has the higher income: you today or your parents in the 1970s, and you or a college student in China.

But it is the quantities of goods and services consumed that determine how well off people are. To consume goods and services, they must be produced. So another way to answer the questions posed is to discover who produces the greater total value of goods and services. Do we produce more per person today than our parents' generation did in the 1970s, and do we produce more per person than the people of China produce? To answer these questions, we need to measure total production.

GDP Defined

Gross domestic product (GDP)
The market value of all the final goods and services produced within a country in a given time period.

We measure total production as **gross domestic product**, or **GDP**, which is the market value of all the final goods and services produced within a country in a given time period. This definition has four parts that we'll examine in turn.

Value Produced

To measure total production, we must add together the production of apples and oranges, computers and popcorn. Just counting the items doesn't get us very far. Which is the greater total production: 100 apples and 50 oranges or 50 apples and 100 oranges?

GDP answers this question by valuing items at their *market value*—at the prices at which each item is traded in markets. If the price of an apple is 10 cents and the price of an orange is 20 cents, the market value of 100 apples plus 50 oranges is $20 and the market value of 50 apples and 100 oranges is $25. So by using market prices to value production, we can add the apples and oranges together.

What Produced

Final good or service
A good or service that is produced for its final user and not as a component of another good or service.

Intermediate good or service
A good or service that is produced by one firm, bought by another firm, and used as a component of a final good or service.

To calculate GDP, we value *all the final goods and services*. A **final good or service** is a good or service that is produced for its final user and not as a component of another good or service. It contrasts with an **intermediate good or service**, which is a good or service that is produced by one firm, bought by another firm, and used as a component of a final good or service. For example, a Ford SUV is a final good, but a Firestone tire on the SUV is an intermediate good.

GDP aims to be a full count of the value of everything that is produced. In practice, with one exception, GDP includes only those items that are traded in markets. It does not include the market value of goods and services that people produce for their own use. For example, GDP includes the value of a car wash that is bought but excludes the value of washing your own car. The exception is the market value of homes that people own. GDP puts a rental value on such homes and pretends that their owners rent them to themselves.

Where Produced

Only goods and services that are produced *within a country* count as part of that country's GDP. Nike Corporation, a U.S. firm, produces sneakers in Vietnam, and the market value of those shoes is part of Vietnam's GDP, not part of U.S. GDP. Toyota, a Japanese firm, produces automobiles in Georgetown, Kentucky, and the value of this production is part of U.S. GDP, not part of Japan's GDP.

When Produced

GDP measures the value of production *during a given time period*. This time period is either a quarter of a year—called the quarterly GDP data—or a year—called the annual GDP data. The Federal Reserve and others use the quarterly GDP data to keep track of the short-term evolution of the economy, and economists use the annual GDP data to examine long-term trends.

GDP measures not only the value of total production but also total income and total expenditure. The circular flow model that you studied in Chapter 2 explains why.

Circular Flows in the U.S. Economy

Four groups buy the final goods and services produced: households, firms, governments, and the rest of the world. Four types of expenditure correspond to these groups:

- Consumption expenditure
- Investment
- Government purchases of goods and services
- Net exports of goods and services

Consumption Expenditure

Consumption expenditure is the expenditure by households on consumption goods and services. It includes expenditures on popcorn and soda, candy and chocolate bars, and dental and dry cleaning services. Consumption expenditure also includes house and apartment rents, including the rental value of owner-occupied housing.

Consumption expenditure
The expenditure by households on consumption goods and services.

Investment

Investment is the purchase of new *capital goods* (tools, instruments, machines, buildings, and other constructions) and additions to inventories. Some firms produce capital goods, and other firms buy them. For example, IBM produces PCs and General Motors buys some of them; Boeing produces airplanes and United Airlines buys some of them.

Investment
The purchase of new *capital goods* (tools, instruments, machines, buildings, and other constructions) and additions to inventories.

Some of a firm's output might remain unsold at the end of a year. For example, if GM produces 4 million cars and sells 3.9 million of them, the other 0.1 million (100,000) cars remain unsold. In this case, GM's inventory of cars increases by 100,000. When a firm adds unsold output to inventory, we count those items as part of investment.

It is important to note that investment does *not* include the purchase of stocks and bonds. In macroeconomics, we reserve the term "investment" for the purchase of new capital goods and the additions to inventories.

Government Purchases of Goods and Services

Government purchases of goods and services The purchases by all levels of government on goods and services.

Government purchases of goods and services are purchases by all levels of government of goods and services from firms. You saw in Chapter 2 (pp. 44–47) that governments buy a wide range of goods and services. For example, the U.S. Defense Department buys missiles and other weapons systems, the State Department buys travel services, the White House buys Internet services, and state and local governments buy cruisers for law-enforcement officers.

Net Exports of Goods and Services

Net exports of goods and services The value of exports of goods and services minus the value of imports of goods and services.

Exports of goods and services Items that firms in the United States produce and sell to the rest of the world.

Imports of goods and services Items that households, firms, and governments in the United States buy from the rest of the world.

Net exports of goods and services is the value of exports of goods and services minus the value of imports of goods and services. **Exports of goods and services** are items that firms in the United States produce and sell to the rest of the world. **Imports of goods and services** are items that households, firms, and governments in the United States buy from the rest of the world. Imports are produced in other countries, so expenditure on imports is not included in expenditure on U.S-produced goods and services. If exports exceed imports, net exports are positive and increase expenditure on U.S.-produced goods and services. If imports exceed exports, net exports are negative and decrease expenditure on U.S.-produced goods and services.

Total Expenditure

Total expenditure on goods and services produced in the United States is the sum of the four items that you've just examined. We call consumption expenditure C, investment I, government purchases of goods and services G, and net exports of goods and services NX. Using these symbols, total expenditure is

$$\text{Total expenditure} = C + I + G + NX.$$

Total expenditure is the total amount received by producers of final goods and services.

Income

Labor earns wages, capital earns interest, land earns rent, and entrepreneurship earns profits. Households receive these incomes. Some part of total income, called *undistributed profit,* is a combination of interest and profit that is not paid out to households. But from an economic viewpoint, undistributed profit is income paid to households and then loaned to firms.

Expenditure Equals Income

Figure 5.1 shows the circular flows of income and expenditure that we've just described. The figure is based on Figures 2.4 and 2.5 (on p. 43 and p. 45), but it includes some more details and additional flows.

We call total income Y and show it by the blue flow from firms to households. When households receive their incomes, they pay some in taxes and save some. Some households receive benefits from governments. *Net taxes* equal taxes paid minus benefits received and are the green flow from households to governments labeled NT. Saving flows from households to financial markets and is the green flow labeled S. These two green flows are not expenditures on goods and services. They are just flows of money.

The red flows show the four expenditure flows described above: consumption expenditure from households to firms, government purchases from governments to firms, and net exports from the rest of the world to firms. Investment flows from the financial markets, where firms borrow, to the firms that produce capital goods.

Because firms pay out everything they receive as incomes to the factors of production, total expenditure equals total income. That is,

$$Y = C + I + G + NX.$$

From the viewpoint of firms, the value of production is the cost of production, which equals income. From the viewpoint of purchasers of goods and services, the value of production is the cost of buying it, which equals expenditure. So

The value of production equals income equals expenditure.

The circular flow and the equality of income and expenditure provide two approaches to measuring GDP that we'll study in the next section.

FIGURE 5.1
The Circular Flow of Income and Expenditure

Practice Online

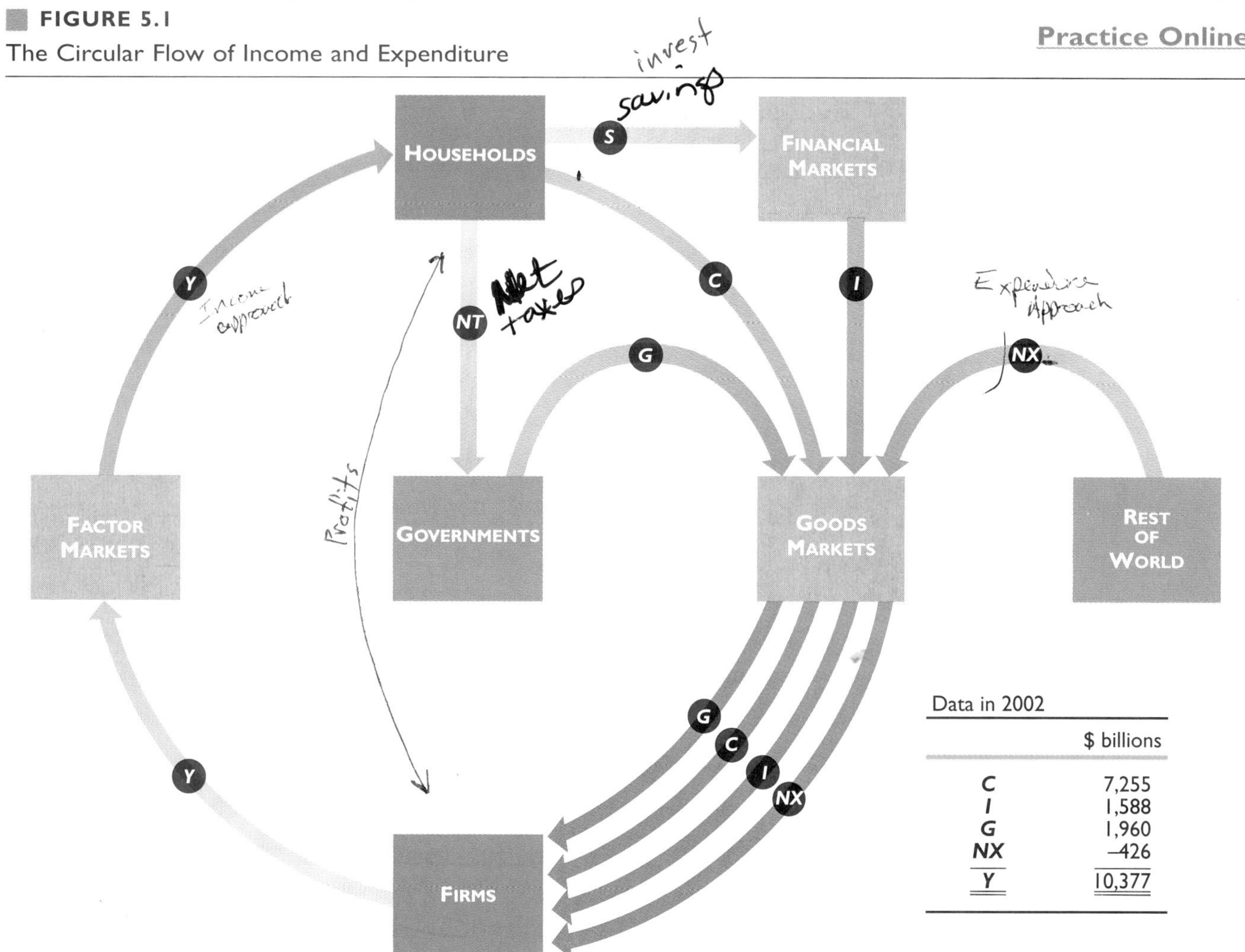

Data in 2002

	$ billions
C	7,255
I	1,588
G	1,960
NX	–426
Y	10,377

In the circular flow, the blue flow (Y) is income and the red flows (C, I, G, and NX) are expenditures on goods and services. The green flows are flows of money: Households pay net taxes (NT) to governments and save (S) some of their income. Firms borrow in financial markets to buy goods (I) from other firms. Expenditure equals income and equals the value of production.

CHECKPOINT 5.1

Study Guide pp. 70–72

Practice Online 5.1

1 Define GDP and explain why the value of production, income, and expenditure are the same for an economy.

Practice Problems 5.1

1. Classify each of the following items as a final good or service or an intermediate good or service:
   - **a.** Banking services bought by a student.
   - **b.** New cars bought by Hertz, the car rental firm.
   - **c.** Newsprint bought by *USA Today* from International Paper.
   - **d.** Ice cream bought by a diner and used to produce sundaes.
2. During 2001 on Lotus Island, net taxes were $10 billion; consumption expenditure was $30 billion; government purchases of goods and services were $12 billion; investment was $15 billion; and net exports were $3 billion. Calculate
   - **a.** Total expenditure.
   - **b.** Total income.
   - **c.** GDP.

Exercises 5.1

1. Classify each of the following items as a final good or service or an intermediate good or service:
   - **a.** The fertilizer bought by a Florida tomato grower.
   - **b.** The *Wall Street Journal* you bought today.
   - **c.** The PlayStation 2 that you bought on eBay.
   - **d.** The aircraft fuel bought by United Airlines.
2. During 2002 on Lotus Island, households spent $60 million of their income on goods and services, saved $20 million, and paid the rest of their income in net taxes; government purchases of goods and services were $15 million; investment was $25 million; and net exports were zero. Calculate
   - **a.** GDP.
   - **b.** Total income.
   - **c.** Total expenditure.
   - **d.** Net taxes.

Solutions to Practice Problems 5.1

1a. A final service—The student is the final user.

1b. Final goods—The new cars that Hertz buys are additions to its capital and as such they are investment.

1c. An intermediate good—Newsprint is a component of the newspaper.

1d. An intermediate good—Ice cream is a component of sundaes.

2a. Total expenditure is $60 billion. Total expenditure = $C + I + G + NX$.
Inserting the values into the equation, we have:
Total expenditure = $(30 + 15 +12 + 3) billion = $60 billion.

2b. Total income = total expenditure = $60 billion.

2c. GDP = total expenditure = $60 billion.

5.2 MEASURING U.S. GDP

U.S. GDP is the market value of all the final goods and services produced within the United States during a year. In 2002, U.S. GDP almost reached the $10.4 trillion mark. The Bureau of Economic Analysis in the U.S. Department of Commerce measures GDP. To do so, it uses two approaches:

- Expenditure approach
- Income approach

The Expenditure Approach

The expenditure approach measures GDP by using data on consumption expenditure, investment, government purchases, and net exports. This approach is like attaching a meter to the circular flow diagram on all the flows running through the markets for goods and services to firms and measuring the magnitudes of those flows. Table 5.1 shows this approach. The first column gives the terms used in the National Income and Product Accounts of the United States. The next column gives the symbol we used in the previous section.

Using the expenditure approach, GDP is the sum of consumption expenditure on goods and services (*C*), investment (*I*), government purchases of goods and services (*G*), and net exports of goods and services (*NX*). The third column gives the expenditures in mid-2002. GDP measured by the expenditure approach was $10,377 billion (annual rate) in the second quarter of 2002.

Net exports were negative in 2002 because imports exceeded exports. Imports were $1,444 billion and exports were $1,018 billion, so net exports—exports minus imports—were –$426 billion as shown in the table.

The fourth column in Table 5.1 shows the relative magnitudes of the expenditures. Consumption expenditure makes up more than half of total expenditure; investment and government purchases are about the same percentage of total expenditure; and net exports is the smallest. In 2002, consumption expenditure was 69.9 percent, investment was 15.3 percent, government purchases were about 18.9 percent each, and net exports were a negative 4.1 percent of GDP.

TABLE 5.1
GDP: The Expenditure Approach

Practice Online

Item	Symbol	Amount in 2002 (billions of dollars)	Percentage of GDP
Consumption expenditure	*C*	7,255	69.9
Investment	*I*	1,588	15.3
Government purchases	*G*	1,960	18.9
Net exports	*NX*	–426	–4.1
GDP	*Y*	10,377	100.0

SOURCE: U.S. Department of Commerce, Bureau of Economic Analysis.

The expenditure approach measures GDP by adding together consumption expenditure (*C*), investment (*I*), government purchases (*G*), and net exports (*NX*). In 2002, GDP measured by the expenditure approach was $10,377 billion.

Expenditures Not in GDP

Total expenditure (and GDP) does not include all the things that people and businesses buy. GDP is the value of *final goods and services*, so spending that is *not* on final goods and services is not part of GDP. Spending on intermediate goods and services is not part of GDP, although it is not always obvious whether an item is an intermediate good or a final good; see Eye on the U.S. Economy. Also, we do not count as part of GDP spending on

- Used goods
- Financial assets

Used Goods

Expenditure on used goods is not part of GDP because these goods were part of GDP in the period in which they were produced and during which time they were new goods. For example, a 1999 automobile was part of GDP in 1999. If the car is traded on the used car market in 2002, the amount paid for the car is not part of GDP in 2002.

Financial Assets

When households buy financial assets such as bonds and stocks, they are making loans, not buying goods and services. The expenditure on newly produced capital goods is part of GDP, but the purchase of financial assets is not.

Eye on the U.S. Economy

Is a Computer Program an Intermediate Good or a Final Good?

When American Airlines buys a new reservations software package, is that like General Motors buying tires? If it is, then software is an *intermediate good* and it is not counted as part of GDP. Airline ticket sales, like GM cars, are part of GDP, but the intermediate goods that are used to produce air transportation or cars are *not* part of GDP.

Or when American Airlines buys new software, is that like General Motors buying a new assembly-line robot? If it is, then the software is a capital good and its purchase is the purchase of a final good. In this case, the software purchase is an *investment* and it *is* counted as part of GDP.

Brent Moulton is a government economist who works in the Bureau of Economic Analysis (BEA). Moulton's recent job was to oversee a periodic adjustment to the GDP estimates to incorporate new data and new ideas about the economy.

The biggest change was in how the purchase of computer software by firms is classified. Before 1999, it was regarded as an *intermediate good*. But since 1999, it has been treated as an *investment*.

How big a deal is this? When GDP in 1996 was recalculated, the change increased the estimate of the 1996 GDP by $115 billion. That is a lot of money. To put it in perspective, GDP in 1996 was $7,662 billion. So the adjustment was 1.5 percent of GDP.

This change is a nice example of the ongoing effort by the BEA to keep the GDP measure as accurate as possible.

The Income Approach

The Bureau of Economic Analysis measures GDP using the income approach by collecting data (from the Internal Revenue Service and other sources) on the incomes that firms pay households for the services of factors of production they hire—wages for labor, interest for the use of capital, rent for the use of land, and profits for entrepreneurship—and summing those incomes. This approach is like attaching a meter to the circular flow diagram on all the flows of factor incomes from firms to households and measuring the magnitudes of those flows. Let's see how the income approach works.

The National Income and Product Accounts divide incomes into five categories:

- Compensation of employees
- Net interest
- Rental income of persons
- Corporate profits
- Proprietors' income

Compensation of Employees

Compensation of employees is the payment for labor services. It includes net wages and salaries plus fringe benefits paid by employers such as health care insurance, social security contributions, and pension fund contributions.

Net Interest

Net interest is the interest households receive on loans they make minus the interest households pay on their own borrowing.

Rental Income of Persons

Rental income of persons is the payment for the use of land and other rented inputs. It includes payments for rented housing and imputed rent for owner-occupied housing. (Imputed rent is an estimate of what homeowners would pay to rent the housing they own and use themselves. By including this item in the national income accounts, we measure the total value of housing services, whether they are owned or rented.)

Corporate Profits

Corporate profits—the profits of corporations—are a combination of interest on capital and profit for entrepreneurship. Corporate profits paid out as dividends and undistributed profits are all counted as income.

Proprietors' Income

Proprietors are people who run their own businesses. Their income is a mixture of the previous four items. It is difficult to split the income earned by the owner-operator of a business into compensation for labor, payment for the use of capital, and profit, so the national income accounts lump all these items into a single category.

TABLE 5.2
GDP: The Income Approach

Practice Online

The sum of all incomes equals net domestic product at factor cost. GDP equals net domestic product at factor cost plus indirect taxes less subsidies plus capital consumption (depreciation). In 2002, GDP measured by the income approach was $10,377 billion. The compensation of employees—labor income—was by far the largest part of aggregate income.

Item	Amount in 2002 (billions of dollars)	Percentage of GDP
Compensation of employees	5,964	57.5
Net interest	678	6.5
Rental income of persons	153	1.5
Corporate profits	785	7.6
Proprietors' income	747	7.2
Net domestic product at factor cost	8,327	80.3
Indirect taxes less subsidies	660	6.4
Capital consumption	1,390	13.3
GDP	10,377	100.0

SOURCE: U.S. Department of Commerce, Bureau of Economic Analysis.

Net domestic product at factor cost
The sum of the five components of incomes—compensation of employees, net interest, rental income of persons, corporate profits, and proprietors' income.

Table 5.2 shows these five components of incomes and their relative magnitudes. These five components of incomes sum to **net domestic product at factor cost**. Net domestic product at factor cost is not GDP. We must make two further adjustments to get to GDP: one from factor cost to market prices and another from net product to gross product.

From Factor Cost to Market Price

The expenditure approach values goods and services at market prices, and the income approach values them at factor cost—the cost of the factors of production used to produce them. Indirect taxes (such as sales taxes) and subsidies (payments by government to firms) make these two values differ. Sales taxes make market prices exceed factor cost, and subsidies make factor cost exceed market prices. To convert the value at factor cost to the value at market prices, we must add indirect taxes and subtract subsidies.

From Gross to Net

Depreciation
The decrease in the value of capital that results from its use and from obsolescence—also called capital consumption.

The expenditure approach measures gross product, and the income approach measures net product. The difference is **depreciation**, the decrease in the value of capital that results from its use and from obsolescence—also called capital consumption. A firm's profit before subtracting the depreciation of capital is its gross profit. And its profit after subtracting the depreciation of capital is its net profit. Income includes net profit, so the income approach gives a *net* measure. Expenditure includes investment, which is the purchase of new capital. Because some new capital is purchased to replace depreciated capital, the expenditure approach gives a *gross* measure. So to get *gross* domestic product from the income approach, we must add depreciation to total income.

Table 5.2 summarizes these adjustments and shows that the income approach gives the same estimate of GDP as the expenditure approach.

Valuing the Output of Industries

The methods that are used to measure GDP can be used to measure the contribution that each industry makes to GDP. To measure the value of production of an industry, we count only the value added by that industry. **Value added** is the value of a firm's production minus the value of the intermediate goods it buys from other firms. Equivalently, a firm's value added equals the sum of the incomes (including profits) that the firm paid for the factors of production it used.

Value added
The value of a firm's production minus the value of the intermediate goods it buys from other firms.

Figure 5.2 illustrates value added by looking at the brief life of a loaf of bread. It starts with the farmer, who hires factors of production and grows wheat. We'll assume that the farmer uses no intermediate goods. The miller buys the wheat (for a loaf) from the farmer for 20¢. The value of the farmer's production is 20¢, and the farmer's value added is 20¢. The farmer's value added equals the incomes that the farmer paid for the factors of production plus the farmer's profit.

The miller hires factors of production to turn the wheat into flour. The baker buys the flour from the miller for 70¢. The miller's value added is 50¢—the value of the flour (70¢) minus the cost of the intermediate good (20¢ for wheat). The miller's value added equals the incomes that the miller paid for the factors of production plus the miller's profit.

The baker adds a further 80¢ of value by turning the flour into bread. The consumer buys the bread for its market price, $1.50. The market price equals the value added by the farmer (20¢), the miller (50¢), and the baker (80¢).

To value output, we count *only* value added because the total of the values added at all stages of production equals expenditure on the final good. By totaling values added, we avoid double counting. In Figure 5.2, the only final good is a loaf of bread. The red bar shows the value of the final good. The blue bars show the value added at each stage, and the sum of the blue bars equals the red bar. The transactions involving intermediate goods, shown by the green bars, are not part of value added and are *not* counted as part of the value of output or of GDP.

FIGURE 5.2
Value Added and Final Expenditure

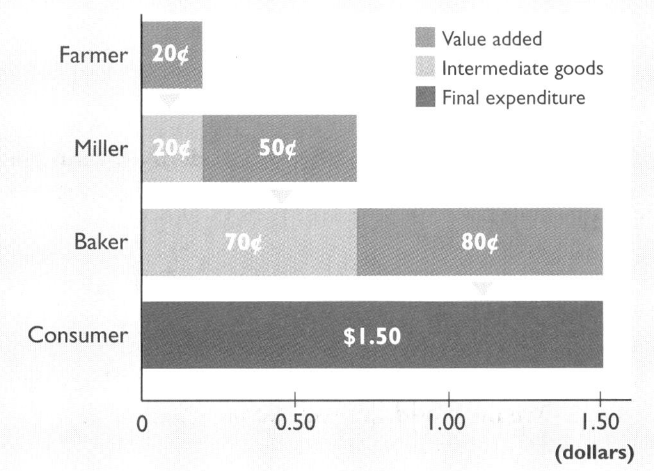

Value added is the value of a firm's production minus the value of the intermediate goods it buys from other firms. The baker's value added is the consumer's expenditure on bread minus the baker's intermediate expenditure on flour. The baker's value added equals the incomes paid, including profit, for the factors of production hired by the baker. The value of the bread (the final good) is equal to the sum of all values added.

CHECKPOINT 5.2

Study Guide pp. 73–75

Practice Online 5.2

2 **Describe how economic statisticians measure GDP in the United States.**

Practice Problem 5.2

Table 1 shows some of the items in the U.S. National Income and Product Accounts in 2001.

a. Calculate U.S. GDP in 2001.
b. Did you use the expenditure approach or the income approach to make this calculation?
c. How much did the U.S. government spend on goods and services in 2001?
d. By how much did capital in the United States depreciate in 2001?

TABLE 1

Item	Amount (billions of dollars)
Compensation of employees	5,875
Consumption expenditure	6,987
Indirect taxes less subsidies	630
Net interest	650
Corporate profits	732
Capital consumption	1,329
Rental income of persons	138
Investment	1,586
Net exports	−349
Proprietors' income	728

Exercises 5.2

1. Table 2 shows some of the items in the U.S. National Income and Product Accounts in 1997.
   a. Use the expenditure approach to calculate U.S. GDP in 1997.
   b. Use the income approach to calculate U.S. net domestic product at factor cost in 1997.
   c. Calculate GDP minus net domestic product at factor cost in 1997.
   d. Calculate indirect taxes less subsidies in 1997.
2. At the American Diner, the price of a mango smoothie is \$3.00. The diner buys the mango for 50¢, skim milk for 20¢, and flavoring for 1¢ from other firms and pays 25¢ for the labor and capital. Calculate the value added by the American Diner when it produces a mango smoothie.

TABLE 2

Item	Amount (billions of dollars)
Consumption expenditure	5,529
Government purchases	1,488
Net interest	424
Corporate profits	834
Rental income of persons	128
Investment	1,391
Net exports	−89
Compensation of employees	4,651
Proprietors' income	581
Capital consumption	1,013

Solution to Practice Problem 5.2

a. GDP = $C + I + G + NX$ (the expenditure approach) and GDP = Compensation of employees + Net interest + Rental income of persons + Corporate profits + Proprietors' incomes + Indirect taxes less subsidies + Capital consumption (the income approach). Inspect the data and notice that Government purchases (G) is missing. So you can't use the expenditure approach. But you can use the income approach. Insert the items in the equation and get

   GDP in billions = \$5,875 + \$650 + \$138 + \$732 + \$728 + \$630 + \$1,329
   = \$10,082 billions.

b. You totaled the incomes for factors of production, so you used the income approach.

c. Use the expenditure approach to calculate G:

   $$\text{GDP} = C + I + G + NX.$$

   Insert the numbers that you know into this equation:

   GDP in billions = \$10,082 = \$6,987 + \$1,586 + G – \$349.

   G = \$10,082 billion – \$8,224 billion = \$1,858 billion.

d. Depreciation equals capital consumption, which in 2001 was \$1,329 billion.

5.3 NOMINAL GDP VERSUS REAL GDP

You've seen that GDP measures total expenditure on final goods and services in a given period. In 2001, GDP was $10,082 billion. In 2002, GDP was $10,377 billion. Because GDP in 2002 was greater than in 2001, we know that one or two things must have happened during that period:

- We produced more goods and services.
- We paid higher prices for our goods and services.

Producing more goods and services contributes to an improvement in our standard of living. Paying higher prices means that our cost of living has increased but our standard of living has not. So it matters a great deal why GDP has increased.

You're going to learn how economists at the Bureau of Economic Analysis split the increase in GDP into two parts: one part that tells us the change in production and another that tells us the change in prices. The method they use has changed in recent years, and we will describe the new method.

We measure the increase in production by a number called real GDP. **Real GDP** is the value of the final goods and services produced in a given year when valued at constant prices. By comparing the value at constant prices of the goods and services produced, we can measure the increase in production.

Real GDP
The value of the final goods and services produced in a given year when valued at constant prices.

Calculating Real GDP

Table 5.3 shows the quantities produced and prices in 2002 for an economy that produces only apples and oranges. The first step toward calculating real GDP is to calculate **nominal GDP**, which is the value of the final goods and services produced in a given year valued at the prices that prevailed in that same year. Nominal GDP is just a more precise name for GDP that we use when we want to make it clear that we are not talking about real GDP.

Nominal GDP
The value of the final goods and services produced in a given year valued at the prices that prevailed in that same year.

Nominal GDP Calculation

To calculate nominal GDP in 2002, sum the expenditures on apples and oranges in 2002 as follows:

Expenditure on apples = 100 apples × $1 = $100.
Expenditure on oranges = 200 oranges × $0.50 = $100.
Nominal GDP in 2002 = $100 + $100 = $200.

Table 5.4 shows the quantities produced and prices in 2003. The quantity of apples produced increased to 160 and the quantity of oranges produced increased to 220. The price of an apple fell to 50¢, and the price of an orange increased to $2.25. To calculate nominal GDP in 2003, sum the expenditures on apples and oranges in 2003 as follows:

Expenditure on apples = 160 apples × $0.50 = $80.
Expenditure on oranges = 220 oranges × $2.25 = $495.
Nominal GDP in 2003 = $80 + $495 = $575.

To calculate real GDP, we choose one year, called the *base year*, against which to compare the other years. The choice of the base year is not important. It is just a common reference point. We'll use 2002 as the base year. By definition, real GDP equals nominal GDP in the base year. So real GDP in 2002 is $200.

TABLE 5.3 GDP DATA FOR 2002

Item	Quantity	Price
Apples	100	$1.00
Oranges	200	$0.50

TABLE 5.4 GDP DATA FOR 2003

Item	Quantity	Price
Apples	160	$0.50
Oranges	220	$2.25

Traditional Real GDP Calculation

The traditional method of calculating real GDP values the quantities produced in each year at the prices of the base year. Table 5.5 summarizes these prices and quantities for 2002 and 2003. The value of the 2003 quantities at the 2002 prices is calculated as follows:

TABLE 5.5 2003 QUANTITIES AND 2002 PRICES

Item	Quantity	Price
Apples	160	$1.00
Oranges	220	$0.50

Expenditure on apples = 160 apples × $1.00 = $160.
Expenditure on oranges = 220 oranges × $0.50 = $110.
Value of the 2003 quantities at 2002 prices = $270.

Using the traditional method, $270 would be recorded as real GDP in 2003.

New Method of Calculating Real GDP

The new method of calculating real GDP builds on the old method but takes a further step. The new method compares the quantities produced in 2002 and 2003 by using not only 2002 prices but also the 2003 prices. It then averages the two sets of numbers in a special way that we'll now describe.

To compare the quantities produced in 2002 and 2003 at 2003 prices, we need to calculate the value of 2002 quantities at 2003 prices. Table 5.6 summarizes these quantities and prices. The value of the 2002 quantities at the 2003 prices is calculated as follows:

TABLE 5.6 2002 QUANTITIES AND 2003 PRICES

Item	Quantity	Price
Apples	100	$0.50
Oranges	200	$2.25

Expenditure on apples = 100 apples × $0.50 = $50.
Expenditure on oranges = 200 oranges × $2.25 = $450.
Value of the 2002 quantities at 2003 prices = $500.

We now have two comparisons between 2002 and 2003. At the 2002 prices, the value of production increased from $200 in 2002 to $270 in 2003. The increase in value is $70, and the percentage increase is ($70 ÷ $200) × 100, which is 35 percent.

At the 2003 prices, the value of production increased from $500 in 2002 to $575 in 2003. The increase in value is $75, and the percentage increase is ($75 ÷ $500) × 100, which is 15 percent.

When we value production in 2002 prices, it increased by 35 percent in 2003. When we value production in 2003 prices, it increased by 15 percent in 2003. The new method of calculating real GDP uses the average of these two percentage increases. The average of 35 percent and 15 percent is (35 + 15) ÷ 2, which equals 25 percent. Real GDP is 25 percent greater in 2003 than in 2002. Real GDP in 2002 is $200, so real GDP in 2003 is $250.

Year	Real GDP	Chain-linked percentage change
2004	$300	+20%
2003	$250	+25%
2002	$200	Base year

Chain Linking

The calculation that we've just described is repeated each year. Each year is compared with its preceding year. So, in 2004, the calculations are repeated but using the prices and quantities of 2003 and 2004. Real GDP in 2004 equals real GDP in 2003 increased by the calculated percentage change in real GDP for 2004. For example, suppose that real GDP for 2004 is calculated to be 20 percent greater than in 2003. You know that real GDP in 2003 is $250. So real GDP in 2004 is 20 percent greater than this value and is $300. In every year, real GDP is valued in base-year (2002) dollars.

By applying the calculated percentage change to the real GDP of the preceding real GDP, each year is linked back to the dollars of the base year like the links in a chain.

Eye on the U.S. Economy

Deflating the GDP Balloon

Nominal GDP increased every year between 1992 and 2002. Part of the increase reflects increased production, and part of it reflects rising prices.

You can think of GDP as a balloon that is blown up by growing production and rising prices. In the figure, the GDP deflator lets the inflation air—the contribution of rising prices—out of the nominal GDP balloon so that we can see what has happened to real GDP. The red balloon for 1992 shows real GDP in that year. The green balloon shows nominal GDP in 2002. The red balloon for 2002 shows real GDP for that year. To see real GDP in 2002, we use the GDP deflator to deflate nominal GDP.

With the inflation air removed, real GDP shows how the total value of production has changed. Production grew from 1992 through 2000, but in 2001, real GDP shrank. Over the 10 years, real GDP grew by 3.1 percent a year, and in 2002, it was 38 percent higher than it was in 1992.

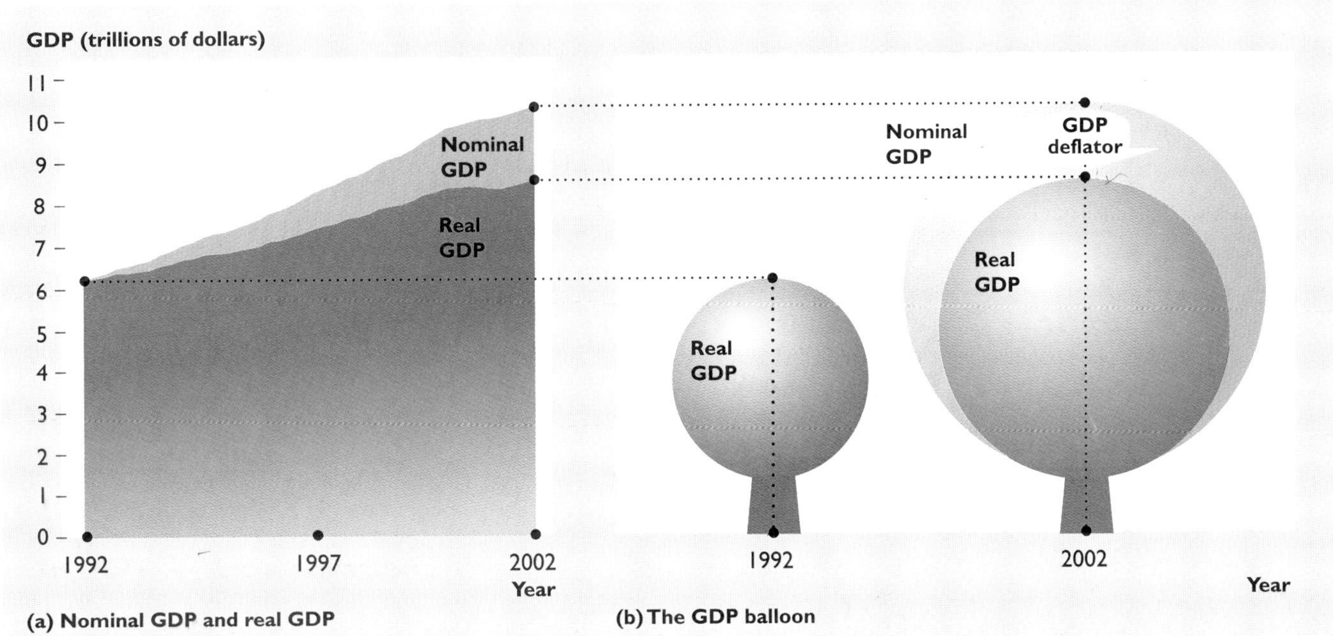

(a) Nominal GDP and real GDP

(b) The GDP balloon

SOURCE: Bureau of Economic Analysis.

Calculating the GDP Deflator

The **GDP deflator** is an average of current prices expressed as a percentage of base-year prices. The GDP deflator measures the price level. We calculate the GDP deflator by using nominal GDP and real GDP in the following formula:

$$\text{GDP deflator} = (\text{Nominal GDP} \div \text{Real GDP}) \times 100.$$

You can see why the GDP deflator is a measure of the price level. If nominal GDP rises but real GDP remains unchanged, it must be that prices have risen. The formula would deliver that result in the form of a higher GDP deflator. The larger the nominal GDP for a given real GDP, the higher are prices and the larger is the GDP deflator.

Table 5.7 shows how the GDP deflator is calculated. In 2002, the deflator is 100. In 2003, it is 230, which equals nominal GDP of $575 divided by real GDP of $250 and then multiplied by 100.

GDP deflator
An average of current prices expressed as a percentage of base-year prices.

TABLE 5.7 CALCULATING THE GDP DEFLATOR

Year	Nominal GDP	Real GDP	GDP Deflator
2002	$200	$200	100
2003	$575	$250	230

CHECKPOINT 5.3

Study Guide pp. 75–77

Practice Online 5.3

3 **Distinguish between nominal GDP and real GDP and define the GDP deflator.**

Practice Problem 5.3

An island economy produces only bananas and coconuts. Table 1 gives the quantities produced and prices in 2001, and Table 2 gives the quantities produced and prices in 2002. The base year is 2001. Calculate

a. Nominal GDP in 2001.
b. Nominal GDP in 2002.
c. The value of 2002 production in 2001 prices.
d. The percentage increase in production when valued at 2001 prices.
e. The value of 2001 production in 2002 prices.
f. The percentage increase in production when valued at 2002 prices.
g. Real GDP in 2001 and 2002 by using the chain-linking method.
h. The GDP deflator in 2002.

TABLE 1

In 2001:

Item	Quantity	Price
Bananas	100	$10 a bunch
Coconuts	50	$12 a bag

TABLE 2

In 2002:

Item	Quantity	Price
Bananas	110	$15 a bunch
Coconuts	60	$10 a bag

Exercise 5.3

An island economy produces only lobsters and crabs. Table 3 gives the quantities produced and the prices in 2001, and Table 4 gives the quantities produced and the prices in 2002. The base year is 2001. Calculate

a. Nominal GDP in 2001.
b. Nominal GDP in 2002.
c. The value of 2002 production in 2001 prices.
d. The percentage increase in production when valued at 2001 prices.
e. The value of 2001 production in 2002 prices.
f. The percentage increase in production when valued at 2002 prices.
g. Real GDP in 2001 and 2002 by using the chain-linking method.
h. The GDP deflator in 2002.

TABLE 3

In 2001:

Item	Quantity	Price
Lobsters	90	$15 each
Crabs	20	$20 each

TABLE 4

In 2002:

Item	Quantity	Price
Lobsters	100	$20 each
Crabs	25	$25 each

Solution to Practice Problem 5.3

a. Nominal GDP in 2001 is $1,600—expenditure is $1,000 on bananas and $600 on coconuts (Table 1).
b. Nominal GDP in 2002 is $2,250—expenditure is $1,650 on bananas and $600 on coconuts (Table 2).
c. The value of 2002 production in 2001 prices is $1,820 (Table 5).
d. In 2001 prices, the value of production increased from $1,600 to $1,820, an increase of $220. The percentage increase is (220 ÷ 1,600) × 100, or 13.75 percent.
e. The value of 2001 production in 2002 prices is $2,000 (Table 6).
f. In 2002 prices, the value of production increased from $2,000 to $2,250, an increase of $250. The percentage increase is (250 ÷ 2,000) × 100, or 12.5 percent.
g. Real GDP in 2001 is $1,600. The average percentage increase in production is (13.75 + 12.5) ÷ 2, which is 13.125 percent. Real GDP in 2002 is 13.125 percent greater than $1,600, which is $1,810.
h. The GDP deflator in 2002 is (nominal GDP ÷ real GDP) × 100, which is 124.3.

TABLE 5

2002 quantities and 2001 prices

Item	Quantity	Price	Expenditure
Bananas	110	$10	$1,100
Coconuts	60	$12	$720
Value in 2001 prices			$1,820

TABLE 6

2001 quantities and 2002 prices

Item	Quantity	Price	Expenditure
Bananas	100	$15	$1,500
Coconuts	50	$10	$500
Value in 2002 prices			$2,000

5.4 REAL GDP AND THE STANDARD OF LIVING

We use estimates of real GDP to compare the standard of living across countries and over time. In 2002, real GDP per person in the United States was $36,000, which (at 2002 prices) is twice what it was in 1965. But are we twice as well off? Does this expansion of real GDP provide a full and accurate measure of the change in our standard of living?

It does not, for two reasons. First, the standard of living depends on *all* goods and services, not only on those included in GDP. Second, the standard of living depends on factors other than the goods and services produced.

Goods and Services Omitted from GDP

GDP measures the value of goods and services that are bought in markets. But it excludes

- Household production
- Underground production
- Leisure time
- Environment quality

Household Production

An enormous amount of production takes place every day in our homes. Preparing meals, cleaning the kitchen, changing a light bulb, cutting the grass, washing the car, and helping a student with homework are all examples of productive activities that do not involve market transactions and are not counted as part of GDP.

Because real GDP omits household production, it underestimates the value of the production of many people, most of them women. But market production is increasingly replacing household production. Two trends point in this direction. One is the number of people who have jobs outside the home, which has increased from 59 percent in 1965 to 67 percent in 2002. The other is the purchase of traditionally home-produced goods and services in the market. For example, more and more families now eat in fast-food restaurants—one of the fastest-growing industries in the United States—and use day-care services. These trends mean that an increasing proportion of food preparation and child care that were once part of household production are now measured as part of GDP. So real GDP grows more rapidly than does real GDP plus home production.

Underground Production

The underground economy is the part of the economy that is hidden from the view of the government either because people want to avoid taxes and regulations or because the goods and services being produced are illegal. Because underground economic activity is unreported, it is omitted from GDP.

The underground economy is easy to describe, even if it is hard to measure. It includes the production and distribution of illegal drugs, production that uses illegal workers who are paid less than the minimum wage, and jobs done for cash to avoid paying income taxes. This last category might be quite large and includes tips earned by cab drivers, hairdressers, and hotel and restaurant workers and a large range of other legal cash transactions.

Edgar L. Feige, an economist at the University of Wisconsin, estimates that the U.S. underground economy peaked at 20 percent of GDP in 1987 and decreased to about 16 percent of GDP during the early 1990s. The underground economy is larger than this in some Eastern European countries, which are making a transition from communist economic planning to a market economy.

Leisure Time

Leisure time is an economic good. Other things remaining the same, the more leisure we have, the better off we are. Our working time is valued as part of GDP, but our leisure time is not. Yet that leisure time must be at least as valuable to us as the wage we earn for working. If it were not, we would work instead. Over the years, leisure time has steadily increased. The workweek has become shorter, more people take early retirement, and the number of vacation days has increased. These improvements in our standard of living are not measured in real GDP.

Environment Quality

An industrial society produces more atmospheric pollution than an agricultural society does. For example, an industrial society burns more coal, oil, and gas. And it depletes resources, clears forests, and pollutes lakes and rivers.

But industrial activity increases wealth, and wealthy people value a clean environment and are better able to devote resources to protecting it. So pollution does not necessarily increase when production increases. Pollution in Germany provides an example. When East Germany, a relatively poor part of the country, opened its borders with West Germany in the late 1980s, it was discovered that East German rivers, lakes, and air were much more severely polluted than those of its richer West German neighbor.

Resources that are used to protect the environment are valued as part of GDP. For example, the production of catalytic converters that help to protect the atmosphere from automobile emissions is part of GDP. But pollution is not subtracted from GDP. If we didn't produce catalytic converters but instead polluted the atmosphere, we would not count the deteriorating atmosphere as a negative part of GDP. So if our standard of living is adversely affected by pollution, our GDP measure does not show this fact.

Other Influences on the Standard of Living

The quantity of goods and services consumed is a major influence on the standard of living. But other influences are

- Health and life expectancy
- Political freedom and social justice

Health and Life Expectancy

Good health and a long life—the hopes of everyone—do not show up directly in real GDP. A higher real GDP enables us to spend more on medical research, health care, a good diet, and exercise equipment. And as real GDP has increased, our life expectancy has lengthened—from 70 years at the end of World War II to nearly 80 years today. Infant deaths and death in childbirth, two scourges of the nineteenth century, have almost been eliminated.

But we face new health and life expectancy problems every year. Diseases such as AIDS and drug abuse are taking young lives at a rate that causes serious concern. When we take these negative influences into account, real GDP growth overstates the improvements in the standard of living.

Political Freedom and Social Justice

A country might have a very large real GDP per person but have limited political freedom and social justice. For example, a small elite might enjoy political liberty and extreme wealth while the majority of people have limited freedom and live in poverty. Such an economy would generally be regarded as having a lower standard of living than one that had the same amount of real GDP but in which everyone enjoyed political freedom. Today, China has rapid real GDP growth but limited political freedom, while Russia has slower real GDP growth and an emerging democratic political system.

Because of the limitations of real GDP, other measures such as the Human Development Index have been proposed (see Eye on the Global Economy).

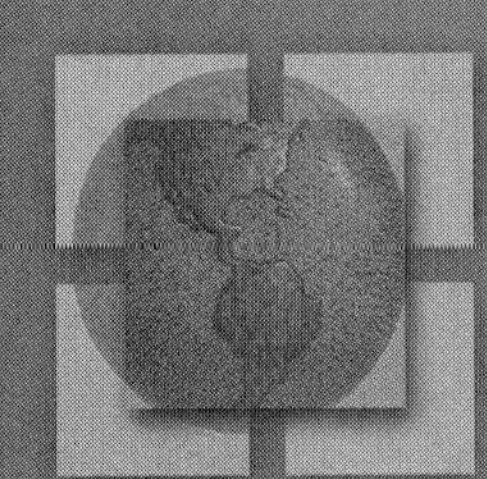

Eye on the Global Economy

The Human Development Index

The limitations of real GDP that we've reviewed in this chapter affect the standard of living of every country. So to make international comparisons of the standard of living, we must look at real GDP and other indicators. Nonetheless, real GDP per person is a major component of international comparisons.

The United Nations has constructed a broader measure called the Human Development Index, or HDI, which combines real GDP, life expectancy and health, and education levels.

The figure shows the relationship between GDP and the HDI. Each dot represents a country. The United States, labeled in the figure, has the highest real GDP per person but the fourth highest HDI. The small African nation of Sierra Leone, also labeled, has the lowest HDI and the lowest real GDP per person.

Why is the United States not the highest-ranked nation on the HDI?

It's because life expectancy at birth in the United States is a bit shorter than it is in Norway, Sweden, and Canada—the three slightly more highly ranked nations.

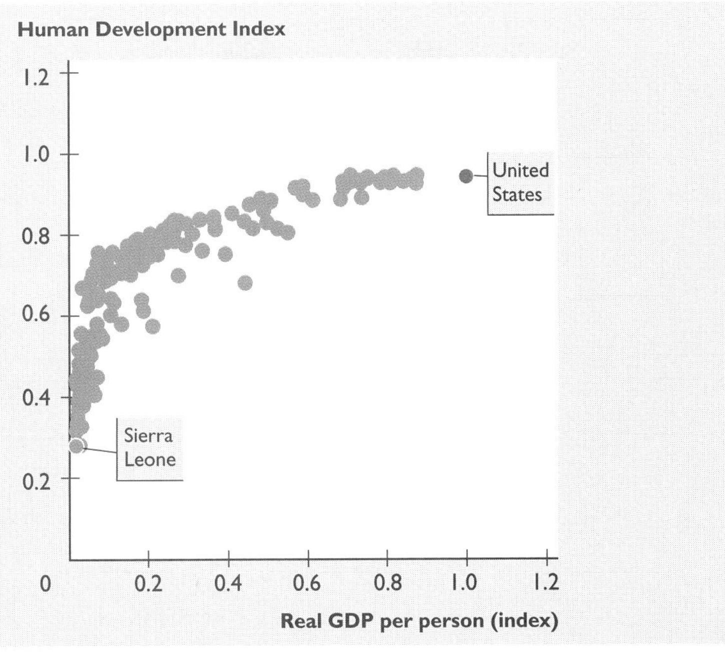

SOURCE: *United Nations Human Development Report*, 2002, http://www.undp.org/hdro/

CHECKPOINT 5.4

Study Guide pp. 77–80

Practice Online 5.4

4 **Explain and describe the limitations of real GDP as a measure of the standard of living.**

Practice Problem 5.4

The United Nations Human Development Report gives the following data for real GDP per person in 2000: China, $3,976; Russia, $8,377; Canada, $27,840; United States, $34,142. Other information suggests that household production is similar in Canada and the United States and smaller in these two countries than in the other two. The underground economy is largest in Russia and China and a similar proportion of the economy in these two cases. Canadians and Americans enjoy more leisure hours than do the Chinese and Russians. Canada and the United States spend significantly more to protect the environment, so air, water, and land pollution is less in those countries than in China and Russia. Given this information and ignoring any other influences on the standard of living

a. In which pair (or pairs) of these four countries is it easiest to compare the standard of living? Why?

b. In which pair (or pairs) of these four countries is it most difficult to compare the standard of living? Why?

c. What more detailed information would we need to be able to make an accurate assessment of the relative standard of living in these four countries?

d. Do you think that real-GDP-per-person differences correctly rank the standard of living in these four countries?

Exercise 5.4

Life expectancy at birth is 78.8 in Canada, 77.0 in the United States, 70.5 in China, and 66.1 in Russia. Freedom House rates political freedom each year, and its ratings are as follows: Canada and the United States, 1.1 (1.0 is the most free); Russia, 4.5; and China, 7.6 (ratings in the 7+ range are the least free). How do these facts change the relative rankings of living standards indicated by differences in real GDP per person?

Solution to Practice Problem 5.4

a. Two pairs—Canada and the United States, and China and Russia—are easy to compare because household production, the underground economy, leisure hours, and the environment are similar in the two countries in each pair.

b. Canada and the United States are the most difficult to compare with China and Russia because household production and the underground economy narrow the differences and leisure hours and the environment widen them.

c. We would need more detailed information on the value of household production, the underground economy, the value of leisure, and the value of environmental differences.

d. Differences in real GDP per person probably correctly rank the standard of living in these four countries because where the gap is small (Canada and the United States), other factors are similar, and where other factors differ, the gaps are huge.

CHAPTER CHECKPOINT

Key Points

1 Define GDP and explain why the value of production, income, and expenditure are the same for an economy.

- GDP is the market value of production of final goods and services in a given time period.
- We can value goods and services either by what it costs to produce (incomes) or by what people are willing to pay (expenditures).
- The value of production equals income equals expenditure.

2 Describe how economic statisticians measure GDP in the United States.

- We measure GDP by summing either expenditures on final goods and services (the expenditure approach) or incomes of all the factors of production (the income approach).
- GDP measures expenditure on final goods and services but excludes expenditure on intermediate goods, used goods, and financial assets.
- To value the output of a sector, we measure only the sector's value added.

3 Distinguish between nominal GDP and real GDP and define the GDP deflator.

- Nominal GDP is the value of production using the prices of the current year and the quantities produced in the current year.
- Real GDP is the value of production using the prices of a base year and the quantities in a current year.
- Changes in real GDP measure changes in production. Changes in nominal GDP combine changes in both production and prices.
- The GDP deflator is the ratio of nominal GDP to real GDP (multiplied by 100).

4 Explain and describe the limitations of real GDP as a measure of the standard of living.

- Real GDP per person is a major indicator of the standard of living.
- Real GDP omits household production, underground production, leisure time, environment quality, health and life expectancy, and political freedom and social justice.
- Broader indexes of the standard of living, such as the Human Development Index, take some of these omitted factors into account.

Key Terms

Consumption expenditure, 113
Depreciation, 120
Exports of goods and services, 114
Final good or service, 112
GDP deflator, 125
Government purchases of goods and services, 114
Gross domestic product (GDP), 112
Imports of goods and services, 114
Intermediate good or service, 112
Investment, 113
Net domestic product at factor cost, 120
Net exports of goods and services, 114
Nominal GDP, 123
Real GDP, 123
Value added, 121

Exercises

FIGURE 1

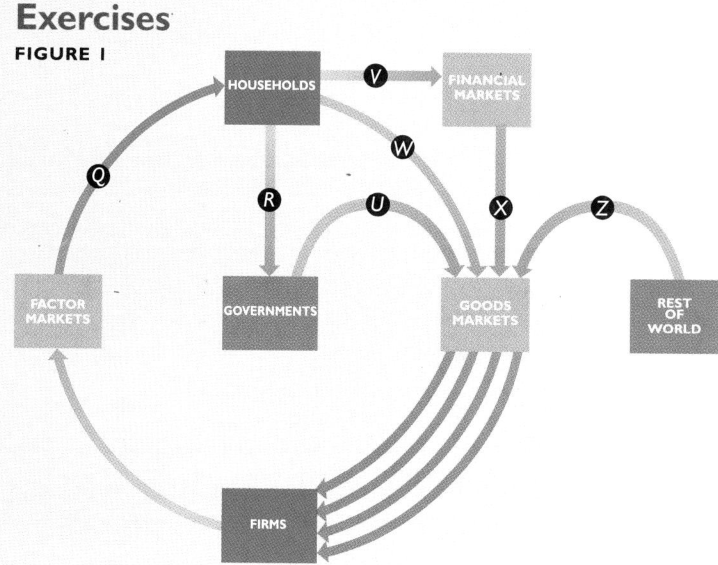

1. In Figure 1, name each of the flows labeled *Q*, *R*, *U*, *V*, *W*, *X*, and *Z*.
2. You are provided with the following data on the economy of Iberia: GDP was \$100 billion, net taxes were \$18 billion, government purchases of goods and services were \$20 billion, household saving was \$15 billion, consumption expenditure was \$67 billion, investment was \$21 billion, and exports of goods and services were \$30 billion.
   a. Find the value of Iberia's import goods and services.
   b. Find Iberia's net exports.
   c. Label all the items in Figure 1 with their values in Iberia.
3. The values of some of the flows shown in Figure 1 in the U. S. economy in 1999 were *U* = \$1.6 trillion, *W* = \$6.2 trillion, *X* = \$1.4 trillion, and *Z* = –\$0.2 trillion. Calculate
   a. *Q*.
   b. *R* + *V*.
   c. GDP.
4. The values of some of the flows shown in Figure 1 in the Canadian economy in 2001 were *Q* = \$1,092 billion, *U* = \$204 billion, *W* = \$621 billion, and *Z* = \$57 billion. Calculate
   a. *X*.
   b. GDP.
   c. Compare Canada's GDP in 2001 with the U.S. GDP of 1999 and comment on the possible sources of the difference.
5. The national income accounts of Parchment Paradise are kept on (you guessed it) parchment. A fire destroyed the national statistics office, and the national income and product accounts are now incomplete. But they contain the following information for 2002: Net domestic product at factor cost was \$2,900; consumption expenditure was \$2,000; indirect taxes less subsidies

was $80; net interest was $200; rental income of persons was $100; investment was $800; government purchases of goods and services were $800; proprietors' income was $200; compensation of employees was $2,000; and net exports were –$200. You've been hired as an economist to reconstruct the missing numbers by calculating for 2002

a. GDP.
b. Corporate profits.
c. Capital consumption.

6. Nominal GDP in the United States in 2001 was $10,082.2 billion, and real GDP (in 1997 dollars) was $9,214.5 billion. Real GDP in 1997 (in 1997 dollars) was $7,813.2 billion.
 a. Calculate the GDP deflator in 2001.
 b. What was the GDP deflator in 1997?
 c. By what percentage did the price level rise between 1997 and 2001?
 d. By what percentage did real GDP rise between 1997 and 2001?
 e. By what percentage did nominal GDP rise between 1997 and 2001?

7. The GDP deflator in the United States in 1990 was 86.5, and real GDP in 1990 (in 1997 dollars) was $6,707.9 billion. The GDP deflator in the United States in 2000 was 106.9, and real GDP in 2000 (in 1997 dollars) was $9,191.4 billion.
 a. Calculate nominal GDP in 1990.
 b. Calculate nominal GDP in 2000.
 c. By what percentage did the price level rise between 1990 and 2000?
 d. By what percentage did real GDP rise between 1990 and 2000?
 e. By what percentage did nominal GDP rise between 1990 and 2000?

8. Use the information provided in Table 1 to calculate
 a. Nominal GDP in 2002.
 b. Nominal GDP in 2003.
 c. Real GDP in 2003 with base year 2002 using the traditional method.
 d. Real GDP in 2003 with base year 2002 using the chain method.
 e. The GDP deflator in 2003.
 f. Comment on the growth rate of real GDP in 2003.
 g. How does the growth rate of nominal GDP in 2003 divide between real GDP growth and inflation?

9. Use the information provided in Tables 1 and 2 to calculate
 a. Nominal GDP in 2004.
 b. Nominal GDP in 2005.
 c. Real GDP in 2004 with base year 2002 using the traditional method.
 d. Real GDP in 2005 with base year 2002 using the traditional method.
 e. Real GDP in 2004 with base year 2002 using the chain method.
 f. Real GDP in 2005 with base year 2002 using the chain method.
 g. The GDP deflator in 2004 and 2005.
 h. Comment on the growth rate of real GDP between 2003 and 2005.
 i. Comment on the changes in the price level between 2003 and 2005.
 j. How much of the growth of nominal GDP between 2002 and 2005 was the result of inflation and how much was the result of real GDP growth?

TABLE 1

(a) In 2002:

Item	Quantity	Price
Fun	40	$2
Food	60	$3

(b) In 2003:

Item	Quantity	Price
Fun	44	$3
Food	72	$2

TABLE 2

(a) In 2004:

Item	Quantity	Price
Fun	50	$3
Food	72	$3

(b) In 2005:

Item	Quantity	Price
Fun	51	$4
Food	80	$6

Critical Thinking

10. In 2002, the oil tanker *Prestige* sank in the Atlantic Ocean and the oil washed ashore on the beaches of Spain . Millions of dollars were spent cleaning up the mess, and much wildlife was killed.
    a. Describe how the effects of this oil spill appear in the national income accounts of Spain.
    b. Does the national accounts treatment of this event properly record the effects of the spill on the standard of living of the people who were affected? Explain why or why not.
11. How do underground economic activities affect the usefulness of the national income accounts for comparing the value of production over time and across countries? What underground economic activities do the national income accounts miss? Do these activities contribute to the standard of living? Do you think that it would be worth expanding the scope of the accounts to include estimates of the value of underground activities?
12. The United Nations Index of Human Development is based on the levels of GDP per person, life expectancy at birth, and indicators of the quality and quantity of education. Do you think the United Nations should expand its index to include items such as pollution, resource depletion, and political freedom? Are there any other factors that influence the standard of living that you think should be included in a comprehensive measure?

Practice Online

Web Exercises

Use the links on your Foundations Web site to work the following exercises.

13. Read the article on one of the great inventions of the twentieth century and the article in the Naples Daily News. Summarize the argument that the national income accounts are one of the great inventions and describe the improvement reported in the news article.
14. Visit the Bureau of Economic Analysis Web site and obtain the most recently released National Income and Product Account data for the United States. For the most recently available quarter,
    a. What are the values of consumption expenditure, investment, government purchases, and net exports?
    b. Check that when you sum the items in part **a**, the total equals GDP.
    c. Find the GDP deflator with the base year of 1997.
    d. Calculate real GDP.
    e. Was the cost of living higher in the most recent quarter than in 1997? Explain your answer.
15. Visit the International Monetary Fund World Economic Outlook Web site and obtain the most recently released real GDP data for the global economy.
    a. In which countries is real GDP growth the fastest?
    b. In which countries is real GDP shrinking?
    c. What is the GDP of the United States as a percentage of world GDP?
    d. On the basis of the growth rates over the past decade, in which regions does the standard of living appear to be improving fastest and in which does it appear to be improving the slowest?

CHAPTER 6

Jobs and Unemployment

CHAPTER CHECKLIST

When you have completed your study of this chapter, you will be able to

1. **Define the unemployment rate and other labor market indicators.**
2. **Describe the trends and fluctuations in the indicators of labor market performance in the United States.**
3. **Describe the sources and types of unemployment, define full employment, and explain the link between unemployment and real GDP.**

Macroeconomics studies three big issues: the standard of living, the cost of living, and economic fluctuations. You've just learned how we measure a main indicator of the standard of living: real GDP. Most of us earn the incomes that make up GDP by working. We become concerned when jobs are hard to find and more relaxed when jobs are plentiful. We also care about the kinds of jobs that are available. We want well-paid and interesting jobs, so we spend time searching for the right job.

In this chapter, we learn how economists track the health of the labor market. First, we'll describe a monthly survey that discovers the labor market status of the population and provides the raw material for job market statistics. Second, we'll describe the trends and fluctuations in the indicators of labor market performance. Third, we'll look at the sources and types of unemployment and learn what we mean by "full employment."

6.1 LABOR MARKET INDICATORS

Every month, 1,600 field interviewers and supervisors working on a joint project between the Bureau of Labor Statistics (or BLS) and the Bureau of the Census survey 50,000 households and ask a series of questions about the age and labor market status of its members. This survey is called the Current Population Survey. Let's look at the types of data collected by this survey.

Current Population Survey

Working-age population
The total number of people aged 16 years and over who are not in jail, hospital, or some other form of institutional care.

Labor force
The number of people employed plus the number unemployed.

Figure 6.1 shows the categories into which the BLS divides the population. It also shows the relationships among the categories. The first category divides the population into two groups: the working-age population and others who are too young to work or who live in institutions and are unable to work. The **working-age population** is the total number of people aged 16 years and over who are not in jail, hospital, or some other form of institutional care. In June 2002, the estimated population of the United States was 287.5 million. In June 2002, the working-age population was 213.8 million and 73.7 million people were under 16 years of age or living in institutions.

The second category divides the working-age population into two groups: those in the labor force and those not in the labor force. The **labor force** is the number of people employed plus the number unemployed. In June 2002, the U.S. labor force was 143.7 million and 70.1 million were not in the labor force. Most of those not in the labor force were in school full time or had retired from work.

The third category divides the labor force into two groups: the employed and the unemployed. In June 2002 in the United States, 135 million were employed and 8.7 million were unemployed.

Population Survey Criteria

The survey counts as employed all persons who, during the week before the survey, either

1. Worked at least 1 hour as paid employees or worked 15 hours or more as unpaid workers in their family business or
2. Were not working but had jobs or businesses from which they were temporarily absent.

The survey counts as unemployed all persons who, during the week before the survey,

1. Had no employment,
2. Were available for work,

and either

1. Had made specific efforts to find employment some time during the previous four weeks or
2. Were waiting to be recalled to a job from which they had been laid off.

People in the working-age population who by the above criteria are neither employed nor unemployed are classified as not in the labor force.

FIGURE 6.1
Population Labor Force Categories

Practice Online

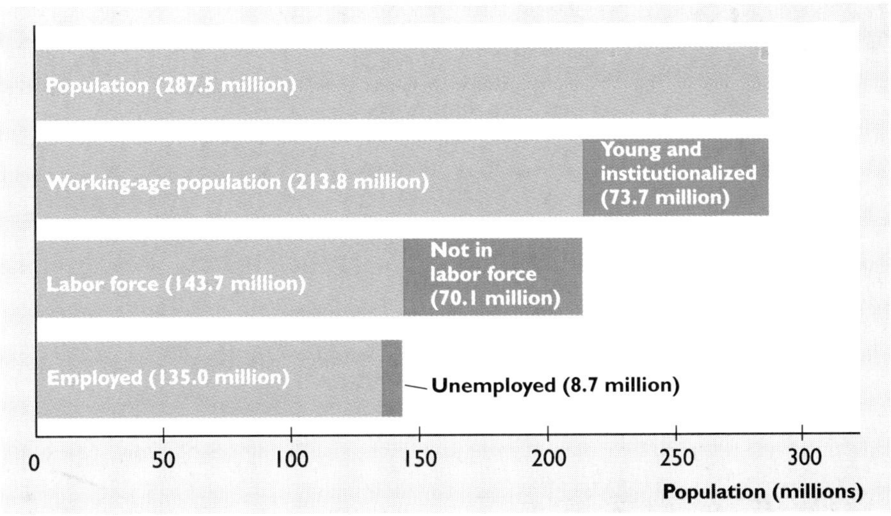

Population (287.5 million)
Working-age population (213.8 million) | Young and institutionalized (73.7 million)
Labor force (143.7 million) | Not in labor force (70.1 million)
Employed (135.0 million) | Unemployed (8.7 million)
0 50 100 150 200 250 300
Population (millions)

SOURCE: Bureau of Labor Statistics.

The U.S. population is divided into the working-age population and the young and institutionalized. The working-age population is divided into the labor force and those not in the labor force. The labor force is divided into the employed and the unemployed. The figure shows the data for June 2002.

Two Main Labor Market Indicators

Using the numbers from the Current Population Survey, the BLS calculates several indicators of the state of the labor market. The two main labor market indicators are

- The unemployment rate
- The labor force participation rate

The Unemployment Rate

The amount of unemployment is an indicator of the extent to which people who want jobs can't find them. It tells us the amount of slack in the labor market. The **unemployment rate** is the percentage of the people in the labor force who are unemployed. That is,

Unemployment rate
The percentage of the people in the labor force who are unemployed.

$$\text{Unemployment rate} = \frac{\text{Number of people unemployed}}{\text{Labor force}} \times 100.$$

In June 2002, the number of people unemployed was 8.7 million and the labor force was 143.7 million. We can use these numbers to calculate the unemployment rate in June 2002, which is

$$\text{Unemployment rate} = \frac{8.7 \text{ million}}{143.7 \text{ million}} \times 100$$
$$= 6.1 \text{ percent}.$$

The Labor Force Participation Rate

Labor force participation rate The percentage of the working-age population who are members of the labor force.

The number of people in the labor force is an indicator of the willingness of people of working age to take jobs. The **labor force participation rate** is the percentage of the working-age population who are members of the labor force. That is

$$\text{Labor force participation rate} = \frac{\text{Labor force}}{\text{Working-age population}} \times 100.$$

In June 2002, the labor force was 143.7 million and the working-age population was 213.8 million. We can use these numbers to calculate the labor force participation rate in June 2000, which is

$$\text{Labor force participation rate} = \frac{143.7\text{ million}}{213.8\text{ million}} \times 100$$

$$= 67.2\text{ percent.}$$

Discouraged Workers

Discouraged worker A person who is available and willing to work but has not made specific efforts to find a job within the previous four weeks.

A **discouraged worker** is a person who does not have a job, is available and willing to work, but has not made specific efforts to find a job within the previous four weeks. Neither the unemployment rate nor the labor force participation rate includes discouraged workers. In June 2002, 5 million people not in the labor force wanted jobs. If we add this group to the labor force and the number unemployed, the unemployment rate becomes 9.2 percent—50 percent higher than the standard definition of the unemployment rate.

Part-Time Workers

Full-time workers People who usually work 35 hours or more a week.

Part-time workers People who usually work less than 35 hours a week.

Involuntary part-time workers People who work 1 to 34 hours per week but who are looking for full-time work.

The Current Population Survey measures the number of full-time workers and part-time workers. **Full-time workers** are those who usually work 35 hours or more a week. **Part-time workers** are those who usually work less than 35 hours a week. Part-time workers are divided into two groups: part time for economic reasons and part time for noneconomic reasons.

Part-time workers for economic reasons, also called **involuntary part-time workers,** are people who work 1 to 34 hours but who are looking for full-time work. These people are unable to find full-time work because of unfavorable business conditions or because of seasonal decreases in the availability of full-time work.

Part-time workers for noneconomic reasons do not want to work full time and are not available for such work. This group includes people with health problems, family or personal responsibilities, or education commitments that limit their availability for work.

The Bureau of Labor Statistics uses the data on full-time and part-time status to calculate the full-time labor force and the part-time labor force as well as the full-time unemployment rate and the part-time unemployment rate.

In June 2002, when the labor force was 143.7 million, the full-time labor force was 122.0 million and the part-time labor force was 21.7 million. An estimated 4.2 million involuntary part-time workers, or 19.4 percent of part-time workers, were looking for full-time work.

Eye on the U.S. Economy

The Current Population Survey

The Bureau of Labor Statistics and the Bureau of the Census go to great lengths to collect accurate labor force data. They constantly train and retrain around 1,600 field interviewers and supervisors. Each month, each field interviewer contacts 37 households and asks basic demographic questions about all persons living at the address and detailed labor force questions about persons aged 15 or over.

Once a household has been selected for the survey, it is questioned for four consecutive months and then again for the same four months a year later. Each month, the addresses that have been in the panel eight times are removed and 6,250 new addresses are added. The rotation and overlap of households provide very reliable information about month-to-month and year-to-year changes in the labor market.

The first time that a household is in the panel, an interviewer, armed with a laptop computer, visits it. If the household has a telephone, most of the subsequent interviews are conducted by phone, many of them from one of the three telephone interviewing centers in Hagerstown, Maryland; Jeffersonville, Indiana; and Tucson, Arizona.

Aggregate Hours

The labor market indicators that we've just examined are useful signs of the health of the economy and directly measure what matters to most people: jobs and whether those jobs are full time or part time. But they don't tell us the *quantity of labor* employed.

The reason the number of people employed does not measure the quantity of labor employed is that jobs are not all the same. You've seen that people in part-time jobs work between 1 and 34 hours a week and people in full-time jobs work 35 or more hours a week. A Starbucks coffee shop might hire six students who work for three hours a day each. Another Starbucks might hire two full-time workers who work nine hours a day each. The total number of people employed is eight, but the total hours worked by six part-time workers is the same as the total hours worked by the two full-time workers.

To determine the total amount of labor employed, we measure labor in hours rather than in jobs. **Aggregate hours** are the total number of hours worked by all the people employed, both full time and part time, during a year and equal the number of people employed multiplied by the average work hours per person.

Aggregate hours
The total number of hours worked by all the people employed, both full time and part time, during a year.

In June 2002, 135 million people worked an average of 34.7 hours per week. With 50 workweeks per year, aggregate hours were

$$\text{Aggregate hours} = 135 \text{ million} \times 34.7 \times 50 = 234.2 \text{ billion.}$$

The measurement of aggregate hours is not very precise. But the estimation of the percentage change in aggregate hours from one month to another is more precise. For this reason, the Bureau of Labor Statistics publishes aggregate hours data as an index number rather than as a number of hours.

CHECKPOINT 6.1

Study Guide **pp. 87–89**

Practice Online 6.1

1 **Define the unemployment rate and other labor market indicators.**

Practice Problem 6.1

The Bureau of Labor Statistics reported that in January 2000, the labor force was 140.9 million, employment was 135.2 million, and the working-age population was 208.6 million. Average weekly hours were 34.5. Calculate for that month the

- **a.** Unemployment rate.
- **b.** Labor force participation rate.
- **c.** Aggregate hours worked in a week.

Exercises 6.1

1. The Bureau of Labor Statistics reported that in July 2002, the labor force was 143.9 million; employment was 135.3 million; and the working-age population was 214 million. Calculate for that month the
- **a.** Unemployment rate.
- **b.** Labor force participation rate.

2. Statistics Canada reported that in January 2002, the Canadian labor force was 16.2 million; Canadian employment was 14.8 million; and the Canadian working-age population was 24.8 million. Calculate for that month the Canadian
- **a.** Unemployment rate.
- **b.** Labor force participation rate.

3. Given the data in exercises 1 and 2, do you think jobs are harder to find in Canada or in the United States? Why?

4. Use the link on the Foundations Web site to obtain data on the labor force, employment, unemployment, and the working-age population for your own state in the most recent month for which data are available. For that month,
- **a.** Calculate your state's unemployment rate.
- **b.** Calculate your state's labor force participation rate.
- **c.** Compare the labor market indicators in your state with the U.S. averages.

Solution to Practice Problem 6.1

a. The unemployment rate is 4.0 percent. The labor force is the sum of the number employed plus the number unemployed. So the number unemployed equals the labor force minus the number employed, which equals 140.9 million – 135.2 million = 5.7 million. The unemployment rate is the number unemployed as a percentage of the labor force, which is (5.7 million ÷ 140.9 million) × 100 = 4.0 percent.

b. The labor force participation rate is 67.5 percent. The labor force participation rate is the percentage of the working-age population who are in the labor force, which equals (140.9 million ÷ 208.6 million) × 100 = 67.5 percent.

c. Aggregate hours worked in a week are 4,664.4 million. In January 2000, average weekly hours were 34.5 and employment was 135.2 million. So the aggregate hours worked in a week were 34.5 × 135.2 million = 4,664.4 million.

6.2 LABOR MARKET TRENDS AND FLUCTUATIONS

What do we learn about the U.S. labor market from changes in the unemployment rate, the labor force participation rate, part-time employment, and aggregate hours? Let's explore the trends and fluctuations in these indicators.

Unemployment

Figure 6.2 shows the U.S. unemployment rate over the 40 years from 1962 to 2002. Over these years, the average U.S. unemployment rate was 5.9 percent—about the same as the 2002 unemployment rate. The 1960s and the late 1990s were years of below-average unemployment, and the 1970s and 1980s were years of above-average unemployment.

During the 1960s, the unemployment rate fell to 3.5 percent. These years saw a rapid rate of job creation partly from the demands placed on the economy by the growth of defense production during the Vietnam War and partly from an expansion of consumer spending encouraged by an expansion of social programs. Another burst of rapid rate of job creation driven by the "new economy"—the high-technology sector driven by the expansion of the Internet—took the unemployment rate below average between 1995 and 2000.

In 2001 and 2002, the unemployment rate increased as the U.S. economy went into a recession. But the unemployment rate remained below or at its average level. In contrast to the 1960s and 1990s, the 1970s and 1980s were years of above average unemployment. The unemployment rate peaked at almost 10 percent during the 1982 recession. The unemployment rate was also high during a mid-1970s recession, which resulted from massive hikes in the world oil price, and in the 1990–1991 recession.

FIGURE 6.2
The U.S. Unemployment Rate: 1962–2002

Practice Online

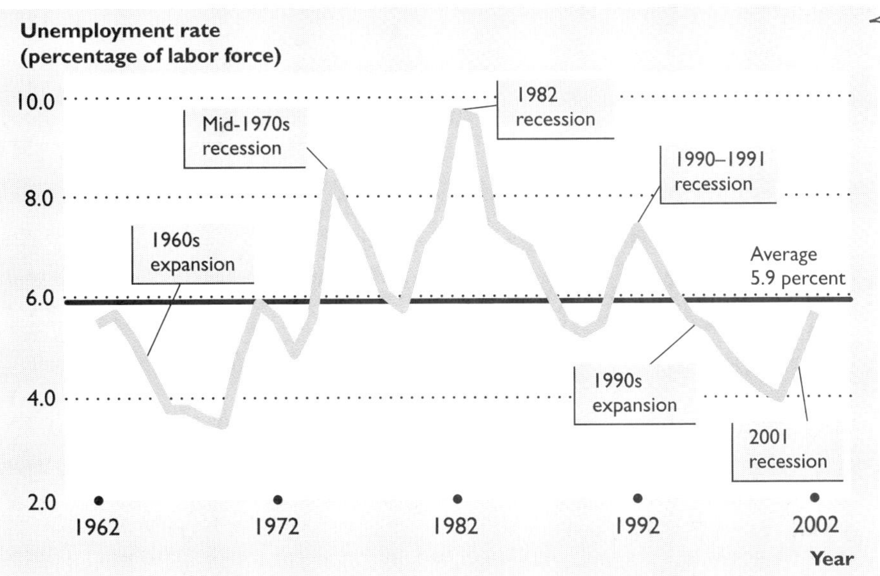

SOURCE: Bureau of Labor Statistics.

The average unemployment rate from 1962 to 2002 was 5.9 percent. The unemployment rate increases in recessions and decreases in expansions. Unemployment fell to an unusually low rate during the expansion of the 1990s and increased during the 2001 recession.

Eye on the U.S. Economy

The Labor Market in the Great Depression

The Great Depression was a period of prolonged and extreme economic hardship that lasted from 1929 until the end of the 1930s.

By 1933, the worst of the Depression years, real GDP had fallen by a huge 30 percent. And, as the figure shows, one in four of the people who wanted jobs couldn't find them.

The horrors of the Great Depression led to the New Deal and shaped political attitudes that persist today.

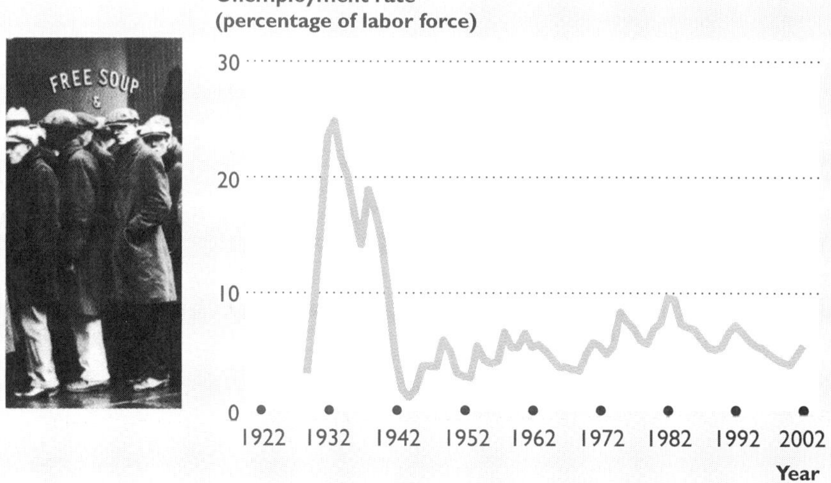

SOURCE: Bureau of Labor Statistics.

The Participation Rate

Figure 6.3 shows the labor force participation rate, which you can see has followed an upward trend. It increased from 59 percent during the 1960s to 67 percent during the 1990s. The cyclical fluctuations in the participation rate are mild and result

FIGURE 6.3

The Changing Face of the Labor Market: 1962–2002

Practice Online

During the past 40 years, the labor force participation rate has increased. The labor force participation rate of men has decreased, and that of women has increased.

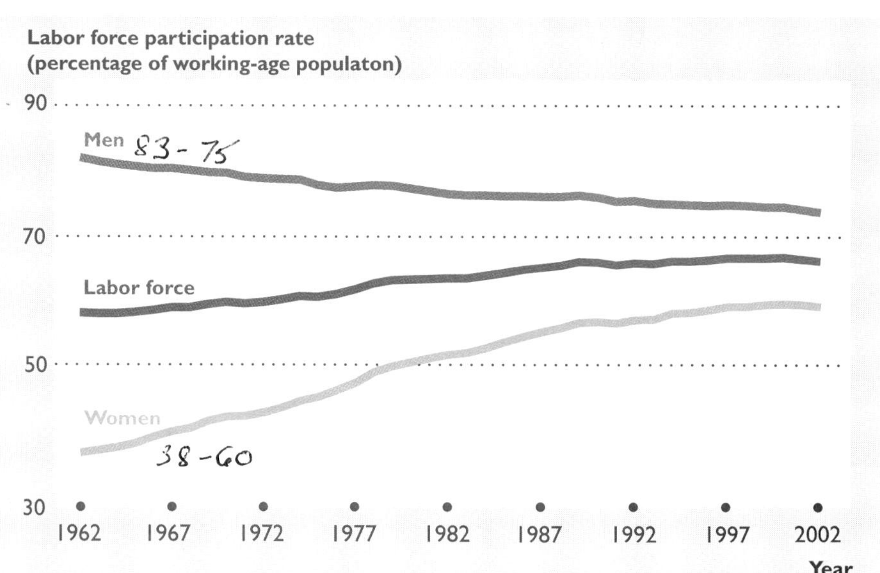

SOURCE: Bureau of Labor Statistics.

Eye on the Global Economy

Unemployment Around the World

In 1992, Canada and the United Kingdom had the highest unemployment rates and Japan the lowest. France, Germany, Italy, and the United States were in the middle of the pack.

Through the 1990s, unemployment rates fell in the United States, United Kingdom, and Canada but increased in Japan.

By 2002, the unemployment rates of the United States, United Kingdom and Japan had converged.

The average unemployment rate of France, Germany, and Italy increased through 1997 and then decreased but has remained the highest among the industrialized countries.

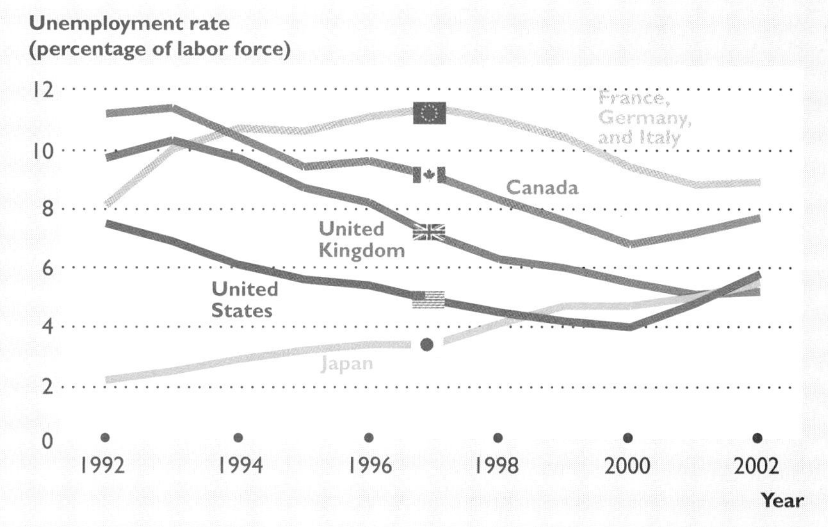

SOURCE: International Monetary Fund, *World Economic Outlook*, September 2002.

from unsuccessful job seekers becoming *discouraged workers*—people who leave the labor force in a recession and reenter in an expansion.

Why has the labor force participation rate increased? The main reason is an increase in the number of women who have entered the labor force. Figure 6.3 shows this increase. Between 1962 and 2002, the participation rate of women increased from 38 percent to 60 percent. This increase is spread across women of all age groups and occurred for four main reasons. First, more women pursued a college education and so increased their earning power. Second, technological change in the workplace created a large number of white-collar jobs with flexible work hours that many women found attractive. Third, technological change in the home increased the time available for paid employment. And fourth, families looked increasingly to a second income to balance tight budgets.

Figure 6.3 also shows another remarkable trend in the U.S. labor force: The participation rate of men *decreased* from 82 percent in 1962 to 74 percent in 2002. Decreased labor force participation by men occurred mostly among older men aged 55 and over. The participation rate of this group fell from 87 percent in 1962 to 67 percent in 2002. Most of this decrease occurred because many men retired at an earlier age. Some of this earlier retirement resulted from an increase in wealth. But some arose from job loss at an age at which finding a new job was difficult. For other men, decreased labor force participation occurred because more remained in full-time education.

Part-Time Workers

A part-time job is attractive to many workers because it enables them to balance family and other commitments with work. Part-time jobs are attractive to employers because they don't have to pay benefits to part-time workers and are less constrained by government regulations. Figure 6.4 shows some interesting facts about part-time workers. First, the percentage of workers who are part time has increased,

FIGURE 6.4
Part-time Workers: 1972–2002

Practice Online

Part-time workers are an increasing proportion of the labor force, up from 15 percent in 1972 to 17 percent in 2002. The percentage of workers who are part time and the percentage of part-time workers who would like full-time work increase in a recession and decrease in an expansion.

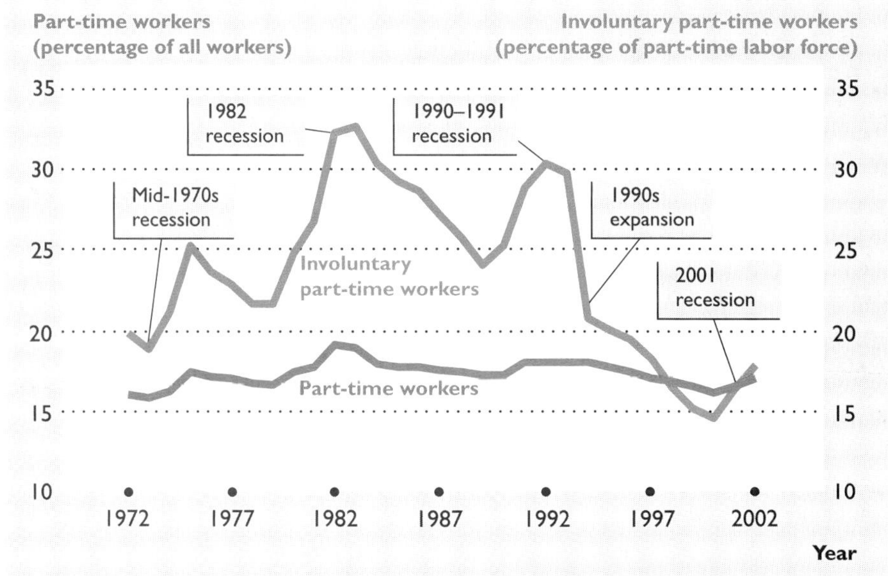

SOURCE: Bureau of Labor Statistics.

but not by much. In 1972, it was 16 percent and in 2002, it was 17 percent. Second, the part-time percentage fluctuates with the business cycle. In the 1982 recession, it reached 19.2 percent, and in the 1990–1991 recession, it reached 18.1 percent. During the expansion years after 1994, the part-time percentage declined.

The involuntary part-time rate—the percentage of part-time workers who want full-time work—has averaged 27 percent. But there are striking and large swings in the involuntary part-time rate. In the 1982 recession, the rate climbed to approach 33 percent. And in the 1990–1991 recession, the rate climbed to 30 percent. During the 1990s expansion, the involuntary part-time rate decreased rapidly, and even after rising again in the 2001 recession, it stood below its 1972 level.

Aggregate and Average Hours

Figure 6.5(a) shows aggregate hours in the U.S. economy from 1962 to 2002. Aggregate hours have an upward trend, but they have not grown as quickly as have the number of people employed. Between 1962 and 2002, the number of people employed in the U.S. economy doubled—an increase of 100 percent. During that same period, aggregate hours increased by 77 percent. Why the difference? Because average hours per worker decreased.

Figure 6.5(b) shows average hours per worker. After hovering at almost 39 hours a week during the early 1960s, average hours per worker decreased to about 34 hours a week during the 1990s. This shortening of the average workweek occurred partly because the average hours worked by full-time workers decreased and partly because the number of part-time jobs increased faster than the number of full-time jobs.

Fluctuations in aggregate hours and average hours per worker line up with the business cycle. Figure 6.5 identifies the four recessions, during which aggregate hours decreased and average hours per worker decreased faster than trend.

FIGURE 6.5
Aggregate Hours: 1962–2002

Practice Online

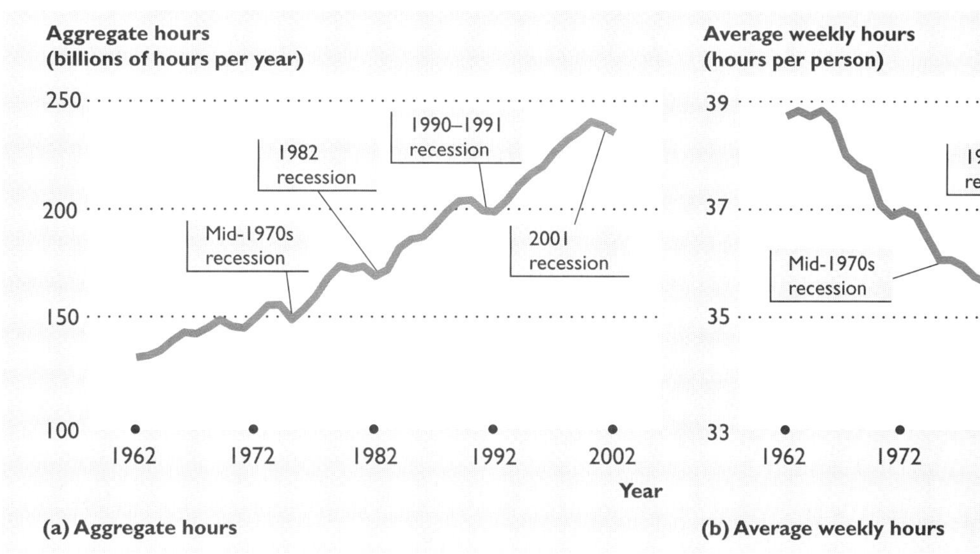

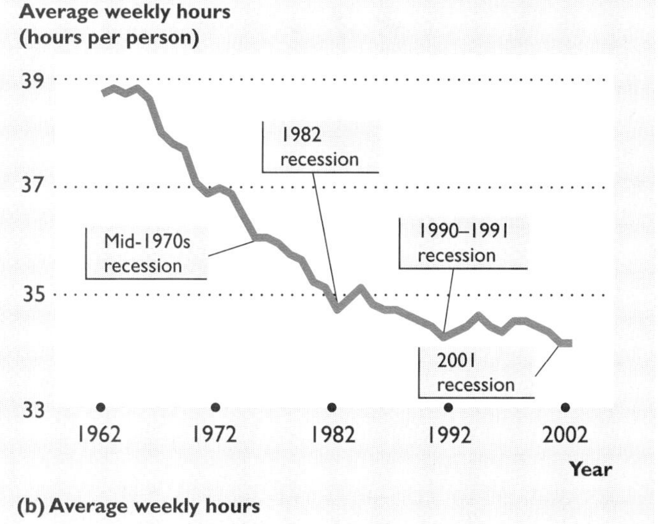

Source: Bureau of Labor Statistics.

In part (a), between 1962 and 2002, aggregate hours increased by an average of 1.5 percent a year. Fluctuations in aggregate hours coincide with business cycle fluctuations.

In part (b), aggregate hours increased at a slower rate than the number of jobs because the average workweek has shortened.

Women in the Labor Force

The participation rate of women in the U.S. labor force has increased from 50 percent in 1980 to 60 percent in 2000. This upward trend is found in most of the world's rich advanced nations.

But the *level* of women's participation in the labor force varies a great deal around the world. Here, we compare seven other countries—Australia, Canada, France, Japan, Spain, Sweden, and the United Kingdom—with the United States.

Among these countries, Sweden's labor force has the largest participation rate of women and the United States comes second. Spain and Japan have the lowest rates.

Cultural factors play a role in determining national differences in women's work choices. But economic factors such as the percentage of women with a college degree will ultimately dominate cultural influences and bring a convergence of outcomes.

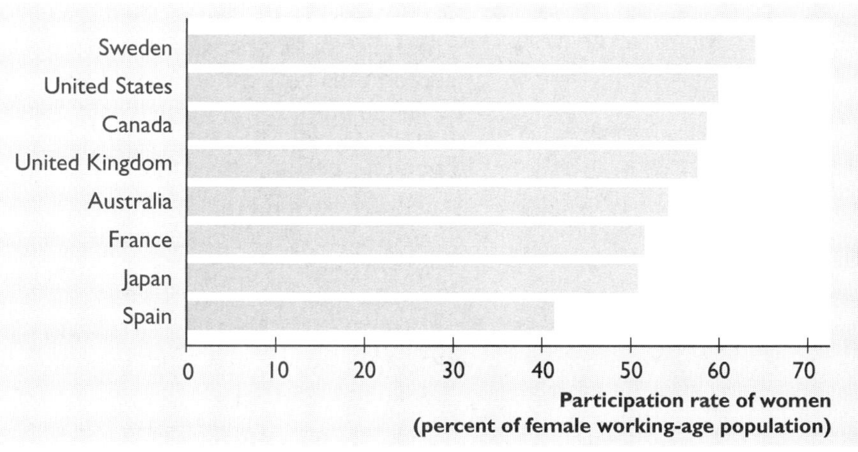

Source: OECD.

CHECKPOINT 6.2

Study Guide pp. 89–92
Practice Online 6.2

2 **Describe the trends and fluctuations in the indicators of labor market performance in the United States.**

Practice Problem 6.2

Use the link on your Foundations Web site and view the data for Figures 6.2, 6.3, 6.4, and 6.5. Then answer the following questions:

a. In which decade—the 1960s, 1970s, 1980s, or 1990s—was the unemployment rate the lowest? What brought low unemployment in that decade?

b. In which decade was the unemployment rate the highest? What brought high unemployment in that decade?

c. Describe the trends in the participation rates of men and women and all workers. Why did these trends occur?

d. Describe the trends and fluctuations in part-time work. Why is part-time work on the increase?

e. Do aggregate hours increase at the same rate as the increase in employment? Explain why or why not.

Exercise 6.2

Use the link on your Foundations Web site and view the data for Figures 6.2, 6.3, 6.4, and 6.5. Then answer the following questions:

a. During which decade—the 1960s, 1970s, 1980s, or 1990s—did the labor force participation rate of women increase most? Suggest some reasons why this rapid increase occurred during that decade.

b. In which decade did the labor force participation rate of men decrease most? Suggest some reasons why this rapid decrease occurred during that decade.

c. Describe the trends in the unemployment rate; the labor force participation rates of men and women, part-time workers, and involuntary part-time workers; and aggregate hours since 1994. Why did these trends occur?

Solution to Practice Problem 6.2

a. The average unemployment rates in each decade were: 1960s, 4.8 percent; 1970s, 6.2 percent; 1980s, 7.3 percent; 1990s, 5.7 percent. The unemployment rate was lowest during the 1960s. Unemployment was low during the 1960s because defense spending on the Vietnam War and an expansion of social programs brought about a rapidly expanding economy.

b. The unemployment rate was highest during the 1980s. A deep recession in 1982 sent the unemployment rate to a peak of almost 10 percent.

c. The participation rate of women increased because (1) better-educated women earn more, (2) more white-collar jobs with flexible work hours were created, (3) people have more time for paid employment and (4) families increasingly needed two incomes to balance their budgets. The participation rate of men decreased because more men remained in school and some men took early retirement. The overall participation rate increased.

d. Part-time work increased because it provides flexible hours for workers and cuts costs for firms.

e. Aggregate hours increase more slowly than employment because average hours per worker fall.

6.3 THE SOURCES AND TYPES OF UNEMPLOYMENT

How do people become unemployed, how long do they remain unemployed, and who is at greatest risk to become unemployed? Let's begin to answer these questions by looking at the events that move people into and out of the labor market and into and out of jobs.

Sources of Unemployment

The labor market is constantly churning. New jobs are created and old ones are destroyed. Some people move into the labor force, and some move out of it. The process of job creation and job destruction and the movement into and out of the labor force create unemployment.

People who become unemployed are

1. Job losers
2. Job leavers
3. Entrants or reentrants

Job Losers

People who are fired or laid off from their jobs, either permanently or temporarily, are called *job losers*. People lose their jobs for a variety of reasons. Some are just not a good match for the job they're doing, and they get fired. Firms fail, so their workers get laid off. And new technology destroys some jobs.

A job loser has two choices: Either look for another job or withdraw from the labor force. A job loser who decides to look for a new job remains in the labor force and becomes unemployed. A job loser who decides to withdraw from the labor force is not counted as being unemployed. Such a person is classified as "not in the labor force." Most job losers decide to look for a new job, and some of them take a long time to find one.

Job Leavers

People who voluntarily quit their jobs are called *job leavers*. Most people who leave their jobs do so for one of two reasons: Either they've gotten a better job or they've decided to withdraw from the labor force. Neither of these types of job leavers becomes unemployed. But a few people quit their jobs because they want to spend time looking for a better one. These job leavers become unemployed.

Entrants and Reentrants

People who have just left school and entered the job market are called *entrants*. Some entrants have a job lined up before leaving school and are never unemployed. But many entrants spend time searching for their first job, and during this period, they are unemployed.

People who have previously had jobs, then quit and left the labor force and have now decided to look for jobs are called *reentrants*. Some reentrants are people who have been out of the labor force rearing children, but most are discouraged workers—people who gave up searching for jobs because they were not able to find suitable ones and who have now decided to look again.

Figure 6.6 shows the magnitudes of the three sources of unemployment. Most of the people unemployed are job losers. Also, their number fluctuates most.

FIGURE 6.6
Unemployment by Reasons: 1982–2002

Practice Online

Everyone who is unemployed is a job loser, a job leaver, or an entrant or reentrant into the labor force. Job losers are the biggest group, and their number fluctuates most. Entrants and reentrants are the second biggest group. Their number also fluctuates. Job leavers are the smallest group.

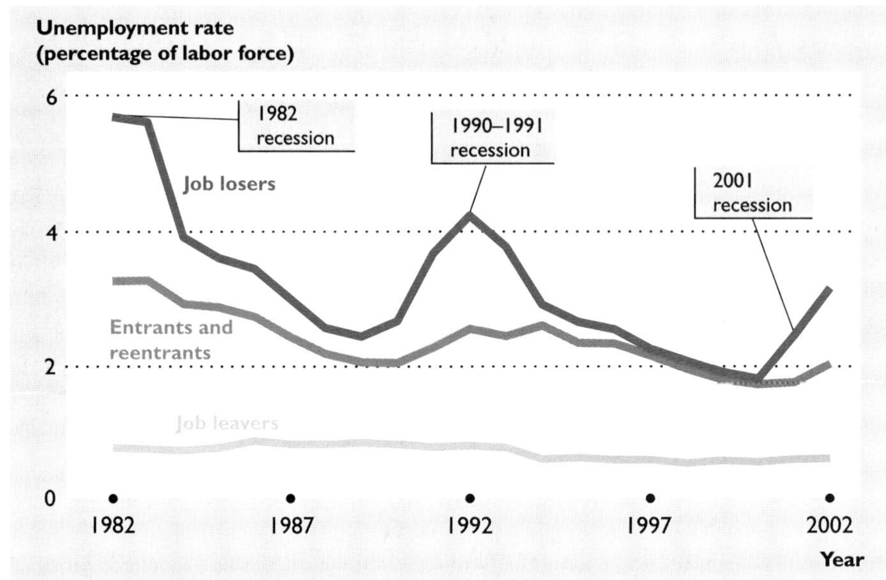

SOURCE: Bureau of Labor Statistics.

Entrants and reentrants are also a large component, and their number also fluctuates. Job leavers are the smallest and most stable source of unemployment.

How Unemployment Ends

People who end a period of unemployment are either

1. Hires and recalls or
2. Withdrawals

Hires and Recalls

People who have been unemployed but have been hired to start a new job are called *hires*. And people who have been temporarily laid off (they are classified as unemployed) and who start work again are called *recalls*. Firms are constantly hiring and recalling workers, so there are always people moving from unemployment to employment.

Withdrawals

People who have been unemployed and who decide to stop looking for jobs are called *withdrawals*. Most of these people are *discouraged workers*. They will most likely reenter the labor force later when they think that job prospects have improved.

Labor Market Flows: A Summary

Figure 6.7 provides a summary of the labor market flows that begin and end a period of unemployment.

FIGURE 6.7
Labor Market Flows

Practice Online

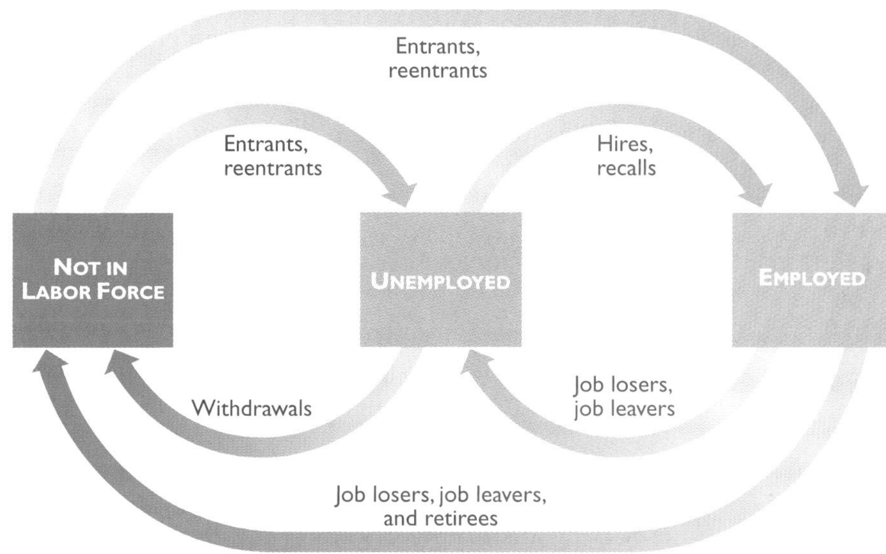

Unemployment results from employed people losing or leaving their jobs (job losers and job leavers) and from people entering the labor force (entrants and reentrants). Unemployment ends because people get hired or recalled or because they withdraw from the labor force.

Types of Unemployment

Unemployment is classified into four types:

- Frictional
- Structural
- Seasonal
- Cyclical

Frictional Unemployment

Frictional unemployment is the unemployment that arises from normal labor turnover—from people entering and leaving the labor force and from the ongoing creation and destruction of jobs. Frictional unemployment is a permanent and healthy phenomenon in a dynamic, growing economy.

The unending flow of people into and out of the labor force and the processes of job creation and job destruction create the need for people to search for jobs and for businesses to search for workers. There are always some businesses with unfilled jobs and some people seeking jobs.

Look in your local newspaper, and you will see that there are always jobs being advertised. Businesses don't usually hire the first person who applies for a job, and unemployed people don't usually take the first job that comes their way. Instead, both firms and workers spend time searching out what they believe will be the best attainable match. By this search process, people can match their own skills and interests with the available jobs and find a satisfying job and income. While these unemployed people are searching, they are frictionally unemployed.

The amount of frictional unemployment depends on the rate at which people enter and reenter the labor force and on the rate at which jobs are created and

Frictional unemployment
The unemployment that arises from normal labor turnover—from people entering and leaving the labor force and from the ongoing creation and destruction of jobs.

destroyed. During the 1970s, the amount of frictional unemployment increased because of the postwar baby boom that began during the 1940s. By the late 1970s, the baby boom created a bulge in the number of people leaving school. As these people entered the labor force, the amount of frictional unemployment increased. Frictional unemployment remained high until the information-age expansion of the mid-1990s. Since 1994, frictional unemployment has decreased.

The amount of frictional unemployment is also influenced by unemployment compensation. The greater the number of unemployed people eligible for benefits and the more generous those benefits, the longer is the average time taken in job search and the greater is the amount of frictional unemployment. Unemployment benefits in Canada and Western Europe exceed those in the United States, and these economies have higher unemployment rates.

Structural Unemployment

Structural unemployment
The unemployment that arises when changes in technology or international competition change the skills needed to perform jobs or change the locations of jobs.

Structural unemployment is the unemployment that arises when changes in technology or international competition change the skills needed to perform jobs or change the locations of jobs. Structural unemployment usually lasts longer than frictional unemployment because workers must retrain and possibly relocate to find a job. For example, when a telephone exchange in Gary, Indiana, is automated, some jobs in that city are destroyed. Meanwhile, new jobs for life-insurance salespeople and retail clerks are created in Chicago, Indianapolis, and other cities. The former telephone operators remain unemployed for several months until they move, retrain, and get one of these jobs. Structural unemployment is painful, especially for older workers for whom the best available option might be to retire early but with a lower income than they had expected.

Sometimes, the amount of structural unemployment is modest. At other times, it is large, and at such times, structural unemployment can become a serious long-term problem. It was especially large during the late 1970s and early 1980s. During those years, oil price hikes and an increasingly competitive international environment destroyed jobs in traditional U.S. industries, such as auto and steel making, and created jobs in new industries, such as information processing, electronics, and bioengineering. Structural unemployment was also present during the early 1990s as many businesses and governments downsized.

Seasonal Unemployment

Seasonal unemployment
The unemployment that arises because of seasonal weather patterns.

Seasonal unemployment is the unemployment that arises because of seasonal weather patterns. Seasonal unemployment increases during the winter months and decreases during the spring and summer. A fruit picker who is laid off after the fall harvest and who gets rehired the following summer experiences seasonal unemployment. A construction worker who gets laid off during the winter and rehired in the spring also experiences seasonal unemployment.

Cyclical Unemployment

Cyclical unemployment
The fluctuating unemployment over the business cycle that increases during a recession and decreases during an expansion.

Cyclical unemployment is the fluctuating unemployment over the business cycle. Cyclical unemployment increases during a recession and decreases during an expansion. An autoworker who is laid off because the economy is in a recession and who gets rehired some months later when the expansion begins has experienced cyclical unemployment.

Duration and Demographics of Unemployment

Some people are unemployed for a week or two and others for a year or more. The longer the period of unemployment, the greater is the personal cost to the unemployed. The average duration of unemployment varies over the business cycle. In a recession, the average duration increases, and during an expansion, the average duration decreases.

Figure 6.8(a) compares the duration of unemployment in 2000 with that in 1983. In 2000, the economy was in a strong expansion and the unemployment rate was low. In 1983, the economy was recovering from a deep recession and the unemployment rate was high. You can see that in 2000, almost all of the unemployed found jobs in less than 14 weeks. But in 1983, almost a quarter of the unemployed took more than 26 weeks to find a job.

Unemployment does not affect all demographic groups in the same way. And the differences between the groups most and least affected by unemployment are large. Figure 6.8(b) shows that during the 1990s black teenagers had the highest unemployment rates, which averaged more than 30 percent. Whites aged 20 years and over had the lowest unemployment rates, which averaged a little more than 4 percent.

Why are teenage unemployment rates so high? There are two reasons. First, young people are still discovering what they are good at and trying different lines of work, so they leave their jobs more frequently than do older workers. Second, firms often hire teenagers on a short-term or trial basis, so the rate of job loss is higher for teenagers than for older workers.

FIGURE 6.8
Unemployment: Duration and Demographics

Practice Online

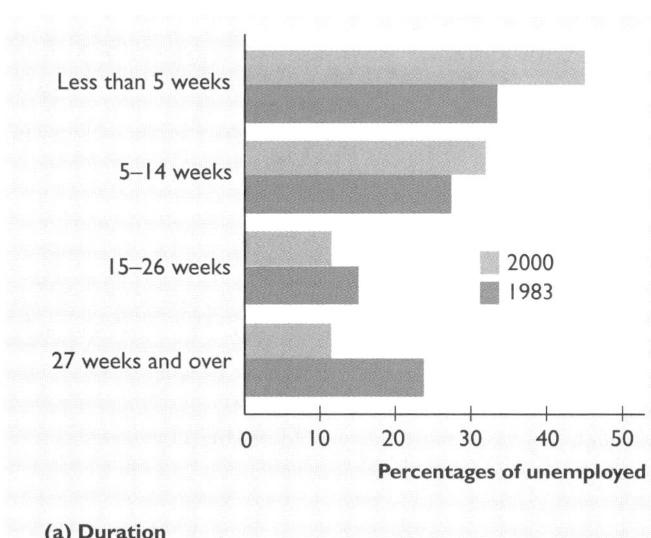

(a) Duration

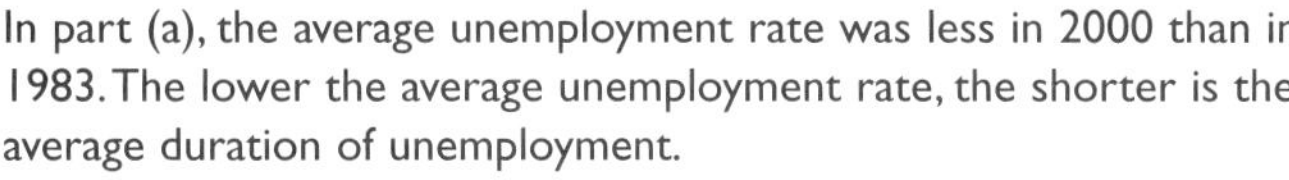

In part (a), the average unemployment rate was less in 2000 than in 1983. The lower the average unemployment rate, the shorter is the average duration of unemployment.

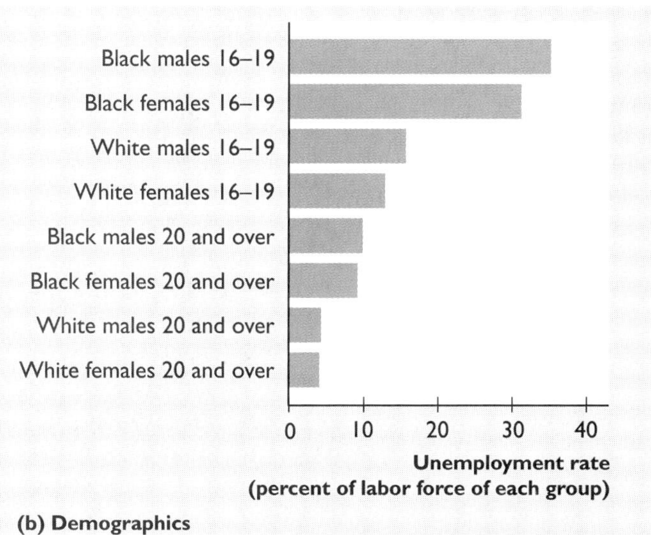

(b) Demographics

SOURCE: Bureau of Labor Statistics.

In part (b), on the average during the 1990s, blacks experienced more than twice the unemployment of whites, and teenagers experienced more than three times the unemployment of workers aged 20 and over.

You've seen that there is always *some* unemployment—someone looking for a job or laid off and waiting to be recalled. Yet one of the goals of economic policy is to achieve full employment. What do we mean by *full employment*?

Full Employment

Full employment
When there is no cyclical unemployment or, equivalently, when all the unemployment is frictional, structural, and seasonal.

Natural unemployment rate
The unemployment rate at full employment.

There can be a lot of unemployment at full employment, and the term "full employment" is an example of a technical economic term that does not correspond with everyday language. **Full employment** occurs when there is no cyclical unemployment or, equivalently, when all the unemployment is frictional, structural, and seasonal. The divergence of the unemployment rate from full employment is cyclical unemployment. The unemployment rate at full employment is called the **natural unemployment rate.** The term "natural unemployment rate" is another example of a technical economic term that does not correspond with everyday language.

Why do economists call a situation with a lot of unemployment one of full employment? And why is the unemployment rate at full employment called the "natural" unemployment rate? The reason is that the U.S. economy is a complex mechanism that undergoes constant change in its players, structure, and direction. For example, in 2002, around 3 million people retired and more than 3 million new workers entered the labor force. Thousands of businesses (including new start-ups) expanded and created jobs while thousands of others downsized or failed and destroyed jobs. This process of change creates frictions and dislocations that are unavoidable—that are natural. And they create unemployment.

Unemployment and Real GDP

Cyclical unemployment is the fluctuating unemployment over the business cycle—unemployment that increases during a recession and decreases during an expansion. At full employment, there is no cyclical unemployment. At a business cycle trough, cyclical unemployment is positive and at a business cycle peak, it is *negative.*

Figure 6.9(a) shows the unemployment rate in the United States between 1982 and 2002. It also shows the natural unemployment rate and cyclical unemployment. In this figure, the natural unemployment rate falls from 7 percent in 1982 to 6 percent in the late 1980s and early 1990s and to 5 percent in the late 1990s and 2000s. This path of the natural unemployment rate is an assumption.

There is not much controversy about the existence of a natural unemployment rate. But economists don't agree about its size or the extent to which it fluctuates. The majority view is that the natural rate changes slowly, and over the long term it averages around 6 percent.

An increasing number of economists think that fluctuations in frictional and structural unemployment bring fluctuations in the natural unemployment rate and that at times of rapid demographic change and rapid structural change, the natural unemployment rate can be high.

But the true natural unemployment rate is unknown and is estimated with a large margin of uncertainty. You will learn more about the uncertain value of the natural rate of unemployment in Chapters 8 and 17.

Cyclical unemployment was positive during most of the 1980s and the early 1990s (shaded red) and negative during the late 1980s and after 1997 (shaded blue).

Potential GDP
The level of real GDP that the economy would produce if it were at full employment.

Figure 6.9(b) shows real GDP in the United States from 1982 to 2002. The figure also shows **potential GDP**, which is the level of real GDP that the economy

FIGURE 6.9
The Relationship Between Unemployment and Real GDP

Practice Online

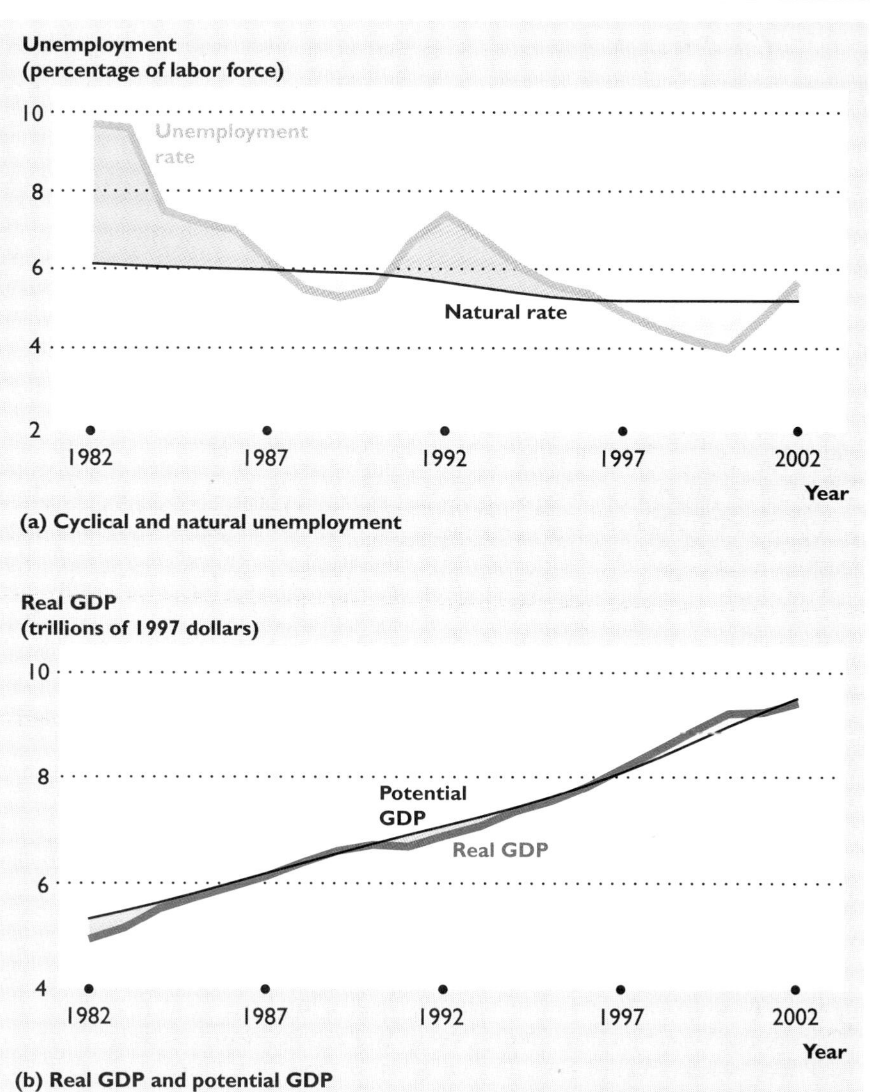

SOURCES: Bureau of Economic Analysis, Bureau of Labor Statistics, and Congressional Budget Office.

As the unemployment rate fluctuates around the natural unemployment rate (part a), real GDP fluctuates around potential GDP (part b).

would produce if it were at full employment. Because the unemployment rate fluctuates around the natural unemployment rate, real GDP fluctuates around potential GDP. When the unemployment rate is above the natural unemployment rate (in part a), real GDP is below potential GDP (in part b); when the unemployment rate is below the natural unemployment rate, real GDP is above potential GDP; and when the unemployment rate equals the natural unemployment rate, real GDP equals potential GDP.

You will learn what determines full employment and potential GDP in Chapter 8. And you'll learn what determines the fluctuations around full employment and potential GDP in Chapters 14 and 15.

CHECKPOINT 6.3

Study Guide pp. 92–95

Practice Online 6.3

3 **Describe the sources and types of unemployment, define full employment, and explain the link between unemployment and real GDP.**

Practice Problem 6.3

A labor force survey in a Polynesian island records the following data for December 31, 2002: employed, 13,500; unemployed, 1,500; not in the labor force, 7,500. The survey also recorded during 2003: hires and recalls, 1,000; job losers, 750; job leavers 300; entrants, 150; reentrants, 450; withdrawals, 500. The working-age population increased during 2003 by 100. (All the job losers, entrants, and reentrants became unemployed.) Calculate for the end of 2003,

a. The unemployment rate.
b. The labor force participation rate.

Exercise 6.3

The Polynesian island labor force survey provides the following information about labor market flows during 2004: hires and recalls, 1,500; job losers, 550; job leavers, 300; entrants, 200; reentrants, 500; withdrawals, 450. The working-age population increased during 2004 by 150. Starting with the situation at the end of 2001 in the practice problem, calculate for the end of 2004:

a. The unemployment rate.
b. The labor force participation rate.
c. What do you predict happened to real GDP in 2004? Why?

Solution to Practice Problem 6.3

a. The number of people unemployed at the end of 2003 equals the number unemployed at the end of 2002, which is 1,500, plus the number of job losers (750), job leavers (300), entrants (150), and reentrants (450) minus the number of hires and recalls (1,000) and withdrawals (500). That is,

$$1{,}500 + 750 + 300 + 150 + 450 - 1{,}000 - 500 = 1{,}650.$$

Now calculate the number of people employed at the end of 2003. It equals the number employed at the end of 2002, which is 13,500, plus the number of hires and recalls (1,000) minus the number of job losers (750) and the number of job leavers (300). That is,

$$13{,}500 + 1{,}000 - 750 - 300 = 13{,}450.$$

Next calculate the labor force, which is the sum of the number unemployed and the number employed, which equals 1,650 + 13,450 = 15,100.

The unemployment rate is the percentage of the labor force who are unemployed, which is (1,650 ÷ 15,100) × 100 = 10.9 percent.

b. The labor force participation rate is the percentage of the working-age population who are in the labor force. The working-age population at the end of 2002 is the sum of number employed (13,500), number unemployed (1,500), and the number not in the labor force (7,500). That is,

$$13{,}500 + 1{,}500 + 7{,}500 = 22{,}500.$$

The working-age population increased during 2003 by 100 so, at the end of 2003, it equals 22,600.

The labor force participation rate is (15,100 ÷ 22,600) × 100 = 66.8 percent.

CHAPTER CHECKPOINT

Key Points

1 Define the unemployment rate and other labor market indicators.

- The unemployment rate is the number of people unemployed as a percentage of the labor force, and the labor force is the sum of the number of people employed and the number unemployed.
- The labor force participation rate is the labor force as a percentage of the working-age population.

2 Describe the trends and fluctuations in the indicators of labor market performance in the United States.

- The unemployment rate fluctuates with the business cycle.
- The female labor force participation rate has increased, and the male labor force participation rate has decreased.
- Aggregate hours trend upward more slowly than employment because average hours decrease. Aggregate hours and average hours fluctuate with the business cycle.

3 Describe the sources and types of unemployment, define full employment, and explain the link between unemployment and real GDP.

- Unemployment arises from the process of job creation and job destruction and from the movement of people into and out of the labor force.
- Unemployment can be frictional, structural, seasonal, or cyclical.
- The duration of unemployment fluctuates over the business cycle.
- Young people and minorities have the highest unemployment rates.
- Full employment occurs when there is no cyclical unemployment; the unemployment rate equals the natural unemployment rate.
- As the unemployment rate fluctuates around the natural unemployment rate, real GDP fluctuates around potential GDP.

Key Terms

Aggregate hours, 139
Cyclical unemployment, 150
Discouraged worker, 138
Frictional unemployment, 149
Full employment, 152
Full-time workers, 138
Involuntary part-time workers, 138
Labor force, 136
Labor force participation rate, 138
Natural unemployment rate, 152
Part-time workers, 138
Potential GDP, 152
Seasonal unemployment, 150
Structural unemployment, 150
Unemployment rate, 137
Working-age population, 136

Exercises

1. A BLS labor market survey interviewer visited four households.

   In the first household, Candy reported that she worked for 20 hours last week trying to get her Internet shopping business up and running. The rest of the week, she filled out application forms and attended two job interviews. Candy's husband Jerry worked for 40 hours at his job at General Motors. Candy and Jerry's 17-year-old daughter, who is still in high school, worked for 10 hours at her weekend convenience store job.

   In the second household, Joey, who works full time in a bank, reported that he was on his annual vacation. Joey's wife, Serena, who wants a full-time job, worked for 10 hours as a part-time checkout clerk.

   In the third household, Ari reported that he had no work last week but was going to be recalled to his regular farm job at the end of the month. Ari's housemate Kosta said that after months of search, he hasn't been able to find a job, so he has stopped looking and is now planning to go back to school.

   In the fourth household, Mimi and Henry reported that they are now senior citizens and are enjoying a well-earned retirement. Hank, their bachelor son who lives with them and is a professional artist, reported that he painted for 12 hours last week and sold one picture.

   a. Classify each of the ten people in these four households by the categories into which the BLS divides the population.
   b. Which of the people are part-time workers and which are full-time workers?
   c. Of the part-time workers, which are involuntary part-time workers?
   d. Calculate for these 10 people the
      i. Unemployment rate.
      ii. Labor force participation rate.
   e. Compare the unemployment rate and labor force participation rate of these four households with the U.S. data. How do these households differ from the average U.S. household?

2. The BLS survey found the following numbers in a small community:

   Total number of persons—320.

   Worked at least 1 hour as paid employees or worked 15 hours or more as unpaid workers in their family business—200.

   Were not working but had jobs or businesses from which they were temporarily absent—20.

   Had no employment—40.

   Were available for work and had made specific efforts to find employment some time during the previous 4 weeks—10.

   Were available for work and were waiting to be recalled to a job from which they had been laid off—6.

   a. Calculate for this community the
      i. Unemployment rate.
      ii. Labor force participation rate.

   b. Compare the unemployment rate and labor force participation rate of this community with that for the households in exercise 1 and with the U.S. data. How does this community differ from the average U.S. household?

3. Describe the trends and fluctuations in the unemployment rate in the United States from 1962 through 2002. In which periods was the unemployment rate above average and in which periods was it below average?

4. Describe the trends and fluctuations in the labor force participation rate in the United States from 1962 through 2002, and contrast and explain the different trends for women and men.

5. What are the labor market flows that create and end a spell of unemployment? Of these flows, which fluctuate most and account for fluctuations in the unemployment rate?

6. Distinguish among the four types of unemployment: frictional, structural, seasonal, and cyclical. Provide an example of each type of unemployment in the United States today.

7. Describe the relationship between the unemployment rate and the natural unemployment rate as real GDP fluctuates around potential GDP. In which periods was real GDP below potential GDP?

Critical Thinking

8. The official measure of the unemployment rate omits many people who don't have a job but would like one. Do you think the omissions make the official unemployment rate an unhelpful indicator of the state of the economy? Or do you think that despite the omissions, the official measure provides useful information? Take a position on this issue and support your argument with examples.

9. If aggregate hours worked provides a more accurate measure of the quantity of labor employed than does the number of persons employed, why doesn't aggregate hours *not worked* provide a more accurate measure of the quantity of unemployment? (Hint: Think about the definition of unemployment.)

10. "Economics is supposed to be about scarcity. But if some labor is always unemployed, how can there be scarcity? All we need to do to produce more goods and services is employ the unemployed people."
    a. Do you agree or disagree with this statement? Why?
    b. Explain why scarcity and unemployment are not incompatible.

11. Most discussion and concern about unemployment arise from unemployed labor. Unemployed capital and land don't generate as much passion. But there is probably much more unemployment of capital and land than of labor.
    a. Provide some examples of unemployed capital and land.
    b. Explain why the unemployment of capital and land does not mean that scarcity isn't a problem.
    c. Can you think of benefits of unemployment that make some unemployment of all factors of production desirable?

Practice Online

Web Exercises

Use the links on your Foundations Web site to work the following exercises.

12. Visit the Bureau of Labor Statistics Web site and find the following labor market data for the United States in the most recent month and for the same month one year ago: the labor force, the number employed, the number unemployed, and the working-age population.
   a. Calculate for the two months the
      i. Unemployment rate.
      ii. Labor force participation rate.
   b. Describe the change in the labor market over the past year.

13. Visit the Bureau of Economic Analysis Web site and find the data on real GDP for the past year through the most recent quarter.
   a. Describe the change in real GDP over the past year.
   b. Explain how the change in real GDP relates to the changes in the labor market that you described in part **b** of exercise 1.

14. Visit the Bureau of Labor Statistics Web site and find labor market data for your own state.
   a. What have been the trends in employment, unemployment, and labor force participation in your own state during the past two years?
   b. On the basis of what you know about your own region, how would you set about explaining these trends?
   c. Try to identify the industries that have expanded most and those that have shrunk.
   d. What are the problems with your own regional labor market that you think need state government action to resolve?
   e. What actions do you think your state government must take to resolve them? Answer this question by using the demand and supply model of the labor market and predict the effects of the actions you prescribe.
   f. Compare the labor market performance of your own state with that of the nation as a whole.
   g. If your state is performing better than the national average, to what do you attribute the success? If your region is performing worse than the national average, to what do you attribute its problems?

15. Visit the Statistics Canada Web site and obtain labor market data for Canada.
   a. What have been the trends in employment, unemployment, and labor force participation in Canada during the past two years?
   b. Compare and contrast Canadian and U.S. labor market trends during these years.
   c. On the basis of what you've learned in this chapter about the types of unemployment, which types of unemployment do you think Canada has more of than the United States? Why?
   d. Is the natural unemployment rate in Canada higher or lower than that in the United States?
   e. To what do you attribute the difference in the natural unemployment rate in the two countries?

CHAPTER 7

The CPI and the Cost of Living

CHAPTER CHECKLIST

When you have completed your study of this chapter, you will be able to

1. **Explain what the Consumer Price Index (CPI) is and how it is calculated.**
2. **Explain the limitations of the CPI as a measure of the cost of living.**
3. **Adjust money values for inflation and calculate real wage rates and real interest rates.**

You learned in Chapter 5 how the Bureau of Economic Analysis measures GDP and in Chapter 6 how economists at the Census Bureau and Bureau of Labor Statistics keep track of developments in the labor market. These economic indicators provide information on the standard of living. In this chapter, we focus on measuring the cost of living.

The main measure of the cost of living is called the Consumer Price Index, or CPI. The Department of Labor publishes new CPI figures each month, and analysts in newspapers and on TV quickly leap to conclusions about the causes of recent changes in prices and the implications of the latest numbers for interest rate actions by the Federal Reserve.

How does the government determine the CPI? How well does it measure the cost of living and the inflation rate?

In this chapter, you will find out how economic statisticians measure the price level and the inflation rate and what the limitations of these measures are. You will also learn how we use price index numbers to strip away the veil of money and dollar values to see the real values that they represent.

7.1 THE CONSUMER PRICE INDEX

Consumer Price Index
A measure of the average of the prices paid by urban consumers for a fixed market basket of consumer goods and services.

The **Consumer Price Index** (CPI) is a measure of the average of the prices paid by urban consumers for a fixed market basket of consumer goods and services. The Bureau of Labor Statistics (BLS) calculates the CPI every month, and we can use these numbers to compare what the fixed market basket costs this month with what it cost in some previous month or other period.

Reading the CPI Numbers

Reference base period
A period for which the CPI is defined to equal 100. Currently, the reference base period is 1982–1984.

The CPI is defined to equal 100 for a period called the **reference base period**. Currently, the reference base period is 1982–1984. That is, the CPI equals 100 on the average, over the 36 months from January 1982 through December 1984.

In September 2002, the CPI was 181. This number tells us that the average of the prices paid by urban consumers for a fixed market basket of consumer goods and services was 81 percent higher in September 2002 than it was on the average during 1982–1984.

In August 2002, the CPI was 180.7. Comparing the September CPI with the August CPI tells us that the average of the prices paid by urban consumers for a fixed market basket of consumer goods and services increased by 0.3 of a percentage point in September 2002.

Constructing the CPI

Constructing the CPI is a huge operation that costs millions of dollars and involves three stages:

- Selecting the CPI basket
- Conducting the monthly price survey
- Calculating the CPI

The CPI Basket

The first stage in constructing the CPI is to select what is called the *CPI basket*. This "basket" contains the goods and services represented in the index and the relative importance attached to each of them. The idea is to make the relative importance of the items in the CPI basket the same as in the budget of an average urban household. For example, people spend more on housing than on bus rides, so the CPI places more weight on the price of housing than on the price of bus rides.

The BLS uses two baskets and calculates two CPIs. One, called CPI-U, measures the average price paid by *all* urban households. The other, called CPI-W, measures the average price paid by urban wage earners and clerical workers. Here, we will focus on CPI-U, the broader measure.

To determine the spending patterns of households and to select the CPI basket, the BLS conducts a Consumer Expenditure Survey. This survey is costly and therefore is undertaken infrequently. Today's CPI is based on data gathered in a survey of 1999–2000. Before 2002, the CPI was based on a 1993–1995 survey. The BLS plans more frequent updates of the CPI basket in the future.

Until recently, the time period covered by the Consumer Expenditure Survey was also the reference base period. But the BLS has now changed the basket on two occasions but retained 1982–1984 as the reference base period.

Figure 7.1 shows the CPI basket at the end of 2002. The basket contains around 80,000 goods and services arranged in the eight large groups shown in the figure. The most important item in a household's budget is housing, which accounts for 41 percent of total expenditure. Transportation comes next at 17 percent. Third in relative importance is food and beverages at 16 percent. These three groups account for almost three quarters of the average household budget. Medical care and recreation each take 6 percent, education and communication takes 6 percent, and apparel (clothing and footwear) takes 4 percent. Another 4 percent is spent on other goods and services.

The BLS breaks down each of these categories into smaller ones. For example, education and communication breaks down into textbooks and supplies, tuition, telephone services, and personal computer services.

As you look at these relatively important numbers, remember that they apply to the average household. Each individual household is spread around the average. Think about your own expenditure and compare it with the average.

The Monthly Price Survey

Each month, BLS employees check the prices of the 80,000 goods and services in the CPI basket in 30 metropolitan areas. Because the CPI aims to measure price changes, it is important that the prices recorded each month refer to exactly the same item. For example, suppose the price of a box of jelly beans has increased but a box now contains more beans. Has the price of a jelly bean increased? The BLS employee must record the details of changes in quality, size, weight, or packaging so that price changes can be isolated from other changes.

Once the raw price data are in hand, the next task is to calculate the CPI.

FIGURE 7.1
The CPI Basket

Practice Online

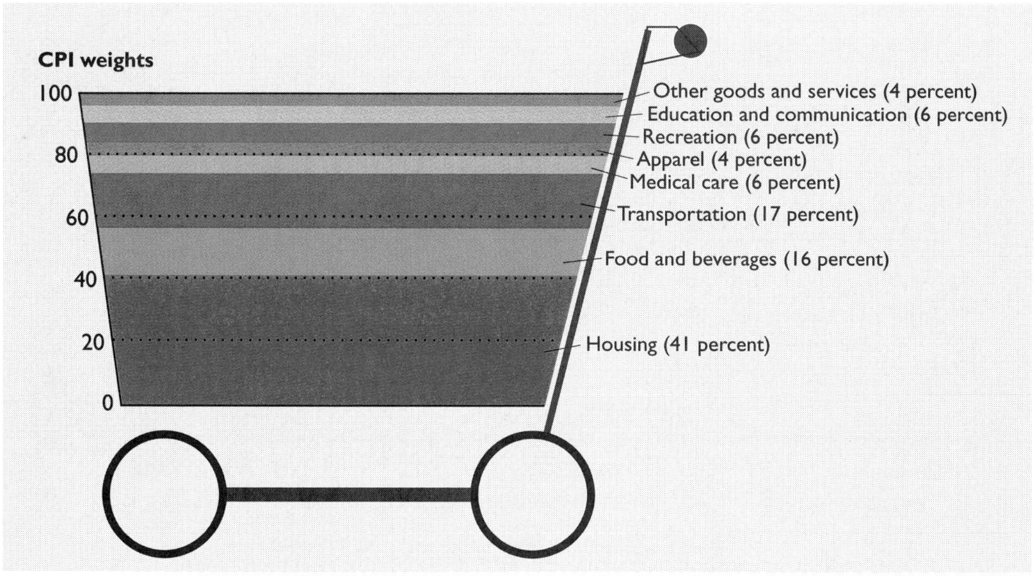

This shopping cart is filled with the items that an average household buys. Housing (41 percent), transportation (17 percent), and food and beverages (16 percent) take 74 percent of household income.

SOURCE: Bureau of Labor Statistics.

Calculating the CPI

The CPI calculation has three steps:

- Find the cost of the CPI basket at base period prices.
- Find the cost of the CPI basket at current period prices.
- Calculate the CPI for the base period and the current period.

We'll work through these three steps for a simple example. Suppose the CPI basket contains only two goods and services: oranges and haircuts. We'll construct an annual CPI rather than a monthly CPI with the reference base period 2000 and the current period 2003.

Table 7.1 shows the quantities in the CPI basket and the prices in the base period and the current period. Part (a) contains the data for the base period. In that period, consumers bought 10 oranges at $1 each and 5 haircuts at $8 each. To find the cost of the CPI basket in the base period prices, multiply the quantities in the CPI basket by the base period prices. The cost of oranges is $10 (10 at $1 each), and the cost of haircuts is $40 (5 at $8 each). So total expenditure in the base period on the CPI basket is $50 ($10 + $40).

Part (b) contains the price data for the current period. The price of an orange increased from $1 to $2, which is a 100 percent increase ($1 ÷ $1 × 100 = 100 percent). The price of a haircut increased from $8 to $10, which is a 25 percent increase ($2 ÷ $8 × 100 = 25 percent).

The CPI provides a way of averaging these price increases by comparing the cost of the basket rather than the price of each item. To find the cost of the CPI basket in the current period, 2003, multiply the quantities in the basket by their 2003 prices. The cost of oranges is $20 (10 at $2 each), and the cost of haircuts is $50 (5 at $10 each) So total expenditure on the fixed CPI basket at current period prices is $70 ($20 + $50).

TABLE 7.1

The Consumer Price Index: A Simplified CPI Calculation

Practice Online

(a) The cost of the CPI basket at base period prices: 2000

	CPI basket		
Item	**Quantity**	**Price**	**Cost of CPI basket**
Oranges	10	$1 each	$10
Haircuts	5	$8 each	$40
	Cost of CPI basket at base period prices		$50

(b) The cost of the CPI basket at current period prices: 2003

	CPI basket		
Item	**Quantity**	**Price**	**Cost of CPI basket**
Oranges	10	$2 each	$20
Haircuts	5	$10 each	$50
	Cost of CPI basket at current period prices		$70

You've now taken the first two steps toward calculating the CPI. The third step uses the numbers you've just calculated to find the CPI for 2000 and 2003. The formula for the CPI is

$$\text{CPI} = \frac{\text{Cost of CPI basket at current period prices}}{\text{Cost of CPI basket at base period prices}} \times 100.$$

In Table 7.1, you established that in 2000, the cost of the CPI basket was \$50 and in 2003, it was \$70. If we use these numbers in the CPI formula, we can find the CPI for 2000 and 2003. The base period is 2000, so for 2000, the CPI is

$$\text{CPI in 2000} = \frac{\$50}{\$50} \times 100 = 100.$$

For 2003, the CPI is

$$\text{CPI in 2003} = \frac{\$70}{\$50} \times 100 = 140.$$

The principles that you've applied in this simplified CPI calculation apply to the more complex calculations performed every month by the BLS.

Figure 7.2(a) shows the CPI in the United States during the 30 years between 1972 and 2002. The CPI increased every year during this period. During the late 1970s and in 1980, the CPI was increasing rapidly, but the rate of increase slowed during the 1980s and 1990s.

Measuring Inflation

A major purpose of the CPI is to measure *changes* in the cost of living and in the value of money. To measure these changes, we calculate the **inflation rate**, which is the percentage change in the price level from one year to the next. To calculate the inflation rate, we use the formula

Inflation rate
The percentage change in the price level from one year to the next.

$$\text{Inflation rate} = \frac{(\text{CPI in current year} - \text{CPI in previous year})}{\text{CPI in previous year}} \times 100.$$

Suppose that the current year is 2003 and the CPI for 2003 is 140. And suppose that in the previous year, 2002, the CPI was 120. Then the inflation rate in 2003 was

$$\text{Inflation rate} = \frac{(140 - 120)}{120} \times 100 = 16.7 \text{ percent}.$$

This inflation rate is very high—much higher than anything that we experience in the United States. You can check the latest inflation rate by visiting the BLS Web site. Let's calculate a recent U.S. inflation rate. In September 2002, the CPI was 181, and in September 2001, it was 178.3. So the inflation rate during the year to September 2002 was

$$\text{Inflation rate} = \frac{(181 - 178.3)}{178.3} \times 100 = 1.5 \text{ percent}.$$

Figure 7.2(b) shows the inflation rate between 1972 and 2002. The two parts of Figure 7.2 are related. When the price *level* in part (a) rises rapidly, the inflation rate in part (b) is high, and when the price level in part (a) rises slowly, the inflation rate in part (b) is low.

FIGURE 7.2
The CPI and the Inflation Rate: 1972–2002

Practice Online

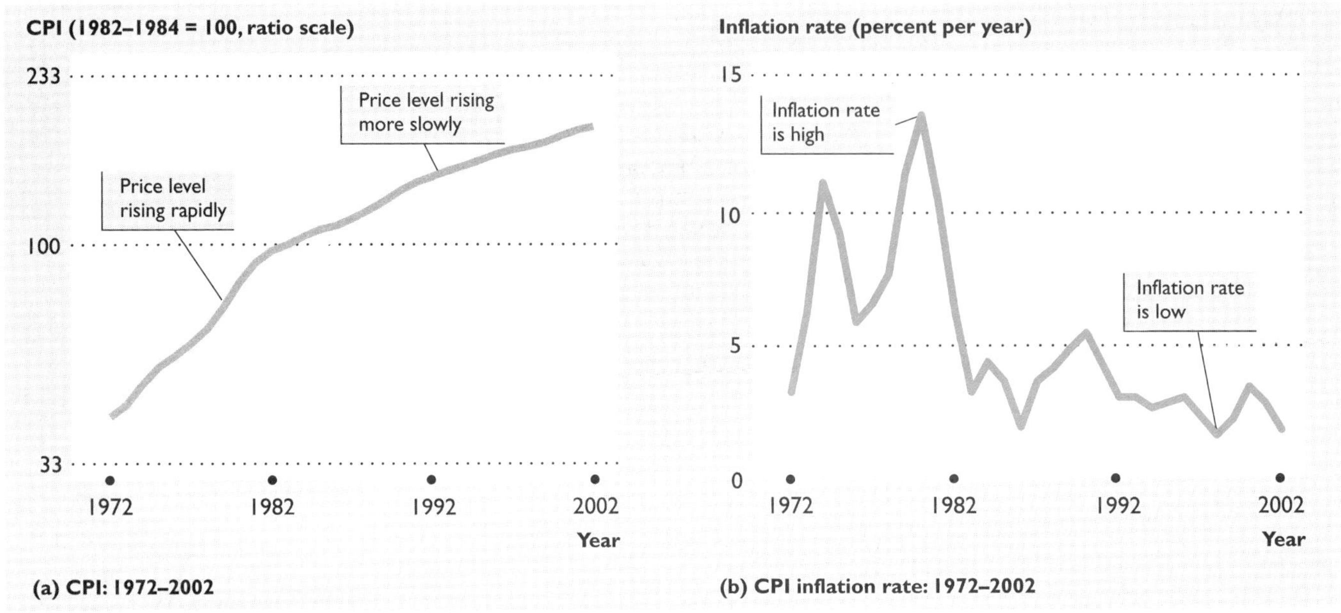

SOURCE: Bureau of Labor Statistics.

In part (a), the CPI (the price *level*) has increased every year. In part (b), the inflation rate has averaged 5 percent a year. During the 1970s and early 1980s, it exceeded 10 percent a year, but since the early 1980s, it has been around 3 percent a year.

700 Years of Inflation and Deflation

These extraordinary data show century averages of inflation in England since the 1300s. There was a burst of inflation during the sixteenth century after Europeans discovered America. But this inflation was less than 2 percent a year—less than we have today—and eventually subsided. During the Industrial Revolution, inflation was less than 1 percent a year. Only in the twentieth century did inflation become a serious problem.

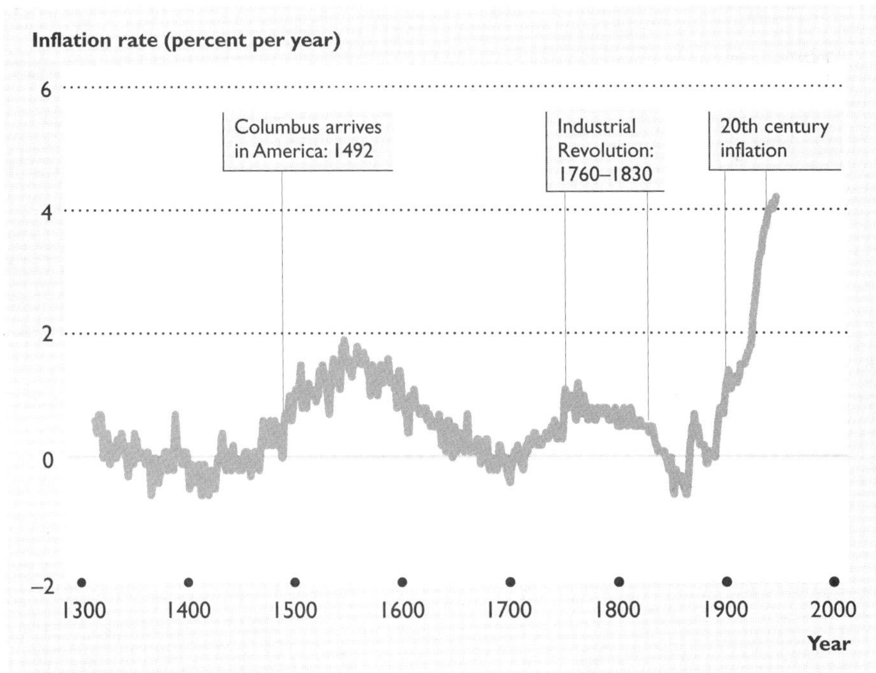

SOURCE: E.H. Phelps Brown and Sheila V. Hopkins, *Economica*, 1955.

CHECKPOINT 7.1

1 Explain what the Consumer Price Index (CPI) is and how it is calculated.

Study Guide pp. 100–103

Practice Online 7.1

Practice Problems 7.1

1. A Consumer Expenditure Survey in Sparta shows that people consume only juice and cloth. In 2003, the year of the Condumer Expenditure Survey and also the reference base year, the average household spent $40 on juice and $25 on cloth. The price of juice in 2003 was $4 a bottle, and the price of cloth was $5 a yard. In the current year, 2004, the price of juice is $4 a bottle and the price of cloth is $6 a yard. Calculate
   a. The CPI basket.
   b. The percentage of household budget spent on juice in the base year.
   c. The CPI in 2004.

2. Table 1 shows the CPI in Russia. Calculate Russia's inflation rate in 2001 and 2002. Did the price level rise or fall in 2002? Did the inflation rate increase or decrease in 2002?

TABLE 1

Year	CPI
2000	225
2001	274
2002	310

Exercise 7.1

A Consumer Expenditure Survey in the city of Firestorm shows that people consume only firecrackers and bandages. In 2002, the year of the Consumer Expenditure Survey and also the reference base year, the average household spent $150 on firecrackers and $15 on bandages. The price of a firecracker in 2002 was $2, and the price of bandages was $1 a pack. In the current year, 2003, the price of a firecracker is $3 and the price of bandages is $1.25 a pack. Calculate

a. The CPI basket.
b. The percentage of a household's budget spent on firecrackers in the base year.
c. The CPI in 2003.
d. The inflation rate in 2003.

Solutions to Practice Problems 7.1

1a. The CPI basket is the quantities bought during the Consumer Expenditure Survey year, 2003. Households spend $40 on juice at $4 a bottle, so the quantity of juice bought was 10 bottles. Households spend $25 on cloth at $5 a yard, so the quantity of cloth bought was 5 yards. The CPI basket is 10 bottles of juice and 5 yards of cloth.

1b. In the reference base year, expenditure on juice was $40 and expenditure on cloth was $25, so the household budget was $65. Expenditure on juice was 61.5 percent of the household budget: ($40 ÷ $65) × 100 = 61.5 percent.

1c. To calculate the CPI in 2004, find the cost of the CPI basket in 2003 and 2004. In 2003, the CPI basket costs $65 ($40 for juice and $25 for cloth). In 2004, the CPI basket costs $40 for juice (10 bottles at $4 a bottle) plus $30 for cloth (5 yards at $6 a yard), which sums to $70. The CPI in 2004 equals ($70/$65) × 100 = 107.7.

2. The inflation rate in 2001 is [(274 – 225) ÷ 225] × 100 = 21.8 percent. The inflation rate in 2002 is [(310 – 274) ÷ 274] × 100 = 13.1 percent. The price level increased and the inflation rate decreased in 2002.

7.2 THE CPI AND THE COST OF LIVING

Cost of living index
A measure of changes in the amount of money that people would need to spend to achieve a given standard of living.

The CPI is sometimes called a cost of living index. The purpose of a **cost of living index** is to measure changes in the amount of money that people would need to spend to achieve a given standard of living. The CPI does not measure the cost of living for two broad reasons.

First, the CPI does not try to measure all the components of the cost of living. For example, a severe winter might cause people to buy more natural gas and electricity to heat their homes. An increase in the prices of these items would increase the CPI, but the increased quantities bought would not change the CPI because the CPI basket is fixed. So part of this increase in spending, which is an increase in the cost of maintaining a given standard of living, would not show up as an increase in the CPI.

Second, even those components of the cost of living that are measured by the CPI are not always measured accurately. The result is that the CPI is possibly a biased measure of changes in the cost of living. Let's look at some of the problems faced by the BLS that might lead to bias in the CPI.

The Biased CPI

The main sources of bias in the CPI are

- New goods bias
- Quality change bias
- Commodity substitution bias
- Outlet substitution bias

New Goods Bias

New goods keep replacing old ones. For example, the PC has replaced the typewriter. The DVD is gradually replacing the videocassette player. The digital camera is replacing the film camera. These are just a few examples of a very long list of new goods to which you can easily add.

If you want to compare the price level in 2003 with that in 1993, you must somehow compare the price of a DVD today with that of a videocassette player in 1993. Because DVDs do a better job than videocassette players, you are better off with the new technology if the prices were the same. But DVDs are more expensive than videocassette players. How much of the higher price is a sign of the higher quality?

The BLS does its best to answer this type of question and employs many experts to help get the correct answer. But there is no sure way of making the necessary adjustment, and most likely, the arrival of new goods puts an upward bias into the CPI and its measure of the inflation rate.

Quality Change Bias

Cars, CD players, and many other items get better every year. For example, central locking, airbags, and antilock braking systems all add to the quality of a car. But they also add to the cost. Is the improvement in quality greater than the increase in cost? Or do car prices rise by more than can be accounted for by quality improvements? To the extent that a price rise is a payment for improved quality, it is not inflation. Again, the BLS does the best job it can to estimate the effects of quality improvements on price changes. But the CPI probably counts too much of any price rise as inflation and so overstates inflation.

Commodity Substitution Bias

Changes in relative prices lead consumers to change the items they buy. People cut back on items that become relatively more costly and increase their consumption of items that become relatively less costly. For example, suppose the price of beef rises while the price of chicken remains constant. Now that beef is more costly relative to chicken, you might decide to buy more chicken and less beef. Suppose that you switch from beef to chicken, spend the same amount on meat as before, and get the same enjoyment as before. Your cost of meat has not changed. But the CPI says that the price of meat has increased because it ignores your substitution between goods in the CPI basket.

Outlet Substitution Bias

When confronted with higher prices, people use discount stores more frequently and convenience stores less frequently. This phenomenon is called *outlet substitution*. Suppose, for example, that gas prices rise by 10 cents a gallon. Instead of buying from your nearby gas station for $1.50 a gallon, you now drive farther to a gas station that charges $1.40 a gallon. Your cost of gas has increased because you must factor in the cost of your time and the gas that you use driving several blocks down the road. But your cost has not increased by as much as the 10 cents a gallon increase in the pump price. However, the CPI says that the price of gas has increased by 10 cents a gallon because it does not measure outlet substitutions.

The growth of online shopping in recent years has provided an alternative to discount stores that makes outlet substitution even easier and potentially makes this source of bias more serious.

The Magnitude of the Bias

You've reviewed the sources of bias in the CPI. But how big is the bias? This question was tackled in 1996 by a Congressional Advisory Commission on the Consumer Price Index chaired by Michael Boskin, an economics professor at Stanford University. This commission said that the CPI overstates inflation by 1.1 percentage points a year. That is, if the CPI reports that inflation is 3.1 percent a year, most likely inflation is actually 2 percent a year. Some economists do not accept the Boskin Commission's conclusion, but most economists agree that there is some bias in the CPI.

To reduce the sources of bias that we've just reviewed, the BLS has decided to increase the frequency of its Consumer Expenditure Survey and to revise the CPI basket every two years.

Two Consequences of the CPI Bias

The bias in the CPI has two main consequences. It

- Distorts private contracts.
- Increases government outlays.

Distortion of Private Contracts

Many wage contracts contain a cost of living adjustment. Suppose that the UAW and General Motors Corporation agree on wage rate of \$28 an hour initially that increases over three years at a rate of 2 percent a year plus the increase in the cost of living. Suppose that over the three years, the CPI increases by 3 percent each year but the true price increase is 1.9 percent a year (a 1.1 percentage point bias in the CPI). Table 7.2 shows the wage rates each year, the wage rates the UAW and GM intended, and the gap between the actual and intended wage rate—the wage bias. At the end of the first year, the wage rate rises by 5 percent to \$29.40 an hour. The intention of the contract was for it to increase by 3.9 percent to \$29.09. There is a 31¢ an hour bias. After the second year, the wage rate rises by a further 5 percent to \$30.87 an hour instead of the intended \$30.23. The bias is now 64¢ an hour. After three years, the workers are receiving \$1.01 an hour more than they would have received if the CPI measured the true increase in prices.

Increases in Government Outlays

Because rising prices decrease the buying power of the dollar, the CPI is used to adjust the incomes of the 48 million Social Security beneficiaries, 22 million food stamp recipients, and 4 million retired former military personnel and federal civil servants (and their surviving spouses) and the budget for 27 million school lunches.

Close to a third of federal government outlays are linked directly to the CPI. If the CPI has a 1.1 percentage point bias, all of these expenditures increase by more than required to compensate for the fall in the buying power of the dollar and, although a bias of 1.1 percent a year seems small, accumulated over a decade, it adds up to almost a trillion dollars of additional government outlays.

The GDP Deflator: A Better Measure?

In Chapter 5, you learned about another measure of average prices: the *GDP deflator*. When we calculate the GDP deflator, we compare the current year's prices with the previous year's prices using the current year's and a previous year's baskets of goods and services. Because it uses current year quantities, the real GDP includes new goods and quality improvements and even allows for substitution effects of both commodities and retail outlets. So in principle, the GDP deflator is not subject to the biases of the CPI.

But in practice, the GDP deflator suffers from some of the CPI's problems. To arrive at its estimate of real GDP, the Commerce Department does not directly measure the physical quantities that are produced. Instead, it estimates quantities

TABLE 7.2
A Three-Year Wage Deal

Practice Online

	Fixed increase (percent)	CPI increase (percent)	Wage rate (dollars per hour)	True price increase (percent)	Intended wage rate (dollars per hour)	Wage bias (dollars per hour)
Initially			28.00		28.00	—
After 1 year	2	3	29.40	1.9	29.09	0.31
After 2 years	2	3	30.87	1.9	30.23	0.64
After 3 years	2	3	32.41	1.9	31.40	1.01

by dividing expenditures by price indexes. And one of these price indexes is the CPI. So the biased CPI injects a bias into the GDP deflator.

Also, the GDP deflator is broader than the CPI. GDP is the sum of expenditures on all final goods and services, not just consumption expenditures. So the GDP deflator reflects the prices of such items as paper mills bought by 3M to make Post-it Notes, nuclear submarines bought by the Defense Department, and Boeing 747s bought by British Airways. So the GDP deflator is not an alternative to the CPI as a measure of the cost of living.

Figure 7.3(a) shows the CPI and the GDP deflator measures of inflation. The two measures move up and down in similar ways, but the CPI measure exceeds the GDP deflator measure and in Figure 7.3(b) they gradually get farther apart.

FIGURE 7.3

Two Measures of Inflation and the Price Level

Practice Online

SOURCES: Bureau of Labor Statistics and Bureau of Economic Analysis.

The two measures of the inflation rate in part (a) fluctuate together, but the CPI rises more rapidly than the GDP deflator, and in part (b), the price levels get farther apart. Both measures probably overstate the inflation rate.

CHECKPOINT 7.2

Study Guide pp. 103–105

Practice Online 7.2

2 **Explain the limitations of the CPI as a measure of the cost of living.**

Practice Problem 7.2

Economists in the Statistics Bureau decide to check the substitution bias in the CPI. To do so, they conduct a Consumer Expenditure Survey in both 2001 and 2002. Table 1 shows the results of the survey. It shows the items that consumers buy and their prices. The Statistics Bureau fixes the reference base year as 2001 and asks you to

a. Calculate the CPI in 2002 using the 2001 CPI basket.
b. Calculate the CPI in 2002 using the 2002 CPI basket.
c. Explain whether there is any substitution bias in the CPI that uses the 2001 basket.

TABLE 1

	2001		2002	
Item	Quantity	Price	Quantity	Price
Broccoli	10	$3.00	15	$3.00
Carrots	15	$2.00	10	$4.00

Exercise 7.2

In Virtual Reality, time travel became possible only in 3002. Economists in the Statistics Bureau decided to conduct a Consumer Expenditure Survey in both 3001 and 3002 to check the substitution bias of the CPI. Table 2 shows the results of the survey. It shows the items that consumers buy and their prices. The Statistics Bureau fixes the reference base year as 3001 and asks you to

a. Calculate the CPI in 3002 using the 3001 CPI basket.
b. Calculate the CPI in 3002 using the 3002 CPI basket.
c. Explain whether there is any substitution bias in the CPI that uses the 3001 basket.

TABLE 2

	3001		3002	
Item	Quantity	Price	Quantity	Price
Games	20	$60	10	$70
Time travel	0	–	20	$8,000

Solution to Practice Problem 7.2

a. Table 3 shows the calculation of the CPI in 2002 using the 2001 basket. The cost of the 2001 basket at 2001 prices is $60, and the cost of the 2001 basket at 2002 prices is $90. So the CPI in 2002 using the 2001 basket is ($90 ÷ $60) × 100 = 150.
b. Table 4 shows the calculation of the CPI in 2002 using the 2002 basket. The cost of the 2002 basket at 2001 prices is $65, and the cost of the 2002 basket at 2002 prices is $85. So the CPI in 2002 using the 2002 basket is ($85 ÷ $65) × 100 = 131.
c. There is some substitution bias in the CPI that uses the 2001 basket. The price of broccoli remains constant, but the price of carrots rises by 100 percent. So consumers cut the quantity of carrots consumed and increase the quantity of broccoli consumed. They end up spending $85 on vegetables. But they would have spent $90 if they had not substituted the now relatively less costly broccoli. The cost of vegetables does not rise by 50 percent as shown by the CPI. Instead, because of substitution, the cost of vegetables increases by only 42 percent ($85 is 42 percent greater than $60). When we calculate the increase in the price of vegetables using the 2002 CPI basket, the increase is only 31 percent ($85 compared with $65). So the CPI is biased upward because it ignores the substitutions that people make in response to changes in the price of one item relative to the price of another.

TABLE 3

Item	2001 basket at 2001 prices	2001 basket at 2002 prices
Broccoli	$30	$30
Carrot	$30	$60
Totals	$60	$90

TABLE 4

Item	2002 basket at 2001 prices	2002 basket at 2002 prices
Broccoli	$45	$45
Carrot	$20	$40
Totals	$65	$85

7.3 NOMINAL AND REAL VALUES

In 2002, it cost 37 cents to mail a first-class letter. One hundred years earlier, in 1902, that same letter would have cost 2 cents to mail. Does it *really* cost you 18.5 times the amount that it cost your great-great-grandmother to mail a letter?

You know that it does not. You know that a dollar today buys less than what a dollar bought in 1902, so the cost of a stamp has not really increased to 18.5 times its 1902 level. But has it increased at all? Did it really cost you any more to mail a letter in 2002 than it cost your great-great-grandmother in 1902?

The CPI can be used to answer questions like these. In fact, that is one of the main reasons for constructing a price index. Let's see how we can compare the price of a stamp in 1902 and the price of a stamp in 2002.

Dollars and Cents at Different Dates

To compare dollar amounts at different dates, we need to know the CPI at those dates. Currently, the CPI has a base of 100 for 1982–1984. That is, the average of the CPI in 1982, 1983, and 1984 is 100. (The numbers for the three years are 96.4, 99.6, and 103.9, respectively. Calculate the average of these numbers and check that it is indeed 100.)

In 2002, the CPI was 180.3, and in 1902, it was 9. By using these two numbers, we can calculate the relative value of the dollar in 1902 and 2002. To do so, we divide the 2002 CPI by the 1902 CPI. That ratio is 180.3 ÷ 9 = 20. That is, prices on the average were 20 times higher in 2002 than in 1902.

We can use this ratio to convert the price of a 2-cent stamp in 1902 into its 2002 equivalent. The formula for this calculation is

$$\text{Price of stamp in 2002 dollars} = \text{Price of stamp in 1902 dollars} \times \frac{\text{CPI in 2002}}{\text{CPI in 1902}}.$$

$$= 2 \text{ cents} \times \frac{180.3}{9} = 40 \text{ cents}.$$

So your great-great-grandmother had a raw deal! It *really* cost her more to mail that first-class letter than it cost you in 2002. She paid the equivalent of 40 cents, and you paid 37 cents.

The calculation that we've just done is an example of converting a *nominal* value into a *real* value. A nominal value is one that is expressed in current dollars. A real value is one that is expressed in the dollars of a given year.

Nominal and Real Values in Macroeconomics

Macroeconomics makes a big issue of the distinction between nominal and real values. You saw that distinction in Chapter 5, where you learned the difference between nominal GDP and real GDP. To calculate real GDP, we use the same idea that you've just used to calculate the real price of a postage stamp. But usually, in macroeconomics, we use the GDP deflator rather than the CPI as our measure of the price level. The reason is that we are dealing with economy totals, of which consumer spending is just one part. So real GDP is equal to nominal GDP divided by the GDP deflator and *not* nominal GDP divided by the CPI.

Eye on the Past

The Nominal and Real Price of a First-Class Letter

The figure shows the cost of a first-class letter since 1902. The green line is the nominal price—the actual price of a stamp in the dollars (cents) of the year in question. The red line is the real price—the price in terms of the 2002 dollar. You can see that the nominal price has gradually increased, but the real price has fluctuated, sometimes rising and sometimes falling. The highest real price, 44 cents, occurred in 1975, and the lowest real price, 18 cents, occurred in 1920.

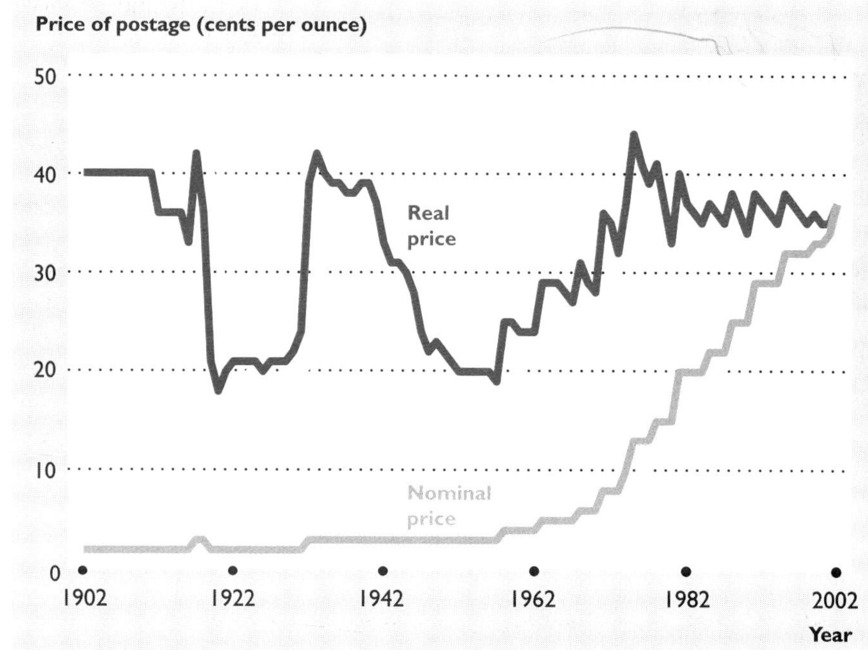

SOURCE: Robert Sahr, Oregon State University, http://www.orst.edu/dept/pol_sci/fac/sahr/stamp.htm.

Two other nominal–real distinctions play a big role in macroeconomics—and in your life. They are the distinctions between

- The nominal wage rate and the real wage rate
- The nominal interest rate and the real interest rate

Let's study these vital distinctions.

Nominal and Real Wage Rates

Nominal wage rate
The average hourly wage rate measured in *current* dollars.

Real wage rate
The average hourly wage rate measured in the dollars of a given reference base year.

The price of labor is the wage rate—the income that an hour of labor earns. In macroeconomics, we are interested in economy-wide performance, so we focus on the *average* hourly wage rate. The **nominal wage rate** is the average hourly wage rate measured in *current* dollars. The **real wage rate** is the average hourly wage rate measured in the dollars of a given reference base year.

To calculate the real wage rate, we divide the nominal wage rate by the CPI and multiply by 100. That is,

$$\text{Real wage rate in 2002} = \frac{\text{Nominal wage rate in 2002}}{\text{CPI in 2002}} \times 100.$$

In June 2002, the nominal wage rate (average hourly wage rate) of production workers was \$14.68 and the CPI was 179.9, so

$$\text{Real wage rate in June 2002} = \frac{\$14.68}{179.9} \times 100 = \$8.16.$$

Because we measure the real wage rate in constant base-year dollars, a change in the real wage rate measures the change in the quantity of goods and services that an hour's work can buy. In contrast, a change in the nominal wage rate measures a combination of a change in the quantity of goods and services that an hour's work can buy and a change in the price level. So the real wage rate takes the effects of inflation out of changes in the nominal wage rate.

The real wage rate is a significant economic variable because it measures the real reward for labor, which is a major determinant of the standard of living. The real wage rate is also significant because it measures the real cost of labor, which influences the quantity of labor that firms are willing to hire.

Figure 7.4 shows what has happened to the nominal wage rate and the real wage rate in the United States between 1972 and 2002. The nominal wage rate is the average hourly earning of production workers. This measure is just one of the several different measures of average hourly earnings that we might have used.

The nominal wage rate increased from \$3.70 an hour in 1972 to \$14.76 an hour in 2002. But the real wage rate decreased. In 1982–1984 dollars (the CPI base period dollars), the real wage rate was \$8.85 in 1972 and \$8.19 in 2002.

The real wage rate decreased as the nominal wage rate increased because the nominal wage rate didn't keep up with inflation. When the effects of inflation are removed from the nominal wage rate, we can see what is happening to the buying power of the average wage rate.

You can also see that the real wage rate has fluctuated. During the late 1970s, the real wage rate increased briefly. It then decreased until the mid-1990s, after which it increased slightly.

FIGURE 7.4

Nominal and Real Wage Rates: 1972–2002

Practice Online

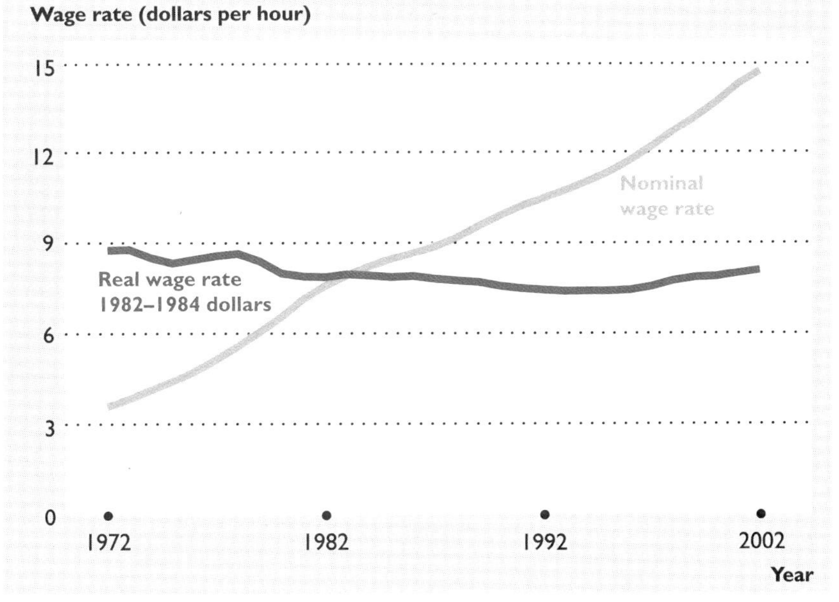

SOURCE: *Economic Report of the President*, 2002.

The nominal wage rate has increased every year since 1972. The real wage rate increased briefly during the late 1970s and then decreased through the mid-1990s, after which it increased slightly again. Over the entire 30-year period, the real wage rate decreased.

Eye on the Past

The Nominal and Real Wage Rates of Presidents of the United States

Does an airline pilot in 2003 earn a higher real wage rate than an airline pilot earned in 1963? Does a coal miner in 2003 earn more than a coal miner earned in 1963? We can use the formula that you've learned in this chapter to calculate the real wage rates of airline pilots and coal miners in 1963 and 2003 and compare them. But the comparison will be imprecise because these jobs have changed a great deal. In 1963, an airline pilot had to make many calculations that in 2003 are done by on-board computers. A 1963 coal miner used much more muscle power than his 2003 counterpart.

One job that has not changed much in more than 200 years is that of President of the United States. The job specification and the level of stress have remained similar over the decades. George Washington faced the challenge of creating a nation, Abraham Lincoln had to cope with civil war, Herbert Hoover with the Great Depression, Franklin Roosevelt with World War II, and George W. Bush with international terrorism.

It is tempting to calculate the real wage rates of U.S. Presidents to establish who was paid the most and who was paid the least.

The figure provides the data. The nominal wage rate (the green line) was set at $25,000 a year in 1789 and remained at that level until 1877, when it was doubled to $50,000 a year. It has increased in jumps to $400,000 in 2001.

The real wage rate (the red line) has followed a remarkable course. Expressed in 2000 dollars, George Washington earned $250,000 a year. The price level was falling during the first half of the nineteenth century, so the real wage rate climbed. It reached $500,000 a year, where it remained through the presidency of Abraham Lincoln. It dipped for Andrew Jackson because a burst of inflation during the Civil War lowered the buying power of his $25,000. The real wage rate then increased through the early 1900s and peaked at $1,500,000 for William Howard Taft.

Throughout the twentieth century, the President's real pay has been on a downward trend. Bill Clinton was the lowest-paid President in U.S. history!

Not counted in the President's salary are the perks that go with the job. The White House is more comfortable today, and presidential travel arrangements are a breeze compared to earlier times. So Bill Clinton probably didn't get such a raw deal.

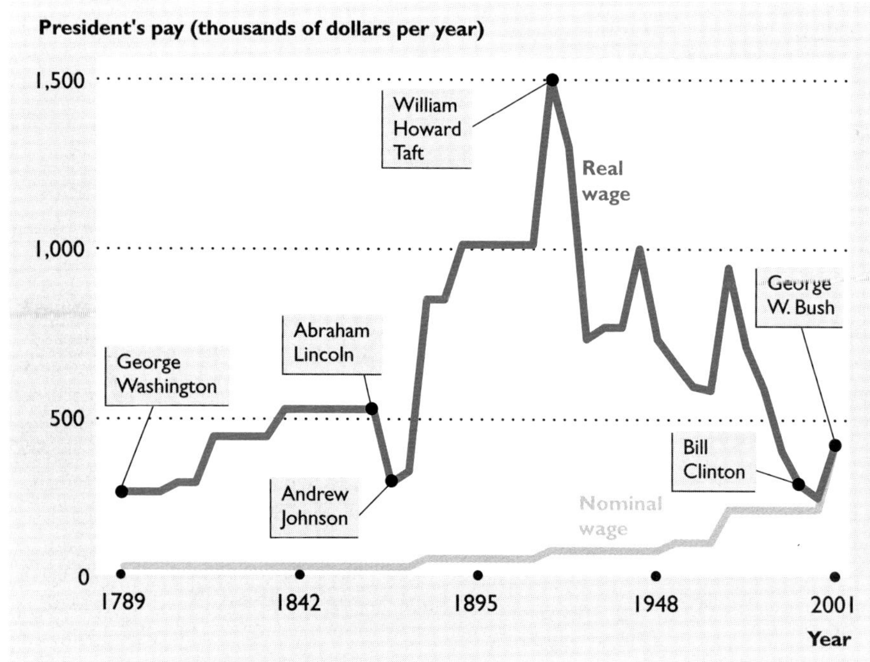

SOURCE: Robert Sahr, Oregon State University, http://www.orst.edu/dept/pol_sci/fac/sahr/sahr.htm.

Nominal and Real Interest Rates

You've just seen that we can calculate real values from nominal values by deflating them using the CPI. And you've seen that to make this calculation, we *divide* the nominal value by a price index. Converting a nominal interest rate to a real interest rate is a bit different. To see why, we'll start with their definitions.

A **nominal interest rate** is the percentage return on a loan, calculated by using dollars. For example, if you deposit $100 in a savings account on which the bank pays a nominal interest of 5 percent a year, you will receive $5 on your deposit.

A **real interest rate** is the percentage return on a loan, calculated by using purchasing power. That is, the real interest rate is the nominal interest rate adjusted for the effects of inflation.

Nominal interest rate
The percentage return on a loan, calculated by using dollars.

Real interest rate
The percentage return on a loan, calculated by using purchasing power—the nominal interest rate adjusted for the effects of inflation.

Suppose that you have $100 in a bank account and that after one year, you take your money out of the bank. The bank pays you the $100 that you deposited plus the $5 interest that you've earned (at 5 percent a year). But suppose that during the year, prices have increased by 3 percent. You've now got $105, but you need $103 just to buy what $100 would have bought when you put your money in the bank. So how much interest have you really earned? You've earned $2, or a real interest rate of 2 percent a year.

To convert a nominal interest rate to a real interest rate, we *subtract* the *inflation rate*. That is,

Real interest rate = Nominal interest rate – Inflation rate.

Plug your numbers into this formula. Your nominal interest rate is 5 percent a year, the inflation rate is 3 percent a year, and your real interest rate is 5 percent minus 3 percent, which equals 2 percent a year.

Figure 7.5 shows the nominal interest rate and the real interest rate in the United States between 1972 and 2002. When the inflation rate was high, during the 1970s and 1980s, the gap between the real interest rate and the nominal interest rate was large. The real interest rate was even negative in the mid-1970s. When the real interest rate is negative, the lender pays the borrower!

FIGURE 7.5
Nominal and Real Interest Rates: 1972–2002

Practice Online

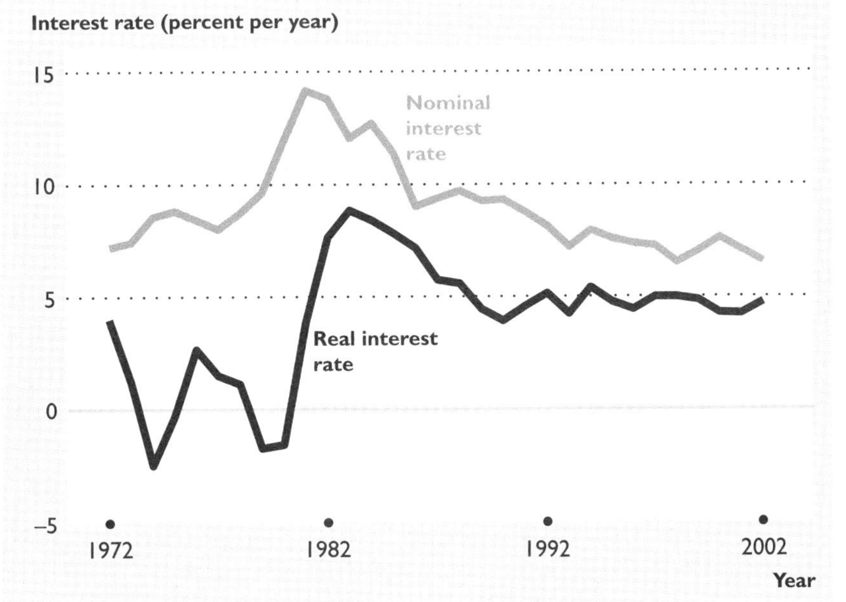

SOURCE: *Economic Report of the President*, 2002.

The real interest rate equals the nominal interest rate minus the inflation rate. During the 1970s, the real interest rate became negative.

CHECKPOINT 7.3

Study Guide pp. 105–108

Practice Online 7.3

3 **Adjust money values for inflation and calculate real wage rates and real interest rates.**

Practice Problems 7.3

1. Table 1 shows some gas prices and the CPI for three years. The reference base period is 1982–1984.
   a. Calculate the real price of gasoline in each year in 1982–1984 dollars.
   b. In which year was gasoline the most costly in real terms?
   c. In which year was gasoline the least costly in real terms?
2. Amazon.com agreed to pay its workers $20 an hour in 1999 and $22 an hour in 2001. The CPI for these years was 166 in 1999 and 180 in 2001.
   a. Calculate the real wage rate in each year.
   b. Did these workers really get a pay raise between 1999 and 2001?
3. Sally worked hard all year so that she could go to school full time the following year. She put her savings into a mutual fund that paid a nominal interest rate of 7 percent a year. The CPI was 165 at the beginning of the year and 177 at the end of the year. What was the real interest rate that Sally earned?

TABLE 1

Year	Price of gasoline (cents per gallon)	CPI
1971	36	40.5
1981	138	90.9
1991	112	136.2

Exercise 7.3

Table 2 shows the nominal interest rate and inflation rate in Japan for several years.

a. Calculate the real interest rate for each year.
b. In which year was the real interest rate the highest?
c. In which year was the real interest rate the lowest?
d. Was the real interest rate in Japan negative in any year?

TABLE 2

Year	Nominal interest rate	Inflation rate
	(percent per year)	
1992	4.6	1.7
1993	3.0	1.2
1994	2.1	0.7
1995	1.2	–0.1
1996	0.4	0.1
1997	0.4	1.7
1998	0.4	0.6
1999	0.1	–0.3
2000	0.1	–0.6
2001	0.1	–0.7
2002	0.1	–0.7

Solutions to Practice Problems 7.3

1a. To calculate the real price of gasoline in 1982–1984 dollars, multiply the nominal price by 100 and divide by the CPI. Table 3 shows the calculations.

1b. Gasoline was the most costly in real terms in 1981, when it was 152 cents (1982–1984 cents) per gallon.

1c. Gasoline was the least costly in real terms in 1991, when it was 82 cents (1982–1984 cents) per gallon.

2a. The real wage rate in 1999, expressed in dollars of the reference base year, was ($20 ÷ 166) × 100 = $12.05. The real wage rate in 2001, expressed in dollars of the reference base year, was ($22 ÷ 180) × 100 = $12.22 an hour.

2b. The real wage of these workers increased between 1999 and 2001.

3. The inflation rate during the year that Sally was working was (177 – 165) ÷ 165 × 100 = 7.3 percent. On the savings that Sally had in the mutual fund for the full year, she earned a real interest rate equal to the nominal interest rate minus the inflation rate, which is 7 – 7.3 = –0.3. Sally's real interest rate was negative. (Sally would have been even worse off if she had just kept her saving in cash. Her nominal interest rate would then have been zero, and her real interest rate would have been –7.3 percent.)

TABLE 3

Year	Price of gasoline (cents per gallon)	CPI	Price of gasoline (1982–1984 cents per gallon)
1971	36	40.5	89
1981	138	90.9	152
1991	112	136.2	82

CHAPTER CHECKPOINT

Key Points

1 Explain what the Consumer Price Index (CPI) is and how it is calculated.

- The Consumer Price Index (CPI) is a measure of the average prices of the goods and services that a typical urban household buys.
- The CPI is calculated by dividing the cost of the CPI basket in the current period by its cost in the base period and then multiplying by 100.

2 Explain the limitations of the CPI as a measure of the cost of living.

- The CPI does not include all the items that contribute to the cost of living.
- The CPI cannot provide an accurate measure of price changes because of new goods, quality improvements, and substitutions that consumers make when relative prices change.

3 Adjust money values for inflation and calculate real wage rates and real interest rates.

- To adjust a money value (also called a nominal value) for inflation, we express the value in terms of the dollar of a given year.
- To convert a dollar value of year *B* to the dollars of year *A*, multiply the value in year *B* by the price level in year *A* and divide by the price level in year *B*.
- The real wage rate equals the nominal wage rate divided by the CPI and multiplied by 100.
- The real interest rate equals the nominal interest rate minus the inflation rate.

Key Terms

Consumer Price Index, 160
Cost of living index, 166
Inflation rate, 163
Nominal interest rate, 175
Nominal wage rate, 172
Real interest rate, 175
Real wage rate, 172
Reference base period, 160

Exercises

1. Looking at some travel magazines, you read that the CPI in Turkey in 2002 was 6,912 and in Russia, it was 670. You do some further investigating and discover that the reference base period in Turkey is 1994 and in Russia it is 1995. The CPI in Russia in 1994 was 34.
   a. By what percentage did prices rise in Turkey between 1994 and 2002?
   b. By what percentage did prices rise in Russia between 1995 and 2002?
   c. By what percentage did prices rise in Russia between 1994 and 1995?
   d. By what percentage did prices rise in Russia between 1994 and 2002?
   e. In which of these two countries did prices rise more between 1994 and 2002?

2. Two countries, Sahara and Arctica, conduct consumer surveys. In Sahara, consumers buy 70 units of bottled water, 20 units of food, and 10 units of housing. In Arctica, consumers buy no bottled water (they suck icicles, which are free), 80 units of housing, and 20 units of food. Both countries use dollars, and prices in these two countries are the same. In the reference base years, water costs $1 a unit, food costs $5 a unit, and housing costs $10 a unit. In the current year, water costs $2 a unit, food costs $6 a unit, and housing costs $11 a unit.
   a. What is the CPI in Sahara in the current year?
   b. What is the CPI in Arctica in the current year?
   c. In which of these two countries did the CPI rise faster?
   d. Why did the CPI rise faster in one country?

3. In Brazil, the reference base period for the CPI is December 1993. In September 2000, prices had risen by 1,565.93 percent since the base period. The inflation rate in Brazil during the year ending September 2001 was 6.46 percent, and during the year ending September 2002, the inflation rate was 7.93 percent.
   a. What is the CPI in Brazil for December 1993?
   b. Calculate Brazil's CPI in September 2000.
   c. Calculate Brazil's CPI in September 2001.
   d. Calculate Brazil's CPI in September 2002.
   e. Is the price level in Brazil rising or falling?
   f. Did Brazil's inflation rate increase or decrease in 2001 and in 2002?
   g. Was the inflation rate in Brazil between 2000 and 2002 greater or less than the inflation rate in the United States?

4. Keep a careful record of your own expenditures during a two-week period. Keep separate data for week 1 and week 2. In particular, record the items that you buy, their prices, and the quantities that you buy. Use these records to calculate
   a. Your own CPI basket based on your week 1 expenditures.
   b. The percentage of your expenditures on each item.
   c. The cost of your CPI basket in week 1.
   d. The cost of your CPI basket in week 2.
   e. Your personal CPI for week 2.
   f. Your personal inflation rate in week 2.

5. On the basis of your observations of your own expenditures in weeks 1 and 2 (recorded in your answer to exercise 4), explain and discuss the way in which your personal CPI is influenced by
   a. New goods
   b. Quality changes
   c. Commodity substitution
   d. Outlet substitution

6. Visit a local supermarket on two dates a month apart. Select 10 items of standard products that the shop always sells. Record the prices of these 10 items on the two dates. Assuming that a consumer buys one of each item in the basket you've chosen, calculate
   a. The cost of the basket in the first month.
   b. The cost of the basket in the second month.
   c. A price index for the second month.
   d. The inflation rate of these 10 prices over the month.

7. On the basis of the price observations recorded in your answer to exercise 6, explain and discuss the way in which commodity substitution and outlet substitution might occur and the effects that these substitutions might have on the inflation rate in your area during the month of observation.

8. In 2002, Annie, an 80-year-old, is telling her granddaughter Suzie about the good old days. She says that in 1932, when she was a child, you could buy a nice house for $15,000 and a jacket for $5. Suzie looks up some current prices and finds that a house that costs $200,000 and a jacket that costs $50 are today's equivalent of the ones that Annie says cost so little when she was a child. Suzie, an economics student, looks up the CPI for 1932 and discovers that it is 13.7. The reference base is 1982–1984. The CPI for 2002 is 180.3.
   a. What is the 2002 price that is equivalent to $15,000 in 1932?
   b. Which is the lower cost: $15,000 in 1932 or $200,000 in 2002?
   c. Which is the lower cost: $5 in 1932 or $50 in 2002?
   d. Is Annie correct about the good old days?

9. Annie and Suzie of exercise 8 continue their conversation. But the subject now changes to wages. Suzie points out that when houses and jackets were cheap, wages were low. Annie recalls that her mother earned 55¢ an hour in 1932, which was the average wage at that time. Suzie seizes on this number and says that the good old days don't sound so good compared to 2002, when the average hourly wage rate was $14.76. Use the information about the CPI provided in exercise 8.
   a. What is the 2002 wage rate that is equivalent to 55¢ in 1932?
   b. Which is the higher wage rate: 55¢ in 1932 or $14.76 in 2002?
   c. How do the calculations in parts **a** and **b** along with those in exercise 8 help to determine whether the good old days were better or worse than today?

10. In 2002, the interest rate was 19 percent a year in Argentina and 0.01 percent a year in Japan. The inflation rate was 39 percent a year in Argentina and –0.9 percent a year in Japan.
    a. What was the real interest rate in Argentina in 2002?
    b. What was the real interest rate in Japan in 2002?

Critical Thinking

11. Imagine that you are given $1,000 to spend and told that you must spend it all buying items from a Sears catalog. But you do have a choice of catalog. You may select from the 1903 catalog or from Sears.com today. You will pay the prices quoted in the catalog that you choose.
   a. Why might you lean toward choosing the 1903 catalog?
   b. Why might you lean toward choosing sears.com?
   c. The bottom line: What is your choice and why? Refer to any biases in the CPI that might be relevant to your choice.

12. "The CPI is too political to be left to governments to calculate. It should be calculated by an independent agency." Argue both sides of this proposition.

Practice Online

Web Exercises

Use the links on your Foundations Web site to work the following exercises.

13. Visit the Web site of the Bureau of Labor Statistics and find the CPI data for the U.S. city and for the region of the country or metropolitan area in which you live.
   a. Is your local CPI higher or lower than the national average?
   b. Explain the deviation of your regional CPI from the national average.

14. Visit the Web site of the Bureau of Labor Statistics and find data on the CPI-U and the CPI-W.
   a. How do these two versions of the CPI differ?
   b. Which version of the CPI showed the faster inflation rate during 2002?
   c. Which of the two CPI measures do you think more closely matches your personal inflation experience?

15. Visit the Web site of Professor Robert Sahr at Oregon State University and find data on the pay of members of Congress in 1900, 1950, and 2000. Also obtain the CPI for those years.
   a. Calculate the real pay of members of Congress in 1900 and 1950 in terms of 2000 dollars.
   b. In which of these years did Congress members receive the highest real earnings?
   c. In which of these years did Congress members receive the lowest real earnings?

16. Download the Excel spreadsheet that provides data on nominal interest rates and inflation rates for the United States and Italy during the 1990s.
   a. Calculate the real interest rate for each country and each year.
   b. In which year and country was the real interest rate higher on the average?
   c. Describe the similarities, if any, and the differences between the real and nominal interest rates for the two countries.

CHAPTER 8

AS-AD and Potential GDP

CHAPTER CHECKLIST

When you have completed your study of this chapter, you will be able to

1 **Preview the aggregate supply–aggregate demand (*AS-AD*) model and explain why real GDP and unemployment fluctuate in a business cycle.**

2 **Explain the forces that determine potential GDP and the distribution of income between labor and other factors of production.**

3 **Explain what creates unemployment when the economy is at full employment and describe the influences on the natural unemployment rate.**

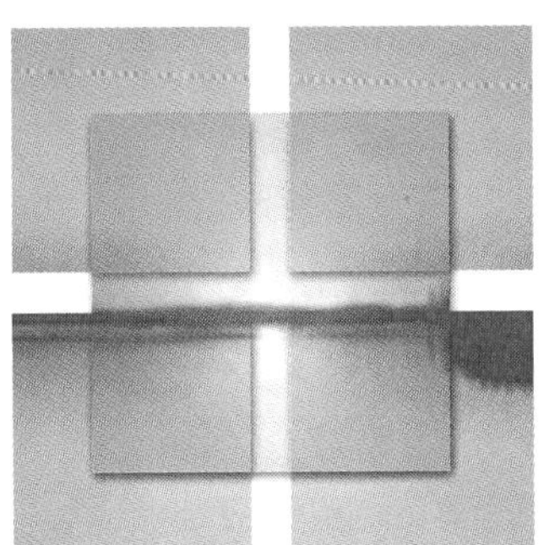

In the three previous chapters, you learned how we define and measure the indicators of macroeconomic performance. You are now going to shift gears and turn from defining and measuring these variables to understanding the forces that determine them.

Why does our economy fluctuate in a business cycle? *Why* is real GDP per person in the United States almost 20 times that in Nigeria? *Why* was real GDP per person in the United States in 2002 around twice the level of 1962? *Why* is the unemployment rate in Spain almost four times that of the United States? *Why* is the inflation rate in Russia six times that of the United States?

This chapter lays the foundation. It begins with a preview of the workhorse model of macroeconomics: the aggregate supply–aggregate demand (or *AS-AD*) model. The chapter then explains the forces that determine real GDP and the unemployment rate when the economy is at full employment.

UNDERSTANDING MACROECONOMIC PERFORMANCE

Macroeconomists have made progress in understanding how the economy works by dividing all the variables that describe macroeconomic performance into two lists:

- Real variables
- Nominal variables

Real variables are items such as real GDP, the real wage rate, the real interest rate, and other real items such as the levels of employment and unemployment. These variables describe the real economy and tell us what is *really* happening to production and consumption, saving and investment, work and leisure, all of which contribute to the standard of living.

Nominal variables are items such as the price level (CPI or GDP deflator) and the inflation rate along with nominal GDP, the nominal wage rate, and the nominal interest rate. These variables describe the nominal economy and tell us how *dollar values* and the cost of living are changing.

This separation of macroeconomic performance into a real part and a nominal part is the basis of a huge discovery called the **classical dichotomy,** which states:

> **When the economy is operating at full employment, the forces that determine the real variables are independent of those that determine the nominal variables.**

In practical terms, the classical dichotomy means that if we want to explain why real GDP per person in the United States is almost 20 times that in Nigeria, we can do so by looking only at the real parts of the two economies and ignoring differences in their price levels and inflation rates. Similarly, to explain why real GDP per person in 2002 was around twice that in 1962, we don't need to consider what happened to the value of the dollar between those two years.

The classical dichotomy describes the economy at full employment. But it does *not* hold over the business cycle as the economy fluctuates around full employment. The forces that shape the real economy and those that shape the nominal economy interact to create the business cycle.

Another practical implication of the classical dichotomy is that it simplifies your task of learning macroeconomics. It allows you to take it in bite-size pieces rather than in one big meal. The subject conveniently divides into the following parts:

- The real economy (Chapters 8–10)
- The money (nominal) economy (Chapters 11–13)
- Economic fluctuations (Chapters 14–18)

In this chapter and the two that follow it, you will learn about the real economy and the process of economic growth. You will then study the nominal economy and the forces that bring inflation. Finally, you will see how real and nominal forces interact to bring about the business cycle. You will also review the ongoing debate about how the government and the Federal Reserve can use policies to improve economic performance. But first, this chapter places the full-employment economy in a broader perspective by previewing the *AS-AD* model.

8.1 THE *AS-AD* MODEL

We are going to begin this chapter with a preview of the aggregate supply–aggregate demand (or *AS-AD*) model, which provides a framework for thinking about all three of the big macroeconomic issues—standard of living, cost of living, and economic fluctuations. What you will learn in this chapter is an outline, the details of which we will fill in as you progress through the rest of your study of macroeconomics. But keeping this outline in view will help you to navigate through the rest of your course.

As its name suggests, the *AS-AD* model applies to the economy as a whole—the aggregate or total economy—the ideas of supply and demand that you studied in Chapter 4. We'll explore the *AS-AD* model by looking at

- Aggregate supply
- Aggregate demand
- Macroeconomic equilibrium

Aggregate Supply

AOL-Time Warner, ExxonMobil, Intel, Boeing, and every other business in the United States, large and small, have wage agreements with their workers that run for a year or more into the future. They also have loan, rental, and long-term supply agreements. Most of these agreements are specified in nominal terms—in dollars. They commit firms to pay agreed dollar amounts.

When firms make long-term commitments to pay agreed dollar amounts, they make bets about the future prices they will be able to obtain for their products. If their bets are accurate and the prices they obtain turn out to be what they expected, each firm operates at its desired output rate and the economy operates at full employment. The level of real GDP that the economy would produce if it were at full employment is called **potential GDP**.

Potential GDP
The level of real GDP that the economy would produce if it were at full employment.

If the prices that firms can obtain for their products fall below the levels they expected, the firms take defensive actions. For some of the firms, the fall in price brings layoffs and a decrease in production. For other firms, the fall in prices is more serious: It shuts the firms down and destroys jobs. Real GDP decreases.

If in a happier time for businesses, the prices that they can obtain for their products rise above the levels they expected, they act to take advantage of the higher prices. Existing firms hire new workers and increase production. New firms set up, hire workers, and start to produce. Real GDP increases.

We've just described the actions of firms that generate **aggregate supply**—the relationship between the quantity of real GDP supplied and the price level when all other influences on production plans remain the same. This relationship can be described as follows:

Aggregate supply
The relationship between the quantity of real GDP supplied and the price level when all other influences on production plans remain the same.

Other things remaining the same, the higher the price level, the greater is the quantity of real GDP supplied, and the lower the price level, the smaller is the quantity of real GDP supplied.

Figure 8.1 illustrates aggregate supply as an aggregate supply schedule and aggregate supply curve. The aggregate supply schedule lists the quantities of real GDP supplied at each price level, and the upward-sloping *AS* curve graphs these points. The figure also shows potential GDP: $10 trillion in the figure.

FIGURE 8.1

Aggregate Supply Schedule and Aggregate Supply Curve

Practice Online

The aggregate supply schedule and aggregate supply curve, *AS*, show the relationship between the quantity of real GDP supplied and the price level when all other influences on production plans remain the same. Each point *A* through *E* on the *AS* curve corresponds to the row identified by the same letter in the schedule.

1. Potential GDP is $10 trillion and when the price level is 110, real GDP equals potential GDP.
2. If the price level is above 110, real GDP exceeds potential GDP.
3. If the price level is below 110, real GDP is less than potential GDP.

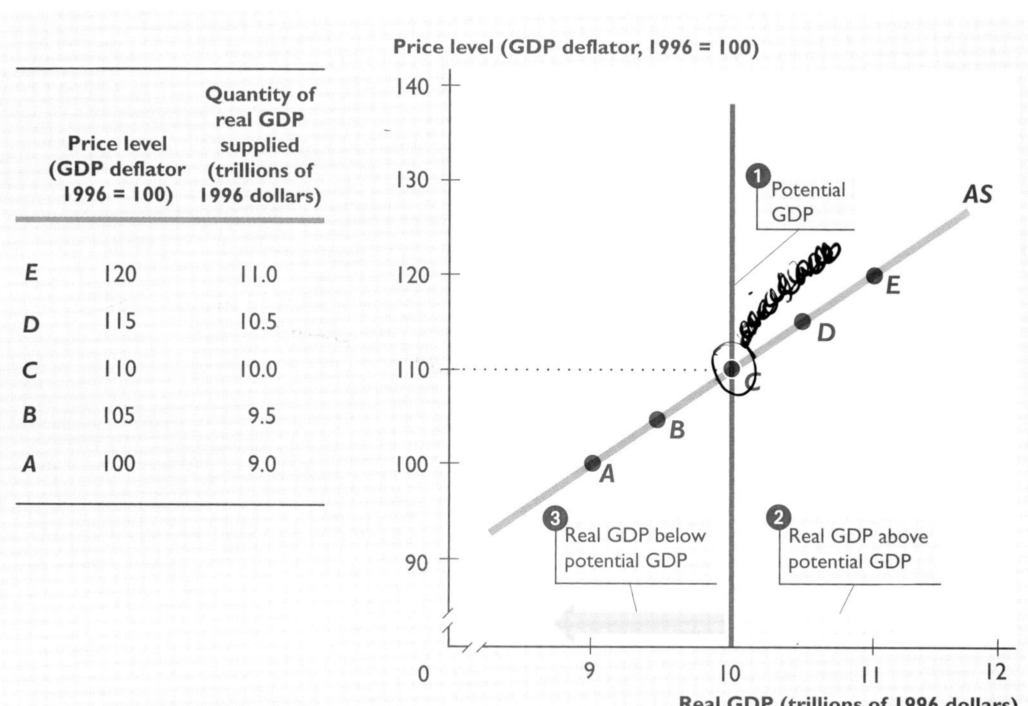

	Price level (GDP deflator 1996 = 100)	Quantity of real GDP supplied (trillions of 1996 dollars)
E	120	11.0
D	115	10.5
C	110	10.0
B	105	9.5
A	100	9.0

When the price level is 110, the quantity of real GDP supplied is $10 trillion, which equals potential GDP (at point *C* on the *AS* curve). If the price level is above 110, the quantity of real GDP supplied exceeds potential GDP; if the price level is below 110, the quantity of real GDP supplied is less than potential GDP. These departures from potential GDP, especially on the upside, can occur only temporarily while firms' money costs are fixed.

Changes in Aggregate Supply

Aggregate supply changes when potential GDP changes. As potential GDP increases, aggregate supply increases and the *AS* curve shifts rightward. Aggregate supply also changes when the money wage rate or any other money costs such as the price of oil changes. A rise in the money wage rate or in the price of oil raises firms' costs, decreases aggregate supply, and shifts the *AS* curve leftward.

Aggregate Demand

You and the other 290 million people in the United States have some money in the bank, some debts, and some available funds on your credit card, all of which influence your spending plans. Firms also have funds available for spending on new capital. All of these funds and lines of credit are set in nominal terms—in dollars.

Suppose that suddenly, the prices that we must all pay for the things that we buy increase. With a fall in the buying power of money, people scale back their consumption expenditure plans and firms scale back their investment plans. Foreigners buy less of our production, so exports decrease.

In a happier time for buyers, the prices that we must pay for the things that we buy decrease. With a rise in the buying power of money, people increase consumption expenditure and businesses increase investment. Foreigners buy more of our production, so exports increase.

We've just described the actions of households, firms, and foreigners that generate **aggregate demand**—the relationship between the quantity of real GDP demanded and the price level when all other influences on expenditure plans remain the same. This relationship can be described as follows:

Aggregate demand
The relationship between the quantity of real GDP demanded and the price level when all other influences on expenditure plans remain the same.

Other things remaining the same, the higher the price level, the smaller is the quantity of real GDP demanded, and the lower the price level, the greater is the quantity of real GDP demanded.

Figure 8.2 illustrates aggregate demand by using an aggregate demand schedule and aggregate demand curve. The aggregate demand schedule lists the quantities of real GDP demanded at each price level, and the downward-sloping *AD* curve graphs these points.

Changes in Aggregate Demand

Many factors change aggregate demand and shift the *AD* curve. Here, we will just list the major ones. A fall in the interest rate, an increase in the quantity of money in the economy, an increase in government purchases or a tax cut, and an increase in real GDP in the rest of the world all stimulate spending and increase aggregate demand. Changes in these variables in the opposite direction decrease aggregate demand. (Chapters 14 and 15 explain these influences.)

FIGURE 8.2
Aggregate Demand Schedule and Aggregate Demand Curve

Practice Online

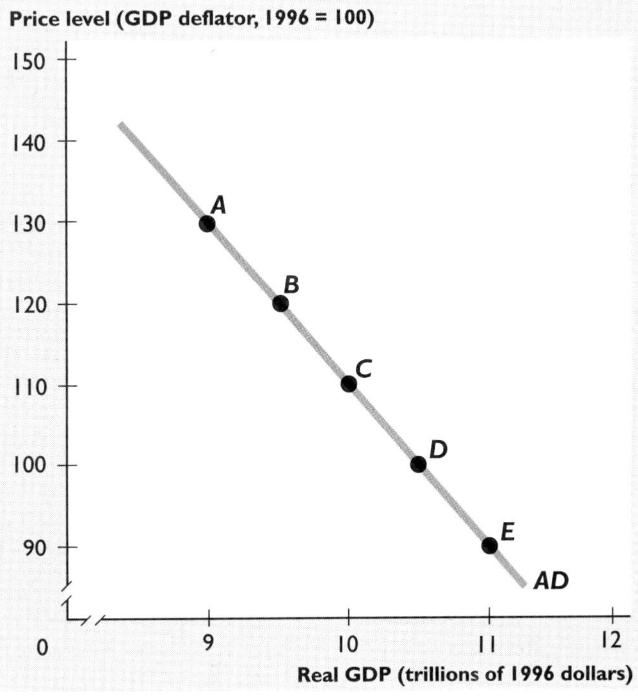

	Price level (GDP deflator 1996 = 100)	Quantity of real GDP demanded (trillions of 1996 dollars)
A	130	9.0
B	120	9.5
C	110	10.0
D	100	10.5
E	90	11.0

The aggregate demand schedule and aggregate demand curve, *AD*, show the relationship between the quantity of real GDP demanded and the price level when all other influences on expenditure plans remain the same. Each point *A* through *E* on the *AD* curve corresponds to the row identified by the same letter in the schedule.

Macroeconomic Equilibrium

Macroeconomic equilibrium
When the quantity of real GDP demanded equals the quantity of real GDP supplied at the point of intersection of the *AD* curve and the *AS* curve.

Aggregate supply and aggregate demand determine real GDP and the price level. **Macroeconomic equilibrium** occurs when the quantity of real GDP demanded equals the quantity of real GDP supplied at the point of intersection of the *AD* curve and the *AS* curve. Figure 8.3(a) shows such an equilibrium at a price level of 110 and real GDP of $10 trillion.

To see why this position is the equilibrium, think about what happens if the price level is something other than 110. Suppose that the price level is 120 and that real GDP is $11 trillion (point *E* on the *AS* curve). The quantity of real GDP demanded is less than $11 trillion, so firms are unable to sell all their output. Unwanted inventories pile up, and firms cut production and prices until they can sell all their output, which occurs only when real GDP is $10 trillion and the price level is 110.

Now suppose the price level is 100 and real GDP is $9 trillion (point *A* on the *AS* curve). The quantity of real GDP demanded exceeds $9 trillion, so firms are unable to meet the demand for their output. Inventories decrease, and customers clamor for goods and services. So firms increase production and raise prices until firms can meet demand, which occurs only when real GDP is $10 trillion and the price level is 110.

FIGURE 8.3
Macroeconomic Equilibrium

Practice Online

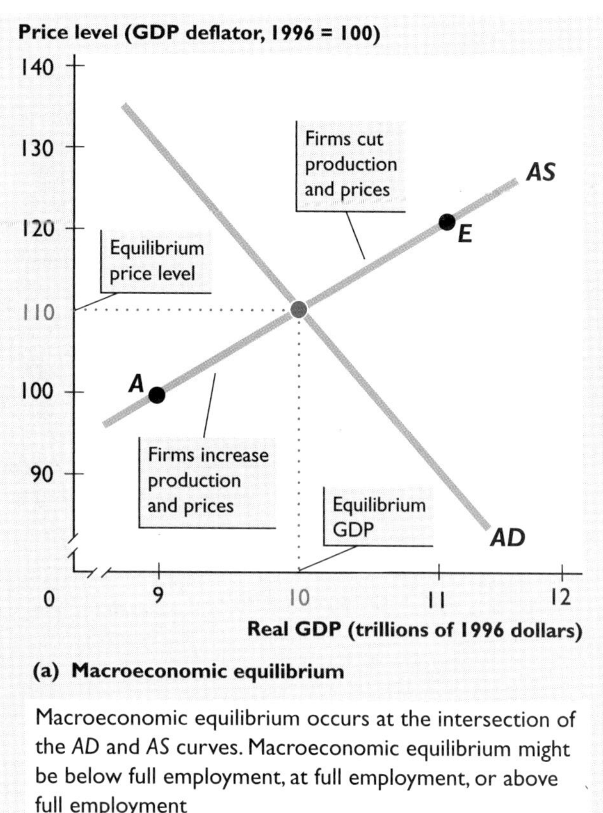

(a) Macroeconomic equilibrium

Macroeconomic equilibrium occurs at the intersection of the *AD* and *AS* curves. Macroeconomic equilibrium might be below full employment, at full employment, or above full employment

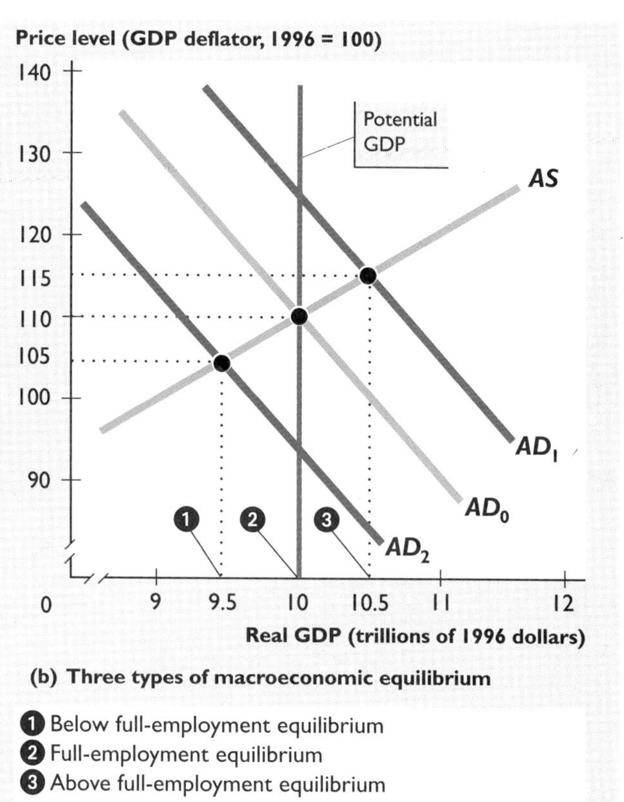

(b) Three types of macroeconomic equilibrium

1. Below full-employment equilibrium
2. Full-employment equilibrium
3. Above full-employment equilibrium

In macroeconomic equilibrium, the economy might be at full employment or above or below full employment, and Figure 8.3(b) shows these three possibilities. **Full-employment equilibrium**—equilibrium real GDP equals potential GDP—occurs where AD_0 intersects the aggregate supply curve AS. Fluctuations in aggregate demand bring fluctuations in real GDP around potential GDP. If aggregate demand increases to AD_1, firms increase production and raise prices until they can meet the higher demand. Real GDP increases to \$10.5 trillion and exceeds potential GDP in an **above full-employment equilibrium**. If aggregate demand decreases to AD_2, firms decrease production and cut prices until they can sell all their output. Real GDP decreases to \$9.5 trillion and is less than potential GDP in a **below full-employment equilibrium**.

Full-employment equilibrium
When equilibrium real GDP equals potential GDP.

Above full-employment equilibrium
When equilibrium real GDP exceeds potential GDP.

Below full-employment equilibrium
When potential GDP exceeds equilibrium real GDP.

Eye on the U.S. Economy

Real GDP Growth, Inflation, and the Business Cycle

Each dot in the figure represents a year. In 1970, potential GDP was \$3.6 trillion. Real GDP was also \$3.6 trillion, and the price level was 29 at the intersection of aggregate demand curve AD_{70} and aggregate supply curve AS_{70}. The economy was in a full-employment equilibrium.

By 2002, potential GDP was \$9.5 trillion. Real GDP was \$9.4 trillion, and the price level was 111 at the intersection of aggregate demand curve AD_{02} and aggregate supply curve AS_{02}. The economy was in a below full-employment equilibrium.

Real GDP grows over time because potential GDP grows. Inflation occurs because aggregate demand increases more rapidly than aggregate supply.

Business cycles occur because aggregate demand and aggregate supply fluctuate. A recession caused by a jump in world oil prices occurred in the mid-1970s. Other recessions occurred in 1982 and 1991–1992. And a very mild recession, not visible in the figure, occurred in 2001.

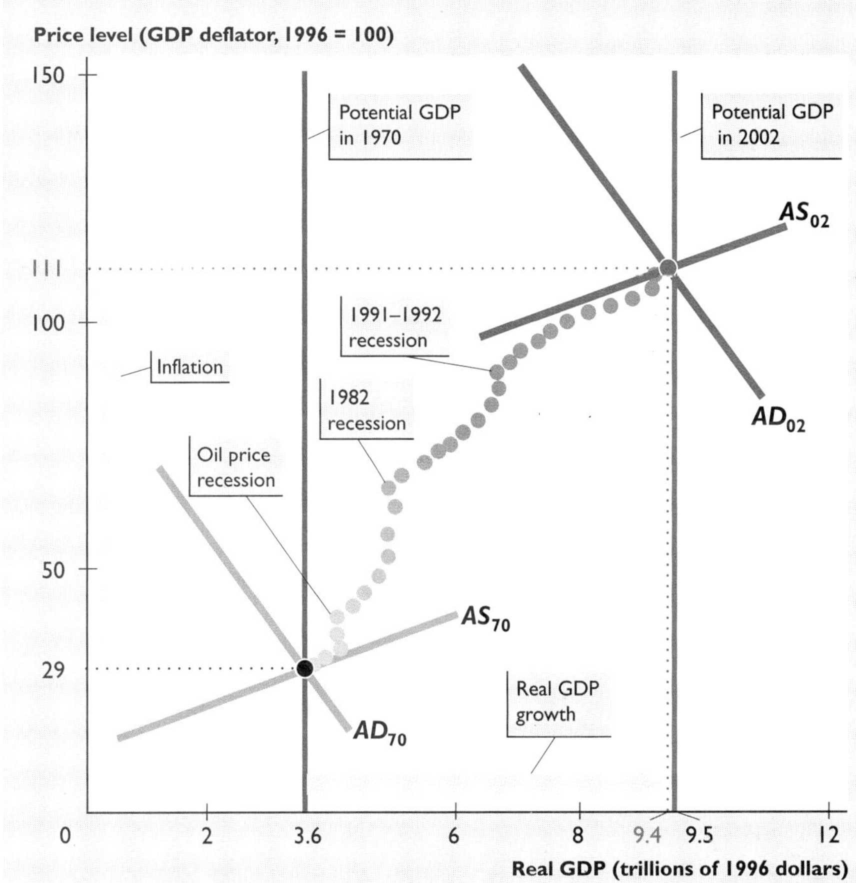

SOURCES: Bureau of Economic Analysis and Congressional Budget Office.

CHECKPOINT 8.1

Study Guide pp. 113–116

Practice Online 8.1

TABLE 1

Price level (GDP deflator)	Real GDP demanded	Real GDP supplied
	(billions of 1995 pounds)	
90	800	650
100	775	700
110	750	750
120	725	800
130	700	850

TABLE 2

Price level (GDP deflator)	Real GDP demanded	Real GDP supplied
	(billions of 1996 dollars)	
95	430	370
105	420	390
115	410	410
125	400	430
135	390	450

FIGURE 1

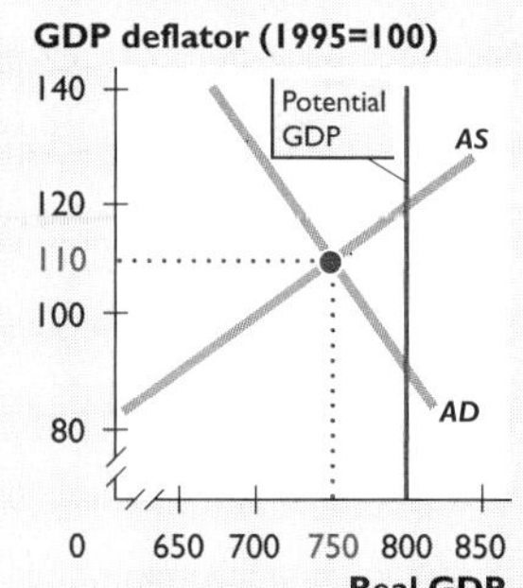

FIGURE 2

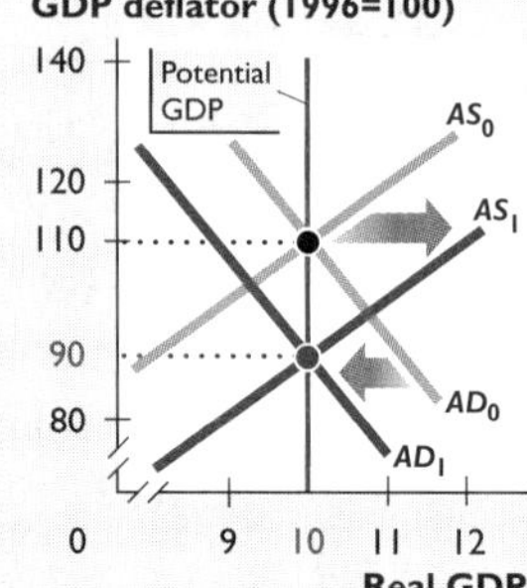

1 **Preview the aggregate supply–aggregate demand (*AS-AD*) model and explain why real GDP and unemployment fluctuate in a business cycle.**

Practice Problems 8.1

1. Table 1 shows aggregate demand and aggregate supply schedules for the United Kingdom.
   a. Plot the aggregate demand curve.
   b. Plot the aggregate supply curve.
   c. What is the macroeconomic equilibrium?
   d. If potential GDP in the United Kingdom is £800 billon, what is the type of macroeconomic equilibrium?
2. The U.S economy is at full employment when the following events occur:
   - A deep recession hits the world economy, and real GDP in the rest of thc world decreases.
   - The world oil price tumbles.

   a. Explain the effect of each event separately on aggregate demand and aggregate supply in the United States.
   b. Explain the combined effect of the two events on the U.S. price level and real GDP.

Exercises 8.1

1. Table 2 shows aggregate demand and aggregate supply schedules for Australia.
   a. Plot the aggregate demand curve.
   b. Plot the aggregate supply curve.
   c. What is the macroeconomic equilibrium?
   d. If potential GDP in Australia is $380 billion, what is the type of macroeconomic equilibrium?
2. The Canadian economy is at full employment when the following events occur:
   - A strong expansion increases real GDP in the United States.
   - The Canadian government cuts taxes.

   a. Explain the effect of each event separately on Canadian aggregate demand and aggregate supply.
   b. Explain the combined effect of the two events on the Canadian price level and real GDP.

Solutions to Practice Problems 8.1

1. Figure 1 shows the *AD* and *AS* curves and potential GDP. Real GDP is less than potential GDP, so the economy is at a below full-employment equilibrium.

2a. A decrease in real GDP in the rest of the world decreases U.S. exports and so decreases U.S. aggregate demand. The *AD* curve shifts leftward. A fall in the world oil price lowers firms' costs and increases aggregate supply. The *AS* curve shifts rightward (Figure 2).

2b. Because *AD* decreases and *AS* increases, the price level falls. But real GDP might increase or decrease depending on which of the two changes is larger (Figure 2).

8.2 POTENTIAL GDP

Potential GDP is the level of real GDP that the economy would produce if it were at full employment (see Chapter 6, p. 152). It is vital to understand the forces that determine potential GDP for three reasons. First, when the economy is *at* full employment, real GDP equals potential GDP; so actual real GDP is determined by the same factors that determine potential GDP. Second, real GDP can exceed potential GDP only temporarily as it approaches and then recedes from a business cycle peak. So potential GDP is the *sustainable* upper limit of production. Third, real GDP fluctuates around potential GDP, which means that on the average over the business cycle, real GDP equals potential GDP.

We produce the goods and services that make up real GDP by using the *factors of production*: labor and human capital, physical capital, land (and natural resources), and entrepreneurship. At any given time, the quantities of capital, land, and entrepreneurship and the state of technology are fixed. But the quantity of labor is not fixed. It depends on the choices that people make about the allocation of time between work and leisure. So with fixed quantities of capital, land, and entrepreneurship and fixed technology, real GDP depends on the quantity of labor employed. To describe this relationship between real GDP and the quantity of labor employed, we use a relationship that is similar to the production possibilities frontier, which is called the production function.

Eye on the U.S. Economy

Potential GDP in the 1960s and 1990s

Back in the 1960s, we had six television channels, black vinyl phonograph records, rotary telephones, roller skates, cars that barely ran 10 miles on a gallon of gasoline, typewriters, and human telephone operators and bank tellers. By the 1990s, we had 600 television channels, MP3 and CDs, cell phones small enough to slip into our shirt pockets and smart enough to remember a hundred numbers, in-line skates, cars that ran 40 miles on a gallon of gasoline, PCs that we could talk to, and ATMs in every shopping mall and main street.

This chapter explains the forces that determined real GDP and the real wage rate on the average during these two decades.

The figure provides a snapshot of the contrasts and a similarity across these decades using some standard macroeconomic indicators.

Real GDP averaged $7.5 trillion (all the dollar values are 1996 dollars) during the 1990s but only $3.0 trillion during the 1960s. Real GDP per working-age person averaged $38,000 during the 1990s but only $23,000 during the 1960s. Real wage rates per hour of work averaged $20 during the 1990s but only $12.25 during the 1960s. But the share of GDP earned by labor was similar in the 1960s and the 1990s.

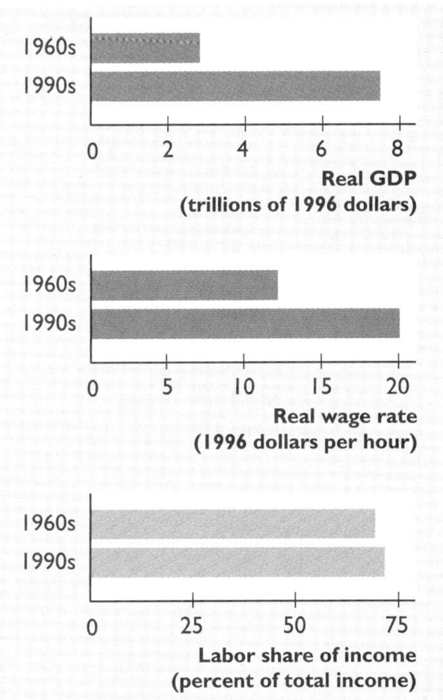

SOURCE: Bureau of Economic Analysis.

The Production Function

Production function
A relationship that shows the maximum quantity of real GDP that can be produced as the quantity of labor employed changes and all other influences on production remain the same.

The **production function** is a relationship that shows the maximum quantity of real GDP that can be produced as the quantity of labor employed changes and all other influences on production remain the same. Figure 8.4 shows a production function, which is the curve labeled *PF*.

In Figure 8.4, when 100 billion labor hours are employed, real GDP is $6 trillion (at point *A*). When 200 billion labor hours are employed, real GDP is $10 trillion (at point *B*). And when 300 billion labor hours are employed, real GDP is $12 trillion (at point *C*).

The production function shares a feature of the *production possibilities frontier* that you studied in Chapter 3 (p. 60). Like the *PPF*, the production function is a boundary between the attainable and the unattainable. It is possible to produce at any point along the production function and beneath it in the shaded area. But it is not possible to produce at points above the production function. Those points are unattainable.

Diminishing returns
The tendency for each additional hour of labor employed to produce a successively smaller additional amount of real GDP.

The production function displays **diminishing returns**—each additional hour of labor employed produces a successively smaller additional amount of real GDP. The first 100 billion hours of labor produces $6 trillion of real GDP. The second 100 billion hours of labor increases real GDP to $10 trillion and so produces only an

FIGURE 8.4
The Production Function

Practice Online

The production function shows the maximum level of real GDP that can be produced as the quantity of labor employed changes and all other influences on production remain the same. The production function separates attainable combinations of labor hours and real GDP from unattainable combinations and displays diminishing returns: Each additional hour of labor produces a successively smaller additional amount of real GDP. In this example, 100 billion hours of labor can produce $6 trillion of real GDP at point *A*, 200 billion hours of labor can produce $10 trillion of real GDP at point *B*, and 300 billion hours of labor can produce $12 trillion of real GDP at point *C*.

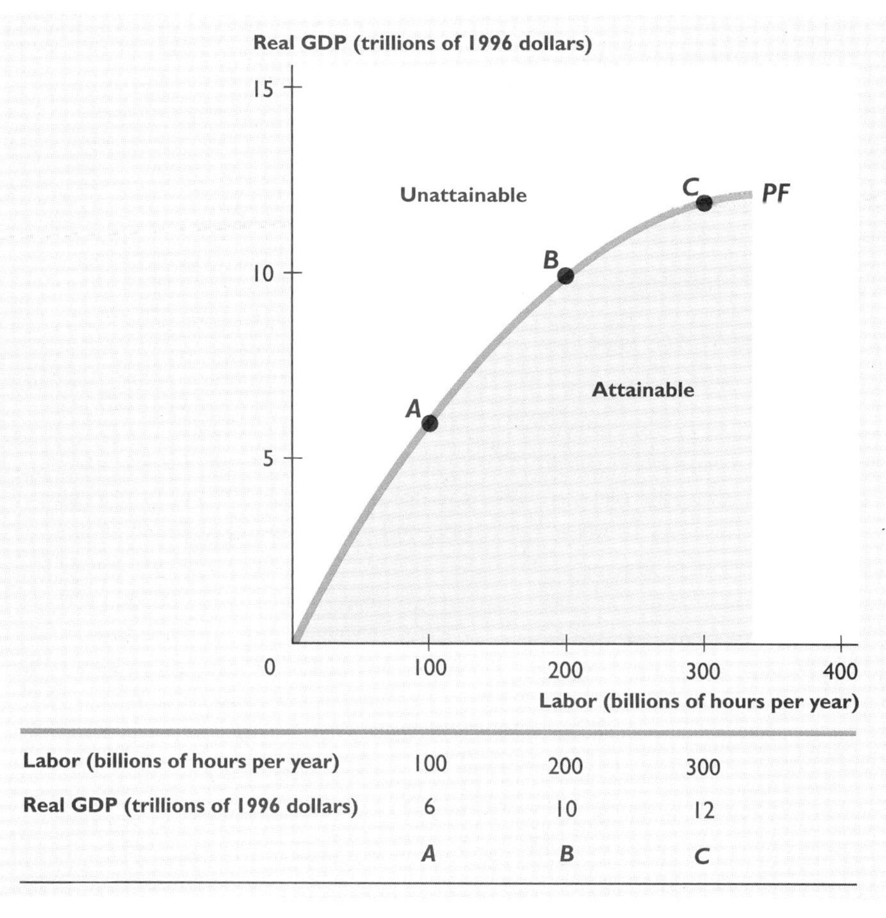

Labor (billions of hours per year)	100	200	300
Real GDP (trillions of 1996 dollars)	6	10	12
	A	B	C

additional $4 trillion of real GDP. The third 100 billion hours of labor increases real GDP to $12 trillion and so produces only an additional $2 trillion of real GDP.

Diminishing returns arise because the quantity of capital (and other factors of production) is fixed. As more labor is hired, the additional output produced decreases because the extra workers have less capital to work with. For example, a forest service has three chain saws and an axe and hires three workers to clear roads and trails of fallen trees and debris during the spring thaw. Hiring a fourth worker will contribute less to the amount cleared than the third worker added and hiring a fifth worker will add even less.

Because real GDP depends on the quantity of labor employed, potential GDP depends on the point on the production function at which the economy operates. To find that point, we must understand what determines the quantity of labor employed.

The Labor Market

You've already studied the tool that we use to determine the quantity of labor employed: demand and supply. In macroeconomics, we apply the concepts of demand, supply, and market equilibrium to economy-wide markets. In the present case, we apply it to the economy-wide labor market.

The quantity of labor employed depends on firms' decisions about how much labor to hire (the demand for labor). It also depends on households' decisions about how to allocate time between employment and other activities (the supply of labor). And it depends on how the labor market coordinates the decisions of firms and households (labor market equilibrium). So we will study

- The demand for labor
- The supply of labor
- Labor market equilibrium

The Demand for Labor

The **quantity of labor demanded** is the total labor hours that all the firms in the economy plan to hire during a given time period at a given real wage rate. The **demand for labor** is the relationship between the quantity of labor demanded and the real wage rate when all other influences on firms' hiring plans remain the same. The lower the real wage rate, the greater is the quantity of labor demanded.

The real wage rate is the *nominal wage rate* (the dollars per hour that people earn on the average) divided by the price level (see Chapter 7, p. 172). We express the real wage rate in constant dollars—today in 1996 dollars. Think about the real wage rate as the quantity of real GDP that an hour of labor earns.

The lower the real wage rate, the greater is the quantity of labor that firms find it profitable to hire. The real wage rate influences the quantity of labor demanded because what matters to firms is not the number of dollars they pay for an hour of labor (the nominal wage rate) but how much output they must sell to earn those dollars. So firms compare the extra output that an hour of labor can produce with the real wage rate.

Firms are in business to maximize profit. So they hire labor as long as each additional hour hired produces at least as much additional output as the real wage rate. When a small quantity of labor is hired, an extra hour of labor produces more output than the real wage rate. But each additional hour of labor produces less additional output than the previous hour. As a firm hires more labor, eventually

Quantity of labor demanded
The total labor hours that all the firms in the economy plan to hire during a given time period at a given real wage rate.

Demand for labor
The relationship between the quantity of labor demanded and real wage rate when all other influences on firms' hiring plans remain the same.

the extra output from an extra hour of labor exactly equals the real wage rate. This equality determines the quantity of labor demanded at the real wage rate.

The Demand for Labor in a Soda Factory You can understand the demand for labor better by thinking about a single firm rather than the economy as a whole. Suppose that the money wage rate is $15 an hour. And suppose that the price of a bottle of soda is $1.50. For the soda factory, the real wage rate is a number of bottles of soda. To find the soda factory's real wage rate, divide the money wage rate by the price of its output—$15 an hour ÷ $1.50 a bottle = 10 bottles of soda an hour. It costs the soda factory 10 bottles of soda to hire an hour of labor. As long as the soda factory can hire labor that produces more than 10 additional bottles of soda an hour, it is profitable to hire more labor. Only when the extra output produced by an extra hour of labor falls to 10 bottles an hour has the factory reached the profit-maximizing quantity of labor.

Labor Demand Schedule and Labor Demand Curve We can represent the demand for labor as either a demand schedule or a demand curve. The table in Figure 8.5 shows part of a demand for labor schedule. It tells us the quantity of labor demanded at three different real wage rates. For example, if the real wage rate is $30 an hour (row *B*), the quantity of labor demanded is 200 billion hours a year. If the real wage rate rises to $50 an hour (row *A*), the quantity of labor demanded decreases to 100 billion hours a year. And if the real wage rate falls to $10 an hour (row *C*), the quantity of labor demanded increases to 300 billion hours a year.

Figure 8.5 shows the demand for labor curve. Points *A*, *B*, and *C* on the demand curve correspond to rows *A*, *B*, and *C* of the demand schedule.

FIGURE 8.5
The Demand for Labor

Practice Online

Firms are willing to hire labor only if it produces more than the real wage rate it costs. So the lower the real wage rate, the more labor firms can profitably hire and the greater is the quantity of labor demanded.

At a real wage rate of $30 an hour, the quantity of labor demanded is 200 billion hours at point *B*.

❶ If the real wage rate rises to $50 an hour, the quantity of labor demanded decreases to 100 billion hours at point *A*.

❷ If the real wage rate falls to $10 an hour, the quantity of labor demanded increases to 300 billion hours at point *C*.

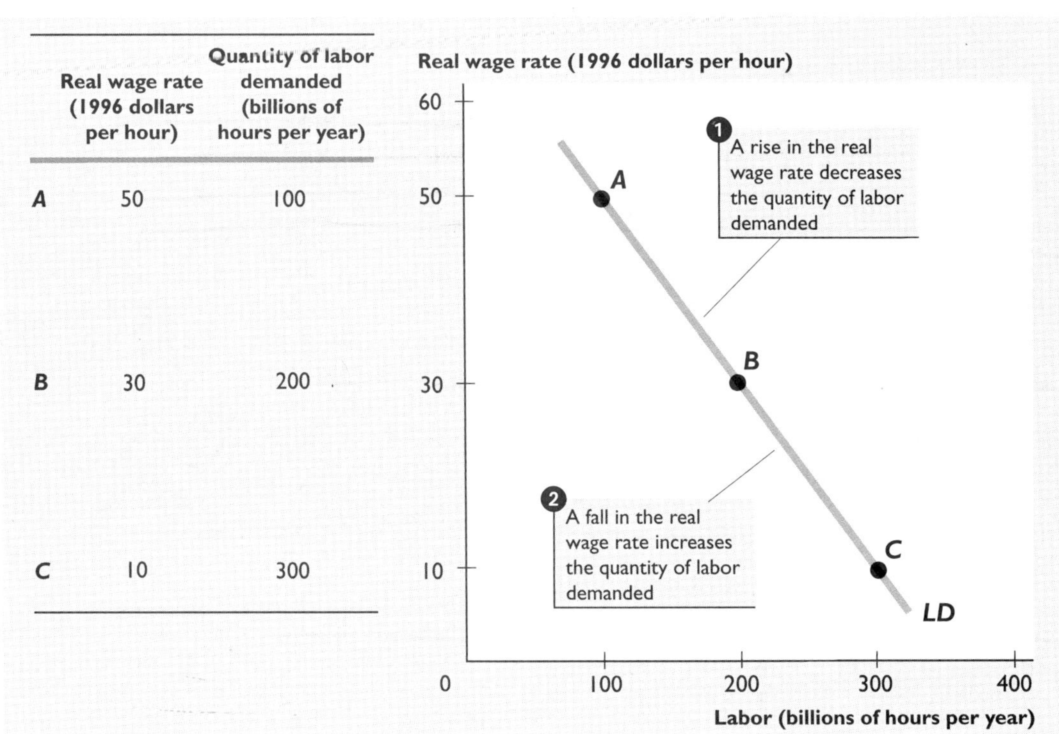

	Real wage rate (1996 dollars per hour)	Quantity of labor demanded (billions of hours per year)
A	50	100
B	30	200
C	10	300

The Supply of Labor

The **quantity of labor supplied** is the number of labor hours that all the households in the economy plan to work during a given time period at a given real wage rate. The **supply of labor** is the relationship between the quantity of labor supplied and the real wage rate when all other influences on work plans remain the same.

Quantity of labor supplied
The number of labor hours that all the households in the economy plan to work during a given time period at a given real wage rate.

Supply of labor
The relationship between the quantity of labor supplied and the real wage rate when all other influences on work plans remain the same.

We can represent the supply of labor as either a supply schedule or a supply curve. The table in Figure 8.6 shows a supply of labor schedule. It tells us the quantity of labor supplied at three different real wage rates. For example, if the real wage rate is $30 an hour (row *B*), the quantity of labor supplied is 200 billion hours a year. If the real wage rate falls to $15 an hour (row *A*) the quantity of labor supplied decreases to 100 billion hours a year. And if the real wage rate rises to $50 an hour (row *C*), the quantity of labor supplied increases to 300 billion hours a year.

Figure 8.6 shows the supply of labor curve. It corresponds to the supply schedule, and the points *A*, *B*, and *C* on the curve correspond to the rows *A*, *B*, and *C* of the supply schedule.

The real wage rate influences the quantity of labor supplied because what matters to people is not the number of dollars they earn but what those dollars will buy.

The quantity of labor supplied increases as the real wage rate increases for two reasons:

- Hours per person increase.
- Labor force participation increases.

FIGURE 8.6
The Supply of Labor

Practice Online

	Real wage rate (1996 dollars per hour)	Quantity of labor supplied (billions of hours per year)
C	50	300
B	30	200
A	15	100

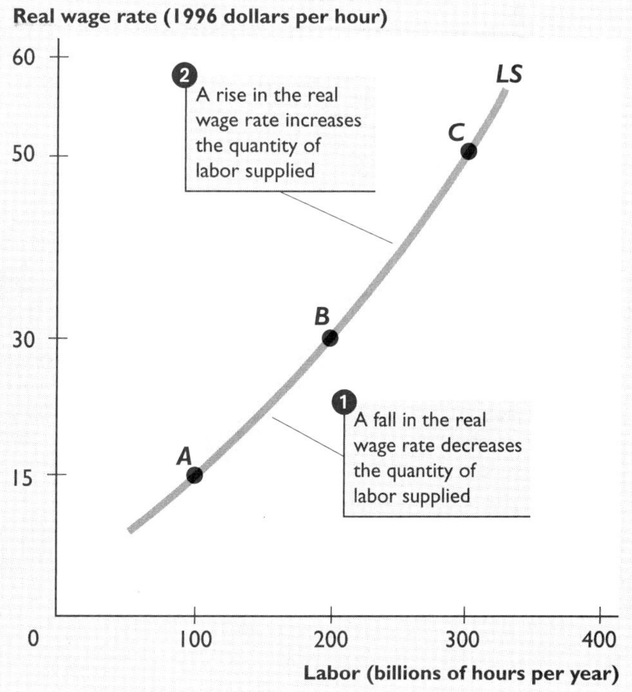

Households are willing to supply labor only if the real wage rate is high enough to attract them from other activities. The higher the real wage rate, the greater is the quantity of labor supplied.

At a real wage rate of $30 an hour, the quantity of labor supplied is 200 billion hours at point *B*. **1** If the real wage rate falls to $15 an hour, the quantity of labor supplied decreases to 100 billion hours at point *A*. **2** If the real wage rate rises to $50 an hour, the quantity of labor supplied increases to 300 billion hours at point *C*.

Hours per Person In choosing how many hours to work, a household considers the opportunity cost of not working. This opportunity cost is the real wage rate. The higher the real wage rate, the greater is the opportunity cost of taking leisure and not working. And as the opportunity cost of taking leisure rises, other things remaining the same, the more the household chooses to work.

But other things don't remain the same. The higher the real wage rate, the greater is the household's income. And the higher the household's income, the more the household wants to consume. One item that it wants to consume more of is leisure.

So a rise in the real wage rate has two opposing effects. By increasing the opportunity cost of leisure, it makes the household want to consume less leisure and to work more. And by increasing the household's income, it makes the household want to consume more leisure and to work fewer hours—an effect called the backward-bending supply response. For most households, the opportunity cost effect is stronger than the income effect. So the higher the real wage rate, the greater is the amount of work that the household chooses to do. That is, the labor supply curve always slopes upward.

Labor Force Participation Most people have productive opportunities outside the labor force and choose to work only if the real wage rate exceeds the value of other productive activities. For example, a parent might spend time caring for her or his child. The alternative is day care. The parent will choose to work only if he or she can earn enough per hour to pay the cost of day care and have enough left to make the work effort worthwhile. The higher the real wage rate, the more likely it is that a parent will choose to work and so the greater is the labor force participation rate.

Labor Supply Response The quantity of labor supplied increases as the real wage rate rises. But the quantity of labor supplied is not highly responsive to the real wage rate. A large percentage change in the real wage rate brings a small percentage change in the quantity of labor supplied.

Let's now see how the labor market determines employment, the real wage rate, and potential GDP.

Labor Market Equilibrium

Figure 8.7(a) shows the labor market equilibrium. The demand curve and the supply curve are the same as those in Figures 8.5 and 8.6. The forces of supply and demand operate in labor markets just as they do in the markets for goods and services. The price of labor is the real wage rate. A rise in the real wage rate eliminates a shortage of labor by decreasing the quantity demanded and increasing the quantity supplied. A fall in the real wage rate eliminates a surplus of labor by increasing the quantity demanded and decreasing the quantity supplied. If there is neither a shortage nor a surplus, the labor market is in equilibrium.

In Figure 8.7(a), if the real wage rate is less than $30 an hour, the quantity of labor demanded exceeds the quantity supplied and there is a shortage of labor. In this situation, the real wage rate rises.

If the real wage rate exceeds $30 an hour, the quantity of labor supplied exceeds the quantity demanded and there is a surplus of labor. In this situation, the real wage rate falls.

If the real wage rate is $30 an hour, the quantity of labor demanded equals the quantity supplied and there is neither a shortage nor a surplus of labor. In this

FIGURE 8.7
Labor Market Equilibrium and Potential GDP

Practice Online

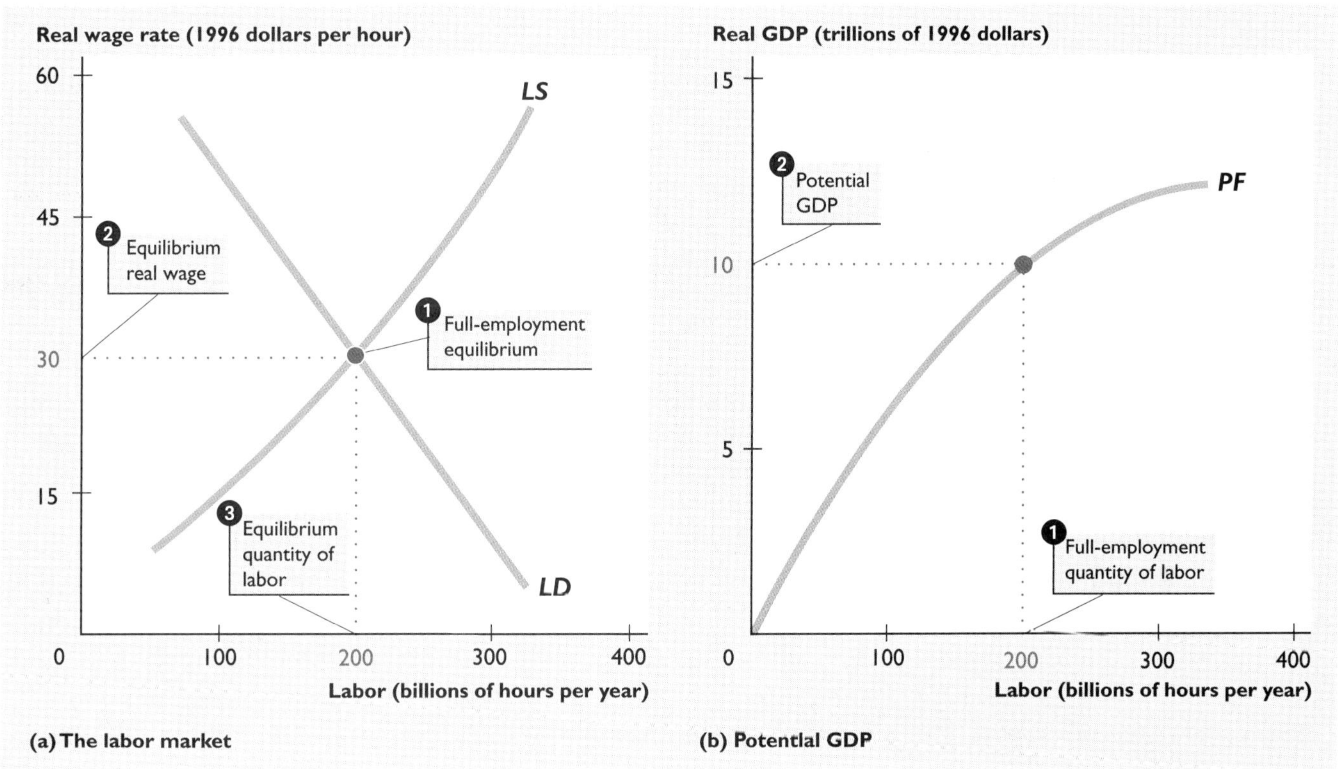

❶ Full employment occurs when the quantity of labor demanded equals the quantity of labor supplied. ❷ The equilibrium real wage rate is \$30 an hour, and ❸ equilibrium employment is 200 billion hours a year.

Potential GDP is the real GDP produced on the production function by the full-employment quantity of labor. ❶ The full-employment quantity of labor, 200 billion hours a year, produces a ❷ potential GDP of \$10 trillion.

situation, the labor market is in equilibrium and the real wage rate remains constant. The equilibrium level of employment is 200 billion hours a year. At the equilibrium level of employment, there is full employment. So full employment is 200 billion hours a year.

Full Employment and Potential GDP

You've seen that the quantity of real GDP depends on the quantity of labor employed. The production function tells us how much real GDP a given amount of employment can produce. Now that we've determined the full-employment quantity of labor, we can find potential GDP.

Figure 8.7(b) shows the relationship between labor market equilibrium and potential GDP. The equilibrium quantity of labor employed in Figure 8.7(a) is 200 billion hours. The production function in Figure 8.7(b) tells us that 200 billion hours of labor produces \$10 trillion of real GDP. This level of real GDP is potential GDP.

When the labor market is in equilibrium, the economy is at full employment and real GDP equals potential GDP.

The Functional Distribution of Income

We can use the full-employment model to explain the *functional distribution of income*—the percentage distribution of income among labor and other factors of production (Chapter 2, p. 39). The quantity of labor employed is 200 billion hours and the wage rate is $30 an hour, so labor earns 200 billion hours multiplied by $30 an hour, which equals $6 trillion. Real GDP is $10 trillion, so the other factors of production earn the remaining $4 trillion. In this economy, labor's share of real GDP is 60 percent and the shares of the other factors of production sum to 40 percent.

Eye on the U.S. Economy

Explaining the Differences Between the 1960s and 1990s

Labor was 90 percent more productive in the 1990s than in the 1960s, so the production function shifted upward from PF_{60s} to PF_{90s}, and the demand for labor curve shifted rightward from LD_{60s} to LD_{90s}. The working-age population was 50 percent larger in the 1990s than in the 1960s, so the labor supply curve shifted rightward from LS_{60s} to LS_{90s}. The real wage rate increased from $12.25 to $20 an hour; the quantity of labor employed increased from 136 billion hours to 214 billion hours a year. Potential GDP increased from $3 trillion to $7.5 trillion.

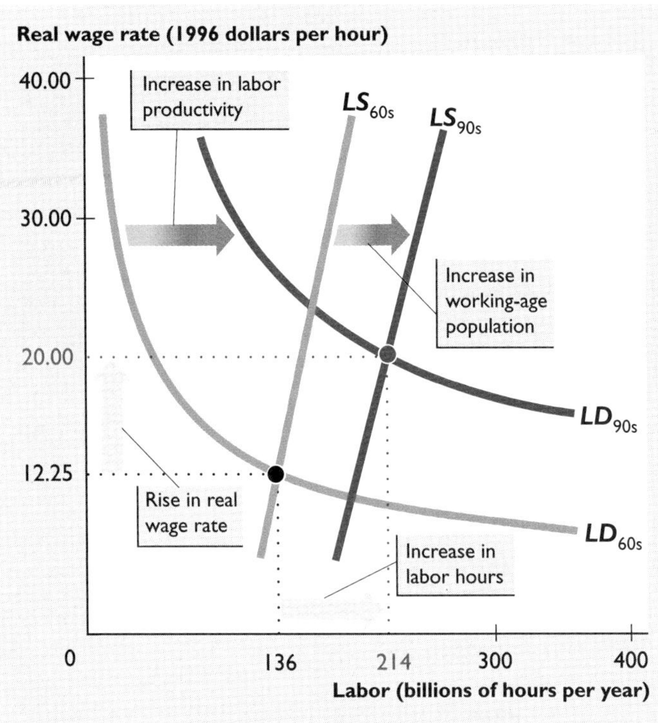

(a) The labor market

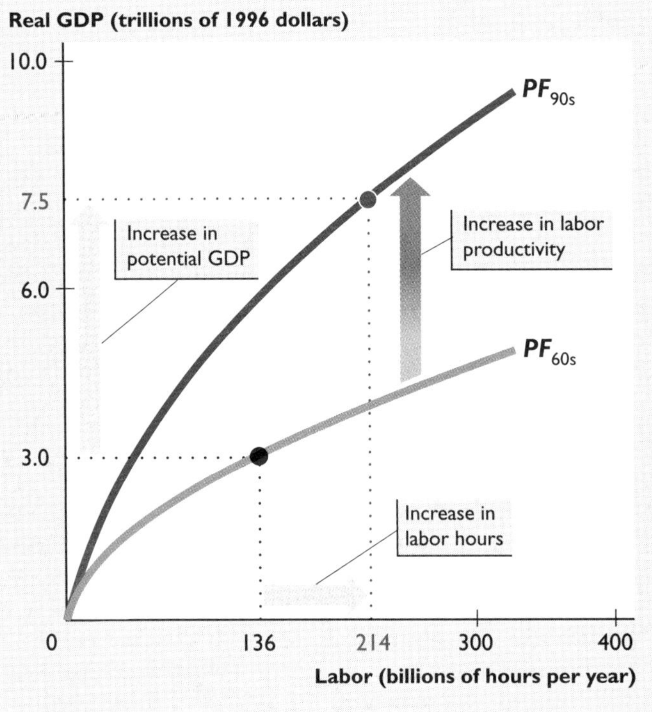

(b) The production function

CHECKPOINT 8.2

2 **Explain the forces that determine potential GDP and the distribution of income between labor and other factors of production.**

Study Guide pp. 116–119

Practice Online 8.2

Practice Problem 8.2

Table 1 describes an economy's production function and its demand for labor.

Table 1

Quantity of labor demanded (billions of hours per year)	0	1	2	3	4
Real GDP (billions of 2001 dollars)	0	40	70	90	100
Real wage rate (2001 dollars per hour)	50	40	30	20	10

Table 2 describes the supply of labor in this economy.

Table 2

Quantity of labor supplied (billions of hours per year)	0	1	2	3	4
Real wage rate (2001 dollars per hour)	10	20	30	40	50

a. Make graphs of the production function and the labor market.
b. Find the equilibrium employment, real wage rate, and potential GDP.
c. What percentage of real GDP does labor earn?

Exercise 8.2

Table 3 describes an economy's production function and its demand for labor.

Table 3

Quantity of labor demanded (billions of hours per year)	0	1	2	3	4	5
Real GDP (billions of 2001 dollars)	0	5	9	12	14	15
Real wage rate (2001 dollars per hour)		5	4	3	2	1

Table 4 describes the supply of labor in this economy.

Table 4

Quantity of labor supplied (billions of hours per year)	0	1	2	3	4	5
Real wage rate (2001 dollars per hour)	1.50	2.00	2.50	3.00	3.50	4.00

a. Make graphs of the production function and the labor market.
b. Find the equilibrium employment, real wage rate, and potential GDP.
c. What percentage of real GDP does labor earn?

FIGURE 1

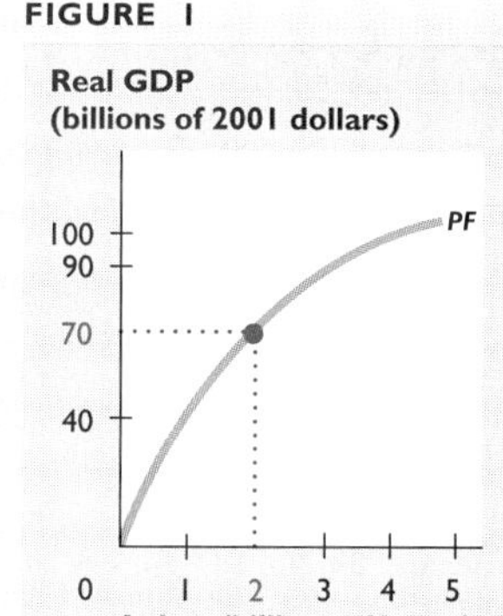

FIGURE 2

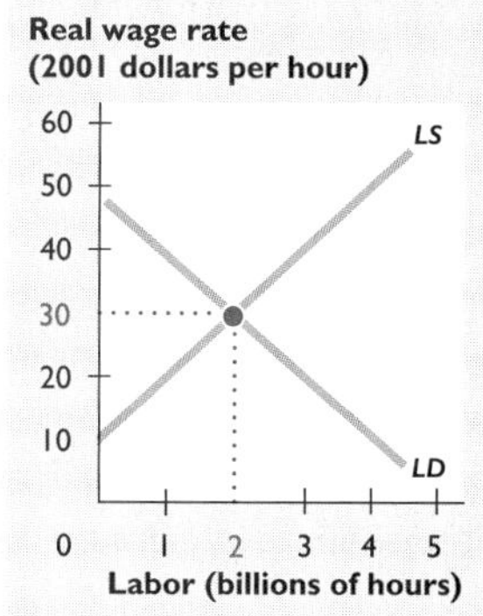

Solution to Practice Problem 8.2

a. The production function is a graph of the first two rows of Table 1 (Figure 1). The demand for labor is a graph of the first and last row of Table 1 and the supply of labor is a graph of the data in Table 2 (Figure 2).

b. Labor market equilibrium occurs when the real wage rate is \$30 an hour and 2 billion hours of labor are employed (Figure 2). Potential GDP is the real GDP produced by the equilibrium quantity of labor (2 billion hours in Figure 2). Potential GDP is \$70 billion (Figure 1).

c. Labor earns \$30 an hour on 2 billion hours, which equals \$60 billion. Real GDP is \$70 billion. So labor earns (\$60 billion ÷ \$70 billion) × 100 = 85.7 percent of real GDP.

8.3 THE NATURAL UNEMPLOYMENT RATE

So far, we've focused on the forces that determine the real wage rate, the quantity of labor employed, and real GDP at full employment. We're now going to bring unemployment into the picture.

You learned in Chapter 6 how unemployment is measured. And you learned how people become unemployed by losing or leaving their jobs and by entering or reentering the labor force. You also learned how we classify unemployment as frictional, structural, seasonal, or cyclical. Finally, you learned that the unemployment rate at full employment, which consists of frictional, structural, and seasonal unemployment, is called the *natural unemployment rate.*

Measuring, describing, and classifying unemployment tell us a lot about it. But these activities do not *explain* the amount of unemployment that exists or why its rate changes over time.

Many forces interact to determine the unemployment rate. Understanding these forces is a challenging task. Economists approach this task in two steps. The first step is to understand what determines the natural unemployment rate—the unemployment rate at full employment. The second step is to understand what makes unemployment fluctuate around the natural unemployment rate. In this chapter, we take the first of these steps. We take the second step in Chapters 14–18 when we study economic fluctuations.

Eye on the Past

Average Unemployment Rates over Five Decades

If we look back at the U.S. economy decade by decade, we can see through the ups and downs of the business cycle and focus on the broad trends. By looking at the average unemployment rates across the decades, we get an estimate of movements in the natural unemployment rate.

The figure shows these averages. During the 1950s and 1960s, the unemployment rate averaged less than 5 percent. During the 1970s, the average unemployment rate climbed to 6 percent, and in the 1980s it climbed to more than 7 percent. The 1990s saw the average unemployment rate fall, but not quite back to the rate of the 1950s and 1960s.

You will be a member of the labor force of the 2000s. And the average unemployment rate of the first decade of the 2000s will have a big effect on your job market success. Will the average unemployment rate of the 2000s fall further to the rate of the 1950s and 1960s? Or will it jump back to the rate of the 1980s? No one knows for sure. But what you learn in this section will help you understand the forces that are at work.

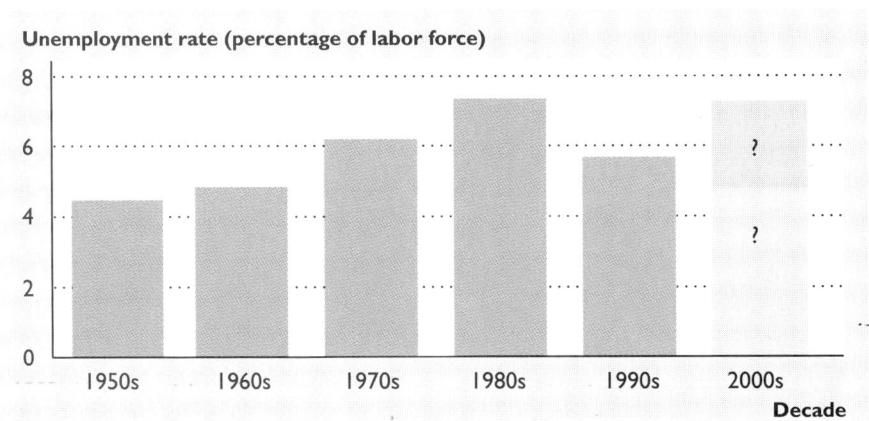

SOURCE: Bureau of Labor Statistics.

To understand the amount of frictional and structural unemployment that exists at the natural unemployment rate, economists focus on two fundamental causes of unemployment that cut across the frictional-structural classification. The two fundamental causes of unemployment are

- Job search
- Job rationing

Job Search

Job search is the activity of looking for an acceptable vacant job. There are always some people who have not yet found suitable jobs and who are actively searching for jobs. The reason is that the labor market is in a constant state of change. The failure of existing businesses destroys jobs. The expansion of existing businesses and the startup of new businesses that use new technologies and develop new markets create jobs. As people pass through different stages of life, some enter or reenter the labor market. Still others leave their jobs to look for better ones, and others retire. This constant churning in the labor market means that there are always some people looking for jobs, and these people are part of the unemployed.

Job search
The activity of looking for an acceptable vacant job.

The amount of job search depends on a number of factors that change over time. The main ones are

- Demographic change
- Unemployment benefits
- Structural change

Demographic Change

An increase in the proportion of the population that is of working age brings an increase in the entry rate into the labor force and an increase in the unemployment rate. This factor was important in the U.S. labor market during the 1970s. The bulge in the birth rate that occurred in the late 1940s and early 1950s increased the proportion of new entrants into the labor force during the 1970s and brought an increase in the unemployment rate.

As the birth rate declined, the bulge moved into higher age groups and the proportion of new entrants declined during the 1980s. During this period, the unemployment rate was decreasing.

Another source of demographic change has been an increase in the number of households with two incomes. When unemployment comes to one of these workers, it is possible, with income still flowing in, to take longer to find a new job. This factor might have increased frictional unemployment.

Unemployment Benefits

The length of time that an unemployed person spends searching for a job depends, in part, on the opportunity cost of job search. An unemployed person who receives no unemployment benefits faces a high opportunity cost of job search. In this situation, the search is likely to be short and the person is likely to accept a less attractive job that is found quickly rather than continue a costly search process. An unemployed person who receives generous unemployment benefits faces a lower opportunity cost of job search. In this situation, the unemployed worker will likely spend a long time searching for the ideal job.

Eye on the Global Economy

Unemployment Benefits and the Natural Unemployment Rate

Before 1980, unemployment rates in the United States and Canada were similar. But during the 1980s, a gap of 3 percentage points opened up and has persisted (see the figure).

We can be reasonably sure that this gap is not cyclical and means that the natural unemployment rate in Canada is higher than that in the United States.

We cannot be sure why this gap exists, but one fact is that Canadian unemployment benefits became more generous during the late 1970s and more widely available than in the United States. Benefit rates are similar in the two countries, but close to 100 percent of the unemployed receive benefits in Canada, compared to 38 percent in the United States. This difference is probably sufficient to account for some of the difference in natural unemployment rates.

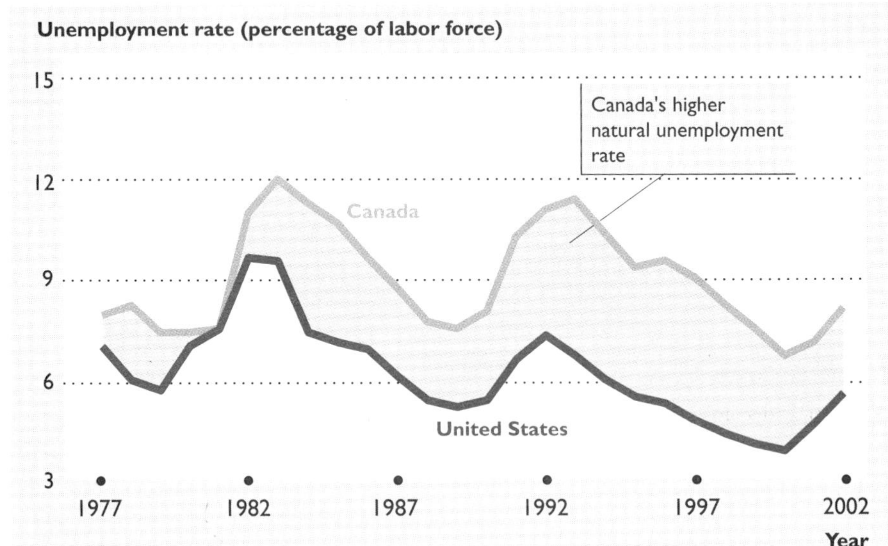

SOURCES: Bureau of Labor Statistics and Statistics Canada.

Structural Change

Labor market flows and unemployment are influenced by the pace and direction of technological change. Sometimes, technological change brings a structural slump, a condition in which some industries die and some regions suffer while other industries are born and other regions flourish. When these events occur, labor turnover is high, job search increases, and the natural unemployment rate is high. At other times, technological change brings a structural boom by creating new jobs that are a good match for the people who are losing their jobs. When these events occur, labor turnover might be high, but job search decreases because new jobs are found quickly, and the natural unemployment rate is low. The Internet economy of the 1990s is an example of a structural boom. Lots of new jobs have been created in every major population center that are a good match for the skills available. As these changes took place, the natural unemployment rate decreased.

Job Rationing

Job rationing
A situation that arises when the real wage rate is above the full-employment equilibrium level.

Job rationing occurs when the real wage rate is above the full-employment equilibrium level. You have learned that markets allocate scarce resources by adjusting the market price to bring buying plans and selling plans into balance. You can think of the market as *rationing* scarce resources. In the labor market, the real wage rate rations employment and therefore rations jobs. Changes in the real wage rate keep the number of people seeking work and the number of jobs available in balance. But the real wage rate is not the only possible instrument for rationing jobs. And in some industries, the real wage rate is set above the full-employment equilibrium level, which brings a surplus of labor. So in these labor markets, jobs are rationed by some other means.

The real wage rate might be set above the full-employment equilibrium level for three reasons:

- Efficiency wage
- Minimum wage
- Union wage

Efficiency Wage

An **efficiency wage** is a real wage rate that is set above the full-employment equilibrium wage rate to induce a greater work effort. The idea is that if a firm pays only the going market average wage, employees have no incentive to work hard because they know that even if they are fired for shirking, they can find a job with another firm at a similar wage rate. But if a firm pays *more* than the going market average wage, employees have an incentive to work hard because they know that if they are fired, they *cannot* expect to find a job with another firm at a similar wage rate.

Efficiency wage
A real wage rate that is set above the full-employment equilibrium wage rate to induce greater work effort.

Further, by paying an efficiency wage, a firm can attract the most productive workers. Also, its workers are less likely to quit their jobs, so the firm faces a lower rate of labor turnover and lower training costs. Finally, the firm's recruiting costs are lower because it always faces a steady stream of available new workers.

Paying an efficiency wage is costly, so only those firms that can't directly monitor the work effort of their employees use this device. But if enough firms pay an efficiency wage, the average real wage rate will exceed the full-employment equilibrium level.

The Minimum Wage

A *minimum wage law* is a government regulation that makes hiring labor for less than a specified wage illegal. If the minimum wage is set below the equilibrium wage, the minimum wage has no effect. The minimum wage law and market forces are not in conflict. But if a minimum wage is set above the equilibrium wage, the minimum wage is in conflict with market forces and unemployment arises.

The current federal minimum wage is $5.15 an hour, and the minimum wage has a major effect in the markets for low-skilled labor. Because skill grows with work experience, teenage labor is particularly affected by the minimum wage.

Union Wage

A **union wage** is a wage rate that results from collective bargaining between a labor union and a firm. Because a union represents a group of workers, it can usually achieve a wage rate that exceeds the level that would prevail in a competitive labor market.

Union wage
A wage rate that results from collective bargaining between a labor union and a firm.

It is estimated that on the average, union wage rates are 30 percent higher than nonunion wage rates. Around that average, the union-nonunion wage difference is close to zero in mining and financial services. In other services, manufacturing, and transportation, the difference lies between 11 and 19 percent. In wholesale and retail trades, the difference is 28 percent, and in construction, it is 65 percent.

But these union-nonunion wage differences probably overstate the effects of unions on wage rates. In some industries, union wages are higher than nonunion wages because union members do jobs that involve greater skill. In these cases, even without a union, those workers would earn a higher wage. To calculate the effects of unions, we must examine the wages of union and nonunion workers who do nearly identical work. The evidence suggests that for comparable skill, the union-nonunion wage difference lies between 10 percent and 25 percent. For example, airline pilots who are members of the Air Line Pilots Association earn about 25 percent more than nonunion pilots with the same level of skill.

Job Rationing and Unemployment

Whether because of efficiency wages, a minimum wage law, or the actions of labor unions, if the real wage rate is above the full-employment equilibrium level, the natural unemployment rate increases. The above-equilibrium real wage rate decreases the quantity of labor demanded and increases the quantity of labor supplied.

Figure 8.8 illustrates job rationing and the frictional and structural unemployment it creates. The full-employment equilibrium real wage rate is $30 an hour, and the equilibrium quantity of labor is 200 billion hours a year. The existence of efficiency wages, the minimum wage, and union wages raises the economy's average real wage rate to $40 an hour. At this wage rate, the quantity of labor demanded decreases to 150 billion hours and the quantity of labor supplied increases to 250 billion hours. Firms ration jobs and choose the workers to hire on the basis of criteria such as education and previous job experience. The labor market is like a game of musical chairs in which a large number of chairs have been removed. So the quantity of labor supplied persistently exceeds the quantity demanded, and additional unemployment arises from job rationing.

FIGURE 8.8

Job Rationing Increases the Natural Unemployment Rate

Practice Online

The full-employment equilibrium real wage rate is $30 an hour. Efficiency wages, the minimum wage, and union wages put the average real wage rate above the full-employment equilibrium level—at $40 an hour.

1. The quantity of labor demanded decreases to 150 billion hours.
2. The quantity of labor supplied increases to 250 billion hours.
3. A surplus of labor arises and increases the natural unemployment rate.

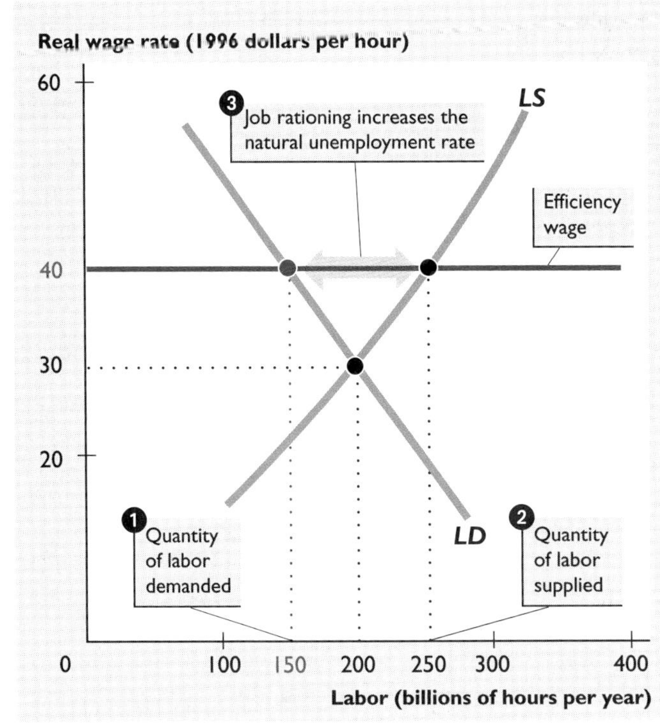

Eye on the U.S. Economy

Unemployment and the Minimum Wage

The Fair Labor Standards Act of 1938 set the federal minimum wage in the United States at 25¢ an hour. Over the years, the federal minimum wage has increased and in 2002, it was $5.15 an hour. Some state governments have passed state minimum wage laws that exceed the federal minimum.

Increases in the minimum wage have occurred at irregular and somewhat infrequent intervals, so the level of the minimum wage has fluctuated between 35 percent and more than 55 percent of the average wage of production workers.

Figure (a) shows the minimum wage as a percentage of the average wage of production workers since 1960. During the 1960s, the minimum wage rate was 52 percent of the average wage. But the minimum wage rate has increased less rapidly than the average wage rate. As a result, the minimum wage rate fell to 46 percent of the average wage during the 1970s and to 40 percent during the 1980s and 1990s.

Figure (b) shows the teenage unemployment rate over the same period. During the 1960s, 15 percent of the teenage labor force was unemployed. The average teenage unemployment rate increased to 17 percent during the 1970s, and to 18 percent during the 1980s. It then fell to 17 percent during the 1990s.

The decade averages of the minimum wage relative to the average wage are not well correlated with the decade average unemployment rates.

Despite the absence of correlation between the minimum wage and the unemployment rate, most economists believe that the minimum wage does contribute to teenage unemployment. Other factors such as the bulge in the number of teenagers during the 1970s mask the effect.

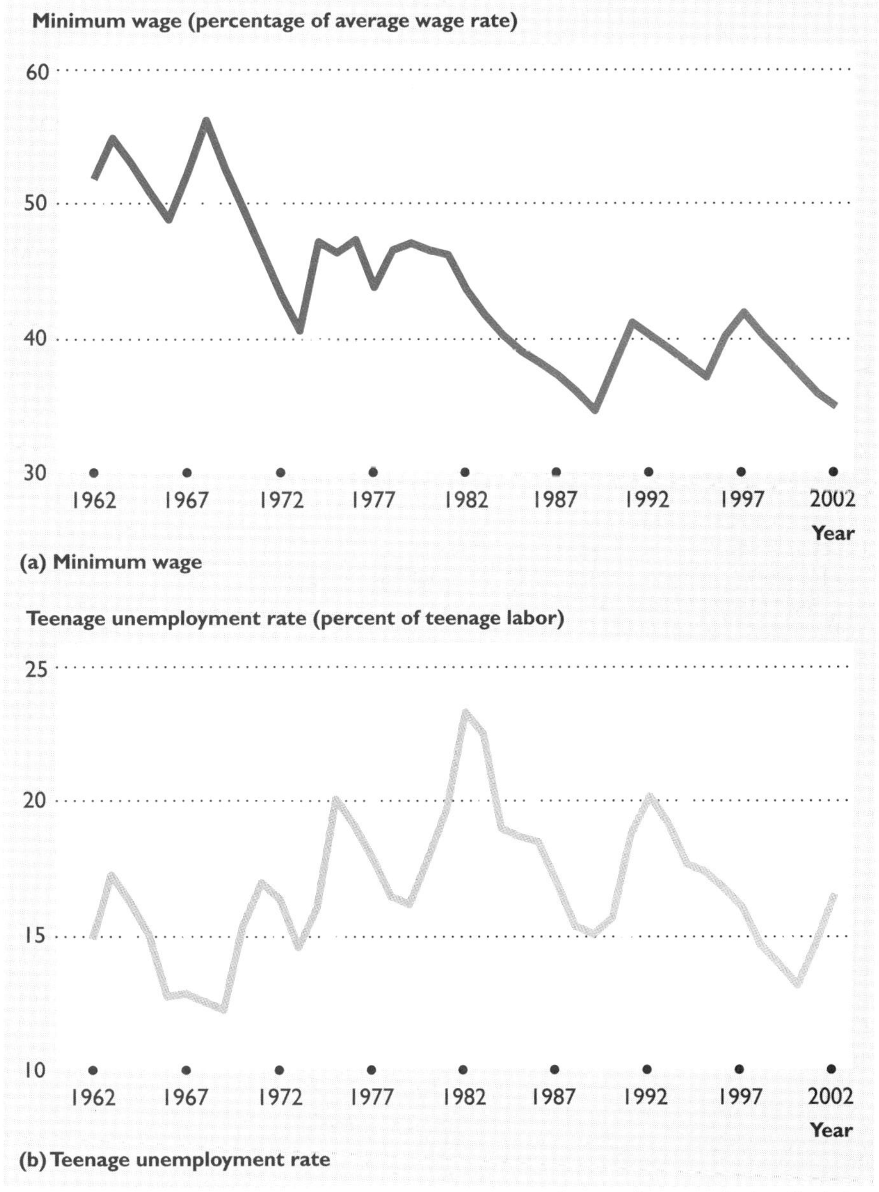

(a) Minimum wage

(b) Teenage unemployment rate

Source: Bureau of Labor Statistics.

CHECKPOINT 8.3

Study Guide pp. 119–122

Practice Online 8.3

3 **Explain what creates unemployment when the economy is at full employment and describe the influences on the natural unemployment rate.**

Practice Problem 8.3

The economy of Singapore has seen huge changes during the past 50 years. It has experienced rapid population growth and has restructured its economy several times to remain at the forefront of the latest technology. Singapore has modest unemployment benefits, no minimum wage, and weak labor unions.

a. Does the unemployment that Singapore experiences arise primarily from job search or job rationing?

b. Which factors mentioned above suggest that Singapore has a higher natural unemployment rate than the United States?

c. Which factors mentioned above suggest that Singapore has a lower natural unemployment rate than the United States?

Exercise 8.3

The economy of Sweden has seen changes during the past 50 years, but the change has been steady and population growth has been modest. Sweden has high unemployment benefits, a high minimum wage, and strong labor unions.

a. Does the unemployment that Sweden experiences arise primarily from job search or job rationing?

b. Which factors mentioned above suggest that Sweden has a higher natural unemployment rate than the United States?

c. Which factors mentioned above suggest that Sweden has a lower natural unemployment rate than the United States?

Solution to Practice Problem 8.3

a. Singapore's unemployment is likely to arise primarily from job search. Of the sources of job rationing (efficiency wages, minimum wages, and union wages) only efficiency wages applies.

b. The factors mentioned above that point toward a higher natural unemployment rate in Singapore than in the United States are rapid population growth and restructuring to remain at the forefront of new technologies, both of which will create a large amount of job search, other things remaining the same.

c. The factors mentioned above that point toward a lower natural unemployment rate in Singapore than in the United States are modest unemployment benefits, which will limit the amount of job search, and the absence of a minimum wage and weak labor unions, which will limit the amount of job rationing.

CHAPTER CHECKPOINT

Key Points

1 Preview the aggregate supply–aggregate demand (*AS-AD*) model and explain why real GDP and unemployment fluctuate in a business cycle.

- A rise in the price level brings an increase in the quantity of real GDP supplied and a decrease in the quantity of real GDP demanded, other influences on production and expenditure remaining the same.
- When the quantity of real GDP supplied equals the quantity of real GDP demanded, real GDP might equal, exceed, or be less than potential GDP.

2 Explain the forces that determine potential GDP and the distribution of income between labor and other factors of production.

- The production function describes the relationship between real GDP and the quantity of labor employed when all other influences on production remain the same. As the quantity of labor increases, real GDP increases.
- The quantity of labor demanded increases as the real wage rate falls, other things remaining the same.
- The quantity of labor supplied increases as the real wage rate rises, other things remaining the same.
- At full-employment equilibrium, the real wage makes the quantity of labor demanded equal the quantity of labor supplied.
- Potential GDP is the level of real GDP that the full-employment quantity of labor produces.

3 Explain what creates unemployment when the economy is at full employment and describe the influences on the natural unemployment rate.

- The unemployment rate at full employment is the natural unemployment rate.
- Unemployment is always present because of job search and job rationing.
- Job search is influenced by demographic change, unemployment benefits, and structural change.
- Job rationing arises from an efficiency wage, the minimum wage, and a union wage.

Key Terms

Above full-employment equilibrium, 187
Aggregate demand, 185
Aggregate supply, 183
Below full-employment equilibrium, 187
Classical dichotomy, 182
Demand for labor, 191
Diminishing returns, 190
Efficiency wage, 201
Full-employment equilibrium, 187
Job rationing, 200
Job search, 199
Macroeconomic equilibrium, 186
Potential GDP, 183
Production function, 190
Quantity of labor demanded, 191
Quantity of labor supplied, 193
Supply of labor, 193
Union wage, 201

Exercises

1. Sort the items in the following list of events into four groups: those that change aggregate supply, those that change aggregate demand, those that change potential GDP, and those that do not change aggregate supply, aggregate demand, or potential GDP in the United States.
   a. The Federal Reserve raises the interest rate.
   b. The U.S. government increases taxes.
   c. The U.S. government increases spending on antiterrorism.
   d. The U.S. price level rises.
   e. An economic slump in the rest of the world decreases U.S. exports.
   f. U.S. real GDP decreases.
   g. The Anaheim Angels win the World Series.
   h. U.S. labor unions negotiate wage hikes that affect all workers.
   i. A huge scientific breakthrough doubles U.S. labor productivity.
   j. Migration to the United States increases the working-age population.
2. Which of the events in exercise 1 increase aggregate supply and which decrease aggregate supply?
3. Which of the events in exercise 1 increase aggregate demand and which decrease aggregate demand?
4. Which of the events in exercise 1 increase potential GDP and which decrease potential GDP?
5. Which of the events in exercise 1 increase real GDP and lower the price level and which increase real GDP and raise the price level?
6. Which of the events in exercise 1 decrease real GDP and lower the price level and which decrease real GDP and raise the price level?
7. You are provided with the following information about the economy of Athabasca:

Labor hours (millions per year)	Real GDP (millions of dollars)	Real wage rate (dollars per hour)	Quantity of labor demanded (millions of hours per year)	Quantity of labor supplied (millions of hours per year)
0	0			
1	10	10	5	1
2	19	9	4	2
3	27	8	3	3
4	34	7	2	4
5	40	6	1	5

Find
a. The quantity of labor employed
b. Potential GDP
c. The real wage rate
d. Total labor income

8. In the economy of Athabasca described in exercise 7, the population increases. In what directions do potential GDP, employment, and the real wage rate change?

9. In the economy of Athabasca described in exercise 7, the labor productivity increases. In what directions do potential GDP, employment, and the real wage rate change?

10. The people of Nautica can work a maximum of 100 hours in total every day. The first 10 hours of work can produce $10 of real GDP. The second 10 hours a day can produce an additional $9 of real GDP. The third 10 hours a day produce an additional $8 of real GDP. Each additional 10 hours of work a day produces additional GDP of $1 a day less than the previous 10 hours. Make a table and a graph of Nautica's production function.

11. Use the information provided in exercise 10 about the economy of Nautica. Also, use the information that the firms in Nautica are willing to hire 10 hours of labor a day for a real wage rate of $1 an hour, 20 hours a day for 90¢ an hour, and an additional 10 hours a day for each 10¢ cut in the real wage rate. The people of Nautica are willing to work 10 hours a day for a real wage rate of 10¢ an hour. And for each 10¢ an hour increase in the real wage, they are willing to work an additional 10 hours a day.
    a. Make a table that shows Nautica's demand for labor schedule and draw Nautica's demand for labor curve.
    b. Make a table that shows Nautica's supply of labor schedule and draw Nautica's supply of labor curve.
    c. Find the full-employment equilibrium real wage rate and quantity of labor in Nautica's economy.
    d. Find Nautica's potential GDP.

12. Two island economies, Cocoa Island and Plantation Island, are identical in every respect except one. A survey tells us that at full employment, people on Cocoa Island spend 1,000 hours a day in job search, while the people on Plantation Island spend 2,000 hours a day in job search.
    a. Which economy has the greater level of potential GDP?
    b. Which economy has the higher real wage rate?
    c. Which economy has the higher natural unemployment rate?

13. On Cocoa Island described in exercise 12, the government introduces a minimum wage that creates an additional 1,000 hours a day of unemployment. On Plantation Island, nothing changes from the situation described in exercise 12.
    a. Which economy now has the greater level of potential GDP?
    b. Which economy now has the higher real wage rate?
    c. Which economy now has the higher natural unemployment rate?
    d. How much unemployment in these two economies results from job search and how much from job rationing?

Critical Thinking

14. Look at the figure in Eye on the U.S. Economy on page 187. Describe the changes in aggregate supply and aggregate demand that brought the changes in real GDP and the price level displayed in that figure. In which periods did *AS* increase fastest relative to *AD* and in which periods did *AD* increase fastest relative to *AS*? What was the type of macroeconomic equilibrium of the U.S. economy in 2002?

15. If the minimum wage were abolished, what do you predict would happen to potential GDP, employment, and the equilibrium real wage rate? Would you favor or oppose the abolition of the minimum wage? Why?

16. How do you think real GDP and potential GDP would change if the United States adopted an unemployment insurance scheme like that of Canada? Refer to Eye on the Global Economy on page 200 for information on the comparison between Canada and the United States. Would you favor or oppose such a change in arrangements?

Practice Online

Web Exercises

Use the links on your Foundations Web site to work the following exercises.

17. Visit the Web site of the Bureau of Economic Analysis and obtain the latest data on real GDP and the price level (the GDP deflator) in the United States. Also visit the International Monetary Fund's World Economic Outlook Database Web site and obtain the latest estimate of the U.S. output gap. Use the *AS-AD* model to organize a description of the influences on and the course of the U.S. economy since 1990. Pay special attention to the changes in aggregate supply and aggregate demand and explain the type of macroeconomic equilibrium that the United States has experienced.

18. Use the Web sites described in exercise 17 and figure out what happened to the macroeconomic *PPF* and to the demand for labor and supply of labor in the United States from 1995 through 2002.

19. Visit some or all of the following Web sites to obtain information about the economy of Russia since 1990:

    CIA World Factbook 2000, Russia section
    IMF World Economic Outlook October 2000, Focus on Transition Economies
    IMF World Economic Outlook October 2002, Data Appendix
    Hoover Institution material on the Russian economy
    Article by the American Enterprise Institute on the Russian economy

    Use the *AS-AD* model to organize a description of the influences on and the course of the Russian economy since 1990. Pay special attention to the changes in aggregate supply and aggregate demand and explain the type of macroeconomic equilibrium that Russia has experienced.

20. Use the Web sites described in exercise 19 and figure out what has happened to the macroeconomic *PPF* and to the demand for labor and supply of labor in Russia since 1990.

CHAPTER 9

Investment and Saving

CHAPTER CHECKLIST

When you have completed your study of this chapter, you will be able to

1. **Define and explain the relationships among capital, investment, wealth, and saving.**

2. **Explain how investment and saving decisions are made and how these decisions interact in financial markets to determine the real interest rate.**

3. **Explain how government influences the real interest rate, investment, and saving.**

You learned in Chapter 8 how real GDP at full employment is determined. And you saw the large differences between the full-employment economies of the 1960s and 1990s. In Chapter 3, you took a quick first look at how the economy gets from one level of real GDP (such as that of the 1960s) to a higher level (such as that of the 1990s). Real GDP expands when the *PPF* shifts rightward. And the *PPF* shifts rightward when the quantity of capital increases and technology advances.

The quantity of capital increases because we save and invest. So the amount of saving and the amount of investment determine the pace at which the quantity of capital increases.

In this chapter, you are going to learn about the choices that businesses, households, and governments make that determine investment and saving. And you're going to see how a global financial market coordinates these choices to determine the quantity of capital and the real interest rate.

9.1 CAPITAL, INVESTMENT, WEALTH, AND SAVING

Physical capital
The tools, instruments, machines, buildings, and other constructions that have been produced in the past and that are used to produce goods and services.

Financial capital
The funds that firms use to buy and operate physical capital.

Capital, or **physical capital,** is the tools, instruments, machines, buildings, and other constructions that have been produced in the past and that are used to produce goods and services. When economists use the term *capital,* they mean physical capital. **Financial capital** is the funds that firms use to buy and operate physical capital. The quantity of physical capital influences our production possibilities and real GDP. But the quantity of financial capital, which depends on the decisions that people and businesses make about spending, saving, borrowing, and lending, influences the quantity of physical capital. We begin by describing the links between the quantity of physical capital and investment.

Capital and Investment

Gross investment
The total amount spent on new capital goods.

Net investment
The change in the quantity of capital—equals gross investment minus depreciation.

Investment and depreciation change the quantity of capital. *Investment* (Chapter 5, p. 113) is the purchase of new capital goods and additions to inventories. *Depreciation* (Chapter 5, p. 120) is the decrease in the value of capital that results from its use and from obsolescence. Also called *capital consumption,* depreciation is part of the opportunity cost of owning and using capital. It is the market price of capital at the beginning of a period minus its market price at the end of a period. The total amount spent on new capital goods is called **gross investment.** The change in the quantity of capital is called net investment. **Net investment** equals gross investment minus depreciation.

Figure 9.1 illustrates these concepts. On January 1, 2003, Tom's DVD Burning, Inc. had DVD recording machines worth $30,000—Tom's initial capital. During 2003, the market value of Tom's machines fell by 67 percent—$20,000. After this depreciation, Tom's machines were valued at $10,000. During 2003, Tom spent $30,000 on new machines. This amount is Tom's gross investment. By December 31, 2003, Tom had capital valued at $40,000, so his capital had increased by $10,000. This amount is Tom's net investment. Tom's net investment equals his gross investment of $30,000 minus depreciation of $20,000.

FIGURE 9.1
Capital and Investment

Practice Online

On January 1, 2003, Tom's DVD Burning, Inc. had DVD recording machines valued at $30,000. During 2003, the value of Tom's machines fell by $20,000—depreciation—and he spent $30,000 on new machines—gross investment. Tom's net investment was $10,000, so at the end of 2003, Tom had capital valued at $40,000.

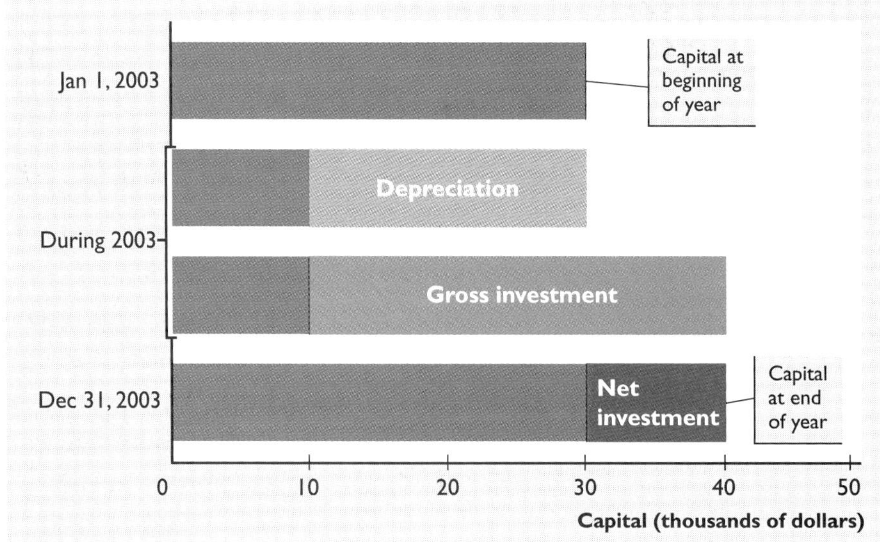

Eye on the U.S. Economy

Investment and Capital, 1971–2001

Gross investment, shown in part (a) of the figure, increases in most years and increased rapidly during the booming 1990s. But it decreases in recession years (highlighted in the figure).

Depreciation, also shown in part (a), increases in most years, but it fluctuates less than gross investment.

Gross investment minus depreciation is net investment. You can see net investment in part (a) as the gap between the two curves.

Part (b) of the figure provides a sharper view of net investment. You can see that it fluctuates a great deal and decreases sharply during a recession. Like gross investment, it increased rapidly during the 1990s expansion.

Although net investment fluctuates, it rarely (and never during the 30 years shown here) becomes negative. Negative net investment would mean that the quantity of capital was shrinking. Because net investment is always positive, the quantity of capital, shown in part (c) of the figure, increases each year.

The quantity of capital grows steadily despite huge swings in net investment. The reason is that net investment is tiny in comparison to the quantity of capital. Between 1971 and 2001, net investment averaged less than 3 percent of the quantity of capital.

(a) Gross investment and depreciation

(b) Net investment

(c) Capital

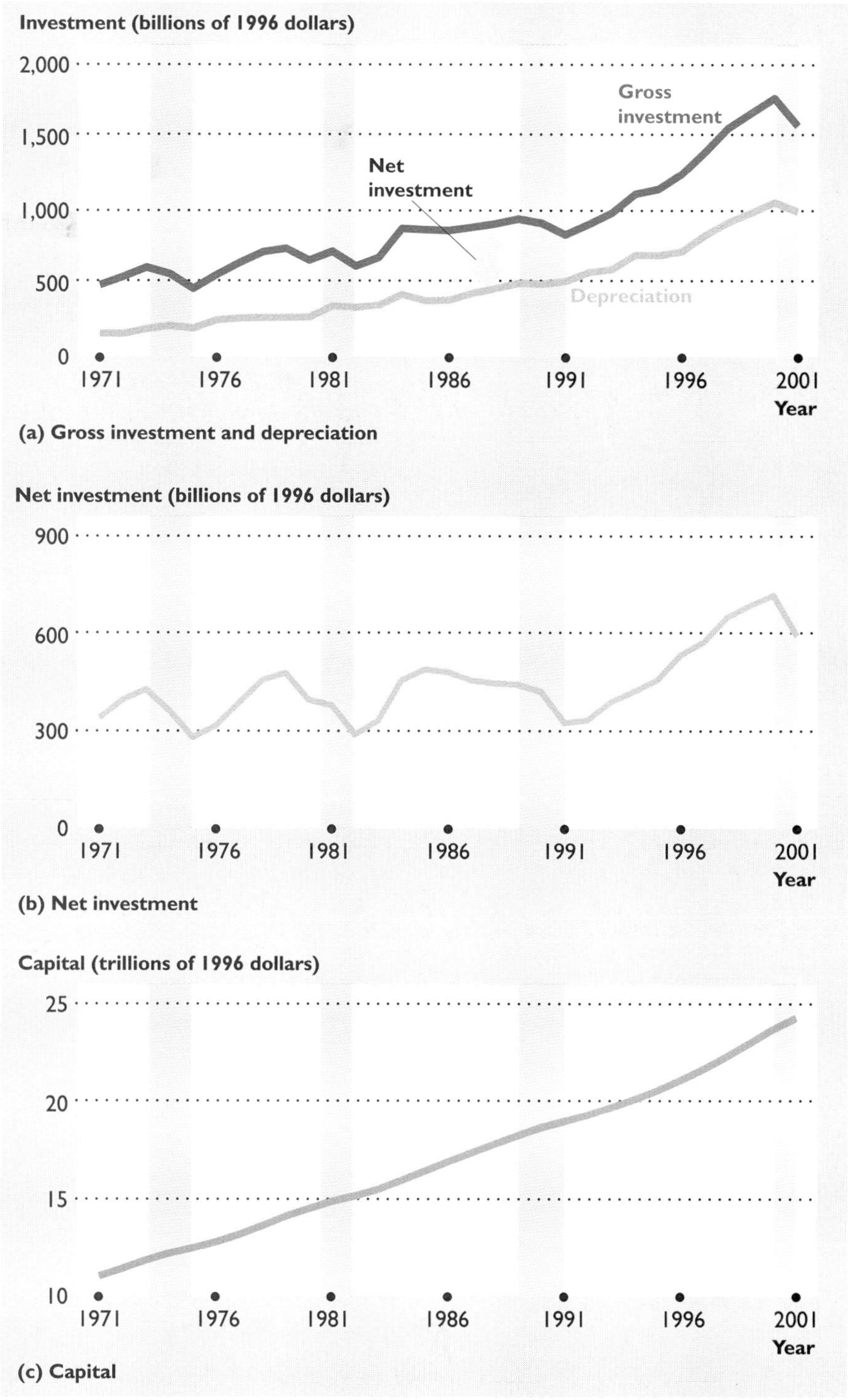

SOURCE: Bureau of Economic Analysis.

Each nation's capital and investment work just like the example of Tom's DVD-recording shop. A nation's capital today equals its capital a year ago plus its net investment during the past year. And a nation's net investment during the past year equals its gross investment minus depreciation. The Eye on the U.S. Economy takes a look at U.S. investment and capital growth from 1971 to 2001.

Wealth and Saving

Wealth
The value of all the things that a person owns.

Saving
The amount of income that is not paid in taxes or spent on consumption goods and services—adds to wealth.

A person's **wealth** is the value of all the things that the person owns. What people *own* is related to what they *earn*. But it is not the same thing. People *earn* an *income*, which is the amount they receive during a given time period from supplying the services of the resources they own. **Saving** is the amount of income that is not paid in taxes or spent on consumption goods and services, and saving adds to wealth. Wealth also increases when the value of assets rises—called *capital gains*.

Suppose that at the end of the school year, you have $250 in a savings account and some textbooks that are worth $300. That's all you own. Your wealth is $550. During the summer, you earn an income (after tax) of $5,000. You spend only $1,000 through the summer on consumption. At the end of the summer, you have $4,250 in your savings account. Your wealth is now $4,550. Your wealth has increased by $4,000, which equals your saving of $4,000. Your saving of $4,000 equals your income of $5,000 minus your consumption expenditure of $1,000.

National wealth and national saving work just like this personal example. The wealth of a nation at the start of a year equals its wealth at the start of the previous year plus its saving during the year. Its saving equals its income minus its consumption expenditure.

Financial Markets

Financial markets
The collection of households, firms, governments, banks, and other financial institutions that lend and borrow.

The **financial markets** are the collections of households, firms, governments, banks, and other financial institutions that lend and borrow. Financial markets are where firms get the funds that they use to buy capital. Firms are demanders and households are suppliers in financial markets. Governments are demanders if they have a budget deficit and suppliers if they have a budget surplus. Banks and other financial institutions help to match the lending plans of households and the borrowing plans of firms. Financial markets determine the price of financial capital, which is expressed as an interest rate (percent per year).

Global Financial Markets

Financial markets are global. Lenders want to earn the highest possible real interest rate. If, for equal risk, they can get a higher real interest rate in Japan than in the United States, they will move their funds to Japan. Borrowers want to pay the lowest possible real interest rate. If they can borrow at a lower interest rate in Europe than in the United States, they will borrow in Europe.

Because funds are free to roam the globe looking for the highest possible real interest rate, and because borrowers are free to seek the lowest possible real interest rate in any country, the financial markets form a single global market.

Financial markets are organized in four groups:

- Stock markets
- Bond markets
- Short-term securities markets
- Loans markets

Stock Markets

Stock
A certificate of ownership and claim to the profits that a firm makes.

When Boeing wanted to raise funds to expand its airplane building business, it issued stock. A **stock** is a certificate of ownership and claim to the profits that a firm makes. Boeing has issued about 900 million shares of its stock. So if you owned 900 Boeing shares, you would own one millionth of Boeing and be entitled to receive one millionth of the company's profits.

A **stock market** is a financial market in which shares in companies' stocks are traded. An example of a stock market is the New York Stock Exchange. The London Stock Exchange (in England) and the Frankfurt Stock Exchange (in Germany) are the main stock markets in Europe. In Asia, the Tokyo and Hong Kong stock exchanges are the dominant ones. You can visit the Web sites of stock markets and see the prices and the quantities of shares that are being traded minute by minute throughout the business day.

Stock market
A financial market in which shares of companies' stocks are traded.

If you buy some Boeing stock today, you pay the current owner of the stock, not Boeing. Boeing received the value of the stock when it first issued it.

Demand and supply in stock markets determine the prices of the individual stocks and the returns on them. The return on a stock is the dividend that the firm pays plus the change in the market value of the stock—the capital gain or loss.

Bond Markets

When Wal-Mart Stores, Inc. planned to expand its business, instead of issuing stock it raised the funds it needed by selling bonds. A **bond** is a promise to pay specified sums of money on specified dates and is a debt for the issuer of the bond. For example, a Wal-Mart bond is a promise to pay $3.4375 every May and October until 2009 and then pay $100 in October 2009. Governments—federal, state, and municipal—also issue bonds. The buyer of a bond from Wal-Mart made a loan to the company and is entitled only to the payments promised by the bond. A bondholder differs from a stockholder and is not a part owner of the firm. When a person buys a newly issued bond, he or she may hold the bond until the borrower repays the amount borrowed or sell it to someone else. The **bond market** is a financial market in which bonds issued by firms and governments are traded. Demand and supply in the bond market determine the prices of bonds and the interest rates on them.

Bond
A promise to pay specified sums of money on specified dates; it is a debt for the issuer.

Bond market
A financial market in which bonds issued by firms and governments are traded.

Short-Term Securities Markets

When General Motors sells $100 million of railway locomotives to Union Pacific, GM wants to be paid as soon as the items are shipped. But Union Pacific doesn't want to pay until the locomotives are operating and earning an income. In this situation, GM might issue a short-term security called a commercial bill. Each bill would be a promise by GM to pay $100 on a date three months in the future. A bank would be willing to buy these bills for an amount less than $100, and the difference between the price paid and $100 would be the interest on the bill. The U.S. Treasury also issues bills of this type, called Treasury bills.

Demand and supply in the short-term securities market determine the price and interest rate on commercial bills and Treasury bills.

Loans Markets

Many businesses finance their short-term capital, such as inventories, with a loan from a bank. Banks and other financial institutions lower the cost of financing firms' capital expenditures by accepting short-term deposits and making longer-term loans. They enable the small savings of millions of individuals to be pooled to finance investment. (You will study banks in some detail in Chapter 11.)

CHECKPOINT 9.1

Study Guide pp. 128–131

Practice Online 9.1

1 Define and explain the relationships among capital, investment, wealth, and saving.

Practice Problems 9.1

1. Michael is an Internet service provider. On December 31, 2000, he bought an existing business with servers and a building worth $400,000. During his first year of operation, his business grew and he bought new servers for $500,000. The market value of some of his older servers fell by $100,000.
   a. What was Michael's gross investment during 2001?
   b. What was Michael's depreciation during 2001?
   c. What was Michael's net investment during 2001?
   d. What was Michael's capital at the end of 2001?

2. Lori is a student who teaches golf on the weekend and in a year earns $20,000 in fees after paying her taxes. At the beginning of 2000, Lori owned $1,000 worth of books, CDs, and golf clubs and she had $5,000 in a savings account at the bank. During 2000, the interest on her savings account was $300 and she spent a total of $15,300 on consumption goods and services. There was no change in the market values of her books, CDs, and golf clubs.
   a. How much did Lori save in 2000?
   b. What was Lori's wealth at the end of 2000?

Exercises 9.1

1. Annie runs a fitness center. On December 31, 2002, she bought an existing business with exercise equipment and a building worth $300,000. During her first year of operation, business was poor. She sold some of her equipment to a competitor for $100,000.
   a. What was Annie's gross investment during 2003?
   b. What was Annie's depreciation during 2003?
   c. What was Annie's net investment during 2003?
   d. What was the value of Annie's capital at the end of 2003?

2. Karrie is a golf pro, and after she paid taxes, her total income from golf and from the stocks and bonds that she owns was $1,500,000 in 2002. At the beginning of 2002, she owned $900,000 worth of stocks and bonds. At the end of 2002, Karrie's stocks and bonds were worth $1,900,000. How much did Karrie save during 2002 and how much did she spend on consumption goods and services?

Solutions to Practice Problems 9.1

1a. Michael's gross investment during 2001 was $500,000.
1b. Michael's depreciation during 2001 was $100,000.
1c. Michael's net investment during 2001 was $400,000.
1d. At the end of 2001, Michael's capital was $800,000.

2a. Lori's saving equals her income (after tax) minus the amount she spent. That is, her saving equaled $20,300 minus $15,300, or $5,000.
2b. Lori's wealth at the end of 2000 was $11,000—the sum of her wealth at the start of 2000 ($6,000) plus her saving during 2000 ($5,000).

9.2 INVESTMENT, SAVING, AND INTEREST

Firms' investment decisions (investment demand) and households' consumption and saving decisions (saving supply) are coordinated in a global financial market to determine the quantity of capital and the real interest rate (financial market equilibrium). You learned how we define and measure the real interest rate in Chapter 7 (p. 175). We're now going to learn how the forces of demand and supply in the global financial market determine the real interest rate. We will study

- Investment demand
- Saving supply
- Financial market equilibrium

Investment Demand

How does Amazon.com decide whether to invest in a new warehouse? How does Chrysler decide whether to build a new car assembly plant? Many details influence business investment decisions like these, but we can summarize them in two factors: the expected rate of profit and the real interest rate.

Other things remaining the same, the higher the real interest rate, the smaller is the quantity of investment demanded; and the lower the real interest rate, the greater is the quantity of investment demanded.

The real interest rate is the opportunity cost of the funds used to finance the purchase of capital, and firms compare the real interest rate with the rate of profit they expect to earn on their new capital. Firms invest only when they expect to earn a rate of profit that exceeds the real interest rate. The higher the real interest rate, the fewer projects that are profitable, so the smaller is the amount of investment demanded.

Suppose that Amazon.com expects to earn \$5 million (before paying its interest costs) if it builds a new \$100 million warehouse. If the real interest rate is 4 percent a year, Amazon's interest bill for this warehouse is \$4 million a year, so the investment earns \$1 million a year. But if the real interest rate is 6 percent a year (other things remaining the same), Amazon's interest bill is \$6 million a year, so the investment incurs a loss of \$1 million a year. Amazon invests in the warehouse at a real interest rate of 4 percent a year but not at 6 percent a year.

To finance investment, a firm either borrows or uses its own funds (retained earnings). The opportunity cost of both sources of funds is the real interest rate because the firm *pays* this interest rate and *forgoes* this interest rate by buying new capital rather than by making a loan.

We summarize the influences on investment decisions in an investment demand curve.

Investment Demand Curve

The relationship between the quantity of investment demanded and the real interest rate, other things remaining the same, is called **investment demand**. If the real interest rate rises, other things remaining the same, the quantity of investment demanded decreases. The table in Figure 9.2 shows an example of this relationship.

Investment demand
The relationship between the quantity of investment demanded and the real interest rate, other things remaining the same.

FIGURE 9.2
Investment Demand

Practice Online

The table shows the quantity of investment demanded at five real interest rates. The graph shows the investment demand curve, *ID*. Points *A* through *E* correspond to the rows of the table.

At a real interest rate of 6 percent a year, the quantity of investment demanded is $10 trillion at point *C*.

1. If the real interest rate rises to 8 percent a year, the quantity of investment demanded decreases to $9 trillion at point *B*.

2. If the real interest rate falls to 4 percent a year, the quantity of investment demanded increases $11 trillion at point *D*.

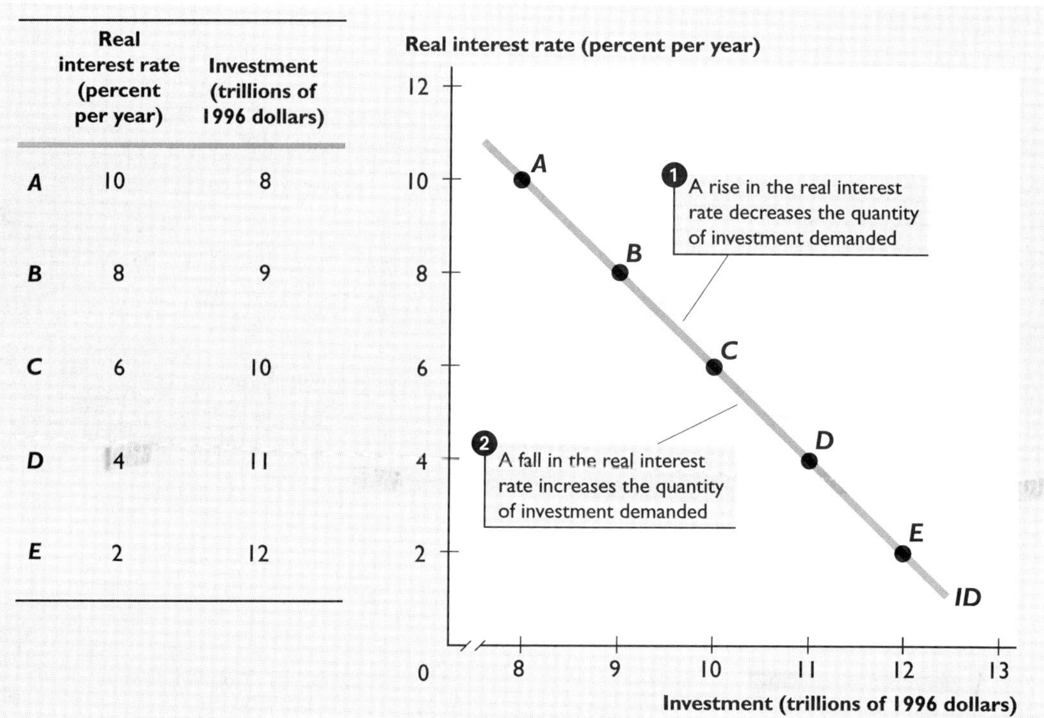

	Real interest rate (percent per year)	Investment (trillions of 1996 dollars)
A	10	8
B	8	9
C	6	10
D	4	11
E	2	12

Figure 9.2 shows an investment demand curve. Each point (*A* through *E*) corresponds to a row in the table. If the real interest rate is 6 percent a year, the quantity of investment demanded is $10 trillion. A change in the real interest rate brings a movement along the investment demand curve. If the real interest rate rises to 8 percent a year, the quantity of investment demanded decreases to $9 trillion; there is a movement up the investment demand curve. If the real interest rate falls to 4 percent a year, the quantity of investment demanded increases to $11 trillion; there is a movement down the investment demand curve.

Changes in Investment Demand

When the expected profit changes, investment demand changes. Other things remaining the same, the greater the expected profit from new capital, the greater is the amount of investment. The many influences on expected profit can be placed in three groups:

- Objective influences such as the phase of the business cycle, technological change, and population growth
- Subjective influences summarized in the phrase "animal spirits"
- Contagion effects summarized in the phrase "irrational exuberance"

Expected profits rise in an expansion and fall in a recession and so bring swings in investment demand over the business cycle. For example, investment soared during the information-based expansion of the late 1990s and sagged during the recession of the early 1990s.

Technological change lowers costs and creates new and profitable products. But to take advantage of new technologies, firms must invest in the equipment that employs them. For example, to produce a new generation of enormously profitable computer chips, Intel Corporation must invest several billion dollars in chip-making equipment that incorporates the latest technology.

Population growth brings a steady increase in the demand for all goods. Greater demand leads to greater profits. But to meet the increased demand and earn the profits available, firms must invest in additional capital.

Because investment decisions are forward looking, they are based on subjective feelings about the future. Sometimes "animal spirits" are optimistic and sometimes pessimistic, and these swings of mood bring swings in investment demand.

Also, mood swings can be contagious. Fed chairman Alan Greenspan has called the contagious optimism of the 1990s "irrational exuberance."

Shifts of the Investment Demand Curve

When investment demand changes, the investment demand curve shifts. Figure 9.3 shows how the investment demand curve depends on expected profit. When firms expect average profits, the investment demand curve is ID_0, which is the same investment demand curve as the one in Figure 9.2.

When the expected profit increases, investment demand increases and the investment demand curve shifts rightward to ID_1. When expected profit decreases, investment demand decreases and the investment demand curve shifts leftward to ID_2.

FIGURE 9.3

Changes in Investment Demand

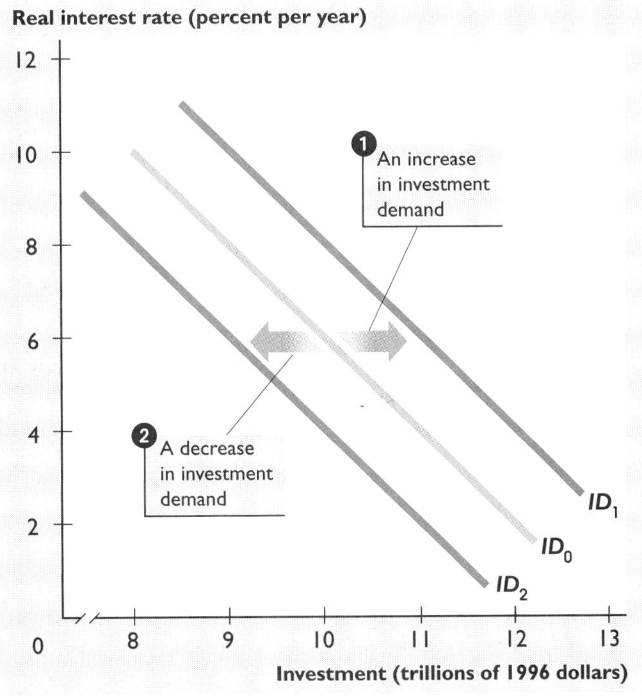

A change in profit expectations shifts the investment demand curve.

1. An increase in the expected profit increases investment demand and shifts the investment demand curve rightward to ID_1.
2. A decrease in the expected profit decreases investment demand and shifts the investment demand curve leftward to ID_2.

Saving Supply

You've graduated and landed a great job that pays you $50,000 a year. How do you decide how much of your income to spend on consumption goods and services and how much to save? Your decision would be influenced by many factors that we'll now review. But we'll begin by focusing on one of them: the real interest rate.

> **Other things remaining the same, the higher the real interest rate, the greater is the quantity of saving supplied; and the lower the real interest rate, the smaller is the quantity of saving supplied.**

The real interest rate is the *opportunity cost* of consumption expenditure. A dollar spent is a dollar not saved, so the interest that could have been earned on that saving is forgone. This opportunity cost arises regardless of whether a person is a lender or a borrower. For a lender, saving less this year means receiving less interest next year. For a borrower, saving less this year means paying less off a loan this year and paying more interest next year.

By thinking about student loans, you can see why the real interest rate influences saving. If the real interest rate on student loans jumped to 20 percent a year, graduates would save more (buying cheaper food and finding lower-rent accommodations) to pay off their loans as quickly as possible and avoid, as much as possible, paying the higher interest cost of their loan. If the real interest rate on student loans fell to 1 percent a year, graduates would save less and take longer to pay off their loan because the interest burden was easier to bear.

Saving Supply Curve

Saving supply
The relationship between the quantity of saving supplied and the real interest rate, other things remaining the same.

The relationship between the quantity of saving supplied and the real interest rate, other things remaining the same, is called **saving supply**.

Figure 9.4 illustrates saving supply. The table shows a saving supply schedule, and the graph shows the saving supply curve. The points *A* through *E* on the saving supply curve *SS* in Figure 9.4 correspond to the rows of the table. For example, point *C* shows that when the real interest rate is 6 percent a year, the quantity of saving supplied is $10 trillion. If the real interest rate rises from 6 percent a year to 8 percent a year, the quantity of saving supplied increases from $10 trillion to $11 trillion and there is a movement along the saving supply curve from *C* to *B*. If the real interest rate falls from 6 percent a year to 4 percent a year, the quantity of saving supplied decreases from $10 trillion to $9 trillion and there is a movement along the saving supply curve from *C* to *D*.

Changes in Saving Supply

When any influence on saving other than the real interest rate changes, saving supply changes. The three main factors that influence saving supply are

- Disposable income
- The buying power of net assets
- Expected future disposable income

Disposable income
Income earned minus net taxes.

Disposable Income A household's **disposable income** is the income earned minus net taxes. The greater a household's disposable income, other things remaining the same, the greater is its saving. For example, a student works part time and earns a disposable income of $10,000. She spends the entire $10,000 on

FIGURE 9.4
Saving Supply

Practice Online

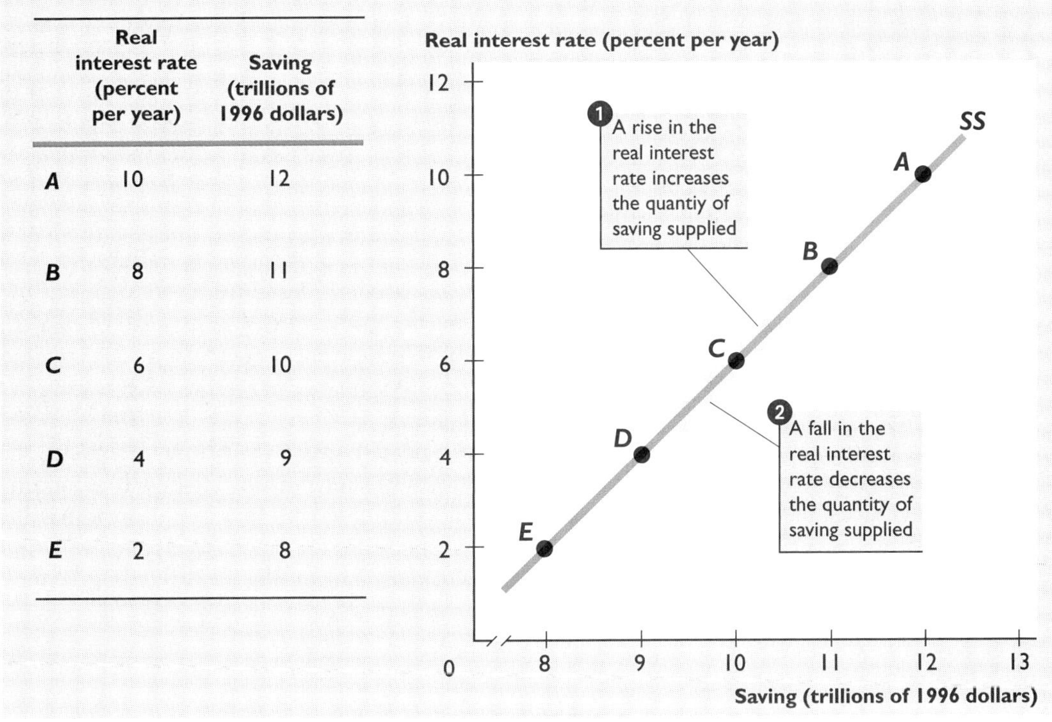

	Real interest rate (percent per year)	Saving (trillions of 1996 dollars)
A	10	12
B	8	11
C	6	10
D	4	9
E	2	8

The table shows the quantity of saving supplied at five real interest rates. The graph shows the saving supply curve, *SS*. Points *A* through *E* correspond to the rows of the table.

At a real interest rate of 6 percent a year, the quantity of saving supplied is $10 trillion at point *C*.

1. If the real interest rate rises to 8 percent a year, the quantity of saving supplied increases to $11 trillion at point *B*.
2. If the real interest rate falls to 4 percent a year, the quantity of saving supplied decreases $9 trillion at point *D*.

consumption and saves nothing. When she graduates as an economics major, her disposable income increases to $35,000 a year. She now saves $10,000 and spends $25,000 on consumption. The increase in disposable income of $25,000 has increased saving by $10,000.

Buying Power of Net Assets A household's net assets are what it owns minus the debts that it owes. The buying power of a household's net assets is the quantity of goods and services that its net assets can buy. The greater the buying power of the net assets a household has accumulated, other things remaining the same, the less it will save.

Patty is a department store executive who earns $50,000 a year. She has been saving $5,000 a year and now has $15,000 in the bank and no debts. With $15,000 in the bank, Patty decides to spend $5,000 on a vacation and save nothing this year. Tony, another department store executive who also earns $50,000, has saved nothing and has an outstanding balance of $10,000 on his credit card. With nothing in the bank and a big debt, Tony feels financially insecure, so he decides to cut his consumption and start saving.

Expected Future Disposable Income The higher a household's expected future disposable income, other things remaining the same, the smaller is its saving today. That is, if two households have the same disposable income in the current year, the household with the larger expected future disposable income will spend a larger portion of current disposable income on consumption goods and services and so save less today.

Look at Patty and Tony again. Patty has just been promoted and will receive a $10,000 pay raise next year. Tony has just been told that he will be fired at the end of the year. On receiving this news, Patty buys a new car—increases her consumption expenditure and cuts her saving—and Tony sells his car and takes the bus—decreases his consumption expenditure and increases his saving.

Most young households expect to have a higher future income for some years and then to have a lower income during retirement. Because of this pattern of income over the life cycle, young people save a small amount, middle-aged people save a lot, and retired people gradually spend their accumulated savings.

Shifts of the Saving Supply Curve

Along the saving supply curve, all the influences on saving other than the real interest rate remain the same. A change in any of these influences on saving changes saving supply and shifts the saving supply curve. An increase in disposable income, a decrease in the buying power of net assets, or a decrease in expected future disposable income increases saving supply. Figure 9.5 shows the effect of this change on the saving supply curve.

Initially, the saving supply curve is SS_0. Then disposable income increases, the buying power of net assets decreases, or expected future disposable income decreases. Saving supply increases, and the saving supply curve shifts rightward from SS_0 to SS_1. Changes in these factors in the opposite direction decrease saving supply and shift the saving supply curve leftward from SS_0 to SS_2.

FIGURE 9.5
Changes in Saving Supply

Practice Online

1 An increase in disposable income, a decrease in the buying power of net assets, or a decrease in expected future disposable income increases saving and shifts the saving supply curve rightward from SS_0 to SS_1.

2 A decrease in disposable income, an increase in the buying power of net assets, or an increase in expected future disposable income decreases saving and shifts the saving supply curve leftward from SS_0 to SS_2.

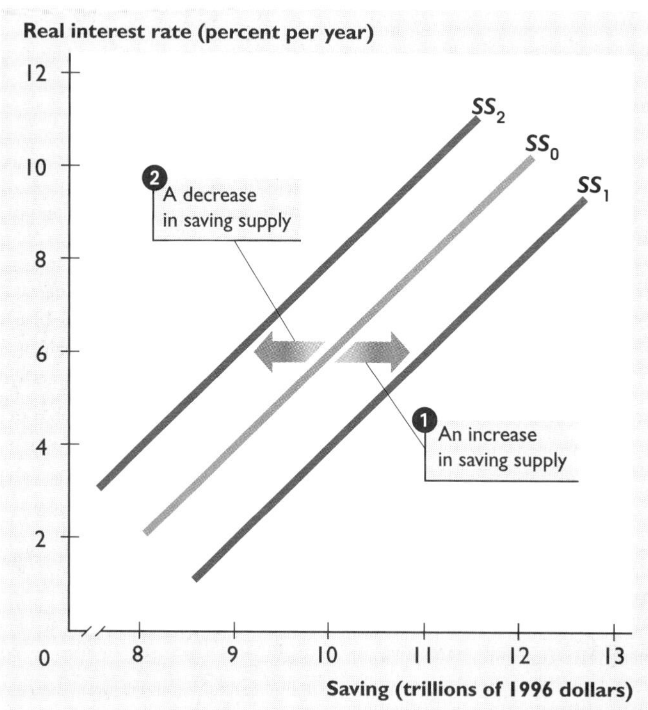

Financial Market Equilibrium

Figure 9.6 shows how the real interest rate is determined. The *ID* curve is the investment demand curve. The *SS* curve is the saving supply curve. The higher the real interest rate, the greater is the amount of saving and the smaller is the amount of investment.

In Figure 9.6, when the real interest rate exceeds 6 percent a year, the quantity of saving supplied exceeds the quantity of investment demanded. There is a surplus of saving. Borrowers have an easy time finding the loans they want, but lenders are unable to lend all the funds they have available. The real interest rate falls, and as it does so, the quantity of investment demanded increases and the quantity of saving supplied decreases.

Alternatively, when the interest rate is less than 6 percent a year, the quantity of saving supplied is less than the quantity of investment demanded. There is a shortage of saving. Borrowers can't find the loans they want, but lenders are able to lend all the funds they have available. So the real interest rate rises. As the real interest rate rises, the quantity of investment demanded decreases and the quantity of saving supplied increases.

Regardless of whether there is a surplus or a shortage of saving, the real interest rate changes and is pulled toward an equilibrium level. In Figure 9.6, this equilibrium is 6 percent a year. At this interest rate there is neither a surplus nor a shortage of saving. Investors can get the funds they demand, and savers can lend all the funds they have available. The plans of savers and investors are consistent with each other.

FIGURE 9.6
Financial Market Equilibrium

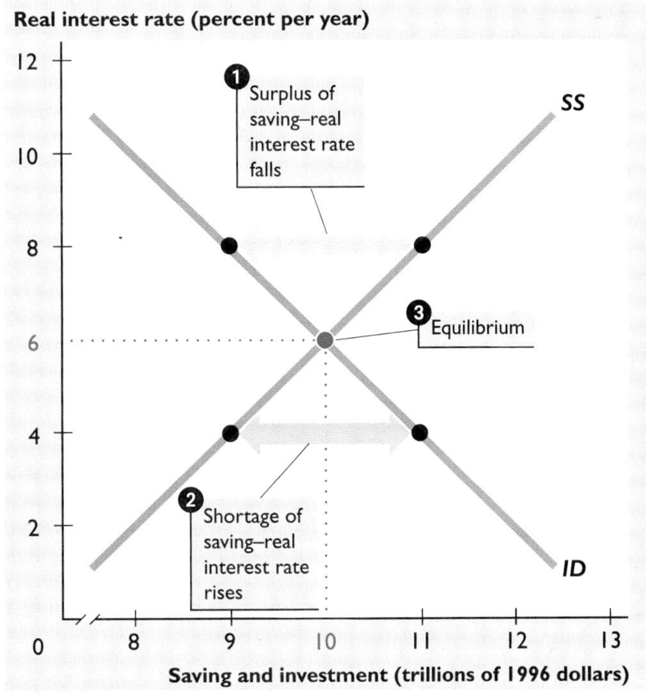

1. If the real interest rate is 8 percent a year, the quantity of investment demanded is less than the quantity of saving supplied. There is a surplus of saving, and the real interest rate falls.
2. If the real interest rate is 4 percent a year, the quantity of investment demanded exceeds the quantity of saving supplied. There is a shortage of saving, and the real interest rate rises.
3. When the real interest rate is 6 percent a year, the quantity of investment demanded equals the quantity of saving supplied. There is neither a shortage nor a surplus of saving, and the real interest rate is at its equilibrium level.

CHECKPOINT 9.2

Study Guide **pp. 131–135**

Practice Online 9.2

2 **Explain how investment and saving decisions are made and how these decisions interact in financial markets to determine the real interest rate.**

Practice Problems 9.2

1. First Call, Inc. is a cellular phone company. It plans to build an assembly plant that costs $10 million if the real interest rate is 6 percent a year. If the real interest rate is 5 percent a year, First Call will build a larger plant that costs $12 million. And if the real interest rate is 7 percent a year, First Call will build a smaller plant that costs $8 million.
   a. Draw a graph of First Call's investment demand curve.
   b. First Call expects its profit from the sale of cellular phones to double next year. If everything else remains the same, explain how this increase in expected profit influences First Call's investment demand.
   c. In 2005, First Call plans to incorporate a new technology into cellular phones. If the demand for its phones increases and other things remain the same, explain the influence of the new technology on First Call's investment demand.
2. In 2002, the King family had a disposable income of $50,000, net assets of $100,000, and an expected future disposable income of $50,000 a year. At a real interest rate of 4 percent a year, the King family would save $10,000 a year; at a real interest rate of 6 percent a year, they would save $12,500 a year; and at a real interest rate of 8 percent a year, they would save $15,000 a year.
   a. Draw a graph of the King family's saving supply curve.
   b. In 2003, the King family expects its future disposable income to increase to $60,000 a year. If other things remain the same, explain how this change influences the King family's saving supply.
   c. In 2004, the stock market booms and the King family's net assets increase in value. If the King family expects its future disposable income to be $50,000 and other things remain the same, explain how this change influences the King family's saving supply.
3. Draw graphs that illustrate how an increase in saving supply and
   a. A decrease in investment demand can lower the real interest rate and leave the equilibrium quantity of saving and investment unchanged.
   b. An even larger increase in investment demand increases the equilibrium quantity of saving and investment and raises the real interest rate.

Exercises 9.2

1. Clean Energy, Inc. is a natural gas company. It plans to build pipelines to metropolitan areas. If the real interest rate is 4 percent a year, it plans to build $25 million of pipelines. If the real interest rate is 6 percent a year, it plans to build $20 million of pipelines. If the real interest rate is 8 percent a year, it plans to build $15 million of pipelines.
   a. Draw a graph of Clean Energy's investment demand curve.
   b. Clean Energy expects the number of households that use gas to increase in the next few years. Explain how this change influences Clean Energy's investment demand curve.

2. In 2002, the Lee family had a disposable income of $80,000, assets of $140,000, and an expected future disposable income of $80,000 a year. At a real interest rate of 4 percent a year, the Lee family would save $15,000 a year; at a real interest rate of 6 percent a year, they would save $20,000 a year; and at a real interest rate of 8 percent, they would save $25,000 a year.
   a. Draw a graph of the Lee family's saving supply curve.
   b. In 2003, the stock market crashes and the Lee family's assets decrease by 50 percent. Explain how this decrease in assets influences the Lee family's saving supply curve.
   c. In 2004, the stock market booms and the Lee family's assets double in value. Explain the influence of this increase in assets on the Lee family's saving supply curve.

3. Draw graphs that illustrate how
   a. A decrease in saving supply and a decrease in investment demand can decrease the equilibrium quantity of saving and investment and leave the real interest rate unchanged.
   b. An increase in investment demand and an even larger increase in saving supply can lower the real interest rate and increase the equilibrium quantity of saving and investment.

FIGURE 1

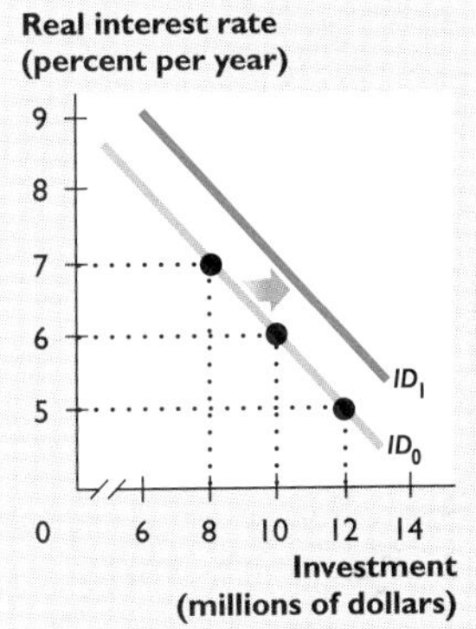

FIGURE 2

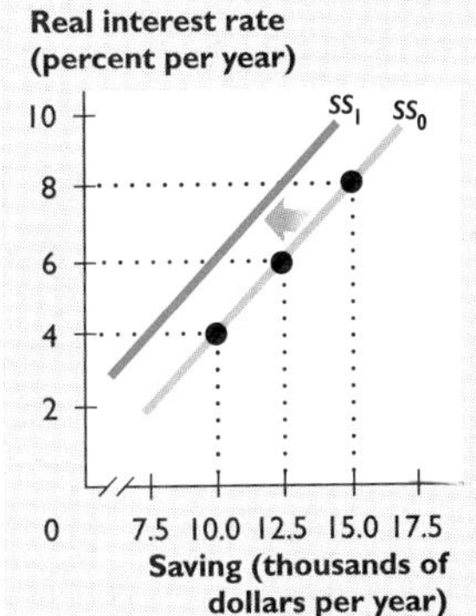

FIGURE 3

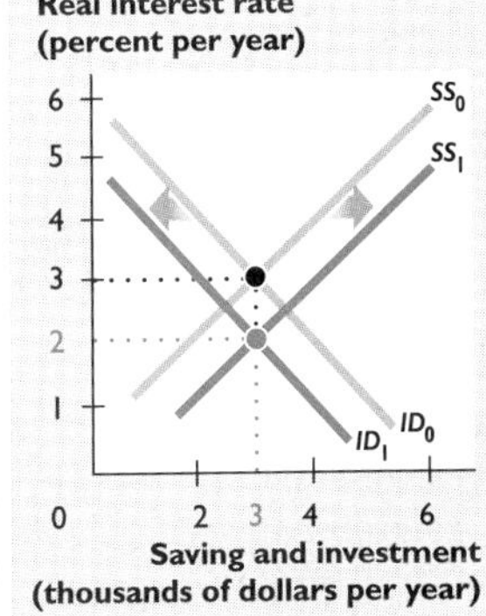

FIGURE 4

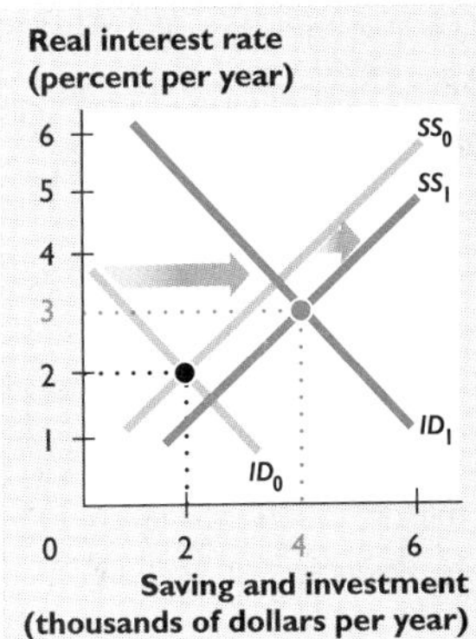

Solutions to Practice Problems 9.2

1a. The investment demand curve is the downward-sloping curve ID_0 and passes through the points highlighted in Figure 1.

1b. An increase in the expected profit increases the amount of investment at each real interest rate. First Call's investment demand increases, and the investment demand curve shifts rightward to ID_1 (Figure 1).

1c. To incorporate the new technology, First Call increases the amount of investment at each real interest rate. First Call's investment demand increases, and the investment demand curve shifts rightward to ID_1 (Figure 1).

2a. The saving supply curve is the upward sloping curve SS_0 and passes through the points highlighted in Figure 2.

2b. An increase in expected future disposable income decreases the amount of saving at each real interest rate. The King family's saving supply decreases, and the saving supply curve shifts leftward to SS_1 (Figure 2).

2c. An increase in the buying power of net assets decreases the amount of saving at each real interest rate. The King family's saving supply decreases, and the saving supply curve shifts leftward to SS_1 (Figure 2).

3a. The increase in saving supply shifts the saving supply curve rightward. The decrease in investment demand shifts the investment demand curve leftward. If the shifts are of the same magnitude, then the real interest rate falls and the equilibrium quantity of saving and investment remains unchanged (Figure 3).

3b. The increase in saving supply shifts the saving supply curve rightward, and the increase in investment demand shifts the investment demand curve rightward, but the investment demand curve shifts farther than the saving supply curve. The real interest rate rises, and the equilibrium quantity of saving and investment increases (Figure 4).

Eye on the Global Economy

Saving, Investment, and the Real Interest Rate Roller Coaster—1973 to 2002

In 1973, the real interest rate was 2 percent a year. But by 1975, it had fallen to *minus* 1 percent a year. This low real interest rate was caused by an increase in saving supply and a decrease in investment demand. The changes in both saving and investment resulted from a single event: a large increase in the price of oil. The suppliers of oil were awash with funds to lend. And the users of oil suffered a big fall in profits and decreased their investment in new capital. Equilibrium saving and investment didn't change much, as part (a) of the figure shows.

By 1984, the real interest rate had increased to 8 percent a year. This increase resulted from a large increase in investment demand accompanied by a smaller increase in saving supply, as part (b) of the figure shows.

Through the 1990s, the real interest rate was around 6 percent a year, and the equilibrium quantity of saving and investment was around twice its mid-1970s level. An increase in the population and in income brought an increase in saving supply. And extraordinary technological advances, especially in communications and information technologies and biotechnologies, brought a large increase in investment demand.

By 2002, an even larger increase in saving supply than the large increase in investment demand lowered the real interest rate to 5 percent a year, as part (c) of the figure shows.

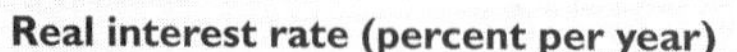

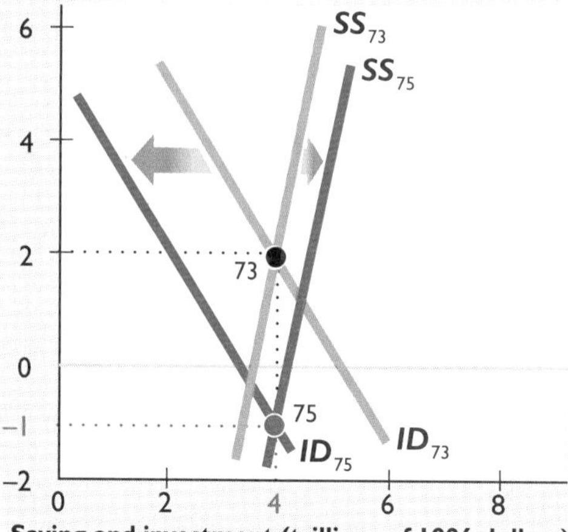

(a) 1973–1975

A large rise in the world price of oil increased saving supply and decreased investment demand.

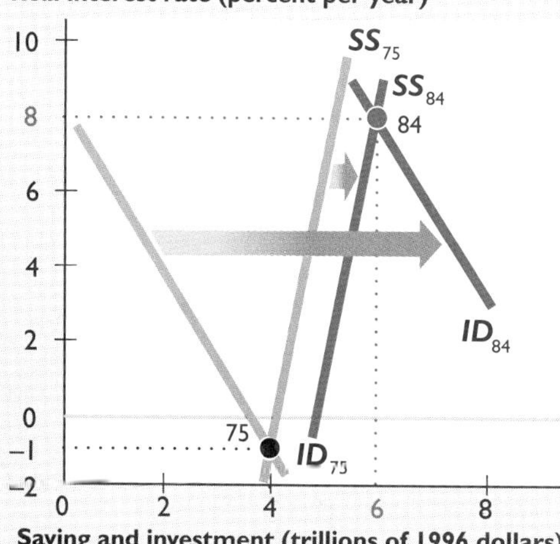

(b) 1975–1984

Slow income growth increased saving supply by less than investment demand and brought a rise in the real interest rate.

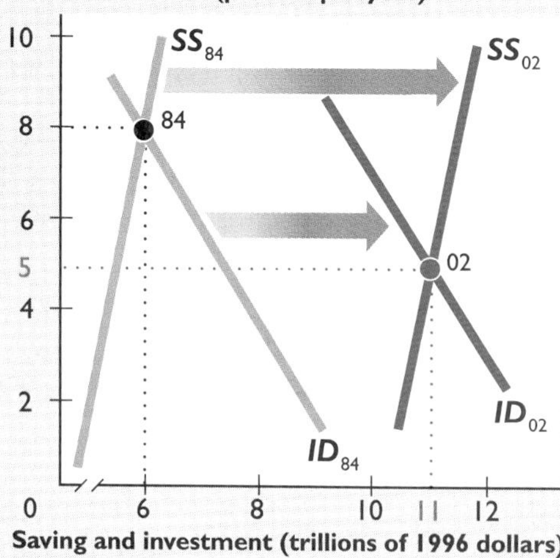

(c) 1984–2002

Rapid income growth increased saving supply by more than investment demand and brought a fall in the real interest rate.

9.3 GOVERNMENT IN THE FINANCIAL MARKET

Part of each nation's saving is government saving, and part of global saving is saving by governments around the world. So government actions that change the saving supply influence the real interest rate and the quantity of investment demanded. To complete our study of the forces that determine the quantity of capital and the real interest rate, we investigate the role played by the government saving.

Government Budget and Government Saving

You learned in Chapter 5 (pp. 114–115) that GDP, Y, equals the sum of consumption expenditure, C; investment, I; government purchases, G; and net exports, NX. Table 9.1 shows data on these variables for 2002. Because we are studying the global financial market, we focus on the global economy, in which net exports are zero. So for the world as a whole,

$$Y = C + I + G.$$

GDP equals total income, which is the sum of consumption expenditure; saving, S; and net taxes, NT. So

$$Y = C + S + NT.$$

By combining these two ways of looking at GDP, you can see that

$$C + I + G = C + S + NT.$$

Because consumption, C, is on both sides of this equation, we can subtract C and simplify the equation to

$$I + G = S + NT.$$

Now subtract government purchases, G, from both sides of this equation to obtain

$$I = S + (NT - G).$$

This equation tells us that investment, I, is financed by private saving, S, and government saving, $NT - G$. Government saving, $NT - G$, is also the government budget surplus. Table 9.2 shows that data for the global economy in 2002.

Total saving equals private saving plus government saving. So when the government has a budget surplus, it contributes toward financing investment. But when the government has a budget deficit, it competes with businesses for private saving and decreases the amount available for investment. Let's study the effects of government saving.

TABLE 9.1 INCOME AND EXPENDITURE IN THE GLOBAL ECONOMY

	Y =	C +	I +	G +	NX
	(trillions of dollars)				
United States	9.2	6.4	1.6	1.6	–0.4
Rest of world	41.4	27.3	6.8	6.9	0.4
Global economy	50.6	33.7	8.4	8.5	0

SOURCES: Bureau of Economic Analysis and International Monetary Fund.

TABLE 9.2 INVESTMENT, SAVING, AND NET TAXES IN THE GLOBAL ECONOMY

	I =	S +	NT –	G –	NX
	(trillions of dollars)				
United States	1.6	1.2	1.6	–1.6	0.4
Rest of world	6.8	8.5	5.6	–6.9	–0.4
Global economy	8.4	9.7	7.2	–8.5	0

SOURCES: Bureau of Economic Analysis and International Monetary Fund.

Effect of Government Saving

A government budget surplus increases total saving supply. To find total saving supply, we must add the government budget surplus to the private saving supply. An increase in total saving supply brings a lower interest rate, which decreases the quantity of private saving supplied and increases the quantity of investment.

Figure 9.7 shows these effects of government saving. The private saving supply curve, PS, shows the relationship between private saving and the real interest rate. The saving supply curve, SS, shows the sum of private saving and government saving. Here, government saving is a constant \$2 trillion at each real interest rate, so the saving supply curve lies \$2 trillion to the right of the private saving supply curve. That is, the horizontal distance between the private saving curve and the saving supply curve is government saving.

The investment demand curve, *ID*, is the same as that in Figure 9.6. In the absence of government saving, the real interest rate would be 6 percent a year and saving and investment would be $10 trillion a year. But with the government saving $2 trillion a year, the equilibrium interest rate falls to 4 percent a year. Investment increases to $11 trillion. Private saving decreases to $9 trillion. Private saving plus government saving equals investment.

So government saving—a government budget surplus—lowers the real interest rate and increases investment.

Government Deficit and Crowding Out

A government budget deficit works in the opposite way to the surplus that we've just examined. It decreases total saving. So to find total saving, we must subtract the government budget deficit from private saving. But a decrease in total saving brings a higher interest rate, which increases the quantity of private saving supplied. So to work out the effects of government saving, we need to find its effects on the interest rate. The private saving supply curve, *PS*, and the investment demand curve, *ID*, are the same as those in Figure 9.7. The horizontal distance between the private saving curve and the saving supply curve is the government budget deficit. In this example, government saving is a negative $2 trillion. That is, the government has a budget deficit of $2 trillion.

The effect of government negative saving (also called dissaving) is to decrease total saving supply and increase the real interest rate. Investment decreases. In

FIGURE 9.7
Government Saving

Practice Online

The investment demand curve is *ID*, and the private saving supply curve is *PS*. With balanced government budgets, the real interest rate is 6 percent a year and investment equals saving at $10 trillion a year.

1. A government budget surplus of $2 trillion is added to private saving to determine the saving supply curve *SS*.
2. The real interest rate falls to 4 percent a year, 3. private saving decreases to $9 trillion, and
4. total saving and investment increase to $11 trillion.

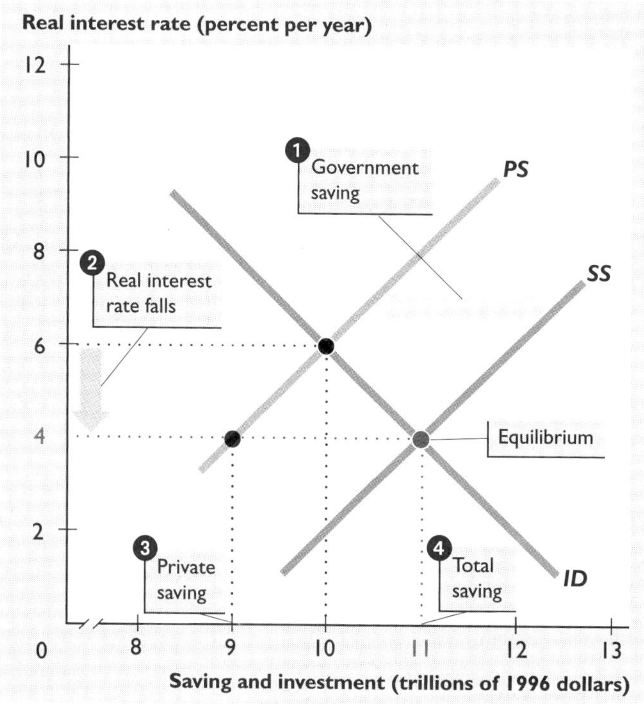

Figure 9.8, with a government budget deficit of $2 trillion, the saving supply curve shifts leftward and the real interest rate rises from 6 percent a year to 8 percent a year. Total saving and investment decrease from $10 trillion to $9 trillion. By raising the real interest rate, the government budget deficit crowds out investment. The tendency for a government budget deficit to decrease investment is called the **crowding-out effect**.

Crowding-out effect
The tendency for a government budget deficit to decrease investment.

Investment does not decrease by the full amount of the government budget deficit because the higher real interest rate induces an increase in private saving. In this example, private saving increases by $1 trillion to $11 trillion. In reality, the increase in private saving might be quite small.

The Ricardo-Barro Effect

First suggested by the English economist David Ricardo in the eighteenth century and refined by Robert J. Barro of Harvard University during the 1980s, the Ricardo-Barro effect holds that the effects we've just shown are wrong and that the government budget deficit has no effect on the real interest rate or investment. The reason is that the private saving supply changes and the private saving supply curve shifts to offset any change in government saving, so the total saving supply is unchanged. It is argued that rational taxpayers can see that a deficit today means that future taxes will be higher and disposable incomes will be smaller. With a smaller expected future disposable income, saving increases. Most economists regard this view as extreme. But there is probably some partial change in private saving supply that goes in the direction suggested by Ricardo and Barro that lessens the effect of the government budget on the real interest rate and investment.

FIGURE 9.8
A Crowding-Out Effect

Practice Online

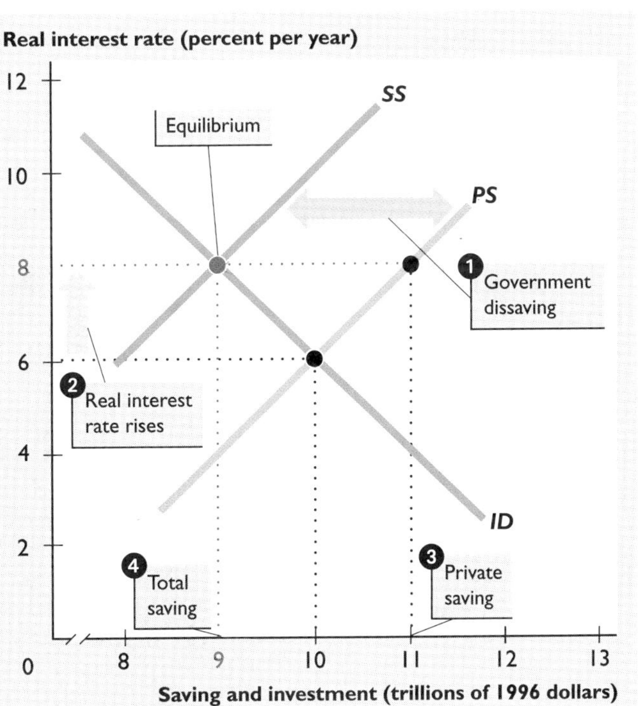

The investment demand curve is *ID*, and the private saving supply curve is *PS*. With balanced government budgets, the real interest rate is 6 percent a year and investment equals saving at $10 trillion a year.

1. A government budget deficit of $2 trillion is subtracted from private saving to determine the saving supply curve *SS*.
2. The real interest rate rises to 8 percent a year, 3. private saving increases to $11 trillion, and 4. total saving and investment decreases to $9 trillion. Investment is crowded out.

CHECKPOINT 9.3

Study Guide pp. 136–138

Practice Online 9.3

3 **Explain how government influences the real interest rate, investment, and saving.**

Practice Problem 9.3

Table 1 shows the investment demand schedule and the supply schedule of private saving.

a. If the government budget surplus is $1 trillion, what are the real interest rate, the quantity of investment, and the quantity of private saving? Is there any crowding out in this situation?

b. If the government budget deficit is $1 trillion, what are the real interest rate, the quantity of investment, and the quantity of private saving? Is there any crowding out in this situation?

c. If the Ricardo-Barro effect occurs, how do your answers to part **a** and part **b** change?

TABLE 1

Real interest rate (percent per year)	Investment	Private saving
	(trillions of 1996 dollars per year)	
4	8.5	5.5
5	8.0	6.0
6	7.5	6.5
7	7.0	7.0
8	6.5	7.5
9	6.0	8.0
10	5.5	8.5

Exercise 9.3

Starting from the situation in Table 1, investment demand increases by $1 trillion at each real interest rate and the supply of private saving increases by $2 trillion at each interest rate.

a. If the government budget has neither a surplus nor a deficit, what are the real interest rate, the quantity of investment, and the quantity of private saving? Is there any crowding out in this situation?

b. If the government budget deficit is $1 trillion, what are the real interest rate, the quantity of investment, and the quantity of private saving? Is there any crowding out in this situation?

c. If governments want to stimulate the quantity of investment and increase it to $9 trillion, what must they do?

FIGURE 1

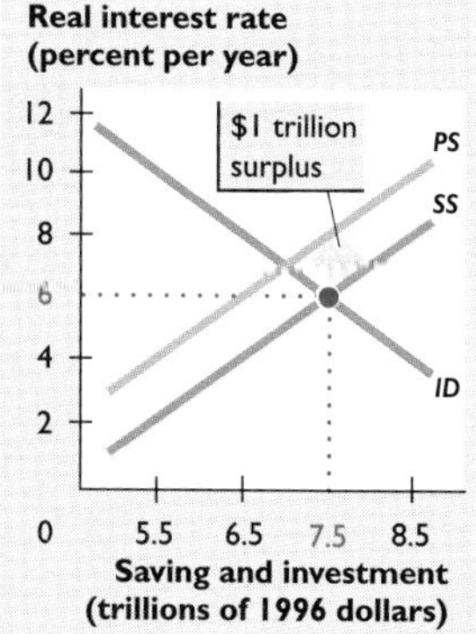

FIGURE 2

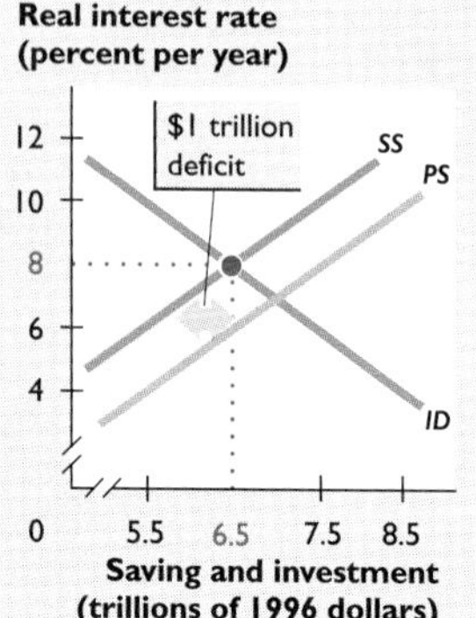

Solution to Practice Problem 9.3

a. If the government budget surplus is $1 trillion, the equilibrium real interest rate is 6 percent a year, the quantity of investment is $7.5 trillion, and the quantity of private saving is $6.5 trillion. There is no crowding out in this situation (Figure 1).

b. If the government budget deficit is $1 trillion, the equilibrium real interest rate is 8 percent a year, the quantity of investment is $6.5 trillion, and the quantity of private saving is $7.5 trillion. There is crowding out in this situation because the deficit increases the real interest rate, which decreases the quantity of investment demanded (Figure 2).

c. If the Ricardo-Barro effect occurs, private saving changes to offset the budget surplus or deficit, and the equilibrium real interest rate equals 7 percent a year. With a balanced government budget, the equilibrium quantity of investment is $7 trillion. There is no crowding out because the government saving or dissaving has no effect on the real interest rate and the quantity of investment.

CHAPTER CHECKPOINT

Key Points

1 Define and explain the relationships among capital, investment, wealth, and saving.

- Firms use financial capital to buy and operate physical capital.
- Gross investment is the total amount spent on physical capital in a given period. Net investment equals gross investment minus depreciation.
- Wealth is the value of what people own; saving is the amount of income that is not spent, and it adds to wealth.
- A financial market (stock, bond, short-term securities, or loans market) is the collection of households, firms, government, banks, and other financial institutions that lend and borrow to finance the purchase of physical capital.

2 Explain how investment and saving decisions are made and how these decisions interact in financial markets to determine the real interest rate.

- Other things remaining the same, the lower the real interest rate or the higher the expected profit rate, the greater is the amount of investment.
- Investment demand changes when the expected profit rate changes.
- Other things remaining the same, the higher the real interest rate, the greater is saving.
- Saving supply changes when disposable income, the buying power of net assets, or expected future disposable income changes.
- Because capital is free to move internationally to seek the highest possible real rate of return, the real interest rate is determined in a global market.
- The equilibrium real interest rate makes global saving equal to global investment.

3 Explain how government influences the real interest rate, investment, and saving.

- Total saving equals private saving plus government saving.
- Government saving equals net taxes minus government purchases.
- A government budget deficit might increase the real interest rate and crowd out private investment.
- A government budget deficit might also increase private saving supply because it decreases expected future disposable income.

Key Terms

Bond, 213
Bond market, 213
Crowding-out effect, 227
Disposable income, 218
Financial capital, 210
Financial markets, 212
Gross investment, 210
Investment demand, 215
Net investment, 210
Physical capital, 210
Saving, 212
Saving supply, 218
Stock, 212
Stock market, 213
Wealth, 212

Exercises

1. On January 1, 2002, Terry's Towing Service owned 4 tow trucks valued at $300,000. During 2002, Terry's bought 2 new trucks that cost a total of $180,000, and at the end of the year, the market value of all the firm's trucks was $400,000.
   a. What was Terry's gross investment during 2002?
   b. What was its depreciation?
   c. What was its net investment?

2. The Bureau of Economic Analysis reported that the U.S. capital stock (in 1996 dollars) was $23.087 billion at the end of 1999, $23,801 billion at the end of 2000, and $24,390 billion at the end of 2001. Depreciation in 2000 was $1,049 billion, and gross investment during 2001 was $1,575 billion (all in 1996 dollars).
   a. What was U.S. net investment during 2000 and 2001?
   b. What was the amount of gross investment during 2000?
   c. What was the amount of depreciation during 2001?
   d. Compare the net investment, gross investment, depreciation, and capital in 2000 and 2001. What do you think these numbers tell us was happening in the U.S. economy during 2001?

3. Mike takes a summer job washing cars. During the summer, he earns an after-tax income of $3,000 and he spends $1,000 on goods and services.
   a. What was Mike's saving during the summer?
   b. What was the change, if any, to Mike's wealth?

4. The numbers in the second column of Table 1 are the Federal Reserve's estimates of the net worth of households and nonprofit organizations at the end of each year. The numbers in the third column are the Bureau of Economic Analysis's estimates of personal saving—disposable income minus consumption expenditure—each year.
   a. In which years did the change in wealth exceed saving?
   b. In which years did saving exceed the change in wealth?
   c. Given the definitions of saving and wealth, how can the change in wealth differ from saving?
   d. What would you estimate was the total value of capital gains during 1997?
   e. What would you estimate was the total value of capital gains during 2001?

TABLE 1 HOUSEHOLDS AND NONPROFIT ORGANIZATIONS

Year	Net worth (billions of 1996 dollars)	Saving (billions of 1996 dollars)
1991	24,342	415
1992	24,695	450
1993	25,340	373
1994	25,487	329
1995	27,700	308
1996	29,713	272
1997	32,854	248
1998	35,681	292
1999	39,810	154
2000	38,353	63
2001	36,450	108

5. What is a financial market? What gets traded in a financial market? What is the price that a financial market determines?

6. Explain why when the real interest rate rises, investment demand does not change but the quantity of investment demanded decreases.

7. A new technology is developed that increases firms' expected profits and creates an increase in investment demand.
   a. Draw a graph to show the effect of this development on the investment demand curve.
   b. Show the effects of this development on the equilibrium real interest rate.

8. Explain why each of the following items changes the private saving supply:
   a. An increase in the buying power of assets.
   b. An increase in expected future disposable income.
   c. A cut in current income taxes.

9. Consider the effects of two developments that occurred during the 1990s:
   i. The invention and use of fiber-optic technologies that required billions of dollars to be spent laying new cables under the oceans and launching communications satellites.
   ii. A stock market boom that increased the buying power of net assets by trillions of dollars.
   a. Draw a graph to illustrate investment demand, saving supply, and equilibrium in the global capital market before the two developments occured.
   b. Show, on your graph, the effects of event **i**.
   c. Show, on your graph, the effects of event **ii**.
   d. Show, on your graph, the combined effects of the two events.
   e. Do the changes that actually occurred during the 1990s correspond to the effects of these two events? If not, what else do you think was happening?

10. During the 1980s and most of the 1990s, governments around the world had large budget deficits. Around 2000, government budget deficits began to turn into surpluses.
   a. Draw a graph to illustrate the global capital market that distinguishes among private saving, government saving, and total saving.
   b. Show, on your graph, the effects of a switch from a government budget deficit to a government budget surplus if there is no Ricardo-Barro effect.
   c. Show, on your graph, the effects of a switch from a government budget deficit to a government budget surplus if there is a complete Ricardo-Barro effect.
   d. Show, on your graph, the effects of a switch from a government budget deficit to a government budget surplus if there is a partial Ricardo-Barro effect.

11. As global tension increased during 2001 and 2002, the defense budgets of the U.S. government and many other governments around the world brought an increase in overall government spending and a decrease in government budget surpluses.
   a. Draw a graph to illustrate the global capital market that distinguishes among private saving, government saving, and total saving.
   b. Show, on your graph, the effects of a decrease in government budget surpluses if there is no Ricardo-Barro effect.
   c. Show, on your graph, the effects of a decrease in government budget surpluses if there is a complete Ricardo-Barro effect.
   d. Show, on your graph, the effects of a decrease in government budget surpluses if there is a partial Ricardo-Barro effect.

Critical Thinking

12. Look at the data provided in Eye on the U.S. Economy on page 211.
    a. What fluctuates most and why: net investment, gross investment, depreciation, or capital?
    b. Why do you think net investment surged upward so strongly during the 1990s?
    c. How might you set about determining whether the swings in net investment were changes in investment demand or changes in the quantity of investment?
    d. Can you think of ways in which the fluctuations in investment might be smoothed?
    e. Do you think it would it be a good idea or a bad idea to smooth the fluctuations? Why?
13. China, India, and Indonesia account for about half the world's population but a small part of world saving and investment. If these economies became wealthier and more similar to the United States, how do you think they would affect the global capital market? Would you expect the real interest rate to rise, fall, or remain close to its current level? Why?
14. During 2001, the Commerce Department reported that the U.S. saving rate was negative. How can the saving rate be negative? Why might a negative saving rate be something to worry about? How do you think saving could be stimulated?

Practice Online

Web Exercises

Use the links on your Foundations Web site to work the following exercises.

15. Visit the Web sites of the New York Stock Exchange and the London Stock Exchange, and PACIFIC.
    a. Find a stock that trades on both exchanges and obtain its current price in New York and London.
    b. Find today's exchange rate between the U.S. dollar and the U.K. pound.
    c. Use today's exchange rate to convert the London price to U.S. dollars.
    d. What is the difference in the two prices? Could you earn a profit by buying in one market and selling in the other?
    e. Why do you think the prices are so similar in the two stock markets?
16. Open the file that provides data on saving rates in the United States and the new industrial economies of East Asia.
    a. Which of the countries has the highest saving rate and which has the lowest?
    b. Of the factors that influence saving, do you think the differences across these economies represent differences in the supply of saving or differences in the quantity of saving supplied? Explain your answer.
    c. Of the influences on the supply of saving, which do you think might account for the differences in saving rates that you've found?

CHAPTER 10

Economic Growth

CHAPTER CHECKLIST

When you have completed your study of this chapter, you will be able to

1. **Define and calculate the economic growth rate, and explain the implications of sustained growth.**
2. **Identify the main sources of economic growth.**
3. **Review the theories of economic growth that explain why growth rates vary over time and across countries.**
4. **Describe policies that might speed economic growth.**

In this chapter, we study the trends in real GDP and the standard of living. Will we have a higher standard of living than our parents did? Will our children have a higher standard of living than we do? Do all countries and regions share in rising living standards, or do some perform better than others? These are among the questions that we'll answer in this chapter.

You learned in Chapter 8 what determines the quantity of labor employed and real GDP when there is full employment. And you learned in Chapter 9 how saving and investment bring an increase in the quantity of capital. This chapter combines the lessons of those two chapters and explains how advancing technology and growing population, labor, and capital expand production possibilities and bring sustained growth in real GDP and the standard of living.

10.1 THE BASICS OF ECONOMIC GROWTH

Economic growth is a sustained expansion of production possibilities measured as the increase in real GDP over a given period. Rapid economic growth maintained over a number of years can transform a poor nation into a rich one. Such has been the experience of Hong Kong, South Korea, Taiwan, and some other Asian economies. Slow economic growth or the absence of growth can condemn a nation to devastating poverty. Such has been the fate of Sierra Leone, Somalia, Zambia, and much of the rest of Africa.

The main goal of this chapter is to help you to understand why some economies expand rapidly and others stagnate. We'll begin by learning how to calculate the economic growth rate and by discovering the magic of sustained growth.

Calculating Growth Rates

Economic growth rate
The annual percentage change of real GDP.

We express the **economic growth rate** as the annual percentage change of real GDP. To calculate this growth rate, we use the formula:

$$\text{Growth rate of real GDP} = \frac{\text{Real GDP in current year} - \text{Real GDP in previous year}}{\text{Real GDP in previous year}} \times 100.$$

For example, if real GDP in the current year is \$8.4 trillion and if real GDP in the previous year was \$8.0 trillion, then

$$\text{Growth rate of real GDP} = \frac{\$8.4 \text{ trillion} - \$8.0 \text{ trillion}}{\$8.0 \text{ trillion}} \times 100 = 5 \text{ percent}.$$

The growth rate of real GDP tells us how rapidly the total economy is expanding. This measure is useful for telling us about potential changes in the balance of economic power among nations. But it does not tell us about changes in the standard of living.

Real GDP per person
Real GDP divided by the population.

The standard of living depends on **real GDP per person**, which is real GDP divided by the population. So the contribution of real GDP growth to the change in the *standard of living* depends on the growth rate of real GDP per person. We use the above formula to calculate this growth rate, replacing real GDP with real GDP per person.

Suppose, for example, that in the current year, when real GDP is \$8.4 trillion, the population is 202 million. Then real GDP per person is \$8.4 trillion divided by 202 million, which equals \$41,584. And suppose that in the previous year, when real GDP was \$8.0 trillion, the population was 200 million. Then real GDP per person in that year was \$8.0 trillion divided by 200 million, which equals \$40,000.

Use these two real GDP per person values with the growth formula to calculate the growth rate of real GDP per person. That is,

$$\text{Growth rate of real GDP per person} = \frac{\$41{,}584 - \$40{,}000}{\$40{,}000} \times 100 = 4 \text{ percent}.$$

The growth rate of real GDP per person can also be calculated by using the formula:

$$\text{Growth rate of real GDP per person} = \text{Growth rate of real GDP} - \text{Growth rate of population}.$$

In the example you've just worked through, the growth rate of real GDP is 5 percent. The population changes from 200 million to 202 million, so

$$\text{Growth rate of population} = \frac{202 \text{ million} - 200 \text{ million}}{200 \text{ million}} \times 100 = 1 \text{ percent},$$

and

$$\text{Growth rate of real GDP per person} = 5 \text{ percent} - 1 \text{ percent} = 4 \text{ percent}.$$

This formula makes it clear that real GDP per person grows only if real GDP grows faster than the population grows. If the growth rate of the population exceeds the growth of real GDP, real GDP per person falls.

The Magic of Sustained Growth

Sustained growth of real GDP per person can transform a poor society into a wealthy one. The reason is that economic growth is like compound interest. Suppose that you put $100 in the bank and earn 5 percent a year interest on it. After one year, you have $105. If you leave that money in the bank for another year, you earn 5 percent interest on the original $100 and on the $5 interest that you earned last year. You are now earning interest on interest! The next year, things get even better. Then you earn 5 percent on the original $100 and on the interest earned in the first year and the second year. Your money in the bank is *growing* at a rate of 5 percent a year. Before too many years have passed, you'll have $200 in the bank. But after *how many* years?

The answer is provided by a powerful and general formula known as the **Rule of 70**, which states that the number of years it takes for the level of any variable to double is approximately 70 divided by the annual percentage growth rate of the variable. Using the Rule of 70, you can now calculate how many years it takes your $100 to become $200. It is 70 divided by 5, which is 14 years.

Rule of 70
The number of years it takes for the level of any variable to double is approximately 70 divided by the annual percentage growth rate of the variable.

The Rule of 70 applies to any variable, so it applies to real GDP per person. Table 10.1 shows the doubling time for a selection of other growth rates. You can see that real GDP per person doubles in 70 years (70 divided by 1)—an average human life span—if the growth rate is 1 percent a year. It doubles in 35 years if the growth rate is 2 percent a year and in just 10 years if the growth rate is 7 percent a year.

TABLE 10.1 GROWTH RATES

Growth rate (percent per year)	Years for level to double
1	70
2	35
3	23
4	18
5	14
6	12
7	10
8	9
9	8
10	7

We can use the Rule of 70 to answer other questions about economic growth. For example, in 2000, U.S. real GDP per person was approximately 8 times that of China. China's recent growth rate of real GDP per person was 7 percent a year. If this growth rate were maintained, how long would it take China's real GDP per person to reach that of the United States in 2000? The answer, provided by the Rule of 70, is 30 years. China's real GDP per person doubles in 10 (70 divided by 7) years. It doubles again to 4 times its current level in another 10 years. And it doubles yet again to 8 times its current level in another 10 years. So after 30 years of growth at 7 percent a year, China's real GDP per person is 8 times its current level and equals that of the United States in 2000.

Eye on the Past

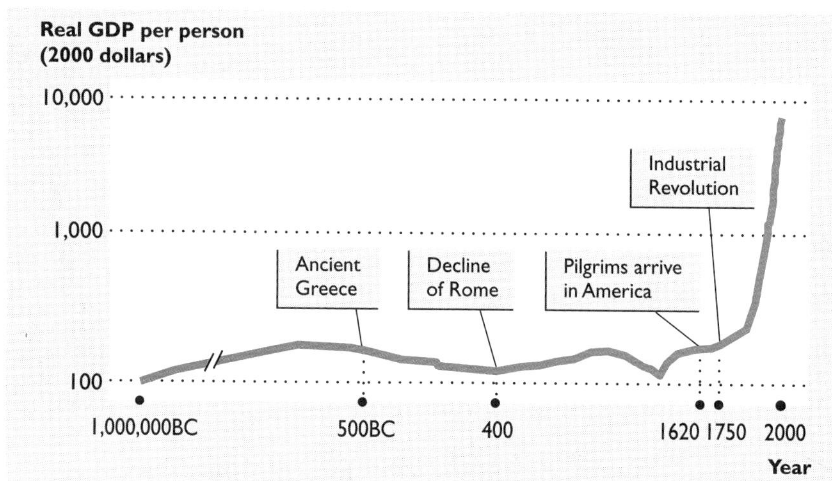

SOURCE: J. Bradford DeLong, *"Estimating World GDP, One Million B.C.–Present."*

How Fast Has Real GDP per Person Grown?

Professor Michael Kremer of Harvard University and Professor J. Bradford DeLong of the University of California, Berkeley, have constructed an extraordinary picture of real GDP in the global economy going back one million years. According to their numbers, human societies lived for a million years with no economic growth.

The top figure shows the numbers using the value of the dollar in 2000 as the measuring rod. Real GDP per person hovered around $100 per year from 1,000,000 BC until 1350! There were some wiggles and wobbles along the way. When Aristotle and Plato were teaching in Athens, around 500 BC, real GDP per person climbed to $175. But it slipped back over the next thousand years, and as the Roman Empire collapsed around 400 AD, it was $120. Even when the Pilgrim Fathers began to arrive in America in the 1620s, real GDP per person was similar to that of Ancient Greece!

Then, beginning around 1750, first in England and then in Europe and the United States, an astonishing change known as the Industrial Revolution occurred. Real GDP per person began to increase, apparently without limit. By 1850, real GDP per person was twice its 1650 level. By 1950, it was more than five times its 1850 level and by 2000, it was four times its 1950 level.

The bottom figure gives you a close-up view of U.S. real GDP per person over the past 100 years. In 1999, real GDP per person was almost six times its level in 1899. It has grown by 2 percent a year. But the growth rate has been uneven. The 1930s saw almost no growth, and the 1960s saw the fastest growth. Measured decade by decade, growth has been slowing since the 1960s.

But if we divide the 1990s into two periods, before and after the Internet (1994), we see a speedup in the growth rate after 1994. Some people think that in the current information age, we are at the beginning of a new increase in economic growth similar to that of the Industrial Revolution. No one knows yet whether this view is correct.

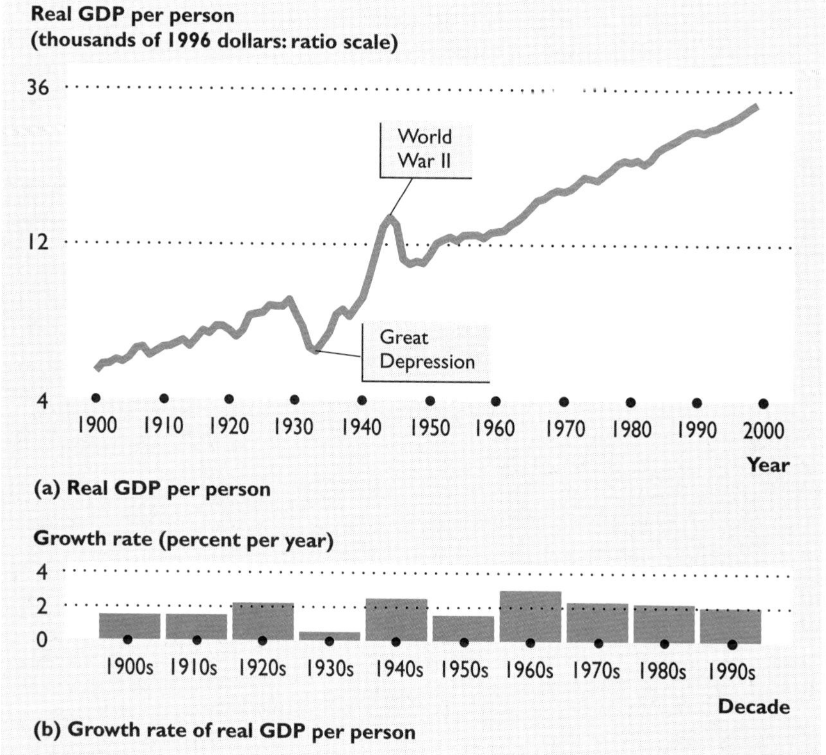

(a) Real GDP per person

(b) Growth rate of real GDP per person

SOURCE: Bureau of Economic Analysis and Bureau of Labor Statistics.

CHECKPOINT 10.1

1 Define and calculate the economic growth rate, and explain the implications of sustained growth.

Study Guide pp. 144–147

Practice Online 10.1

Practice Problem 10.1

Mexico's real GDP was 1,448 billion pesos in 1998 and 1,501 billion pesos in 1999. Mexico's population growth rate in 1999 was 1.8 percent. Calculate

- **a.** Mexico's economic growth rate in 1999.
- **b.** The growth rate of real GDP per person in Mexico in 1999.
- **c.** The approximate number of years it takes for real GDP per person in Mexico to double if the 1999 economic growth rate and population growth rate are maintained.
- **d.** The approximate number of years it takes for real GDP per person in Mexico to double if the 1999 economic growth rate is maintained but the population growth rate slows to 1 percent a year.

Exercise 10.1

Canada's real GDP was $1,012 billion in 2000 and $1,028 billion in 2001. Canada's population was 30.8 million in 2000 and 31.1 million in 2001. Calculate

- **a.** Canada's economic growth rate in 2001.
- **b.** The growth rate of real GDP per person in Canada in 2001.
- **c.** The approximate number of years it takes for real GDP per person in Canada to double if the 2001 economic growth rate and population growth rate are maintained.
- **d.** The approximate number of years it takes for real GDP per person in Canada to double if the economic growth rate rises to 6 percent a year but the population growth rate remains the same as it was in 2001.

Solution to Practice Problem 10.1

- **a.** Mexico's economic growth rate in 1999 was 3.7 percent. The economic growth rate equals the percentage change in real GDP:
  [(Real GDP in 1999 – Real GDP in 1998)/Real GDP in 1998] × 100.
  When we substitute the numbers, Mexico's economic growth rate equals [(1,501 billion – 1,448 billion)/1,448 billion] × 100, which is 3.7 percent.
- **b.** The growth rate of real GDP per person in Mexico in 1999 was 1.9 percent. The growth rate of real GDP per person equals the growth rate of real GDP minus the population growth rate. When we substitute the numbers, the growth rate of real GDP per person equals 3.7 percent – 1.8 percent, or 1.9 percent.
- **c.** It will take approximately 37 years for real GDP per person in Mexico to double. The Rule of 70 tells us that the level of a variable that grows at 1.9 percent a year will double in 70/1.9 years, which is approximately 37 years.
- **d.** If Mexico's population growth rate falls to 1.0 percent a year, real GDP per person in Mexico will increase to 2.7 percent a year. The Rule of 70 tells us that real GDP in Mexico will double in 70/2.7 years, which is approximately 26 years.

10.2 THE SOURCES OF ECONOMIC GROWTH

Real GDP grows when the quantities of the factors of production grow or when persistent advances in technology make them increasingly productive. To understand what determines the growth rate of real GDP, we must understand what determines the growth rates of the factors of production and rate of increase in their productivity. We've already seen that saving and investment determine the growth rate of physical capital. We're now going to see how the growth of physical capital and human capital and advances in technology interact to determine the economic growth rate.

We are interested in real GDP growth because it contributes to improvements in our standard of living. But our standard of living improves only if we produce more goods and services with each hour of labor. So our main concern is to understand the forces that make our labor more productive. For this reason, we begin by dividing all the influences on real GDP growth into those that increase

- Aggregate hours
- Labor productivity

Aggregate Hours

Over time, aggregate hours increase. This growth in aggregate hours comes from growth in the labor force rather than from growth in average hours per worker. As you saw in Chapter 6 (pp. 144–145), average hours per worker have *decreased* over the past decades. This decrease—and an associated *increase* in average leisure hours—is one of the benefits of economic growth.

The labor force depends on the population and the *labor force participation rate* (see Chapter 6, p. 138). While the participation rate has increased over the past few decades, it has an upper limit, and most of the growth of aggregate hours comes from population growth. So population growth is the only source of growth in aggregate labor hours that can be sustained over long periods.

Population growth brings economic growth, but it does not bring growth in real GDP per person unless labor hours become more productive.

Labor Productivity

Labor productivity
The quantity of real GDP produced by one hour of labor.

The quantity of real GDP produced by one hour of labor is called **labor productivity**. It is calculated by using the formula:

$$\text{Labor productivity} = \frac{\text{Real GDP}}{\text{Aggregate hours}}.$$

For example, if real GDP is \$8,000 billion and if aggregate hours are 200 billion, then we can calculate labor productivity as

$$\text{Labor productivity} = \frac{\$8{,}000 \text{ billion}}{200 \text{ billion hours}} = \$40 \text{ an hour.}$$

You can turn this formula around and see that

$$\text{Real GDP} = \text{Aggregate hours} \times \text{Labor productivity}.$$

When labor productivity grows, real GDP per person grows. So the growth in labor productivity is the basis of rising living standards. The growth of labor productivity depends on three things:

- Saving and investment in physical capital
- Expansion of human capital
- Discovery of new technologies

These three sources of growth in labor productivity interact and are the primary sources of the extraordinary growth in productivity during the past 200 years. Let's look at each in turn.

Saving and Investment in Physical Capital

Saving and investment in physical capital increase the amount of capital per worker and increase labor productivity. Labor productivity took a dramatic upturn when the amount of capital per worker increased during the Industrial Revolution. Production processes that use hand tools can create beautiful objects, but production methods that use large amounts of capital per worker, such as auto plant assembly lines, enable workers to be much more productive. The accumulation of capital on farms, in textile factories, in iron foundries and steel mills, in coal mines, on building sites, in chemical plants, in auto plants, in banks, and in insurance companies has added incredibly to the productivity of our labor.

A strong and experienced farm worker of 1830, using a scythe, could harvest 3 acres of wheat in a day. A farm worker of 1831, using a mechanical reaper, could harvest 15 acres in a day. And a farm worker of today, using a combine harvester, can harvest and thresh 100 acres a day.

The next time you see a movie set in the old West, look carefully at the small amount of capital around. Try to imagine how productive you would be in such circumstances compared with your productivity today.

Expansion of Human Capital

Human capital—the accumulated skill and knowledge of people—comes from two sources:

- Education and training
- Job experience

A hundred years ago, most people attended school for around eight years. A hundred years before that, most people had no formal education at all. Today, 90 percent of Americans complete high school and more than 60 percent go to college or university. Our ability to read, write, and communicate effectively contributes enormously to our productivity.

While formal education is productive, school is not the only place where people acquire human capital. We also learn from on-the-job experience—from *learning by doing*. One carefully studied example illustrates the importance of learning by doing. Between 1941 and 1944 (during World War II), U.S. shipyards produced 2,500 Liberty Ships—a cargo ship built to a standardized design. In 1941, it took 1.2 million person-hours to build a ship. By 1942, it took 600,000, and by 1943, it took only 500,000. Not much change occurred in the physical capital employed during these years. But an enormous amount of human capital was accumulated. Thousands of workers and managers learned from experience and more than doubled their productivity in two years.

The expansion of human capital is the most fundamental source of economic growth because it directly increases labor productivity and is the source of the discovery of new technologies.

Discovery of New Technologies

The growth of physical capital and human capital has made a large contribution to economic growth. But the discovery and application of new technologies have made an even greater contribution.

The development of writing, one of the most basic human skills, was the source of some of the earliest productivity gains. The ability to keep written records made it possible to reap ever-larger gains from specialization and trade. Imagine how hard it would be to do any kind of business if all the accounts, invoices, and agreements existed only in people's memories.

Later, the development of mathematics laid the foundation for the eventual extension of knowledge in physics, chemistry, and biology. This base of scientific knowledge was the foundation for the technological advances of the Industrial Revolution 200 years ago and of today's Information Revolution.

Since the Industrial Revolution, technological change has become a part of everyday life. Firms routinely conduct research to develop technologies that are more productive, and partnerships between business and the universities are commonplace in fields such as biotechnology and electronics.

To reap the benefits of technological change, capital must increase. Some of the most powerful and far-reaching technologies are embodied in human capital—for example, language, writing, and mathematics. But most technologies are embodied in physical capital. For example, to reap the benefits of the internal combustion engine, millions of horse-drawn carriages had to be replaced by automobiles and trucks; more recently, to reap the benefits of computerized word processing, millions of typewriters had to be replaced by PCs and printers.

Sources of Growth: A Summary

Figure 10.1 summarizes the sources of economic growth. Your next task is to learn how these sources combine and how we identify the separate contributions of capital growth and the other influences on labor productivity.

FIGURE 10.1
The Sources of Economic Growth

Practice Online

Real GDP depends on aggregate labor hours and labor productivity. Labor productivity depends on the amount of physical capital and human capital and the state of technology. Growth in aggregate hours and growth in labor productivity bring real GDP growth.

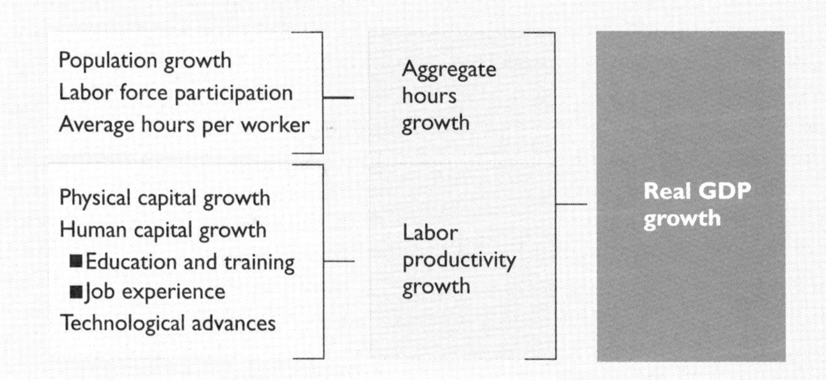

The Productivity Curve

The **productivity curve** is a relationship between real GDP per hour of labor and the quantity of capital per hour of labor with a given state of technology. Figure 10.2 illustrates the productivity curve. Capital per hour of labor, measured on the *x*-axis, is physical capital valued in 1996 dollars. (Remember that even though we use dollar values to measure capital, we are talking about *physical capital*.) Labor productivity (real GDP per hour of labor) is measured on the *y*-axis. The figure shows two productivity curves, one labeled PC_0 and the other labeled PC_1.

Productivity curve
The relationship between real GDP per hour of labor and the quantity of capital per hour of labor with a given state of technology.

An increase in the quantity of capital per hour of labor increases labor productivity, which is shown by a movement along a productivity curve. For example, on PC_0, when capital per hour of labor is \$30, labor productivity is \$20 an hour. If capital per hour of labor increases to \$60, labor productivity increases to \$25 an hour.

At a given amount of capital per hour of labor, labor productivity increases if human capital increases or technology advances. An upward shift of the productivity curve illustrates these influences on labor productivity. For example, if capital per hour of labor is \$30 and a technological change increases labor productivity from \$20 to \$25, the productivity curve shifts upward from PC_0 to PC_1. Similarly, if capital per hour of labor is \$60, the same technological change increases labor productivity from \$25 to \$32 and shifts the productivity curve upward from PC_0 to PC_1.

FIGURE 10.2
How Labor Productivity Grows

Practice Online

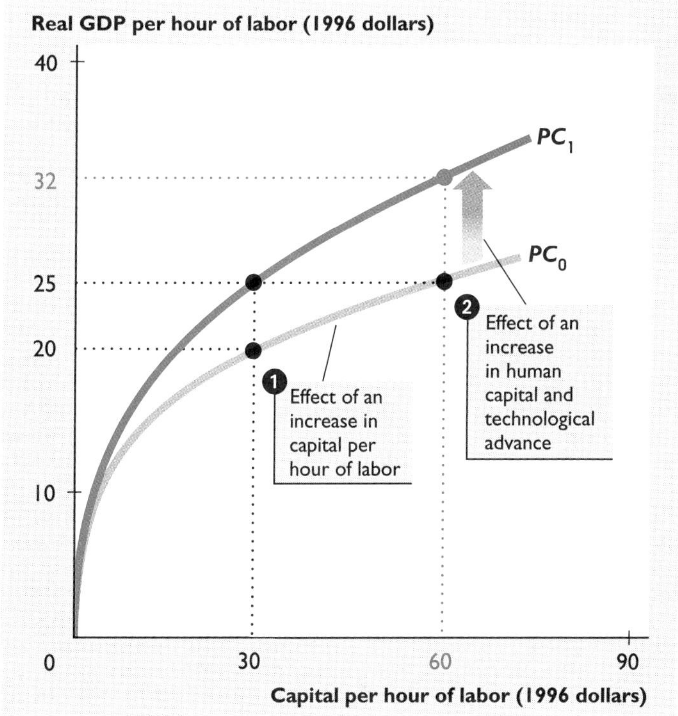

Labor productivity, which is measured by real GDP per hour of labor, can grow for two reasons:

1. An increase in capital per hour of labor brings a movement along the productivity curve PC_0. When capital per hour of labor increases from \$30 to \$60, real GDP per hour of labor increases from \$20 to \$25.
2. An increase in human capital and a technological advance shift the productivity curve upward from PC_0 to PC_1. With this increase in human capital and technological advance, real GDP per hour of labor increases from \$20 to \$25 when there is \$30 of capital per hour of labor and from \$25 to \$32 when there is \$60 of capital per hour of labor.

With constant average hours per worker and a constant labor force participation rate, aggregate hours grow at the same rate as the population. The capital stock grows at a rate determined by saving and investment. If the capital stock grows faster than the population, capital per hour of labor increases. If the capital stock grows slower than the population, capital per hour of labor decreases. And if the capital stock grows at the same rate as the population, capital per hour of labor is constant. The faster the growth rate of capital per hour of labor, the higher is the growth rate of real GDP per person.

But growth from capital alone is limited by diminishing returns.

Diminishing Returns

The shape of the productivity curve displays *diminishing returns*—each additional unit of capital per hour of labor produces a successively smaller additional amount of real GDP per hour of labor. For example, along productivity curve PC_0, if capital per hour of labor increases from zero to \$30, real GDP per hour of labor increases by \$20. But when capital per hour of labor increases by another \$30 to \$60, real GDP per hour of labor increases by only \$5 to \$25. Diminishing returns to capital are similar to diminishing returns to labor that you met in Chapter 8 (see pp. 190–191). You can see why diminishing returns apply to both capital and labor by thinking about Larry's Lawn Services, which owns one lawn mower and employs two workers. If Larry hires one more worker—a 50 percent increase in

Eye on the U.S. Economy

Labor Productivity and Economic Growth since 1962

The figure on this page shows that labor productivity growth was most rapid during the 1960s. It slowed after 1969 and slowed further after 1974. It speeded up again after 1995. But despite the spread of the personal computer and the expansion of the Internet, by the late 1990s labor productivity growth had not returned to that of the 1960s.

Why does labor productivity growth fluctuate? The figure on the next page provides a first look at the answer. The

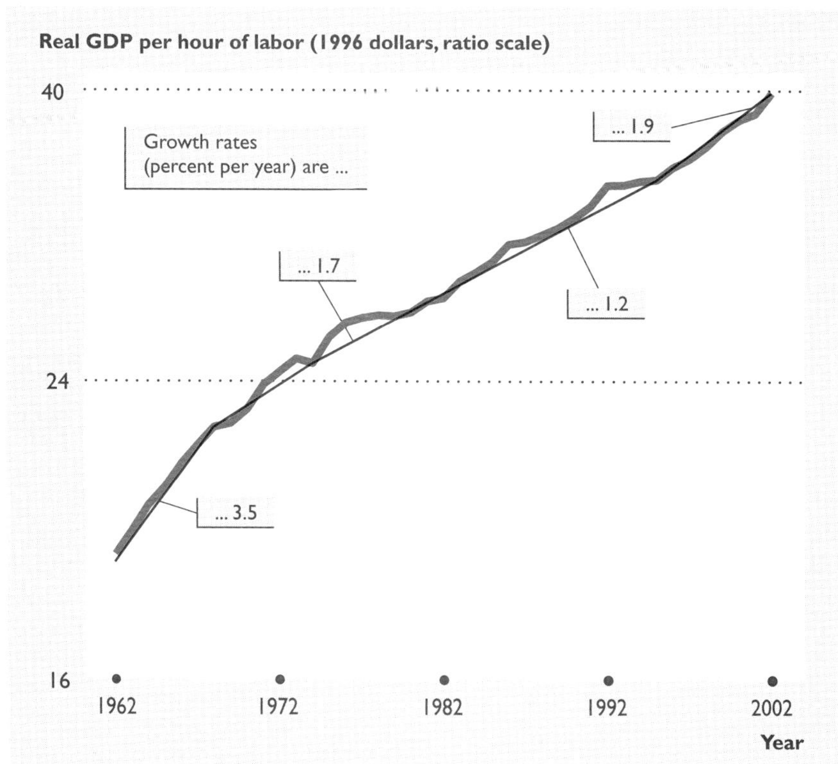

SOURCE: Bureau of Economic Analysis and Bureau of Labor Statistics.

labor—he gets more lawns mown, but not 50 percent more. Similarly, if Larry buys an extra lawn mower—a 100 percent increase in capital—he gets more lawns mown, but not 100 percent more.

More generally, one hour of labor working with $40 worth of capital produces less than twice the output of one hour of labor working with $20 worth of capital. But how much less? The answer is given by the one third rule.

The One Third Rule

To identify the contribution of capital growth to labor productivity growth, we use a feature of the productivity curve discovered by Robert Solow of MIT. By studying growth in the U.S. economy, Solow noticed a **one third rule**: On the average, with no change in human capital and technology, a *one percent* increase in capital per hour of labor brings a *one third percent* increase in labor productivity.

One third rule
The observation that on the average, with no change in human capital and technology, a *one percent* increase in capital per hour of labor brings a *one third percent* increase in labor productivity.

We can use the one third rule to identify the contribution of capital growth to labor productivity growth. Suppose, for example, that in a year, capital per hour of labor grows by 3 percent and labor productivity grows by 2.5 percent. The one third rule tells us that capital growth has contributed one third of 3 percent, which is 1 percent.

Labor productivity growth that is not attributed to capital growth arises from human capital growth and technological change. In the above example in which labor productivity grows by 2.5 percent and capital growth contributed 1 percent, the remaining 1.5 percent growth of labor productivity comes from human capital growth and technological change.

contribution of human capital growth and technological change fluctuated. But why did it fluctuate?

The 1960s enjoyed a period of rapid technological change based on spillovers from World War II and on the plastics revolution.

The contribution of human capital growth and technological change slowed during the 1970s because

(1) Its focus changed from increasing productivity to coping with energy price increases. Oil price hikes in 1973–1974 and 1979–1980 diverted research toward saving energy rather than increasing labor productivity. Airplanes became more fuel efficient, but they didn't operate with smaller crews. Real GDP per gallon of fuel increased faster but real GDP per hour of labor increased slower.

(2) More resources were devoted to protecting the environment and improving the quality of the workplace. The benefits of these activities—a cleaner environment and safer factories—are not counted as part of GDP. So the growth of these benefits was not counted as part of productivity growth.

(3) Taxes and government regulation expanded during the late 1960s and 1970s, so incentives were weakened and growth slowed.

(4) Rapid inflation distorted saving and investment decisions and shortened the horizon over which firms made their borrowing and lending plans.

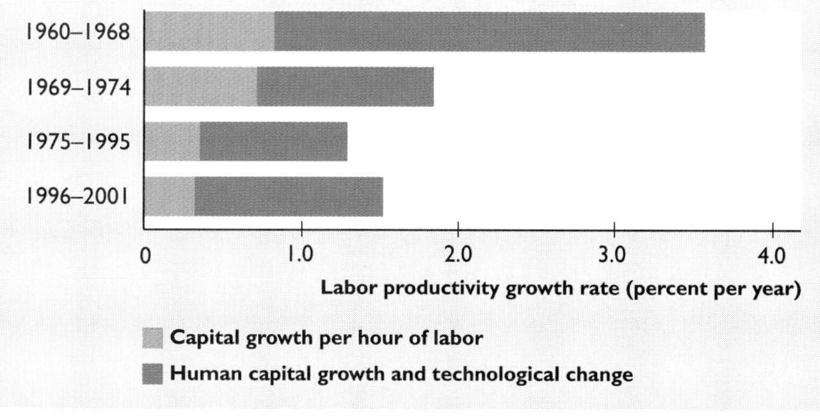

SOURCE: Bureau of Economic Analysis and Bureau of Labor Statistics.

CHECKPOINT 10.2

Study Guide pp. 147–150

Practice Online 10.2

2 **Identify the main sources of economic growth.**

Practice Problem 10.2

The table provides some data on the Canadian economy in 1998 and 1999.

Item	1998	1999
Aggregate hours (billions)	25.0	25.2
Real GDP (billions of 1992 dollars)	840	880
Capital per hour of labor (1992 dollars)	127	130

a. Calculate the growth rate of real GDP in 1999.
b. Calculate labor productivity in 1998 and 1999.
c. Calculate the growth rate of labor productivity in 1999.
d. If the one third rule applies in Canada, what were the sources of labor productivity growth in 1999? Explain your answer.

Exercise 10.2

The table provides some data on the U.S. economy in 2000 and 2001.

Item	2000	2001
Aggregate hours (billion)	240.6	238.8
Real GDP (billions of 1996 dollars)	9,191	9,215
Capital per hour of labor (1996 dollars)	98.91	102.13

a. Calculate the growth rate of real GDP in 2001.
b. Calculate labor productivity in 2000 and 2001.
c. Calculate the growth rate of labor productivity in 2001.
d. If the one third rule applies in the United States, what were the sources of labor productivity growth in 2001? Explain your answer.

Solution to Practice Problem 10.2

a. The growth rate of real GDP in 1999 was [($880 billion – $840 billion)/$840 billion] × 100, which equals 4.8 percent.
b. Labor productivity equals real GDP per hour of labor. In 1998, labor productivity was $840 billion/25 billion, which equals $33.60 per hour of labor. In 1999, labor productivity was $880 billion/25.2 billion hours, which equals $34.92 per hour of labor.
c. The growth rate of labor productivity in 1999 is [($34.92 – $33.60)/$33.60] × 100, which equals 3.93 percent.
d. The one third rule identifies the contribution of capital growth to labor productivity growth. Capital per hour of labor grew by [($130 – $127)/$127] × 100, which equals 2.36 percent.
So the one third rule tells us that 1/3 of the 2.36 percent of labor productivity growth, which is 0.79 percent, came from capital growth. The remainder of labor productivity growth, which is 3.14 percent, came from human capital growth and technological change.

10.3 THEORIES OF ECONOMIC GROWTH

We've seen that real GDP grows when the quantities of labor, capital, and human capital grow and when technology advances. Does this mean that all these factors *cause* economic growth? It might. But there are other possibilities. One of these factors might be the cause of real GDP growth and the others the effect. We must try to discover how the influences on economic growth interact with each other to make some economies grow quickly and others grow slowly. And we must probe the reasons why a country's long-term growth rate sometimes speeds up and sometimes slows down.

Growth theories are designed to study the interactions among the several factors that contribute to growth and to disentangle cause and effect. They are also designed to enable us to study how the various factors influence each other.

Growth theories are also designed to be universal. They are not theories about the growth of poor countries only or of rich countries only. They are theories about why and how poor countries become rich and rich countries become richer.

We're going to study three theories of economic growth, each of which gives some insights into the process of economic growth. But none provides a definite answer to the basic questions: What causes economic growth and why do growth rates vary? Economics has some way to go before it can provide a definite answer to these most important of questions.

We study three growth theories:

- Classical growth theory
- Neoclassical growth theory
- New growth theory

Classical Growth Theory

Classical growth theory predicts that the clash between an exploding population and limited resources will eventually bring economic growth to an end. According to classical growth theory, labor productivity growth is temporary. When labor productivity rises and lifts real GDP per person above the subsistence level, which is the minimum real income needed to maintain life, a population explosion occurs. Eventually, the population grows so large that labor productivity falls and returns real GDP per person back to the subsistence level.

Classical growth theory
The theory that the clash between an exploding population and limited resources will eventually bring economic growth to an end.

Adam Smith, Thomas Robert Malthus, and David Ricardo, the leading economists of the late eighteenth and early nineteenth centuries, proposed this theory, but the view is most closely associated with Malthus and is sometimes called the **Malthusian theory**. It is also sometimes called the Doomsday theory.

Malthusian theory
Another name for classical growth theory—named for Thomas Robert Malthus.

Many people today are Malthusians. They say that if today's global population of 6.3 billion explodes to 11 billion by 2200, we will run out of resources and return to a primitive standard of living. We must act, say the Malthusians, to contain the population growth.

The Basic Idea

To understand the basic idea of classical growth theory, let's transport ourselves back to the world of 1776. Adam Smith's *Wealth of Nations* has just been published, the Industrial Revolution is under way in Britain, and the United States of America is not yet born. Most of the 2.5 million people who live in the not yet independent United States of America work on farms or on their own land and perform their tasks using simple tools and animal power. They earn an average of 2 shillings (a bit less than $12 dollars in today's money) for working a ten-hour day.

Then advances in farming technology bring new types of plows and seeds that increase farm productivity. As farm productivity increases, farm production increases and some farm workers move from the land to the cities, where they get work producing and selling the expanding range of farm equipment. Real GDP per person rises, and people are prospering. But will the prosperity last? Classical growth theory says that it will not. The prosperity will induce a population explosion. And the population explosion will decrease real GDP per person.

Classical Theory of Population Growth

When the classical economists were developing their ideas about population growth, an unprecedented population explosion was under way. In Britain and other Western European countries, improvements in diet and hygiene had lowered the death rate while the birth rate remained unchanged. For several decades, population growth was extremely rapid.

For example, after being relatively stable for several centuries, the population of Britain increased by 40 percent between 1750 and 1800 and by another 50 percent between 1800 and 1830. At the same time, an estimated 1 million people (about 20 percent of the 1750 population) left Britain for America and Australia before 1800, and outward migration continued on a similar scale through the nineteenth century. This historical population explosion was the basis for the classical theory of population growth.

To explain the high rate of population growth, the classical economists used the idea of a subsistence real income. If the actual real income is less than the subsistence real income, some people cannot survive and the population decreases. In classical theory, when real income exceeds the subsistence real income, the population grows. But the increasing population decreases the amount of capital per hour of labor. So labor productivity and real GDP per person eventually decrease. And no matter how much technological change occurs, real GDP per person is always pushed back toward the subsistence level. This dismal implication led to economics being called the dismal science.

Productivity Curve Illustration

Figure 10.3 illustrates the classical growth theory, using the productivity curve. Initially, the productivity curve is PC_0. The economy is producing at point *A*, and real GDP per hour is just high enough for people to earn a subsistence real income.

Now capital per hour increases, which moves the economy along the productivity curve to point *B*. And technology advances, which shifts the productivity curve to PC_1 and moves the economy to point *C*. Real GDP per hour of labor is now above the level that provides a subsistence level of real income. So the population increases, and labor hours grow. Capital per hour of labor decreases and real GDP per hour of labor decreases as the economy moves down along the productivity curve PC_1. As long as real GDP per hour of labor exceeds the subsistence level, population growth brings a decrease in capital per hour of labor. Eventually, real GDP per hour of labor returns to the subsistence level at point *D*.

The economy has grown—real GDP has increased—but a larger population is earning only the subsistence real GDP per person.

FIGURE 10.3
Classical Growth Theory

Practice Online

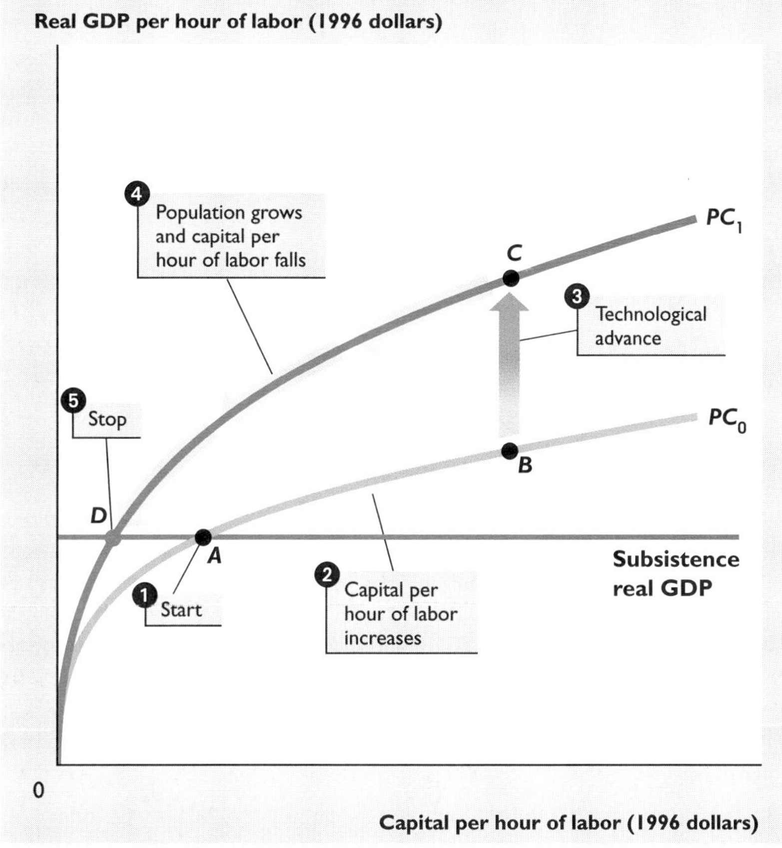

1. The economy starts out at point *A* on productivity curve PC_0 with real GDP per hour of labor at the subsistence level and the population constant.
2. The economy moves to point *B* as capital per hour of labor increases and real GDP per hour of labor increases above the subsistence level.
3. The economy moves to point *C* as technological advance (and the accumulation of human capital) increase productivity and the productivity curve shifts upward to PC_1.
4. With real GDP per hour of labor above the subsistence level, the economy moves toward point *D* as the population grows and capital per hour of labor decreases.
5. At point *D*, the economy is back at the subsistence level of real GDP per hour of labor.

Neoclassical Growth Theory

Neoclassical growth theory (developed by Robert Solow of MIT during the 1960s) predicts that real GDP per person will increase as long as technology keeps advancing. Real GDP will grow at a rate equal to the population growth rate plus the rate of productivity growth induced by technological change and the accumulation of human capital. So according to the neoclassical theory, growth will persist.

Neoclassical growth theory
The theory that real GDP per person will increase as long as technology keeps advancing.

Neoclassical growth theory asserts that population growth and the pace of technological change determine, but are not themselves influenced by, the growth rate of real GDP. Let's briefly examine the neoclassical view of population growth and technological change.

Population Growth

The population explosion of eighteenth century Europe that created the classical theory eventually ended. The birth rate fell, and the population growth rate slowed. This slowdown in population growth seemed to make the classical theory increasingly less relevant. And the slowdown in population growth eventually led to the development of a new economic theory of population growth.

Economists began to realize that although the population growth rate is influenced by economic factors, that influence is not the one identified by the classical economists. Key among the economic influences on population growth is the opportunity cost of a woman's time. As women's wage rates increase and their job opportunities expand, the opportunity cost of having children increases. Faced with a higher opportunity cost, families choose to have fewer children and the birth rate falls.

A second economic influence lowers the death rate. The technological advances that increase labor productivity also bring advances in health care that extend lives.

So two opposing economic forces influence population growth. As incomes increase, the birth rate decreases and the death rate decreases. It turns out that these opposing forces are offsetting, so the rate of population growth is independent of the rate of economic growth.

The historical population trends contradict the views of the classical economists and call into question the contemporary Doomsday conclusion that one day we will be swamped with too many people for the planet to feed.

Technological Change

In the neoclassical theory, the rate of technological change influences the rate of economic growth, but economic growth does not influence the pace of technological change. It is assumed that technological change results from chance. When we get lucky, we have rapid technological change; and when bad luck strikes, the pace of technological advance slows.

The Basic Idea

To understand the basic idea of neoclassical growth theory, imagine the world of the mid-1950s. Americans are enjoying post–World War II prosperity. Real GDP per person is around $12,000 a year in today's money. The population is growing at about 1 percent a year, and people are saving and investing enough to make capital grow at a similar rate. So real GDP per person is not growing much.

Then technology advances at a more rapid pace across a range of activities. The transistor revolutionizes an emerging electronics industry. New plastics revolutionize the manufacture of household appliances. Jet airliners start to replace piston engine airplanes and speed transportation. And Elvis and the Beatles change the face of popular music!

These technological advances bring new profit opportunities. Businesses expand and new businesses are created to exploit the new technologies. Investment and saving increase, so capital per hour of labor increases. The economy enjoys increased prosperity and growth. But will the prosperity last? And will the growth last? Neoclassical growth theory says that the prosperity will last but the growth will not unless technology keeps advancing.

The prosperity persists because no population explosion occurs to lower real GDP per person. But growth stops if technology stops advancing because capital accumulation brings diminishing returns, which slow the growth rate of real GDP and slow the level of saving and investment. Eventually, the growth rate of capital slows to that of the population and real GDP per person stops growing.

A Problem with Neoclassical Growth Theory

Neoclassical growth theory predicts that real GDP per person will grow at a rate that is determined by the pace of technological change. But the theory does not explain what determines technological change. In the neoclassical theory, technological change is like the weather—it rains down on us at a pace that we must simply accept. In reality, the pace of technological change results from choices. The new growth theory, which we'll now study, emphasizes the role of these choices.

New Growth Theory

New growth theory predicts that our unlimited wants will lead us to ever greater productivity and perpetual economic growth. According to new growth theory, real GDP per person grows because of the choices people make in the pursuit of profit. Paul Romer of the University of California at Berkeley developed this theory during the 1980s, but the new growth theory builds on ideas developed by Joseph Schumpeter during the 1930s and 1940s.

New growth theory
The theory that our unlimited wants will lead us to ever greater productivity and perpetual economic growth.

Choices and Innovation

The new growth theory emphasizes three facts about market economies:

- Human capital grows because of choices.
- Discoveries result from choices.
- Discoveries bring profit, and competition destroys profit.

Human Capital Growth and Choices People decide how long to remain in school, what to study, and how hard to study. And when they graduate from school, people make more choices about job training and on-the-job learning. All these choices govern the speed at which human capital grows.

Discoveries and Choices When people discover a new product or technique, they consider themselves lucky. They are right. But the pace at which new discoveries are made—and at which technology advances—is not determined by chance. It depends on how many people are looking for a new technology and how intensively they are looking.

Discoveries and Profits Profit is the spur to technological change. The forces of competition squeeze profits, so to increase profit, people constantly seek either lower-cost methods of production or new and better products for which people are willing to pay a higher price. Inventors can maintain a profit for several years by taking out a patent or copyright. But eventually, a new discovery is copied, and profits disappear.

Two other facts play a key role in the new growth theory:

- Many people can use discoveries at the same time.
- Physical activities can be replicated.

Discoveries Used by All Once a profitable new discovery has been made, everyone can use it. For example, when Marc Andreeson created Mosaic, the Web browser that led to the creation of Netscape Navigator and Microsoft's Internet Explorer, everyone who was interested in navigating the Internet had access to a new and more efficient tool. One person's use of a Web browser does not prevent others from using it. This fact means that as the benefits of a new discovery spread, socially free resources become available. These resources are free because nothing is given up when an additional person uses them. They have a zero opportunity cost.

Replicating Activities Production activities can be replicated. For example, there might be 2, 3, or 53 identical firms making fiber-optic cable by using an identical assembly line and production technique. If one firm increases its capital and output, that *firm* experiences diminishing returns. But the economy can increase its capital and output by adding another identical fiber cable factory, and the *economy* does not experience diminishing returns.

The assumption that capital does not experience diminishing returns is the central novel proposition of the new growth theory. And the implication of this simple and appealing idea is astonishing. As capital accumulates, labor productivity grows indefinitely as long as people devote resources to expanding human capital and introducing new technologies.

Perpetual Motion

Figure 10.4 illustrates new growth theory in terms of a perpetual motion machine. Economic growth is driven by insatiable wants that lead us to pursue profit and innovate. New and better products result from this process, which lead to new firms starting up and old firms going out of business. As firms start up and die, jobs are created and destroyed. New and better jobs lead to more leisure and more

FIGURE 10.4
A Perpetual Motion Machine

Practice Online

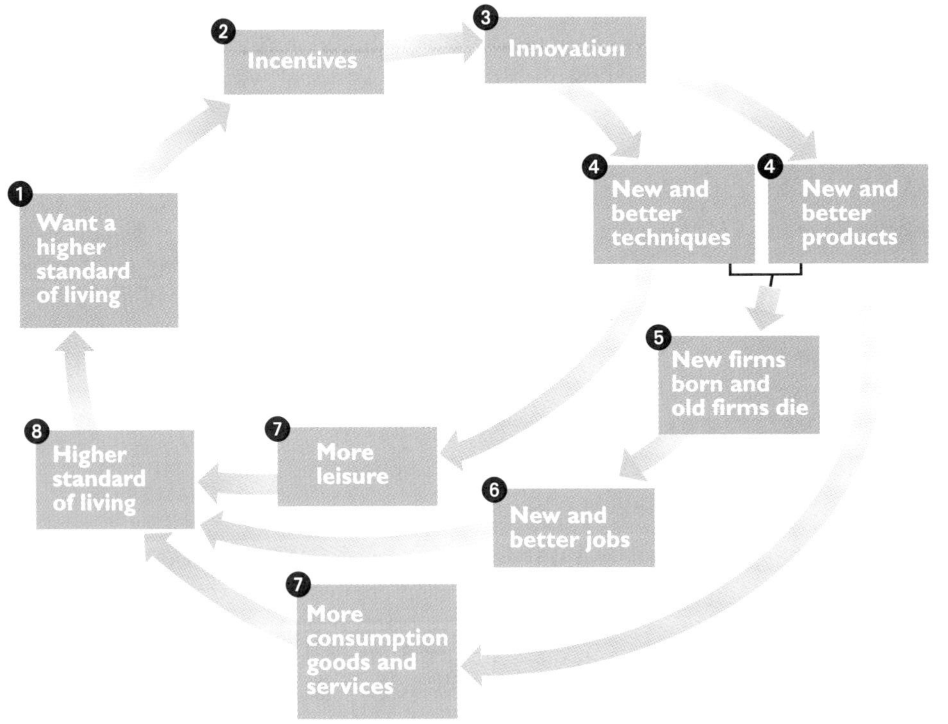

❶ People want a higher standard of living and are spurred by ❷ profit incentives to make the ❸ innovations that lead to ❹ new and better techniques and new and better products, which in turn lead to ❺ the birth of new firms and the death of some old firms, ❻ new and better jobs, and ❼ more leisure and more consumption goods and services. The result is ❽ a higher standard of living. But people want a yet higher standard of living, and the growth process continues.

Based on a similar figure in *These Are the Good Old Days: A Report on U.S. Living Standards*, Federal Reserve Bank of Dallas 1993 Annual Report.

consumption. But our insatiable wants are still there, so the process continues, going round and round a circle of wants, profit incentives, innovation, and new products. The growth rate depends on people's ability to innovate and the incentives to do so. Over the years, the ability to innovate has changed. The invention of language and writing (the two most basic human capital tools), and later the development of the scientific method and the establishment of universities and research institutions, brought a huge increase in profit opportunities. Today, a deeper understanding of genes is bringing profit in a growing biotechnology industry. And astonishing advances in computer technology are creating an explosion of profit opportunities in a wide range of new information-age industries.

Productivity Curve and New Growth Theory

Figure 10.5 illustrates new growth theory by using the productivity curve. According to this theory, capital increases and technology advances together to bring unending growth. The economy starts out on the productivity curve PC_0 at point *A*. Capital per hour of labor increases, which brings a movement along the productivity curve and increases labor productivity. At the same time, technology advances and human capital grows, which shifts the productivity curve upward to PC_1. So, for a second reason, labor productivity increases. The economy moves to point *B*. This process repeats indefinitely and takes the economy next to point *C* and then beyond.

FIGURE 10.5
New Growth Theory

Practice Online

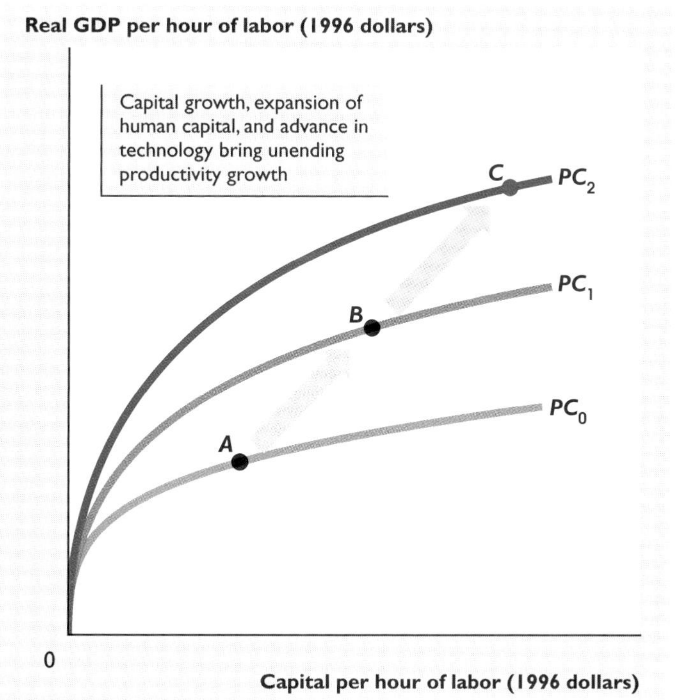

The economy starts out at point *A* on the productivity curve PC_0. An increase in capital per hour of labor brings a movement along the productivity curve PC_0 and the expansion of human capital and technological change increase labor productivity and shift the productivity curve upward to PC_1. The economy moves to point *B*.

The process repeats. The economy moves to point *C* and then to points of yet greater capital per hour of labor and labor productivity.

Eye on the U.S. Economy

Labor Productivity and Capital per Hour: 1960–2001

New growth theory is supported by the performance of the U.S. economy. In the figure, each dot represents a year from 1960 to 2001 and shows the U.S. data on labor productivity and capital per hour of labor. The two curves are the productivity curves of 1960 and 2001 based on the one third rule.

You can see that advances in technology and the expansion of human capital have shifted the productivity curve upward and overcome diminishing returns.

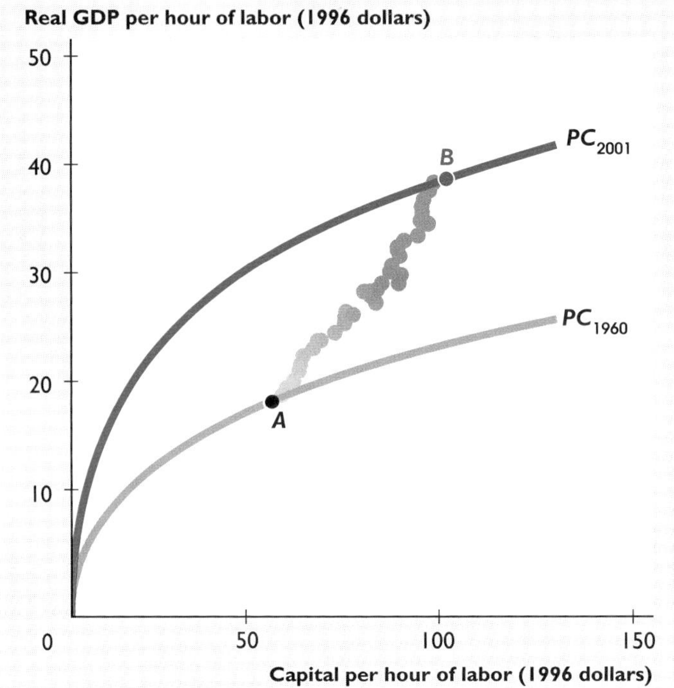

SOURCE: Bureau of Economic Analysis and Bureau of Labor Statistics.

Growth in the Global Economy

Economic growth is a global phenomenon, not just a national one. And the three growth theories make strikingly different predictions about the growth patterns that we should find in the global economy.

Classical growth theory predicts that the global economy will stagnate under the pressure of population growth. It also implies that the richest nations will be the ones with the fastest population growth and therefore they will be the first to stagnate. These predictions are resoundingly rejected by the experience of the world economy over the past few decades.

Neoclassical growth theory predicts that the global economy will grow and at a rate that is determined by the pace of technological change. All economies have access to the same technologies, and capital is free to roam the globe seeking the highest available profits. So neoclassical theory predicts that national levels of real GDP and national growth rates will converge. There is some sign of convergence among the rich countries. But convergence is slow, and it does not appear to be imminent for all countries (see Eye on the Global Economy).

New growth theory predicts that national growth rates depend on national incentives to save, invest, accumulate human capital, and innovate. Because these incentives depend on factors that are special to each country, national growth rates will not necessarily converge. Some real GDP per person gaps among rich countries and gaps between rich and poor countries might persist. Other gaps might close as poorer nations create better incentives to boost capital accumulation and technological change. New growth theory fits the facts more closely than do the other two theories.

Eye on the Global Economy

Persistent Gaps or Convergence?

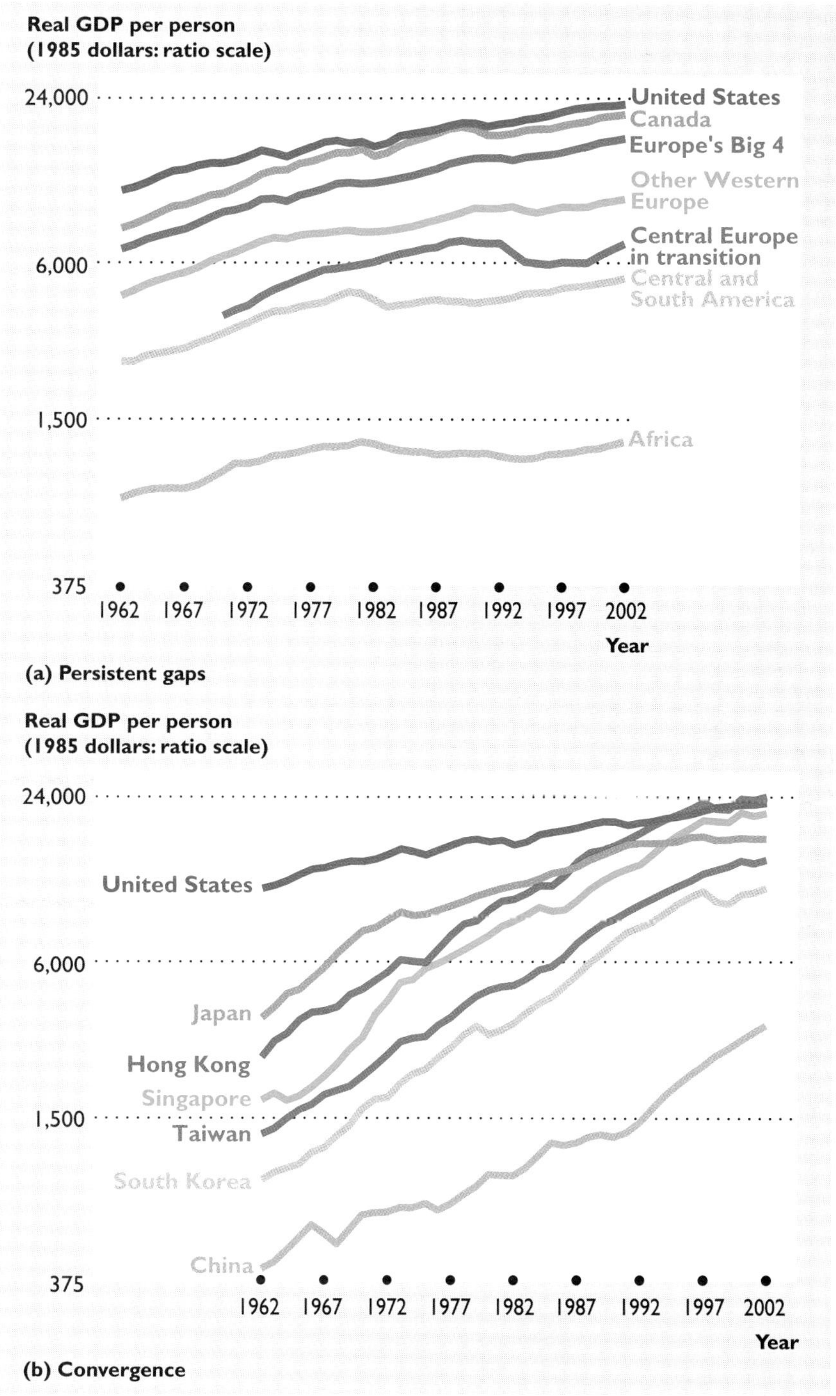

The figure shows real GDP per person in the United States and in other countries and regions from 1962 to 2002.

Part (a) shows persistent gaps in real GDP per person. Growth rates in Canada and Europe's Big 4 (France, Germany, Italy, and the United Kingdom) have been similar to that of the United States, so the gaps between these countries haven't changed much.

Other Western European countries grew faster than the United States before 1975, slowed to the U.S. growth rate during the 1980s, and fell behind during the 1990s. After a brief period of catch-up, the former Communist countries of Central Europe fell increasingly behind the United States.

Africa and Central and South America persistently grew more slowly than the United States, so the gaps between the United States and these regions widened.

Part (b) of the figure tells a different story. It shows how real GDP per person in the East Asian economies has converged on that in the United States.

In 1962, Hong Kong, Singapore, Taiwan, and South Korea had levels of real GDP per person that ranged from 10 percent to 25 percent of that in the United States. By 2002, real GDP per person in Hong Kong equaled that in the United States. Singapore was close behind, and the two others were converging fast. These four small Asian countries are like fast trains running on the same track at similar speeds and with a roughly constant gap between them. Hong Kong is the lead train and runs about 10 years in front of South Korea, which is the last train. Real GDP per person in South Korea in 1992 was similar to that in Hong Kong in 1982, ten years earlier. Between 1962 and 2002, Hong Kong transformed itself from a poor developing country into one of the world's richest countries.

Part (b) of the figure also shows that China is catching up, but more slowly and from a very long way behind.

(a) Persistent gaps

(b) Convergence

SOURCE: Alan Heston and Robert Summers, *Penn World Tables* 5.6 and *World Economic Outlook*.

CHECKPOINT 10.3

Study Guide pp. 150–152

Practice Online 10.3

3 **Review the theories of economic growth that explain why growth rates vary over time and across countries.**

Practice Problems 10.3

1. What does classical growth theory say will eventually end economic growth? Does the evidence of history support the prediction of the classical growth theory?
2. What does neoclassical growth theory say about the source of persistent growth in real GDP per person?
3. Why does neoclassical growth theory predict that national levels of real GDP and national growth rates will converge?
4. What is the driving force of growth according to new growth theory?
5. What does new growth theory imply about growth in the global economy?

Exercises 10.3

1. Contrast the modern theory of population growth with the classical growth theory.
2. What is the main limitation of neoclassical growth theory?
3. What are the three facts about market economies that new growth theory emphasizes and how do those facts influence the economic growth rate? Provide examples of each.
4. Why don't diminishing returns limit growth in new growth theory?
5. Families in China are permitted to have only one child. Predict the effects of this policy according to classical, neoclassical, and new growth theories.

Solutions to Practice Problems 10.3

1. Classical growth theory predicts that real GDP per person will be persistently pulled toward the subsistence level. When real GDP per person exceeds the subsistence level, the population grows and real GDP per person decreases. The evidence of history does not support the prediction that economic growth will eventually end.
2. Neoclassical growth theory says that technological advance is the source of persistent growth in real GDP per person.
3. Neoclassical growth theory predicts convergence because all countries have access to the same technology and capital is free to roam the globe.
4. The driving force of growth according to new growth theory is a persistent incentive to innovate and an absence of diminishing returns.
5. New growth theory implies that national growth rates depend on national incentives to save, invest, and innovate so that gaps between rich and poor nations might persist.

10.4 ACHIEVING FASTER GROWTH

Why did it take more than a million years of human life before economic growth began? Why are some countries even today still barely growing? Why don't *all* societies save and invest in new capital, expand human capital, and discover and apply new technologies on a scale that brings rapid economic growth? What actions can governments take to encourage growth?

Preconditions for Economic Growth

The key reason why economic growth is either absent or slow is that some societies lack the incentive system that encourages growth-producing activities. And economic freedom is the fundamental precondition for creating the incentives that lead to economic growth.

Economic Freedom

Economic freedom is present when people are able to make personal choices, their private property is protected, and they are free to buy and sell in markets. The rule of law, an efficient legal system, and the ability to enforce contracts are essential foundations for creating economic freedom. Impediments to economic freedom are corruption in the courts and government bureaucracy; barriers to trade, such as import bans; high tax rates; stringent regulations on business, such as health, safety, and environmental regulation; restrictions on banks; labor market regulations that limit a firm's ability to hire and fire workers; and illegal markets, such as those that violate intellectual property rights.

Economic freedom
A condition in which people are able to make personal choices, their private property is protected, and they are free to buy and sell in markets.

No unique political system is necessary to deliver economic freedom. Democratic systems do a good job. But the rule of law, not democracy, is the key requirement for creating economic freedom. Nondemocratic political systems that respect the rule of law do a good job too. Hong Kong is the best example of a country with little democracy but a lot of economic freedom—and a lot of economic growth. No country with a high level of economic freedom is economically poor. But many countries with low levels of economic freedom stagnate.

Property Rights

Economic freedom requires the protection of private property—the factors of production and goods that people own. The social arrangements that govern the protection of private property are called **property rights**. They include the rights to physical property (land, buildings, and capital equipment), to financial property (claims by one person against another), and to intellectual property (such as inventions). Clearly established and enforced property rights provide people with the incentive to work and save. If someone attempts to steal their property, a legal system will protect them. Such property rights also assure people that government itself will not confiscate their income or savings.

Property rights
The social arrangements that govern the protection of private property.

Markets

Economic freedom also requires free markets. Buyers and sellers get information and do business with each other in *markets*. And market prices send signals to buyers and sellers that create incentives to increase or decrease the quantities demanded and supplied. Markets enable people to trade and to save and invest. But markets cannot operate without property rights.

Property rights and markets create incentives for people to specialize and trade, to save and invest, to expand their human capital, and to discover and apply new technologies. Early human societies based on hunting and gathering did not experience economic growth because they lacked property rights and markets. Economic growth began when societies evolved the institutions that create incentives. But the presence of an incentive system and the institutions that create it do not guarantee that economic growth will occur. They permit economic growth but do not make it inevitable.

Growth begins when the appropriate incentive system exists because people can specialize in the activities at which they have a comparative advantage and trade with each other. You saw in Chapter 3 how everyone gains from such activity. By specializing and trading, everyone can acquire goods and services at the lowest possible cost. Consequently, people can obtain a greater volume of goods and services from their labor.

As an economy moves from one with little specialization to one that reaps the gains from specialization and trade, its production and consumption grows. Real GDP per person increases, and the standard of living rises.

But for growth to be persistent, people must face incentives that encourage them to pursue the three activities that generate *ongoing* economic growth: saving and investment, expansion of human capital, and the discovery and application of new technologies.

Policies to Achieve Faster Growth

To achieve faster economic growth, we must either increase the growth rate of capital per hour of labor or increase the growth rate of human capital or the pace of technological advance. The main actions that governments can take to achieve these objectives are

- Create incentive mechanisms.
- Encourage saving.
- Encourage research and development.
- Encourage international trade.
- Improve the quality of education.

Create Incentive Mechanisms

Economic growth occurs when the incentive to save, invest, and innovate is strong enough. And these incentives require property rights enforced by a well-functioning legal system. Property rights and a legal system are key missing ingredients in many societies. For example, they are absent throughout much of Africa. The first priority for growth policy is to establish these institutions so that incentives to save, invest, and innovate exist. Russia is a leading example of a country that is striving to take this step toward establishing the conditions in which economic growth can occur.

Encourage Saving

Saving finances investment, which brings capital accumulation. So encouraging saving can increase the growth of capital and stimulate economic growth. The East Asian economies have the highest saving rates and highest growth rates. Some African economies have the lowest saving rates and the lowest growth rates.

Tax incentives can increase saving. Individual Retirement Accounts (IRAs) are an example of a tax incentive to save. Economists claim that a tax on consumption rather than on income provides the best incentive to save.

Encourage Research and Development

Everyone can use the fruits of basic research and development efforts. For example, all biotechnology firms can use advances in gene-splicing technology. Because basic inventions can be copied, the inventor's profit is limited and so the market allocates too few resources to this activity.

Governments can direct public funds toward financing basic research, but this solution is not foolproof. It requires a mechanism for allocating public funds to their highest-valued use. The National Science Foundation is one possibly efficient channel for allocating public funds to universities and public research facilities to finance and encourage basic research. Government programs such as national defense and space exploration also lead to innovations that have wide use. Laptop computers and Teflon coatings are two prominent examples of innovations that came from the U.S. space program.

Encourage International Trade

Free international trade stimulates economic growth by extracting all the available gains from specialization and trade. The fastest-growing nations today are those with the fastest-growing exports and imports. The creation of the North American Free Trade Agreement and the integration of the economies of Europe through the formation of the European Union are examples of successful actions that governments have taken to stimulate economic growth through trade.

Improve the Quality of Education

The free market would produce too little education because it brings social benefits beyond the benefits to the people who receive the education. By funding basic education and by ensuring high standards in skills such as language, mathematics, and science, governments can contribute enormously to a nation's growth potential. Education can also be expanded and improved by using tax incentives to encourage improved private provision. Singapore's Information Technology in Education program is one of the best examples of a successful attempt to stimulate growth through education.

How Much Difference Can Policy Make?

It is easy to make a list of policy actions that could increase a nation's economic growth rate. It is hard to convert that list into acceptable actions that make a big difference.

Societies are the way they are because they balance the interests of one group against the interests of another group. Change brings gains for some and losses for others. So change is slow. And even when change occurs, if the economic growth rate can be increased by even as much as half a percentage point, it takes many years for the full benefits to accrue.

A well-intentioned government cannot dial up a big increase in the economic growth rate. But it can pursue policies that will nudge the economic growth rate upward. And over time, the benefits from these policies will be large.

CHECKPOINT 10.4

Study Guide **pp. 152–154**

Practice Online 10.4

4 **Describe policies that might speed economic growth.**

Practice Problems 10.4

1. What are the preconditions for economic growth?
2. Why does much of Africa experience slow economic growth?
3. Why is economic freedom crucial for achieving economic growth?
4. What role do property rights play in encouraging economic growth?
5. Explain why, other things remaining the same, a country with a well-educated population has a faster economic growth rate than a country that has a poorly educated population.

Exercises 10.4

1. What is the key reason why economic growth is either absent or slow in some societies?
2. Why does Russia experience slow economic growth?
3. Is economic freedom the same as democracy? Can you think of a country that enjoys economic freedom and achieves rapid economic growth but does not have democracy?
4. Why are markets a necessary precondition for economic growth?
5. Explain why, other things remaining the same, a country that adopts free international trade (for example, Hong Kong) has a faster economic growth rate than a country that restricts international trade (for example, Myanmar).

Solutions to Practice Problems 10.4

1. The preconditions for economic growth are economic freedom, private property rights, and markets. Without these preconditions, people have little incentive to undertake the actions that lead to economic growth.
2. Some African countries experience slow economic growth because they lack economic freedom, private property rights are not enforced, and markets do not function well. People in these countries have little incentive to specialize and trade or to accumulate both physical and human capital.
3. Economic freedom is crucial for achieving economic growth because economic freedom allows people to make choices and gives them the incentives to pursue growth-producing activities.
4. Clearly defined private property rights and a legal system to enforce them give people the incentives to work, save, invest, and accumulate human capital.
5. A well-educated population has more skills and greater labor productivity than a poorly educated population. A well-educated population can contribute to the research and development that create new technology.

CHAPTER CHECKPOINT

Key Points

1 Define and calculate the economic growth rate, and explain the implications of sustained growth.

- Economic growth is the sustained expansion of production possibilities. The annual percentage change in real GDP measures the economic growth rate.
- Real GDP per person must grow if the standard of living is to rise.
- Sustained economic growth transforms poor nations into rich ones.
- The Rule of 70 tells us the number of years in which real GDP doubles—70 divided by the percentage growth rate of real GDP.

2 Identify the main sources of economic growth.

- Real GDP grows when aggregate hours and labor productivity grow.
- Real GDP per person grows when labor productivity grows.
- Saving, investment in physical capital and human capital, and technological advance bring labor productivity growth.
- The productivity curve shows how labor productivity changes when capital per hour of labor changes, other things remaining the same.
- The productivity curve shifts when human capital expands and technology advances.

3 Review the theories of economic growth that explain why growth rates vary over time and across countries.

- Classical growth theory predicts that economic growth will end because a population explosion will lower real GDP per person to its subsistence level.
- Neoclassical theory predicts that economic growth will persist at a rate that is determined by the pace of technological change.
- New growth theory predicts that capital accumulation, human capital growth, and technological change respond to incentives and can bring persistent growth in labor productivity.

4 Describe policies that might speed economic growth.

- Economic growth requires an incentive system created by economic freedom, property rights, and markets.
- It might be possible to achieve faster growth by encouraging saving, subsidizing research and education, and encouraging international trade.

Key Terms

Classical growth theory, 245
Economic freedom, 255
Economic growth rate, 234
Labor productivity, 238
Malthusian theory, 245
Neoclassical growth theory, 247
New growth theory, 249
One third rule, 243
Productivity curve, 241
Property rights, 255
Real GDP per person, 234
Rule of 70, 235

Exercises

1. Explain why sustained growth of real GDP per person can transform a poor country into wealthy one.

2. In Ireland, the growth rate of real GDP per person averaged 10 percent a year during the 1990s. If this growth rate were to continue, in what year would real GDP per person be twice what it was in 2000?

3. Describe how U.S. real GDP per person has changed over the last 100 years.

4. Explain how the amount of capital increases, how human capital increases, and how technology advances.

5. What is the link between labor hours, labor productivity, and real GDP?

6. What is a productivity curve? Draw a graph of a productivity curve.

7. Explain how saving and investment in new capital, increases in human capital, and advances in technology change labor productivity. Use the productivity curve to illustrate your answer.

8. What is the one third rule? Who discovered the one third rule? How is the one third rule used?

9. If labor productivity grows by 5 percent when capital per hour of labor grows by 6 percent, what is capital's contribution to labor productivity growth? What else contributes to labor productivity growth and what is its contribution?

10. The following information has been discovered about the economy of Longland. The table provides data on the economy's productivity curve.

Capital per hour of labor (1996 dollars per hour)	Real GDP per hour of labor (1996 dollars per hour)
10	3.80
20	5.70
30	7.13
40	8.31
50	9.35
60	10.29
70	11.14
80	11.94

Does this economy conform to the one third rule? If so, explain why. If not, explain why not and explain what rule, if any, it does conform to. Explain how you would do the growth accounting for this economy.

11. In Longland, described in exercise 10, capital per hour of labor in 2001 was $40 and real GDP per hour of labor was $8.31. In 2003, capital per hour of labor had increased to $50 and real GDP per hour of labor had increased to $10.29 an hour.
    a. Does Longland experience diminishing returns? Explain why or why not.
    b. Use growth accounting to find the contribution of the growth of capital between 2001 and 2003 to the growth of labor productivity in Longland.
    c. Use growth accounting to find the contribution of technological change between 2001 and 2003 to the growth of labor productivity in Longland.

12. The following information has been discovered about the economy of Cape Despair. Subsistence real GDP is $15 an hour. Whenever real GDP per hour of labor rises above this level, the population grows, and when real GDP per hour of labor falls below this level, the population falls. The table provides data on the productivity curve in Cape Despair.

Capital per hour of labor (1996 dollars per hour)	Real GDP per hour of labor (1996 dollars per hour)
20	8
40	15
60	21
80	26
100	30
120	33
140	35
160	36

    Initially, the population of Cape Despair is constant and real GDP per hour of labor is at its subsistence level. Then a technological advance shifts the productivity curve upward by $7 at each level of capital per hour of labor.
    a. What are the initial capital per hour of labor and real GDP per hour of labor in Cape Despair?
    b. What happens to real GDP per hour of labor immediately following the technological advance?
    c. What happens to the population growth rate following the technological advance?
    d. What is the eventual quantity of capital per hour of labor in Cape Despair?

13. What do the classical, neoclassical, and new growth theories predict about growth in the global economy and which theory best fits the facts?

14. List five actions that governments can take to encourage economic growth, and provide an example of each.

Critical Thinking

15. What can governments in Africa do to encourage economic growth and raise their living standards?
16. Why do you think the standard of living in Asian economies has increased in the last decade by so much more than the standard of living in the United States?
17. What are the ingredients of economic freedom and how does each ingredient make economic growth more likely? Provide examples of nations that do not enjoy political freedom and that have a low economic growth rate and examples of nations that do enjoy political freedom and have a high economic growth rate. Are there any notable examples that contradict the view that economic freedom and economic growth go together?
18. Why might high taxes hold back economic growth? Would you recommend any changes in the U.S. tax laws to encourage faster growth? How would the changes that you recommend work?
19. Critically evaluate the two following contradictory statements.

    (1) Economic growth results from technological change, which results from creative people responding to incentives. A larger population has more creative people, so it brings faster technological advance. So population growth brings faster growth of real GDP per person.

    (2) Economic growth can be sustained only if we conserve natural resources. A larger population places strain on natural resources. So population growth brings slower growth of real GDP per person.
20. An increasing number of Chinese citizens who are educated in the United States are returning to China to work. How do you think this development might influence economic growth in China? Do you think the Chinese government would be wise to adopt policies that encourage more of its students attending foreign universities to return to China when they have completed their studies?

Practice Online

Web Exercises

Use the links on your Foundations Web site to work the following exercises.

21. Visit the IMF's World Economic Outlook database and obtain data on growth rates of real GDP per person for the United States, China, South Africa, and Mexico since 1990.
    a. Draw a graph of the data.
    b. Which country has the lowest real GDP per person and which has the highest?
    c. Which country has experienced the fastest growth rate since 1990 and which has experienced the slowest?
    d. Explain why the growth rates in these four countries are ranked in the order you have discovered.
22. Visit the Web site of the Penn World Tables and obtain data for any four countries (but not those of the previous exercise) that interest you. Describe and explain the patterns that you find for these countries.

CHAPTER 11

Money and the Monetary System

CHAPTER CHECKLIST

When you have completed your study of this chapter, you will be able to

1. **Define money and describe its functions.**
2. **Describe the monetary system and explain the functions of banks and other monetary institutions.**
3. **Describe the functions of the Federal Reserve System.**

You are now going to study the role of money in the economy. In this chapter and in Chapters 12 and 13, we address two main questions. First, what brings a persistent rise in the cost of living? Second, how does the Fed control the quantity of money and how do the Fed's actions influence interest rates and spending? This second question sets the scene for your study of economic fluctuations and stabilization policy in Part 5.

The quick answer to the first question is that many factors cause changes in the cost of living. But one factor dominates in the long run. The cost of living rises when the *quantity* of money grows more quickly than real GDP. But what exactly is money? The present chapter answers this question and describes the institutions of the monetary system. How does money get "created" so that its quantity grows? And how is the quantity of money controlled? Chapter 12 answers these questions. What happens when the quantity of money increases? And how does the creation of too much money bring a rising cost of living? Chapter 13 answers these questions.

11.1 WHAT IS MONEY?

Money, like fire and the wheel, has been around for a very long time. An incredible array of items has served as money. North American Indians used wampum (beads made from shells), Fijians used whales' teeth, and early American colonists used tobacco. Cakes of salt served as money in Ethiopia and Tibet. What do wampum, whales' teeth, tobacco, and salt have in common? Why are they examples of money? Today, when we want to buy something, we use coins or notes (dollar bills), write a check, send an e-check, present a credit or debit card, or use a "smart card." Are all these things that we use today money? To answer these questions, we need a definition of money.

Definition of Money

Money
Any commodity or token that is generally accepted as a means of payment.

Money is any commodity or token that is generally accepted as a *means of payment*. This definition has three bits that we'll examine in turn.

A Commodity or Token

Money is always something that can be recognized and that can be divided up into small parts. So money might be an actual commodity, such as a bar of silver or gold. But it might also be a token, such as a quarter or a $10 bill. Money might also be a virtual token, such as an electronic record in a bank's database (more about this type of money later).

Generally Accepted

Money is *generally* accepted, which means that it can be used to buy anything and everything. Some tokens can be used to buy some things but not others. For example, a phone card is accepted as payment for a phone call. But you can't use your phone card to buy toothpaste. So a phone card is not money. In contrast, you can use a $5 bill to buy either a phone call or toothpaste—or anything else that costs $5 or less. So a $5 bill is money.

Means of Payment

Means of payment
A method of settling a debt.

A **means of payment** is a method of settling a debt. When a payment has been made, there is no remaining obligation between the parties to a transaction. The deal is complete. Suppose that Gus buys a car from his friend Ann. Gus doesn't have enough money to pay for the car right now, but he will have enough three months from now, when he gets paid. Ann agrees that Gus may pay for the car in three months' time. Gus buys the car with a loan from Ann and then pays off the loan. The loan that Ann made to Gus isn't money. Money is what Gus uses to pay off the loan.

So what wampum, whales' teeth, tobacco, and salt have in common is that they have served as a generally accepted means of payment, and that is why they are examples of money.

Money performs three vital functions. It serves as a

- Medium of exchange
- Unit of account
- Store of value

Medium of Exchange

A **medium of exchange** is an object that is generally accepted in return for goods and services. Money is a medium of exchange. Without money, you would have to exchange goods and services directly for other goods and services—an exchange called **barter**. Barter requires a *double coincidence of wants*. For example, if you want a soda and have only a paperback novel to offer in exchange for it, you must find someone who is selling soda and who also wants your paperback novel. Money guarantees that there is a double coincidence of wants because people with something to sell will always accept money in exchange for it. So money acts as a lubricant that smoothes the mechanism of exchange. It enables you to specialize in the activity at which you have a comparative advantage (see Chapter 3, pp. 70–72) instead of searching for a double coincidence.

Medium of exchange
An object that is generally accepted in return for goods and services.

Barter
The direct exchange of goods and services for other goods and services, which requires a double coincidence of wants.

Unit of Account

A **unit of account** is an agreed-upon measure for stating the prices of goods and services. To get the most out of your budget, you have to figure out whether going to a rock concert is worth its opportunity cost. But that cost is not dollars and cents. It is the number of movies, cappuccinos, ice-cream cones, or local phone calls that you must give up to attend the concert. It's easy to do such calculations when all these goods have prices in terms of dollars and cents (see Table 11.1). If a rock concert costs $32 and movie costs $8, you know right away that going to the concert costs you 4 movies. If a cappuccino costs $2, going to the concert costs 16 cappuccinos. You need only one calculation to figure out the opportunity cost of any pair of goods and services. For example, the opportunity cost of the rock concert is 128 local phone calls ($32.00 ÷ 25¢ = 128).

Now imagine how troublesome it would be if the rock concert ticket agent posted its price as 4 movies, and if the movie theater posted its price as 4 cappuccinos, and if the coffee shop posted the price of a cappuccino as 2 ice-cream cones, and if the ice-cream shop posted its price as 4 local phone calls! Now how much running around and calculating do you have to do to figure out how much that rock concert is going to cost you in terms of the movies, cappuccino, ice cream, or phone calls that you must give up to attend it? You get the answer for movies right away from the sign posted by the ticket agent. But for all the other goods, you're going to have to visit many different places to establish the price of each commodity in terms of another and then calculate prices in units that are relevant for your own decision. Cover up the column labeled "price in money units" in Table 11.1 and see how hard it is to figure out the number of local phone calls it costs to attend a rock concert. It's enough to make a person swear off rock! How much simpler it is using dollars and cents.

Unit of account
An agreed-upon measure for stating the prices of goods and services.

TABLE 11.1 A UNIT OF ACCOUNT SIMPLIFIES PRICE COMPARISONS

Good	Price in money units	Price in units of another good
Rock concert	$32.00	4 movies
Movie	$8.00	4 cappuccinos
Cappuccino	$2.00	2 ice-cream cones
Ice-cream cone	$1.00	4 local phone calls
Local phone call	$0.25	

Store of Value

Any commodity or token that can be held and exchanged later for goods and services is called a **store of value**. Money acts as a store of value. If it did not, it would not be accepted in exchange for goods and services. The more stable the value of a commodity or token, the better it can act as a store of value and the more useful it is as money. No store of value is completely stable. The value of a physical object, such as a house, a car, or a work of art, fluctuates over time. The value of the commodities and tokens that we use as money also fluctuates, and when there is inflation, money persistently falls in value.

Store of value
Any commodity or token that can be held and exchanged later for goods and services.

Money Today

Fiat money
Objects that are money because the law decrees or orders them to be money.

Money in the world today is called **fiat money**. *Fiat* is a Latin word that means "Let it be done." The modern word "fiat" means decree or order. So today's money is money because the law decrees or orders it to be money. The objects that we use as money today are

- Currency
- Deposits at banks and other financial institutions

Currency

Currency
Notes (dollar bills) and coins.

The notes (dollar bills) and coins that we use in the United States today are known as **currency**. Notes are money because the government declares them to be with the words printed on every dollar bill, "This note is legal tender for all debts, public and private."

Deposits

Deposits at banks, credit unions, savings banks, and savings and loan associations are also money. Deposits are money because they can be used directly to make payments.

Currency in a Bank Is Not Money

Bank deposits are one form of money, and currency *outside the banks* is another form. Currency *inside* the banks is not money. When you get some cash from the ATM, you convert your bank deposit into currency. You change the form of your money, but there is no change in the quantity of money. Deposits decrease, and currency increases. If we counted both bank deposits and currency inside the banks as money, when you get cash at the ATM, the quantity of money would *appear* to decrease—your currency would increase, but *both* deposits *and* currency inside the banks would decrease. You can see that counting deposits *and* currency inside the banks as money would be counting the same thing twice—called double counting.

Deposits Are Money but Checks Are Not

Checks are not money. To see why, think about what happens when Colleen buys some inline skates from Rocky's Rollers. Colleen has $500 in her deposit account, and Rocky has $3,000 in his deposit account. Both of them bank at the Laser Bank. The total bank deposits of Colleen and Rocky are $3,500.

To pay for her skates, Colleen writes a check for $200. Rocky takes the check to the bank and deposits it. The Laser Bank now credits Rocky's account and debits Colleen's account. Rocky's deposit increases from $3,000 to $3,200, and Colleen's deposit decreases from $500 to $300. The total deposits of Colleen and Rocky are still the same as before: $3,500. Rocky now has $200 more, and Colleen has $200 less than before.

This transaction has transferred money from Colleen to Rocky. The check itself was never money. There wasn't an extra $200 worth of money while the check was in circulation. The check only instructs the bank to transfer money from Colleen to Rocky. Figure 11.1 shows these transactions.

FIGURE 11.1
Paying by Check

Practice Online

When you pay by check, you tell your bank to take some money from your deposit and put it into someone else's deposit. The deposit is money, but the check is not money.

LASER BANK 123 Dakota Street, Andover, MA 01810 (508) 555-3937

Date	Item	Debit	Credit	Balance
June 1 2001	Opening balance			$500.00
June 11 2001	Rocky's Rollers	$200.00		$300.00

(a) Colleen's account

LASER BANK 123 Dakota Street, Andover, MA 01810 (508) 555-3937

Date	Item	Debit	Credit	Balance
June 1 2001	Opening balance			$3,000.00
June 11 2001	Colleen's check		$200.00	$3,200.00

(b) Rocky's Rollers's account

In the example, Colleen and Rocky use the same bank. The same story, but with additional steps, describes what happens if Colleen and Rocky use different banks. In that case, the check must be cleared and a payment made by Colleen's bank to Rocky's bank. We explain the details of the process of check clearing in Chapter 12, pp. 293–294. This process can take a few days, but the principles are the same as when two people use the same bank.

Credit Cards, Debit Cards, E-Checks, and E-Cash

We've seen that checks are not money, but what about credit cards, debit cards, e-checks, and e-cash? Are they money?

Credit Cards

A credit card is not money. It is a special type of ID card. To see why, suppose that Colleen uses her credit card to buy her inline skates. Colleen signs a credit card slip and leaves the store with her new skates. But she has not yet *paid* for the skates. She has taken a loan from the bank that issued her credit card. Rocky's bank credits his account with $200 (minus the bank's charge) and sends a charge to the bank that issued Colleen's credit card. Colleen eventually gets her credit card bill, which she pays, using money.

If you pay by check, you are often asked to show your driver's license. Your driver's license is obviously not money. It's just an ID card. A credit card is also an

ID card but one that enables you to get a loan at the instant you buy something. So when you use a credit card to buy something, the bank that issued your credit card pays for the goods and you pay later. The credit card is not the means of payment, and it is not money.

Debit Cards

A debit card is not money. To see why, think about what happens if Colleen uses her debit card to buy her inline skates. When the sales clerk swipes Colleen's card in Rocky's store, the Laser Bank's computer gets a message: Take $200 from Colleen's account and put it in the account of Rocky's Rollers. The transactions shown in Figure 11.1 are done in a flash. But again, the bank deposits are the money and the debit card is the tool that causes money to move from Colleen to Rocky.

E-Checks

Electronic check (or e-check) An electronic equivalent of a paper check.

An **electronic check** (or **e-check**) is an electronic equivalent of a paper check. A group of more than 90 banks and other financial institutions have formed the Financial Services Technology Consortium to collaborate on developing the electronic check. First Virtual offers an Internet e-check system via email. Like a paper check, an e-check is not money. The deposit transferred is money.

E-Cash

Electronic cash (or e-cash) An electronic equivalent of paper notes and coins.

Electronic cash (or **e-cash**) is an electronic equivalent of paper notes and coins. It is an electronic currency, and for people to be willing to use it, e-cash has to work like money. People use physical currency because it is portable, recognizable, transferable, untraceable, and anonymous and can be used to make change. The designers of e-cash aim to reproduce all of these features of notes and coins. Today's e-cash is portable, untraceable, and anonymous. But it has not yet reached the level of recognition that makes it universally accepted as a means of payment, so it doesn't meet the definition of money.

Like notes and coins, e-cash can be used in shops. It can also be used over the Internet. To use e-cash in a shop, the buyer uses a smart card that stores some e-cash and the shop uses a smart card reader. When a transaction is made, e-cash is transferred from the smart card directly to the shop's bank account. Users of smart cards receive their e-cash by withdrawing it from a bank account by using a special ATM or a special cell phone.

There are several versions of e-cash in U.S. dollars, euros, and many other currencies available from issuing banks on the Internet. Mondex, a firm owned by MasterCard International, is a prominent e-cash provider. But there are many others, one of which is the CYPHERMINT™ Pay Cash System, an e-cash system from Russia that is being marketed throughout the world.

A handy advantage of e-cash over paper notes arises when you lose your wallet. If it is stuffed with dollar bills, you're out of luck. If it contains e-cash recorded on your smart card, your bank can cancel the e-cash stored in the card and issue you replacement e-cash.

Although e-cash is not sufficiently widely accepted to serve as money today, it is likely that its use will grow and that it will gradually replace physical forms of currency.

Official Measures of Money: M1 and M2

Figure 11.2 shows the items that make up two official measures of money. **M1** consists of currency held outside banks and traveler's checks plus checkable deposits owned by individuals and businesses. M1 does not include currency inside the banks. **M2** consists of M1 plus savings deposits and small time deposits (less than $100,000), money market funds, and other deposits. Time deposits are deposits that can be withdrawn only after a fixed term. Money market funds are deposits that are invested in short-term securities that pay a higher interest rate than bank deposits.

M1
Currency held outside banks and traveler's checks plus checkable deposits owned by individuals and businesses.

M2
M1 plus savings deposits and small time deposits, money market funds, and other deposits.

Are M1 and M2 Really Money?

Money is a generally accepted means of payment. So the test of whether something is money is whether it serves this purpose. Currency passes the test. Checkable deposits also pass the test because they can be transferred from one person to another by writing a check. Because M1 consists of currency plus checkable deposits and each is a means of payment, M1 is money.

But what about M2? Some of the savings deposits in M2 are just as much a means of payment as the checkable deposits in M1. You can use the ATM at the grocery store checkout or gas station to transfer funds directly from your savings account to pay for your purchase. But other savings deposits, time deposits, and money market funds are *not* means of payment. Technically, they are not money. So all of M1 is money, but only part of M2 is money.

FIGURE 11.2
Two Measures of Money: September 2002

Practice Online

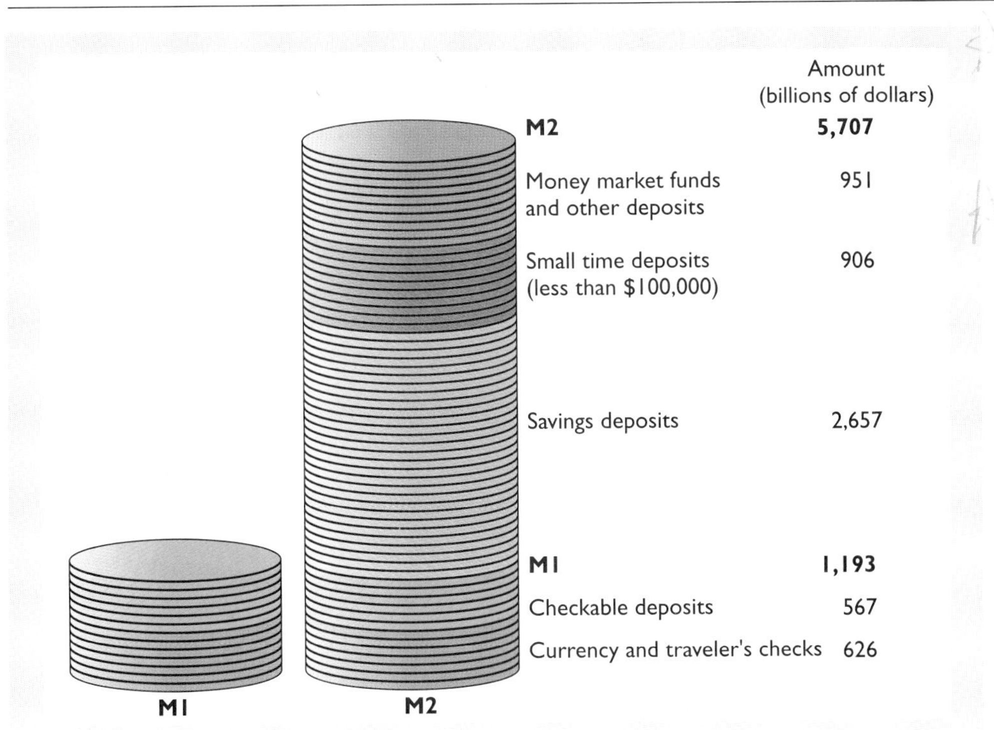

M1 Currency held outside banks and traveler's checks plus checkable deposits owned by individuals and businesses.

M2 M1 plus savings deposits plus small time deposits plus money market funds and other deposits.

SOURCE: Federal Reserve.

Eye on the Global Economy

The U.S. Dollar Abroad

At the end of 1999, there were around $500 billion worth of U.S. dollar bills in circulation. Of these, somewhere between $250 billion and $350 billion were circulating abroad.

The figure shows the growth of U.S. dollars held abroad. Russia is the biggest foreign user of U.S. dollars. Argentina is another big user. U.S. dollars are used extensively through the Middle East and Asia.

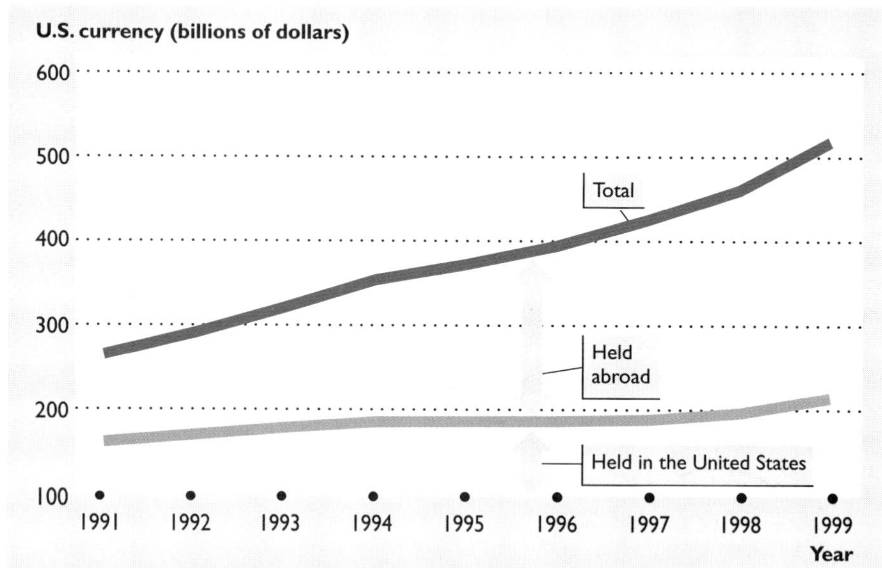

SOURCE: U.S. Department of the Treasury, *The Use and Counterfeiting of United States Currency Abroad*, January 2000.

Figure 11.3 shows the changing composition of money in the United States. Currency decreased in relative importance between 1962 and 1986 but became increasingly important during the 1990s. Checkable deposits decreased in relative importance but made a temporary comeback during the mid-1990s.

FIGURE 11.3
The Changing Face of Money in the United States

Practice Online

The proportion of money held as checkable deposits has been falling. The proportion of money held as currency fell slightly from 1962 through 1986 but then increased, mainly because the amount of U.S. currency abroad increased.

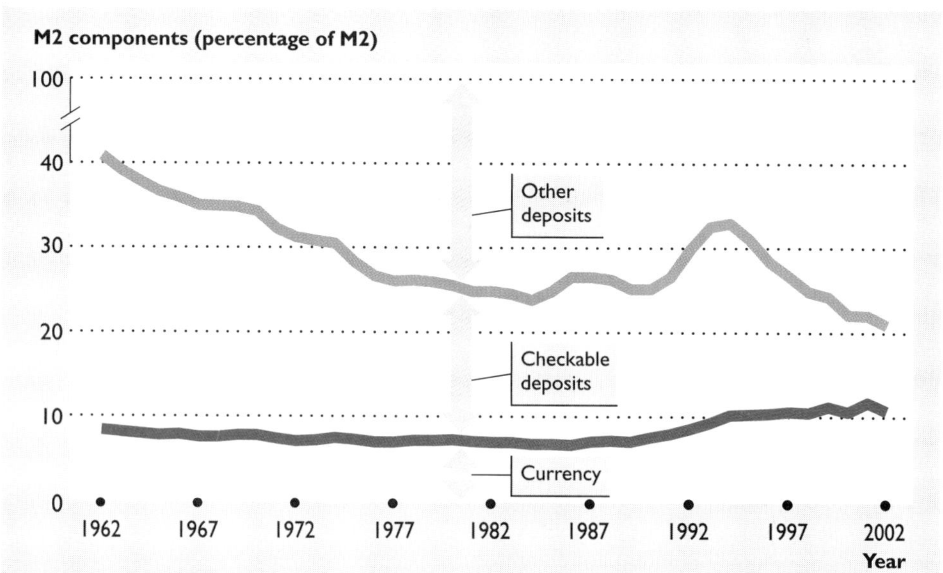

SOURCE: Federal Reserve.

CHECKPOINT 11.1

1 Define money and describe its functions.

Study Guide pp. 160–162

Practice Online 11.1

Practice Problems 11.1

1. In the United States today, money includes which of the following items?
   a. Your Visa card
   b. The quarters inside public phones
   c. U.S. dollar bills in your wallet
   d. The check that you have just written to pay for your rent
   e. The loan you took out last August to pay for your school fees

2. In January 2001, currency held by individuals and businesses was $534.9 billion; traveler's checks were $8.1 billion; checkable deposits owned by individuals and businesses were $559.3 billion; savings deposits were $1,889.7 billion; small time deposits were $1,052.6 billion; and money market funds and other deposits were $952 billion.
   a. What was M1 in January 2001?
   b. What was M2 in January 2001?

Exercises 11.1

1. Which of the following items are money?
   a. Checkable deposits at First Boston Bank
   b. General Motors stock held by individuals
   c. A Sacagawea dollar coin
   d. U.S. government securities
   e. Money market funds

2. Sara withdraws $2,000 from her time deposit account at Bank of America, keeps $100 in cash, and deposits the balance in her checking account at Citibank. What is the immediate change in M1 and M2?

3. In December 2001, currency held by individuals and businesses was $580.5 billion; traveler's checks in circulation were $7.7 billion; checkable deposits owned by individuals and businesses were $580.5 billion; savings deposits were $2,304.5 billion; time deposits were $970.1 billion; and money market funds and other deposits were $996.6 billion.
   a. What was M1 in December 2001?
   b. What was M2 in December 2001?

Solutions to Practice Problems 11.1

1. Money is defined as a means of payment. Only items **b** and **c** (the quarters inside public phones and U.S. dollar bills in your wallet) are money.

2a. M1 is the sum of currency held by individuals and businesses, $534.9 billion; traveler's checks, $8.1 billion; and checkable deposits owned by individuals and businesses, $559.3 billion. M1 is $1,102.3 billion.

2b. M2 is the sum of M1 ($1,102.3 billion), savings deposits ($1,889.7 billion), small time deposits ($1,052.6 billion), and money market funds and other deposits ($952 billion). M2 is $4,996.6 billion.

11.2 THE MONETARY SYSTEM

Monetary system
The Federal Reserve and the banks and other institutions that accept deposits and provide the services that enable people and businesses to make and receive payments.

The **monetary system** consists of the Federal Reserve and the banks and other institutions that accept deposits and that provide the services that enable people and businesses to make and receive payments. Figure 11.4 illustrates the institutions of the monetary system. Sitting at the top of the figure, the Federal Reserve (or Fed) sets the rules and regulates and influences the activities of the banks and other institutions. Three types of financial institutions accept the deposits that are part of the nation's money:

- Commercial banks
- Thrift institutions
- Money market funds

In this section, we describe the functions of these institutions, and in the final section of the chapter, we describe the structure and functions of the Fed.

Commercial Banks

Commercial bank
A firm that is chartered by the Comptroller of the Currency in the U.S. Treasury (or by a state agency) to accept deposits and make loans.

A **commercial bank** is a firm that is chartered by the Comptroller of the Currency in the U.S. Treasury (or by a state agency) to accept deposits and make loans. About 8,600 commercial banks operate in the United States today, down from 13,000 a few years ago. The number of banks has shrunk because in 1997, the rules under which banks operate were changed, permitting them to open branches in every state. A wave of mergers followed this change of rules.

Types of Deposit

A commercial bank accepts three broad types of deposit: checkable deposits, savings deposits, and time deposits. A bank pays a low interest rate (sometimes zero) on checkable deposits, and it pays the highest interest rate on time deposits.

FIGURE 11.4
The Institutions of the Monetary System

Practice Online

The Federal Reserve regulates and influences the activities of the commercial banks, thrift institutions, and money market funds, whose deposits make up the nation's money.

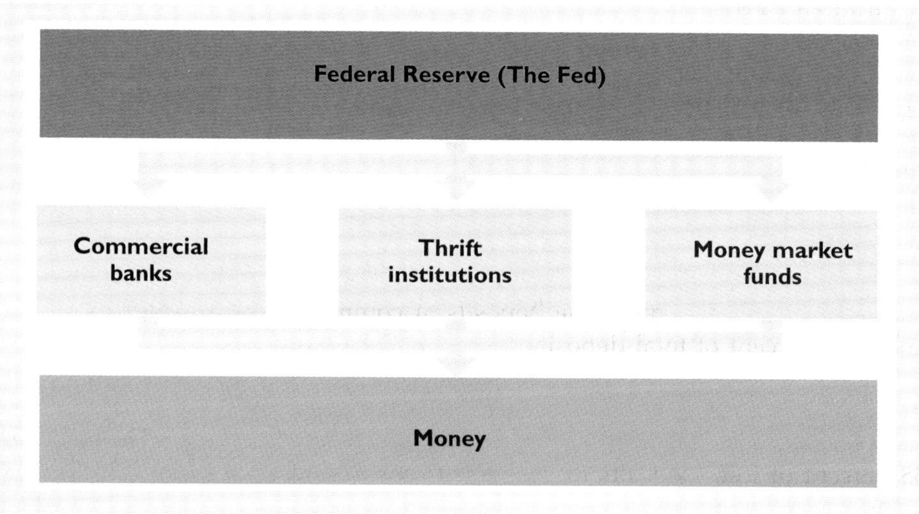

Profit and Prudence: A Balancing Act

The goal of a commercial bank is to maximize its stockholders' long-term wealth. To achieve this goal, a bank makes loans at a higher interest rate than the interest rate it pays on deposits. But lending is risky. The more a bank ties up its deposits in high-risk, high-interest rate loans, the bigger is the risk that it will not be able to pay its depositors when they want to withdraw funds. And if depositors perceive this risk, mass withdrawals might create a crisis for the bank. So a bank must perform a balancing act. It must be prudent in the way it uses the depositors' funds and balance security for the depositors against profit for its stockholders. To achieve security for its depositors, a bank divides its assets into four parts: cash assets, interbank loans, securities, and loans.

Cash Assets

A bank's *cash assets* consist of its reserves and funds that are due from other banks as payments for checks that are being cleared. A bank's **reserves** consist of currency in its vaults plus the balance on its reserve account at a Federal Reserve Bank. The currency in a bank's vaults is a reserve to meet its depositors' withdrawals. It replenishes the ATM every time you and your friends have raided it for cash for a midnight pizza. A commercial bank's deposit at a Federal Reserve Bank is similar to your own bank deposit. The bank uses its reserve account at the Fed to receive and make payments to other banks and to obtain currency. The Fed requires banks to hold a minimum percentage of deposits as reserves, called the **required reserve ratio** (Table 11.2 on p. 282). Reserves that exceed those needed to meet the required reserve ratio are called **excess reserves**.

Reserves
The currency in the bank's vaults plus the balance on its reserve account at a Federal Reserve Bank.

Required reserve ratio
The minimum percentage of deposits that banks and other financial institutions must hold in reserves.

Excess reserves
Bank reserves that exceed those needed to meet the required reserve ratio.

Interbank Loans

Banks that have excess reserves can lend them, and banks with a shortage of reserves can borrow them in an interbank loans market called the federal funds market. The interest rate in this market, called the **federal funds rate**, is the central target of the Fed's monetary policy actions.

Federal funds rate
The interest rate on interbank loans (loans made in the federal funds market).

Securities and Loans

Securities are bonds issued by the U.S. government and by other large, safe organizations. These bonds are traded every day on the bond market. A bank earns a moderate interest rate on securities, but it can sell them quickly if it needs cash. Loans are the provision of funds to businesses and individuals that earn the bank a high interest rate but that cannot be called in before the agreed date. A bank earns the highest interest rate on unpaid credit card balances, which are loans to its credit card holders.

Bank Deposits and Assets: The Relative Magnitudes

In the United States, checkable deposits at commercial banks (part of M1) are about 13 percent of total deposits. The other 87 percent of deposits are savings deposits and time deposits (part of M2). After performing their profit versus prudence balancing acts, the banks on the average keep about 6.5 percent of total deposits in cash assets and another 6.5 percent in interbank loans. The banks use 38 percent of total deposits to buy government bonds and 49 percent to make loans. Figure 11.5 summarizes the numbers in 2002.

FIGURE 11.5
Commercial Banks' Deposits and Assets

Practice Online

In 2002, commercial banks had $600 billion in checkable deposits and $3,900 in other deposits. They loaned $2,300 billion of these deposits, placed $1,600 billion in securities, and made $300 billion in interbank loans and kept $300 billion in cash assets.

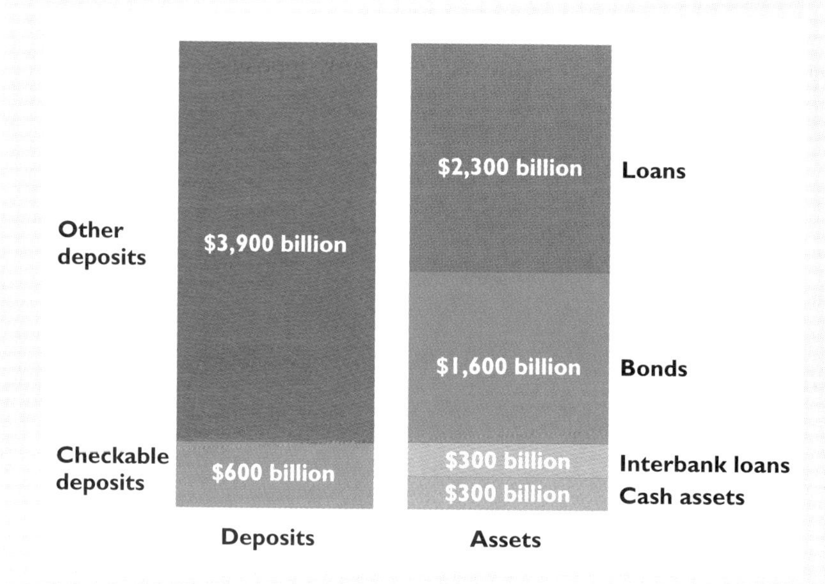

SOURCE: Federal Reserve.

Thrift Institutions

The three types of thrift institutions are savings and loan associations, savings banks, and credit unions. A **savings and loan association** (S&L) is a financial institution that accepts checkable deposits and savings deposits and that makes personal, commercial, and home-purchase loans. A **savings bank** is a financial institution that accepts savings deposits and makes mostly consumer and home-purchase loans. The depositors own some savings banks (called mutual savings banks). A **credit union** is a financial institution owned by a social or economic group, such as a firm's employees, that accepts savings deposits and makes mostly consumer loans.

Savings and loan association
A financial institution that accepts checkable deposits and savings deposits and that makes personal, commercial, and home-purchase loans.

Savings bank
A financial institution that accepts savings deposits and makes mostly consumer and home-purchase loans.

Credit union
A financial institution owned by a social or economic group such as a firm's employees, that accepts savings deposits and makes mostly consumer loans.

Like commercial banks, the thrift institutions hold reserves and must meet minimum reserve ratios set by the Fed.

The total deposits of thrift institutions in 2002 were $1,100 billion. Of these, $120 billion were checkable deposits included in M1 and $980 billion were savings deposits and time deposits included in M2.

Money Market Funds

Money market fund
A financial institution that obtains funds by selling shares and uses these funds to buy assets such as U.S. Treasury bills.

A **money market fund** is a financial institution that obtains funds by selling shares and uses these funds to buy assets such as U.S. Treasury bills. Money market fund shares act like bank deposits. Shareholders can write checks on their money market fund accounts. But there are restrictions on most of these accounts.

For example, the minimum deposit accepted might be $2,500 and the smallest check a depositor is permitted to write might be $500.

In 2002, the value of money market funds included in M2 was $950 billion.

Relative Size of Monetary Institutions

Commercial banks provide most of the nation's bank deposits. In Figure 11.6, we show the relative contributions of commercial banks, thrift institutions, and money market funds. Part (a) shows that checkable deposits at commercial banks are 41 percent of M1, in contrast to the 10 percent of the thrift institutions. Currency represents 49 percent (almost one half) of M1.

Part (b) shows that M1 is 22 percent of M2. The savings deposits and time deposits at commercial banks are another 43 percent of M2. Money market funds and other deposits provide 19 percent of M2, and deposits at thrift institutions provide 16 percent.

On the basis of these numbers, you can see that commercial banks are the dominant financial institutions in the monetary system.

FIGURE 11.6
The Deposits Behind M1 and M2

Practice Online

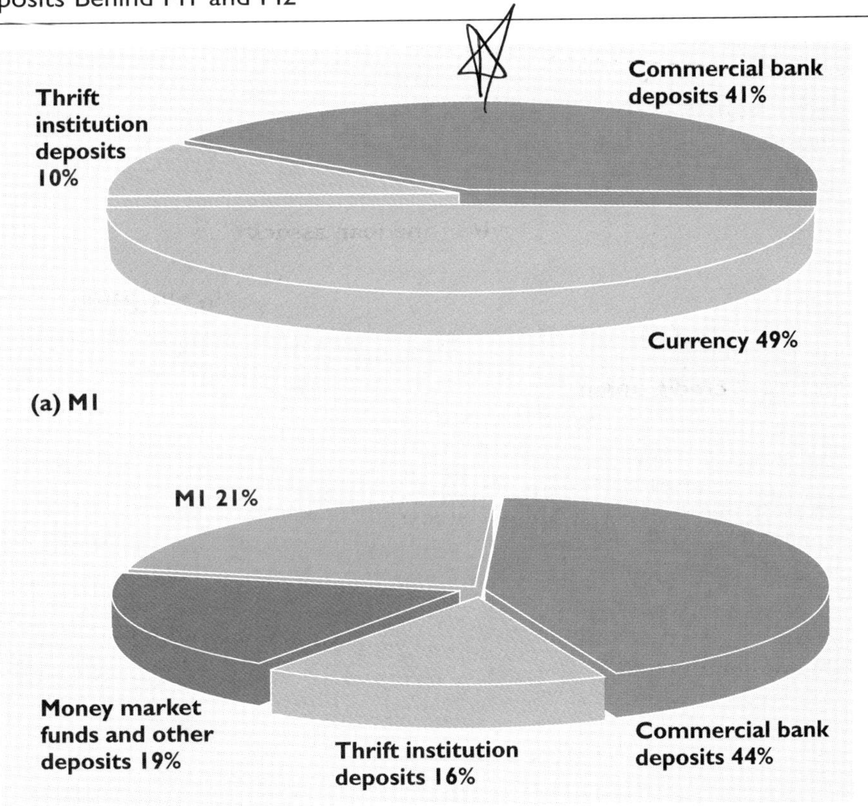

Deposits in commercial banks account for a much larger percentage of the nation's money than do the deposits in thrift institutions and money market funds.

SOURCE: Federal Reserve.

The Economic Functions of Monetary Institutions

The institutions of the monetary system earn their incomes by performing four economic functions that people are willing to pay for. They are

- Create liquidity
- Lower the costs of lending and borrowing
- Pool risks
- Make payments

Create Liquidity

Liquid asset
An asset that can be easily, and with certainty, converted into money.

A **liquid asset** is an asset that can be easily and with certainty converted into money. Some bank* deposits *are* money. Other deposits are almost money and can be converted into money instantly and safely—they are liquid assets.

A bank creates liquid assets by borrowing short and lending long. Borrowing short means accepting deposits and standing ready to repay them whenever the depositor requests the funds. Lending long means making loan commitments for a long term.

For example, a bank might have accepted $1 million in checkable deposits that could be withdrawn at any time and loaned $1 million to a startup Coffee Shop business for an agreed-upon 5 years. The bank earns part of its income by being able to charge a higher interest rate on a 5-year loan than the interest rate it must pay on a checkable account.

Lower Costs

Banks lower the costs of lending and borrowing funds. People with funds to lend can easily find a bank and make a deposit. Because banks offer a range of types of deposit, it is easy to find the type of deposit that best matches the plans of the depositor.

People who want to borrow can do so by using the facilities offered by banks. Business and personal loans can be tailored to match the cash flows of borrowers. And consumers can obtain instant loans by using credit card facilities.

Again, banks make profits because people are willing to make deposits at much lower interest rates than those available to the banks on their loans. Interest rates on credit card loans are especially high and so are profitable for the banks.

Pool Risks

Lending funds, as banks do, is risky. Some loans don't get repaid. By lending to a large number of businesses and individuals, a bank lowers the average risk it faces. The bank knows the odds of a loan not being repaid like a lottery operator knows the odds of having to pay out on a winning number. The lottery operator offers odds that ensure it ends up with a profit. Similarly, the market for bank loans determines an interest rate that ensures that the amount earned on the loans that do get repaid is sufficiently high to pay for the losses on the ones that don't get repaid.

---

* We'll use the term "bank" to mean any institution that accepts deposits when there is no gain from distinguishing among these institutions.

Make Payments

Bank deposits are money because they can be transferred from one person or business to another at low cost. The banks provide the payments system that enables these transfers of ownership to occur.

The check-clearing system is the main mechanism provided by the banks. Think of this system as a giant delivery service like FedEx that, instead of moving packages overnight to anywhere in the nation, moves checks and calculates the amounts that each bank must pay or receive based on the totals of the checks paid by and received by their customers. The banks collect a fee for these check-clearing activities.

The credit card payments system is another major payments mechanism operated by the banks. When you buy a new pair of jeans and the checkout clerk swipes your Visa card, a signal goes to the bank that issued your card to get approval for and place a hold on the amount that you are about to spend. Later that day, when the jeans store has some spare time, it transmits the accumulated day's credit card information from its card reader to its own bank and gets its account credited for the day's takings. At that same moment, a message goes from the jeans store's bank to your card-issuing bank (and the banks of all its other customers) that places the charge for your purchase on your credit card account (and likewise for the other customers). All these electronic transactions are performed automatically. The banks collect fees for all these credit card payment activities.

Big Banks

Before 1997, U.S. banks were not permitted to operate in more than one state. In 1997, that restriction was lifted, and since then, bank mergers and failures have decreased the number of banks from 13,000 to 8,600.

The largest U.S. banks are huge. But only two of the big U.S. banks, Citigroup and JP Morgan Chase, made the world's top 10 list in 2002.

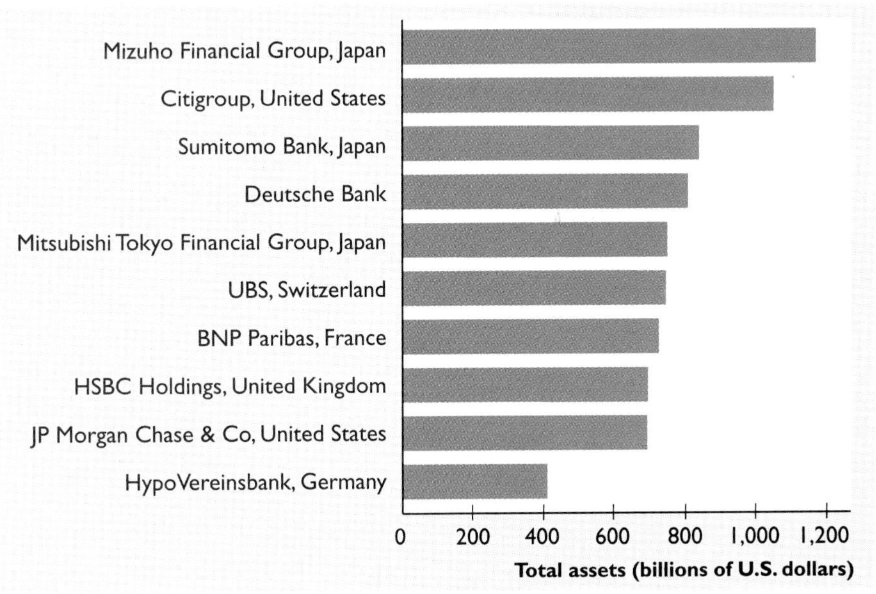

SOURCE: *The Banker*, July 2002.

CHECKPOINT 11.2

Study Guide **pp. 163–165**

Practice Online 11.2

2 **Describe the monetary system and explain the functions of banks and other monetary institutions.**

Practice Problems 11.2

1. What are the institutions that make up the monetary system?
2. What is a bank's "balancing act"?
3. A bank has the following deposits and assets: $320 in checkable deposits, $896 in savings deposits, $840 in small time deposits, $990 in loans to businesses, $400 in outstanding credit card balances, $634 in government securities, $2 in currency, and $30 in its reserve account at the Fed. Calculate the bank's
   a. Total deposits
   b. Deposits that are part of M1
   c. Deposits that are part of M2
   d. Loans
   e. Securities
   f. Reserves

Exercises 11.2

1. Explain how a bank makes a profit.
2. A savings and loan association has $550 in checkable deposits, $1,600 in home loans, $900 in savings deposits, $600 in government securities, $800 in time deposits, $50 in currency, and no deposit at the Fed. Calculate
   a. Total deposits
   b. Deposits that are part of M1
   c. Deposits that are part of M2
   d. Loans
   e. Reserves
3. On which items does the S&L in exercise 2 pay interest (borrow short) and on which items does it receive interest (lend long)?

Solutions to Practice Problems 11.2

1. The institutions that make up the monetary system are the Fed, commercial banks, thrift institutions, and money market funds.
2. A bank makes a profit by borrowing from depositors at a low interest rate and lending at a higher interest rate. The bank earns no interest on reserves, but it must hold enough reserves to meet withdrawals. The bank's "balancing act" is to balance the risk of loans against the safety of reserves.

3a. Total deposits are $320 + $896 + $840 = $2,056.
3b. Deposits that are part of M1 are checkable deposits, $320.
3c. Deposits that are part of M2 include all deposits, $2,056.
3d. Loans are $990 + $400 = $1,390.
3e. Securities are $634.
3f. Reserves are $30 + $2 = $32.

11.3 THE FEDERAL RESERVE SYSTEM

The **Federal Reserve System**, which is organized into 12 Federal Reserve districts shown in Figure 11.7, is the central bank of the United States. A **central bank** is a public authority that provides banking services to banks and regulates financial institutions and markets. A central bank does not provide banking services to businesses and individual citizens. Its only customers are banks such as Bank of America and Citibank and the U.S. government.

The Fed conducts the nation's **monetary policy**, which means that it adjusts the quantity of money in the economy. The Fed's goals are to keep inflation in check, maintain full employment, moderate the business cycle, and contribute toward achieving economic growth. Complete success in the pursuit of these goals is impossible, and the Fed's more modest goal is to improve the performance of the economy and to move it closer to the goals than a hands-off approach would achieve. There is a range of opinion on whether the Fed succeeds in improving economic performance.

Federal Reserve System
The central bank of the United States.

Central bank
A public authority that provides banking services to banks and regulates financial institutions and markets.

Monetary policy
Adjusting the quantity of money in the economy.

The Structure of the Federal Reserve

The key elements in the structure of the Federal Reserve are

- The Board of Governors
- The Regional Federal Reserve Banks
- The Federal Open Market Committee

FIGURE 11.7
The Federal Reserve Districts

Practice Online

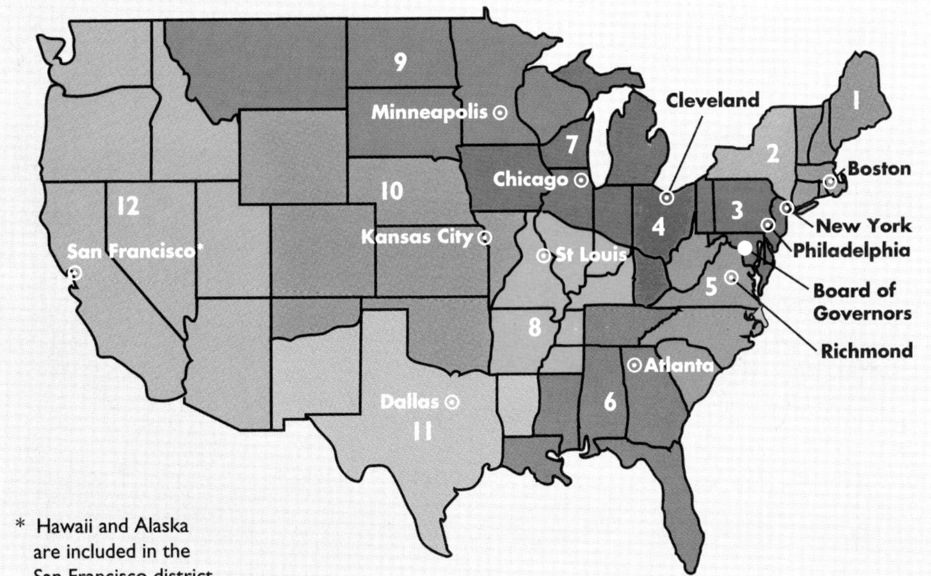

SOURCE: *Federal Reserve Bulletin.*

The nation is divided into 12 Federal Reserve districts, each having a Federal Reserve Bank. (Some of the larger districts also have branch banks.) The Board of Governors of the Federal Reserve System is located in Washington, D.C.

The Board of Governors

The Board of Governors has seven members, who are appointed by the President of the United States and confirmed by the Senate, each for a 14-year term. The terms are staggered so that one seat on the board becomes vacant every two years. The President appoints one of the board members as Chairman for a term of four years, which is renewable.

The Regional Federal Reserve Banks

There are 12 regional Federal Reserve Banks, one for each of 12 Federal Reserve districts shown in Figure 11.7. Each regional Federal Reserve Bank has nine directors, three of whom are appointed by the Board of Governors and six of whom are elected by the commercial banks in the Federal Reserve district. The directors of the regional Federal Reserve Banks appoint the bank's president, and the Board of Governors approves this appointment.

The Federal Reserve Bank of New York (known as the New York Fed) occupies a special place because it implements some of the Fed's most important policy decisions.

The Federal Open Market Committee

Federal Open Market Committee
The Fed's main policy-making committee.

The **Federal Open Market Committee** (FOMC) is the Fed's main policy-making committee (see Figure 11.8). The FOMC consists of the following twelve members:

- The chairman and the other six members of the Board of Governors
- The president of the Federal Reserve Bank of New York
- Four presidents of the other regional Federal Reserve Banks (on a yearly rotating basis)

The FOMC meets approximately every six weeks to review the state of the economy and to decide the actions to be carried out by the New York Fed.

FIGURE 11.8
The Structure of the FOMC

Practice Online

The Board of Governors sets required reserve ratios and, on the proposal of the regional Federal Reserve Banks, sets the discount rate. The Board of Governors and rotating presidents of the regional Federal Reserve Banks sit on the FOMC to determine open market operations.

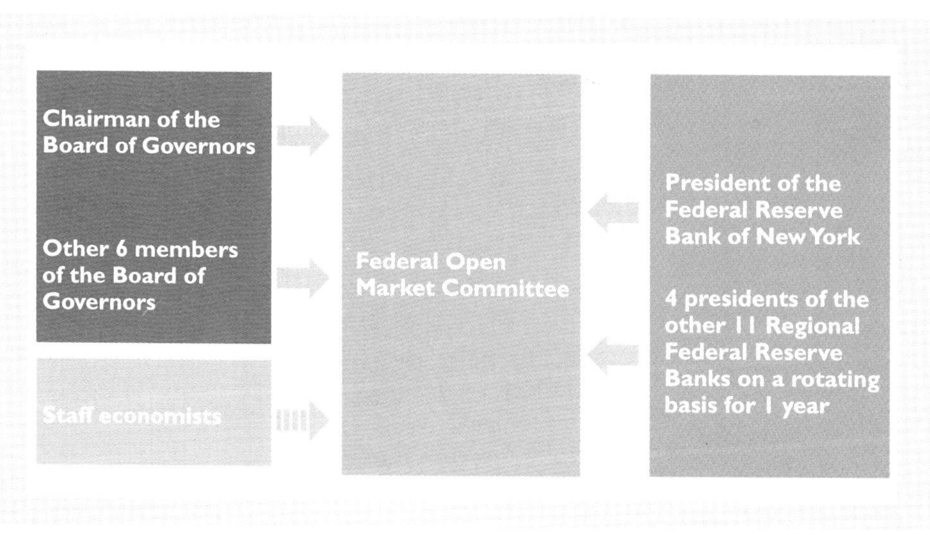

FOMC meeting

The Fed's Power Center

A description of the formal structure of the Fed gives the impression that power in the Fed resides with the Board of Governors. In practice, it is the chairman of the Board of Governors who has the largest influence on the Fed's monetary policy actions. Some remarkable people have been Fed chairmen.

The current chairman of the Board of Governors (in 2003) is Alan Greenspan, who was appointed by President Reagan in 1987 and reappointed by President Bush in 1992 and by President Clinton in 1996 and 2000. Alan Greenspan succeeded another influential chairman, Paul Volcker, who was appointed in 1979 by President Carter and reappointed in 1983 by President Reagan. Volcker ended the 1970s inflation but helped to create one of the most severe post–World War II recessions.

The chairman's power and influence stem from three sources. First, it is the chairman who controls the agenda and who dominates the meetings of the FOMC. Second, day-to-day contact with a large staff of economists and other technical experts provides the chairman with detailed background briefings on monetary policy issues. Third, the chairman is the spokesperson for the Fed and the main point of contact of the Fed with the President and government and with foreign central banks and governments.

The Fed's Policy Tools

The Federal Reserve has many responsibilities, but we'll examine its single most important one: regulating the amount of money floating around in the United States. How does the Fed control the quantity of money? It does so by adjusting the reserves of the banking system. Also, by adjusting the reserves of the banking system and standing ready to make loans to banks, the Fed is able to prevent bank failures. The Fed uses three main policy tools to achieve its objectives:

- Required reserve ratios
- Discount rate
- Open market operations

TABLE 11.2 REQUIRED RESERVE RATIOS

Type of Deposit	Percent
Checkable deposits up to $41.3 million	3
Checkable deposits above $41.3 million	10
All other deposits	0

SOURCE: Federal Reserve.

Required Reserve Ratios

Banks hold reserves. These reserves are currency in the institutions' vaults and ATMs plus deposits held with other banks or with the Fed itself. Banks and thrifts are required to hold a minimum percentage of deposits as reserves. This minimum percentage is known as a *required reserve ratio*. The Fed determines a required reserve ratio for each type of deposit. In 2002, banks were required to hold minimum reserves equal to 3 percent of checkable deposits up to $41.3 million and 10 percent of these deposits in excess of this amount. The required reserves on other types of deposits were zero—see Table 11.2.

Discount rate
The interest rate at which the Fed stands ready to lend reserves to commercial banks.

Discount Rate

The **discount rate** is the interest rate at which the Fed stands ready to lend reserves to commercial banks. A change in the discount rate begins with a proposal to the FOMC by at least one of the 12 Federal Reserve Banks. If the FOMC agrees that a change is required, it proposes the change to the Board of Governors for its approval.

Open market operation
The purchase or sale of government securities—U.S. Treasury bills and bonds—by the Federal Reserve in the open market.

Open Market Operations

An **open market operation** is the purchase or sale of government securities—U.S. Treasury bills and bonds—by the Federal Reserve in the open market. When the Fed conducts an open market operation, it makes a transaction with a bank or some other business but it does not transact with the federal government.

To understand how the Fed's policy tools work, you need to know about the monetary base.

The Monetary Base

Monetary base
The sum of coins, Federal Reserve notes, and banks' reserves at the Fed.

The **monetary base** is the sum of coins, Federal Reserve notes, and banks' reserves at the Fed. The monetary base is so called because it acts like a base that supports the nation's money. The larger the monetary base, the greater is the quantity of money that it can support. Chapter 12 explains how a change in the monetary base leads to a change in the quantity of money.

In September 2002, the monetary base was $670 billion. Figure 11.9 shows how this amount was distributed among its three components: Coins were $30 billion; banks' deposits at the Fed were $10 billion; and the bulk of the monetary base, $630 billion, was made up of Federal Reserve notes.

Federal reserve notes and banks' reserves at the Fed are *liabilities* of the Fed. The Fed's *assets* are

- Gold and deposits in other central banks
- U.S. government securities
- Loans to banks

The Fed holds gold that it could sell if it needed or wished to. It also has deposits in other central banks such as the Bank of Japan and the Bank of England that it can withdraw if it needs to. The Fed holds U.S. government securities that it can sell. Finally, the Fed makes loans to banks, which it can call in. (These loans are usually very small). The Fed charges the banks the discount rate on these loans.

FIGURE 11.9
The Monetary Base and Its Composition

Practice Online

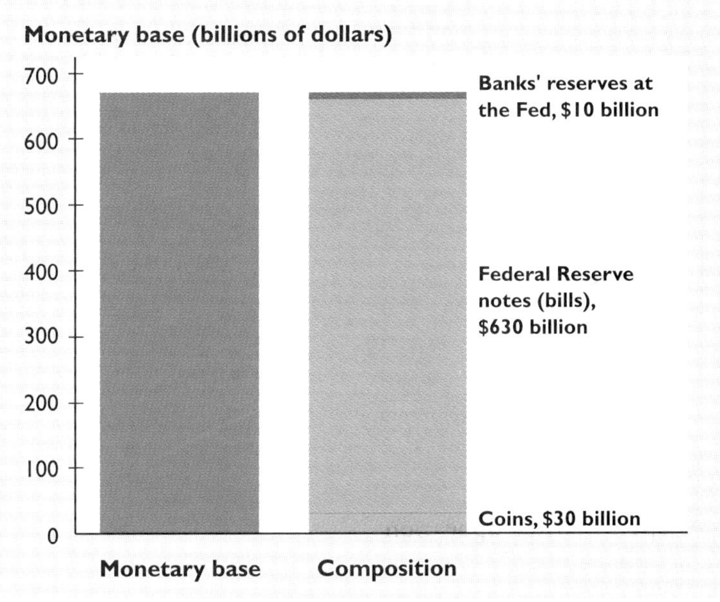

SOURCE: Federal Reserve.

The monetary base is the sum of banks' reserves at the Fed, coins, and Federal Reserve notes (bills). Most of the monetary base consists of Federal Reserve notes.

Why Are Dollar Notes a Liability of the Fed?

You might be wondering why Federal Reserve notes (dollar bills) are a liability of the Fed. When bank notes were invented, they gave their owner a claim on the gold reserves of the issuing bank. These notes were *convertible paper money* and their holders could convert them into gold. So when a bank issued a note, it held itself liable to convert it into gold. The notes were "backed" by gold.

Federal Reserve notes are nonconvertible. A *nonconvertible note* is a bank note that is not convertible into gold and that obtains its value by government fiat—hence the term *fiat money*. These notes are the legal liability of the Fed, and they are "backed" by the Fed's assets. If everyone turned in their dollar bills and banks withdrew their reserves, the Fed would pay out by selling its assets.

How the Fed's Policy Tools Work: A Quick First Look

The next chapter explains how the Fed's policy tools work and how they change the quantity of money. Here, we'll take a quick first look at the basic ideas.

By increasing the required reserve ratio, the Fed can force the banks to hold a larger quantity of monetary base. By raising the discount rate, the Fed can make it more costly for the banks to borrow reserves—borrow monetary base. And by selling securities in the open market, the Fed can decrease the monetary base. All of these actions decrease the quantity of money, other things remaining the same.

Similarly, by decreasing the required reserve ratio, the Fed can permit the banks to hold a smaller quantity of monetary base. By lowering the discount rate, the Fed can make it less costly for the banks to borrow monetary base. And by buying securities in the open market, the Fed can increase the monetary base. All of these actions increase the quantity of money, other things remaining the same.

CHECKPOINT 11.3

Study Guide pp. 165–167

Practice Online 11.3

3 **Describe the functions of the Federal Reserve System.**

Practice Problems 11.3

1. What is the Fed?
2. What is the FOMC?
3. What is the Fed's "power center"?
4. What are the Fed's main policy tools?
5. What is the monetary base?
6. Suppose that at the end of December 2005, the monetary base in the United States is $700 billion, Federal Reserve notes are $650 billion, and banks' reserves at the Fed are $20 billion. Calculate the quantity of coins.

Exercises 11.3

1. What is a central bank?
2. What is the central bank in the United States?
3. Suppose that at the end of December 2004, the monetary base in the United States is $750 billion, Federal Reserve bills are $700 billion, and currency in circulation is $40 billion. What are the commercial banks' deposits at the Fed?
4. Suppose that at the end of December 2005, the monetary base in Canada is $85 billion, Bank of Canada bills are $75 billion, and there is $3 billion of currency in circulation. What are the deposits of the Canadian banks at the Bank of Canada?

Solutions to Practice Problems 11.3

1. The Federal Reserve (Fed) is the central bank in the United States. The central bank in the United States is a public authority that provides banking services to banks and the U.S. government and that regulates the quantity of money and the monetary system.
2. The FOMC is the Federal Open Market Committee. The FOMC is the Fed's main policy-making committee.
3. The Fed's power center is the chairman of the Board of Governors. In 2003, that chairman is Alan Greenspan.
4. The Fed's main policy tools are required reserve ratios, the discount rate, and open market operations.
5. The monetary base is the sum of coins, Federal Reserve notes (dollar bills), and banks' reserves at the Fed.
6. To calculate the quantity of coins at the end of December 2005, we use the definition of the monetary base: coins plus Federal Reserve notes plus banks' reserves at the Fed. Coins equal the monetary base minus Federal Reserve notes minus banks' reserves at the Fed. If at the end of December 2005, the monetary base in the United States is $700 billion, Federal Reserve notes are $650 billion, and bank's reserves at the Fed are $20 billion, so the quantity of coins is $700 billion – $650 billion – $20 billion = $30 billion.

CHAPTER CHECKPOINT

Key Points

1 Define money and describe its functions.

- Money is anything that serves as a generally accepted means of payment.
- Money serves as a medium of exchange, a unit of account, and a store of value.
- M1 consists of currency, travelers' checks, and checkable deposits. M2 consists of M1 plus savings deposits, small time deposits, and money market funds.

2 Describe the monetary system and explain the functions of banks and other monetary institutions.

- Commercial banks, S&Ls, savings banks, credit unions, and money market funds are financial institutions whose deposits are money.
- Banks borrow short term and lend long term and make a profit on the spread between the interest rates that they pay and receive.
- Banks lend most of the funds they receive as deposits and hold only a small amount as reserves.
- Banks can borrow and lend reserves in the interbank federal funds market.

3 Describe the functions of the Federal Reserve System.

- The Federal Reserve is the central bank of the United States.
- The Fed influences the economy by setting the required reserve ratio for banks, by setting the discount rate, and by open market operations.

Key Terms

Barter, 265
Central bank, 279
Commercial bank, 272
Credit union, 274
Currency, 266
Discount rate, 282
Electronic cash (e-cash), 268
Electronic check (e-check), 268
Excess reserves, 273
Federal funds rate, 273
Federal Open Market Committee, 280
Federal Reserve System, 279
Fiat money, 266
Liquid asset, 276
M1, 269
M2, 269
Means of payment, 264
Medium of exchange, 265
Monetary base, 282
Monetary policy, 279
Monetary system, 272
Money, 264
Money market fund, 274
Open market operation, 282
Required reserve ratio, 273
Reserves, 273
Savings and loan association, 274
Savings bank, 274
Store of value, 265
Unit of account, 265

Exercises

1. What is money? Would you classify any of the following items as money?
   a. Store coupons for cat food
   b. A $100 Amazon.com gift certificate
   c. An S&L saving deposit
   d. Frequent Flier Miles
   e. Credit available on your Visa card
   f. The dollar coins that a coin collector owns
   g. Postage stamps issued to commemorate the 2002 Winter Olympic Games
2. What are the three vital functions that money performs? Which of the following items perform some but not all of these functions, and which perform all of these functions? Which of the items are money?
   a. A blank check
   b. A checkable deposit at the Bank of America
   c. A dime
   d. An antique clock
   e. Plastic sheets used to make Visa cards
   f. The coins in the Fed's museum
   g. Government bonds
3. Monica transfers $10,000 from her savings account at the Bank of Alaska to her money market fund. What is the immediate change in M1 and M2?
4. Naomi buys $1,000 worth of American Express travelers' checks and charges the purchase to her American Express card. What is the immediate change in M1 and M2?
5. Terry takes $100 from his checking account and deposits the $100 in his savings account. What is the immediate change in M1 and M2?
6. Vincenzo goes shopping. First, he visits an ATM, where he gets $200 from his savings account. Then he visits a clothing store, where he buys a shirt for $50 using his Visa card. At lunchtime, he meets Donna, his Italian girlfriend, who has just arrived from Rome and has only euros (the money of Italy) in her purse. Donna uses some of her euros to buy $100 from Vincenzo. Donna buys lunch and pays with the $100 that she got from Vincenzo. Did any of the transactions done by Vincenzo and Donna change the quantity of money?
7. In December 2002, banks in Australia had deposits of $500 billion, a required reserve ratio of 4 percent, and no excess reserves. The banks had $15 billion in currency. How much did the banks have in deposits at the Reserve Bank of Australia (the Australian central bank)?
8. In Canada in December 2005, the Bank of Canada (the central bank of Canada) had
   Gold and foreign exchange: $4 billion
   Banks' deposits: $3 billion
   Government securities: $10 billion
   Currency in circulation: $11 billion

The Canadian banks had
Checkable deposits: $400 billion
Savings deposits and time deposits: $600 billion
Currency inside the banks: $1 billion.
Calculate

a. The banks' reserves
b. The monetary base
c. M1
d. M2

9. In Mexico in January 2004, the Banco de México (the central bank of Mexico) reported that bills and coins outside the banks were 175 billion pesos. The Mexican banks had checkable deposits of 418 billion pesos and savings deposits and time deposits of 1782 billion pesos. Currency inside the banks was 28 billion pesos. The Mexican banks had deposits at the Banco de México of 186 billion pesos. Calculate
   a. The banks' reserves
   b. The monetary base
   c. M1
   d. M2

10. What are the main differences and similarities among commercial banks, thrift institutions, and money market funds? How do these institutions earn a profit? What are the main risks they face? How do they manage their exposure to risk?

11. List the policy tools of the Fed and sketch the way in which each tool works to change the quantity of money.

Critical Thinking

12. The President of the United States has no formal authority over the Federal Reserve. In contrast, in some countries, the government directs the central bank and decides what its interest rate policy shall be. Provide some reasons why the central bank should be independent of the government as it is in the United States.

13. Suppose that e-cash issued by private online banks becomes so popular that it completely replaces physical cash and no one has any use for notes issued by the Fed and coins issued by the U.S. mint. What role do you think the Fed could play in such a world?

14. If banks are required to hold reserves at the Fed, doesn't that mean that the required reserves are not really reserves at all and that the only true reserves the banks hold are their excess reserves?

Practice Online

Web Exercises

Use the links on your Foundations Web site to work the following exercises.

15. Visit the Web site of the Federal Reserve. For the most recent week,
    a. What is M1?
    b. What is M2?
    c. What is the monetary base?
    d. What is the percentage increase in M1 over the past year?
    e. What is the percentage increase in M2 over the past year?
    f. What is the percentage increase in the monetary base over the past year?

16. Visit the page of the Federal Reserve Web site that provides data on the assets and liabilities of the commercial banks in the United States. For the most recent week and the same week a year earlier,
    a. What is the total amount of deposits?
    b. What is the total amount of cash assets?
    c. What is the total amount of loans?
    d. What is the percentage increase in deposits over the past year?
    e. What is the percentage increase in cash assets over the past year?
    f. What is the percentage increase in loans over the past year?

17. Visit the Web site of the Federal Reserve. For the most recent week,
    a. What is the total amount of reserves?
    b. What are the total borrowed reserves as a percentage of total reserves?
    c. What are excess reserves as a percentage of total reserves?

18. Visit the Open Market Operations page of the Federal Reserve Web site.
    a. What is the current target for the federal funds rate?
    b. How has the target for the federal funds rate changed over the past year?
    c. What do you think the Fed has been trying to do with the changes in the federal funds rate over the past year?

CHAPTER 12

Money Creation and Control

CHAPTER CHECKLIST

When you have completed your study of this chapter, you will be able to

1. **Explain how banks create money by making loans.**
2. **Explain how the Fed controls the quantity of money.**

Making imitation dollar bills is a serious crime. But creating billions of dollars' worth of money is a perfectly legal activity that banks perform every day. In this chapter, you're going to learn how banks create money by making loans.

This chapter builds on what you learned in Chapter 11. There, you saw that most of the money in the United States today is deposits in commercial banks and thrift institutions. You also learned about the structure of the Fed and the tools it uses to control the quantity of money that circulates in the United States.

You're now going to see exactly how money gets created and how the Fed controls its quantity. Understanding these processes is crucial to understanding how inflation occurs and how it can be kept under control. It is also crucial to understanding how the Fed tries to smooth the business cycle.

First, we'll study the links between the banks' reserves, the quantity of loans that banks make, and the quantity of deposits that they create. Then we'll learn how the Fed uses open market operations and other tools to influence the quantity of money.

12.1 HOW BANKS CREATE MONEY

Banks* create money out of thin air! But this doesn't mean that they have smoke-filled back rooms in which counterfeiters are busily working. Remember, most money is bank deposits, not currency. Banks create deposits, and they do so by making loans. But they cannot create any amount of money they wish. The amount of deposits they can create is limited by their reserves.

Creating a Bank

The easiest way to see how banks create money is to work through the process of creating a bank. Suppose that you and your friends decide to create the Virtual College Bank, an Internet bank that specializes in banking services for college students. You will need to go through the following eight steps:

- Obtain a charter to operate a commercial bank
- Raise some financial capital
- Buy some equipment and computer programs
- Accept deposits
- Establish a reserve account at a Federal Reserve Bank
- Clear checks
- Buy government securities
- Make loans

Obtaining a Charter

Your first task is to obtain a charter to operate a commercial bank. You apply to the Comptroller of the Currency for this charter and establish a federally chartered bank. (If you wanted to establish a state commercial bank, you would apply to your state treasurer's office.)

Raising Financial Capital

Balance sheet
A statement that summarizes assets (amounts owned) and liabilities (amounts owed).

Your next task is to get some funds. You figure that you can open your bank with $200,000, so Virtual College Bank creates 2,000 shares, each worth $100, and sells these shares in your local community. Your bank now has a **balance sheet**—a statement that summarizes its assets and liabilities. The bank's assets are what it owns, and its liabilities are the claims against it, or what it owes, and its owners' equity. Table 12.1 shows your new bank's first balance sheet.

TABLE 12.1
Virtual College Bank's Balance Sheet #1

Assets		Liabilities	
Cash	$200,000	Owners' equity	$200,000

You are now ready to take your third step.

*In this chapter, we'll use the term "bank" to include commercial banks and thrift institutions whose deposits are part of the money supply.

Eye on the Past

The "Invention" of Banking

Goldsmiths and their customers stumbled upon a brilliant idea that led to the creation of the first banks. You will gain useful insights into modern banks and the way they create money by looking at these early banks.

Because gold is valuable and easy to steal, the goldsmiths of sixteenth century Europe had well-guarded safes in which to keep their own gold. They also rented space in their safes to artisans and others who wanted to put their gold in safekeeping. The goldsmiths issued a receipt to the owners of the gold entitling them to reclaim their "deposits" on demand. These receipts were similar to the coat check token you get at a theater or museum.

Isabella has a gold receipt that shows that she has deposited 100 ounces of gold with Samuel Goldsmith. She is going to use her gold to buy some land from Henry. Isabella can make this transaction in one of two ways: She can visit Samuel, collect her gold, and hand the gold to Henry. Or she can give Henry her gold receipt, which will then enable Henry to claim the 100 ounces of gold from Samuel Goldsmith.

It is obviously much more convenient to pass the receipt to Henry. It is a simpler and safer transaction. When Henry wants to use the gold to buy something, he too can pass the receipt on to someone else.

So Samuel Goldsmith's gold receipt is circulating as a means of payment. It is money!

After some years, Samuel notices that the gold that people have placed in his safekeeping never leaves his vault. The receipts circulate, and the gold simply sits in the safe.

Samuel realizes that he can lend people gold receipts and charge them interest on the receipts. So he writes some receipts for gold that he doesn't have and lends these receipts.

After some further years, when many goldsmiths are doing what Samuel is doing, they begin to compete with each other for gold deposits, and instead of charging rent to gold owners, they start to pay interest on gold deposits.

Samuel and his fellow goldsmiths have made the transition from being goldsmiths to being bankers.

As long as they don't issue too many gold receipts, they will always be able to honor requests from depositors who wish to reclaim their gold.

Buying Equipment

You buy some office equipment, a server, banking database software, and a high-speed Internet connection. These items cost you $200,000. Table 12.2 shows your bank's new balance sheet.

TABLE 12.2
Virtual College Bank's Balance Sheet #2

Assets		Liabilities	
Cash	$0		
Equipment	$200,000	Owners' equity	$200,000

Accepting Deposits

You are now ready to start accepting deposits. You pass the word around that you are offering the best terms available and the lowest charges on checkable deposits. Deposits begin to roll in. After a hectic day of business, you have accepted $120,000 of deposits. Table 12.3 shows Virtual College Bank's new balance sheet.

TABLE 12.3
Virtual College Bank's Balance Sheet #3

Assets		Liabilities	
Cash	$120,000	Checkable deposits	$120,000
Equipment	$200,000	Owners' equity	$200,000

The deposits at Virtual College Bank are now part of the money supply. But the quantity of money in the economy has not increased. People have deposited either currency or checks drawn on other banks. To keep the story simple, we'll suppose that all these deposits are currency. So currency outside the banks has decreased by $120,000, and checkable deposits have increased by $120,000.

Establishing a Reserve Account

Now that Virtual College Bank has deposits, it must establish a reserve account at its local Federal Reserve Bank. We'll suppose that your virtual bank is in College Station, Texas, in the Dallas Federal Reserve District. Virtual College Bank now opens an account at the Dallas Fed and deposits in that account all its cash. Table 12.4 shows Virtual College Bank's new balance sheet.

TABLE 12.4
Virtual College Bank's Balance Sheet #4

Assets		Liabilities	
Cash	$0		
Reserves at the Dallas Fed	$120,000	Checkable deposits	$120,000
Equipment	$200,000	Owners' equity	$200,000

Reserves: Actual and Required You saw in Chapter 11 that banks don't keep $100 in bills for every $100 that people have deposited with them. In fact, a typical bank today has reserves of a bit less than $1 for every $100 of deposits. But there's no need for panic. These reserve levels are adequate for ordinary business needs.

The proportion of a bank's total deposits that are held in reserves is called the *reserve ratio.* Virtual College Bank's reserves are $120,000 and deposits are $120,000, so its reserve ratio is 100 percent.

The *required reserve ratio* is the ratio of reserves to deposits that banks are required, by regulation, to hold. We'll suppose that the required reserve ratio for virtual banks operated by college students is 25 percent, a much higher percentage than that for U.S. commercial banks (see Chapter 11, p. 282).

A bank's *required reserves* are equal to its deposits multiplied by the required reserve ratio. So Virtual College Bank's required reserves are

$$\text{Required reserves} = \$120,000 \times 25 \div 100 = \$30,000.$$

Actual reserves minus required reserves are *excess reserves*. Virtual College Bank's excess reserves are

$$\text{Excess reserves} = \$120{,}000 - \$30{,}000 = \$90{,}000.$$

Whenever banks have excess reserves, they are able to make loans. But before Virtual College Bank takes that step, it needs to learn how to clear checks.

Clearing Checks

Virtual College Bank's depositors want to be able to make and receive payments by check. So when Virtual College depositor Jay writes a check for $20,000 to buy some computers from Hal's PCs, which has a checkable deposit at the First American Bank, funds must move from Jay's account at your bank to Hal's account at First American. In the process, Virtual College loses reserves and First American gains reserves. Figure 12.1 tracks the balance sheet changes that occur.

When Hal's PCs banks Jay's check, First American sends the check to the Dallas Fed for collection. The Dallas Fed increases First American's reserves and decreases Virtual College's reserves by $20,000—see Figure 12.1(a). First American now has an extra $20,000 in its reserves at the Dallas Fed, and it increases Hal's PCs' checkable deposit by $20,000. First American's assets and liabilities have both increased by $20,000 in Figure 12.1(b). The Dallas Fed returns the cleared check to Virtual College. Virtual College now has $20,000 less in its reserve account, and it decreases Jay's checkable deposit by $20,000. Virtual College's assets and liabilities have both decreased by $20,000 in Figure 12.1(c).

FIGURE 12.1
Clearing a Check

Practice Online

Federal Reserve Bank of Dallas

Assets		Liabilities	
		First American reserves	+$20,000
		Virtual College reserves	–$20,000

(a) Change in Dallas Fed's balance sheet

First American Bank

Assets		Liabilities	
Reserves at the Dallas Fed	+$20,000	Checkable deposits	+$20,000

(b) Change in First American Bank's balance sheet

Virtual College Bank

Assets		Liabilities	
Reserves at the Dallas Fed	–$20,000	Checkable deposits	–$20,000

(c) Change in Virtual College Bank's balance sheet

(a) First American sends a $20,000 check for collection to the Dallas Fed. The Dallas Fed increases First American's reserves by $20,000 and decreases Virtual College's reserves by $20,000.

(b) First American increases Hal's PCs' checkable deposit by $20,000. First American's assets and liabilities have both increased by $20,000.

(c) Virtual College decreases Jay's checkable deposit by $20,000. Virtual College's assets and liabilities have both decreased by $20,000.

The quantity of money is unaffected by these transactions. Checkable deposits have increased at First American and decreased at Virtual College, but total deposits are unchanged. Total bank reserves are also unaffected. First American's reserves have increased and Virtual College's reserves have decreased by the same amount.

Virtual College Bank is now ready to use some of its reserves to earn an income. It buys some government securities.

Buying Government Securities

Government securities provide Virtual College with an income and a safe asset that is easily converted back into reserves when necessary. Suppose that Virtual College decides to buy $60,000 worth of government securities. On the same day, First American decides to sell $60,000 of government securities to Virtual College. In reality, a bond broker will match the First American sale with Virtual College's purchase.

Figure 12.2 tracks the effects of this transaction on the balance sheets of the two banks and the Dallas Fed. Virtual College gives First American a check for $60,000, and First American transfers the government bonds to Virtual College. First American sends the check to the Dallas Fed for collection. The Dallas Fed

FIGURE 12.2
Making Interbank Loans and Buying Government Securities

Practice Online

(a) Virtual College buys $60,000 worth of government securities from First American and pays by check. The Dallas Fed increases First American's reserves by $60,000 and decreases Virtual College's reserves by the same amount.

(b) First American's reserves have increased and its government securities have decreased by $60,000.

(c) Virtual College's reserves have decreased and its government securities have increased by the $60,000.

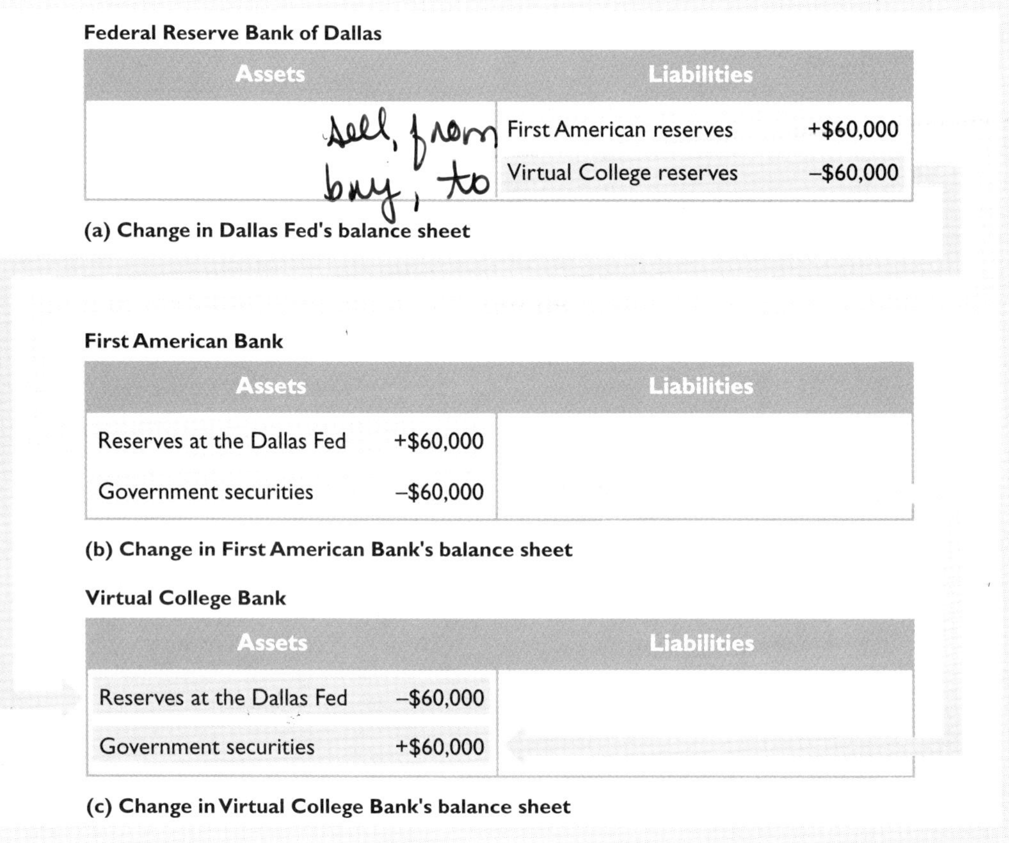

Federal Reserve Bank of Dallas

Assets		Liabilities	
		First American reserves	+$60,000
		Virtual College reserves	–$60,000

(a) Change in Dallas Fed's balance sheet

First American Bank

Assets		Liabilities
Reserves at the Dallas Fed	+$60,000	
Government securities	–$60,000	

(b) Change in First American Bank's balance sheet

Virtual College Bank

Assets		Liabilities
Reserves at the Dallas Fed	–$60,000	
Government securities	+$60,000	

(c) Change in Virtual College Bank's balance sheet

increases First American's reserves by $60,000 and decreases Virtual College's reserves by the same amount in Figure 12.2(a).

First American's reserves have increased and its government securities have decreased by the same $60,000 in Figure 12.2(b). Virtual College's reserves have decreased and its government securities have increased by the same $60,000 in Figure 12.2(c).

After all the transactions we've just followed in Figures 12.1 and 12.2, Virtual College's balance sheet looks like that in Table 12.5.

TABLE 12.5

Virtual College Bank's Balance Sheet #5

Assets		Liabilities	
Reserves at the Dallas Fed	$40,000	Checkable deposits	$100,000
Government securities	$60,000	Owners' equity	$200,000
Equipment	$200,000		
Total assets	$300,000	Total liabilities	$300,000

With deposits of $100,000 and a required reserve ratio of 25 percent, Virtual College must hold a minimum of $25,000 in reserves. Because it currently has $40,000 in reserves, Virtual College can make some loans.

Making Loans

With reserves of $40,000 and required reserves of $25,000, Virtual College has excess reserves of $15,000. So the bank decides to make loans of this amount. Table 12.6 shows the bank's balance sheet on the day the bank makes these loans. Loans of $15,000 are added to the bank's assets. Loans are an asset to the bank because the borrower is committed to repaying the loan on an agreed-upon schedule. The bank places the $15,000 loaned in the checkable deposit accounts of the borrowers. So the bank's checkable deposits increase by $15,000 to $115,000.

TABLE 12.6

Virtual College Bank's Balance Sheet #6

Assets		Liabilities	
Reserves at the Dallas Fed	$40,000	Checkable deposits	$115,000
Government securities	$60,000	Owners' equity	$200,000
Loans	$15,000		
Equipment	$200,000		
Total assets	$315,000	Total liabilities	$315,000

The bank has now created some money. Checkable deposits have increased by the amount of the loans, so the quantity of money has increased by $15,000. And although Virtual College has made loans equal to its excess reserves of $15,000, it still has those reserves! Because its deposits have increased, its required reserves have also increased. They are now 25 percent of $115,000, or $28,750. So the bank now has excess reserves of $11,250.

Before you get too excited and decide to lend another $11,250, let's see what happens when the borrowers of the $15,000 that you've just loaned start to spend their loans.

Spending a Loan To spend their loans, the borrowers write checks on their checkable deposits. Let's assume that they spend the entire $15,000. Most likely, the people to whom these checks are paid do not bank at Virtual College. That's what we'll assume. So when these checks are cleared, transactions like those that we described above take place. The receiving banks send the checks to the Dallas Fed for collection. The Fed increases the reserves of the receiving banks by $15,000 and decreases the reserves of Virtual College by $15,000. Virtual College's balance sheet now looks like that in Table 12.7.

TABLE 12.7
Virtual College Bank's Balance Sheet #7

Assets		Liabilities	
Reserves at the Dallas Fed	$25,000	Checkable deposits	$100,000
Government securities	$60,000	Owners' equity	$200,000
Loans	$15,000		
Equipment	$200,000		
Total assets	$300,000	Total liabilities	$300,000

Both reserves and deposits have decreased by $15,000 because this amount has been paid to people with accounts in other banks. If some of the checks drawn were paid to customers of Virtual College, deposits and reserves would have fallen by less than the full $15,000 and the bank would still have some excess reserves. But in the situation shown in Table 12.7, the bank is fully loaned—its reserves are just sufficient to meet the required reserve ratio.

But the banks that received the deposits that Virtual College has lost have also received reserves. These banks now have excess reserves, so they can make some loans. And these loans will create some more money. Also, when Virtual College bought government securities from First American, the reserves of First American increased by $60,000. So other banks now have reserves of $75,000 that they didn't have before that they could now lend. So yet more money can be created.

If you told the loan officer at your own bank that she creates money, she wouldn't believe you. People who work in banks see themselves as lending the money they receive from others, but (unless they've studied economics) they don't see the entire process, so they don't realize that they create money. But in fact, even though each bank lends only what it receives, the banking system creates money. To see how, let's see what happens in the entire banking system when one bank receives some new reserves.

The Limits to Money Creation

Figure 12.3 is going to keep track of what is happening in the process of money creation by a banking system in which each bank has a required reserve ratio of 25 percent. We'll start the process off with every bank holding exactly its required reserves. Then Al Capone, after years of shady dealing, decides to go to school. He takes $100,000 of notes from under his mattress and deposits them at Virtual College Bank. Virtual College now has $100,000 of new deposits and $100,000 of new reserves. With a required reserve ratio of 25 percent, the bank's required reserves are $25,000. So the bank makes a loan of $75,000 to Amy. Then Amy writes a check for $75,000 to buy a copy-shop franchise from Barb. At this point,

Virtual College has a new deposit of $100,000, a new loan of $75,000, and new reserves of $25,000. You can see this situation in Figure 12.3.

For Virtual College, that is the end of the story. But it's not the end of the story for the banking system. Barb deposits her check for $75,000 in First American, where deposits and reserves increase by $75,000. First American puts 25 percent of its increase in deposits ($18,750) into reserves and lends $56,250 to Bob. And Bob writes a check to Carl to pay off a business loan.

Figure 12.3 shows the state of play at the end of round 2. Total bank reserves have increased by $43,750 ($25,000 plus $18,750), total loans have increased by $131,250 ($75,000 plus $56,250), and total deposits have increased by $175,000 ($100,000 plus $75,000).

When Carl takes his check to Fleet PC, its deposits and reserves increase by $56,250. Fleet PC keeps $14,063 in reserves and lends $42,187. This process continues until there are no excess reserves in the banking system. But the process

FIGURE 12.3
The Multiple Creation of Bank Deposits

Practice Online

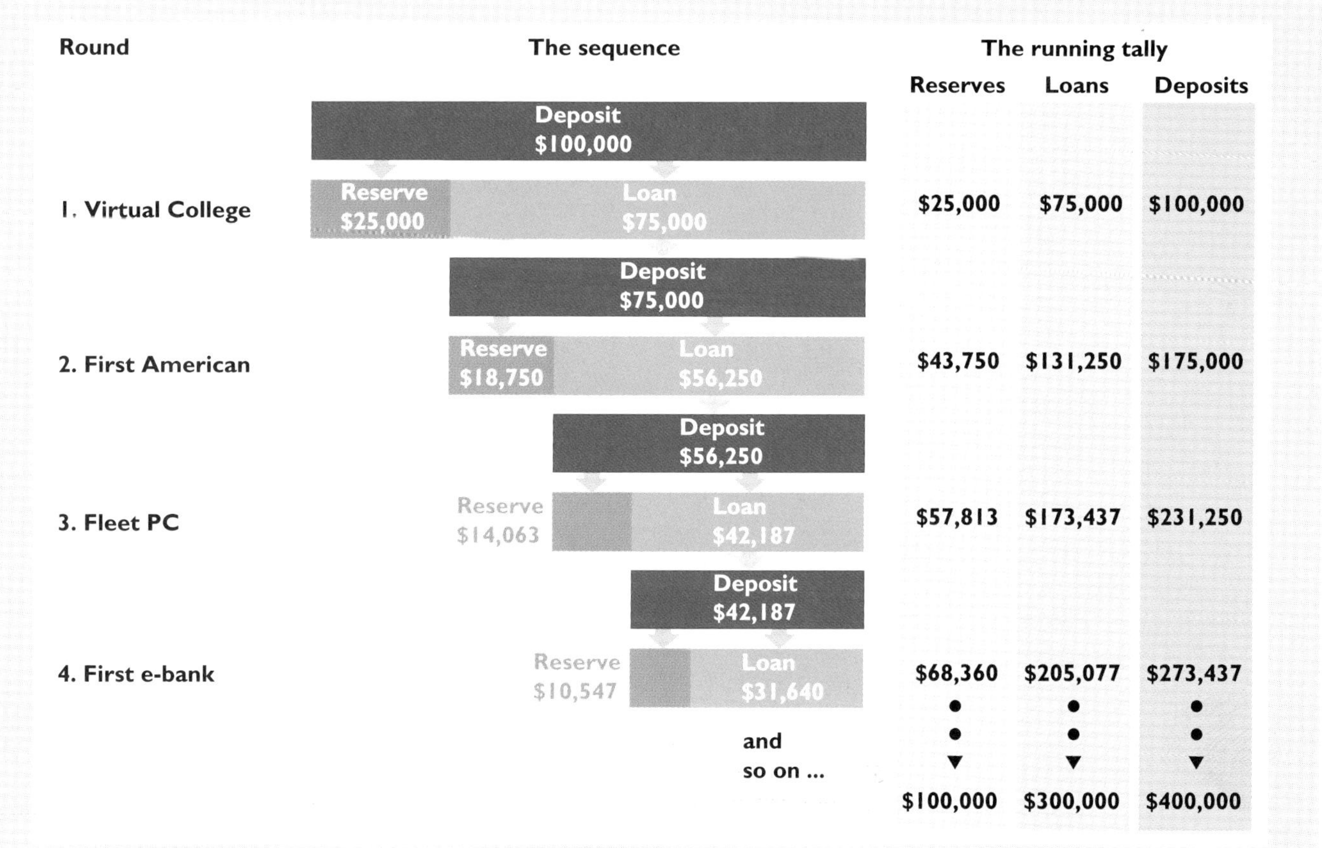

When a bank receives deposits, it keeps 25 percent in reserves and lends 75 percent. The amount loaned becomes a new deposit at another bank. The next bank in the sequence keeps 25 percent and lends 75 percent, and the process continues until the banking system has created enough deposits to eliminate its excess reserves. The running tally tells us the deposits and loans created at each stage. At the end of the process, an additional $100,000 of reserves creates an additional $400,000 of deposits.

takes a lot of further steps. Figure 12.3 shows one additional step. The figure also shows the final tallies: Reserves increase by $100,000, loans increase by $300,000, and deposits increase by $400,000.

The sequence in Figure 12.3 is the first four rounds of the process. To work out the entire process, look closely at the numbers in the figure. At each stage, the loan is 75 percent (0.75) of the previous loan and the deposit is 0.75 of the previous deposit. Let's call that proportion L ($L = 0.75$). The complete sequence is

$$1 + L + L^2 + L^3 + L^4 + \ldots.$$

Remember, L is a fraction, so at each stage in this sequence, the amount of new loans and new deposits gets smaller. The total increase in deposits when the process ends is the sum of the above sequence multiplied by the initial increase in reserves, which is

$$\frac{1}{1 - L} \times \text{Initial increase in reserves.}$$

If we use the numbers from the example, the total increase in deposits is

$$\$100{,}000 + 75{,}000 + 56{,}250 + 42{,}187 + \ldots$$

$$= \$100{,}000 \times (1 + 0.75 + 0.5625 + 0.42187 + \ldots)$$

$$= \$100{,}000 \times (1 + 0.75 + 0.75^2 + 0.75^3 + \ldots)$$

$$= \$100{,}000 \times \frac{1}{(1 - 0.75)}$$

$$= \$100{,}000 \times \frac{1}{0.25}$$

$$= \$100{,}000 \times 4.$$

$$= \$400{,}000.$$

So even though each bank lends only the money it receives, the banking system as a whole does create money by making loans.

The Deposit Multiplier

Deposit multiplier
The number by which an increase in bank reserves is multiplied to find the resulting increase in bank deposits.

The **deposit multiplier** is the number by which an increase in bank reserves is multiplied to find the resulting increase in bank deposits. That is,

$$\text{Change in deposits} = \text{Deposit multiplier} \times \text{Change in reserves.}$$

In the example that we've just worked through, the deposit multiplier is 4. The $100,000 increase in reserves brought a $400,000 increase in deposits. The deposit multiplier is linked to the required reserve ratio by the following equation:

$$\text{Deposit multiplier} = \frac{1}{\text{Required reserve ratio}}.$$

In the example, the required reserve ratio is 25 percent, or 0.25. That is,

$$\text{Deposit multiplier} = \frac{1}{0.25} = 4.$$

CHECKPOINT 12.1

1 Explain how banks create money by making loans.

Study Guide pp. 172–175

Practice Online 12.1

Practice Problems 12.1

1. How do banks create new deposits by making loans, and what factors limit the amount of deposits and loans they can create?
2. The required reserve ratio is 0.1, and banks have no excess reserves. Jamie deposits $100 in his bank. Calculate
   a. The bank's excess reserves as soon as Jamie makes the deposit.
   b. The maximum amount of loans that the banking system can make.
   c. The maximum amount of new money that the banking system can create.

Exercises 12.1

1. Your bank manager tells you that he does not create money. He just lends the money that people deposit in the bank. Explain to him how he does create money.
2. If the banking system receives new deposits of $200 million, what determines the maximum amount of new money that the banks can create?
3. If a multibank system has a required reserve ratio of 0.05 and Erin deposits $50 in her bank, calculate
   a. The bank's excess reserves as soon as Erin makes her deposit.
   b. The maximum amount of loans that the banking system can make.
   c. The maximum amount of new money that the banking system can create.

Solutions to Practice Problems 12.1

1. Banks can make loans when they have excess reserves—reserves in excess of those required. When a bank makes a loan, it creates a new deposit for the person who receives the loan. The bank uses its excess reserves to create new deposits. The amount of loans that the bank can make, and therefore the amount of new deposits that it can create, is limited by two things: the amount of excess reserves and the required reserve ratio.

2a. The bank's excess reserves are $90. When deposits increase by $100, the bank is required to keep 10 percent of the deposit as reserves. That is, required reserves increase by $10 and the bank has $90 of excess reserves.

2b. The maximum amount of loans that the banking system can make is $900. When reserves increase by $100, the deposit multiplier determines the maximum increase in deposits that the banking system can have. Deposits increase to make the bank's required reserves increase by $100. The deposit multiplier equals 1/Required reserve ratio, which is 1/0.1 or 10. With the $100 increase in reserves, deposits can increase to $1,000. Jamie deposited $100, so the banking system can create an additional $900 of deposits. It does so by making loans of $900.

2c. The maximum amount of new money that can be created is $900. When a bank makes loans, it creates new money. The maximum amount of new money created by the banking system equals the maximum amount of loans that it can make.

12.2 INFLUENCING THE QUANTITY OF MONEY

The Fed constantly monitors and adjusts the quantity of money in the economy. To change the quantity of money, the Fed can use any of its three tools:

- Required reserve ratios
- Discount rate
- Open market operations

Let's see how these three tools work.

How Required Reserve Ratios Work

If the Fed increases the required reserve ratio, the banks must increase their reserves and decrease their lending, which decreases the quantity of money. If the Fed decreases the required reserve ratio, the banks can decrease their reserves and increase their lending, which increases the quantity of money. The Fed changes the required reserve ratio infrequently because a small change in the ratio would have a drastic effect on bank lending and the Fed has more refined tools at its disposal.

How the Discount Rate Works

If the Fed increases the discount rate, the banks must pay a higher price for any reserves that they borrow from the Fed. Faced with higher cost of reserves, the banks are less willing to borrow reserves and prefer to decrease their lending. So when the discount rate increases, the quantity of money decreases. Similarly, if the Fed decreases the discount rate, the banks pay a lower price for reserves that they borrow from the Fed. Faced with a lower cost of reserves, the banks are more willing to borrow reserves and increase their lending. So when the discount rate decreases, the quantity of money increases. The discount rate has limited effect because the banks rarely borrow from the Fed.

How an Open Market Operation Works

Open market operations are the Fed's major policy tool. When the Fed buys securities in an open market operation, it pays for them with newly created bank reserves and money. With more reserves in the banking system, the supply of interbank loans increases, the demand for interbank loans decreases, and the federal funds rate—the interest rate in the interbank loans market—falls. Similarly, when the Fed sells securities in an open market operation, buyers pay for the securities with bank reserves and money. With smaller reserves in the banking system, the supply of interbank loans decreases, the demand for interbank loans increases, and the federal funds rate rises. The Fed sets a target for the federal funds rate and conducts open market operations on the scale needed to hit its target.

A change in the federal funds rate is only the first stage in an adjustment process that follows an open market operation. If banks' reserves increase, the banks can increase their lending and create even more money. If banks' reserves decrease, the banks must decrease their lending, which decreases the quantity of money. We'll study the effects of open market operations in some detail, beginning with an open market purchase.

The Fed Buys Securities

Suppose the Fed buys $100 million of U.S. government securities in the open market. There are two cases to consider, depending on who sells the securities. A bank might sell some of its securities, or a person or business that is not a commercial bank—the general public—might sell. The outcome is essentially the same in the two cases, but you might need to be convinced of this fact. So we'll study the two cases, starting with the simpler case in which a commercial bank sells securities. (The seller will be someone who thinks the Fed is offering a good price for securities so that it is profitable to make the sale.)

A Commercial Bank Sells When the Fed buys $100 million of securities from the Manhattan Commercial Bank, two things happen:

1. The Manhattan Commercial Bank has $100 million less in securities, and the Fed has $100 million more in securities.
2. To pay for the securities, the Fed increases the Manhattan Commercial Bank's reserve account at the New York Fed by $100 million.

Figure 12.4 shows the effects of these actions on the balance sheets of the Fed and the Manhattan Commercial Bank. Ownership of the securities passes from the commercial bank to the Fed, so the bank's securities decrease by $100 million and the Fed's securities increase by $100 million, as shown by the red-to-blue arrow running from the Manhattan Commercial Bank to the Fed. The Fed increases the Manhattan Commercial Bank's reserves by $100 million, as shown by the green arrow running from the Fed to the Manhattan Commercial Bank. This action increases the monetary base and increases the reserves of the banking system.

The commercial bank's total assets remain constant, but their composition changes. Its holdings of government securities decrease by $100 million, and its reserves increase by $100 million. The bank can use these additional reserves to make loans. When the bank makes loans, the quantity of money increases by the process that we described in the previous section.

FIGURE 12.4
The Fed Buys Securities from a Commercial Bank

Practice Online

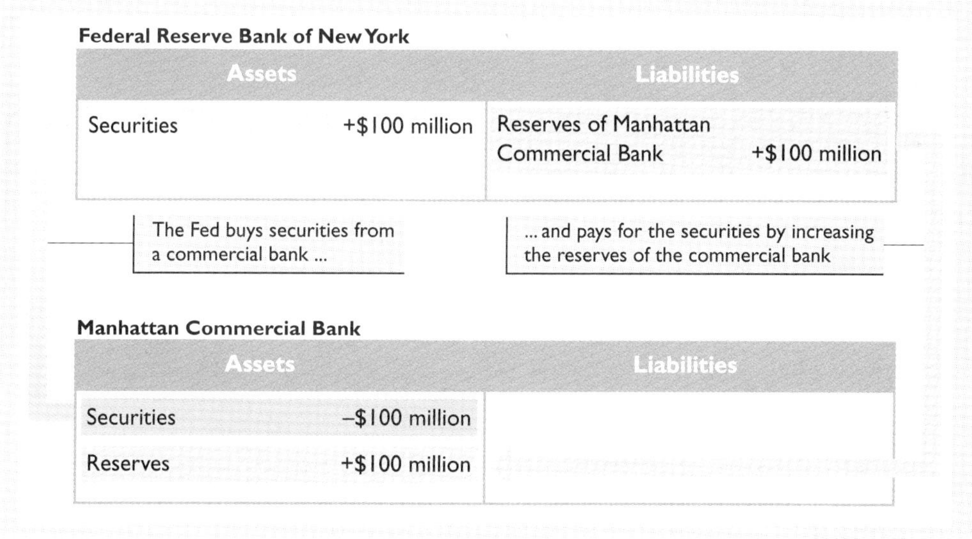

We've just seen that when the Fed buys government securities from a bank, the bank's reserves increase. What happens if the Fed buys government securities from the public—say, from Goldman Sachs, a financial services company?

The Nonbank Public Sells When the Fed buys $100 million of securities from Goldman Sachs, three things happen:

1. Goldman Sachs has $100 million less in securities, and the Fed has $100 million more in securities.
2. The Fed pays for the securities with a check for $100 million drawn on itself, which Goldman Sachs deposits in its account at the Manhattan Commercial Bank.
3. The Manhattan Commercial Bank collects payment of this check from the Fed, and the Manhattan Commercial Bank's reserves increase by $100 million.

Figure 12.5 shows the effects of these actions on the balance sheets of the Fed, Goldman Sachs, and the Manhattan Commercial Bank. Ownership of the securities passes from Goldman Sachs to the Fed, so Goldman Sachs's securities decrease by $100 million and the Fed's securities increase by $100 million (red-to-blue arrow). The Fed pays for the securities with a check payable to Goldman Sachs, which Goldman Sachs deposits in the Manhattan Commercial Bank. This payment increases Manhattan's reserves by $100 million (green arrow). It also

FIGURE 12.5
The Fed Buys Securities from the Public

Practice Online

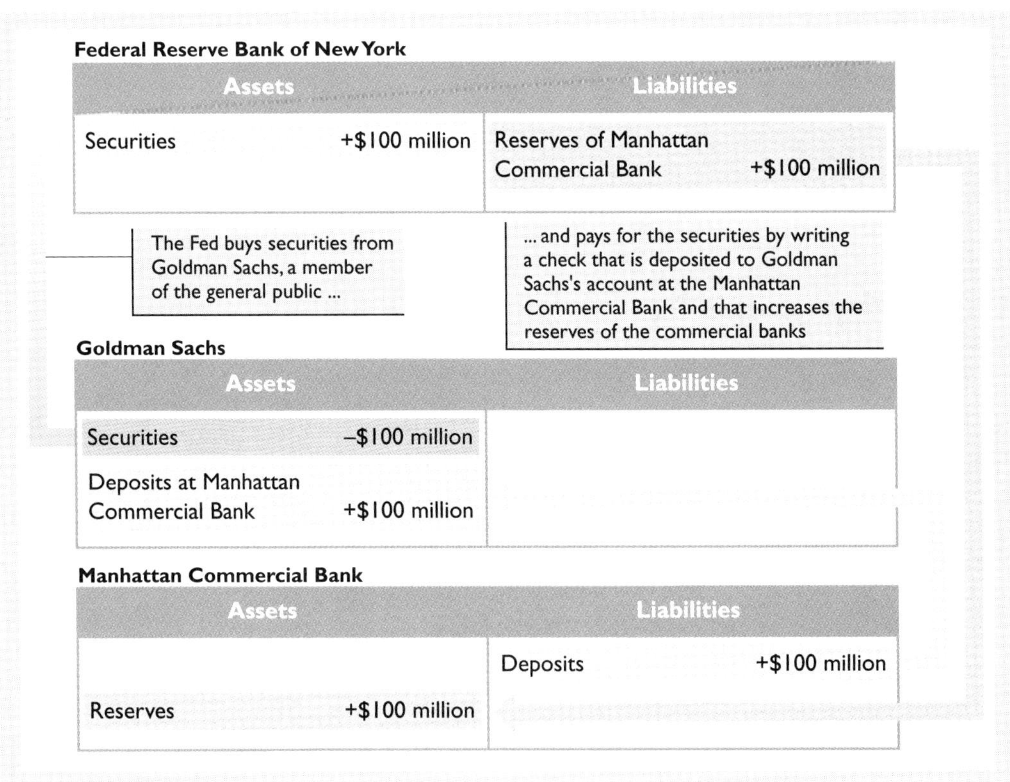

increases Goldman Sachs's deposit at the Manhattan Commercial Bank by $100 million (blue arrow). Just as when the Fed buys securities from a bank, this action increases the monetary base and increases the reserves of the banking system.

Goldman Sachs has the same total assets as before, but their composition has changed. It now has more money and fewer securities. The Manhattan Commercial Bank's reserves increase, and so do its deposits—both by $100 million. Because bank reserves and deposits have increased by the same amount, the bank has excess reserves, which it can use to make loans. When it makes loans, the quantity of money increases by the process that we described in the previous section.

We've worked through what happens when the Fed buys government securities from either a bank or the public. When the Fed sells securities, the transactions that we've just traced operate in reverse.

The Fed Sells Securities

If the Fed sells $100 million of U.S. government securities in the open market, most likely a person or business other than a bank buys them. (A bank would buy them only if it had excess reserves and it couldn't find a better use of its funds.)

When the Fed sells $100 million of securities to Goldman Sachs, three things happen:

1. Goldman Sachs has $100 million more in securities, and the Fed has $100 million less in securities.
2. Goldman Sachs pays for the securities with a check for $100 million drawn on its deposit account at the Manhattan Commercial Bank.
3. The Fed collects payment of this check from the Manhattan Commercial Bank by decreasing its reserves by $100 million.

These actions decrease the monetary base and decrease the reserves of the banking system. The Manhattan Commercial Bank is now short of reserves and must borrow in the federal funds market to meet its required reserve ratio.

The changes in the balance sheets of the Fed and the banks that we've just described are not the end of the story about the effects of an open market operation; they are just the beginning. A multiplier effect on the quantity of money now begins. To study this multiplier effect of an open market operation on the quantity of money, we build on the link between bank reserves and bank deposits that you studied in the previous section.

The Multiplier Effect of an Open Market Operation

An open market purchase that increases bank reserves also increases the *monetary base*. The increase in the monetary base equals the amount of the open market purchase, and initially, it equals the increase in bank reserves. To see why, recall that the *monetary base is the sum of Federal Reserve notes, coins, and banks' reserves at the Fed*. An open market purchase increases the banks' reserves at the Fed by the amount of the open market purchase. Nothing else changes, so the monetary base increases by the amount of the open market purchase.

If the Fed buys securities from the banks, the quantity of deposits (and quantity of money) does not change. If the Fed buys securities from the public, the quantity of deposits (and quantity of money) increases by the same amount as the increase in bank reserves. Either way, the banks have excess reserves that they now start to lend.

Figure 12.6 illustrates the multiplier effect of an open market purchase of securities from the banks. The following sequence of events takes place:

- An open market purchase creates excess reserves.
- Banks lend excess reserves.
- Bank deposits increase.
- The quantity of money increases.
- New money is used to make payments.
- Some of the new money is held as currency—a currency drain.
- Some of the new money remains in deposits in banks.
- Banks' required reserves increase.
- Excess reserves decrease but remain positive.

This sequence is similar to the one you studied in the previous section of this chapter but with one addition: the currency drain. When banks use excess reserves to make loans, bank deposits increase but currency held outside the banks also increases. An increase in currency held outside the banks is called the **currency drain**. The currency drain does not change the monetary base. Bank reserves decrease, currency increases, and the monetary base remains the same. But a currency drain decreases the amount of money that banks can create from a given increase in the monetary base because currency drains from their reserves and decreases the excess reserves available.

Currency drain
An increase in currency held outside the banks.

The sequence of rounds described in Figure 12.6 repeats, but each round begins with a smaller quantity of excess reserves than did the previous one. The process ends when excess reserves have been eliminated.

FIGURE 12.6
A Round in the Multiplier Process Following an Open Market Operation

Practice Online

❶ An open market purchase increases bank reserves and ❷ creates excess reserves. ❸ Banks lend the excess reserves, ❹ new deposits are created, and ❺ the quantity of money increases. ❻ New money is used to make payments. ❼ Households and firms receiving payments keep some on deposit in banks and some in the form of currency—❽ a currency drain. The increase in bank deposits increases banks' reserves but also ❾ increases banks' required reserves. Required reserves increase by less than actual reserves, so the banks still have some excess reserves, though less than before. The process repeats until excess reserves have been eliminated.

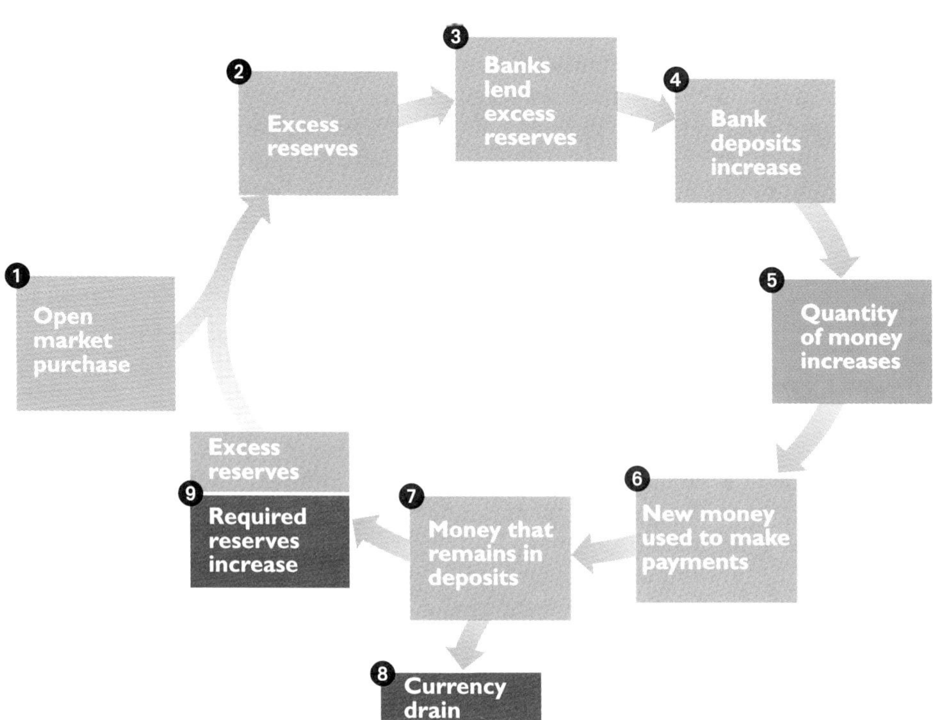

Figure 12.7 keeps track of the magnitudes of the increases in reserves, loans, deposits, currency, and money that result from an open market purchase of \$100,000. In this figure, the currency drain is 33.33 percent of money and the required reserve ratio is 10 percent of deposits. These numbers are assumed to keep the arithmetic simple.

The Fed buys \$100,000 of securities from the banks. The banks' reserves increase by this amount, but deposits do not change. The banks have excess reserves of \$100,000, and they lend those reserves. When the banks lend \$100,000 of excess reserves, \$66,667 remains in the banks as deposits and \$33,333 drains off and is held outside the banks as currency. The quantity of money has now increased by \$100,000—the increase in deposits plus the increase in currency holdings.

The increased bank deposits of \$66,667 generate an increase in required reserves of 10 percent of that amount, which is \$6,667. Actual reserves have increased by the same amount as the increase in deposits—\$66,667. So the banks now have excess reserves of \$60,000. At this stage, we have gone around the circle shown in Figure 12.6 once. The process that we've just described repeats but begins with excess reserves of \$60,000. Figure 12.7 shows the next two rounds. At the end of the process, the quantity of money has increased by a multiple of the increase in the monetary base. In this case, the increase is \$250,000, which is 2.5 times the increase in the monetary base.

An open market *sale* works similarly to an open market *purchase*, but the sale *decreases* the quantity of money. (Trace the process again but with the Fed *selling* and the banks or public *buying* securities.)

FIGURE 12.7
The Multiplier Effect of an Open Market Operation

Practice Online

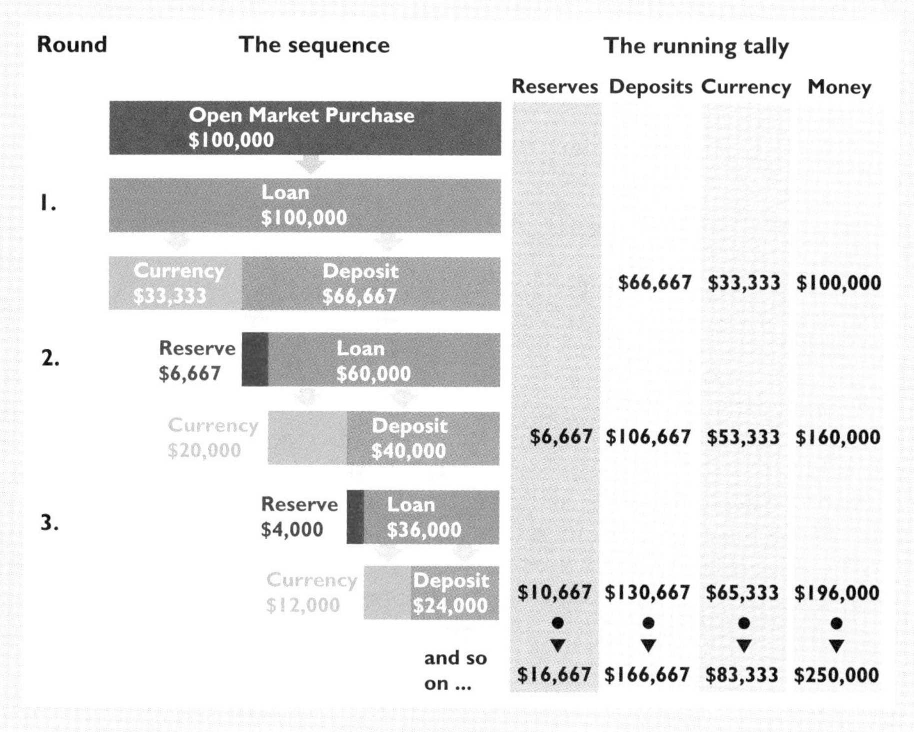

When the Fed provides the banks with \$100,000 of additional reserves in an open market purchase, the banks lend those reserves. Of the amount loaned, \$33,333 (33.33 percent) leaves the banks in a currency drain and \$66,667 remains on deposit. With additional deposits, required reserves increase by \$6,667 (10 percent required reserve ratio) and the banks lend \$60,000. Of this amount, \$20,000 leaves the banks in a currency drain and \$40,000 remains on deposit. The process repeats until the banks have created enough deposits to eliminate their excess reserves. An additional \$100,000 of reserves creates \$250,000 of money.

The Money Multiplier

Money multiplier
The number by which a change in the monetary base is multiplied to find the resulting change in the quantity of money.

In the example we've just worked through, the quantity of money increases by 2.5 times the increase in the monetary base. The **money multiplier** is the number by which a change in the monetary base is multiplied to find the resulting change in the quantity of money. That is,

$$\text{Change in quantity of money} = \text{Money multiplier} \times \text{Change in monetary base.}$$

In the example, the change in monetary base is the size of the open market purchase, which is \$100,000, so

$$\text{Change in quantity of money} = 2.5 \times \$100{,}000 = \$250{,}000.$$

The money multiplier is determined by the banks' required reserve ratio and by the currency drain. In the above example, the required reserve ratio is 10 percent of deposits and the currency drain is 33.33 percent of money. So when the banks lend their initial \$100,000 of excess reserves, \$33,333 drains off as currency and \$66,667 remains in the banks as reserves and deposits.

With an additional \$66,667 of deposits and a 10 percent required reserve ratio, the banks' required reserves increase by \$6,667, so their excess reserves are \$60,000. Notice that \$60,000 is 0.6 of the original \$100,000 of excess reserves. That is, in the second round of lending, the banks lend 0.6 of the amount they loaned in the first round. Call this proportion L ($L = 0.6$). In the third round, the banks lend $0.6^2 = 0.36$ of the original amount (\$36,000 in Figure 12.7).

Because L is a fraction, at each stage in this sequence the amounts of new loans and new money created get smaller. The total amount of new money created at the end of the process is

$$\text{Quantity of money created} = \frac{1}{1 - L} \times \text{Open market purchase.}$$

If we use the numbers from the example, the total increase in the quantity of money is

$$\begin{aligned}\text{Quantity of money created} &= \$100{,}000 \times \frac{1}{(1 - 0.6)} \\ &= \$100{,}000 \times \frac{1}{0.4} \\ &= \$100{,}000 \times 2.5 \\ &= \$250{,}000.\end{aligned}$$

The proportion L can be calculated from the currency drain and required reserve ratio. Call the currency drain C and the required reserve ratio R. So $C = 0.33$ and $R = 0.1$.

When the banks lend \$1, \$$C$ is held as currency and \$$(1 - C)$ remains on deposit. Banks must hold \$$R$ of reserves for each \$1 of deposits, so they are free to lend \$$(1 - R)$ of each dollar on deposit. When \$$(1 - C)$ remains on deposit, banks can lend \$$(1 - C) \times (1 - R)$. That is, the proportion L is

$$L = (1 - C) \times (1 - R).$$

Eye on the U.S. Economy

The Money Multiplier

We can measure the money multiplier in the United States by using the following formula:

Money multiplier = Quantity of money ÷ Monetary base.

Because there are two main definitions of money, M1 and M2, there are two money multipliers: the M1 multiplier and the M2 multiplier.

Also, there are two measures of the currency drain and bank reserve ratios. Part (a) shows the currency drain measures: the ratio of currency to M1 and the ratio of currency to M2.

Notice the increase in the ratio of currency to M1, which arises mainly from a surge in holdings of U.S. currency abroad.

In part (b), you can see that the reserve ratios have fallen as required reserve ratios have been decreased.

In part (c), you can see the two money multipliers. The M2 multiplier increased through the 1980s because required reserves decreased. This multiplier decreased during the 1990s because the currency drain increased. In 2002, this multiplier was about 8.

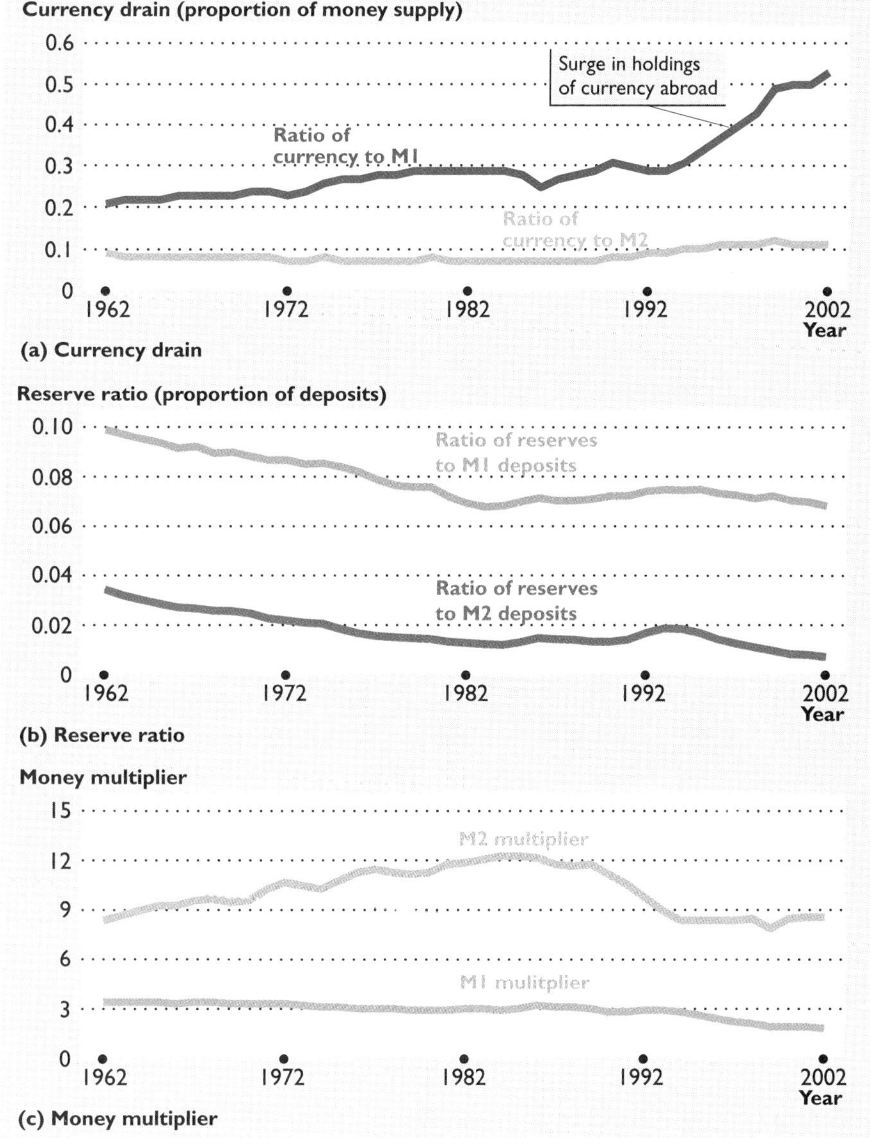

The M1 multiplier decreased from close to 4 in 1960 to about 2 in 2000.

The increasing currency drain is the main influence on this multiplier.

In terms of the numbers in our example,

$$L = (1 - 0.33) \times (1 - 0.1)$$

$$= (0.67) \times (0.9) = 0.6.$$

The larger the currency drain and the larger the required reserve ratio, the smaller is the money multiplier.

CHECKPOINT 12.2

Study Guide pp. 175–179

Practice Online 12.2

2 **Explain how the Fed controls the quantity of money.**

Practice Problems 12.2

1. Which of the Fed's tools does it use most often?
2. What is the money multiplier? What determines its magnitude?
3. If the Fed makes an open market purchase of $1 million of securities,
   a. Who can sell the securities to the Fed in an open market operation? Does it matter from whom the Fed buys the securities?
   b. What initial changes occur in the economy if the Fed buys from a bank?
   c. What is the process by which the quantity of money changes?
   d. What factors determine how much the quantity of money changes?

Exercises 12.2

1. What is an open market operation? How do open market operations influence the monetary base?
2. Explain how the banking system creates money when the Fed conducts an open market operation.
3. If the Fed makes an open market sale of $1 million of securities,
   a. What initial changes occur in the economy?
   b. What is the process by which the quantity of money in the economy changes?
   c. By how much does the quantity of money change?
   d. What is the magnitude of the money multiplier?

Solutions to Practice Problems 12.2

1. The Fed's most used tool is the open market operation.
2. The money multiplier is the number by which a change in the monetary base is multiplied to find the resulting change in the quantity of money. The currency drain and the banks' required reserve ratio determine its magnitude.

3a. The Fed buys securities from banks or the public. The Fed does not buy securities from the government. It does not matter from whom the Fed buys the securities. The change in the monetary base is the same.

3b. The monetary base increases by $1 million. Ownership of the securities passes from the bank to the Fed. As a result, the Fed's assets increase by $1 million. When the Fed pays for the securities, it increases the bank's deposit with the Fed by $1 million. The Fed's liabilities increase by $1 million. The bank's assets are the same, but their composition has changed. The bank has $1 million more in reserves and $1 million less in securities.

3c. The bank's reserves have increased by $1 million and its deposits have not changed, so it has excess reserves of $1 million. The bank makes loans and creates new deposits. The new deposits are new money.

3d. The required reserve ratio and the currency drain determine the increase in the quantity of money. The larger the required reserve ratio or the currency drain, the smaller is the increase in the quantity of money.

CHAPTER CHECKPOINT

Key Points

1 Explain how banks create money by making loans.

- Banks create money by making loans.
- Banks hold a proportion of their deposits as reserves to meet the *required reserve ratio.*
- Reserves that exceed the required reserve ratio are *excess reserves,* which banks loan.
- The quantity of reserves and the required reserve ratio limit the total quantity of deposits that the banks can create.
- The deposit multiplier is the number by which an increase in bank reserves is multiplied to give the increase in bank deposits.
- The deposit multiplier equals one divided by the required reserve ratio.

2 Explain how the Fed controls the quantity of money.

- The Fed has three tools for controlling the quantity of money: required reserve ratios, the discount rate, and open market operations.
- An increase in the required reserve ratio forces the banks to hold more reserves and decreases the quantity of money that can be supported by a given amount of monetary base.
- An increase in the discount rate makes the banks pay a higher price for borrowed reserves, makes them less willing to borrow reserves, and decreases the quantity of money.
- When the Fed *buys* securities in an open market operation, it pays for them with newly created bank reserves. When the Fed *sells* securities in an open market operation, people pay for them with money and banks pay for them with reserves.
- An open market purchase increases the monetary base and creates the following sequence of events: banks lend excess reserves; the quantity of money increases; new money is used to make payments; some of the new money is held as currency—a currency drain; some of the new money remains on deposit in banks; banks' required reserves increase; excess reserves decrease. This sequence repeats until excess reserves are eliminated.
- The money multiplier determines the amount of money that banks can create from a given increase in the monetary base.
- The money multiplier is determined by the banks' required reserve ratio and by the currency drain.

Key Terms

Balance sheet, 290
Currency drain, 304
Deposit multiplier, 298
Money multiplier, 306

Exercises

1. If the banking system receives new deposits of $2 million, the required reserve ratio is 0.1, and there is no currency drain, calculate
   a. The bank's excess reserves as soon as the deposit is made.
   b. The maximum amount of loans that the banking system can make.
   c. The maximum amount of new money that the banking system can create.
2. If the banking system loses deposits of $3 million, the required reserve ratio is 0.1, and there is no currency drain, calculate
   a. The bank's excess reserves as soon as the deposit withdrawal occurs.
   b. The amount of loans that the banking system must call in.
   c. The amount of money that the banking system must destroy.
3. The required reserve ratio is 5 percent and the currency drain is 20 percent. If the Fed makes an open market purchase of $1 million of securities,
   a. What is the change in the monetary base?
   b. Which components of the monetary base change?
   c. By how much does the quantity of money change?
   d. How much of the new money is currency and how much is bank deposits?
4. Initially, the banking system has $2 trillion of deposits and no excess reserves. If the Fed lowers the required reserve ratio from 0.1 to 0.05, calculate the change in
   a. Reserves.
   b. Deposits.
   c. The quantity of money.
5. The First Student Bank has the following balance sheet (in millions of dollars).

Assets		Liabilities	
Reserves at the Fed	25	Demand deposits	90
Cash in ATMs	15	Savings deposits	110
Government securities	60		
Loans	100		

   The required reserve ratio on all deposits is 5 percent.
   a. What, if any, are the bank's excess reserves?
   b. What is the bank's deposit multiplier?
   c. How much will the bank loan?
   d. If there is no currency drain and if all the funds loaned are deposited in the First Student Bank, what are the bank's excess reserves, if any, after the loans made in part **c**?
   e. If there is no currency drain and if all the funds loaned remain deposited in the First Student Bank, what is the quantity of loans and total deposits when the bank has no excess reserves?
   f. If the required reserve ratio is decreased to 2 percent and if there is no currency drain and all the funds loaned remain deposited in the First Student Bank, what is the quantity of loans and total deposits when the bank has no excess reserves?

6. The Second Student Bank has the following balance sheet (in millions of dollars).

Assets		Liabilities	
Reserves at the Fed	3	Demand deposits	90
Cash in ATMs	2	Savings deposits	110
Government securities	60		
Loans	100		

The required reserve ratio on all deposits is 5 percent.

a. Does the bank have any excess reserves?
b. Does the bank have a shortage of reserves?
c. How much of the outstanding loans will the bank not renew?
d. If there is no currency drain and if all the loans that are repaid are paid out of deposits in the Second Student Bank, what is the bank's shortage of reserves, if any, after the loans are repaid in part **c**?
e. If there is no currency drain and if all the loans are repaid come from deposits in the Second Student Bank, what is the quantity of loans and total deposits when the bank has no excess reserves?

7. If the Fed wants to decrease quantity of money, what type of open market operation might it undertake? Explain the process by which the quantity of money decreases.

8. Suppose that the currency drain is 10 percent and the required reserve ratio is 1 percent. If the Fed sells $100,000 of securities on the open market, calculate the first round changes in

a. Excess reserves.
b. Deposits.
c. Currency in circulation.

9. What can the Fed do to increase the quantity of money and keep the monetary base constant? Explain why the Fed would or would not do each of the following:

a. Change the currency drain
b. Change the required reserve ratio
c. Change the discount rate
d. Conduct an open market operation

10. The commercial banks have the following balance sheet (in billions of dollars).

Assets		Liabilities	
Reserves	10	Deposits	200
Government securities	50		
Loans	150		

The required reserve ratio is 5 percent, there is no currency drain, and the Fed conducts an open market purchase of securities of $1 billion.

a. What is the initial change in the reserves of the banks?
b. By how much do loans increase?
c. By how much do deposits increase?

Critical Thinking

11. An early goldsmith banker earned a profit (and sometimes a large profit) simply by writing notes to certify that a person had deposited a certain amount of gold in his vault. By writing more notes than the amount of gold held, the goldsmith could lend the notes and charge interest on them.
    a. Did the goldsmith bankers make money out of thin air in a form of legal theft?
    b. Should the goldsmith bankers have been regulated to ensure that the amount of gold in their vaults equaled the value of the notes they created?
    c. What were the main benefits from the activities of the goldsmith bankers?

12. In the United States today, the Federal Reserve is the only bank that is permitted to create bank notes.
    a. Do you think that Citigroup and JP Morgan Chase should be permitted to issue their own private bank notes in competition with the Fed?
    b. Do you think the Fed should be the only bank that is permitted to issue e-cash?

13. Bank deposits are insured against the risk of bank failure. Can you think of any bad side effects of this arrangement?

Practice Online

Web Exercises

Use the links on your Foundations Web site to work the following exercises.

14. Visit the Web site of JP Morgan Chase and obtain the most recent balance sheet data for this bank.
    a. What is the total amount of deposits?
    b. What is the total amount of loans?
    c. What is the total amount of reserves held?
    d. What is the reserve ratio?
    e. Why can't you determine from the published balance sheet the deposits that are part of M1 and the deposits that are part of M2?

15. Visit the Web sites of JP Morgan Chase and Citigroup and obtain the most recent earnings data for these large banks.
    a. What are their profits during the most recent year?
    b. Explain how these banks earn such large profits.

16. Visit the Web site of the Federal Reserve and obtain the most recent data on the monetary base, M1, M2, and the composition of money and calculate for the most recent month
    a. The currency drain (using both M1 and M2).
    b. The banks' reserve ratio (using both the M1 deposits and the M2 deposits).
    c. The money multiplier (for both M1 and M2).

17. Visit the Web site of the Federal Reserve and obtain the most recent information on "Factors Affecting Reserve Balances of Depository Institutions."
    a. Have the reserves of depository institutions increased or decreased?
    b. Has the Fed increased or decreased the amount that it has loaned to depository institutions?

CHAPTER 13

Money, Interest, and Inflation

CHAPTER CHECKLIST

When you have completed your study of this chapter, you will be able to

1 **Explain what determines the demand for money and how the demand for money and the supply of money determine the *nominal* interest rate.**

2 **Explain how in the long run, the quantity of money determines the price level and money growth brings inflation.**

3 **Identify the costs of inflation and the benefits of a stable value of money.**

You know what money is, how banks create it, and how the Fed controls its quantity. In this chapter, you are going to learn about the effects of money on the economy.

First, you'll see how, on any given day, the quantity of money determines the interest rate. The effect of money on the interest rate is one of the channels through which the Fed influences expenditure plans and the business cycle. You'll learn more about these aspects of money in subsequent chapters.

Second, you'll see how, when we smooth out the influence of the business cycle and look at the long-term trends, the quantity of money determines the price level and money growth in excess of potential GDP growth brings inflation.

Finally, you'll see why inflation—ongoing *changes* in the price level—can have a big influence on people's lives.

WHERE WE ARE AND WHERE WE'RE HEADING

Before we explore the effects of money on the interest rate and the inflation rate, let's take stock of what we've learned and preview where we are heading.

The Real Economy

Real factors that are independent of the price level determine potential GDP and the natural unemployment rate (Chapter 8). The demand for labor and supply of labor determine the quantity of labor employed and the real wage rate at full employment. The full-employment equilibrium quantity of labor and the production function determine potential GDP. At full employment, real GDP equals potential GDP and the unemployment rate equals the natural unemployment rate.

Real GDP and the unemployment rate are independent of the price level only at full employment. Away from potential GDP, aggregate supply and aggregate demand determine equilibrium real GDP and the price level, and fluctuations in aggregate supply and aggregate demand bring fluctuations around full employment (Chapter 8).

Investment demand and saving supply determine the levels of investment and saving and the real interest rate (Chapter 9). Investment and saving along with population growth, human capital growth, and technological change determine the growth rate of real GDP (Chapter 10).

The Money Economy

Money—the economy's means of payment—consists of currency and bank deposits (Chapter 11). Banks create deposits by making loans, and the Fed controls the quantity of money through its open market operations, which determine the monetary base and the federal funds rate—the interest rate on interbank loans (Chapter 12).

The effects of money on the economy, which we explore in this chapter, are complex and to explain and understand them, we proceed in three steps. We take these steps in an order that might seem strange but that turns out to be the most effective.

Step one looks at the immediate effect of the Fed's actions. This effect is on the short-term nominal interest rate. The Fed raises and lowers the short-term nominal interest rate by changing the quantity of money.

Step two looks at the long-term effects of the Fed's actions. These effects are on the price level and the inflation rate. The Fed lowers or raises the price level by decreasing or increasing the quantity of money. And the Fed lowers or raises the inflation rate by slowing down or speeding up the rate at which the quantity of money grows. We take these two steps in the current chapter.

Step three provides the blow-by-blow story of how the Fed's actions ripple through the economy and ultimately change the price level and the inflation rate. This story is a long one that needs to be broken down into manageable bites, and we explore it in the chapters of Part 5.

Some people approach a novel in this order: first, read the introduction, then the conclusion, and then the steps in between. Try it! It sometimes helps to know where you are going.

13.1 MONEY AND THE INTEREST RATE

To understand the Fed's short-run influence on the interest rate, we must understand what determines the demand for money, the supply of money, and the forces that bring equilibrium in the market for money. We'll begin by studying the demand for money.

The Demand for Money

The amount of money that households and firms choose to hold is the **quantity of money demanded**. What determines the quantity of money demanded? The answer is a benefit–opportunity cost calculation. The quantity of money that households and firms choose to hold is the quantity that balances the benefit of holding an additional dollar of money against the opportunity cost of doing so. But just what are the benefit and opportunity cost of holding money?

Quantity of money demanded
The amount of money that households and firms choose to hold.

Benefit of Holding Money

You've seen that money is the means of payment and that it serves as a medium of exchange, unit of account, and store of value (Chapter 11, pp. 264–265). You don't need any money to use it as a unit of account. You can keep financial records in dollars and cents even if you don't have any money. You don't need money to store your wealth. You can store it in the form of bonds, stocks, and mutual funds. Money and other financial assets are substitute stores of value. But you do need money to make payments and do transactions. These two features of money are the sources of benefit from holding money. The more money you hold, the easier it is for you to make payments and transactions.

The marginal benefit of holding money is the change in total benefit that results from holding one more dollar as money. The marginal benefit of holding money diminishes as the quantity of money held increases. If you hold only a few dollars in money, holding one more dollar brings large benefits—you can buy a cup of coffee, take a bus ride, or use a pay phone. If you hold enough money to make your normal weekly payments, holding one more dollar brings only a small benefit because you're not very likely to want to spend it. Holding even more money brings only a small additional benefit. You barely notice the difference in the benefit of having $1,000 versus $1,001 in your bank account.

To get the most out of your assets, you hold money only up to the point at which its marginal benefit equals its opportunity cost. But what is the opportunity cost of holding money?

Opportunity Cost of Holding Money

The opportunity cost of holding money is the interest rate forgone on an alternative asset. If you can earn 8 percent a year on a mutual fund account, then holding an additional $100 in money costs you $8 a year. Your opportunity cost of holding $100 in money is the goods and services worth $8 that you must forgo.

A fundamental principle of economics is that if the opportunity cost of something increases, people seek substitutes for it. Money is no exception. Other assets such as a mutual fund account are substitutes for money. And the higher the opportunity cost of holding money—the higher the interest income forgone by not holding other assets—the smaller is the quantity of money demanded.

Opportunity Cost: *Nominal* Interest Is a *Real* Cost

The opportunity cost of holding money is the nominal interest rate. In Chapter 7, (p. 175) you learned the distinction between the *nominal* interest rate and the *real* interest rate and that

Nominal interest rate = Real interest rate + Inflation rate.

We can use this equation to find the real interest rate for a given nominal interest rate and inflation rate. For example, if the nominal interest rate on a mutual fund account is 8 percent a year and the inflation rate is 2 percent a year, the real interest rate is 6 percent a year. Why isn't the real interest rate of 6 percent a year the opportunity cost of holding money? That is, why isn't the opportunity cost of holding $100 in money only $6 worth of goods and services forgone?

The answer is that if you hold $100 in money rather than in a mutual fund, your buying power decreases by $8, not by $6. With inflation running at 2 percent a year, on each $100 that you hold as money and that earns no interest, you lose $2 worth of buying power a year. On each $100 that you put into your mutual fund account, you gain $6 worth of buying power a year. So if you hold money rather than a mutual fund, you lose the buying power of $6 plus $2, or $8—equivalent to the nominal interest rate on the mutual fund, not the real interest rate.

Because the opportunity cost of holding money is the nominal interest rate on an alternative asset,

Other things remaining the same, the higher the nominal interest rate, the smaller is the quantity of money demanded.

This relationship describes the money holding decisions of individuals and firms. It also describes money holding decisions for the economy—the sum of the decisions of every individual and firm.

We summarize the influence of the nominal interest rate on money holding decisions in a demand for money schedule and curve.

The Demand for Money Schedule and Curve

Demand for money
The relationship between the quantity of money demanded and the nominal interest rate, when all other influences on the amount of money that people wish to hold remain the same.

The **demand for money** is the relationship between the quantity of money demanded and the nominal interest rate, when all other influences on the amount of money that people wish to hold remain the same. We illustrate the demand for money with a demand for money schedule and a demand for money curve, such as those in Figure 13.1. If the interest rate is 5 percent a year, the quantity of money demanded is $1 trillion. The quantity of money demanded decreases to $0.98 trillion if the interest rate rises to 6 percent a year and increases to $1.02 trillion if the interest rate falls to 4 percent a year.

The demand for money curve is *MD*. When the interest rate rises, everything else remaining the same, the opportunity cost of holding money rises and the quantity of money demanded decreases—there is a movement up along the demand for money curve. When the interest rate falls, the opportunity cost of holding money falls and the quantity of money demanded increases—there is a movement down along the demand for money curve.

FIGURE 13.1
The Demand for Money

Practice Online

	Nominal interest rate (percent per year)	Quantity of money demanded (trillions of dollars)
A	6	0.98
B	5	1.00
C	4	1.02

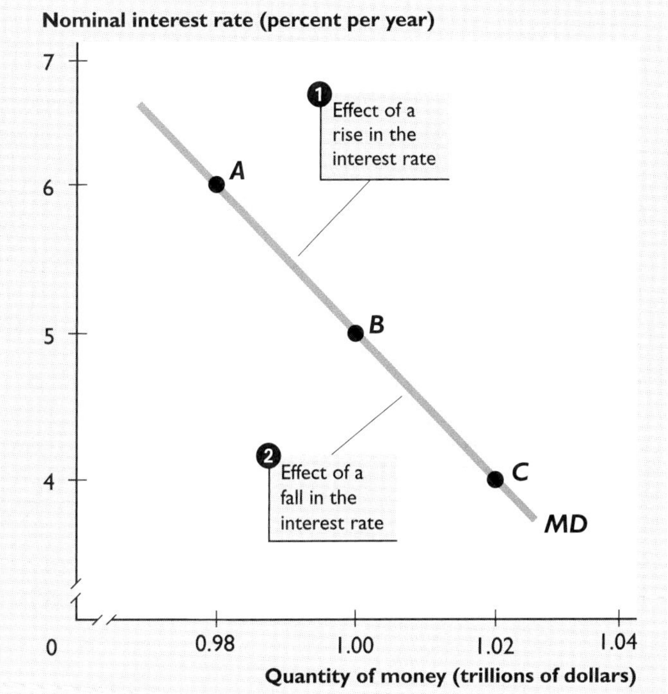

The demand for money schedule is graphed as the demand for money curve, *MD*. Rows *A*, *B*, and *C* in the table correspond to points *A*, *B*, and *C* on the curve. The nominal interest rate is the opportunity cost of holding money.

1 Other things remaining the same, an increase in the nominal interest rate decreases the quantity of money demanded, and 2 a decrease in the nominal interest rate increases the quantity of money demanded.

Changes in the Demand for Money

A change in the nominal interest rate brings a change in the quantity of money demanded and a movement along the demand for money curve. A change in any other influence on money holding changes the demand for money. The three main influences on the demand for money are

- The price level
- Real GDP
- Financial technology

The Price Level

The demand for money is proportional to the price level—an x percent rise in the price level brings an x percent increase in the quantity of money demanded at each nominal interest rate. The reason is that we hold money to make payments: If the price level changes, the quantity of dollars that we need to make payments changes in the same proportion.

Real GDP

The demand for money increases as real GDP increases. The reason is that expenditures and incomes increase when real GDP increases. So households and firms must hold larger average inventories of money to make the increased expenditures and income payments.

Financial Technology

Changes in financial technology change the demand for money. Most changes in financial technology come from advances in computing and record keeping. Some advances increase the quantity of money demanded, and some decrease it.

Daily interest checking deposits and automatic transfers between checking and savings deposits enable people to earn interest on money, lower the opportunity cost of holding money, and increase the demand for money. Automatic teller machines, debit cards, and smart cards, which have made money easier to obtain and use, have increased the marginal benefit of money and increased the demand for money.

Credit cards have made it easier for people to buy goods and services on credit and pay for them when their credit card account becomes due. This development has decreased the demand for money.

Shifts in the Demand for Money Curve

A change in any influence on money holdings other than the interest rate changes the demand for money and shifts the demand for money curve, as you can see in Figure 13.2. A rise in the price level, an increase in real GDP, or an advance in financial technology that lowers the opportunity cost of holding money or makes money more useful increases the demand for money and shifts the demand curve rightward from MD_0 to MD_1. A fall in the price level, a decrease in real GDP, or a technological advance that creates a substitute for money has the opposite effect. It decreases the demand for money and shifts the demand curve leftward from MD_0 to MD_2.

FIGURE 13.2
Changes in the Demand for Money

Practice Online

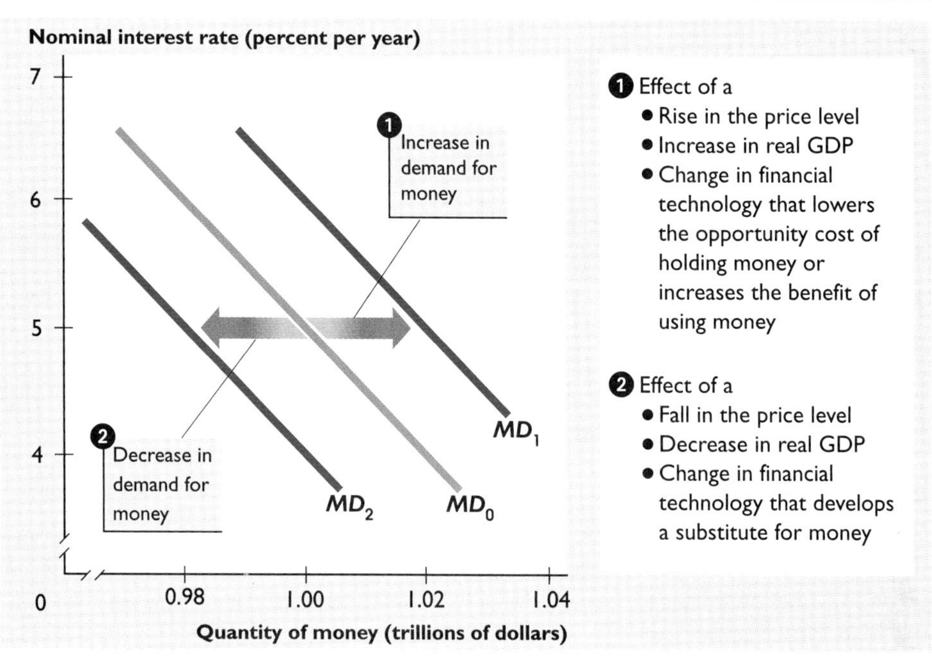

The Nominal Interest Rate

People hold some of their financial wealth as money and some in the form of other financial assets. You have seen that the amount that people hold as money depends on the nominal interest rate that they can earn on other financial assets. Demand and supply determine the nominal interest rate. We can study the forces of demand and supply in either the market for financial assets or the market for money. Because the Fed influences the quantity of money, we focus on the market for money.

Figure 13.3 shows the market for money. The quantity of money supplied is determined by the actions of the banking system and the Fed. On any given day, there is a fixed quantity of money supplied. In Figure 13.3, that quantity is $1 trillion. The **supply of money**, which is the relationship between the quantity of money supplied and the nominal interest rate, is shown by the vertical line *MS*.

Supply of money
The relationship between the quantity of money supplied and the nominal interest rate.

Also, on any given day, the price level, real GDP, and the state of financial technology are fixed. Because these influences on the demand for money are fixed, the demand for money curve is given and is the curve *MD* in Figure 13.3.

The interest rate is the only influence on the quantity of money demanded that is free to fluctuate. And every day, the interest rate adjusts to make the quantity of money demanded equal the quantity of money supplied—to achieve money market equilibrium. In Figure 13.3, the equilibrium interest rate is 5 percent a year. At any interest rate above 5 percent a year, the quantity of money demanded is less than the quantity of money supplied. At any interest rate below 5 percent a year, the quantity of money demanded exceeds the quantity of money supplied.

FIGURE 13.3
Money Market Equilibrium

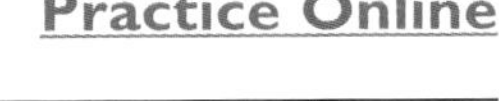

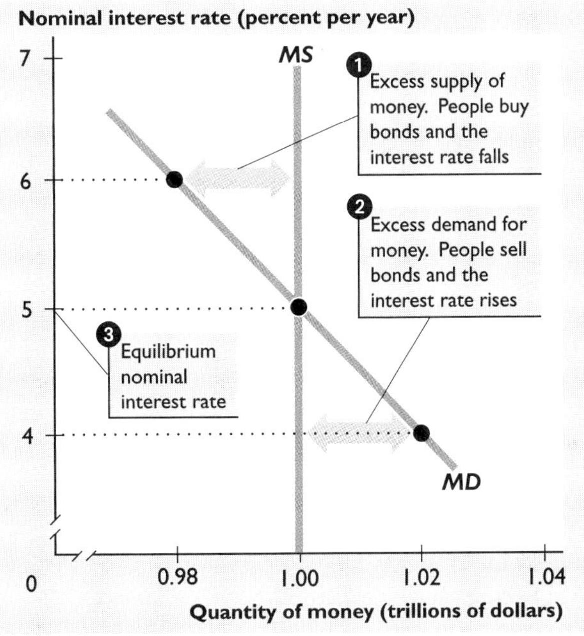

The supply of money curve is *MS*, and the demand for money curve is *MD*.

1. If the interest rate is 6 percent a year, the quantity of money held exceeds the quantity demanded. People buy bonds, the price of a bond rises, and the interest rate falls.
2. If the interest rate is 4 percent a year, the quantity of money held falls short of the quantity demanded. People sell bonds, the price of a bond falls, and the interest rate rises.
3. If the interest rate is 5 percent a year, the quantity of money held equals the quantity demanded. The money market is in equilibrium.

Eye on the U.S. Economy

Money and Credit Cards

The quantity of M1 money has decreased as a percentage of GDP. Part (a) of the figure shows that M1 fell from 20 percent of GDP in 1970 to less than 12 percent in 2002.

In sharp contrast to the use of M1 money, credit card ownership and use has expanded strongly. Part (b) of the figure shows the upward trend. In 1970, 16 percent (one in six) of families had a credit card. By 1999, 72 percent of families had a credit card. And by 2005, it is projected that 80 percent of families will use a credit card.

Most people use their credit card account as a substitute for money. When they buy goods or services, they use their credit card. And when the monthly bill arrives, many people pay off some of the outstanding balance, but not all of it. In 1998, 42 percent of credit card holders had an outstanding balance after making their most recent payment, and the average card balance was $4,000.

The changing financial technology has led to a steady decrease in the demand for money and a leftward shift of the demand for money curve. Part (c) of the figure shows the shifts in the demand curve for M1. Here, we're measuring the quantity of M1 as a percentage of GDP so that you can see the influence of the interest rate and financial technology on the demand for money.

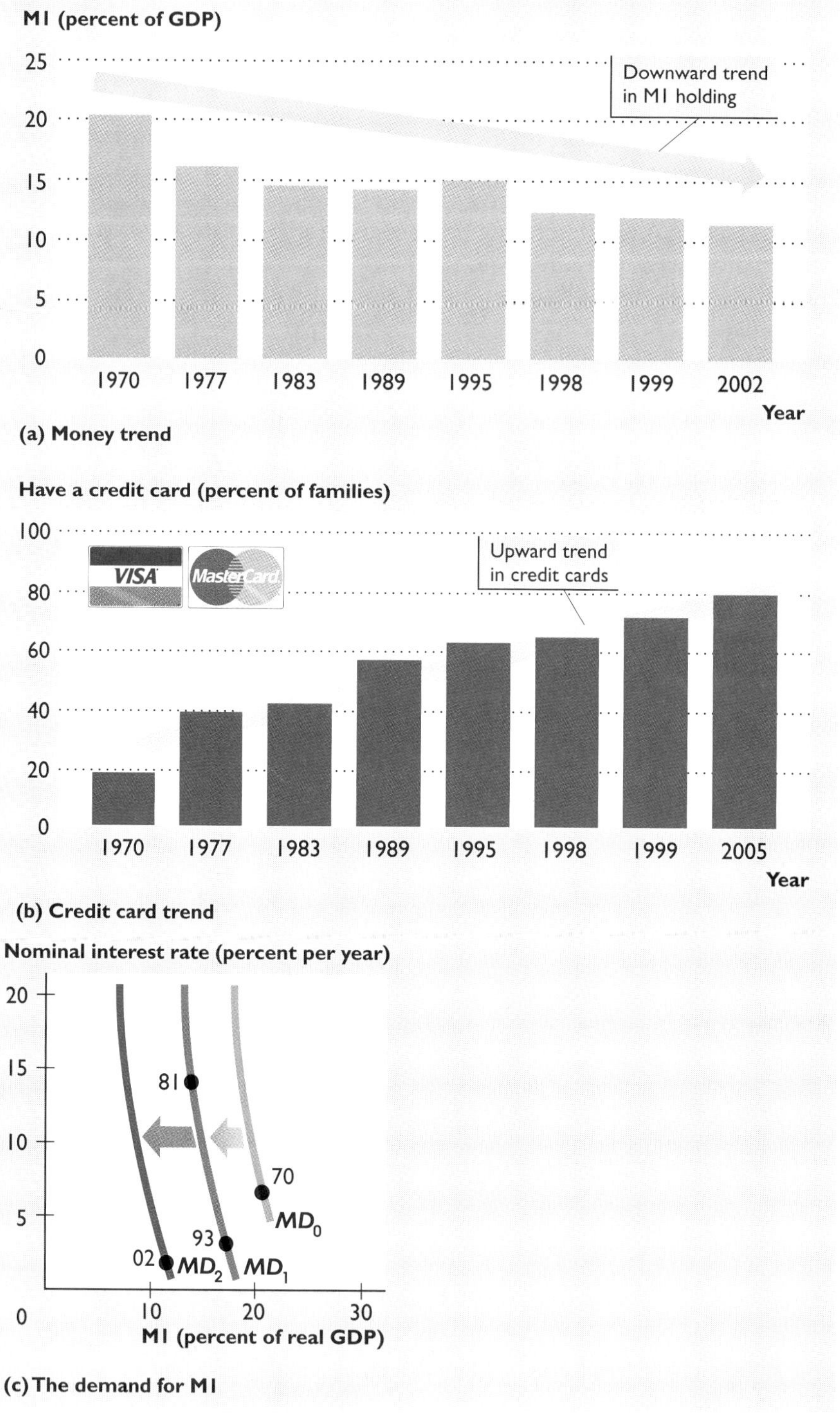

M1 (percent of GDP)
25
20
15
10
5
0
Downward trend in M1 holding
1970 1977 1983 1989 1995 1998 1999 2002
Year

(a) Money trend

Have a credit card (percent of families)
100
80
60
40
20
0
VISA
MasterCard
Upward trend in credit cards
1970 1977 1983 1989 1995 1998 1999 2005
Year

(b) Credit card trend

Nominal interest rate (percent per year)
20
15
10
5
0
81
70
93
02
MD_0
MD_1
MD_2
10 20 30
M1 (percent of real GDP)

(c) The demand for M1

SOURCE: The Federal Reserve.

The Interest Rate and Bond Price Move in Opposite Directions When the government issues a bond, it specifies the dollar amount of interest that it will pay each year on the bond. Suppose that the government issues a bond that pays $100 of interest a year. The interest *rate* that you receive on this bond depends on the price that you pay for it. If the price is $1,000, the interest rate is 10 percent a year—$100 is 10 percent of $1,000.

If the price of the bond *falls* to \$500, the interest rate *rises* to 20 percent a year. The reason is that you still receive an interest payment of \$100, but this amount is 20 percent of the \$500 price of the bond. If the price of the bond *rises* to \$2,000, the interest rate *falls* to 5 percent a year. Again, you still receive an interest payment of \$100, but this amount is 5 percent of the \$2,000 price of the bond.

Interest Rate Adjustment If the interest rate is above its equilibrium level, people would like to hold less money than they are actually holding. So they try to get rid of money by buying other financial assets such as bonds. The demand for financial assets increases, the prices of these assets rise, and the interest rate falls. The interest rate keeps falling until the quantity of money that people want to hold increases to equal the quantity of money supplied.

Conversely, when the interest rate is below its equilibrium level, people are holding less money than they would like to hold. So they try to get more money by selling other financial assets. The demand for financial assets decreases, the prices of these assets fall, and the interest rate rises. The interest rate keeps rising until the quantity of money that people want to hold decreases to equal the quantity of money supplied.

Changing the Interest Rate

To change the interest rate, the Fed changes the quantity of money. Figure 13.4 illustrates two changes. The demand for money curve is *MD*. If the Fed increases the quantity of money to \$1.02 trillion, the supply of money curve shifts rightward from MS_0 to MS_1 and the interest rate falls to 4 percent a year. If the Fed decreases the quantity of money to \$0.98 trillion, the supply of money curve shifts leftward from MS_0 to MS_2 and the interest rate rises to 6 percent a year.

FIGURE 13.4
Interest Rate Changes

Practice Online

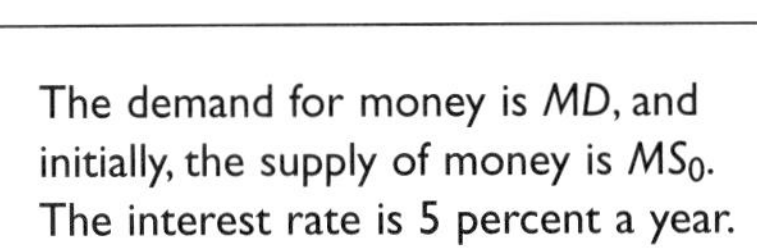

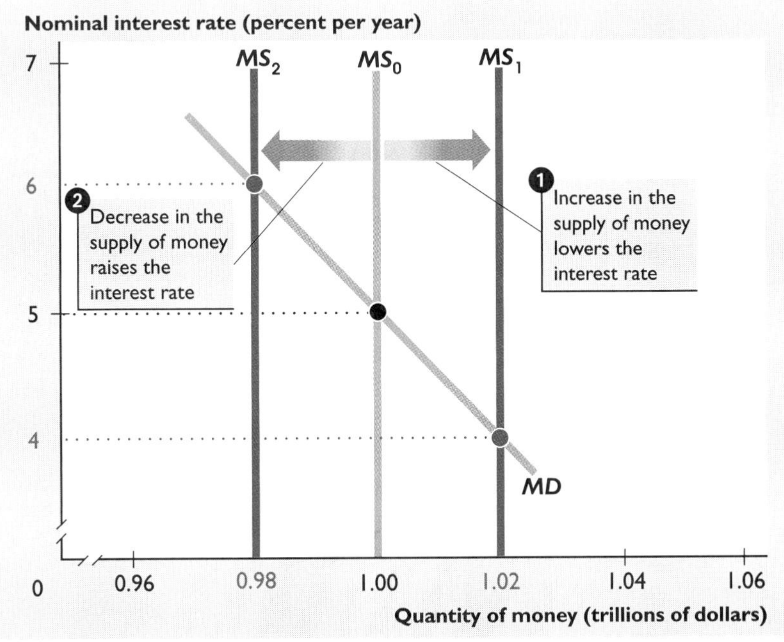

The demand for money is *MD*, and initially, the supply of money is MS_0. The interest rate is 5 percent a year.

1. The Fed increases the quantity of money and the supply of money curve shifts to MS_1. The interest rate falls to 4 percent a year.

2. The Fed decreases the quantity of money and the supply of money curve shifts to MS_2. The interest rate rises to 6 percent a year.

CHECKPOINT 13.1

Study Guide pp. 184–187

Practice Online 13.1

1 **Explain what determines the demand for money and how the demand for money and the supply of money determine the *nominal* interest rate.**

Practice Problems 13.1

1. Figure 1 shows the demand for money curve.
   a. If the quantity of money is $4 trillion, what is the nominal interest rate?
   b. If real GDP increases, how will the interest rate change? Explain the process that brings about the change in the interest rate.
   c. In part **a**, the Fed decreases the quantity of money to $3.9 trillion. Will bond prices rise or fall? Why? What happens to the nominal interest rate?
2. Suppose that the banks increase the fee they charge for credit cards, introduce a user fee on every credit card purchase, and increase the interest rate on outstanding credit card balances.
   a. How would the demand for money change?
   b. How would the nominal interest rate change?

FIGURE 1

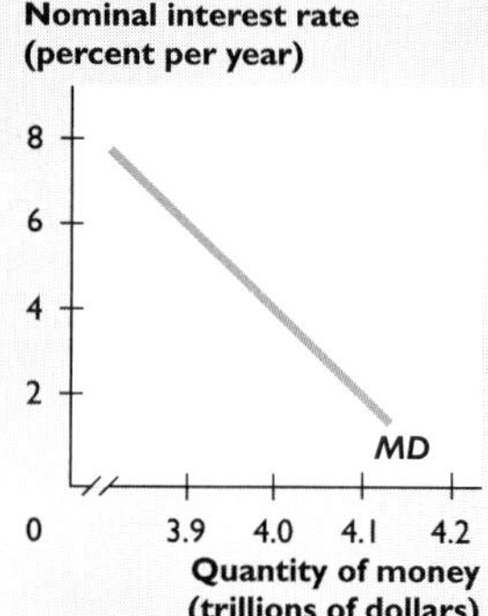
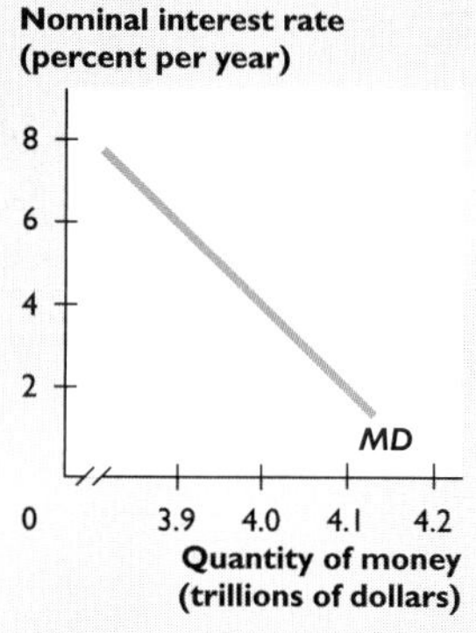

Exercises 13.1

1. Figure 1 shows the demand for money curve.
   a. If the quantity of money supplied is $3.9 trillion, what is the nominal interest rate?
   b. If real GDP decreases, how will the interest rate change? Explain what happens in the market for bonds as the market returns to equilibrium.
   c. In part **a**, the Fed increases the quantity of money to $4.0 trillion. What is the change in the nominal interest rate? What happens to the price of bonds?
2. Suppose that the banks launch an aggressive marketing campaign to get everyone to use credit cards for every conceivable transaction. They offer prizes to new cardholders and slash the interest rate on outstanding credit card balances.
   a. How would the demand for money change?
   b. How would the nominal interest rate change?

FIGURE 2

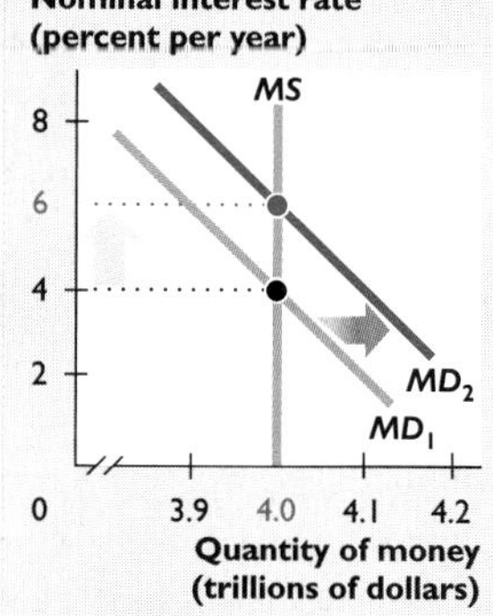

Solutions to Practice Problems 13.1

1a. The interest rate is 4 percent a year, at the intersection of MD_1 and *MS* (Figure 2).

1b. The demand for money increases and the demand for money curve shifts from MD_1 to MD_2. At an interest rate of 4 percent a year, people want to hold more money so they sell bonds. The price of a bond falls and the interest rate rises (Figure 2).

1c. At an interest rate at 4 percent a year, people would like to hold $4 trillion. With only $3.9 trillion of money available, they sell bonds. The price of a bond falls, and the interest rate rises. The new equilibrium nominal interest rate is 6 percent a year (Figure 3).

FIGURE 3

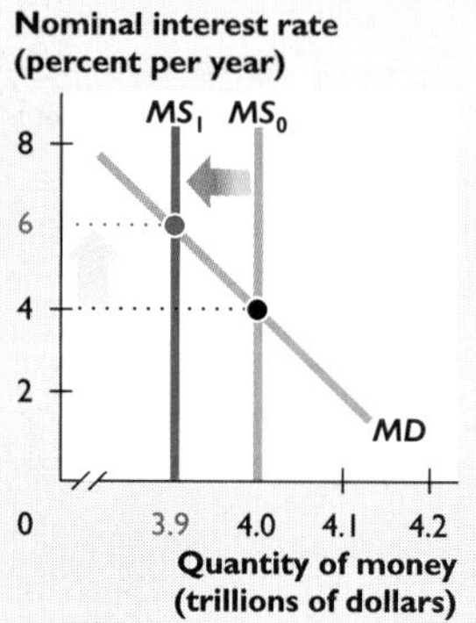

2a. The demand for money would increase as people use their credit cards less and use money for more transactions.

2b. With an increase in the demand for money, the nominal interest rate would rise.

13.2 MONEY, THE PRICE LEVEL, AND INFLATION

Each day, the price level and real GDP are at levels that have resulted from previous decisions. When the Fed conducts an open market operation to change the quantity of money, the nominal interest rate is the only variable that is free to adjust to make the quantity of money demanded equal the quantity of money supplied. You've seen that if the Fed decreases the quantity of money, the interest rate rises, and if the Fed increases the quantity of money, the interest rate falls.

These changes in the nominal interest rate also change the real interest rate. The reason is that the inflation rate is slow to adjust. It does not change every time the Fed changes the quantity of money.

Changes in the real interest rate influence spending plans. If the real interest rate falls, firms borrow and invest more and households borrow and spend more on consumption goods, especially on big-ticket items such as homes and automobiles. Similarly, if the real interest rate rises, firms borrow and invest less and households borrow and spend less on consumption goods.

These changes in spending change production and prices. The details of the adjustment process are complex, and we explore them in the next two chapters. But the place where the adjustment process comes to rest is easier to describe. We're now going to explain the long-run outcome of a change in the quantity of money and a change in the growth rate of money.

The Money Market in the Long Run

The *long run* refers to the economy at full employment or when we smooth out the effects of the business cycle. Potential GDP, the current state of financial technology, the price level, and the nominal interest rate determine the quantity of money demanded at full employment. The actions of the Fed and the banking system determine the quantity of money supplied. In the short run, the nominal interest rate adjusts to bring equilibrium in the market for money, but in the long run, the price level does the adjusting. To see why, let's see what determines the other influences on the quantity of money demanded.

Potential GDP and Financial Technology

Potential GDP and the state of financial technology, two influences on the quantity of money demanded, are determined by real factors and are independent of the price level. You studied the forces that determine potential GDP in Chapter 8. It is the real GDP produced by the full-employment quantity of labor. This quantity is determined by the equilibrium real wage rate at which the quantity of labor demanded equals the quantity of labor supplied. Potential GDP is independent of the price level.

Financial technology is determined by the state of knowledge and the quantity of capital (computers, ATMs, and so on) that banks have installed. Like potential GDP, financial technology is independent of the price level.

The Nominal Interest Rate in the Long Run

In 2001, businesses in the United States could borrow at a nominal interest rate of around 7 percent a year. Businesses in Russia paid a nominal interest rate of 60 percent a year, and businesses in Turkey paid 80 percent a year. Although the U.S. nominal interest rate has never been as high as these two cases, U.S. businesses faced a nominal interest rate of 16 percent a year during the 1980s.

Nominal interest rates vary across countries and over time for many reasons, but the dominant one is differences in inflation rates. The equilibrium nominal interest rate equals the equilibrium real interest rate plus the inflation rate. That is, the nominal interest rate exceeds the real interest rate by the inflation rate.

You studied the global financial market, which determines investment, saving, and the equilibrium real interest rate in Chapter 9. The real interest rate, like potential GDP, is independent of the price level. It is also independent of the inflation rate in the long run.

But the nominal interest rate depends directly on the inflation rate. Borrowers are willing to pay a high nominal interest rate when there is inflation because the real value of loans decreases over time. And lenders insist on receiving a high nominal interest rate because the money with which they are repaid buys less than what the money they loaned would have bought.

An Example Suppose that when there is no inflation, investment equals saving at a real interest rate of 3 percent a year. Walt Disney Corporation is willing to pay an interest rate of 3 percent a year to get the funds it needs to pay for its new theme parks. Sue (along with millions of others) is willing to save and lend Disney the amount it needs for its theme parks at a real interest rate of 3 percent a year.

Now imagine that the inflation rate is steady at 2 percent a year. All dollar amounts, including theme park profits and car prices, are rising by 2 percent a year. If Disney was willing to pay 3 percent a year in interest when there was no inflation, it is now willing to pay 5 percent a year. Its profits are rising by 2 percent a year, so it is really paying only 3 percent a year. Similarly, if Sue was willing to lend at 3 percent a year when there was no inflation, she is now willing to lend only if the interest rate is 5 percent a year. The price of the car that Sue is planning to buy is rising by 2 percent a year, so she is really getting an interest rate of only 3 percent a year.

Because borrowers are willing to pay the higher rate and lenders are willing to lend only if they receive the higher rate when inflation is present, the nominal interest rate increases by an amount equal to the inflation rate.

We'll explain how the inflation rate is determined later in this chapter.

Money Market Equilibrium in the Long Run

You've seen how all of the influences on the quantity of money demanded except the price level are determined. Money market equilibrium determines the price level. Figure 13.5 illustrates how.

Part (a) emphasizes the idea that the demand for money depends on the price level and, for a given quantity of money, the equilibrium nominal interest rate depends on the price level. It looks at three *possible* short-run situations. Real GDP equals potential GDP in each of them. First, if the price level were 100, the demand for money would be MD_0. In this case, the equilibrium nominal interest rate would be 5 percent a year. Second, if the price level were 102, the demand for money would be MD_1 and the equilibrium nominal interest rate would be 6 percent a year. Finally, if the price level were 98, the demand for money would be MD_2 and the equilibrium nominal interest rate would be 4 percent a year.

Which of these three *possible* short-run situations describes the long run? Part (b) provides the answer. Saving and investment decisions determine the long-run equilibrium real interest rate, which we'll assume to be 3 percent a year. The nominal interest rate is the real interest rate plus the inflation rate. We'll assume that

FIGURE 13.5
Long-Run Equilibrium

Practice Online

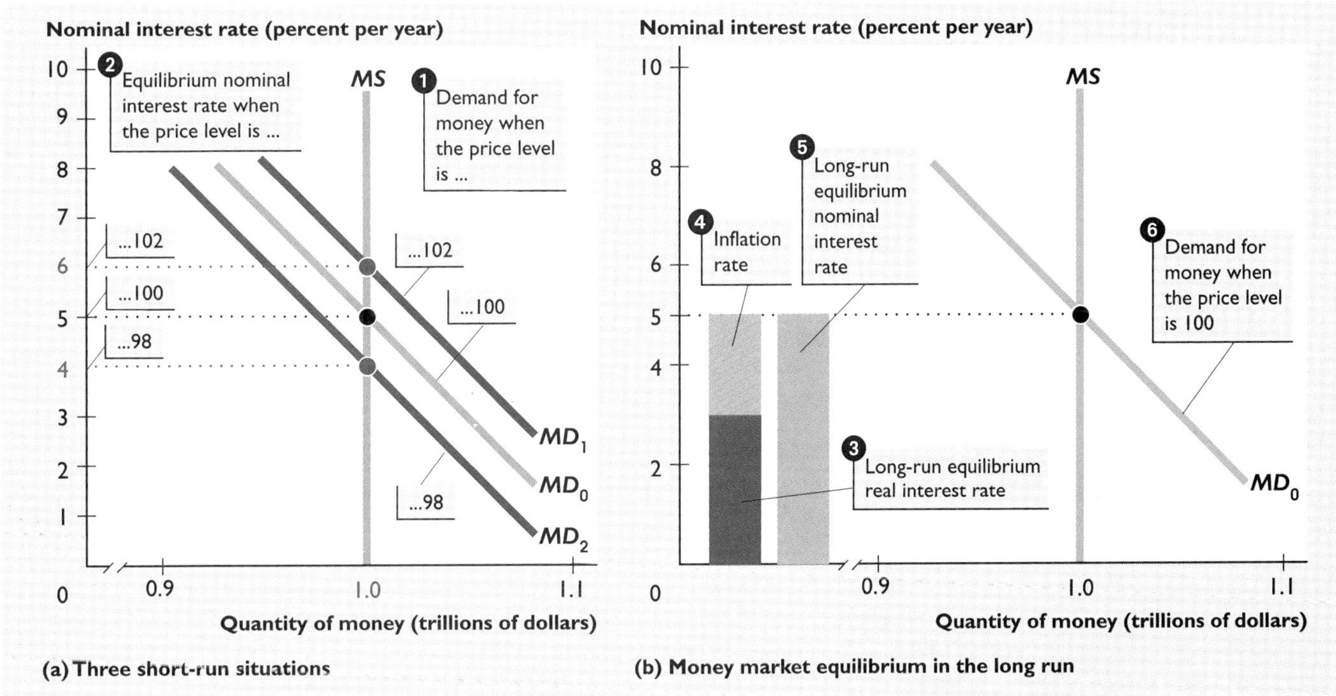

❶ The demand for money depends on the price level, so ❷ the equilibrium nominal interest rate also depends on the price level.

❸ The long-run equilibrium real interest rate (determined in the global financial market) plus ❹ the inflation rate determines the ❺ long-run equilibrium nominal interest rate.

❻ The price level adjusts to 100 to achieve money market equilibrium at the long-run equilibrium interest rate.

the inflation rate is 2 percent a year. So the long-run equilibrium nominal interest rate is 5 percent a year. Only one of the *possible* equilibrium situations shown in part (a) is consistent with the long-run equilibrium nominal interest rate. It is the situation in which the price level is 100, the demand for money is MD_0, and the nominal interest rate is 5 percent a year.

You will see how this long-run equilibrium comes about by considering what happens if the Fed changes the quantity of money.

A Change in the Quantity of Money

Suppose that the quantity of money is initially \$1 trillion and the Fed then increases it by 2 percent to \$1.02 trillion. In the short run, the greater quantity of money lowers the nominal interest rate. With a lower interest rate, aggregate demand increases and the price level rises. Eventually, a new long-run equilibrium is reached at which the price level has increased in proportion to the increase in the quantity of money.

Because the quantity of money increased by 2 percent from \$1 trillion to \$1.02 trillion, the price level rises by 2 percent from 100 to 102.

Figure 13.6 illustrates these events. Initially, the supply of money curve is MS_0, the demand for money curve is MD_0, the nominal interest rate is at its long-run equilibrium level of 5 percent a year, and the price level that lies behind MD_0 is 100.

The quantity of money then increases and the supply of money curve shifts rightward to MS_1. Initially, the price level remains at 100, so the demand for money curve remains at MD_0. The nominal interest rate falls below its long-run equilibrium level to 4 percent a year. The lower interest rate brings increased spending, which eventually raises the price level to 102. The demand for money increases as the price level rises, and the interest rate rises. Eventually, the economy is back at its long-run equilibrium interest rate but at a higher price level.

You've just seen a key proposition about money and the price level:

In the long run and other things remaining the same, a given percentage change in the quantity of money brings an equal percentage change in the price level.

The Price Level in a Baby-Sitting Club

It is hard to visualize a long-run equilibrium and even harder to visualize and compare two long-run equilibrium situations. So an example of a simpler situation might help.

In an isolated neighborhood, there are no teenagers, but lots of young children and parents can't find any babysitters. So they form a club and sit for each other. The deal is that each time a parent sits for someone else, he or she receives a token that can be used to buy one sit from another member of the club. The organizer

FIGURE 13.6

A Change in the Price Level

Practice Online

1. The quantity of money increases by 2 percent from $1 trillion to $1.02 trillion and the supply of money curve shifts from MS_0 to MS_1.
2. In the short run, the interest rate falls to 4 percent a year.
3. In the long run, the price level rises by 2 percent from 100 to 102, the demand for money curve shifts from MD_0 to MD_1, and the nominal interest rate returns to its long-run equilibrium level.

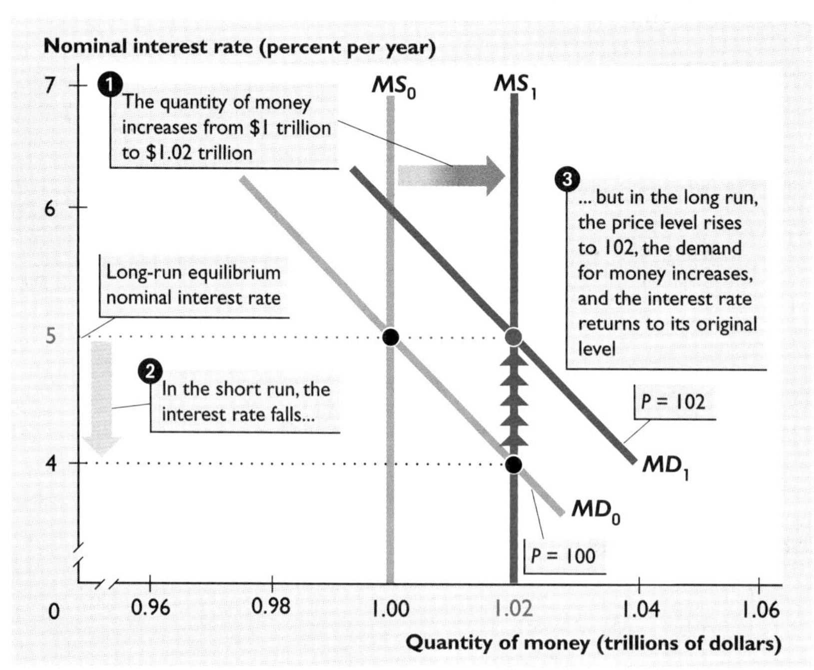

notices that the club is inactive. Every member has a few unspent tokens, but they spend them infrequently. To make the club more active, the organizer decides to issue every member one token for each token that is currently held, so the supply of tokens doubles.

With more tokens to spend, parents start to plan more evenings out. Suddenly, the phones are ringing as parents seek babysitters. Every member of the club wants a sitter. But there are no more sitters than before. After making a few calls and finding no sitters available, anxious parents who really do need a sitter start to offer a higher price: two tokens per session. That does the trick. At the higher price, the quantity of baby-sitting services demanded decreases and the quantity supplied increases. Equilibrium is restored. Nothing real has changed, but the quantity of tokens and the price level have doubled.

Think of the equilibrium quantity of baby-sitting services as potential GDP, the quantity of tokens as the quantity of money, and the price of a baby-sitting session as the price level. You can then see how a given percentage change in the quantity of money at full employment brings an equal percentage change in the price level.

The Quantity Theory of Money

The proposition that when real GDP equals potential GDP, an increase in the quantity of money brings an equal percentage increase in the price level is called the **quantity theory of money**. We've derived this proposition by looking at equilibrium in the money market in the long run. Another way of seeing the relationship between the quantity of money and the price level uses the concepts of *the velocity of circulation* and *the equation of exchange*. We're now going to explore this alternative approach. We're then going to see how ongoing money growth brings inflation and see what determines the inflation rate in the long run.

Quantity theory of money
The proposition that when real GDP equals potential GDP, an increase in the quantity of money brings an equal percentage increase in the price level.

The Velocity of Circulation and Equation of Exchange

The **velocity of circulation** is the number of times in a year that the average dollar of money gets used to buy final goods and services. The value of final goods and services is nominal GDP, which is real GDP, Y, multiplied by the price level, P. If we call the quantity of money M, then the velocity of circulation is determined by the equation:

Velocity of circulation
The number of times in a year that the average dollar of money gets used to buy final goods and services.

$$V = (P \times Y) \div M.$$

In this equation, P is the GDP deflator divided by 100. For example, if the GDP deflator is 125, the price level is 1.25. If the price level is 1.25, real GDP, Y, is \$8 trillion, and the quantity of money, M, is \$2 trillion, then the velocity of circulation is calculated as

$$V = (1.25 \times \$8 \text{ trillion}) \div \$2 \text{ trillion, or}$$

$$V = 5.$$

That is, with \$2 trillion of money, the average dollar gets used 5 times so that \$2 trillion × 5 = \$10 trillion of goods and services are bought.

The **equation of exchange** states that the quantity of money, M, multiplied by the velocity of circulation, V, equals the price level P, multiplied by real GDP, Y. That is,

Equation of exchange
An equation that states that the quantity of money multiplied by the velocity of circulation equals the price level multiplied by real GDP.

$$M \times V = P \times Y.$$

The equation of exchange is *always* true because it is implied by the definition of the velocity of circulation. That is, if you multiply both sides of the equation on page 327 that defines the velocity of circulation by M, you get the equation of exchange.

Using the above numbers—a price level of 1.25, real GDP, Y, of \$8 trillion, the quantity of money, M, of \$2 trillion, and the velocity of circulation of 5—you can see that

$$M \times V = \$2 \text{ trillion} \times 5 = \$10 \text{ trillion},$$

and

$$P \times Y = 1.25 \times \$8 \text{ trillion} = \$10 \text{ trillion}.$$

So,

$$M \times V = P \times Y = \$10 \text{ trillion}.$$

The Quantity Theory Prediction

We can rearrange the equation of exchange to isolate the price level on the left side. To do so, divide both sides of the equation of exchange by real GDP, Y, to obtain

$$P = M \times V \div Y.$$

On the left side is the price level. And on the right side are all the things that influence the price level. But this equation is still just an implication of the definition of the velocity of circulation. To turn the equation into a theory of what determines the price level, we use two other facts: (1) At full employment, real GDP equals potential GDP, which is determined only by real factors and not by the quantity of money; and (2) the velocity of circulation is relatively stable and does not change when the quantity of money changes.

So if M increases with V and Y constant, P must increase, and by the same percentage that M increased.

We can use the above numbers to illustrate this prediction. Real GDP, Y, is \$8 trillion, the quantity of money, M, is \$2 trillion, and the velocity of circulation, V, is 5. Put these values into the equation:

$$P = M \times V \div Y$$

to obtain

$$P = \$2 \text{ trillion} \times 5 \div \$8 \text{ trillion} = 1.25.$$

Now increase the quantity of money from \$2 trillion to \$2.4 trillion. The percentage increase in the quantity of money is

$$(\$2.4 \text{ trillion} - \$2 \text{ trillion}) \times 100 \div \$2 \text{ trillion} = 20 \text{ percent}.$$

Now find the new price level. It is

$$P = \$2.4 \text{ trillion} \times 5 \div \$8 \text{ trillion} = 1.50.$$

The price level rises from 1.25 to 1.50. The percentage increase in the price level is

$$(1.50 - 1.25) \times 100 \div 1.25 = 20 \text{ percent}.$$

The price level and the quantity of money increase by the same 20 percent.

Inflation and the Quantity Theory of Money

The equation of exchange tells us about the price *level,* the quantity of money, the level of real GDP and the level of the velocity of circulation. We can turn the equation into one that tells us about rates of change or growth rates. We do this because the inflation rate is the rate of change in the price level, and we want to know what determines the inflation rate.

In rates of change or growth rates,

$$\text{Money growth} + \text{Velocity growth} = \text{Inflation} + \text{Real GDP growth.}$$

For example, in Figure 13.7 in period 1, the quantity of money is growing at a rate of 4 percent a year and velocity is growing at a rate of 1 percent a year. So $M \times V$ is growing at a rate of 5 percent a year. But $M \times V = P \times Y$, so $P \times Y$ is growing at 5 percent a year. Real GDP is growing at 3 percent a year, so the inflation rate is 2 percent a year. That is,

$$\text{4 percent a year} + \text{1 percent a year} = \text{Inflation rate} + \text{3 percent a year,}$$

so,

$$\text{Inflation rate} = \text{4 percent a year} + \text{1 percent a year} - \text{3 percent a year,}$$

or,

$$\text{Inflation rate} = \text{2 percent a year.}$$

FIGURE 13.7
Money Growth and Inflation

Practice Online

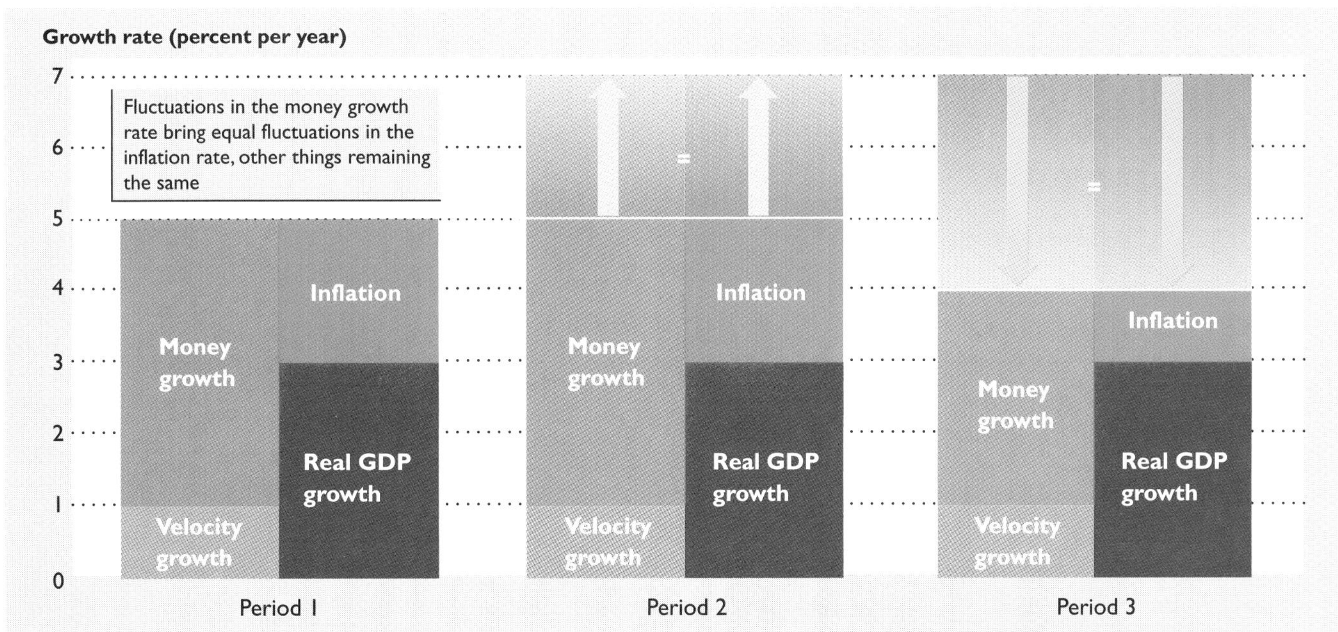

The velocity of circulation grows at 1 percent a year, and real GDP grows at 3 percent a year. In period 1, the quantity of money grows at 4 percent a year and the inflation rate is 2 percent a year. In period 2, money growth increases to 6 percent a year and the inflation rate rises to 4 percent a year. In period 3, money growth slows to 3 percent a year and the inflation rate slows to 1 percent a year.

Changes in the Inflation Rate

Recall two facts that turn the equation of exchange into a theory of what determines the price level: (1) At full employment, real GDP equals potential GDP, which is determined only by real factors and not by the quantity of money; and (2) the velocity of circulation is relatively stable and does not change when the quantity of money changes. In terms of growth rates, potential GDP growth and velocity growth are not influenced by the growth rate of the quantity of money. If the growth rate of the quantity of money changes, velocity growth and real GDP growth remain the same, the inflation rate changes by the same amount as the change in the money growth rate.

Figure 13.7 illustrates both an increase and a decrease in money growth and inflation. In each period, real GDP growth and velocity growth remain constant. In period 2, the money growth rate increases from 4 percent to 6 percent a year and the inflation rate increases from 2 percent to 4 percent a year. In period 3, the money growth rate decreases from 6 percent to 3 percent a year and the inflation rate decreases from 4 percent to 1 percent a year.

In reality, the inflation rate influences velocity and real GDP, so the link between money growth and inflation is not as precise as that shown in Figure 13.7. Velocity increases when the inflation rate speeds up. And faster inflation reduces potential GDP and slows real GDP growth. But these effects are small and are dominated by the main direct effect of money growth on the inflation rate.

Eye on the U.S. Economy

The Quantity Theory of Money in Action

During the 1960s, M2 velocity was constant, real GDP grew at 4.4 percent a year, the quantity of M2 grew at 6.7 percent a year, and the inflation rate was 2.3 percent a year.

During the 1970s, M2 growth climbed, real GDP growth shrank, and the inflation rate increased to 6.6 percent a year. During the 1980s and 1990s, M2 growth slowed and so did inflation. But during the 1990s, an increase in the velocity of circulation of M2 kept the inflation rate higher than it would otherwise have been by almost 2 percent a year.

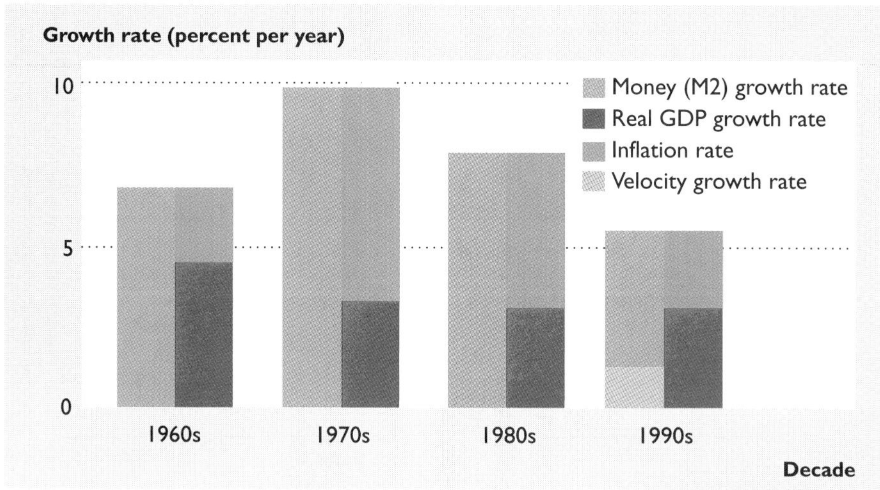

SOURCE: Federal Reserve.

Hyperinflation

When the inflation rate exceeds 50 percent *a month*, the inflation is called **hyperinflation**. Hyperinflation occurs when a government's expenditures exceed the sum of what it can collect in tax revenue and borrow. In such a situation, the government prints money and the quantity of money increases at an extraordinarily rapid rate. This phenomenon is rare but not unknown (see Eye on the Past below). The highest inflation rates in the world today, in the African nations of Angola and Zimbabwe, exceed 100 percent a year but are not considered hyperinflation.

Hyperinflation
Inflation at a rate that exceeds 50 percent *a month*.

Eye on the Past

Hyperinflation in Germany in the 1920s

An international treaty signed in 1919 required Germany to pay large amounts as compensation for war damage to other countries in Europe. To meet its obligations, Germany started to print money. The German money supply increased by 24 percent in 1921, by 220 percent in 1922, and by 43 *billion* percent in 1923!

Not surprisingly, the price level increased rapidly. The figure shows you how rapidly. In November 1923, when the hyperinflation reached its peak, the price level was more than doubling every day. Wages were paid twice a day, and people spent their morning's wages at lunchtime to avoid the loss in the value of money that the afternoon would bring.

In 1923, bank notes were more valuable as fire kindling than as money, and the sight of people burning Reichmarks (the name of Germany's money at that time) was a common one.

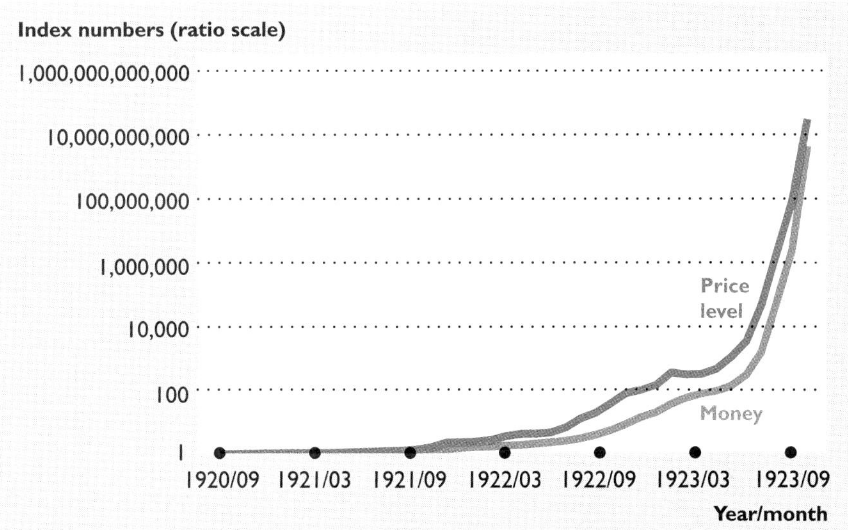

SOURCE: Phillip Cagan, "The Monetary Dynamics of Hyperinflation," in Milton Friedman (editor), *Studies in the Quantity Theory of Money*, University of Chicago Press, 1956.

CHECKPOINT 13.2

Study Guide pp. 187–189

Practice Online 13.2

2 Explain how in the long run, the quantity of money determines the price level and money growth brings inflation.

Practice Problems 13.2

1. In 1999, the Canadian economy was at full employment. Real GDP was $886 billion, the nominal interest rate was around 6 percent per year, the inflation rate was 2 percent a year, the price level was 110, and the velocity of circulation was constant at 10.
   a. Calculate the real interest rate.
   b. If the real interest rate remains unchanged when the inflation rate increases to 4 percent a year, explain how the nominal interest rate changes.
   c. What was the quantity of money in Canada?
2. If the quantity of money grows at a rate of 10 percent a year and potential GDP grows at 3 percent a year, what is the inflation rate in the long run?

Exercises 13.2

1. In 2002, the United Kingdom was at full employment. Nominal GDP was £850 billion, the real interest rate was 5 percent per year, the inflation rate was 6 percent a year, and the price level was 120.
   a. Calculate the nominal interest rate.
   b. If the real interest rate remains unchanged when the inflation rate in the long run decreases to 3 percent a year, explain how the nominal interest rate changes.
2. In 2003, the United Kingdom was at full employment. Nominal GDP was £900 billion, the nominal interest rate was 8 percent per year, the price level was 130, and the velocity of circulation was constant at 2. What was the quantity of money in the United Kingdom?
3. In exercise 2, if the velocity of circulation remains at 2, money grows at 8 percent a year, and real GDP grows at 5 percent a year in the long run, what is the inflation rate in the long run?

Solutions to Practice Problems 13.2

1a. The real interest rate equals the nominal interest rate minus the inflation rate. That is, the real interest rate equals 6 percent a year minus 2 percent a year, which equals 4 percent a year.

1b. The nominal interest rate rises from 6 percent a year to 8 percent a year.

1c. Velocity of circulation (V) = Nominal GDP ($P \times Y$) ÷ Quantity of money (M). Rewrite this equation as: Quantity of money (M) = Nominal GDP ($P \times Y$) ÷ Velocity of circulation (V). Nominal GDP is $886 billion × 110, or $975 billion. Quantity of money is $975 billion ÷ 10, which equals $97.5 billion.

2. With velocity constant, velocity growth is zero. So the inflation rate in the long run equals the money growth rate minus the real GDP growth rate, which is 10 percent a year minus 3 percent a year, or 7 percent a year.

13.3 THE COST OF INFLATION

Inflation decreases potential GDP, slows economic growth, and consumes leisure time. These outcomes occur for four reasons that we classify as the four costs of inflation. They are

- Tax costs
- Shoe-leather costs
- Confusion costs
- Uncertainty costs

Tax Costs

We've seen that inflation occurs when the quantity of money grows more rapidly than real GDP. But why would we ever want to make this happen? Why don't we keep the quantity of money growing at the same pace as real GDP grows? One part of the answer is that the government gets revenue from inflation.

Inflation Is a Tax

Inflation is a tax on holding money. To see how the inflation tax gets paid, suppose that the Coca-Cola Company keeps $100,000 in money on the average. With inflation at 10 percent a year, that money will buy only $90,000 of goods and services after one year. So Coca-Cola loses $10,000 a year—it pays $10,000 a year in inflation tax.

You've seen how Coca-Cola *pays* the inflation tax. But how does the government get *revenue* from it? The answer is by selling government securities that end up being held by the Federal Reserve. When the government issues securities, it must pay interest on them. But paying interest to the Fed costs the government nothing because it owns the Fed and gets the Fed's profits. So when the government issues securities that end up at the Fed, the government gets the value of those securities to spend. But when the Fed buys government securities, the quantity of money grows and money growth brings inflation.

So inflation is a tax. If this were the end of the story, the inflation tax would not be a problem. It would be just one more way for the government to collect revenue—an alternative to the income tax or the sales tax. Inflation would transfer resources from households and businesses to the government, but it would not be a cost to society. Some would pay and others would benefit, and the two actions would cancel each other out.

Inflation Tax, Saving, and Investment

The inflation tax is bigger than the tax on money holding, and it interacts with the income tax to lower saving and investment. The core of the problem is that inflation increases the nominal interest rate, and because income taxes are paid on nominal interest income, the true income tax rate rises with inflation. Let's consider an example.

Suppose that the real interest rate is 4 percent a year and the income tax rate is 50 percent. With no inflation, the nominal interest rate is also 4 percent a year and 50 percent of this rate is taxed. The real after-tax interest rate is 2 percent a year (50 percent of 4 percent). Now suppose the inflation rate is 4 percent a year, so the nominal interest rate is 8 percent a year. The after-tax nominal rate is 4 percent a year (50 percent of 8 percent). Now subtract the 4 percent inflation rate from this amount, and you see that the after-tax real interest rate is zero! The true income tax rate is 100 percent.

The higher the inflation rate, the higher is the true income tax rate on income from capital. And the higher the tax rate, the higher is the interest rate paid by borrowers and the lower is the after-tax interest rate received by lenders.

With a low after-tax real interest rate, the incentive to save is weakened and the supply of saving decreases. With a high cost of borrowing, the amount of investment decreases. And with a fall in saving and investment, the pace of capital accumulation slows and so does the long-term growth rate of real GDP.

Shoe-Leather Costs

The "shoe-leather costs" of inflation are costs that arise from an increase in the velocity of circulation of money and an increase in the amount of running around that people do to try to avoid incurring losses from the falling value of money.

When money loses value at a rapid anticipated rate, it does not function well as a store of value and people try to avoid holding it. They spend their incomes as soon as they receive them, and firms pay out incomes—wages and dividends—as soon as they receive revenue from their sales. The velocity of circulation increases.

During the 1990s, when inflation in Brazil was around 80 percent a year, people would end a taxi ride at the ATM closest to their destination, get some cash, pay the driver, and finish their journey on foot. The driver would deposit the cash in his bank account before looking for the next customer.

During the 1920s when inflation in Germany exceeded 50 percent a month—hyperinflation—wages were paid and spent twice in a single day!

Imagine the inconvenience of spending most of your time figuring out how to keep your money holdings close to zero.

One way of keeping money holdings low is to find other means of payment such as tokens, commodities, or even barter. All of these are less efficient than money as a means of payment. For example, in Israel during the 1980s, when inflation reached 1,000 percent a year, the U.S. dollar started to replace the increasingly worthless shekel. Consequently, people had to keep track of the exchange rate between the shekel and the dollar hour by hour and had to engage in many additional and costly transactions in the foreign exchange market.

Confusion Costs

We make economic decisions by comparing marginal cost and marginal benefit. Marginal cost is a real cost—an opportunity forgone. Marginal benefit is a real benefit—a willingness to forgo an opportunity. Although costs and benefits are real, we use money as our unit of account and standard of value to calculate them. Money is our measuring rod of value. Borrowers and lenders, workers and employers, all make agreements in terms of money. Inflation makes the value of money change, so it changes the units on our measuring rod.

Does it matter that our units of value keep changing? Some economists think it matters a lot. Others think it matters only a little.

Economists who think it matters a lot point to the obvious benefits of stable units of measurement in other areas of life. For example, suppose that we had not invented an accurate time-keeping technology and clocks and watches gained 5 to 15 minutes a day. Imagine the hassle you would have arriving at class on time or catching the start of the ball game. For another example, suppose that a tailor used an elastic tape measure. You would end up with a jacket that was either too tight or too sloppy, depending on how tightly the tape was stretched.

For a third example, recall the crash of the Mars Climate Orbiter.

> "Mars Climate Orbiter . . . failed to achieve Mars orbit because of a navigation error. . . . Spacecraft operating data needed for navigation were provided . . . in English units rather than the specified metric units. This was the direct cause of the failure." (Mars Program Independent Assessment Team Summary Report, March 14, 2000)

If rocket scientists can't make correct calculations that use just two units of measurement, what chance do ordinary people and business decision makers have of making correct calculations that involve money when its value keeps changing?

These examples of confusion and error that can arise from units of measurement don't automatically mean that a changing value of money is a big problem. But they raise the possibility that it might be.

Uncertainty Costs

A high inflation rate brings increased uncertainty about the long-term inflation rate. Will inflation remain high for a long time or will price stability be restored? This increased uncertainty makes long-term planning difficult and gives people a shorter-term focus. Investment falls, and so the growth rate slows.

But this increased uncertainty also misallocates resources. Instead of concentrating on the activities at which they have a comparative advantage, people find it more profitable to search for ways of avoiding the losses that inflation inflicts. As a result, inventive talent that might otherwise work on productive innovations works on finding ways of profiting from the inflation instead.

Uncertainty about inflation makes the economy behave a bit like a casino in which some people gain and some lose and no one can predict where the gains and losses will fall. Gains and losses occur because of unpredictable changes in the value of money. In a period of rapid, unpredictable inflation, resources get diverted from productive activities to forecasting inflation. It becomes more profitable to forecast the inflation rate correctly than to invent a new product. Doctors, lawyers, accountants, farmers—just about everyone—can make themselves better off, not by specializing in the profession for which they have been trained but by spending more of their time dabbling as amateur economists and inflation forecasters and managing their investment portfolios.

From a social perspective, this diversion of talent resulting from inflation is like throwing scarce resources onto the garbage heap. This waste of resources is a cost of inflation.

How Big Is the Cost of Inflation?

The cost of inflation depends on its rate and its predictability. The higher the rate, the greater is the cost. And the more unpredictable the rate, the greater is the cost. Peter Howitt of Brown University, building on work by Robert Barro of Harvard University, has estimated that if inflation is lowered from 3 percent a year to zero, the growth rate of real GDP will rise by between 0.06 and 0.09 percentage points a year. These numbers might seem small. But they are growth rates. After 30 years, real GDP would be 2.3 percent higher and the accumulated value of all the additional future output would be worth 85 percent of current GDP, or $8.5 trillion!

In hyperinflation, the costs are much greater. Hyperinflation is rare, but there have been some spectacular examples of it. Several European countries experienced hyperinflation during the 1920s after World War I and again during the 1940s after World War II. But hyperinflation is more than just a historical curiosity. It occurs in today's world. In 1994, the African nation of Zaire had a hyperinflation that peaked at a monthly inflation rate of 76 percent. Also in 1994, Brazil almost reached the hyperinflation stratosphere with a monthly inflation rate of 40 percent. A cup of coffee that cost 15 cruzeiros in 1980 cost 22 billion cruzeiros in 1994. And Russia has had a near hyperinflation experience in recent years.

CHECKPOINT 13.3

Study Guide pp. 189–192

Practice Online 13.3

3 Identify the costs of inflation and the benefits of a stable value of money.

Practice Problem 13.3

Suppose that you have $1,000 in your savings account and the bank pays an interest rate of 5 percent a year. The inflation rate is 3 percent a year. The government taxes the interest that you earn on your deposit at 20 percent.

a. Calculate the nominal after-tax interest rate that you earn.
b. Calculate the real after-tax interest rate that you earn.

Exercise 13.3

Sally has a credit card balance of $4,000. The credit card charges a nominal interest rate of 18 percent a year on unpaid balances. The inflation rate is 3 percent a year.

a. Calculate the real interest rate that Sally pays the credit card company.
b. If the inflation rate falls to 2 percent a year and the credit card company keeps the nominal interest rate at 18 percent a year, calculate the real interest rate that Sally pays.

Solution to Practice Problem 13.3

a. You earn $50 of interest and the government takes $10 of the interest in tax, so the interest income you earn after tax is $40. The nominal after-tax interest rate is 4 percent a year.
b. The real after-tax interest rate equals the nominal after-tax interest rate minus the inflation rate, which is 1 percent a year.

CHAPTER CHECKPOINT

Key Points

1 Explain what determines the demand for money and how the demand for money and the supply of money determine the *nominal* interest rate.

- The demand for money is the relationship between the quantity of money demanded and the nominal interest rate, other things remaining the same—the higher the nominal interest rate, other things remaining the same, the smaller is the quantity of money demanded.
- Increases in real GDP increase the demand for money. Some advances in financial technology increase the demand for money, and some advances decrease it.
- Each day, the price level, real GDP, and financial technology are given and money market equilibrium determines the nominal interest rate.
- To lower the interest rate, the Fed increases the supply of money. To raise the interest rate, the Fed decreases the supply of money.

2 Explain how in the long run, the quantity of money determines the price level and money growth brings inflation.

- In the long run, real GDP equals potential GDP and the real interest rate is the level that makes the quantity of investment demanded equal the quantity of saving supplied in the global financial market.
- The nominal interest rate in the long run equals the equilibrium real interest rate plus the inflation rate.
- Money market equilibrium in the long run determines the price level.
- An increase in the quantity of money, other things remaining the same, increases the price level by the same percentage.
- The inflation rate in the long run equals the growth rate of the quantity of money minus the growth rate of potential GDP.
- The equation of exchange and the velocity of circulation provide an alternative way of viewing the relationship between the quantity of money and the price level (and money growth and inflation).

3 Identify the costs of inflation and the benefits of a stable value of money.

- Inflation has four costs: tax costs, shoe-leather costs, confusion costs, and uncertainty costs.
- The higher the inflation rate, the greater are these four costs.

Key Terms

Demand for money, 316
Equation of exchange, 327
Hyperinflation, 331
Quantity of money demanded, 315
Quantity theory of money, 327
Supply of money, 319
Velocity of circulation, 327

Exercises

1. Review the factors that influence the quantity of money that people plan to hold and
   a. Draw a graph to illustrate the demand for money curve.
   b. Show the new demand for money curve that results from an increase in real GDP.
   c. Illustrate on your graph the effects of a change in the interest rate.
   d. Show the effects of an increase in the number of families that have a credit card.
   e. Explain how the spread of ATMs has influenced the demand for money.
2. The Fed decreases the quantity of money. Explain the effects of this action in the short run and the long run on
   a. The quantity of money demanded.
   b. The nominal interest rate.
   c. The real interest rate.
   d. Real GDP.
   e. The price level.
3. The Fed conducts an open market purchase of securities. [Hint: Check back with Chapter 12 if you need a reminder about the effects of an open market operation.] Explain the effects of this action in the short run and the long run on
   a. The quantity of money.
   b. The quantity of money demanded.
   c. The nominal interest rate.
   d. The real interest rate.
   e. Real GDP.
   f. The price level.
4. In 2000, the United States was at full employment. The quantity of money was growing at 8.3 percent a year, the nominal interest rate was 9.5 percent a year, real GDP grew at 5 percent a year, and the inflation rate was 3.1 percent a year.
   a. Calculate the real interest rate.
   b. Use the information given along with the quantity theory of money to see whether the velocity of circulation was constant. If it was not constant, how did it change? And if it changed, why might it have changed?
5. Suppose the government passes a new law that sets a limit on the interest rate that credit card companies can charge on overdue balances. As a result, the nominal interest rate charged by credit card companies falls from 15 percent a year to 7 percent a year. If the average income tax rate is 30 percent, explain how the real after-tax interest rate on overdue credit card balances changes.
6. Draw a graph of the money market to illustrate equilibrium in both the short run and the long run.
   a. Explain what happens to the real interest rate and the nominal interest rate in the short run.
   b. Explain what happens to the real interest rate and the nominal interest rate in the long run.
   c. Explain why the short-run effects are different from the long-run effects.

7. What is the quantity theory of money?

8. Define the velocity of circulation and explain how is it measured.

9. If the quantity of money is \$3 trillion, real GDP is \$10 trillion, the price level is 0.9, the real interest rate is 2 percent a year, and the nominal interest rate is 7 percent a year,
   a. What is the velocity of circulation?
   b. What is value of $M \times V$?
   c. What is the value of nominal GDP?

10. If the velocity of circulation is constant, real GDP is growing at 3 percent a year, the real interest rate is 2 percent a year, and the nominal interest rate is 7 percent a year,
    a. What is the inflation rate?
    b. What is the growth rate of money?
    c. What is the growth rate of nominal GDP?

11. If the velocity of circulation is growing at a rate of 1 percent a year, the real interest rate is 2 percent a year, the nominal interest rate is 7 percent a year, and the growth rate of real GDP is 3 percent a year,
    a. What is the inflation rate?
    b. What is the growth rate of money?
    c. What is the growth rate of nominal GDP?

12. List the costs of inflation and provide an example of each type of cost.

13. Explain what the costs of inflation were for Brazilians when inflation hit 40 percent a month in Brazil.

14. Explain why businesses paid workers twice a day during the hyperinflation in Germany after World War II and why workers spent their incomes as soon as they were paid.

Critical Thinking

15. With the spread of credit cards, debit cards, and e-cash, people will want to hold less and less money. Eventually, no one will want to hold any money and the Federal Reserve will have no role. Critically evaluate this view.

16. The Federal Reserve could easily eliminate inflation by making the quantity of money grow at a rate equal to the growth rate of real GDP minus the growth rate of the velocity of circulation. Do you think the Fed should pursue this objective? Explain why or why not.

17. The Federal Reserve could peg the interest rate by making the quantity of money adjust to match the quantity of money demanded at the chosen interest rate. Do you think the Fed should pursue this objective? Explain why or why not.

18. Do you think the Federal Reserve could simultaneously pursue a fixed interest rate and a money growth rate equal to the growth rate of real GDP minus the growth rate of the velocity of circulation? Explain why or why not.

Practice Online

Web Exercises

Use the links on your Foundations Web site to work the following exercises.

19. Visit the Web sites of the Federal Reserve and the Bureau of Economic Analysis and obtain the latest data on the quantity of M1 and M2, real GDP, and the price level.
    a. Calculate the inflation rate, the growth rate of the two money aggregates, and the growth rate of real GDP.
    b. Use the information you calculated in part **a** to determine whether the velocity of circulation was constant. If it was not constant, how did it change? If it changed, why might it have changed?
    c. Given the information that you obtained in part **a**, do you think the Fed is trying to slow inflation, speed up inflation, or neither? If neither, what do you think the Fed is trying to do?

20. Visit the European Central Bank Web site.
    a. Obtain data on money supply growth rates and inflation rates for the euro area.
    b. Is the money supply in the euro area growing faster or slower than in the United States?
    c. Would you expect inflation in the euro area to be higher, lower, or about the same as in the United States? Explain why.

21. Visit the International Monetary Fund's World Economic Outlook database Web site.
    a. Obtain data on money supply growth rates and inflation rates for Advanced Economies and the Developing Economies.
    b. Use a spreadsheet program (Excel or Lotus 1-2-3) to make a scatter diagram of the data placing money growth on the x-axis and inflation on the y-axis.
    c. Do these data support or contradict the quantity theory of money?

CHAPTER 14

AS-AD and the Business Cycle

CHAPTER CHECKLIST

When you have completed your study of this chapter, you will be able to

1. **Provide a technical definition of recession and describe the history of the U.S. business cycle.**
2. **Explain the influences on aggregate supply.**
3. **Explain the influences on aggregate demand.**
4. **Explain how fluctuations in aggregate demand and aggregate supply create the business cycle.**

From 1991 to 2001, our economy expanded. Then, in 2001, we had a recession. In 2002, a new expansion was under way, but people wondered whether it would persist or whether another "double-dip" recession was imminent.

In this chapter, we're going to use the aggregate supply–aggregate demand, or *AS-AD,* model to study the business cycle—the recessions and expansions that alternate through our economic history. You had a sneak preview of the *AS-AD* model in Chapter 8, where you met the concepts of aggregate supply, aggregate demand, and macroeconomic equilibrium. You saw that the persistent expansion of potential GDP increases aggregate supply and brings economic growth. You also saw that persistent growth in the quantity of money increases aggregate demand and brings inflation. You've filled in a lot of the details about economic growth (in Chapters 9 and 10) and inflation (in Chapters 11–13). Now we're filling in the details on the business cycle.

We begin with some definitions and a bit of business-cycle history.

14.1 BUSINESS-CYCLE DEFINITIONS AND FACTS

We defined the *business cycle* in Chapter 1 (p. 5) as a periodic but irregular up-and-down movement in production and jobs. A business cycle has two phases, expansion and recession, and two turning points, a peak and a trough. An expansion runs from a trough to a peak, and a recession runs from a peak to a trough.

Over the business cycle, real GDP fluctuates around trend. When real GDP is below trend, resources are *under*used—some labor is unemployed and capital is underemployed. When real GDP is above trend, resources are *over*used—people work longer hours than they are willing to put up with in the long run, capital is worked so intensively that it is not maintained in prime condition, delivery times lengthen, bottlenecks occur, and backorders increase.

Dating Business-Cycle Turning Points

The task of identifying and dating business-cycle phases and turning points is performed not by the U.S. government, but by a private research organization, the National Bureau of Economic Research (NBER). The NBER's Business Cycle Dating Committee meets after an obvious turning point and determines the exact month in which it occurred. The committee declared in November 2001 that a business-cycle peak occurred in March 2001. In November 2002, the committee reported that it was too early to say whether a trough had occurred.

Recession
A decrease in real GDP that lasts for at least two quarters (six months) or a period of significant decline in total output, income, employment, and trade, usually lasting from six months to a year, and marked by widespread contractions in many sectors of the economy.

To date the business-cycle turning points, the NBER needs a definition of recession. A standard definition of **recession** is a decrease in real GDP that lasts for at least two quarters (six months). The NBER uses a broader definition. It defines a recession as "a period of significant decline in total output, income, employment, and trade, usually lasting from six months to a year, and marked by widespread contractions in many sectors of the economy."

In this definition of recession, total output and income are the same thing as real GDP. You've seen that employment fluctuations closely match fluctuations in real GDP. Because real GDP measures production in all sectors of the economy, a decrease in real GDP means that many sectors of the economy are experiencing falling production. So although the NBER looks beyond real GDP to date the turning points precisely, a two-quarter decrease in real GDP is a good practical indicator of recession and gives almost the same dating as the more refined method of the NBER.

U.S. Business-Cycle History

The NBER has identified 32 complete cycles starting from a trough in December 1854. (In 2001, we entered the 33rd recession.) Over all 32 complete cycles, the average length of an expansion is 35 months (almost 3 years), the average length of a recession is 18 months, and the average time from trough to trough is 53 months (almost 4½ years). So over the 147 years since 1854, the U.S. economy has been in recession for about one third of the time and in expansion for about two thirds of the time.

The 147-year averages that we've just reviewed hide significant changes that have occurred in the length of a cycle and the relative length of the recession and expansion phases. Figure 14.1 shows these changes by dividing U.S. business-cycle history into three periods: 1854–1919 (before and during World War I);

FIGURE 14.1
Recession, Expansion, and Cycle Length: A Summary

Practice Online

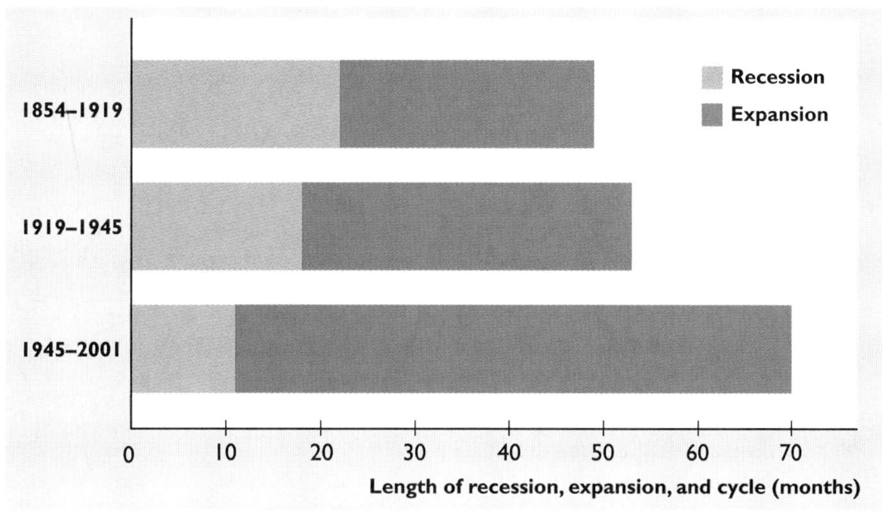

SOURCE: National Bureau of Economic Research.

During the nineteenth century and through World War I, recessions were almost as long as expansions. During the twentieth century, recessions have shortened, expansions have lengthened, and complete cycles have lengthened.

1919–1945 (between the two World Wars and through World War II); and 1945–2001 (the post–World War II years).

The figure shows that before 1919, recessions lasted for 22 months and expansions for 27 months on the average. So during this period, recession was almost as common an experience as expansion.

During the years between the wars and through World War II, the average recession shortened to 18 months and the average expansion lengthened to 35 months. (It is a coincidence that these durations are the same as the overall averages for the entire period since 1854.) One recession during this period, the Great Depression, was enormous and lasted for 43 months.

During the years since World War II, the average recession has shortened to 11 months and the average expansion has lengthened to 59 months (almost 5 years). The longest ever expansion is the one that began in March 1991 and ended in March 2001.

Recent Cycles

The current cycle began at a trough that followed a recession that ran from July 1990 to March 1991. The economy expanded from March 1991 until March 2001, an expansion that lasted for 120 months and was the longest in U.S. history. The previous record expansion was 106 months and ran from February 1961 to December 1969. The next longest expansion was 92 months and ran from November 1982 to July 1990.

Figure 14.2 shows three features of the recent cycles: real GDP fluctuations around potential GDP, the unemployment rate, and the inflation rate. The dates in the three parts of the figure are aligned above each other so that you can see the relationship between the three variables. The two most recent recessions are highlighted in all three parts.

FIGURE 14.2
The Current Cycle

Practice Online

The last two recessions (highlighted in all three parts) began in mid-1990 and the first quarter of 2001. The expansion that followed the 1990–1991 recession was the longest in U.S. history. When real GDP decreases in a recession (part a), the unemployment rate increases (part b), and a little later, the inflation rate decreases (part c). As real GDP increases toward potential GDP, the unemployment rate falls toward the natural rate and the inflation rate falls.

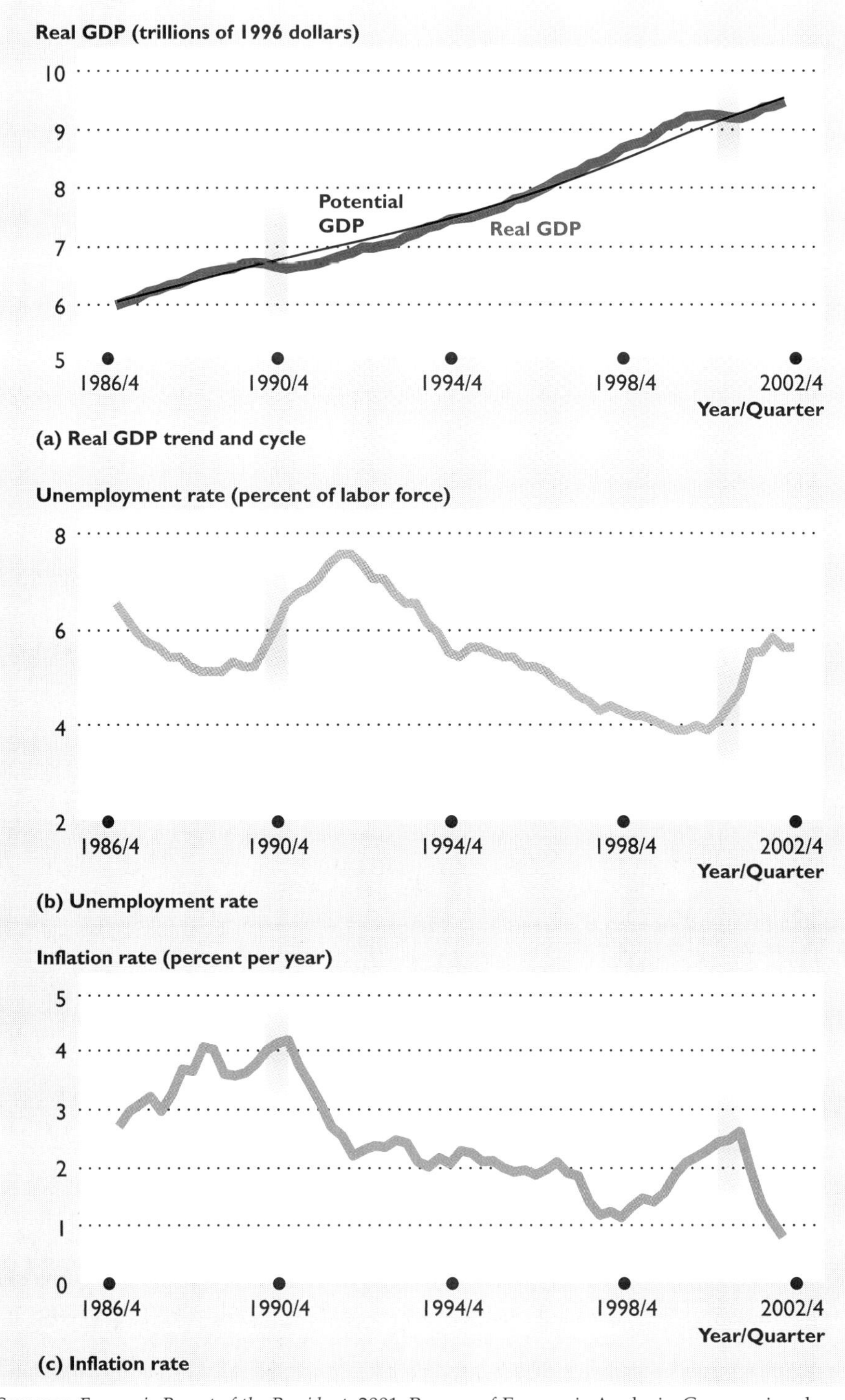

SOURCES: *Economic Report of the President*, 2001. Bureau of Economic Analysis, Congressional Budget Office, and Bureau of Labor Statistics.

In part (a), you can see that real GDP fell from a peak in mid-1990 to a trough in the first quarter of 1991, and it fell from a peak at the end of 2000 to a trough in the third quarter of 2001. In a recession, real GDP moves from above to below potential GDP. From the trough, real GDP begins its long expansion. In the expansion of the 1990s, real GDP reached potential GDP in 1998 and then moved above potential.

In part (b), you can see that the unemployment rate increased during the recession. It kept increasing after the recession was over but then began a long and steady decline. At its peak, the unemployment rate exceeded the natural rate. The natural unemployment rate decreased during the 1990s (see Chapter 17, pp. 435–437), but at its lowest level, in 2000, the unemployment rate was below the natural rate.

In part (c), the inflation rate reached a peak during the 1990 recession and then fell steadily until 1998. It then began to increase as real GDP moved above potential GDP. So the business cycle is not confined to the real economy. The money economy cycles alongside the real economy. The inflation rate decreases when real GDP is below potential GDP and increases when real GDP is above potential GDP.

CHECKPOINT 14.1

1 **Provide a technical definition of recession and describe the history of the U.S. business cycle.**

Study Guide **pp. 198–200**

Practice Online 14.1

Practice Problem 14.1

Table 1 shows real GDP in Canada from the first quarter of 1989 to the fourth quarter of 1993.

a. In which quarter was Canada at a business-cycle peak?
b. In which quarter was Canada at a business-cycle trough?
c. Did Canada experience a recession during these years?
d. In what periods did Canada experience an expansion?

TABLE 1

Billions of 1996 dollars

Year	Quarter 1	2	3	4
1989	700	703	705	706
1990	711	709	705	698
1991	689	691	694	696
1992	696	697	699	702
1993	708	712	716	722

Exercise 14.1

Table 2 shows real GDP in Mexico from the first quarter of 1994 to the last quarter of 1996.

a. In which quarters was Mexico at a business-cycle peak?
b. In which quarters was Mexico at a business-cycle trough?
c. Did Mexico experience a recession during these years?
d. In what years did Mexico experience an expansion?

TABLE 2

Trillions of 1993 pesos

Year	Quarter 1	2	3	4
1994	1.25	1.19	1.29	1.27
1995	1.21	1.16	1.28	1.27
1996	1.27	1.29	1.25	1.37

Solution to Practice Problem 14.1

a. Canada was at a business-cycle peak in the first quarter of 1990.
b. Canada was at a business-cycle trough in the first quarter of 1991.
c. The recession ran from the first quarter of 1990 to the first quarter of 1991.
d. Expansions ran from the first quarter 1989 to the first quarter of 1990 and from the first quarter of 1991 to the fourth quarter of 1993.

14.2 AGGREGATE SUPPLY

We introduced the concept of *aggregate supply* in Chapter 8 (pp. 183–184). You learned that aggregate supply is the relationship between the quantity of real GDP supplied and the price level when all other influences on production plans remain the same. Other things remaining the same, the higher the price level, the greater is the quantity of real GDP supplied, and the lower the price level, the smaller is the quantity of real GDP supplied. We illustrate aggregate supply with an upward-sloping aggregate supply curve.

In Chapter 8, we described the influence of the price level on the quantity of real GDP supplied, but we didn't explain *why* it occurs. Here, we'll explain the reasons. We'll also explore the link between aggregate supply and potential GDP, and we'll study the factors that make aggregate supply change.

Aggregate Supply Basics

The *quantity of real GDP supplied* (*Y*), depends on

- The quantity of labor employed
- The quantities of capital and human capital and the technologies they embody
- The quantities of land and natural resources used
- The amount of entrepreneurial talent available

At full employment, the real wage rate makes the quantity of labor demanded equal the quantity of labor supplied, and the quantity of real GDP supplied equals potential GDP. Over the business cycle, the quantity of real GDP supplied fluctuates around potential GDP and the quantity of labor employed fluctuates. The quantities of capital and human capital grow, technology advances, and the amount of entrepreneurial talent increases as the population increases. These changes are the sources of economic growth, but they occur gradually and do not fluctuate much over the business cycle.

Aggregate Supply and Potential GDP

Figure 14.3 shows an aggregate supply curve, *AS*, and a potential GDP line. Along the aggregate supply curve, the only influence on production plans that changes is the price level. A rise in the price level brings an increase in the quantity of real GDP supplied and a movement up along the aggregate supply curve; a fall in the price level brings a decrease in the quantity of real GDP supplied and a movement down along the aggregate supply curve. All the other influences on production plans remain constant. Among these other influences are

- The money wage rate
- The money prices of other resources

In contrast, along the potential GDP line, when the price level changes, the money wage rate and the money prices of other resources change by the same percentage as the change in the price level to keep the real wage rate (and other real prices) at the full-employment equilibrium level.

FIGURE 14.3

A Change in the Quantity of Real GDP Supplied

Practice Online

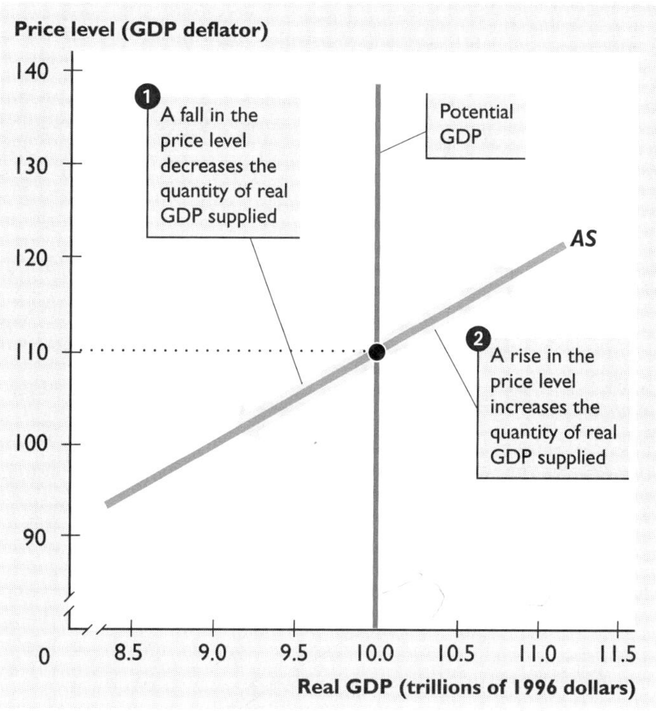

The aggregate supply (*AS*) curve shows the relationship between the quantity of real GDP supplied and the price level when the money wage rate, other resource prices, and potential output remain the same. The quantity of real GDP supplied ❶ decreases when the price level falls and ❷ increases when the price level rises.

Why the *AS* Curve Slopes Upward

Why does the quantity of real GDP supplied increase when the price level rises and decrease when the price level falls? The answer is that a movement along the *AS* curve brings a change in the real wage rate (and changes in the real cost of other resources whose money prices are fixed). If the price level rises, the real wage rate falls, and if the price level falls, the real wage rate rises.

Think about a concrete example. Suppose Microsoft has a contract with its programmers to pay them $200 an hour. Microsoft sells copies of Windows to computer makers (such as Dell Computer Corporation) for $100 a copy. The real wage rate of a programmer is 2 copies of Windows. That is, Microsoft must sell 2 copies of Windows to buy one hour of programming labor. Now suppose the price of a copy of Windows falls to $50. The real wage rate of a programmer has increased to 4 copies of Windows—Microsoft must now sell 4 copies of the program to buy one hour of programming labor.

If the price of a copy of Windows increased, the real wage rate of a programmer would fall. For example, if the price increased to $200 a copy, the real wage rate would be one copy of Windows—Microsoft would need to sell only one copy of the software to buy one hour of programmer time.

A change in the real wage rate means that the cost of labor changes relative to the revenue that an hour of labor can produce, and it changes a firm's profit. A rise in the real wage rate cuts into a firm's profit, and a fall in the real wage rate boosts a firm's profit. Firms respond to a change in the real wage rate and their profit in one of three possible ways:

- Go out of business or start up in business.
- Shut down temporarily or restart production.
- Change their output rate.

Business Failure and Startup New businesses are born and some existing businesses die every day. Real GDP changes when the number of firms in business changes. And the price level influences this number in the short run.

People create businesses in the hope of earning a profit. When profits are generally high, more firms start up and fewer existing firms fail. So the number of firms in business increases. When profits are squeezed or when losses arise, fewer new firms start up and more existing firms fail. So the number of firms in business decreases.

The price level relative to wage and other costs influences the number of firms in business. If the price level rises relative to costs, profits increase, the number of firms in business increases, and the quantity of real GDP supplied increases. If the price level falls relative to costs, profits fall, the number of firms in business decreases, and the quantity of real GDP supplied decreases.

In a severe recession, business failure can be contagious. The failure of one firm puts pressure on both its suppliers and its customers and can bring a flood of failures and a large decrease in the quantity of real GDP supplied.

Temporary Shutdowns and Restarts A firm that is incurring a loss might foresee a profit in the future. So rather than going out of business, such a firm might decide to shut down temporarily and lay off its workers.

The price level relative to costs is an influence on temporary shutdown decisions. If the price level rises relative to costs, fewer firms will decide to shut down temporarily; so more firms operate and the quantity of real GDP supplied increases. If the price level falls relative to costs, a larger number of firms find that they cannot earn enough to pay the wage bill and so temporarily shut down. The quantity of real GDP supplied decreases.

Changes in Output Rate The price level relative to costs influences even those firms that remain profitable and keep producing. You know that to produce more output, a firm must hire more labor. It is profitable to hire more labor if the additional labor brings in more revenue than it costs. If the price level rises and the money wage rate doesn't change, an extra hour of labor that was previously unprofitable becomes profitable. So when the price level rises and the money wage rate doesn't change, the quantity of labor demanded increases and production increases. For the economy as a whole, the quantity of real GDP supplied increases.

Production at a Pepsi Plant

A Pepsi bottling plant produces the quantity of Pepsi that maximizes profit. The production plant is fixed, but Pepsi can increase production by hiring more labor and working the plant harder. But each additional hour of labor hired produces fewer additional bottles of Pepsi than the previous hour produces. So Pepsi increases the quantity of labor hired and increases production only if the real wage rate falls. But if the price of Pepsi rises and wage rates and other costs don't change, the real wage rate *does* fall. Similarly, if the price of Pepsi falls and wage rates and other costs don't change, the real wage rate *rises*. In this situation, Pepsi decreases the quantity of labor demanded and decreases production.

What is true for Pepsi bottlers is true for the producers of all goods and services. So when the price level rises and the money wage rate and other resource prices remain constant, the quantity of labor demanded increases and the quantity of real GDP supplied increases.

Changes in Aggregate Supply

You saw in Figure 14.3 that a change in the price level changes the quantity of real GDP supplied and brings a movement along the aggregate supply curve. But it does not change aggregate supply.

Aggregate supply changes when any influence on production plans other than the price level changes. In particular, aggregate supply changes when

- Potential GDP changes.
- The money wage rate changes.
- The money prices of other resources change.

Changes in Potential GDP

Anything that changes potential GDP—real GDP at full employment—changes aggregate supply and shifts the aggregate supply curve. Figure 14.4 shows these changes. You can think of point *C* as an anchor point. The *AS* curve and potential GDP line are anchored at this point, and when potential GDP changes, *AS* changes along with it. Point *C* shifts to point *C'*, and the aggregate supply curve and potential GDP line shift rightward together. When potential GDP increases from $10 trillion to $11 trillion, the *AS* curve shifts from AS_0 to AS_1.

FIGURE 14.4
An Increase in Potential GDP

Practice Online

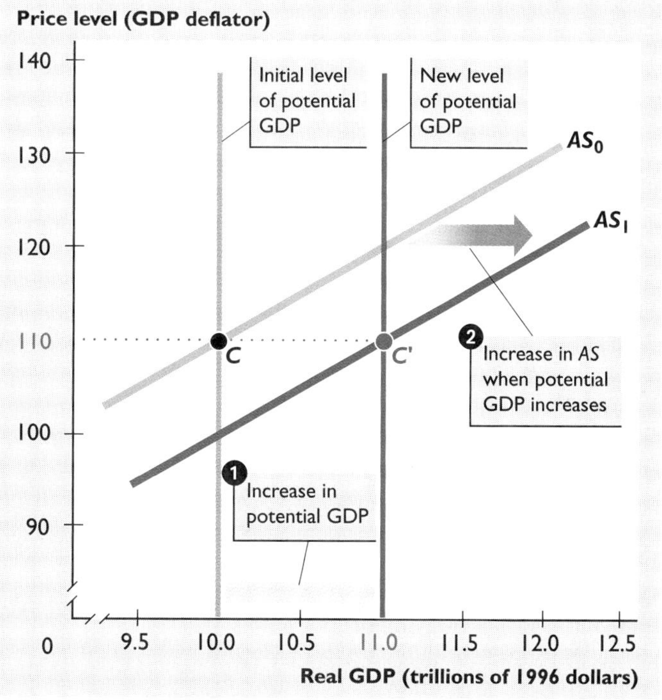

❶ An increase in potential GDP increases aggregate supply. ❷ The aggregate supply curve shifts rightward from AS_0 to AS_1.

Changes in Money Wage Rate and Other Resource Prices

A change in the money wage rate or in the money price of another resource changes aggregate supply because it changes firms' costs. The higher the money wage rate or the price of another resource, the higher are firms' costs and the smaller is the quantity that firms are willing to supply at each price level. So an increase in the money wage rate or the price of another resource decreases aggregate supply.

Suppose that the money wage rate is $33 an hour and the price level is 110. Then the real wage rate is $30 an hour ($33 × 100 ÷ 110 = $30). If the full-employment equilibrium real wage rate is $30 an hour, the economy is at full employment and real GDP equals potential GDP. In Figure 14.5, the economy is at point *C* on the aggregate supply curve AS_0. The money wage rate is $33 an hour at all points on AS_0.

Now suppose the money wage rate rises to $36 an hour but the full-employment equilibrium real wage rate remains at $30 an hour. Real GDP now equals potential GDP when the price level is 120, at point *D* on the aggregate supply curve AS_2. (If the money wage rate is $36 an hour and the price level is 120, the real wage rate is $36 × 100 ÷ 120 = $30 an hour.) The money wage rate is $36 an hour at all points on AS_2. The rise in the money wage rate *decreases* aggregate supply and shifts the aggregate supply curve leftward from AS_0 to AS_2.

A change in the money wage rate does not change potential GDP. The reason is that potential GDP depends only on the economy's real ability to produce and on the full-employment quantity of labor, which occurs at the equilibrium *real* wage rate. The equilibrium real wage rate can occur at any money wage rate.

FIGURE 14.5
A Change in the Money Wage Rate

Practice Online

A rise in the money wage rate decreases aggregate supply. The aggregate supply curve shifts leftward from AS_0 to AS_2. A rise in the money wage rate does not change potential GDP.

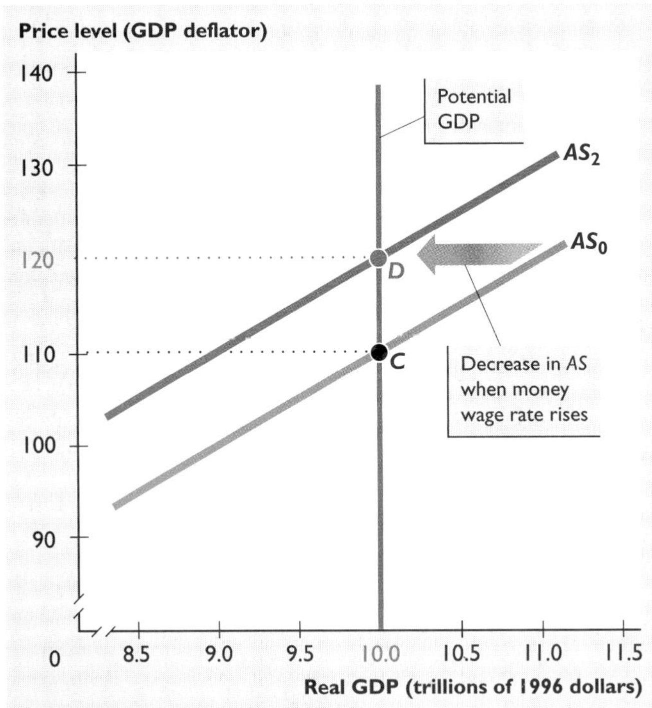

CHECKPOINT 14.2

2 Explain the influences on aggregate supply.

Study Guide **pp. 200–202**

Practice Online 14.2

Practice Problem 14.2

In May 2000, armed men took over the Parliament in Fiji and held the Prime Minister and other people as hostages. This action led to many other events. Explain the effect of each of the following events on Fiji's aggregate supply.

a. Downtown Suva (the capital of Fiji) was heavily looted and businesses were destroyed.
b. Dock workers in Australia refused to handle cargo to and from Fiji, including raw material going to Fiji's garment industry.
c. The number of tourists fell and many hotels closed.
d. As unemployment increased, the workweek was shortened.
e. The fresh tuna industry boomed with increased sales to Japan and the United States.
f. With widespread shortages, suppose that the unionized workers demanded higher wages and got them.

Exercise 14.2

Many events have followed the ending of apartheid in South Africa. Explain the effect of each of the following events on South Africa's aggregate supply.

a. Businesses around the world have established branches in South Africa.
b. More South Africans have access to education.
c. Trade sanctions ended.
d. Unemployment decreased.
e. Tourism increased and many new hotels were built.
f. AIDS became more prevalent.

Solution to Practice Problem 14.2

a. As businesses closed, real GDP supplied at the current price level decreased. The *AS* curve shifted leftward (Figure 1).
b. As Fiji's garment industry ran out of raw materials, production in the garment industry decreased and the quantity of real GDP supplied at the current price level decreased. The *AS* curve shifted leftward (Figure 1).
c. As many hotels closed, the quantity of tourist services supplied decreased and the quantity of real GDP supplied at the current price level decreased. The *AS* curve shifted leftward (Figure 1).
d. As employers cut the workweek and shared jobs among workers, production decreased and the *AS* curve shifted leftward (Figure 1).
e. As the tuna industry continued to expand, production increased. In isolation, its effect shifted the *AS* curve rightward (Figure 2).
f. As the wage rate increased, businesses that became unprofitable closed and real GDP produced at the current price level decreased. The *AS* curve shifted leftward (Figure 1).

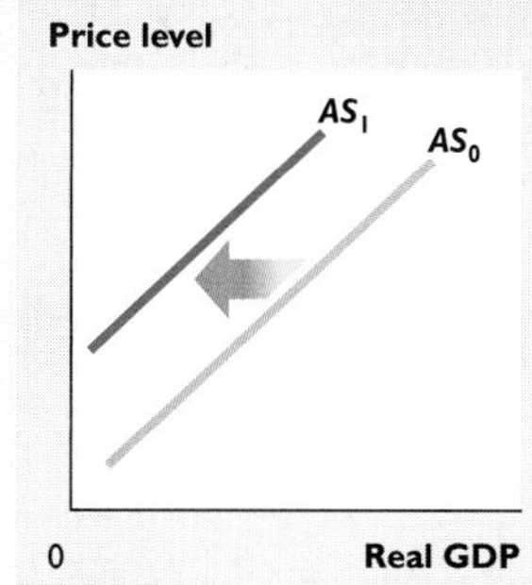

FIGURE 2

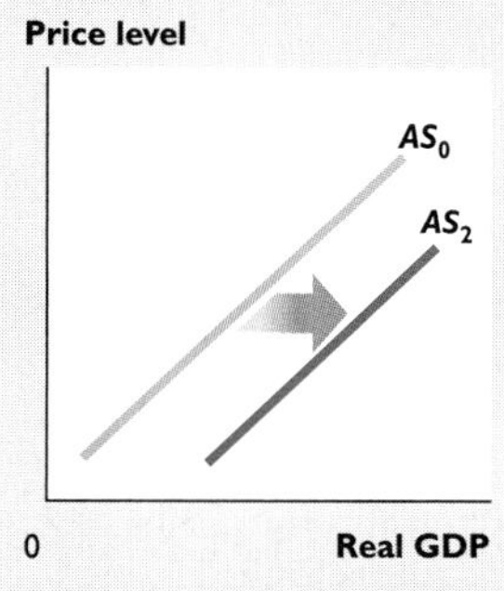

14.3 AGGREGATE DEMAND

We introduced the concept of *aggregate demand* in Chapter 8 (pp. 184–185). Aggregate demand is the relationship between the quantity of real GDP demanded and the price level when all other influences on expenditure plans remain the same. Other things remaining the same, the higher the price level, the smaller is the quantity of real GDP demanded, and the lower the price level, the greater is the quantity of real GDP demanded. We illustrate aggregate demand with a downward-sloping aggregate demand curve.

In Chapter 8, we described the influence of the price level on the quantity of real GDP demanded, but we didn't explain *why* it occurs. Here, we'll explain the reasons.

Aggregate Demand Basics

The *quantity of real GDP demanded* is the total amount of final goods and services produced in the United States that people, businesses, governments, and foreigners plan to buy. This quantity is the sum of the real consumption expenditure (C), investment (I), government purchases (G), and exports (X) minus imports (M). That is,

$$Y = C + I + G + X - M.$$

Many factors influence expenditure plans; to study aggregate demand, we divide them into two groups: the price level and everything else. We'll first consider the influence of the price level on expenditure plans and then consider the other influences.

Aggregate Demand and the *AD* Curve

Figure 14.6 shows an aggregate demand curve, *AD*. Along the aggregate demand curve, the only influence on expenditure plans that changes is the price level. A rise in the price level decreases the quantity of real GDP demanded and brings a movement up along the aggregate demand curve; a fall in the price level increases the quantity of real GDP demanded and brings a movement down along the aggregate demand curve.

The price level influences the quantity of real GDP demanded because a change in the price level brings changes in

- The buying power of money
- The real interest rate
- The real prices of exports and imports

The Buying Power of Money

A rise in the price level lowers the buying power of money and decreases the quantity of real GDP demanded. To see why, think about the buying plans of Anna, who lives in Moscow, Russia. She has worked hard all summer and saved 20,000 rubles (the ruble is the currency of Russia), which she plans to spend attending graduate school when she has finished her economics degree. So Anna's money holding is 20,000 rubles. Anna has a part-time job, and her income from this job pays her expenses. The price level in Russia rises by 100 percent. Anna needs 40,000 rubles to buy what 20,000 rubles once bought. To make up some of

FIGURE 14.6

A Change in the Quantity of Real GDP Demanded

Practice Online

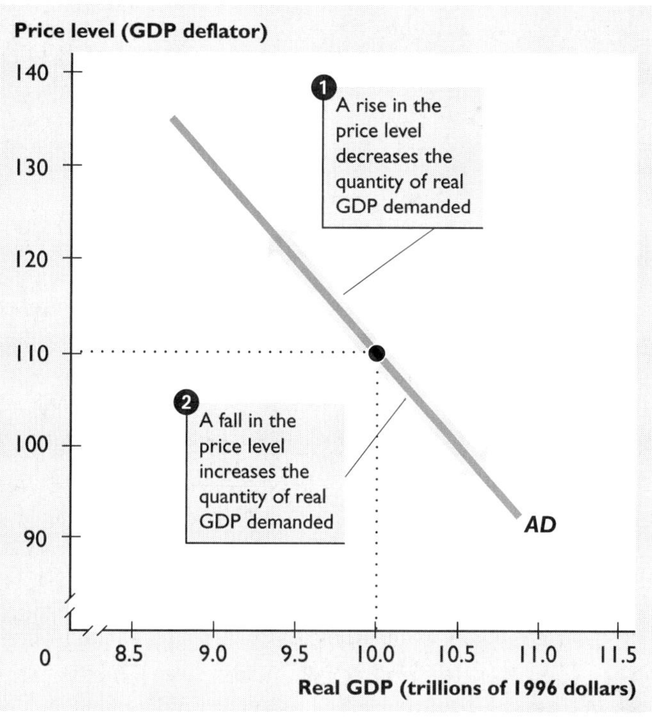

The aggregate demand curve (*AD*) shows the relationship between the quantity of real GDP demanded and the price level when all other influences on expenditure plans remain the same. The quantity of real GDP demanded ❶ decreases when the price level rises and ❷ increases when the price level falls.

the fall in the buying power of her money, Anna slashes her spending.

Similarly, a fall in the price level, other things remaining the same, brings an increase in the quantity of real GDP demanded. To see why, think about the buying plans of Mika, who lives in Tokyo, Japan. She too has worked hard all summer and saved 200,000 yen (the yen is the currency of Japan), which she plans to spend attending school next year. The price level in Japan falls by 10 percent; now Mika needs only 180,000 yen to buy what 200,000 yen once bought. With a rise in what her money buys, Mika decides to buy a DVD player.

The Real Interest Rate

When the price level rises, the real interest rate rises. You saw in Chapter 13 (pp. 317–318) that an increase in the price level increases the amount of money that people want to hold—increases the demand for money. When the demand for money increases, the nominal interest rate rises. In the short run, the inflation rate doesn't change, so a rise in the nominal interest rate brings a rise in the real interest rate. Faced with a higher real interest rate, businesses and people delay plans to buy new capital and consumer durable goods and cut back on spending. So the quantity of real GDP demanded decreases.

Anna and Mika Again Think about Anna and Mika again. Both of them want to buy a computer. In Moscow, a rise in the price level increases the demand for money and raises the real interest rate. At a real interest rate of 5 percent a year,

Anna was willing to borrow to buy the new computer. But at a real interest rate of 10 percent a year, she decides that the payments would be too high, so she delays buying it. The rise in the price level decreases the quantity of real GDP demanded.

In Tokyo, a fall in the price level lowers the real interest rate. At a real interest rate of 5 percent a year, Mika was willing to borrow to buy a low-performance computer. But at a real interest rate of close to zero, she decides to buy a fancier computer that costs more: The fall in the price level increases the quantity of real GDP demanded.

The Real Prices of Exports and Imports

When the U.S. price level rises and other things remain the same, the prices in other countries do not change. So a rise in the U.S. price level makes U.S.-made goods and services more expensive relative to foreign-made goods and services. This change in real prices encourages people to spend less on U.S.-made items and more on foreign-made items. For example, if the U.S. price level rises relative to the foreign price level, foreigners buy fewer U.S.-made cars (U.S. exports decrease) and Americans buy more foreign-made cars (U.S. imports increase).

Anna's and Mika's Imports In Moscow, Anna is buying some new shoes. With a sharp rise in the Russian price level, the Russian-made shoes that she planned to buy are too expensive, so she buys a less expensive pair imported from Brazil. In Tokyo, Mika is buying a CD player. With the fall in the Japanese price level, a Sony CD player made in Japan looks like a better buy than one made in Taiwan.

In the long run, when the price level changes by more in one country than in other countries, the exchange rate changes. The exchange rate change neutralizes the price level change, so this international price effect on buying plans is a short-run effect only. But in the short run, it is a powerful effect.

Changes in Aggregate Demand

A change in any factor that influences expenditure plans other than the price level brings a change in aggregate demand. When aggregate demand increases, the aggregate demand curve shifts rightward, which Figure 14.7 illustrates as the rightward shift of the *AD* curve from AD_0 to AD_1. When aggregate demand decreases, the aggregate demand curve shifts leftward, which Figure 14.7 illustrates as the leftward shift of the *AD* curve from AD_0 to AD_2. The factors that change aggregate demand are

- Expectations about the future
- Fiscal policy and monetary policy
- The state of the world economy

Expectations

An increase in expected future income increases the amount of consumption goods (especially big-ticket items such as cars) that people plan to buy and increases aggregate demand.

An increase in expected future inflation increases aggregate demand because people decide to buy more goods and services before their prices rise.

An increase in expected future profit increases the investment that firms plan to undertake and increases aggregate demand.

FIGURE 14.7
Changes in Aggregate Demand

Practice Online

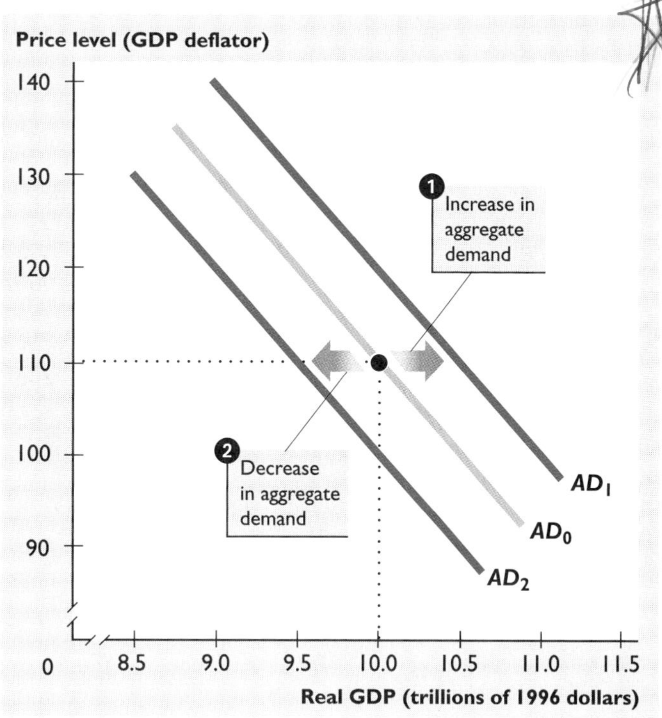

Aggregate demand:

❶ *Increases if*

- Expected future income, inflation, or profits increase.
- The government or the Federal Reserve takes steps that increase planned expenditure.
- The exchange rate falls or the global economy expands.

❷ *Decreases if*

- Expected future income, inflation, or profits decrease.
- The government or the Federal Reserve takes steps that decrease planned expenditure.
- The exchange rate rises or the global economy contracts.

Fiscal Policy and Monetary Policy

We study the effects of policy actions on aggregate demand in Chapter 16. Here, we'll just briefly note that the government can influence aggregate demand by setting and changing taxes, transfer payments, and government purchases of goods and services. And the Federal Reserve can influence aggregate demand by changing the quantity of money and the interest rate.

A tax cut or an increase in either transfer payments or government purchases increases aggregate demand. A cut in the interest rate or an increase in the quantity of money increases aggregate demand.

The World Economy

Two main influences that the world economy has on aggregate demand are the foreign exchange rate and foreign income. The foreign exchange rate is the amount of a foreign currency that you can buy with a U.S. dollar. Other things remaining the same, a rise in the foreign exchange rate decreases aggregate demand. To see how the foreign exchange rate influences aggregate demand, suppose that $1 exchanges for 100 Japanese yen. A Fujitsu phone made in Japan costs 12,500 yen, and an equivalent Motorola phone made in the United States costs $110. In U.S. dollars, the Fujitsu phone costs $125, so people around the world buy the cheaper U.S. phone. Now suppose the exchange rate rises to 125 yen per dollar. At 125 yen per dollar, the Fujitsu phone costs $100 and is now cheaper than the Motorola phone. People will switch from the U.S. phone to the Japanese phone.

U.S. exports will decrease and U.S. imports will increase, so U.S. aggregate demand will decrease.

An increase in foreign income increases U.S. exports and increases U.S. aggregate demand. For example, an increase in income in Japan and Germany increases Japanese and German consumers' and producers' planned expenditures on U.S.-made goods and services.

The Aggregate Demand Multiplier

The aggregate demand multiplier is an effect that magnifies changes in expenditure plans and brings potentially large fluctuations in aggregate demand. When any influence on aggregate demand changes expenditure plans, the change in expenditure changes income; and the change in income induces a change in consumption expenditure. The increase in aggregate demand is the initial increase in expenditure plus the induced increase in consumption expenditure.

Figure 14.8 illustrates this multiplier effect. Initially, the aggregate demand curve is AD_0. Investment then increases by \$0.4 trillion (ΔI) and the purple curve $AD_0 + \Delta I$ now describes aggregate spending plans at each price level. An increase in income induces an increase in consumption expenditure of \$0.6 trillion, and the aggregate demand curve shifts rightward to AD_1. Chapter 15 (pp. 384–388) explains the expenditure multiplier in detail.

FIGURE 14.8
The Aggregate Demand Multiplier

Practice Online

❶ An increase in investment increases aggregate demand and increases income. ❷ The increase in income induces an increase in consumption expenditure, so ❸ aggregate demand increases by more than the initial increase in investment.

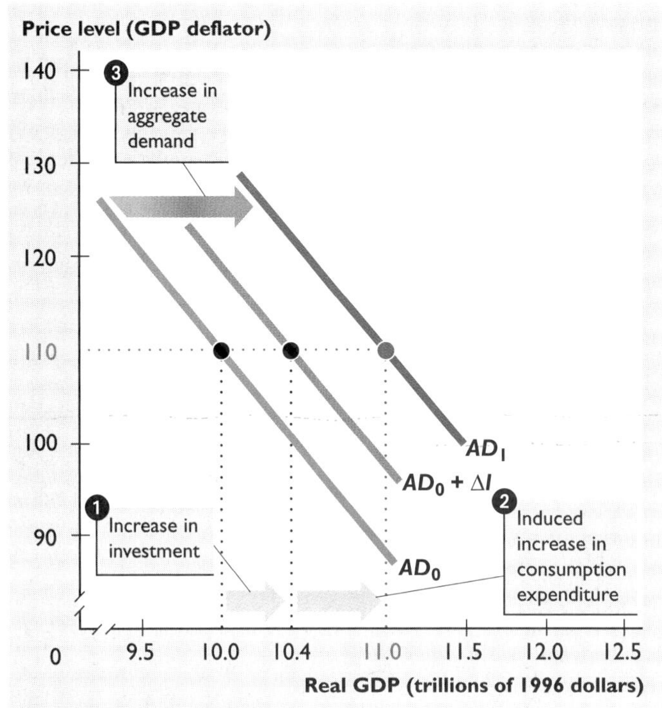

CHECKPOINT 14.3

3 Explain the influences on aggregate demand.

Study Guide pp. 203–205

Practice Online 14.3

Practice Problem 14.3

Mexico has signed free trade agreements with many countries, including the United States, Canada, and the European Union. Explain the effect of each of the following events on Mexico's aggregate demand in the short run.

a. The price level in Mexico increases faster than that in its trading partners.
b. The government of Mexico cuts taxes.
c. The United States and Canada experienced strong economic growth.
d. The European Union goes into a recession.
e. The Mexican government sets new environmental standards that require factories to upgrade their production facilities.
f. Mexico adopts an expansionary monetary policy and increases the quantity of money.

Exercise 14.3

Explain the effect on Japan's aggregate demand in the short run of each of the following events, one at a time.

a. The price level in Japan is constant, and the price level in its trading partners increases.
b. The price level in Japan rises.
c. The rest of Asia goes into recession.
d. The Asian economies experience very strong growth.
e. The yen strengthens against the U.S. dollar.
f. Japan adopts an expansionary fiscal policy and cuts taxes.

Solution to Practice Problem 14.3

a. As Mexico's price level increases faster than that of its trading partners, its exports become relatively more expensive. The quantity demanded of Mexican real GDP by its trading partners decreases. Mexico's aggregate demand does not change—there is a movement up along the *AD* curve (Figure 1).
b. A tax cut in Mexico increases Mexico's aggregate demand. The *AD* curve shifts rightward (Figure 2).
c. Strong economic growth in Canada and the United States increases the demand for Mexican real GDP and increases aggregate demand in Mexico. The *AD* curve shifts rightward (Figure 2).
d. A recession in the European Union decreases European demand for goods and services from Mexico. So Mexico's exports decrease, and its aggregate demand decreases. The *AD* curve shifts leftward (Figure 3).
e. As factories upgrade their production facilities, investment increases. Aggregate demand in Mexico increases, and the *AD* curve shifts rightward (Figure 2).
f. An increase in the quantity of money increases aggregate demand, and the *AD* curve shifts rightward (Figure 2).

FIGURE 1

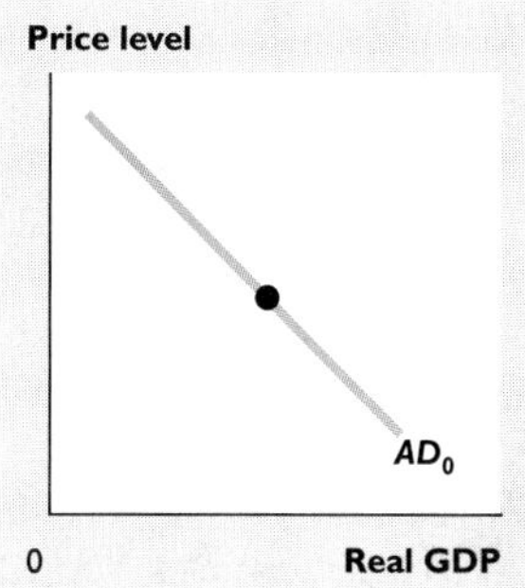

FIGURE 2

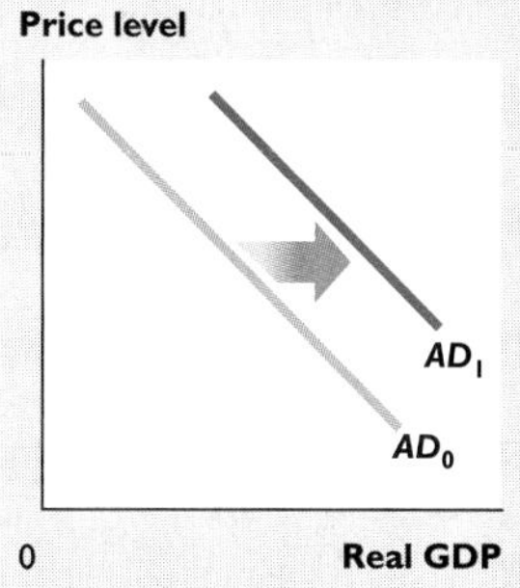

FIGURE 3

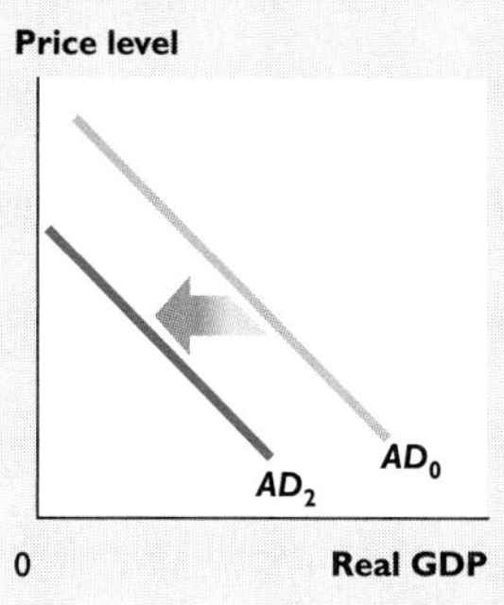

14.4 UNDERSTANDING THE BUSINESS CYCLE

Aggregate supply and aggregate demand determine real GDP and the price level (see Chapter 8, p. 186). And changes in aggregate demand and aggregate supply bring changes in real GDP and the price level. These changes generate the business cycle.

The business cycle is an irregular cycle because the changes in aggregate demand and aggregate supply occur at irregular intervals and are of variable magnitude. And these changes initiate adjustments that are spread out over time.

To study the business cycle, we're first going to consider the effects of fluctuations in aggregate demand. Then we'll examine the effects of fluctuations in aggregate supply. Finally, we'll look at the adjustments that keep real GDP returning toward potential GDP when aggregate demand or aggregate supply shocks occur.

Aggregate Demand Fluctuations

We're going to describe a business cycle that results from fluctuations in aggregate demand with no changes in aggregate supply. In the U.S. economy, potential GDP grows and the full-employment price level rises over a business cycle. To focus on the cycle, we'll ignore economic growth and inflation. We'll suppose that potential GDP remains constant and that the full-employment price level is also constant.

Figure 14.9 illustrates the sequence of events. Throughout the cycle, potential GDP is $10 trillion and the full-employment price level is 110. Aggregate supply is shown by the *AS* curve, which does not change. Part (a) shows the changes in aggregate demand that bring an expansion, and part (c) tracks real GDP.

The economy starts out at a trough at point *A* at the intersection of AD_0 and *AS*. Real GDP is $9.5 trillion, and the price level is 105. Expecting high future profits, firms increase investment, and aggregate demand increases. The *AD* curve shifts rightward to AD_1, and the economy moves to point *B*. There is now full employment. The aggregate demand multiplier kicks in and increases in consumption expenditure keep *AD* increasing. The *AD* curve shifts further rightward to AD_2, and the economy moves to a cycle peak at point *C*. There is now above-full employment.

Figure 14.9(b) shows the changes in aggregate demand that bring a recession, and part (c) continues to track real GDP. The economy is at a peak at point *C* at the intersection of AD_2 and *AS*. Real GDP is $10.5 trillion, and the price level is 115. Now, expecting low future profits, firms decrease investment, and aggregate demand decreases. The *AD* curve shifts leftward to AD_3, and the economy moves to point *D*. There is full employment again. The aggregate demand multiplier decreases consumption expenditure and keeps *AD* decreasing. The *AD* curve shifts further leftward to AD_4, and the economy moves to a new cycle trough at point *E*.

Here, changes in profit expectations drive changes in investment and aggregate demand to create the business cycle. This factor is frequently the one at work. But sometimes other factors initiate a change in aggregate demand, and any of the factors that influence expenditure plans that we reviewed above (on pp. 354–356) could be at work. For smaller countries, a change in exports is frequently the initiating factor and the source of an international business cycle.

FIGURE 14.9
An Aggregate Demand Cycle

Practice Online

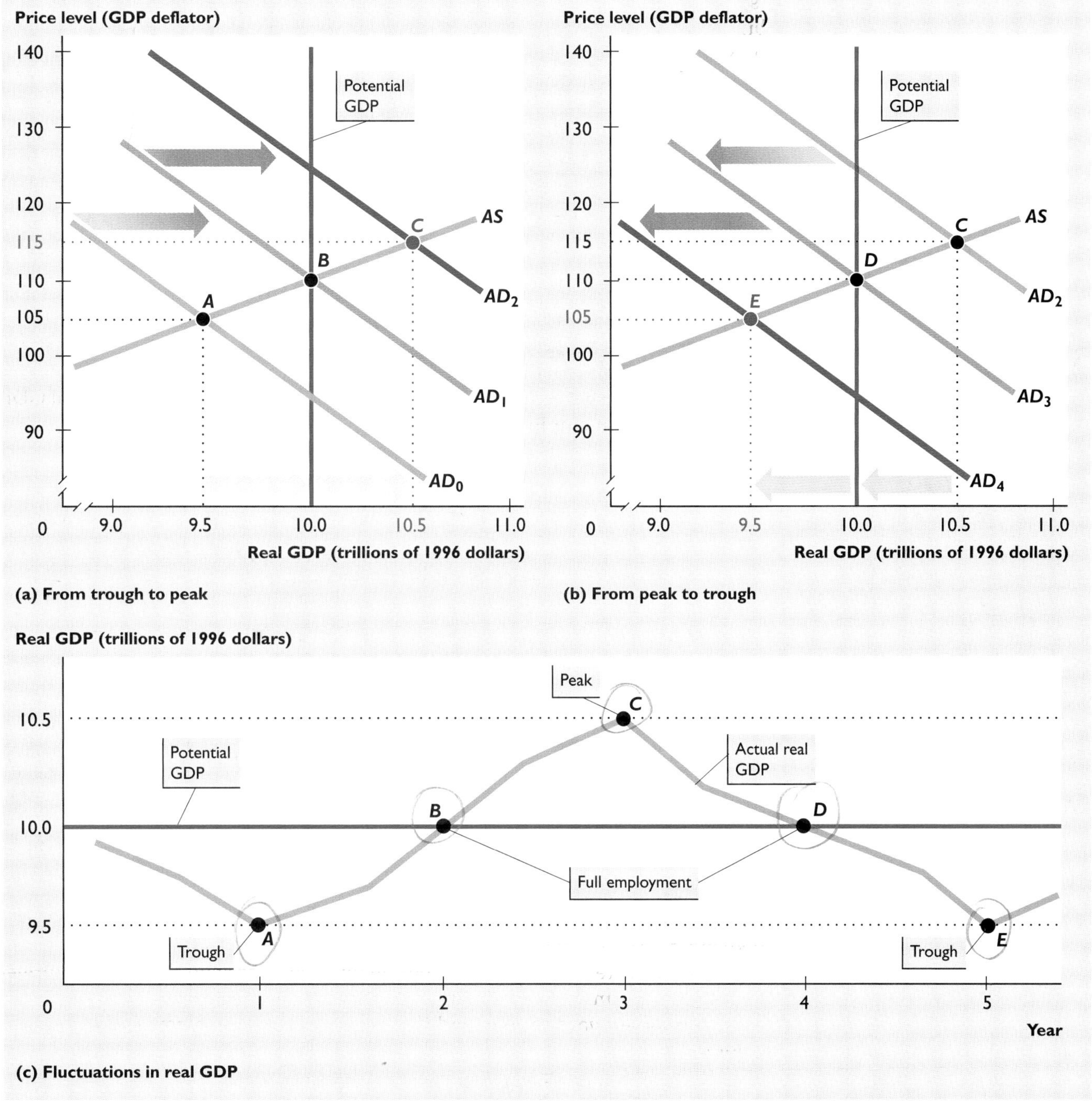

Real GDP is \$9.5 trillion at the intersection of *AS* and AD_0 in part (a), and the economy is in a trough at point *A* in part (c). An increase in investment increases aggregate demand through AD_1 to AD_2. The economy moves from *A* through full employment at *B* to a cycle peak at *C*. A decrease in investment decreases aggregate demand through AD_3 to AD_4 in part (b). The economy moves from *C* through full employment at *D* to a new trough at *E*.

Aggregate Supply Fluctuations

Aggregate supply can fluctuate for two types of reasons. First, potential GDP grows at an uneven pace. During a period of rapid technological change and capital accumulation, potential GDP grows rapidly and above its long-term trend. The second half of the 1990s experienced this type of expansion.

Second, a change in the money price of a major resource, such as crude oil, might change. Oil is used so widely throughout the economy that a large change in its price affects almost every firm and impacts the aggregate economy.

Figure 14.10 shows how a large change in the price of oil can bring recession and expansion. In part (a), the aggregate demand curve is *AD* and initially, the aggregate supply curve is AS_0. Equilibrium real GDP is $10 trillion, which equals potential GDP, and the price level is 110. Then the price of oil rises. Faced with higher energy and transportation costs, firms decrease production. Aggregate supply decreases, and the aggregate supply curve shifts leftward to AS_1. The price level rises to 115, and real GDP decreases to $9.75 trillion. Because real GDP decreases, the economy experiences recession. Because the price level increases, the economy experiences inflation. A combination of recession and inflation, called **stagflation**, actually occurred in the United States and the global economy in the mid-1970s and early 1980s. But events like this are infrequent.

Stagflation
A combination of recession (falling real GDP) and inflation (rising price level).

FIGURE 14.10
An Oil Price Cycle

Practice Online

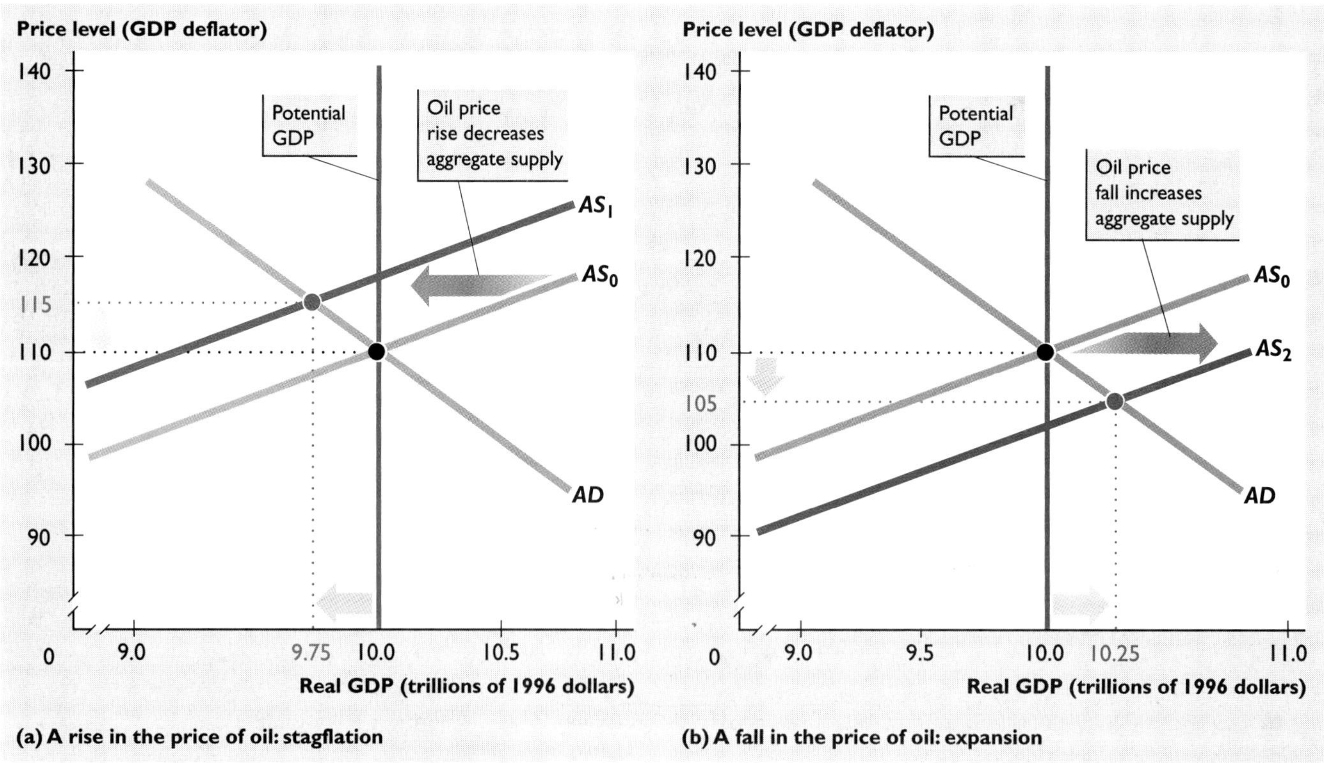

(a) A rise in the price of oil: stagflation

(b) A fall in the price of oil: expansion

In part (a), a decrease in aggregate supply shifts the *AS* curve leftward to AS_1. Real GDP decreases, and the price level rises.

In part (b), an increase in aggregate supply shifts the *AS* curve rightward to AS_2. Real GDP increases, and the price level falls.

In Figure 14.10(b), starting from the same full-employment equilibrium as before, the price of oil falls. With lower energy and transportation costs, firms increase production and the aggregate supply curve shifts rightward to AS_2. The price level falls to 105, and real GDP increases to \$10.25 trillion. The economy experiences expansion and moves above full employment, but the price level falls. Similar events occurred in the United States and global economies during the mid-1980s, bringing strong economic expansion. The price level didn't fall, but inflation slowed, so the price level was lower than it otherwise would have been.

Oil Price Cycles in the U.S. and Global Economies

In 1973, a barrel of crude oil cost around \$3.50—a bit more than \$11.50 in 1996 dollars (see figure). Most of the world's crude oil came from a handful of nations mainly located in the Persian Gulf region, and the large producer nations were (and still are) members of an international cartel known as OPEC—the Organization of Petroleum Exporting Countries. (A cartel is an organization that seeks to control the supply and the price of a commodity and is illegal in the United States.)

In September 1973, OPEC cut the production of crude oil and raised its price to \$10 a barrel—about \$28 in 1996 dollars. This near tripling of the price of crude oil sent the United States, Europe, Japan, and the developing nations into recession.

Through the rest of the 1970s, the price of oil drifted upward slightly. Then, in 1980, OPEC delivered its second jolt to the global economy by again cutting production and then raising the price to \$37 a barrel—\$65 in 1996 dollars.

The global economy experienced another recession. But this recession was much more severe than that of the mid-1970s because the oil price shock was accompanied by a large decrease in aggregate demand that resulted from the Fed's monetary policy.

With the very high price of oil, it did not take long for OPEC to be joined by many other producers. Canada and the United States intensified exploration and increased North American oil production. Britain and Norway developed oil resources in the North Sea. And Mexico stepped up its production.

As these additional sources of supply came onstream, the price of oil tumbled. By 1998, it had fallen to \$14 a barrel.

This gradual fall in the price of oil aided the expansion of the U.S. and global economies during the 1980s and 1990s.

During the late 1990s, the price of oil again increased and by 2001, it was back at its 1974 level in real terms.

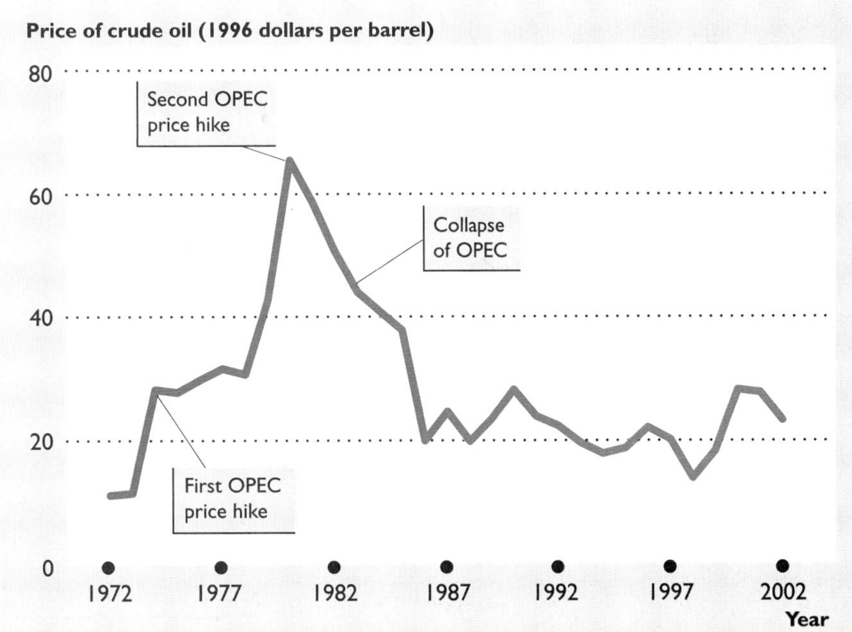

SOURCES: *International Financial Statistics*, International Monetary Fund and Bureau of Economic Analysis.

Adjustment Toward Full Employment

When the economy is away from full employment, forces begin to operate that move it back toward full employment. In Figure 14.11(a), aggregate supply is AS_0 and an increase in aggregate demand from AD_0 to AD_1 moves real GDP above full employment. There is now an **inflationary gap**—a gap that brings a rising price level. Workers have experienced a fall in the buying power of their wages, and firms' profits have increased. Workers demand higher wages, and firms, anxious to maintain their employment and output levels in the face of a labor shortage, meet those demands. As the money wage rate rises, aggregate supply decreases and the aggregate supply curve shifts leftward. Eventually, it will reach AS_1, where real GDP is back at potential GDP.

Inflationary gap
A gap that exists when real GDP exceeds potential GDP and that brings a rising price level.

In Figure 14.11(b), aggregate supply is AS_1 and a decrease in aggregate demand from AD_1 to AD_2 moves real GDP below full employment. There is a **deflationary gap**—a gap that brings a falling price level. The people who are lucky enough to have jobs see the buying power of their wages rise and firms' profits shrink. In these circumstances, and with a labor surplus, the money wage rate gradually falls and the aggregate supply curve shifts rightward. Eventually, it reaches AS_2, where real GDP is back at potential GDP.

Deflationary gap
A gap that exists when potential GDP exceeds real GDP and that brings a falling price level.

FIGURE 14.11
Adjustments Toward Full Employment

Practice Online

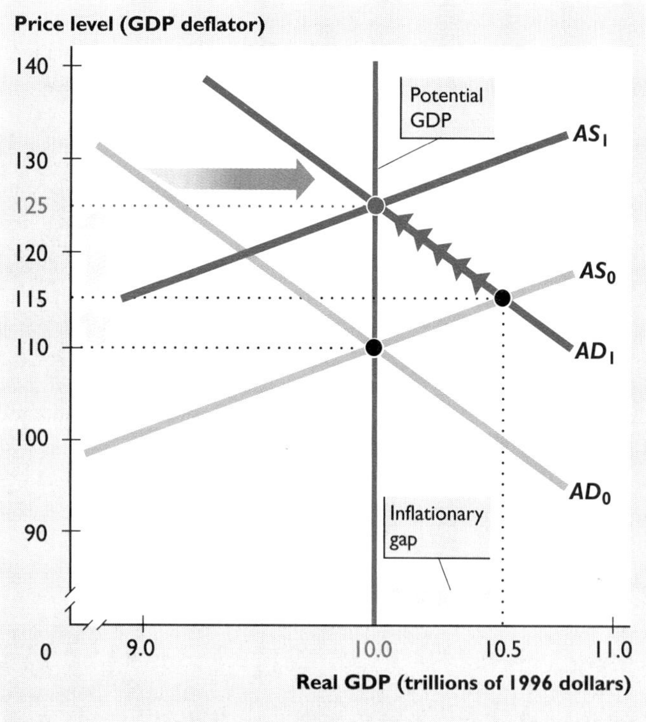

(a) Adjustment to full employment from increase in *AD*

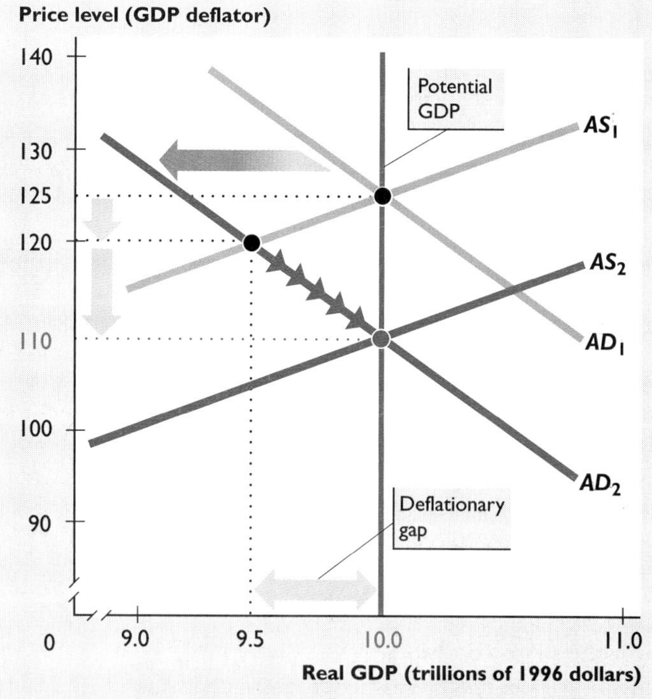

(b) Adjustment to full employment from decrease in *AD*

In part (a), real GDP exceeds potential GDP—an inflationary gap. The money wage rate rises, aggregate supply decreases, real GDP decreases, and the price level rises.

In part (b), potential GDP exceeds real GDP—a deflationary gap. The money wage rate falls, aggregate supply increases, real GDP increases, and the price level falls.

Eye on the U.S. Economy

The National Bureau Calls a Recession

The NBER's Business Cycle Dating Committee announced in November 2001 that a peak in business activity occurred in the U.S. economy in March 2001. So, according to the NBER committee, the expansion that began in March 1991 ended in March 2001 and a recession began. The expansion lasted exactly 10 years and was the longest that the NBER has observed.

To identify the date of the cycle peak, the NBER committee looked at industrial production, employment, real income, and wholesale and retail sales. But they paid most attention to employment.

You can see the employment cycle in part (a) of the figure, which shows that employment peaked in March 2001. The other factors considered by the NBER didn't peak in March but didn't contradict the employment numbers, so the committee was clear that March was the peak month.

Part (a) of the figure also shows that employment reached a trough in April 2002. But the trough was shallow, and in November 2002, the NBER reported that it was not yet ready to define the month of the business cycle trough.

The committee says that it gives relatively little weight to real GDP because it is measured only quarterly and is subject to ongoing and sometimes large revisions. Nonetheless, it is interesting to see what real GDP tells us. And long enough after the event, the revisions to real GDP are complete, so the numbers do provide a good indicator of the overall level of economic activity.

Part (b) of the figure shows the real GDP cycle. You can see that through 2000, real GDP exceeded potential GDP and there was an inflationary gap. Real GDP was shrinking during the first quarter of 2001, before the NBER says the recession began. In June 2001, real GDP was close to potential GDP, and after June, a deflationary gap opened up.

The real GDP trough occurred between the third and fourth quarters of 2001, after which the economy was expanding. But the expansion was not strong enough to eliminate the deflationary gap, which persisted through 2002.

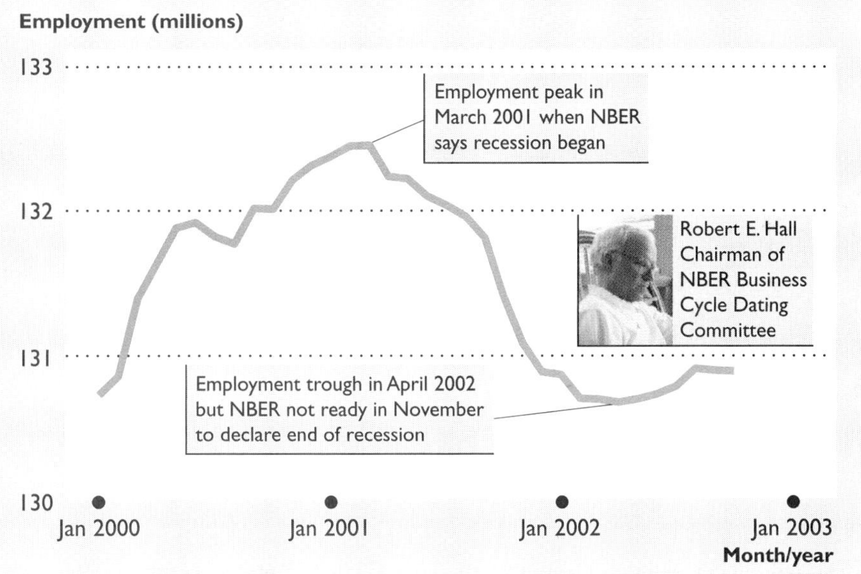

(a) The employment cycle

(b) The real GDP cycle

SOURCES: Bureau of Labor Statistics, Bureau of Economic Analysis, and Congressional Budget Office.

CHECKPOINT 14.4

Study Guide **pp. 205–208**

Practice Online 14.4

4 **Explain how fluctuations in aggregate demand and aggregate supply create the business cycle.**

Practice Problem 14.4

In the U.S economy, real GDP equals potential GDP. Then the following events occur one at a time:

- A deep recession hits the world economy.
- The world oil price rises by a large amount.
- U.S. businesses expect future profits to fall.

a. Explain the effect of each event on aggregate demand and aggregate supply in the United States.

b. Explain the effect of each event separately on the U.S. real GDP and price level.

c. Explain the combined effect of all the events together on the U.S. real GDP and price level.

d. Which event, if any, brings stagflation?

Exercise 14.4

In the Canadian economy, real GDP equals potential GDP. Then the following events occur one at a time:

- The world economy goes into a strong expansion.
- World oil price tumbles.
- Canadian businesses expect future profits to rise.

a. Explain the effect of each event on aggregate demand and aggregate supply in Canada.

b. Explain the effect of each event separately on Canadian real GDP and price level.

c. Explain the combined effect of all the events together on Canadian real GDP and price level.

FIGURE 1

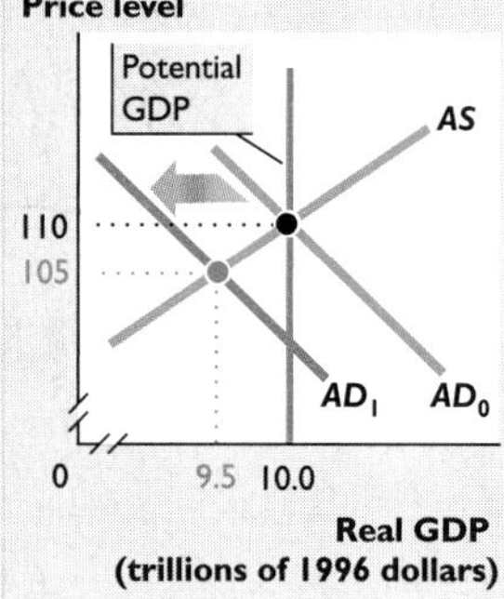

FIGURE 2

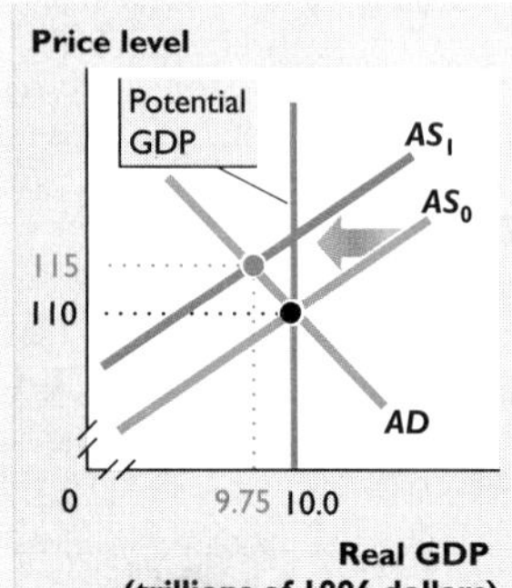

Solution to Practice Problem 14.4

a. A deep recession in the world economy decreases U.S. aggregate demand. A rise in the world oil price decreases U.S. aggregate supply. A fall in expected future profits decreases U.S. aggregate demand.

b. A deep recession in the world economy decreases U.S. aggregate demand. The *AD* curve shifts leftward. U.S. real GDP decreases, and the price level falls (Figure 1). A rise in the world oil price decreases U.S. aggregate supply. The *AS* curve shifts leftward. U.S. real GDP decreases, and the price level rises (Figure 2). A fall in expected future profits decreases U.S. aggregate demand. The *AD* curve shifts leftward. U.S. real GDP decreases, and the price level falls (Figure 1).

c. All three events decrease U.S. real GDP. The deep recession in the world economy and the fall in expected future profits decrease the price level. The rise in the world oil price increases the price level.

d. The oil price increase brings stagflation because it decreases aggregate supply, lowers equilibrium real GDP, and raises the price level.

CHAPTER CHECKPOINT

Key Points

1 Provide a technical definition of recession and describe the history of the U.S. business cycle.

- A recession is a decrease in real GDP that lasts for at least two quarters.
- U.S. recessions have been getting shorter, and expansions have been getting longer.

2 Explain the influences on aggregate supply.

- The aggregate supply curve slopes upward because with a given money wage rate, a rise in the price level lowers the real wage rate, increases the quantity of labor demanded, and increases the quantity of real GDP supplied.
- A change in potential GDP, a change in the money wage rate, or a change in the money price of other resources changes aggregate supply.

3 Explain the influences on aggregate demand.

- The aggregate demand curve slopes downward because a rise in the price decreases the buying power of money, raises the real interest rate, and raises the real price of domestic goods compared with foreign goods, and decreases the quantity of real GDP demanded.
- A change in expected future income, inflation, and profits, a change in fiscal policy and monetary policy, and a change in the foreign exchange rate and foreign real GDP change aggregate demand—the aggregate demand curve shifts.

4 Explain how fluctuations in aggregate demand and aggregate supply create the business cycle.

- Aggregate demand and aggregate supply determine real GDP and the price level.
- Business cycles occur because aggregate demand and aggregate supply fluctuate.
- Away from full employment, gradual adjustment of the money wage rate moves real GDP toward potential GDP.

Key Terms

Exercises

FIGURE 1

1. Figure 1 shows real GDP in Germany from the first quarter of 1991 to the last quarter of 1994.
   a. In which quarter was Germany at a business-cycle peak?
   b. In which quarter was Germany at a business-cycle trough?
   c. Did Germany experience a recession during these years?
   d. In what years did Germany experience an expansion?

2. Over the course of the most recent U.S. business cycles, real GDP and the unemployment rate fluctuated in opposite directions. (See p. 344.)
   a. Did real GDP reach a peak at the same time that the unemployment rate reached its lowest level?
   b. Did real GDP reach a trough at the same time that the unemployment rate reached its highest level?
   c. Which of these two indicators begins to signal recession first?
   d. Which of these two indicators begins to signal expansion first?

3. Over the course of the most recent U.S. business cycles, real GDP and the inflation rate fluctuated together. (See p. 344.)
   a. Did real GDP reach a peak at the same time that the inflation rate reached its peak?
   b. Did real GDP reach a trough at the same time that the inflation rate reached its trough?
   c. Which of these two indicators begins to signal recession first?
   d. Which of these two indicators begins to signal expansion first?

4. At the beginning of 2001, the United States was at full employment.
   a. Suppose that in 2001, major union wage settlements pushed the money wage rate upward by 10 percent and that all other influences on aggregate supply remained the same. Explain the effect of the rise in the money wage rate on aggregate supply.
   b. Suppose that in 2001, the price level increased and all other influences on aggregate supply remained the same. Explain the effect of the rise in the price level on aggregate supply.
   c. Over time, potential GDP grows. Explain the effect of the increase in potential GDP on aggregate supply.

5. In 2004, the United States is at full employment. Then in 2005,
   a. The Fed cuts the quantity of money, and all other influences on aggregate demand remain the same. Explain the effect of the cut in the quantity of money on aggregate demand in the short run.
   b. The federal government cuts taxes, and all other influences on aggregate demand remain the same. Explain the effect of the tax cut on aggregate demand in the short run.
   c. The world economy goes into recession. Explain the effect of the world recession on U.S. aggregate demand in the short run.
   d. The U.S. price level rises faster than the price level in the world economy. Explain the effect of U.S. inflation on U.S. aggregate demand in the short run.

6. In 2003, the Japanese economy is at a below full-employment equilibrium.
   a. Compare the amount of unemployment in Japan with Japan's natural unemployment.
   b. Compare Japan's real GDP with its potential GDP.
   c. What policies could Japan adopt to restore full employment?
   d. In your answer to exercise **6c**, would any of the policies create inflation? Explain.

7. Table 1 gives Canada's aggregate demand and aggregate supply schedules in 2004.
   a. Plot the aggregate demand curve.
   b. Plot the aggregate supply curve.
   c. What is the macroeconomic equilibrium?
   d. If potential GDP in Canada is $800 billion, what is the type of macroeconomic equilibrium?

TABLE 1

Price level (GDP deflator)	Real GDP demanded	Real GDP supplied
	(billions of 1992 dollars)	
90	900	600
100	850	700
110	800	800
120	750	900
130	700	1,000

8. Use the information provided in Table 1 together with the information that potential GDP is $800 billion to draw an *AS-AD* graph of the economy of Canada and then
   a. Show the effect of a rise in the world oil price on your *AS-AD* graph. Does it change aggregate supply or aggregate demand, and in what direction?
   b. Following the increase in the world price of oil, what is the new short-run equilibrium?
   c. What is the adjustment process that now begins to restore full employment? Do you expect that process to work slowly or rapidly? Why?

9. Use the information provided in Table 1 together with the information that potential GDP is $800 billion to draw an *AS-AD* graph of the economy of Canada and then
   a. Show the effect of a rise in the quantity of money in Canada on your *AS-AD* graph. Does it change aggregate supply or aggregate demand, and in what direction?
   b. Following the increase in the quantity of money, what is the new short-run equilibrium?
   c. What is the adjustment process that now begins to restore full employment? Do you expect that process to work slowly or rapidly? Why?

10. Use the information provided in Table 1 together with the information that potential GDP is $800 billion to draw an *AS-AD* graph of the economy of Canada and then
   a. Show the effect of a global recession on your *AS-AD* graph. Does the global recession change aggregate supply or aggregate demand, and in what direction?
   b. Following the onset of the global recession, what is the new short-run equilibrium?
   c. What is the adjustment process that now begins to restore full employment? Do you expect that process to work slowly or rapidly? Why?

11. For each of the events you analyzed in exercises 8 to 10, explain what happens to the unemployment rate and the real wage rate
   a. In the move to the initial short-run equilibrium.
   b. In the adjustment toward the new long-run equilibrium.

Critical Thinking

12. Review the NBER committee's task of identifying the correct date for the onset of recession in 2001.
    a. Do you think the committee got the date of the onset of recession right?
    b. Do you think the committee was correct in November 2002 to wait for more evidence before declaring the recession over?
    c. Do you think the government rather than the NBER should determine the dates of recessions and expansions?
13. Because fluctuations in the world oil price make our economy fluctuate, someone suggests that we should vary the tax rate on oil, lowering the tax when the world oil price rises and increasing the tax when the world oil price falls, to stabilize the oil price in the U.S. market.
    a. How do you think such an action would influence aggregate demand?
    b. How do you think such an action would influence aggregate supply?
    c. Lay out the arguments for and against such a policy.
14. Recessions have been getting shorter, and expansions have been getting longer.
    a. When did the change in average length of recessions and expansions occur?
    b. Can you think of some reasons why this change in the business cycle might have occurred?
    c. What do you think of the view that policy actions designed to stabilize aggregate demand are responsible for this change in the business cycle?

Practice Online

Web Exercises

Use the links on your Foundations Web site to work the following exercises.

15. Visit the Web site of the National Bureau of Economic Research and read the announcements of November 2001 and November 2002 (and any later announcements made after this book was published).
    a. What factors did the NBER committee consider to determine the onset of the 2001 recession?
    b. Did the NBER committee look at real GDP? Why or why not?
    c. Why did the NBER committee have a hard time determining when the 2001–2002 recession ended?
    d. Where in the phases of the business cycle is the U.S. economy today (the day on which you are working this exercise).
16. Visit the Web site of the Economic Cycle Research Institute and obtain information on the dates of recessions and expansions in three countries other than the United States that interest you.
    a. Compare the cycles dates in the countries you've chosen with those in the United States.
    b. Compare the recessions in the three countries you've chosen and the United States.
    c. In which country do you think aggregate demand fluctuates most?
    d. The Economic Cycle Research Institute uses two definitions of the business cycle, one that is the same as the NBER definition and one called a "growth rate cycle." What is the difference between these two definitions? Which definition gives the higher frequency of recession?

CHAPTER 15

Aggregate Expenditure

CHAPTER CHECKLIST

When you have completed your study of this chapter, you will be able to

1. **Distinguish between autonomous expenditure and induced expenditure and explain how real GDP influences expenditure plans.**
2. **Explain how real GDP adjusts to achieve equilibrium expenditure.**
3. **Describe and explain the expenditure multiplier.**
4. **Derive the *AD* curve from equilibrium expenditure.**

Our economy grows, bringing ever-higher living standards, and inflation persists, bringing an ever-rising cost of living. But economic growth and inflation don't proceed at a constant pace. Instead, they ebb and flow in a business cycle. For example, we had a recession in 1991 when real GDP shrank for nine months. The rest of the 1990s brought a strong expansion. We had another recession that began in March 2001. The Fed repeatedly cut the interest rate in an attempt to keep spending growing and avoid recession. But firms cut employment, and recession began.

This chapter continues your exploration of the business cycle by studying the aggregate expenditure model—a model of the forces that make aggregate demand fluctuate. You will also explore the connection between aggregate expenditure and aggregate demand.

A QUICK REVIEW AND PREVIEW

Before we begin our exploration of the aggregate expenditure model, let's take stock of what we've learned and preview where we are heading.

The Economy at Full Employment

At full employment, real GDP equals potential GDP and the unemployment rate equals the natural unemployment rate. Potential GDP and the natural unemployment rate are determined by *real* factors and are independent of the price level.

The quantity of money and potential GDP determine the price level. Changes in the quantity of money change the price level, but they have no effect on potential GDP.

This description of the forces that determine real GDP and the price level applies only to the full-employment economy. Away from potential GDP, real and monetary factors interact to determine real GDP and the price level. But potential GDP is like an anchor around which the economy fluctuates in the business cycle.

Departures from Full Employment

We studied aggregate supply and aggregate demand and the *AS-AD* model in Chapter 14. Aggregate supply and aggregate demand determine equilibrium real GDP and the price level. And fluctuations in aggregate supply and aggregate demand bring fluctuations around full employment.

Our economy is like an ocean. Movements in the full-employment economy are the tides, and fluctuations around full employment are the waves. The forces that make the tides—the position of the moon and its gravitational pull—are like the real and money forces that determine potential GDP and the price level. The forces that make the waves—the interaction of the moon and wind—are like the interactions of real and money forces that make the economy fluctuate.

We're now going to learn more about the forces that bring fluctuations to aggregate demand.

Fixed Price Level

The interaction of aggregate demand and aggregate supply determine equilibrium real GDP and the price level simultaneously. But the forces that we want to isolate and put in clear view are hard to see if we consider the *simultaneous* adjustment of real GDP and the price level. So in the aggregate expenditure model, the price level is fixed. The model explains what determines the quantity of real GDP demanded and changes in that quantity *at a given price level*.

The aggregate expenditure model was originally designed to explain what happens in an economy in deep recession when firms can't cut their prices any further but can increase production without raising their prices, so the price level is actually fixed. But you can also think about this model as telling us about the forces that determine the quantity of real GDP demanded at any given price level.

15.1 EXPENDITURE PLANS AND REAL GDP

You've seen from the circular flows of income and expenditure (Chapter 5, p. 114–115) that aggregate expenditure equals the sum of

- Consumption expenditure, C
- Investment, I
- Government purchases of goods and services, G
- Net exports, NX

That is,

$$\text{Aggregate expenditure} = C + I + G + NX.$$

Planned and Unplanned Expenditures

Motorola decides to produce 11 million cell phones this year. The factors of production that it hires to produce these phones cost \$550 million. So the incomes generated and the value of production is \$550 million. Households, other firms, governments, and people in the rest of the world make their expenditure plans. Suppose they decide to buy 9 million Motorola phones. Their total expenditure on phones is \$450 million. Motorola plans to sell 10 million phones and add 1 million to its inventory. (Firms need inventories to smooth out short-term fluctuations in production and sales.) But at the end of the year Motorola is left with 2 million phones in inventory. Valuing this inventory at the cost of production, Motorola has invested \$100 million in an inventory of phones. Total expenditure on phones, including Motorola's investment in inventories, equals the value of phones produced and equals the incomes paid to produce the phones. But *planned* expenditure on phones is less than the value of the phones produced because Motorola planned to invest only \$50 million in new inventory.

This account of a year in the life of Motorola can be extended to the economy as a whole. Aggregate expenditure equals aggregate income and real GDP. But aggregate *planned* expenditure might not equal real GDP because firms can end up with larger or smaller inventories than they had intended. Firms make their production plans, the aggregate value of which is real GDP. They pay incomes that equal the value of production, so aggregate income equals real GDP. Households and governments make their planned purchases of goods and services, and net exports are as planned. Firms make their planned purchases of new buildings, plant, and equipment and their *planned* inventory changes. The total of all these spending plans is **aggregate planned expenditure**.

Aggregate planned expenditure
Planned consumption expenditure plus planned investment plus planned government purchases plus planned exports minus planned imports.

If aggregate planned expenditure equals real GDP, the change in firms' inventories is the planned change. But if aggregate planned expenditure exceeds real GDP, firms' inventories are smaller than planned; and if aggregate planned expenditure is less than real GDP, firms' inventories are larger than planned. Notice that *actual* expenditure, which equals *planned* expenditure plus the *unplanned* change in firms' inventories, always equals real GDP and aggregate income.

Unplanned changes in firms' inventories lead to changes in production and incomes. If unwanted inventories have piled up, firms decrease production, which decreases real GDP. If inventories have fallen below their target levels, firms increase production, which increases real GDP.

Autonomous Expenditure and Induced Expenditure

Continuing the story of Motorola, when the firm decreases production in 2004, the incomes of its workers and suppliers of other factors of production decrease. If most firms share Motorola's experience, aggregate income falls, and with lower incomes, people decrease their expenditures on all types of goods and services—including cell phones. So in 2004, Motorola sells even fewer phones than it sold in 2003. Where does this process end?

To begin to answer this question, we must again extend the Motorola story to the economy as a whole. Just as lower incomes bring a decrease in expenditure on cell phones, so lower *aggregate* income—lower real GDP—brings a decrease in expenditure on a wide range of goods and services. We divide aggregate expenditure into two components: autonomous expenditure and induced expenditure. **Autonomous expenditure** is the part of aggregate expenditure that does not respond to changes in real GDP. It equals investment plus government purchases, plus exports, plus the components of consumption expenditure and imports that are not influenced by real GDP. **Induced expenditure** is the part of aggregate expenditure that changes in response to a change in real GDP. It equals consumption expenditure minus imports (excluding the elements of consumption and imports that are part of autonomous expenditure).

Autonomous expenditure
The components of aggregate expenditure that do not change when real GDP changes.

Induced expenditure
The components of aggregate expenditure that change when real GDP changes.

Your next task is to learn more about the influence of real GDP on induced expenditure. We start with its influence on consumption expenditure.

The Consumption Function

The **consumption function** is the relationship between consumption expenditure and disposable income, other things remaining the same. *Disposable income* is aggregate income—GDP—minus net taxes. (Net taxes are taxes paid to the government minus transfer payments received from the government.)

Consumption function
The relationship between consumption expenditure and disposable income, other things remaining the same.

Households must either spend their disposable income on consumption or save it. A decision to spend a dollar on consumption is a decision not to save a dollar. The consumption decision and the saving decision is one decision.

Consumption Plans

For households and the economy as a whole, as disposable income increases, planned consumption expenditure increases. But the increase in planned consumption is less than the increase in disposable income. The table in Figure 15.1 shows a consumption schedule. It lists the consumption expenditure that people plan to undertake at each level of disposable income.

Figure 15.1 shows a consumption function based on the consumption schedule. Along the consumption function, the points labeled *A* through *F* correspond to the rows of the table. For example, point *E* shows that when disposable income is $8 trillion, consumption expenditure is $7.5 trillion. Along the consumption function, as disposable income increases, consumption expenditure increases.

At point *A* on the consumption function, consumption expenditure is $1.5 trillion even though disposable income is zero. This consumption expenditure is called *autonomous consumption*, and it is the amount of consumption expenditure that would take place in the short run, even if people had no current income. This consumption expenditure would be financed either by spending past savings or by borrowing.

FIGURE 15.1

The Consumption Function

Practice Online

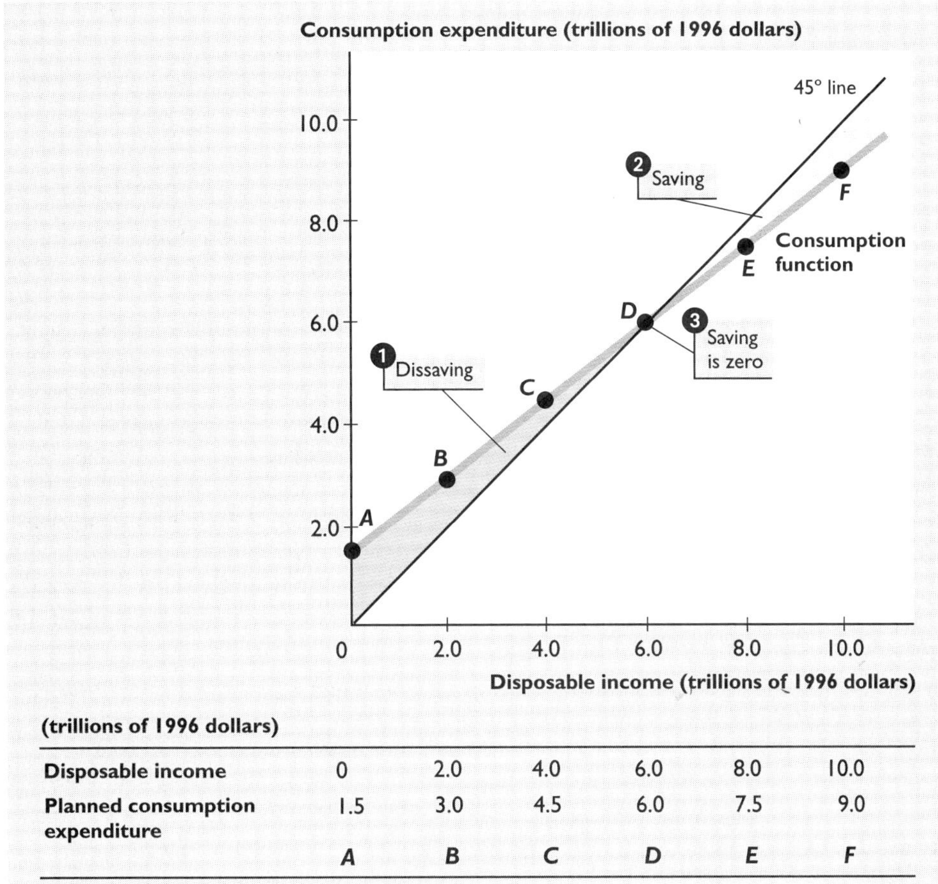

(trillions of 1996 dollars)						
Disposable income	0	2.0	4.0	6.0	8.0	10.0
Planned consumption expenditure	1.5	3.0	4.5	6.0	7.5	9.0
	A	*B*	*C*	*D*	*E*	*F*

The table shows consumption expenditure (and saving) plans at various levels of disposable income. The figure graphs these data as the consumption function. The figure also shows a 45° line along which consumption expenditure equals disposable income.

1. When the consumption function is above the 45° line, saving is negative (dissaving occurs).
2. When the consumption function is below the 45° line, saving is positive.
3. At the point where the consumption function intersects the 45° line, all disposable income is consumed and saving is zero.

Figure 15.1 also shows a 45° line. Because the scale on the x-axis measures disposable income and the scale on the y-axis measures consumption expenditure, and because the two scales are equal, along the 45° line consumption expenditure equals disposable income. So the 45° line serves as a reference line for comparing consumption expenditure and disposable income. Between *A* and *D*, consumption expenditure exceeds disposable income; between *D* and *F*, disposable income exceeds consumption expenditure; and at point *D*, consumption expenditure equals disposable income.

You can see saving in Figure 15.1. When consumption expenditure exceeds disposable income (and the consumption function is above the 45° line), saving is negative—called *dissaving*. When consumption expenditure is less than disposable income (the consumption function is below the 45° line), saving is positive. And when consumption expenditure equals disposable income (the consumption function intersects the 45° line), saving is zero.

When consumption expenditure exceeds disposable income, past savings are used to pay for current consumption. Such a situation cannot last forever, but it can and does occur if disposable income falls temporarily.

Marginal Propensity to Consume

Marginal propensity to consume
The fraction of a change in disposable income that is spent on consumption—the change in consumption expenditure divided by the change in disposable income that brought it about.

The **marginal propensity to consume** (*MPC*) is the fraction of a change in disposable income that is spent on consumption. It is calculated as the change in consumption expenditure divided by the change in disposable income that brought it about. That is,

$$MPC = \frac{\text{Change in consumption expenditure}}{\text{Change in disposable income}}.$$

Suppose that when disposable income increases from \$6 trillion to \$8 trillion, consumption expenditure increases from \$6 trillion to \$7.5 trillion. The \$2 trillion increase in disposable income increases consumption expenditure by \$1.5 trillion. Using these numbers in the formula to calculate the *MPC*,

$$MPC = \frac{\$1.5 \text{ trillion}}{\$2.0 \text{ trillion}} = 0.75.$$

The marginal propensity to consume tells us that when disposable income increases by \$1, consumption expenditure increases by 75¢.

Figure 15.2 shows that the *MPC* equals the slope of the consumption function. A \$2 trillion increase in disposable income from \$4 trillion to \$6 trillion is the base of the red triangle. The increase in consumption expenditure that results from this increase in income is \$1.5 trillion and is the height of the triangle. The slope of the consumption function is given by the formula "slope equals rise over run" and is \$1.5 trillion divided by \$2 trillion, which equals 0.75—the *MPC*.

FIGURE 15.2
Marginal Propensity to Consume

Practice Online

The marginal propensity to consume, *MPC*, is equal to the change in consumption expenditure divided by the change in disposable income, other things remaining the same. The slope of the consumption function measures the *MPC*.

In the figure, ❶ a \$2 trillion change in disposable income brings ❷ a \$1.5 trillion change in consumption expenditure, so ❸ the *MPC* equals \$1.5 trillion ÷ \$2.0 trillion = 0.75.

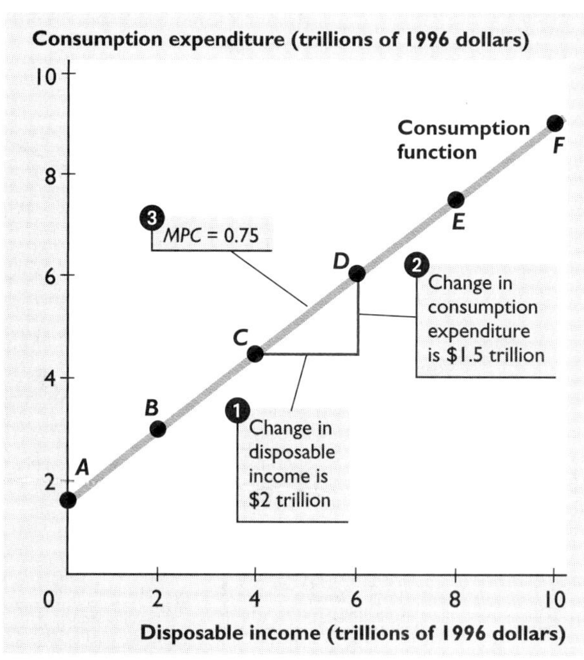

Other Influences on Consumption

Chapter 9 lists the factors that influence saving plans (see p. 218), and these same factors influence planned consumption expenditure. They are

- Disposable income
- Real interest rate
- The buying power of net assets
- Expected future disposable income

A change in disposable income leads to a change in consumption expenditure and a movement along the consumption function. A change in any of the other influences *shifts* the consumption function. For example, when the real interest rate falls or when the buying power of money or expected future income increases, consumption expenditure increases. Figure 15.3 shows the effects of these changes on the consumption function, which shifts upward from CF_0 to CF_1. Such a shift occurs during the expansion phase of the business cycle if a stock market boom increases the buying power of net assets and expected future income increases. A shift such as this occurred during the strong expansion of the late 1990s.

When the real interest rate rises or when the buying power of net assets or expected future income decreases, consumption expenditure decreases. Figure 15.3 also shows the effects of these changes on the consumption function, which shifts downward from CF_0 to CF_2. Such a shift occurs during a recession if a stock market crash decreases the buying power of net assets and expected future income decreases. A shift such as this occurred during the Great Depression of the 1930s.

FIGURE 15.3
Shifts in the Consumption Function

Practice Online

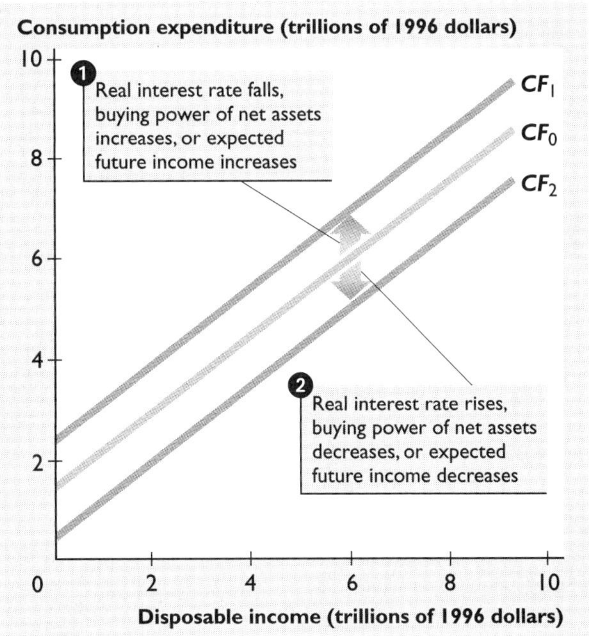

1. A fall in the real interest rate or an increase in either the buying power of net assets or expected future income increases consumption expenditure and shifts the consumption function upward from CF_0 to CF_1.
2. A rise in the real interest rate or a decrease in either the buying power of net assets or expected future income decreases consumption expenditure and shifts the consumption function downward from CF_0 to CF_2.

The U.S. Consumption Function

Each blue dot in the figure represents consumption expenditure and disposable income in the United States for a year between 1960 and 2002 (labeled at five-year intervals).

The line labeled CF_0 is an estimate of the U.S. consumption function for the period from 1960 to 1990. The line labeled CF_1 is an estimate of the U.S. consumption function in 2000.

The slope of the U.S. consumption function—the marginal propensity to consume—is 0.87, which means that a $1 increase in disposable income brings an 87¢ increase in consumption expenditure.

The consumption function shifted upward during the 1990s as influences on consumption expenditure other than disposable income changed. Of these other influences, rising expected future income and the rising stock market were the most important. They brought a steady upward shift in the consumption function.

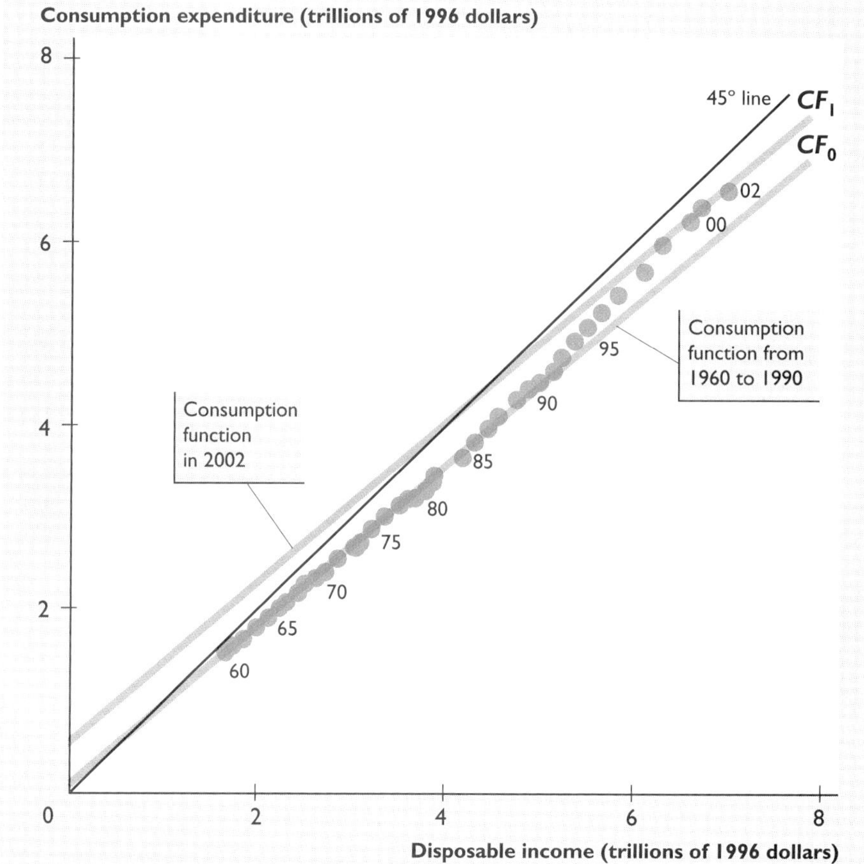

Source: Bureau of Economic Analysis

Imports and GDP

Imports are the other major component of induced expenditure. Many factors influence U.S. imports, but in the short run, one factor dominates: U.S. real GDP. Other things remaining the same, an increase in U.S. real GDP brings an increase in U.S. imports. The reason for this influence is that an increase in real GDP is also an increase in income. As incomes increase, people increase their expenditures on most goods and services. Because many goods and services are imported, an increase in incomes brings an increase in imports.

Marginal propensity to import
The fraction of an increase in real GDP that is spent on imports—the change in imports divided by the change in real GDP.

The relationship between imports and real GDP is described by the **marginal propensity to import**, which is the fraction of an increase in real GDP that is spent on imports.

$$\text{Marginal propensity to import} = \frac{\text{Change in imports}}{\text{Change in real GDP}}.$$

For example, if, with other things remaining the same, a $2 trillion increase in real GDP increases imports by $0.3 trillion, then the marginal propensity to import is 0.15.

CHECKPOINT 15.1

1 Distinguish between autonomous expenditure and induced expenditure and explain how real GDP influences expenditure plans.

Study Guide pp. 214–217

Practice Online 15.1

Practice Problems 15.1

1. If the marginal propensity to consume is 0.8 and if disposable income increases by $0.5 trillion, by how much will consumption expenditure change?
2. If Americans decrease the fraction of each dollar of disposable income they spend on consumption, how will the U.S. consumption function change?
3. If Americans decide to decrease consumption expenditure by a fixed number of dollars, how will the U.S. consumption function change?
4. Suppose that expected future disposable income increases. Explain how this change in expectation will influence the consumption function.
5. Figure 1 shows the Canadian consumption function. Calculate the marginal propensity to consume and autonomous consumption in Canada.

FIGURE 1

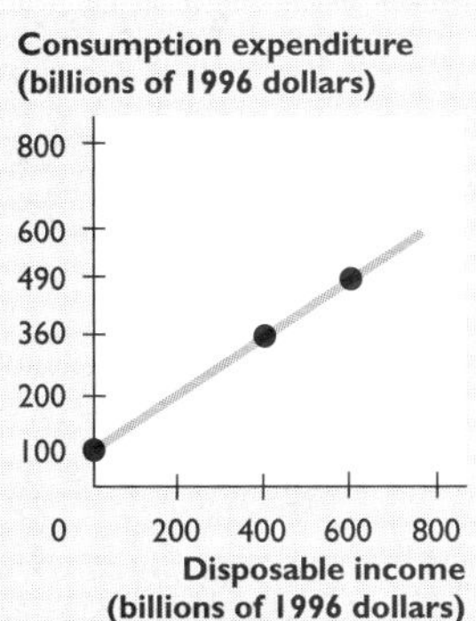

Exercises 15.1

1. The marginal propensity to consume in Japan is less than that in the United States, and for any amount of real GDP, Americans spend more on consumption than do the Japanese. Compare the consumption functions in Japan and the United States.
2. As China becomes richer, we expect that the marginal propensity to consume in China will decrease. What effect will this decrease have on the consumption function in China?
3. Suppose that the real interest rate in Japan rises. Explain how this change will influence the Japanese consumption function.
4. In 2002, autonomous consumption in the United Kingdom was £150 billion and the marginal propensity to consume was 0.9. Plot the U.K. consumption function.
5. The marginal propensity to import is higher in Singapore than it is in the United States. The growth rate of real GDP in Singapore exceeds that in the United States. Which country's imports grow more quickly and why?

Solutions to Practice Problems 15.1

1. Consumption expenditure will increase by $0.4 trillion, which is 0.8 multiplied by the change in disposable income of $0.5 trillion.
2. The marginal propensity to consume will decrease, so the slope of the consumption function will become less steep.
3. Autonomous consumption decreases, so the consumption function shifts downward.
4. Consumption expenditure will increase, and the consumption function will shift upward.
5. When disposable income increases by $200 billion, consumption expenditure increases by $130 billion. The *MPC* is $130 billion ÷ $200 billion = 0.65. Autonomous consumption (consumption expenditure that is independent of disposable income) equals the *y*-axis intercept and is $100 billion (Figure 2).

FIGURE 2

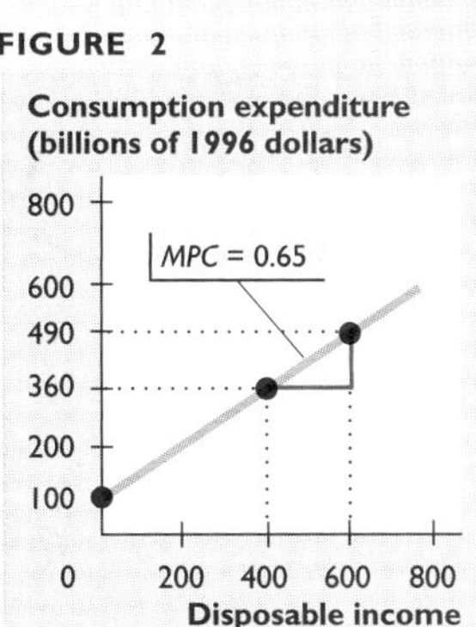

15.2 EQUILIBRIUM EXPENDITURE

You are now going to discover how, with a fixed price level, aggregate expenditure plans interact to determine real GDP. First we will study the relationship between aggregate planned expenditure and real GDP. Then we'll study the forces that make aggregate planned expenditure and actual expenditure equal.

An aggregate expenditure schedule and an aggregate expenditure curve describe the relationship between aggregate planned expenditure and real GDP.

Aggregate Planned Expenditure and Real GDP

You've seen that consumption expenditure increases when disposable income increases. Disposable income equals aggregate income—real GDP—minus net taxes, so disposable income and consumption expenditure increase when real GDP increases. We use this link between consumption expenditure and real GDP to determine equilibrium expenditure.

The table in Figure 15.4 sets out an aggregate expenditure schedule together with the components of aggregate planned expenditure. All the variables are measured in real (constant dollar) values. To calculate aggregate planned expenditure at a given real GDP, we add the various components together.

The first column of the table shows real GDP, and the second column shows the consumption expenditure generated by each level of real GDP. A $3 trillion increase in real GDP generates a $2.25 trillion increase in consumption expenditure—the *MPC* is 0.75. The next three columns show investment, government purchases of goods and services, and exports. These items do not depend on real GDP. They are autonomous expenditure. Investment is $2 trillion, government purchases are $1 trillion, and exports are $1.5 trillion. The next column shows imports, which increase as real GDP increases. A $3 trillion increase in real GDP generates a $0.75 trillion increase in imports. The marginal propensity to import is 0.25.

The final column shows aggregate planned expenditure—the sum of planned consumption expenditure, investment, government purchases of goods and services, and exports minus imports.

Figure 15.4 plots an aggregate expenditure curve. Real GDP is shown on the *x*-axis, and aggregate planned expenditure is shown on the *y*-axis. The aggregate expenditure curve is the red line *AE*. Points *A* through *F* on that curve correspond to the rows of the table. The *AE* curve is a graph of aggregate planned expenditure (the last column) plotted against real GDP (the first column).

Figure 15.4 also shows the components of aggregate expenditure. The horizontal lines in the figure show the constant components of aggregate expenditure—investment (*I*), government purchases of goods and services (*G*), and exports (*X*). The line labeled $C + I + G + X$ adds consumption expenditure to the constant components.

Finally, to construct the *AE* curve, subtract imports (*M*) from the $C + I + G + X$ line. Aggregate expenditure is expenditure on U.S.-made goods and services. But $C + I + G + X$ includes expenditure on imported goods and services. For example, if a student buys a Honda motorbike that is made in Japan, the student's expenditure is part of *C*, but it is not an expenditure on a U.S.-produced good. To find the expenditure on U.S.-produced goods, we subtract the value of the imported motorbike.

Figure 15.4 shows that aggregate planned expenditure increases as real GDP increases. But notice that for each $1 increase in real GDP, aggregate planned

FIGURE 15.4
Aggregate Expenditure

Practice Online

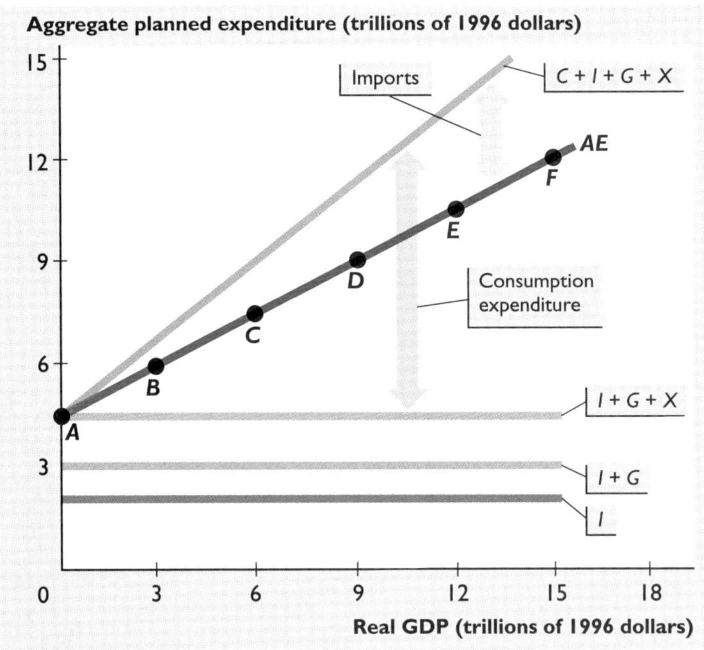

The aggregate expenditure schedule shows the relationship between aggregate planned expenditure and real GDP. For example, in row *B* of the table, when real GDP is \$3 trillion, aggregate planned expenditure is \$6 trillion (\$2.25 + \$2 + \$1 + \$1.5 – \$0.75). As real GDP increases, aggregate planned expenditure increases.

This relationship is graphed as the aggregate expenditure curve *AE*. The components of aggregate expenditure that increase with real GDP are consumption expenditure and imports. The other components–investment, government purchases, and exports–do not vary with real GDP.

	Real GDP (*Y*)	Consumption expenditure (*C*)	Investment (*I*)	Government purchases (*G*)	Exports (*X*)	Imports (*M*)	Aggregate planned expenditure (*AE* = *C* + *I* + *G* + *X* – *M*)
		Planned expenditure (trillions of 1996 dollars)					
A	0	0	2.00	1.00	1.50	0	4.50
B	3.00	2.25	2.00	1.00	1.50	0.75	6.00
C	6.00	4.50	2.00	1.00	1.50	1.50	7.50
D	9.00	6.75	2.00	1.00	1.50	2.25	9.00
E	12.00	9.00	2.00	1.00	1.50	3.00	10.50
F	15.00	11.25	2.00	1.00	1.50	3.75	12.00

expenditure increases by less than \$1. For example, when real GDP increases from \$9 trillion to \$12 trillion (row *D* to row *E* of the table), aggregate planned expenditure increases from \$9 trillion to \$10.5 trillion. A \$3 trillion increase in real GDP brings a \$1.5 trillion increase in aggregate planned expenditure. So a \$1 increase in real GDP brings a 50¢ increase in aggregate planned expenditure. This feature of the *AE* curve is important and plays a big role in determining equilibrium expenditure and the effect of a change in autonomous expenditure.

The *AE* curve summarizes the relationship between aggregate planned expenditure and real GDP. But what determines the point on the *AE* curve at which the economy operates? What determines actual aggregate expenditure?

Equilibrium Expenditure

Equilibrium expenditure
The level of aggregate expenditure that occurs when aggregate planned expenditure equals real GDP.

Equilibrium expenditure occurs when aggregate *planned* expenditure equals real GDP. In Figure 15.5(a) aggregate planned expenditure equals real GDP at all the points on the 45° line. Equilibrium occurs where the *AE* curve intersects the 45° line at point *D* with real GDP at $9 trillion. If real GDP is less than $9 trillion, aggregate planned expenditure exceeds real GDP; and if real GDP exceeds $9 trillion, aggregate planned expenditure is less than real GDP.

FIGURE 15.5
Equilibrium Expenditure

Practice Online

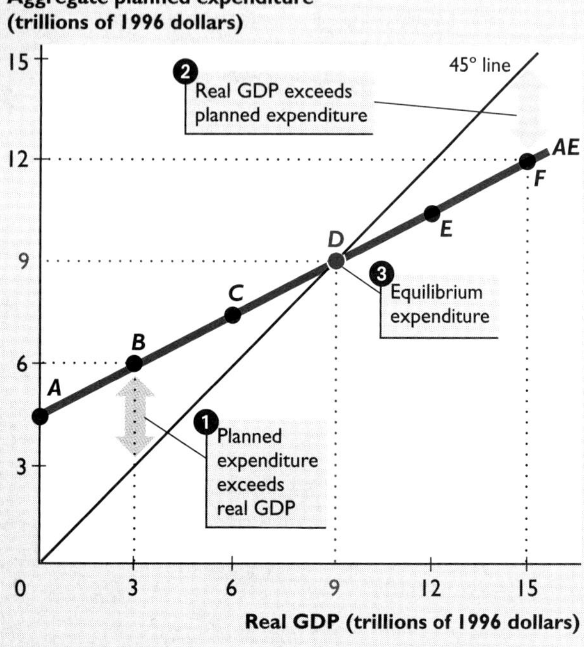

(a) Equilibrium expenditure

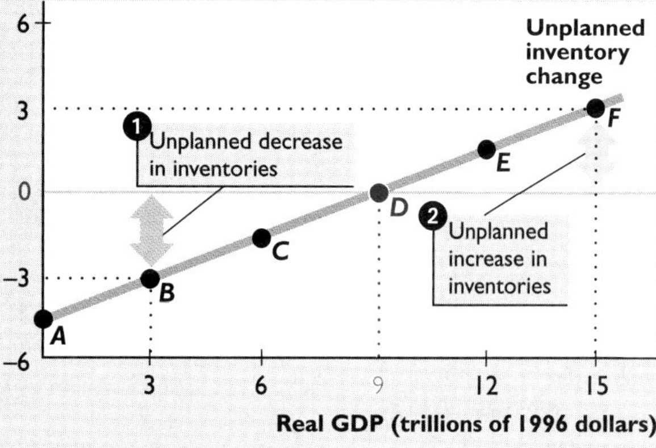

(b) Unplanned inventory change

	Real GDP	Aggregate planned expenditure	Unplanned inventory change
	(trillions of 1996 dollars)		
A	0	4.5	–4.5
B	3.0	6.0	–3.0
C	6.0	7.5	–1.5
D	9.0	9.0	0.0
E	12.0	10.5	1.5
F	15.0	12.0	3.0

The table shows expenditure plans and unplanned changes in inventories at different levels of real GDP. Part (a) illustrates equilibrium expenditure, and part (b) shows the unplanned inventory changes that bring changes in real GDP.

❶ When aggregate planned expenditure exceeds real GDP, an unplanned decrease in inventories occurs. Firms increase production, and real GDP increases.

❷ When real GDP exceeds aggregate planned expenditure, an unplanned increase in inventories occurs. Firms decrease production, and real GDP decreases.

❸ When aggregate planned expenditure equals real GDP, there are no unplanned inventory changes and real GDP remains at its equilibrium level.

Convergence to Equilibrium

At equilibrium expenditure, production plans and spending plans agree, and there is no reason for production or spending to change. But when aggregate planned expenditure and actual aggregate expenditure are unequal, production plans and spending plans are misaligned, and a process of convergence toward equilibrium expenditure occurs. Throughout this convergence process, real GDP adjusts.

What are the forces that move aggregate expenditure toward equilibrium? To answer this question, we look at a situation in which aggregate expenditure is away from equilibrium. Suppose that in Figure 15.5, real GDP is $3 trillion. With real GDP at $3 trillion, actual aggregate expenditure is also $3 trillion. But aggregate planned expenditure is $6 trillion (point *B* in Figure 15.5a). Aggregate planned expenditure exceeds actual expenditure. When people spend $6 trillion and firms produce goods and services worth $3 trillion, firms' inventories decrease by $3 trillion (point *B* in Figure 15.5b). Because the change in inventories is part of investment, the decrease in inventories decreases actual investment. So actual investment is $3 trillion less than planned investment.

Real GDP doesn't remain at $3 trillion for long. Firms have inventory targets based on their sales. When inventories fall below target, firms increase production. Suppose that they increase production by $3 trillion. Real GDP increases by $3 trillion to $6 trillion. At this real GDP, aggregate planned expenditure rises to $7.5 trillion (point *C* in Figure 15.5a). The unplanned decrease in inventories is now $1.5 trillion, so firms increase production yet again. Suppose that they increase production by another $3 trillion to $9 trillion. At this real GDP, aggregate planned expenditure rises to $9 trillion (point *D* in Figure 15.5a). The unplanned inventory change is zero, and firms have no reason to change production. Real GDP and aggregate expenditure are in equilibrium.

You can do a thought experiment similar to the one we've just done but starting with a level of real GDP greater than equilibrium expenditure. In this case, planned expenditure is less than actual expenditure, inventories pile up, and firms cut production. Real GDP decreases, and it will continue to decrease until it reaches its equilibrium level of $9 trillion.

Back at Motorola

You can now answer the question about Motorola that we left dangling earlier in this chapter. Recall that faced with unwanted inventories, Motorola and most other firms cut production in 2004. So Motorola sells even fewer phones in 2004 than in 2003. We asked: Where does this process end? It ends when equilibrium expenditure is reached. The economy arrives at equilibrium expenditure because a $1 increase in real GDP brings a less than $1 increase in aggregate planned expenditure (and a $1 decrease in real GDP brings a less than $1 decrease in aggregate planned expenditure).

When aggregate planned expenditure exceeds real GDP, firms increase production and real GDP increases. Aggregate planned expenditure increases, but real GDP increases by more than planned expenditure, so eventually the gap between planned expenditure and actual expenditure closes. Similarly, when aggregate planned expenditure is less than real GDP, firms cut production and real GDP decreases. Aggregate planned expenditure decreases, but real GDP decreases by more than planned expenditure, so again, eventually, the gap between planned expenditure and actual expenditure is closed.

Eye on the Past

Say's Law and Keynes' Principle of Effective Demand

During the Industrial Revolution, which began around 1760 and lasted for 70 years, technological change was rapid. People have talked about the "new economy" of the 1990s. But the 1990s was just another phase of a process that began in the truly new economy of the late 1700s. The pace of change in economic life during those years was unprecedented. Never before had old jobs been destroyed and new jobs created on such a scale. In this environment of rapid economic change, people began to wonder whether the economy could create enough jobs and a high enough level of demand to ensure that people would buy all the things that the new industrial economy could produce.

A French economist, Jean-Baptiste Say, provided the assurance that people were looking for. Born in 1767 (he was 9 years old when Adam Smith's *Wealth of Nations* was published—see Chapter 1, p. 10), Say suffered the wrath of Napoleon for his conservative call for smaller and leaner government and was the most famous economist of his era. His book *A Treatise on Political Economy (Traité d'économie politique)*, published in 1803, became the best-selling university economics textbook in both Europe and America.

In this book, Say reasoned that *supply creates its own demand*—an idea that came to be called *Say's Law.*

You've seen Say's Law at work in the full-employment economy. The real wage rate adjusts to ensure that the quantity of labor demanded equals the quantity of labor supplied and real GDP equals potential GDP. The real interest rate adjusts to ensure that the quantity of investment demanded equals the quantity of saving supplied. Because saving equals income minus consumption expenditure, the equilibrium real interest rate ensures that consumption expenditure plus investment exactly equals potential GDP.

Say's Law came under attack at various times during the nineteenth century. But it came under an onslaught during the Great Depression of the 1930s. With a quarter of the labor force unemployed and real GDP at around three quarters of potential GDP, it seemed like a stretch to argue that supply creates its own demand. But there was no simple principle or slogan with which to replace Say's Law.

In the midst of the Great Depression, in 1936, a British economist, John Maynard Keynes, provided the catchphrase that the world was looking for: *effective demand.*

Born in England in 1883, Keynes was one of the outstanding people of the twentieth century. He was a prolific writer on economic issues, represented Britain at the Versailles peace conference at the end of World War I, and played a prominent role in creating the International Monetary Fund, which monitors the global macroeconomy today.

Keynes revolutionized macroeconomic thinking by turning Say's Law on its head. Supply does *not* create its own demand, and *effective demand* determines real GDP. If businesses fail to spend on new capital the amount that people plan to save, aggregate demand will be less than potential GDP. Prices and wages are sticky, and resources can become unemployed and remain unemployed indefinitely.

The aggregate expenditure model that you're studying in this chapter is the modern distillation of Keynes' idea.

Jean-Baptiste Say

John Maynard Keynes

CHECKPOINT 15.2

2 **Explain how real GDP adjusts to achieve equilibrium expenditure.**

Study Guide pp. 218–220

Practice Online 15.2

Practice Problem 15.2

Table 1 is a spreadsheet that gives the components of real GDP in billions of dollars.

a. Calculate aggregate planned expenditure when real GDP is $200 billion.
b. Calculate aggregate planned expenditure when real GDP is $600 billion.
c. Calculate equilibrium expenditure.
d. If real GDP is $200 billion, explain the process that moves the economy toward equilibrium expenditure.
e. If real GDP is $600 billion, explain the process that moves the economy toward equilibrium expenditure.

TABLE 1

	A	B	C	D	E	F	G
1		*Y*	*C*	*I*	*G*	*X*	*M*
2	*A*	100	110	50	60	60	15
3	*B*	200	170	50	60	60	30
4	*C*	300	230	50	60	60	45
5	*D*	400	290	50	60	60	60
6	*E*	500	350	50	60	60	75
7	*F*	600	410	50	60	60	90

Exercise 15.2

Figure 1 shows aggregate planned expenditure.

a. Calculate aggregate planned expenditure when real GDP is $8 billion.
b. Calculate aggregate planned expenditure when real GDP is $2 billion.
c. Calculate equilibrium expenditure.
d. If real GDP is $8 billion, explain the process that moves the economy toward equilibrium expenditure.
e. If real GDP is $2 billion, explain the process that moves the economy toward equilibrium expenditure.

FIGURE 1

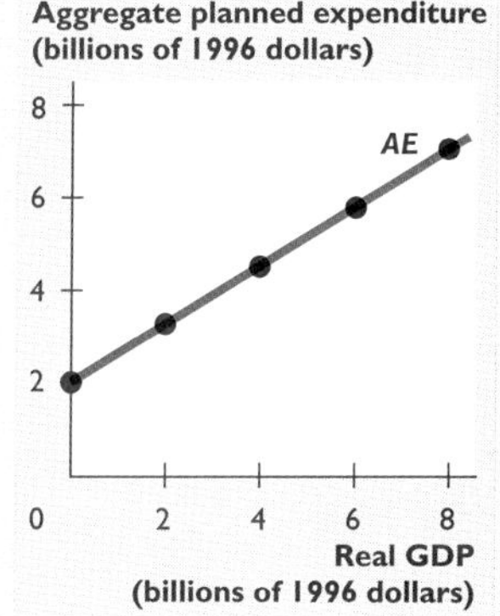

Solution to Practice Problem 15.2

a. Aggregate planned expenditure equals $C + G + I + X - M$. When real GDP is $200 billion, aggregate planned expenditure (in billions) equals $170 + $50 + $60 + $60 – $30, which equals $310 billion (row *B* of Table 1).

b. Aggregate planned expenditure equals $C + G + I + X - M$. When real GDP is $600 billion, aggregate planned expenditure (in billions) equals $410 + $50 + $60 + $60 – $90, which equals $490 billion (row *F* of Table 1).

c. Equilibrium expenditure occurs when aggregate planned expenditure equals real GDP. Equilibrium expenditure is $400 billion (row *D* of Table 1).

d. If real GDP is $200 billion, aggregate planned expenditure is $310 billion. Aggregate planned expenditure exceeds real GDP, so firms' inventories decrease. Expenditure plans are not fulfilled. Firms increase production to restore their inventories, and real GDP increases. As long as aggregate planned expenditure exceeds real GDP, firms will increase production to restore their inventories to their target level and real GDP will increase.

e. If real GDP is $600 billion, aggregate planned expenditure is $490 billion. Aggregate planned expenditure is less than real GDP, so firms' inventories increase. Firms cut production and try to reduce their inventories. Real GDP decreases. As long as aggregate planned expenditure is less than real GDP, firms' inventories will increase. Firms will cut production and try to reduce their inventories to their target level. Real GDP decreases.

15.3 THE EXPENDITURE MULTIPLIER

Multiplier
The amount by which a change in any component of autonomous expenditure is magnified or multiplied to determine the change that it generates in equilibrium expenditure and real GDP.

When investment increases, aggregate expenditure and real GDP also increase. But the increase in real GDP is larger than the increase in investment. The **multiplier** is the amount by which a change in investment (or any other component of autonomous expenditure) is magnified or multiplied to determine the change that it generates in equilibrium expenditure and real GDP.

The Basic Idea of the Multiplier

The growth of the Internet during the 1990s brought a large increase in investment in personal computers, servers, fiber-optic cables, satellites, and other communication and computing equipment. These investment expenditures increased aggregate expenditure and real GDP.

The increase in real GDP increased disposable income. The increase in disposable income increased consumption expenditure. And the increased consumption expenditure added even more to aggregate expenditure. Real GDP and disposable income increased further, and so did consumption expenditure.

The initial increase in investment brought an increase in aggregate expenditure that exceeded the increase in investment because it induced an increase in consumption expenditure.

The multiplier determines the magnitude of the increase in aggregate expenditure that results from an increase in investment or another component of autonomous expenditure.

Consumption expenditure decisions, imports, and income taxes that open a gap between disposable income and real GDP all influence the multiplier. But we can understand the basic idea of the multiplier more clearly if we temporarily ignore the effects of imports and income taxes and focus on the role of consumption expenditure.

Figure 15.6 illustrates the multiplier. The table shows an initial aggregate expenditure schedule, and the initial *AE* curve is AE_0. With this *AE* schedule and curve, equilibrium expenditure and real GDP are $9 trillion. You can see this equilibrium in row *B* of the table and where the curve AE_0 intersects the 45° line at point *B* in the figure.

Now suppose that investment increases by $0.5 trillion. What happens to equilibrium expenditure? Figure 15.6 shows the answer. When this increase in investment is added to the initial aggregate planned expenditure, aggregate planned expenditure increases by $0.5 trillion at each level of real GDP. The new *AE* curve is AE_1. The new equilibrium expenditure, highlighted in the table (row *D*'), occurs where AE_1 intersects the 45° line and is $11 trillion (point *D*'). At this real GDP, aggregate planned expenditure equals real GDP. The increase in equilibrium expenditure ($2 trillion) is larger than the increase in investment that brought it about ($0.5 trillion).

We've just analyzed the effects of an *increase* in investment. The same analysis applies to a *decrease* in investment. If initially the *AE* curve is AE_1, equilibrium expenditure and real GDP are $11 trillion. A decrease in investment of $0.5 trillion shifts the *AE* curve downward by $0.5 trillion to AE_0. Equilibrium expenditure decreases from $11 trillion to $9 trillion. The decrease in equilibrium expenditure ($2 trillion) is larger than the decrease in investment that brought it about ($0.5 trillion).

FIGURE 15.6
The Multiplier

Practice Online

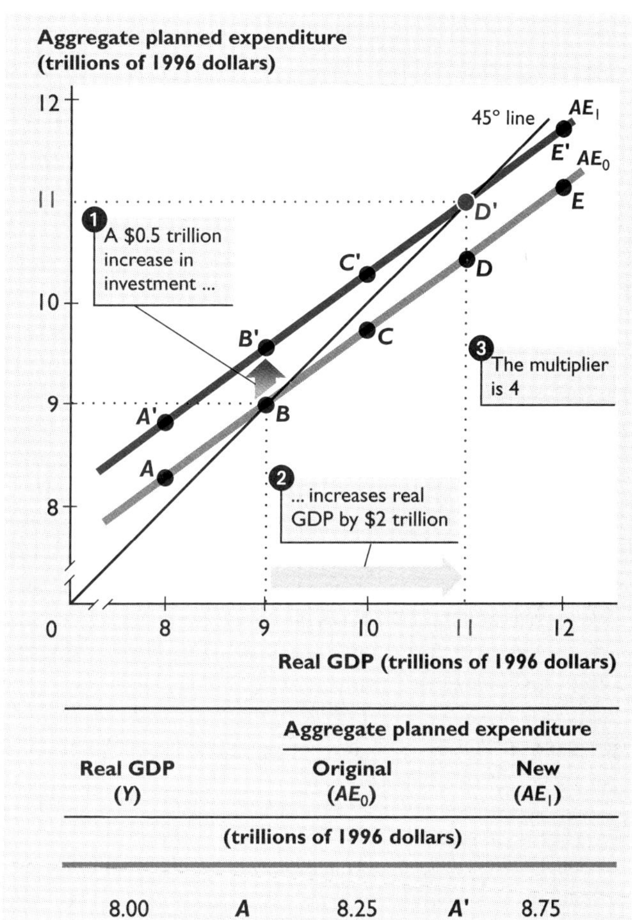

Real GDP (Y)		Aggregate planned expenditure: Original (AE_0)		Aggregate planned expenditure: New (AE_1)
		(trillions of 1996 dollars)		
8.00	*A*	8.25	*A'*	8.75
9.00	*B*	**9.00**	*B'*	9.50
10.00	*C*	9.75	*C'*	10.25
11.00	*D*	10.50	*D'*	**11.00**
12.00	*E*	11.25	*E'*	11.75

1. A $0.5 trillion increase in investment shifts the *AE* curve upward by $0.5 trillion from AE_0 to AE_1.
2. Equilibrium expenditure increases by $2 trillion from $9 trillion to $11 trillion.
3. The increase in equilibrium expenditure is 4 times the increase in autonomous expenditure, so the multiplier is 4.

The Size of the Multiplier

The multiplier is the amount by which a change in autonomous expenditure is multiplied to determine the change in equilibrium expenditure that it generates. To calculate the multiplier, we divide the change in equilibrium expenditure by the change in autonomous expenditure that generated it. That is,

$$\text{Multiplier} = \frac{\text{Change in equilibrium expenditure}}{\text{Change in autonomous expenditure}}.$$

The change in equilibrium expenditure also equals the change in real GDP, which we'll call ΔY. In Figure 15.6, the change in autonomous expenditure is a change in investment, which we'll call ΔI. The multiplier is

$$\text{Multiplier} = \frac{\Delta Y}{\Delta I}.$$

In Figure 15.6, equilibrium expenditure increases by \$2 trillion (ΔY = \$2 trillion) and investment increases by \$0.5 trillion (ΔI = \$0.5 trillion), so the multiplier is

$$\text{Multiplier} = \frac{\Delta Y}{\Delta I} = \frac{\$2 \text{ trillion}}{\$0.5 \text{ trillion}} = 4.$$

The multiplier is 4—real GDP changes by 4 times the change in investment.

Why Is the Multiplier Greater Than 1?

The multiplier is greater than 1 because an increase in autonomous expenditure induces further increases in aggregate expenditure—induced expenditure increases. If General Motors spends \$10 million on a new car assembly line, aggregate expenditure and real GDP immediately increase by \$10 million. Engineers and construction workers now have more income, and they spend part of the extra income on cars, microwave ovens, vacations, and a host of other goods and services. Real GDP now increases by the initial \$10 million plus the extra consumption expenditure induced by the \$10 million increase in income. The producers of cars, microwave ovens, vacations, and other goods now have increased incomes, and they in turn spend part of the increase in their incomes on consumption goods and services. Additional income induces additional expenditure, which creates additional income.

The Multiplier and the *MPC*

The magnitude of the muliplier depends on the marginal propensity to consume. To see why, let's do a calculation. Remember that we are temporarily ignoring imports and income taxes. The change in real GDP (ΔY) equals the change in consumption expenditure (ΔC) plus the change in investment (ΔI). That is,

$$\Delta Y = \Delta C + \Delta I.$$

But the change in consumption expenditure is determined by the change in real GDP and the marginal propensity to consume. It is

$$\Delta C = MPC \times \Delta Y.$$

Now substitute $MPC \times \Delta Y$ for ΔC in the previous equation:

$$\Delta Y = MPC \times \Delta Y + \Delta I.$$

Now solve for ΔY as

$$(1 - MPC) \times \Delta Y = \Delta I,$$

and rearrange the equation:

$$\Delta Y = \frac{1}{(1 - MPC)} \Delta I.$$

Finally, divide both sides of the previous equation by ΔI to give

$$\text{Multiplier} = \frac{\Delta Y}{\Delta I} = \frac{1}{(1 - MPC)}.$$

In Figure 15.6, the *MPC* is 0.75. So if we use the numbers in this figure,

$$\text{Multiplier} = \frac{\Delta Y}{\Delta I} = \frac{1}{(1 - 0.75)} = \frac{1}{0.25} = 4.$$

The greater the marginal proposity to consume, the larger is the multiplier. For example, if the marginal propensity to consume is 0.9, the multiplier is 10. (Use the above formula to check this proposition.) So far, we've ignored the effects of imports and income taxes on the multiplier. Let's now look at the influence of these two factors.

Imports and Income Taxes

The size of the multiplier depends, in general, not only on consumption decisions but also on imports and income taxes. Imports make the multiplier smaller than it otherwise would be. To see why, think about what happens following an increase in investment. The increase in investment increases real GDP, which in turn increases consumption expenditure. But part of the increase in expenditure is on imported goods and services, not U.S.-produced goods and services. Only expenditure on U.S.-produced goods and services increases U.S. real GDP. The larger the marginal propensity to import, the smaller is the change in U.S. real GDP that results from a change in autonomous expenditure.

Income taxes also make the multiplier smaller than it otherwise would be. Again, think about what happens following an increase in investment. The increase in investment increases real GDP. But with increased incomes, income tax payments increase and disposable income increases by less than the increase in real GDP. Because disposable income influences consumption expenditure, the increase in consumption expenditure is less than it would be if income tax payments had not changed.

Marginal tax rate
The fraction of a change in real GDP that is paid in income taxes—the change in tax payments divided by the change in real GDP.

The marginal tax rate determines the extent to which income tax payments change when real GDP changes. The **marginal tax rate** is the fraction of a change in real GDP that is paid in income taxes. The larger the marginal tax rate, the smaller are the changes in disposable income and real GDP that result from a given change in autonomous expenditure.

The marginal propensity to import and the marginal tax rate together with the marginal propensity to consume determine the multiplier. And their combined influence determines the slope of the *AE* curve. The general formula for the multiplier is

$$\text{Multiplier} = \frac{\Delta Y}{\Delta I} = \frac{1}{(1 - \text{Slope of } AE \text{ curve})}.$$

Figure 15.7 compares two situations. In Figure 15.7(a), there are no imports and no taxes. The slope of the *AE* curve equals the *MPC*, which is 0.75, so the multiplier is 4 (as we calculated above). In Figure 15.7(b), imports and income taxes decrease the slope of the *AE* curve to 0.5. So in this case,

$$\text{Multiplier} = \frac{\Delta Y}{\Delta I} = \frac{1}{(1 - 0.5)} = 2.$$

Over time, the value of the multiplier changes as the marginal tax rate, the marginal propensity to consume, and the marginal propensity to import change. These ongoing changes make the multiplier hard to predict. But they do not change the fundamental fact that an initial change in autonomous expenditure leads to a magnified change in equilibrium expenditure.

FIGURE 15.7
The Multiplier and the Slope of the *AE* Curve

Practice Online

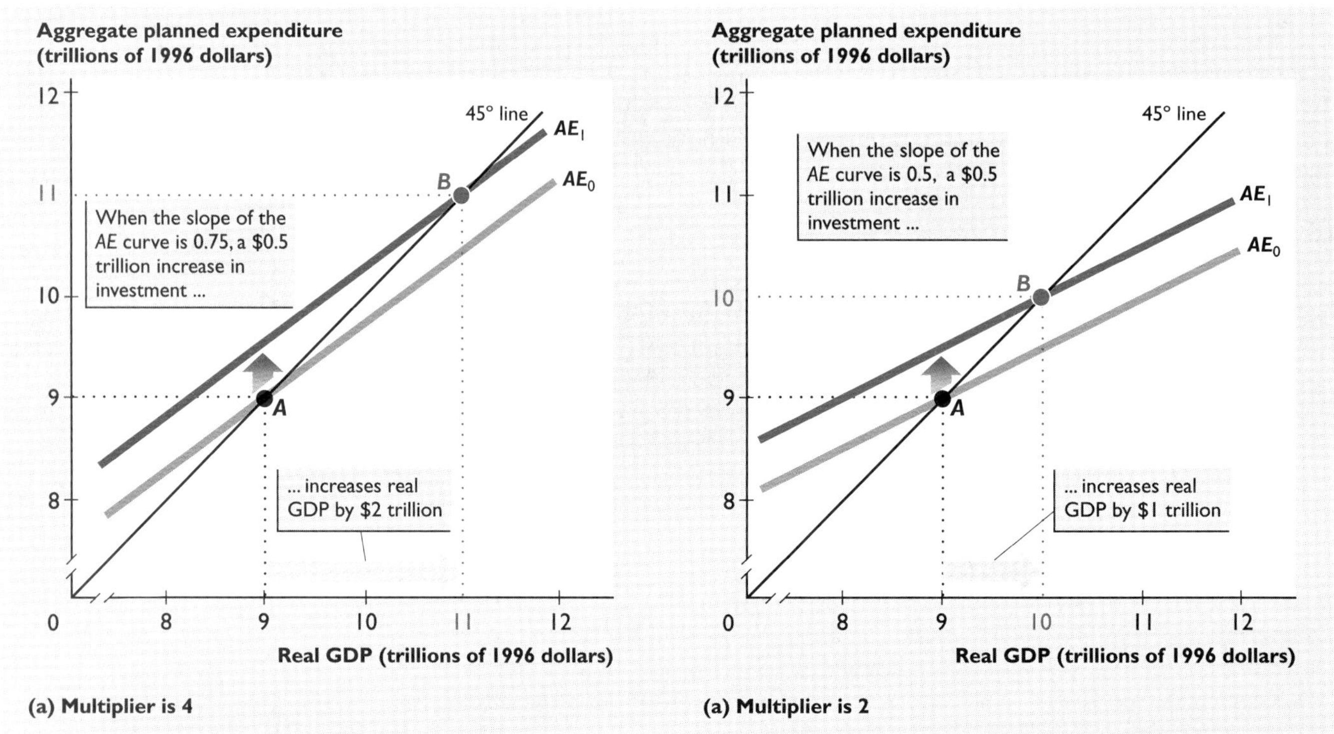

In part (a), with no imports and income taxes, the slope of the *AE* curve equals the marginal propensity to consume, which in this example is 0.75. The multiplier is 4.

In part (b), with imports and income taxes, the slope of the *AE* curve is less than the marginal propensity to consume. In this example, the slope of the *AE* curve is 0.5 and the multiplier is 2.

Business-Cycle Turning Points

Let's use what we've just learned to gain some insights into what happens at business-cycle turning points.

An expansion is triggered by an increase in autonomous expenditure. At the moment the economy turns the corner into expansion, aggregate planned expenditure exceeds real GDP. In this situation, firms see their inventories taking an unplanned dive. The expansion now begins. To meet their inventory targets, firms increase production, and real GDP begins to increase. This initial increase in real GDP brings higher incomes, and the higher incomes stimulate consumption expenditure. The multiplier process kicks in, and the expansion picks up speed.

The process works in reverse at a business cycle peak. A recession is triggered by a decrease in autonomous expenditure. At the moment the economy turns the corner into recession, real GDP exceeds aggregate planned expenditure. In this situation, firms see unplanned inventories piling up. The recession now begins. To reduce their inventories, firms cut production, and real GDP begins to decrease. This initial decrease in real GDP brings lower incomes, which cut consumption expenditure. The multiplier process reinforces the initial cut in autonomous expenditure, and the recession takes hold.

CHECKPOINT 15.3

3 **Describe and explain the expenditure multiplier.**

Study Guide pp. 220–223

Practice Online 15.3

Practice Problems 15.3

1. An economy has no imports or taxes, the *MPC* is 0.80, and real GDP is $150 billion. Businesses increase investment by $5 billion.
   a. Calculate the multiplier.
   b. Calculate the change in real GDP.
   c. Calculate the new level of real GDP.
   d. Explain why real GDP increases by more than $5 billion.

2. An economy has no imports or taxes. An increase in autonomous expenditure of $2 trillion increases equilibrium expenditure by $8 trillion.
   a. Calculate the multiplier.
   b. Calculate the marginal propensity to consume.
   c. What happens to the multiplier if an income tax is introduced in this economy?

Exercises 15.3

1. An economy has no imports or taxes. The marginal propensity to consume is 0.60, and real GDP is $100 billion. Businesses decrease investment by $10 billion.
   a. Calculate the multiplier.
   b. Calculate the change in real GDP.
   c. Calculate the new level of real GDP.
   d. Explain why real GDP decreases by more than $10 billion.

2. An economy has no imports or taxes. The multiplier is 1.25, and autonomous expenditure increases by $2 trillion.
   a. Calculate the change in real GDP.
   b. Calculate the marginal propensity to consume.
   c. If the government decides to open the country up to international trade, explain how international trade influences the multiplier.

Solutions to Practice Problems 15.3

1a. The multiplier equals 1/(1 – *MPC*). *MPC* is 0.8, so the multiplier is 5.

1b. Real GDP increases by $25 billion. The increase in investment increases real GDP by the multiplier (5) times the change in investment ($5 billion).

1c. Real GDP increases from $150 billion to $175 billion.

1d. Real GDP increases by more than $5 billion because the increase in investment induces an increase in consumption expenditure.

2a. The multiplier is the increase in equilibrium expenditure ($8 trillion) divided by the increase in autonomous expenditure ($2 trillion). The multiplier is 4.

2b. The marginal propensity to consume is 0.75. The multiplier = 1/(1 – *MPC*). So 4 = 1/(1 – *MPC*), and *MPC* is 0.75.

2c. If the government introduces an income tax, the slope of the *AE* curve becomes smaller and the multiplier becomes smaller.

15.4 THE *AD* CURVE AND EQUILIBRIUM EXPENDITURE

In this chapter, we've studied the aggregate expenditure model, in which firms change production when sales and inventories change but they don't change their prices. The aggregate expenditure model determines equilibrium expenditure and real GDP at a given price level. In Chapter 14, we studied the simultaneous determination of real GDP and the price level using the *AS-AD* model. The aggregate demand curve and equilibrium expenditure are related, and this section shows you how.

Deriving the *AD* Curve from Equilibrium Expenditure

The *AE* curve is the relationship between aggregate planned expenditure and real GDP when all other influences on expenditure plans remain the same. A movement along the *AE* curve arises from a change in real GDP.

The *AD* curve is the relationship between the quantity of real GDP demanded and the price level when all other influences on expenditure plans remain the same. A movement along the *AD* curve arises from a change in the price level.

Equilibrium expenditure depends on the price level. When the price level rises, other things remaining the same, aggregate planned expenditure decreases and equilibrium expenditure decreases. And when the price level falls, other things remaining the same, aggregate planned expenditure increases and equilibrium expenditure increases. The reason is that a change in the price level changes the buying power of money, the real interest rate, and the real prices of exports and imports (see Chapter 14, pp. 352–354).

When the price level rises, each of these effects decreases aggregate planned expenditure at each level of real GDP. So the *AE* curve shifts downward. A fall in the price level has the opposite effect. When the price level falls, the *AE* curve shifts upward.

Figure 15.8(a) shows the shifts of the *AE* curve. When the price level is 110, the *AE* curve intersects the 45° line at point *B*. Equilibrium expenditure is $10 trillion. If the price level rises to 130, the *AE* curve shifts downward and equilibrium expenditure is $9 trillion at point *A*. If the price level falls to 90, the *AE* curve shifts upward and equilibrium expenditure is $11 trillion at point *C*.

The price level changes that shift the *AE* curve and change equilibrium expenditure bring movements along the *AD* curve. Figure 15.8(b) shows these movements. At a price level of 110, the quantity of real GDP demanded is $10 trillion—point *B* on the *AD* curve. If the price level rises to 130, the quantity of real GDP demanded decreases to $9 trillion at point *A*. If the price level falls to 90, the quantity of real GDP demanded increases to $11 trillion at point *C*.

The two parts of Figure 15.8 are connected and illustrate the relationship between the *AE* curve and the *AD* curve. Each point of equilibrium expenditure corresponds to a point on the *AD* curve. The equilibrium expenditure points *A*, *B*, and *C* (part a) correspond to the points *A*, *B*, and *C* on the *AD* curve (part b).

FIGURE 15.8

Equilibrium Expenditure and Aggregate Demand

Practice Online

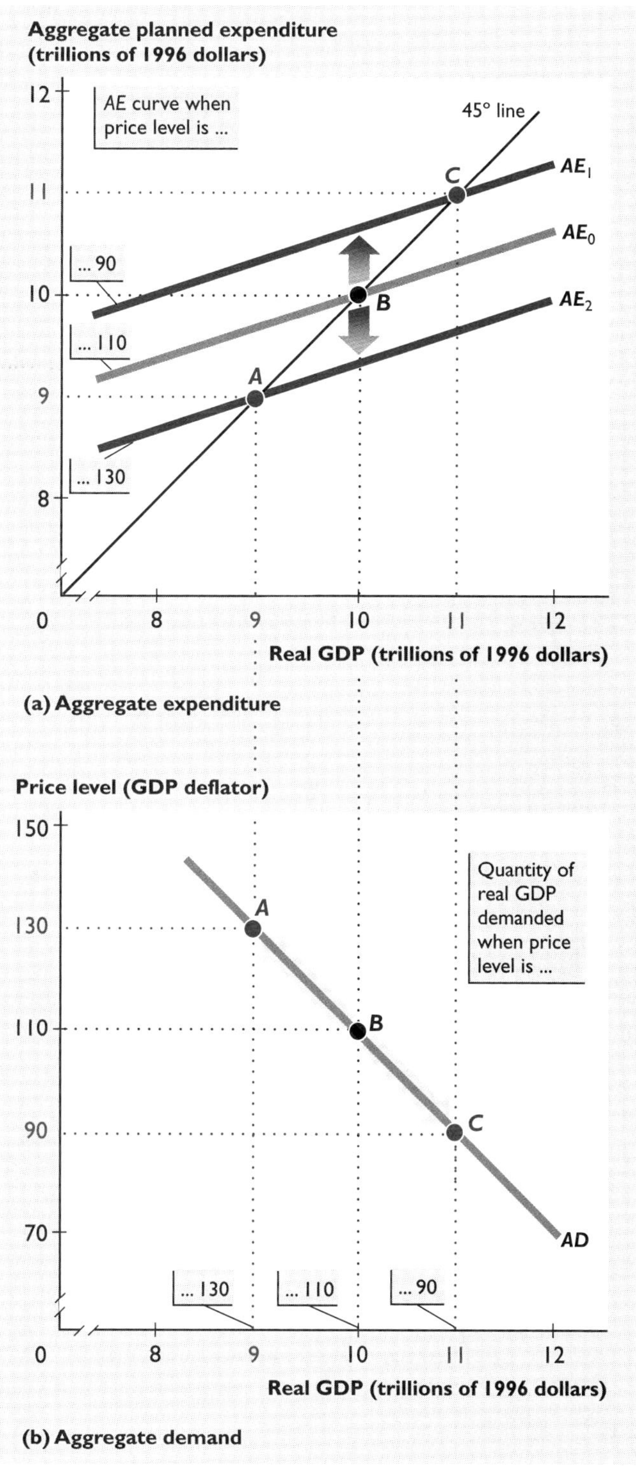

A change in the price level shifts the *AE* curve and results in a movement along the *AD* curve. When the price level is 110, equilibrium expenditure is $10 trillion at point *B*. When the price level is 130, equilibrium expenditure is $9 trillion at point *A*. When the price level is 90, equilibrium expenditure is $11 trillion at point *C*. Points *A*, *B*, and *C* on the *AD* curve in part (b) correspond to the equilibrium expenditure points *A*, *B*, and *C* in part (a).

CHECKPOINT 15.4

Study Guide pp. 223–226

Practice Online 15.4

4 Derive the *AD* curve from equilibrium expenditure.

Practice Problem 15.4

An economy has the following aggregate expenditure schedules:

Real GDP (trillions of 1996 dollars)	Aggregate planned expenditure in trillions of 1996 dollars when the price level is		
	110	100	90
0	1.0	1.5	2.0
1	1.5	2.0	2.5
2	2.0	2.5	3.0
3	2.5	3.0	3.5
4	3.0	3.5	4.0
5	3.5	4.0	4.5
6	4.0	4.5	5.0

a. Make a graph to show three *AE* curves.
b. Find equilibrium expenditure at each price level.
c. Construct the aggregate demand schedule and plot the aggregate demand curve.

FIGURE 1

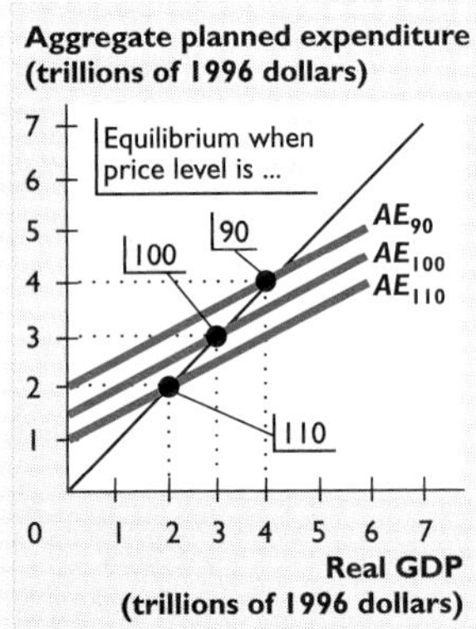

FIGURE 2

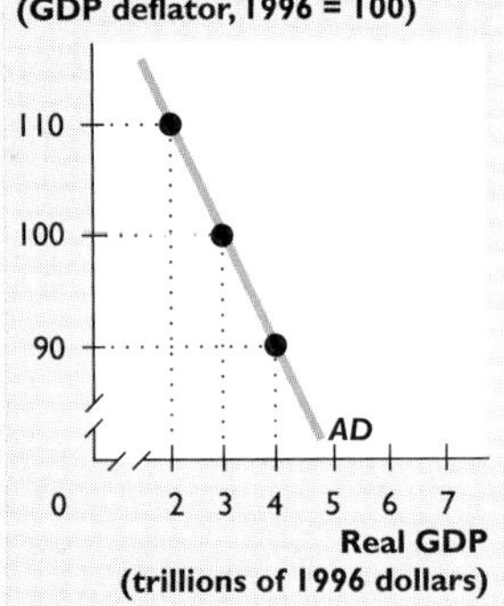

Exercise 15.4

In the economy described in the practice problem, autonomous expenditure increases by $0.5 trillion.
a. Make a graph to show three new *AE* curves.
b. Find equilibrium expenditure at each price level.
c. Construct the aggregate demand schedule and plot the aggregate demand curve.
d. What is the magnitude of the multiplier?

Solution to Practice Problem 15.4

a. Figure 1 shows the three *AE* curves.
b. Figure 1 shows the three equilibrium levels of aggregate expenditure. When the price level is 90, equilibrium expenditure is $4 trillion. When the price level is 100, equilibrium expenditure is $3 trillion. When the price level is 110, equilibrium expenditure is $2 trillion.
c. The table below shows the aggregate demand schedule, and Figure 2 shows the aggregate demand curve.

Price level	Quantity of real GDP demanded (trillions of 1996 dollars)
90	4
100	3
110	2

CHAPTER CHECKPOINT

Key Points

1 Distinguish between autonomous expenditure and induced expenditure and explain how real GDP influences expenditure plans.

- Investment plus government purchases plus exports, which real GDP does *not* influence directly, plus the components of consumption expenditure and imports that are not influenced by real GDP is called autonomous expenditure.
- The components of consumption expenditure and imports, which real GDP influence, are called induced expenditure.
- Consumption expenditure varies with disposable income and real GDP and depends on the marginal propensity to consume.
- Imports vary with real GDP and depend on the marginal propensity to import.

2 Explain how real GDP adjusts to achieve equilibrium expenditure.

- Actual aggregate expenditure equals real GDP and differs from planned expenditure when firms have unplanned inventory changes.
- If aggregate planned expenditure exceeds real GDP, firms increase production and real GDP increases. If real GDP exceeds aggregate planned expenditure, firms decrease production and real GDP decreases.
- Real GDP changes until aggregate planned expenditure equals real GDP.

3 Describe and explain the expenditure multiplier.

- When autonomous expenditure changes, equilibrium expenditure changes by a larger amount: There is a multiplier.
- The multiplier is greater than 1 because a change in autonomous expenditure changes induced expenditure.
- The larger the marginal propensity to consume, the larger is the multiplier.
- Income taxes and imports make the multiplier smaller.

4 Derive the *AD* curve from equilibrium expenditure.

- The *AD* curve is the relationship between the quantity of real GDP demanded and the price level when all other influences on expenditure plans remain the same.
- The quantity of real GDP demanded on the *AD* curve is the equilibrium real GDP when aggregate planned expenditure equals real GDP.

Key Terms

Aggregate planned expenditure, 371
Autonomous expenditure, 372
Consumption function, 372
Equilibrium expenditure, 380
Induced expenditure, 372
Marginal propensity to consume, 374
Marginal propensity to import, 376
Marginal tax rate, 387
Multiplier, 384

Exercises

1. The table shows disposable income and saving in the global economy.

Disposable income (trillions of dollars)	0	10	20	30	40	50
Saving (trillions of dollars)	–5	–3	–1	1	3	5

   a. Calculate consumption expenditure at each level of disposable income.
   b. Over what range of disposable income is there dissaving?
   c. Estimate the level of disposable income at which saving is zero.
   d. Calculate the marginal propensity to consume.
   e. If buying power of net assets increased by $10 trillion, in which direction would the consumption function that you've found change?

2. The table shows some values of real GDP, *Y*, consumption expenditure, *C*, investment, *I*, government purchases, *G*, exports, *X*, imports, *M*, and aggregate planned expenditure, *AE*, in millions of dollars in an economy in which taxes are constant.

	Planned expenditure					
Y	*C*	*I*	*G*	*X*	*M*	*AE*
0	2.0	1.75	1.0	1.25	0.0	6.0
2	**Q**	1.75	1.0	1.25	0.4	6.8
4	4.4	**R**	1.0	1.25	0.8	7.6
6	5.6	1.75	**S**	1.25	1.2	8.4
8	6.8	1.75	1.0	**T**	1.6	9.2
10	8.0	1.75	1.0	1.25	**U**	10.0
12	9.2	1.75	1.0	1.25	2.4	**V**

   a. Find the value of *Q*, *R*, *S*, *T*, *U*, and *V*.
   b. Make a graph of the components of aggregate planned expenditure similar to Figure 15.4.
   c. Calculate the marginal propensity to consume.
   d. Calculate the marginal propensity to import.
   e. Find equilibrium expenditure.

3. In the economy described in exercise 2, investment crashes to $0.55 trillion but nothing else changes.
   a. What now is equilibrium expenditure?
   b. What is the multiplier?

4. In an economy with no exports and imports, autonomous consumption is $1 trillion, the marginal propensity to consume is 0.8, investment is $5 trillion, and government purchases are $4 trillion. Taxes are $4 trillion and do not vary with real GDP.
   a. Calculate disposable income when real GDP is $30 trillion.
   b. Calculate consumption expenditure when real GDP is $30 trillion.
   c. Calculate aggregate planned expenditure when real GDP is $30 trillion.
   d. Calculate equilibrium expenditure.

e. If real GDP is $30 trillion, explain the process that takes the economy to equilibrium expenditure.
f. If real GDP is $40 trillion, explain the process that takes the economy to equilibrium expenditure.

5. In exercise 4, investment increases by $0.5 trillion. Calculate
   a. The size of the shift of the *AE* curve.
   b. The size of the multiplier.
   c. The change in equilibrium expenditure.

6. The Mexican government has just cut the marginal income tax rate. Explain how this cut will change
   a. Consumption expenditure in Mexico.
   b. Equilibrium expenditure in Mexico.
   c. The multiplier in Mexico.

7. In the global economy, when the price level is 100, aggregate planned expenditure would be $10 trillion if real GDP were zero; when the price level is 90, aggregate planned expenditure would be $11 trillion if real GDP were zero; and when the price level is 110, aggregate planned expenditure would be $9 trillion if real GDP were zero. For each $1 increase in real GDP, aggregate planned expenditure increases by 75¢, and this relationship between expenditure plans and real GDP is the same at every price level.
   a. Calculate aggregate planned expenditure when the price level is 100 at real GDP levels of $35 trillion, $40 trillion, and $45 trillion.
   b. Calculate aggregate planned expenditure when the price level is 110 at real GDP levels of $35 trillion, $40 trillion, and $45 trillion.
   c. Calculate aggregate planned expenditure when the price level is 90 at real GDP levels of $35 trillion, $40 trillion, and $45 trillion.
   d. Calculate equilibrium expenditure at price levels of 90, 100, and 110.
   e. Make graphs of the *AE* curves at price levels of 90, 100, and 110 and the *AD* curve.

8. In exercise 7, global investment increases by $1 trillion.
   a. Calculate aggregate planned expenditure when the price level is 100 at real GDP levels of $35 trillion, $40 trillion, and $45 trillion.
   b. Calculate aggregate planned expenditure when the price level is 110 at real GDP levels of $35 trillion, $40 trillion, and $45 trillion.
   c. Calculate aggregate planned expenditure when the price level is 90 at real GDP levels of $35 trillion, $40 trillion, and $45 trillion.
   d. Calculate equilibrium expenditure at price levels of 90, 100, and 110.
   e. Make graphs of the new *AE* curve at price levels of 90, 100, and 110 and the *AD* curve.

9. Compare the *AD* curve of exercise 7 with that of exercise 8.
   a. Does the *AD* curve shift leftward or rightward? Explain the direction of the shift.
   b. Does the *AD* curve shift by the same $1 trillion increase in investment, by more than that amount, or by less than that amount? Explain the magnitude of the shift.

Critical Thinking

10. The Japanese economy is in a recession, and economists have suggested that the Japanese government increase its purchases of goods and services but not change taxes. Explain how such a policy change will influence equilibrium expenditure. Would such a policy change help to turn the economy from recession to expansion?
11. It is 2005, and real GDP in the U.S. economy is decreasing. Consumption and other components of aggregate expenditure are also decreasing. Explain how these events will influence
    a. The U.S. consumption function.
    b. The U.S. aggregate expenditure curve.
    c. Equilibrium expenditure in the United States.
    d. Autonomous expenditure in Mexico and Canada.
    e. The consumption functions of Mexico and Canada.
    f. The aggregate expenditure curves of Mexico and Canada.
    g. Equilibrium expenditure in Mexico and Canada.
12. Throughout the 1990s, the economy of Russia was in a prolonged recession—a depression. Use the aggregate expenditure model to illustrate the state of the Russian economy during its depression. Then explain how the following events might have influenced aggregate expenditure and equilibrium expenditure.
    a. The booming U.S. economy.
    b. Tax increases in Russia.
    c. Cuts in government purchases of goods and services in Russia.

Practice Online

Web Exercises

Use the links on your Foundations Web site to work the following exercises.

13. Visit the Bureau of Economic Analysis Web site and obtain annual data on real GDP, real consumption expenditure, real investment, real government purchases, real exports, and real imports since 1990.
    a. Load the data into a spreadsheet.
    b. Calculate the annual growth rates of each expenditure item.
    c. Make a graph of the annual growth rates of each expenditure item.
    d. Which component of aggregate expenditure fluctuates most and which fluctuates least?
    e. Which components of aggregate expenditure appear to have fluctuations that move in a similar way to the fluctuations in real GDP?
    f. Which components of aggregate expenditure appear to have fluctuations that are independent of real GDP?
    g. Which components of aggregate expenditure appear to be autonomous and which appear to be induced?
14. Use the data on real GDP and real consumption expenditure that you obtained in exercise 13.
    a. Make a graph to show consumption as a function of real GDP.
    b. Make an estimate of the marginal propensity to consume.
    c. Does the consumption function seem to have shifted? In which direction has it shifted? Can you think of reasons why it might have shifted?

Fiscal and Monetary Policy Effects

CHAPTER 16

CHAPTER CHECKLIST

When you have completed your study of this chapter, you will be able to

1. **Describe the federal budget process and explain the effects of fiscal policy.**
2. **Describe the Federal Reserve's monetary policy process and explain the effects of monetary policy.**

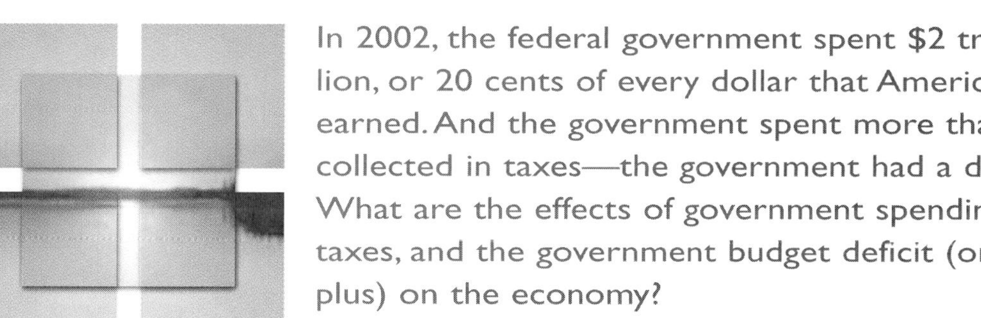

In 2002, the federal government spent $2 trillion, or 20 cents of every dollar that Americans earned. And the government spent more than it collected in taxes—the government had a deficit. What are the effects of government spending, taxes, and the government budget deficit (or surplus) on the economy?

Every six weeks or so, the Federal Open Market Committee (FOMC) meets at the Fed's Washington, D.C., headquarters. The eyes of Wall Street and the nation's financial managers focus on this event, looking for signs of changes in the interest rate. What are the effects of the Fed's actions on the economy?

In this chapter, we build on what you have learned about aggregate demand and aggregate supply, aggregate expenditures, and money to explore the tools used by the federal government and the Federal Reserve to influence aggregate demand and counteract the forces that push the economy away from full employment. Our focus in this chapter is on the effects of these tools. The next two chapters examine questions about priorities and strategies in using these tools.

16.1 THE FEDERAL BUDGET AND FISCAL POLICY

Fiscal policy
The use of the federal budget to smooth the business cycle and encourage economic growth.

Federal budget
An annual statement of the expenditures, tax receipts, and surplus or deficit of the government of the United States.

Budget surplus
The budget balance when tax receipts exceed expenditures.

Budget deficit
The budget balance when expenditures exceed tax receipts.

Balanced budget
The budget balance when tax receipts equal expenditures.

Fiscal policy is the use of the federal budget to smooth the business cycle and encourage economic growth. We begin our study of fiscal policy by describing the federal budget and the process that creates it.

The Federal Budget

The **federal budget** is an annual statement of the expenditures, tax receipts, and the surplus or deficit of the government of the United States. The government's surplus or deficit is equal to its tax receipts minus its expenditures. That is,

Budget surplus (+)/deficit (–) = Tax receipts – Expenditures.

The government has a **budget surplus** if tax receipts exceed expenditures, a **budget deficit** if expenditures exceed tax receipts, and a **balanced budget** if tax receipts equal expenditures. The government borrows to finance a budget deficit and repays its debt when it has a surplus. The amount of debt outstanding that arises from past budget deficits is called *national debt*.

A Personal Analogy The government's budget and the national debt are like a student's budget and debt—only bigger. If you take a student loan each year to go to school, you have a budget deficit and a growing debt. If after graduating and getting a job, you repay some of your loan each year, you have a budget surplus and a shrinking debt.

Budget Time Line

The President and Congress make the federal budget on the annual time line shown in Figure 16.1. Although the President proposes and ultimately approves

FIGURE 16.1
The Federal Budget Time Line for Fiscal 2004

Practice Online

The federal budget process begins with the President's proposals in February. Congress debates and amends these proposals and enacts a budget before the start of the fiscal year on October 1. The President signs the Budget Act into law but may exercise a line-item veto. Throughout the fiscal year, Congress might pass supplementary budget laws. The budget outcome is calculated after the end of the fiscal year.

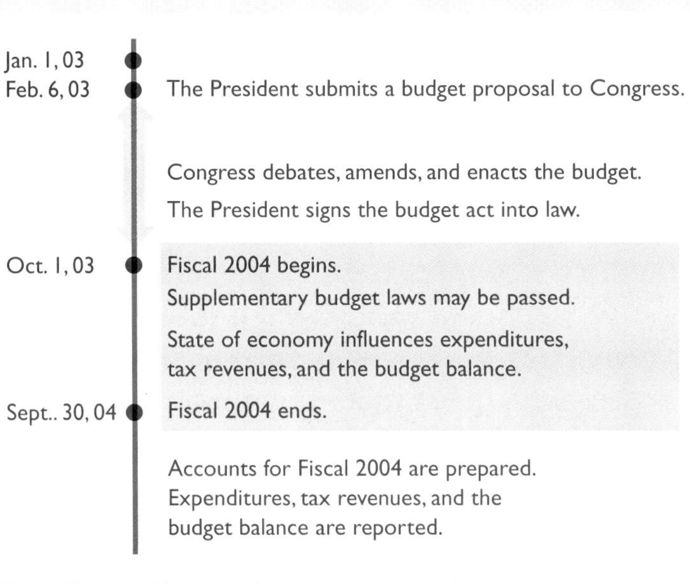

Eye on the Past

Federal Receipts and Expenditures

In 1902, the federal government collected \$562 million in taxes, spent \$485 million, and had a budget surplus of \$77 million. In 2002, revenues were projected to be \$1,950 billion, expenditures to be \$2,050 billion, and the budget *deficit* to be \$100 billion.

Expressed as percentages of GDP, tax revenues increased from 2.6 percent of GDP in 1902 to 18.6 percent of GDP in 2002. Expenditures grew from 2.3 percent of GDP in 1902 to 19.7 percent of GDP in 2002.

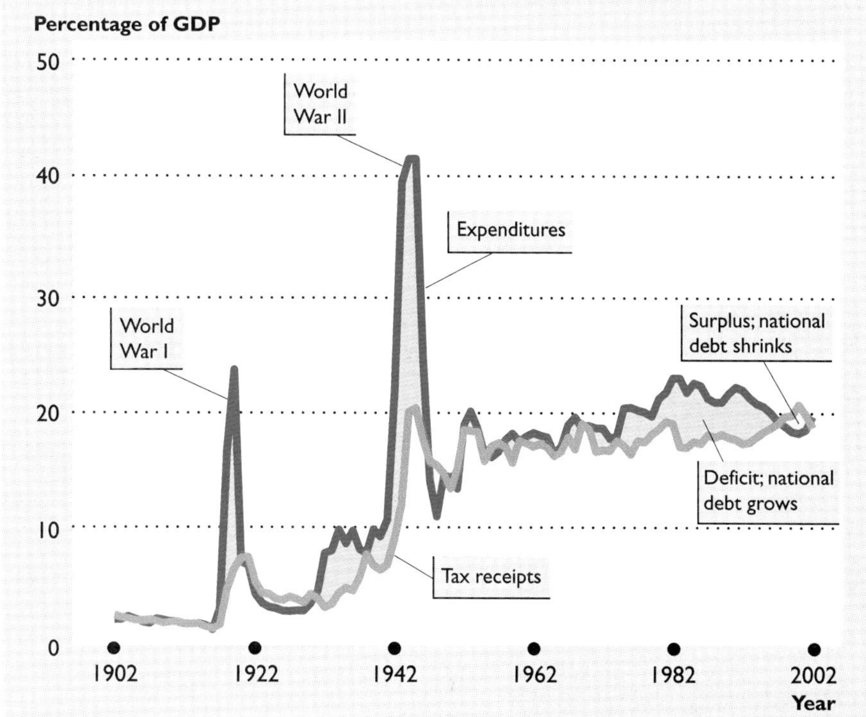

SOURCE: Office of Management and Budget, Historical Tables, Budget of the United States Government, Fiscal Year 2003.

Eye on the Global Economy

The U.S. Budget in Global Perspective

Summing the budgets of all the governments in the world, the IMF estimates that budgets were in deficit by 3.4 percent of world GDP in 2002.

Japan had one of the biggest deficits at more than 7 percent of GDP. But the developing countries of Asia, which include China and India, had large deficits.

Canada was the only major advanced economy with a surplus in 2002.

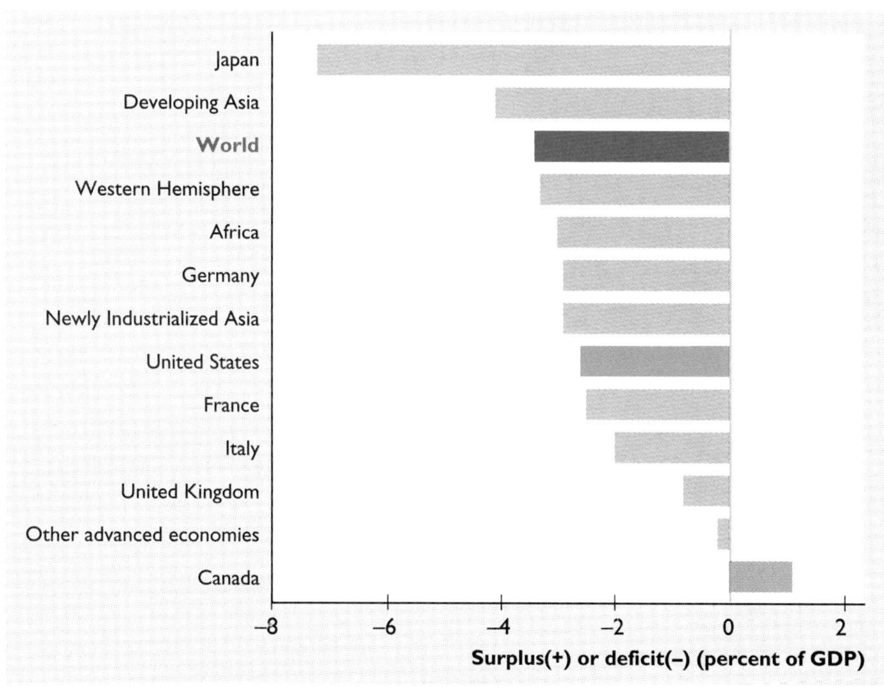

SOURCE: International Monetary Fund, *World Economic Outlook*, September 2002.

the budget, Congress makes the tough decisions on spending and taxes. The House of Representatives and the Senate develop their budget ideas in their respective Budget Committees, and conferences between the two houses resolve differences of view and draft the bills that become the Budget Act. The fiscal year is a year that runs from October 1 to September 30 of the next calendar year. Fiscal 2004 is the fiscal year that *ends* on September 30, 2004.

R. Glenn Hubbard

The Employment Act of 1946

Fiscal policy operates within the framework of the landmark Employment Act of 1946, in which Congress declared that

> it is the continuing policy and responsibility of the Federal Government to use all practicable means . . . to coordinate and utilize all its plans, functions, and resources . . . to promote maximum employment, production, and purchasing power.

This act recognized a role for government actions to keep unemployment low, the economy expanding, and inflation in check. The *Full Employment and Balanced Growth Act of 1978*, more commonly known as the *Humphrey-Hawkins Act*, went further than the 1946 employment act and set a specific target of 4 percent for the unemployment rate, but this target has never been an unwavering policy goal.

Council of Economic Advisers and National Economic Council

Stephen Friedman

The 1946 Employment Act established the President's Council of Economic Advisers, which writes an annual *Economic Report of the President*, a handy review of the current state of the economy. The Council consists of economists who are usually on leave from university jobs. R. Glenn Hubbard of Columbia University is the Chairman of President George W. Bush's Council of Economic Advisers.

The creation of the National Economic Council in 1993 has limited the role of the Council of Economic Advisers. The chairman of the National Economic Council, currently Stephen Friedman, formerly Chairman of Goldman Sachs, a leading global investment bank, is the President's chief economic adviser. The National Economic Council coordinates economic policy and attempts to ensure that the President's economic policy agenda is implemented.

Types of Fiscal Policy

Fiscal policy can be either

- Discretionary or
- Automatic

Discretionary fiscal policy
A fiscal policy action that is initiated by an act of Congress.

Discretionary Fiscal Policy A fiscal action that is initiated by an act of Congress is called **discretionary fiscal policy**. It requires a change in a spending program or in a tax law. For example, an increase in defense spending or a cut in the income tax rate is a discretionary fiscal policy.

Automatic fiscal policy
A fiscal policy action that is triggered by the state of the economy such as an increase in payments to the unemployed and a decrease in tax receipts triggered by recession.

Automatic Fiscal Policy A fiscal action that is triggered by the state of the economy is called **automatic fiscal policy**. For example, an increase in unemployment induces an increase in payments to the unemployed. A fall in incomes induces a decrease in tax receipts.

Discretionary Fiscal Policy: Demand-Side Effects

Discretionary fiscal policy influences both aggregate demand and aggregate supply. We'll look first at the demand-side effects. Changes in government purchases and changes in taxes have multiplier effects on aggregate demand similar to the multiplier that you studied in Chapters 14 and 15.

The Government Purchases Multiplier

The **government purchases multiplier** is the magnification effect of a change in government purchases of goods and services on aggregate demand. Government purchases are a component of aggregate expenditure, so when government purchases change, aggregate demand changes. Real GDP changes and induces a change in consumption expenditure, which brings a further change in aggregate expenditure. A multiplier process like the one described in Chapter 15 (pp. 384-388) ensues.

Government purchases multiplier
The magnification effect of a change in government purchases of goods and services on aggregate demand.

A Homeland Security Multiplier The terrorist attacks of September 11, 2001, brought a reappraisal of the nation's homeland security requirements and an increase in government purchases. This increase in purchases initially increased the incomes of producers of airport and border security equipment and security workers. Better-off security workers increased their consumption expenditures. With rising revenues, other businesses in all parts of the nation boomed and expanded their payrolls. A second round of increased consumption expenditures increased incomes yet further. The increase in security expenditures and its multiplier effect helped to end the 2001 recession.

The Tax Multiplier

The **tax multiplier** is the magnification effect of a change in taxes on aggregate demand. A *decrease* in taxes *increases* disposable income, which increases consumption expenditure. A decrease in taxes works like an increase in government purchases. But the magnitude of the tax multiplier is smaller than the government purchases multiplier. The reason is that a $1 tax cut generates *less than* $1 of additional expenditure. The marginal propensity to consume determines the increase in expenditure induced by a tax cut. For example, if the marginal propensity to consume is 0.75, then a $1 tax cut increases consumption expenditure by only 75 cents. In this case, the tax multiplier is 0.75 times the magnitude of the government purchases multiplier.

Tax multiplier
The magnification effect of a change in taxes on aggregate demand.

A Bush Tax Cut Multiplier Congress enacted the Bush tax cut package that lowered taxes in 2002. These tax cuts had a multiplier effect. With more disposable income, people increased consumption expenditure. This spending increased other people's incomes, which spurred yet more consumption expenditure. Like the increase in security expenditures, the tax cut and its multiplier effect helped to end the 2001 recession.

The Balanced Budget Multiplier

The **balanced budget multiplier** is the magnification effect on aggregate demand of a *simultaneous* change in government purchases and taxes that leaves the budget balance unchanged. The balanced budget multiplier is positive because a $1 increase in government purchases increases aggregate demand by more than a $1 increase in taxes decreases aggregate demand. So when both government purchases and taxes increase by $1, aggregate demand increases.

Balanced budget multiplier
The magnification effect on aggregate demand of a *simultaneous* change in government purchases and taxes that leaves the budget balance unchanged.

Discretionary Fiscal Stabilization

If real GDP is below potential GDP, discretionary fiscal policy might be used in an attempt to restore full employment. The government might increase its purchases of goods and services, cut taxes, or do some of both. These actions would increase aggregate demand. If they were timed correctly and were of the correct magnitude, they could restore full employment. Figure 16.2 shows how.

In Figure 16.2(a), potential GDP is \$10 trillion. Real GDP is \$9 trillion and the price level is 105. There is a \$1 trillion *deflationary gap* (see Chapter 14, p. 362).

To eliminate the deflationary gap and restore full employment, the government takes a discretionary fiscal policy action. An increase in government purchases or a tax cut increases aggregate expenditure by ΔE. If this were the only change in spending plans, the *AD* curve would become $AD_0 + \Delta E$ in Figure 16.2(b). But the increase in government purchases or the tax cut sets off a multiplier process, which increases consumption expenditure. As the multiplier process plays out, aggregate demand increases and the *AD* curve shifts rightward to AD_1.

With no change in the price level, the economy would move from the initial equilibrium point *A* to point *B* on AD_1. But the increase in aggregate demand combined with the upward-sloping aggregate supply curve brings a rise in the price level. So the economy moves to a new equilibrium at point *C*. The price level rises to 110, and real GDP increases to \$10 trillion. Full employment is restored.

FIGURE 16.2
Expansionary Fiscal Policy

Practice Online

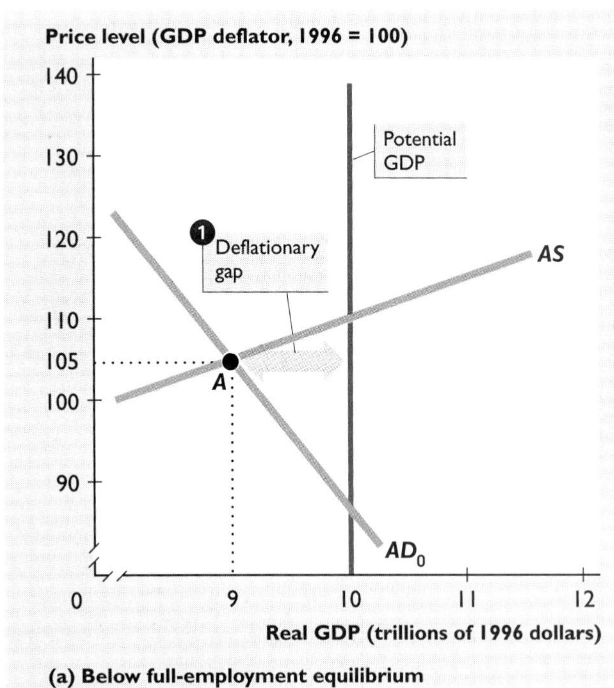

(a) Below full-employment equilibrium

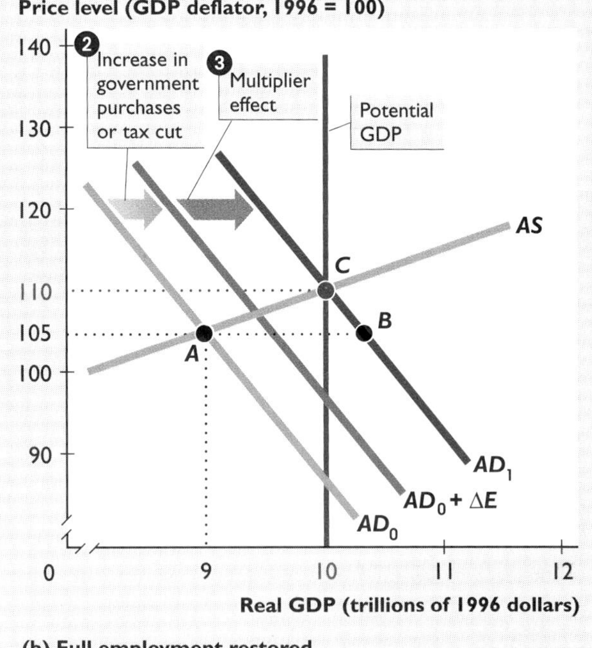

(b) Full employment restored

Potential GDP is \$10 trillion, real GDP is \$9 trillion, and (1) there is a \$1 trillion deflationary gap. (2) An increase in government purchases or a tax cut increases expenditure by ΔE. (3) The multiplier increases induced expenditure. The *AD* curve shifts rightward to AD_1, the price level rises to 110, real GDP increases to \$10 trillion, and the deflationary gap is eliminated.

If an inflationary gap exists, discretionary fiscal policy can be used to decrease aggregate demand, restore full employment, and eliminate inflationary pressure. In this case, the government decreases its purchases of goods and services, raises taxes, or does some of both. These two actions decrease aggregate demand, decrease real GDP, and lower the price level. Figure 16.3 illustrates these effects.

In Figure 16.3(a), potential GDP is $10 trillion and equilibrium occurs at a real GDP of $11 trillion and a price level of 115. There is a $1 trillion *inflationary gap.*

To eliminate the inflationary gap and restore full employment, the government takes a discretionary fiscal policy action. A decrease in government purchases or a rise in taxes decreases aggregate expenditure by ΔE. If this were the only change in spending plans, the *AD* curve would become $AD_0 - \Delta E$. But the initial decrease in aggregate expenditure sets off a multiplier process, which decreases consumption expenditure. As the multiplier process plays out, aggregate demand decreases and the *AD* curve shifts leftward to AD_1.

With no change in the price level, the economy would move from the initial equilibrium point *A* to point *B* on AD_1 in Figure 16.3(b). But the decrease in aggregate demand combined with the upward-sloping *AS* curve brings a fall in the price level. So the economy moves to a new equilibrium at point *C*. The price level falls to 110, and real GDP decreases to $10 trillion. The inflationary gap has been eliminated, inflation has been avoided, and the economy is back at full employment.

FIGURE 16.3

Contractionary Fiscal Policy

Practice Online

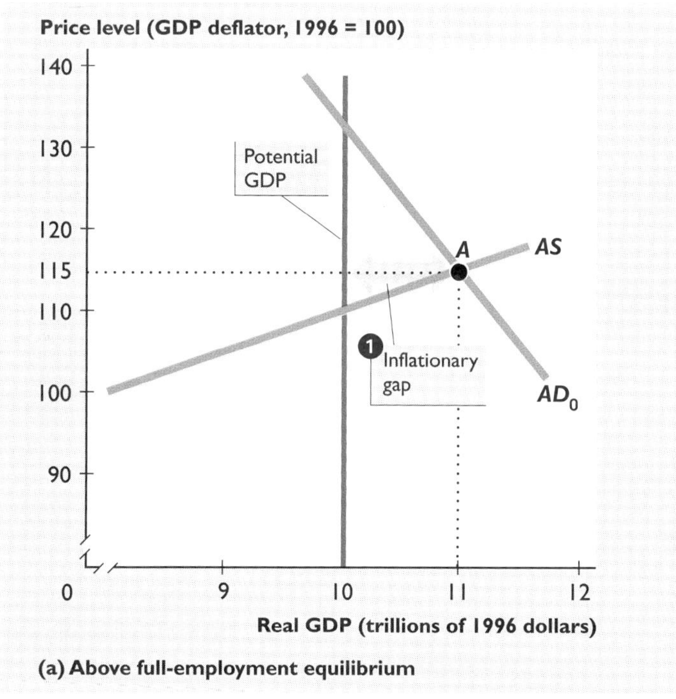

(a) Above full-employment equilibrium

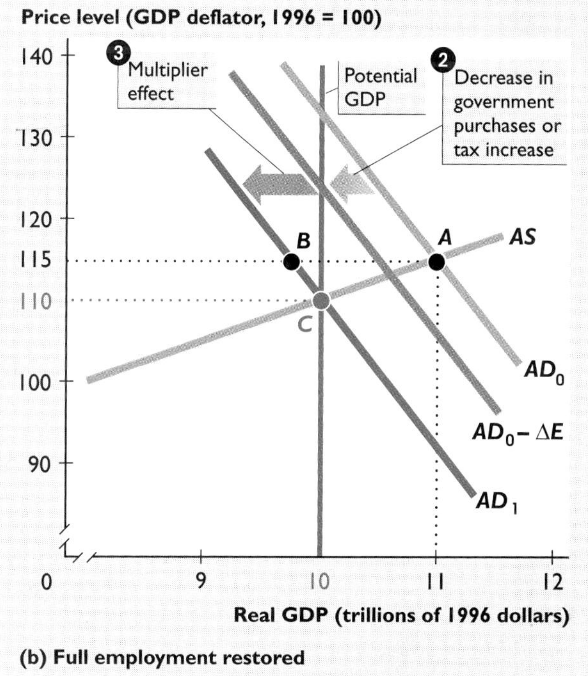

(b) Full employment restored

Potential GDP is $10 trillion, real GDP is $11 trillion, and ❶ there is a $1 trillion inflationary gap. ❷ A decrease in government purchases or a tax increase decreases expenditure by ΔE. ❸ The multiplier decreases induced expenditure. The *AD* curve shifts leftward to AD_1, the price level falls to 110, real GDP decreases to $10 trillion, and the inflationary gap is eliminated.

Discretionary Fiscal Policy: Supply-Side Effects

Both government purchases and taxes influence aggregate supply, and we now look at the supply-side effects of fiscal policy.

Supply-Side Effects of Government Purchases

Government provides services such as law and order, public education, and public health that increase production possibilities. For example, one of the reasons why we are more productive than the citizens of the poor developing countries is that we are better educated and healthier than they are. Government also provides social infrastructure capital such as highways, bridges, tunnels, and dams that increase our production possibilities. The interstate highway system that was begun during the 1950s is an example of the contribution that government purchases can make to the nation's production possibilities.

Government services and capital could be overprovided to the point at which they no longer increase production possibilities. But it is unlikely that we have reached such a point.

An *increase* in government purchases that increase the quantities of productive services and capital increases potential GDP and increases aggregate supply. A *decrease* in government purchases that decrease the quantities of productive services and capital decreases potential GDP and decreases aggregate supply.

Supply-Side Effects of Taxes

To pay for the productive services and capital that the government provides, it collects taxes. All taxes create disincentives to work, save, and provide entrepreneurial services.

Taxes on labor income decrease the supply of labor. And a smaller supply of labor means a higher equilibrium real wage rate and smaller equilibrium quantity of labor employed. With a smaller quantity of labor employed, potential GDP and aggregate supply are smaller than they would otherwise be.

Taxes on the income from capital decrease saving and decrease the supply of capital. A smaller supply of capital means a higher equilibrium real interest rate and a smaller equilibrium quantity of investment and capital employed. With a smaller quantity of capital, potential GDP and aggregate supply are smaller than they would otherwise be.

Taxes on the incomes of entrepreneurs weaken the incentive to take risks and create new businesses. With a smaller number of firms, the quantities of labor and capital employed are lower and potential GDP and aggregate supply are smaller than they would otherwise be.

An *increase* in taxes strengthens the disincentive effects that we've just described. It decreases the supply of labor, capital, and entrepreneurial services; decreases potential GDP; and decreases aggregate supply. And a tax cut has the opposite effects. It strengthens the incentives to work, save, and provide entrepreneurial services. So a tax cut increases potential GDP and aggregate supply.

Balanced Budget Supply-Side Effects

The supply-side effects of a balanced budget change in the scale of government are not clear. More productive spending increases potential GDP, but higher taxes to pay for the spending decreases potential GDP. So an increase in both taxes and government purchases might increase or decrease potential GDP and aggregate supply depending on which effect is stronger. Some economists (and politicians) believe that a larger scale of government increases potential GDP and aggregate supply despite the weakened incentives from higher tax rates. Others believe that the incentive effects are so powerful that smaller government is more productive and brings a greater potential GDP and aggregate supply.

Supply-Side Effects on the *AS* Curve

Figure 16.4 illustrates the effects of fiscal policy on aggregate supply. An increase in government purchases of productive services and capital or a tax cut increases potential GDP, and the aggregate supply curve shifts rightward from AS_0 to AS_1. A decrease in government purchases of productive services and capital or a tax rise decreases potential GDP, and the aggregate supply curve shifts leftward from AS_0 to AS_2.

Combined Demand and Supply Effects

When we combine the supply-side and demand-side effects, we see that an increase in government purchases or a tax cut increases equilibrium real GDP but might raise, lower, or have no effect on the price level. Figure 16.5 illustrates two cases for an expansionary fiscal policy.

FIGURE 16.4

The Effects of Fiscal Policy on Aggregate Supply

Practice Online

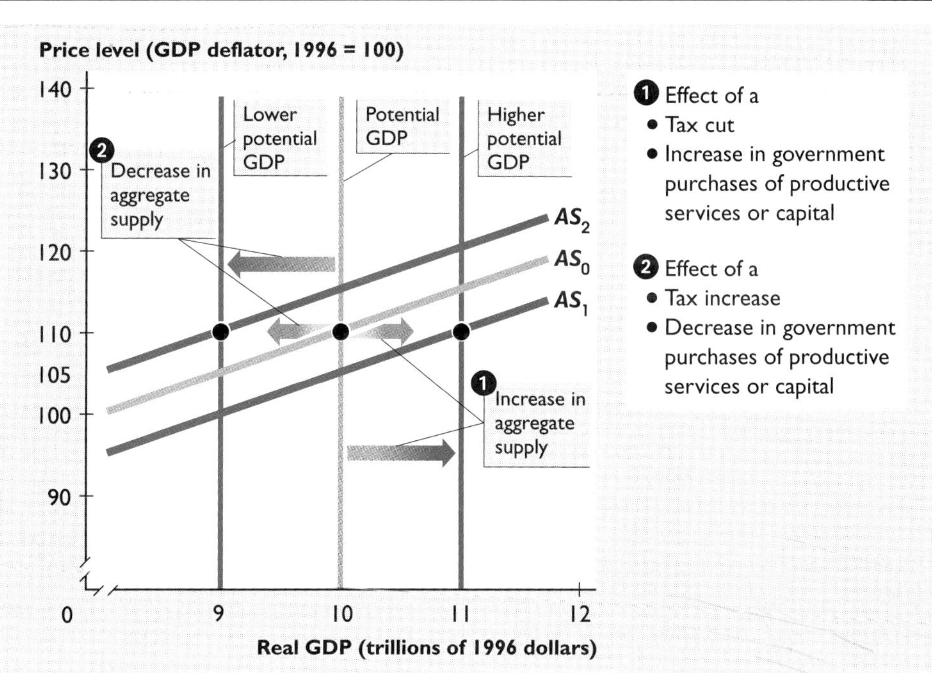

Figure 16.5(a) shows the case in which an expansionary fiscal policy increases aggregate demand by a large amount and shifts the *AD* curve from AD_0 to AD_1. The same fiscal actions also increase aggregate supply but this effect is small, so the *AS* curve shifts by a small amount, from AS_0 to AS_1. The combination of a large increase in aggregate demand and a small increase in aggregate supply increases real GDP and raises the price level.

Figure 16.5(b) shows the case in which an expansionary fiscal policy increases aggregate supply by a large amount, so the *AS* curve shifts from AS_0 to AS_1. The same fiscal actions increase aggregate demand but by a smaller amount and shift the *AD* curve from AD_0 to AD_1. The combination of a large increase in aggregate supply and a small increase in aggregate demand increases real GDP and *lowers* the price level. If the increase in aggregate demand and aggregate supply were equal, real GDP would increase and the price level would remain constant.

The outcome that actually occurs depends on the details of the fiscal policy. Some tax-cut packages would have larger supply-side effects than demand-side effects, and some would have larger demand-side effects than supply-side effects.

Some economists believe that the supply-side effects might be so powerful that a tax cut would end up *increasing* tax revenue. This outcome would occur if real GDP increased by a larger percentage than the percentage cut in tax rates so that when the lower tax rate is applied to the larger income, the total amount of tax revenue increases. There are no examples of this situation actually occurring.

FIGURE 16.5

The Combined Demand-Side and Supply-Side Effects of Fiscal Policy

Practice Online

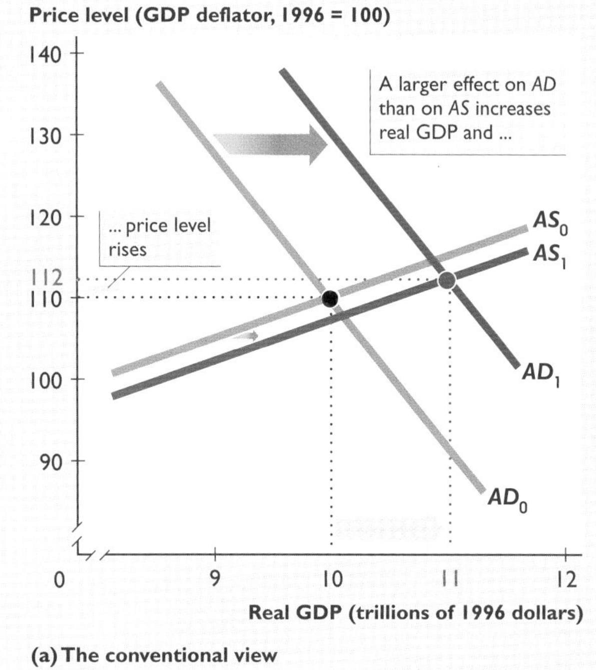

(a) The conventional view

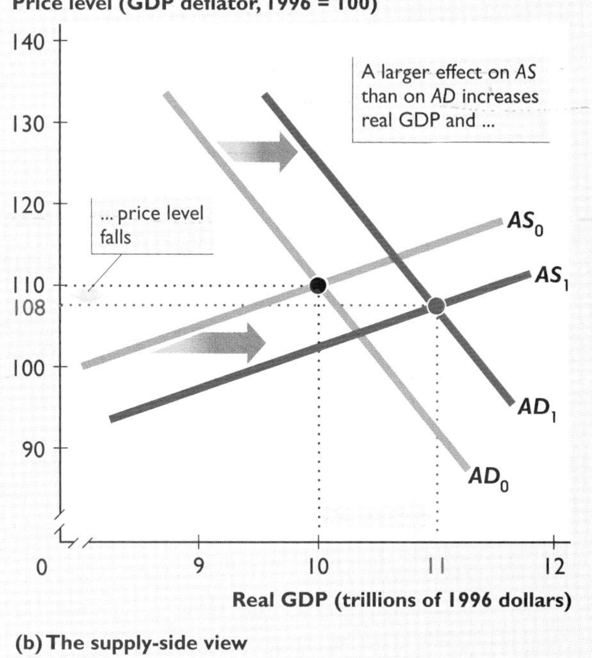

(b) The supply-side view

The conventional view (part a) is that an expansionary fiscal policy increases aggregate demand by more than it increases aggregate supply. Real GDP increases and the price level rises.

The supply-side view (part b) is that an expansionary fiscal policy increases aggregate supply by more than it increases aggregate demand. Real GDP increases and the price level falls.

The 2003 Stimulus Package

At the beginning of 2003, it appeared that real GDP would be about $9,730 billion—some $130 billion below potential GDP—by the end of 2003. In the figure, aggregate demand curve AD_0 and aggregate supply curve AS_0 are consistent with this consensus view.

Concerned about the deflationary gap, President Bush proposed in January 2003 a tax cut of $100 billion in 2003 and $670 billion over the ten years through 2012.

The major tax change proposed was the abolition of personal income taxes on corporate profits paid to stockholders as dividends. This tax cut would lower the opportunity cost of funds to firms, increase investment in new capital, and increase both potential GDP and aggregate supply.

Aggregate demand curve AD_1 and aggregate supply curve AS_1 illustrate a good outcome for the President's plan.

For this outcome to occur the tax multiplier must be 1.3 and the supply-side effects of the tax cuts must equal the demand-side effects.

It is unlikely that these conditions will be met. The tax multiplier will probably be small because most of the lower taxes go to people with high incomes who will save a large part of their increased disposable income. So the increase in aggregate demand will be smaller than that shown in the figure. And the supply-side effects, which probably will be large, are not likely to occur quickly. So the increase in aggregate supply during 2003 will be smaller than that shown in the figure.

Most likely, real GDP will remain below potential GDP through 2003.

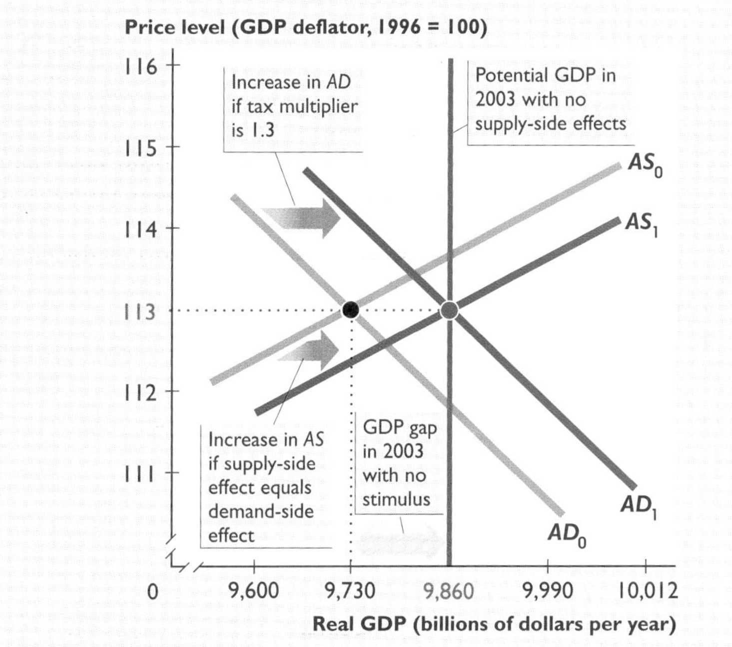

Limitations of Discretionary Fiscal Policy

Figures 16.2 and 16.3 make fiscal policy look easy. Calculate the deflationary gap or the inflationary gap, calculate the multiplier, and determine the magnitude of the change in government purchases or taxes that, with the multiplier effect, will eliminate the gap. In reality, things are not that easy. The use of discretionary fiscal policy is seriously hampered by three factors:

- Law-making time lag
- Estimating potential GDP
- Economic forecasting

Law-Making Time Lag

The law-making time lag is the amount of time it takes Congress to pass the laws needed to change taxes or spending. This process takes time because each member of Congress has a different idea about what is the best tax or spending program to change, so long debates and committee meetings are needed to reconcile conflicting views. The economy might benefit from fiscal stimulation today, but by the time Congress acts, a different fiscal medicine might be needed.

Estimating Potential GDP

It is not easy to tell whether real GDP is below, above, or at potential GDP. So a discretionary fiscal action might move real GDP *away* from potential GDP instead of toward it. This problem is a serious one because too much fiscal stimulation brings inflation and too little might bring recession.

Economic Forecasting

Fiscal policy changes take a long time to enact in Congress and yet more time to become effective. So fiscal policy must target forecasts of where the economy will be in the future. Economic forecasting has improved enormously in recent years, but it remains inexact and subject to error. So for a second reason, discretionary fiscal action might move real GDP *away* from potential GDP and create the very problems it seeks to correct.

Let's now look at automatic fiscal policy.

Automatic Fiscal Policy

Automatic stabilizers
Features of fiscal policy that stabilize real GDP without explicit action by the government.

Automatic fiscal policy is a consequence of tax receipts and expenditures that fluctuate with real GDP. These features of fiscal policy are called **automatic stabilizers** because they work to stabilize real GDP without explicit action by the government. Their name is borrowed from engineering and conjures up images of shock absorbers, thermostats, and sophisticated devices that keep airplanes and ships steady in turbulent air and seas.

Induced Taxes

Induced taxes
Taxes that vary with real GDP.

On the receipts side of the budget, tax laws define tax *rates*, not tax *dollars*. Tax dollars paid depend on tax rates and incomes. But incomes vary with real GDP, so tax receipts depend on real GDP. Taxes that vary with real GDP are called **induced taxes**. When real GDP increases in an expansion, wages and profits rise, so the taxes on these incomes—induced taxes—rise. When real GDP decreases in a recession, wages and profits fall, so the induced taxes on these incomes fall.

Needs-Tested Spending

Needs-tested spending
Spending on programs that entitle suitably qualified people and businesses to receive benefits—benefits that vary with need and with the state of the economy.

On the expenditure side of the budget, the government creates programs that pay benefits to suitably qualified people and businesses. The spending on such programs is called **needs-tested spending**, and it results in transfer payments that depend on the economic state of individual citizens and businesses. When the economy is in a recession, unemployment is high and the number of people experiencing economic hardship increases, but needs-tested spending on unemployment benefits and food stamps also increases. When the economy expands, unemployment falls, the number of people experiencing economic hardship decreases, and needs-tested spending decreases.

Induced taxes and needs-tested spending decrease the multiplier effects of changes in autonomous expenditure (such as investment and exports). So they moderate both expansions and recessions and make real GDP more stable. They achieve this outcome by weakening the link between real GDP and disposable income and so reduce the effect of a change in real GDP on consumption expenditure. When real GDP increases, induced taxes increase and needs-tested spending decreases, so disposable income does not increase by as much as the increase in real GDP. As a result, consumption expenditure does not increase by as much as it otherwise would have done and the multiplier effect is reduced.

CHECKPOINT 16.1

1 **Describe the federal budget process and explain the effects of fiscal policy.**

Study Guide pp. 232–236

Practice Online 16.1

Practice Problems 16.1

1. Classify each of the following as discretionary fiscal policy or automatic fiscal policy or neither.
   a. A decrease in tax receipts in a recession
   b. Additional expenditure to upgrade highways
   c. An increase in the public education budget
   d. A purchase of $1 billion of medicines to treat AIDS sufferers in Africa
   e. A cut in funding for NASA during an expansion
2. Explain the change in aggregate demand when
   a. Government purchases increase by $100 billion, which the government spends on national defense.
   b. Taxes are increased by $100 billion.
   c. Both parts **a** and **b** occur simultaneously.

Exercises 16.1

1. Classify each of the following as discretionary fiscal policy or automatic fiscal policy or neither.
   a. Huge fines are imposed on the tobacco companies
   b. A cut in the gas tax
   c. A cut in cross-border (custom) taxes
   d. The cost of refurnishing the White House basement
   e. An increase in payments to unemployed people
2. Illustrate, using an *AD-AS* graph, the effects of
   a. A $100 billion decrease in government purchases.
   b. A $100 billion decrease in taxes.
   c. Both parts **a** and **b** occurring simultaneously.

Solutions to Practice Problems 16.1

1a. A decrease in tax receipts in a recession is an automatic fiscal policy.
1b. Expenditure to upgrade highways is a discretionary fiscal policy.
1c. An increase in the public education budget is discretionary fiscal policy.
1d. A purchase of $1 billion of medicines is a discretionary fiscal policy.
1e. A cut in funding for NASA is a discretionary fiscal policy.

2a. Aggregate demand increases by more than $100 billion because the increase in government purchases has a multiplier effect that increases induced expenditure.
2b. Aggregate demand decreases by more than $100 billion because the tax increase has a multiplier effect that decreases induced expenditure.
2c. Aggregate demand increases because the increase in part **a** is larger than the decrease in part **b**.

16.2 THE FEDERAL RESERVE AND MONETARY POLICY

You learned about the structure of the Federal Reserve in Chapter 11, how the Fed controls the quantity of money in Chapter 12, and how the quantity of money influences interest rates in Chapter 13. Here, we're going to see how the Fed monitors the economy and examine the effects of its policy actions on aggregate demand and how the effects of those actions ripple through the economy to influence real GDP and the price level.

The Monetary Policy Process

The Fed makes monetary policy in a process that has three main elements:

- Monitoring economic conditions
- Meetings of the Federal Open Market Committee (FOMC)
- Monetary Policy Report to Congress

Monitoring Economic Conditions

Beige Book
A report that summarizes current economic conditions in each Federal Reserve district and each sector of the economy.

Each Federal Reserve Bank constantly gathers information on its district by talking with business leaders, economists, market experts, and others. The Fed brings the results together in the **Beige Book**, which is published eight times a year. The Beige Book serves as a background document for the members of the Federal Open Market Committee.

The Beige Book is a public document that is easily accessible on the Fed's Web site and is a good source of current information for businesses and anyone who wants to be well informed about the current state of the economy.

Meetings of the Federal Open Market Committee (FOMC)

The FOMC, which meets eight times a year, makes the monetary policy decisions. The FOMC's first and fourth meetings of the year run for two days (the other six meetings run for one day) and are opportunities for the committee to assess the longer-term outlook as well as the current period's open market operations.

After each meeting, the FOMC announces its decisions and describes its view of the likelihood that its goals of price stability and sustainable economic growth will be achieved. The FOMC publishes the minutes of its meetings after they have been confirmed as a correct record of the meeting at the next scheduled meeting. For example, the minutes of the first meeting of the year are published after the second meeting of the year.

Full transcripts of FOMC meetings are published with a five-year time lag. This delay enables the members of the FOMC to have a frank exchange of views without worrying about how their discussions might be interpreted by the traders in financial markets. The eventual publication of the transcripts permits a detailed public scrutiny of the FOMC's decision-making process.

Monetary Policy Report to Congress

Twice a year, in February and July, the Fed prepares a Monetary Policy Report to Congress, and the Fed chairman testifies before the House of Representatives Committee on Financial Services. The report and the chairman's testimony review the monetary policy and economic developments of the past year and the economic outlook for the coming year.

Influencing the Interest Rate

When the FOMC announces a policy change, its press release talks about the federal funds interest rate, the interest rate at which banks borrow reserves from each other, or the discount rate, the interest rate at which banks borrow reserves from the Fed. The press release does not talk about the quantity of money or the size of the open market operations it plans to conduct. This focus on interest rates makes it appear as though the Fed determines interest rates rather than the quantity of money. But this impression is misleading for two reasons: a long-run reason and a short-run reason.

In the Long Run

In the long run, saving supply and investment demand determine the real interest rate in global financial markets (see Chapter 9, pp. 215–221). The inflation rate, along with the real interest rate, determines the nominal interest rate (Chapter 13, p. 316). The inflation rate in the long run is determined by the growth rate of the quantity of money that results from the Fed's actions.

So in the long run, the Fed *influences* the nominal interest rate by the effects of its policies on the inflation rate. But it does not directly control the nominal interest rate, and it has no control over the real interest rate.

In the Short Run

In the short run, the Fed influences both the nominal interest rate and the real interest rate. To change the nominal interest rate, the Fed undertakes an open market operation that changes the quantity of money. It is by changing the quantity of money that the Fed achieves its target for the federal funds rate. The expected inflation rate doesn't change every time the Fed changes the nominal interest rate. So an open market operation changes the real interest rate in the short run.

The Fed Raises the Interest Rate

Suppose that the Fed fears inflation and decides it must to take action to decrease aggregate demand. The FOMC announces that it will raise the short-term interest rate. How does the Fed achieve this goal?

The FOMC instructs the New York Fed to sell securities in the open market. This action mops up bank reserves. Some banks are short of reserves and seek to borrow reserves from other banks. The federal funds interest rate rises. With fewer reserves, the banks make a smaller quantity of new loans each day until the quantity of loans outstanding has fallen to a level that is consistent with the new lower level of reserves. The quantity of money decreases.

The demand for money determines the quantity of money that will achieve the FOMC's interest rate target. The Fed could, if it chose, fix the quantity of money and let the interest rate adjust to its equilibrium level. Or the Fed can, and does, fix the interest rate and adjust the quantity of money to the level that makes the chosen interest rate the equilibrium rate.

Suppose, for example, that the short-term nominal interest rate is 5 percent a year and the FOMC decides that it needs to rise to 6 percent a year. Figure 16.6(a) illustrates what the Fed must do. The demand for money is *MD*, so when the interest rate is 5 percent a year, the quantity of money is $1 trillion. The Fed

FIGURE 16.6
Interest Rate Changes

Practice Online

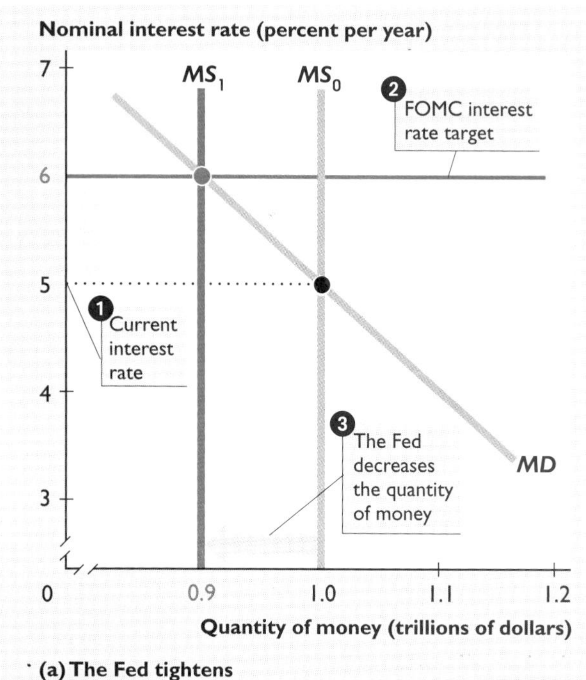

(a) The Fed tightens

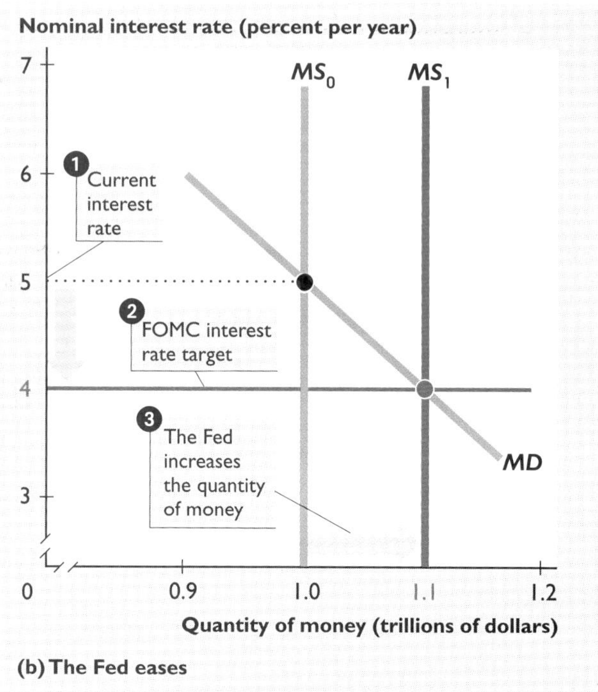

(b) The Fed eases

❶ The current interest rate is 5 percent a year, and ❷ the FOMC's target is 6 percent a year. To raise the interest rate to the target, the Fed must sell securities in the open market and ❸ decrease the quantity of money to $0.9 trillion.

❶ The current interest rate is 5 percent a year, and ❷ the FOMC's target is 4 percent a year. To lower the interest rate to the target, the Fed must buy securities in the open market and ❸ increase the quantity of money to $1.1 trillion.

conducts an open market sale on a sufficiently large scale to decrease the quantity of money from $1 trillion to $0.9 trillion. When the quantity of money is $0.9 trillion, the nominal interest rate is 6 percent a year, the FOMC's target level.

The Fed Lowers the Interest Rate

If the Fed fears recession, it acts to increase aggregate demand. The FOMC announces that it will lower the short-term interest rate. To achieve this goal, the FOMC instructs the New York Fed to buy securities in the open market. This action increases bank reserves. Flush with reserves, banks now seek to lend reserves to other banks. The federal funds rate falls. With more reserves, the banks increase their lending and the quantity of money increases.

Again, the demand for money determines the change in the quantity of money that achieves the Fed's interest rate target. Suppose the FOMC wants to lower the interest rate from 5 percent a year to 4 percent a year. Figure 16.6(b) shows what it must do. When the interest rate is 5 percent a year, the quantity of money is $1 trillion. The Fed conducts an open market purchase on a sufficiently large scale to increase the quantity of money from $1 trillion to $1.1 trillion. When the quantity of money is $1.1 trillion, the nominal interest rate is 4 percent a year, the FOMC's target level.

The Ripple Effects of the Fed's Actions

Suppose that the Fed increases the interest rate. What happens next?

Three main events follow:

- Investment and consumption expenditure decrease.
- The dollar rises, and net exports decrease.
- A multiplier process induces a further decrease in consumption expenditure and aggregate demand.

Investment and Consumption Expenditure

The interest rate influences investment and consumption expenditure. When the Fed increases the nominal interest rate, the real interest rate rises temporarily, and investment and expenditure on consumer durables decrease. The reason is that the interest rate is the *opportunity cost* of the funds used to finance investment and the purchase of big-ticket consumer items. So when the opportunity costs of buying capital and consumer goods rise, the quantities bought and expenditures on these items decrease.

The Dollar and Net Exports

A rise in the interest rate, other things remaining the same, means that the U.S. interest rate rises relative to the interest rates in other countries. Some people will want to move funds into the United States from other countries to take advantage of the higher interest rate they can now earn on their U.S. bank deposits and bonds. When money is moved into the United States, people buy dollars and sell other currencies, such as Japanese yen or British pounds. With more dollars demanded, the price of the dollar rises on the foreign exchange market.

The higher price of the dollar means that foreigners must now pay more for U.S.-made goods and services. So the quantity demanded and the expenditure on U.S.-made items decrease. U.S. exports decrease. Similarly, the higher price of the dollar means that Americans now pay less for foreign-made goods and services. So the quantity demanded and the expenditure on foreign-made items increase. U.S. imports increase.

The Multiplier Process

Because investment, consumption expenditure, and net exports are all interest-sensitive components of expenditure, a rise in the interest rate brings a decrease in aggregate expenditure.

You already know the rest of the story, because it is the same as that of the fiscal policy multipliers. The decrease in expenditure decreases incomes, and the decrease in income induces a decrease in consumption expenditure. The decreased consumption expenditure lowers aggregate expenditure. Real GDP and disposable income decrease further, and so does consumption expenditure. Real GDP growth slows, and the inflation rate slows.

If the Fed lowers the interest rate, the events that we've just described occur in the opposite directions, so real GDP growth and the inflation rate speed up.

Figure 16.7 summarizes the process that we've just described. It begins with the Fed's open market operations that change the quantity of money and interest rate and ends with the effects on real GDP and the price level.

FIGURE 16.7
Ripple Effects of the Fed's Actions

Practice Online

The Fed's open market operations change the quantity of money and the interest rate. Expenditure plans eventually change, and so does aggregate demand. Eventually, the Fed's open market operation has ripple effects that change real GDP and the price level.

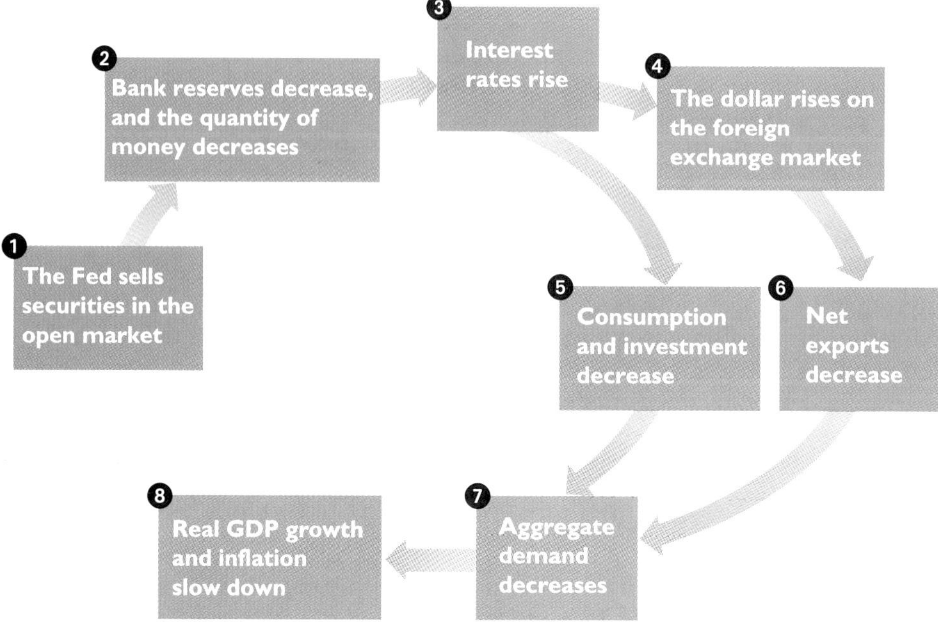

(a) The Fed tightens

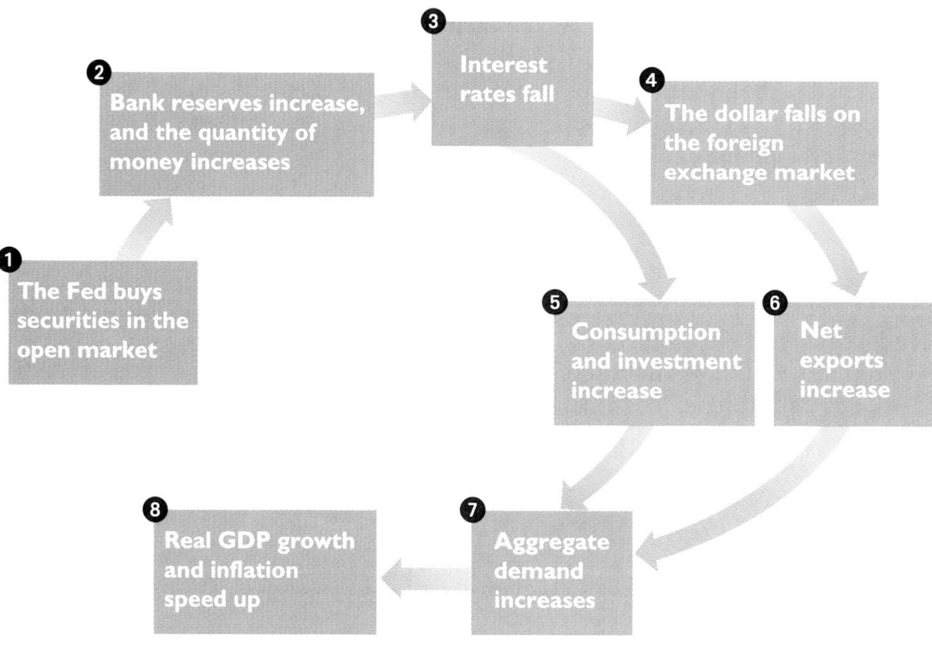

(b) The Fed eases

Monetary Stabilization in the *AS-AD* Model

We've described the broad outline of how the Fed's actions influence the economy. Let's now see how monetary policy might be used to stabilize real GDP.

The Fed Tightens to Fight Inflation

In Figure 16.8, part (a) shows investment demand and part (b) shows aggregate demand and aggregate supply. Initially, the interest rate is 5 percent a year and the quantity of investment is $2 trillion. At this level of investment (think of investment demand as representing all the interest-sensitive components of aggregate expenditure), aggregate demand is AD_0 in part (b). The aggregate supply curve is *AS*, so equilibrium real GDP is $11 trillion, which exceeds potential GDP.

The Fed now conducts an open market sale that increases the interest rate to 6 percent a year. The quantity of investment demand decreases to $1.5 trillion. If this were the only change in aggregate expenditure, aggregate demand would be $AD_0 - \Delta I$. But the multiplier decreases aggregate demand and the aggregate demand curve shifts leftward to AD_1.

The Fed's actions have eliminated an inflation threat, brought real GDP to equal potential GDP, and lowered the price level. In reality, real GDP is growing and the price level is rising, so the Fed's actions would slow real GDP growth and slow inflation rather than decrease real GDP and the price level.

FIGURE 16.8

Monetary Stabilization: Avoiding Inflation

Practice Online

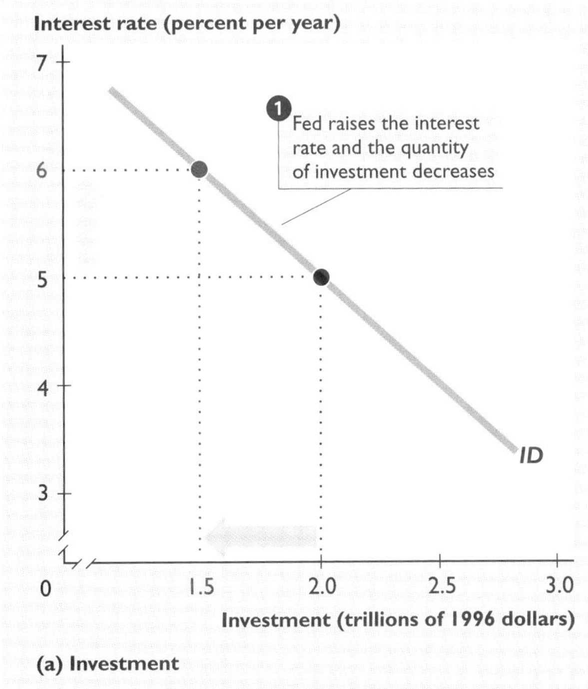

(a) Investment

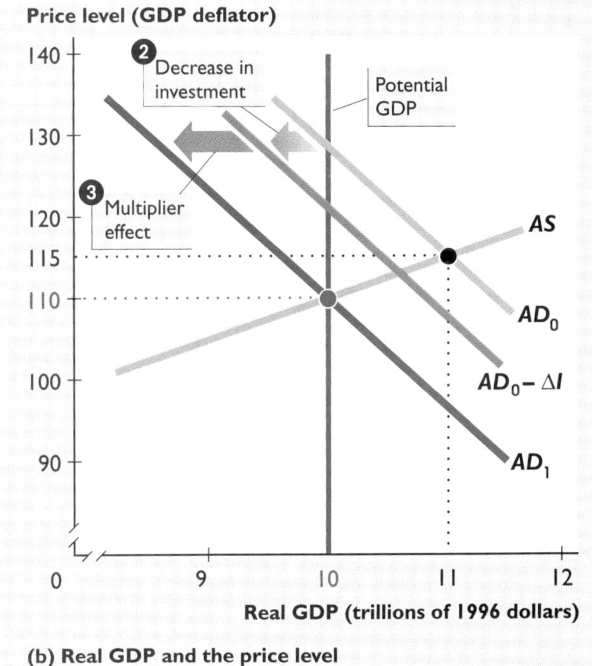

(b) Real GDP and the price level

Real GDP exceeds potential GDP (part b). To avoid inflation, ❶ the Fed raises the interest rate (part a). ❷ Expenditure decreases by ΔI, and ❸ the multiplier induces additional expenditure cuts. The aggregate demand curve shifts to AD_1, real GDP decreases to potential GDP, and inflation is avoided.

The Fed Eases to Fight Recession

Figure 16.9 is similar to Figure 16.8, which you've just examined. The starting point in part (a) is the same. The interest rate is 5 percent a year, and the quantity of investment demanded is \$2 trillion. But the starting point in part (b) is different. Now, at the equilibrium level of investment (and other components of aggregate expenditure), aggregate demand is AD_0 in part (b). The aggregate supply curve is *AS*, so equilibrium real GDP is \$9 trillion, which is less than potential GDP.

The Fed now conducts an open market purchase that lowers the interest rate to 4 percent a year. The quantity of investment increases to \$2.5 trillion. Other interest-sensitive expenditure items (not shown in the figure) also increase. If this were the only change, aggregate demand would increase to $AD_0 + \Delta I$.

With an increase in aggregate expenditure, the multiplier increases aggregate demand. The aggregate demand curve shifts to AD_1. The Fed's actions have eliminated a recession and brought real GDP to equal potential GDP at \$10 trillion and the price level to 110.

The Size of the Multiplier Effect

The size of the multiplier effect of monetary policy depends on the sensitivity of expenditure plans to the interest rate The larger the effect of a change in the interest rate on aggregate expenditure, the greater is the multiplier effect and the smaller is the change in the interest rate that achieves the Fed's objective.

FIGURE 16.9

Monetary Stabilization: Avoiding Recession

Practice Online

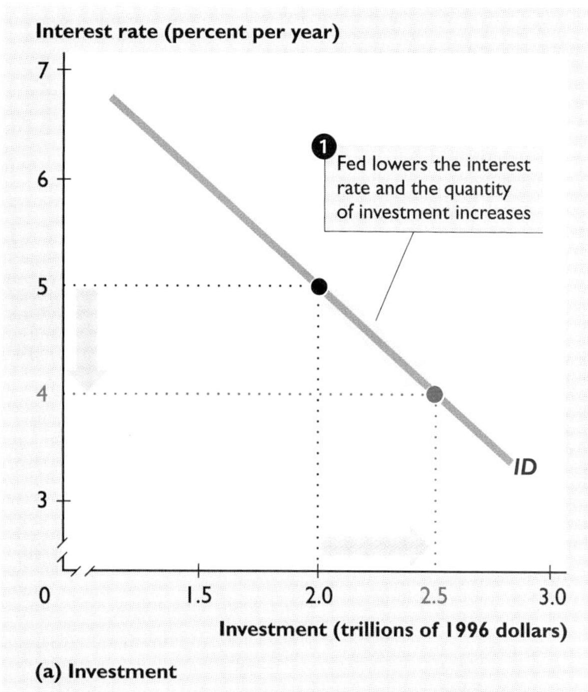

(a) Investment

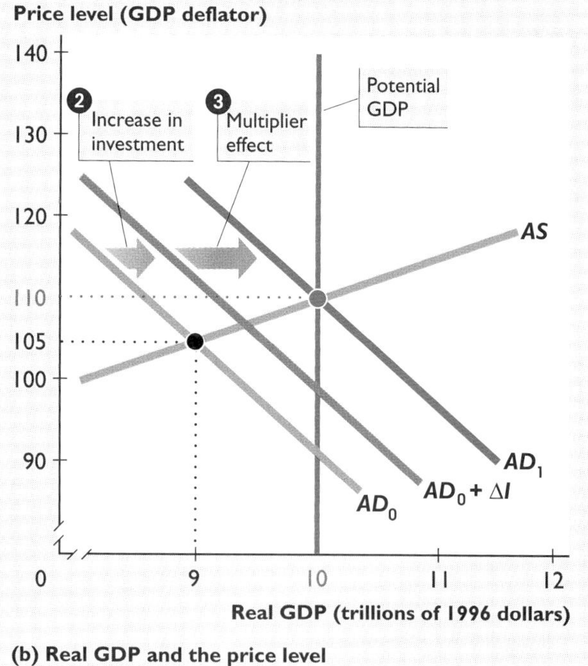

(b) Real GDP and the price level

Real GDP is less than potential GDP (part b). To avoid recession, ❶ the Fed lowers the interest rate (part a). ❷ Expenditure increases by ΔI, and ❸ the multiplier induces additional expenditure. The aggregate demand curve shifts to AD_1, real GDP increases to potential GDP, and recession is avoided.

Limitations of Monetary Stabilization Policy

Monetary policy has an advantage over fiscal policy because it cuts out the law-making time lags. The FOMC meets eight times a year and can conduct telephone meetings between its scheduled meetings if the need arises. And the actual actions that change the quantity of money are daily actions taken by the New York Fed operating under the guidelines decided by the FOMC. So monetary policy is a continuous policy process and is not subject to the long decision lag and the need to create a broad political consensus that confronts fiscal policy.

But monetary policy shares the other two limitations of fiscal policy: Estimating potential GDP is hard, and economic forecasting is error-prone. Monetary policy suffers an additional limitation: Its effects are indirect and depend on how private decisions respond to a change in the interest rate. These responses are themselves hard to forecast and vary from one situation to another in unpredictable ways. A related problem is that the time lags in the operation of monetary policy are longer than those for fiscal policy. So the forecasting horizon must be longer.

In this chapter, we've described the fiscal and monetary policy processes and explained the effects of stabilization policies on real GDP and the price level. In the next two chapters, we study policy tradeoffs and alternative policy strategies.

Eye on the U.S. Economy

The Fed in Action

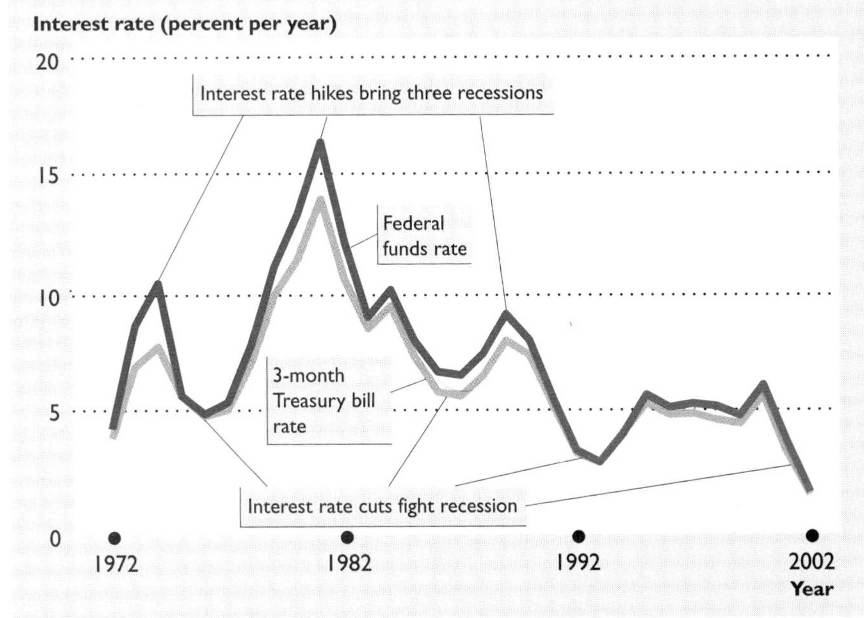

SOURCE: Federal Reserve Board.

The figure shows the federal funds rate and the 3-month Treasury bill rate between 1972 and 2002. The 3-month Treasury bill rate is a good general indicator of the cost of short-term loans to the federal government and large firms.

Notice how closely these interest rates move together. The federal funds rate, which the Fed directly targets, is the main influence on the short-term interest rate at which the government and businesses borrow.

Interest rate hikes brought three recessions: in the mid-1970s, early 1980s, and early 1990s. Through most of the 1990s, the Fed tried to keep the economy expanding while avoiding inflation. So interest rates and money growth were kept steady.

In 2000, the Fed raised short-term interest rates. But fearing recession, the Fed lowered rates aggressively during 2001 and 2002 to an unusually low 1.7 percent a year.

CHECKPOINT 16.2

Study Guide pp. 236–239

Practice Online 16.2

2 **Describe the Federal Reserve's monetary policy process and explain the effects of monetary policy.**

Practice Problems 16.2

1. If the Fed cuts the quantity of money, explain how each of the following items changes.
   a. Businesses' purchases of new capital equipment
   b. Households' purchases of new cars and houses
   c. Foreigners' purchases of U.S.-made goods and services
   d. Americans' purchases of Canadian-made goods and services
2. What is the multiplier effect of monetary policy? How does it work? How does the size of the expenditure multiplier influence the size of the multiplier effect of monetary policy?

Exercises 16.2

1. If the Fed lowers the interest rate, explain how each of the following items changes.
   a. U.S exports
   b. U.S. imports
   c. Investment
   d. The value of the dollar on the foreign exchange market
2. Explain the process by which the Fed's monetary policy influences aggregate demand in the United States.
3. Compare the effectiveness of monetary policy and fiscal policy for stabilizing U.S real GDP and employment.

Solutions to Practice Problems 16.2

1a. When the Fed cuts the quantity of money, the interest rate rises and businesses delay their purchases of new capital equipment.

1b. Households will delay their purchases of new cars and houses.

1c. As the U.S. interest rate rises and foreign interest rates remain the same, the dollar strengthens. U.S.-made goods and services become relatively more expensive for foreigners to buy. Foreigners' purchases of U.S.-made goods and services decrease.

1d. As the dollar strengthens, Canadian-made goods become cheaper for Americans to buy. Americans' purchases of Canadian-produced goods increase.

2. When the Fed increases the quantity of money, interest rates fall and the foreign exchange value of the dollar falls. As interest rates fall, aggregate expenditure increases because investment, consumption expenditure, and net exports increase. The multiplier effect of monetary policy is the increase in aggregate expenditure divided by the increase in the quantity of money.
When the interest rate changes, part of autonomous expenditure changes and the expenditure multiplier determines the change in aggregate demand. The larger the expenditure multiplier, the larger is the multiplier effect of monetary policy.

CHAPTER CHECKPOINT

Key Points

1 Describe the federal budget process and explain the effects of fiscal policy.

- The federal budget is an annual statement of the expenditures, tax receipts, and surplus or deficit of the government of the United States.
- Fiscal policy is the use of the federal budget to finance the federal government and to stabilize the economy.
- Fiscal policy can be either discretionary or automatic.
- Changes in government purchases and changes in taxes have multiplier effects on aggregate demand and can be used to try to keep real GDP at potential GDP.
- In practice, law-making time lags, the difficulty of estimating potential GDP, and the limitations of economic forecasting seriously hamper discretionary fiscal policy.
- Automatic stabilizers arise because tax receipts and expenditures fluctuate with real GDP.

2 Describe the Federal Reserve's monetary policy process and explain the effects of monetary policy.

- The Fed makes monetary policy in an open and transparent process that involves three main elements: the Beige Book, meetings of the Federal Open Market Committee, and the Monetary Policy Report to Congress.
- When the FOMC announces a policy change, it is in terms of the interest rate, not the quantity of money.
- In the long run, the Fed influences the nominal interest rate by the effects of its policies on the inflation rate. But it does not directly control the nominal interest rate, and it has no control over the real interest rate.
- In the short run, the Fed can determine the nominal interest rate, but to do so, it must undertake open market operations that change the quantity of money.
- When the Fed changes the interest rate, the effects ripple through the economy by changing aggregate demand.
- The size of the multiplier effect of monetary policy depends on the sensitivity of expenditure plans to the interest rate.
- Monetary policy has no law-making time lag, but its effects are indirect and depend on how the interest rate influences private decisions.

Key Terms

Exercises

1. How did the role of fiscal policy change in 1946? What are the main provisions of the landmark act that changed it? What further change occurred in 1978?
2. Sort the following items into those that are discretionary fiscal policy actions, those that are automatic fiscal policy actions, and those that are not fiscal policy.
   a. An increase in expenditure on homeland security
   b. An increase in unemployment benefits paid during the 2001 recession
   c. The Bush tax cuts
   d. An open market operation
   e. The fall in taxes paid by corporations because their profits fell in 2001
   f. Increased expenditures on national defense arising from the war against terrorism
   g. A rise in the federal funds rate
   h. An increase in Medicaid expenditure brought about by a flu epidemic
   i. The changes in farm subsidies arising from the 2002 Farm Bill
   j. A fall in customs revenue that resulted from a decrease in U.S. imports
3. Suppose that the U.S. government increases its expenditure on highways and bridges by $100 billion in 2003. Explain the effect that this expenditure would have on
   a. Autonomous expenditure.
   b. Aggregate demand.
   c. Real GDP.
   d. Needs-tested spending.
   e. The government's budget surplus.
4. Suppose that Congress passes additional tax cuts that total $100 billion in 2004. Explain the effect that this tax cut would have on
   a. Consumption expenditure before any change in real GDP occurs.
   b. Consumption expenditure induced by a change in real GDP.
   c. Aggregate demand.
   d. Real GDP.
   e. The government's budget surplus.
5. The income tax rate is higher in Sweden than it is in the United States. Also, Sweden has more generous payments to the unemployed and others who fall on hard economic times. And the percentage of expenditure on imported goods and services is much larger in Sweden than in the United States. Which country, Sweden or the United States, do you think is likely to have
   a. The larger government purchases multiplier?
   b. The larger tax multiplier?
   c. The more effective automatic stabilizers?
   d. The greater fluctuations in real GDP over the business cycle?
   e. The greater fluctuations in the government budget balance over the business cycle?
   f. The larger supply-side effects of fiscal policy?

6. Describe the supply-side effects of fiscal policy and explain how a tax cut or an increase in government purchases might influence
   a. Potential GDP.
   b. Aggregate supply.
   c. Equilibrium real GDP and the price level.

   Use an aggregate supply–aggregate demand graph to illustrate the effects you've described.
7. Suppose that the Fed sees an expansion slowing and forecasts a recession in the near future. What change in its monetary policy would lessen the effect of the recession? Use appropriate graphs to explain and illustrate the effect of the Fed's actions on
   a. Interest rates.
   b. The quantity of money.
   c. Investment.
   d. The foreign exchange value of the dollar.
   e. Net exports.
   f. Aggregate demand.
   g. Real GDP and the price level.
8. Suppose that the Fed sees the current expansion gaining too much steam and forecasts an increase in inflation in the near future. What change in its monetary policy would lessen the likelihood of inflation? Use appropriate graphs to explain and illustrate the effect of the Fed's actions on
   a. Interest rates.
   b. The quantity of money.
   c. Investment.
   d. The foreign exchange value of the dollar.
   e. Net exports.
   f. Aggregate demand.
   g. Real GDP and the price level.
9. Explain why monetary policy is used more often than fiscal policy to stabilize the economy.
10. Explain the effect of a decrease in the quantity of money on aggregate demand. What determines how big the change in aggregate demand will be?
11. If the U.S. government wanted to increase investment, would it encourage the Fed to change its monetary policy or would the government change its fiscal policy? Explain why. What effect would the policy change have on the price level?
12. If the U.S. government wanted to increase exports, would it encourage the Fed to change its monetary policy or would the government change its fiscal policy? Explain why. What effect would the policy change have on the composition of aggregate expenditure?

Critical Thinking

13. Suppose that Bill Frist (Republican) and Tom Daschle (Democrat) are debating the effects of fiscal policy on real GDP and the price level. Bill Frist says that a tax cut will increase real GDP and keep the price level stable. Tom Daschle says that the tax cut will only line the pockets of the rich and have no effects on output or the price level.
    a. Using the aggregate supply–aggregate demand model, provide an explanation of what Bill Frist says will happen.
    b. Using the aggregate supply–aggregate demand model, provide an explanation of what Tom Daschle says will happen.
    c. Highlight the differences in assumptions about how the economy works and sketch a research project that could settle the debate.
14. Review the main limitations of discretionary fiscal policy and contrast those limitations with the benefits of automatic fiscal policy.
15. In the U.S. recession of 2001, government purchases increased and taxes were cut. Explain how the government's actions
    a. Changed aggregate demand.
    b. Changed the budget surplus and outstanding government debt.
16. Describe and critically evaluate the effects of the actions taken by the Federal Reserve and the federal government during 2002 to stimulate the U.S. economy and lift it from recession.

Practice Online

Web Exercises

Use the links on your Foundations Web site to work the following exercises.

17. Visit the Office of Management and Budget Web site and review the history of the budget surplus/deficit and the national debt. What events have led to the greatest increases in the national debt? In which periods has the debt been paid down? Looking at the history of the U.S. federal budget, do you think the current plan to pay off the national debt will be carried out? Why or why not?
18. Visit the Federal Reserve's Web site and review the current state of the U.S. economy using the latest issue of the Beige Book. In light of what you discover about real GDP, inflation, and the unemployment rate, set out your policy recommendations to
    a. The FOMC.
    b. Congress.
19. Visit the IMF World Economic Outlook Web site to review the current state of the global economy. [Change the 2002 in this URL to the current year and change 02 to 01 before October.] In light of what you discover about real GDP growth and inflation, set out your policy advice to the governments of the major countries.

CHAPTER 17

The Short-Run Policy Tradeoff

CHAPTER CHECKLIST

When you have completed your study of this chapter, you will be able to

1. **Describe the short-run tradeoff between inflation and unemployment.**
2. **Distinguish between the short-run and the long-run Phillips curves and describe the shifting tradeoff between inflation and unemployment.**
3. **Explain how the Fed can influence the expected inflation rate and how expected inflation influences the short-run tradeoff.**

The task of this chapter is to explore a tradeoff that we face in implementing fiscal and monetary stabilization policies.

We want low unemployment and low inflation. But can we have both at the same time? Must we pay the cost of a bit more inflation to obtain the benefits of a bit less unemployment—or the cost of a bit more unemployment to obtain the benefits of a bit less inflation? That is, do we face a tradeoff between unemployment and inflation?

If we do face a tradeoff, what is it like? Is it a permanent or a temporary tradeoff? That is, must we pay the cost of a permanently higher unemployment rate to obtain the benefits of permanently lower inflation? Or do we have to pay for a limited time to secure a permanent benefit?

And how harsh is the tradeoff? Must we pay a high cost in terms of unemployment for a small gain in lower inflation? Or can we get a big drop in inflation at a small unemployment cost? This chapter answers these questions.

17.1 THE SHORT-RUN PHILLIPS CURVE

Short-run Phillips curve
A curve that shows the relationship between the inflation rate and the unemployment rate when the natural unemployment rate and the expected inflation rate remain constant.

The **short-run Phillips curve** is a curve that shows the relationship between the inflation rate and the unemployment rate when the natural unemployment rate and the expected inflation rate remain constant. The short-run Phillips curve is a downward-sloping curve along which an increase in the unemployment rate is associated with a decrease in the inflation rate.

Figure 17.1 illustrates a short-run Phillips curve. In this example, the natural unemployment rate is 6 percent and the expected inflation rate is 3 percent a year. If the economy were at full employment, the unemployment rate would equal the natural unemployment rate and the inflation rate would equal the expected inflation rate at point *B*. This point is the anchor point for the short-run Phillips curve.

An expansion that takes the economy above full-employment decreases the unemployment rate and increases the inflation rate. In an expansion, the economy might move to a point such as *A*, where the unemployment rate is 5 percent and the inflation rate is 4 percent a year. A recession that takes the economy below full employment increases the unemployment rate and lowers the inflation rate. In a recession, the economy might move to a point such as *C*, where the unemployment rate is 7 percent and the inflation rate is 2 percent a year.

The short-run Phillips curve presents a *tradeoff* between inflation and unemployment because, along a given curve, a lower unemployment rate can be achieved only by paying the cost of a higher inflation rate, and a lower inflation rate can be achieved only by paying the cost of a higher unemployment rate. For example, in Figure 17.1, a decrease in the unemployment rate from 6 percent to 5

FIGURE 17.1
A Short-Run Phillips Curve

Practice Online

The short-run Phillips curve (*SRPC*) shows the relationship between inflation and unemployment at a particular natural unemployment rate and expected inflation rate. Here, if the unemployment rate is 6 percent, the inflation rate is 3 percent a year. Higher unemployment rates bring lower inflation rates, and lower unemployment rates bring higher inflation rates.

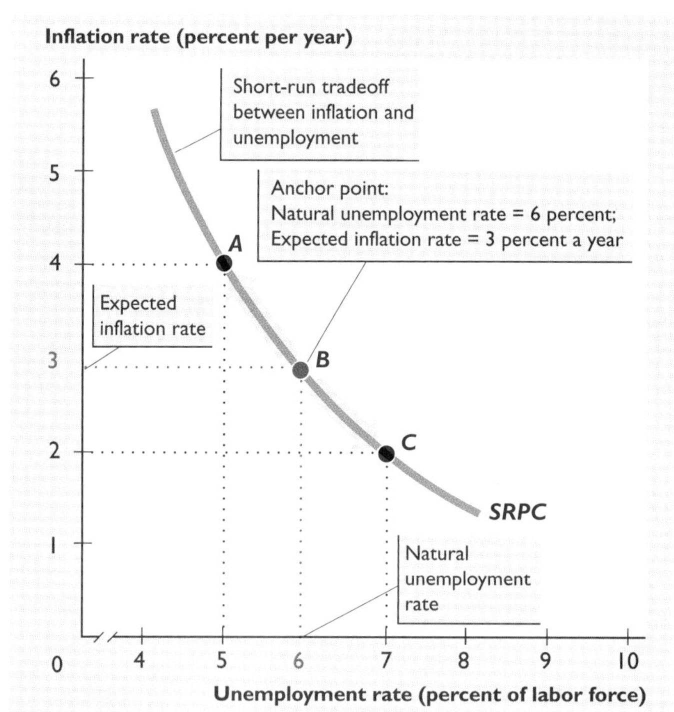

percent costs a 1-percentage point increase in the inflation rate from 3 percent a year to 4 percent a year.

The short-run Phillips curve describes a *short-run* tradeoff because the tradeoff changes when the expected inflation rate or the natural unemployment rate changes. We'll explore the effects of these changes later in this chapter.

Aggregate Supply and the Short-Run Phillips Curve

The *AS-AD* model explains the negative relationship between unemployment and inflation along the short-run Phillips curve. The short-run Phillips curve is another way of looking at the upward-sloping aggregate supply curve. Both curves arise because the money wage rate is sticky in the short run. When the price level changes but the money wage rate doesn't change, the real wage rate changes and so does the quantity of labor demanded and the quantity of real GDP supplied. (Chapter 8, pp. 183–184, provides a brief account of this process, and Chapter 14, pp. 347–349, provides a detailed account.) A change in real GDP also changes the unemployment rate, and a change in the price level also changes the inflation rate. Let's explore the connections between the variables used in the *AS-AD* model and the short-run Phillips curve a bit more closely.

Unemployment and Real GDP

In a given period, with a fixed amount of capital and given state of technology, real GDP depends on the quantity of labor employed. At full employment, the quantity of real GDP is *potential GDP* and the unemployment rate is the natural unemployment rate. If real GDP exceeds potential GDP, employment exceeds its full-employment level and the unemployment rate falls below the natural unemployment rate. Similarly, if real GDP is less than potential GDP, employment is less than its full-employment level and the unemployment rate rises above the natural unemployment rate.

The quantitative relationship between the unemployment rate and real GDP was first estimated by economist Arthur M. Okun and is called **Okun's Law**. Okun's Law states that for each percentage point that the unemployment rate is above the natural unemployment rate, there is a 2 percent gap between real GDP and potential GDP. If the natural unemployment rate is 6 percent and potential GDP is $10 trillion, then when the actual unemployment rate is 7 percent, real GDP is $9.8 trillion—98 percent of potential GDP, or 2 percent below potential GDP. When the actual unemployment rate is 5 percent, real GDP is $10.2 trillion—102 percent of potential GDP, or 2 percent above potential GDP. Table 17.1 summarizes this relationship.

Okun's Law
For each percentage point that the unemployment rate is above the natural unemployment rate, there is a 2 percent gap between real GDP and potential GDP.

TABLE 17.1

	Unemployment rate (percent)	Real GDP (trillions of 1996 dollars)
A	5	10.2
B	6	10.0
C	7	9.8

Inflation and the Price Level

The inflation rate is defined as the percentage change in the price level. So starting from last period's price level, the higher the inflation rate, the higher is the current period's price level. Suppose that last year, the price level was 100. If in the current year, the inflation rate is 2 percent, the price level rises to 102; if the inflation rate is 3 percent, the price level rises to 103; and if the inflation rate is 4 percent, the price level rises to 104.

With these relationships between the unemployment rate and real GDP and between the inflation rate and the price level, we can establish the connection between the short-run Phillips curve and the aggregate supply curve. Figure 17.2 shows this connection.

If in the current year, the economy expands along its full-employment path, real GDP equals potential GDP of $10 trillion and the unemployment rate equals the natural unemployment rate of 6 percent in Figure 17.2. Point *B* on the short-run Phillips curve in part (a) and point *B* on the aggregate supply curve in part (b) show this situation. The inflation rate is 3 percent a year (its expected rate) in part (a) and the price level is 103 (also its expected level) in part (b).

If instead of expanding along its full-employment path, the economy expands more strongly, real GDP might be $10.2 trillion at point *A* on the aggregate supply curve in part (b). In this case, the unemployment rate is 5 percent at point *A* in part (a). The inflation rate is 4 percent a year (higher than expected) in part (a), and the price level is 104 (also higher than expected) in part (b).

Finally, if instead the economy expands by less than potential GDP, real GDP might be $9.8 trillion at point *C* on the aggregate supply curve in part (b). In this case, the unemployment rate is 7 percent at point *C* in part (a). The inflation rate is 2 percent a year (lower than expected) in part (a), and the price level is 102 (also lower than expected) in part (b).

FIGURE 17.2

The Short-Run Phillips Curve and the Aggregate Supply Curve

Practice Online

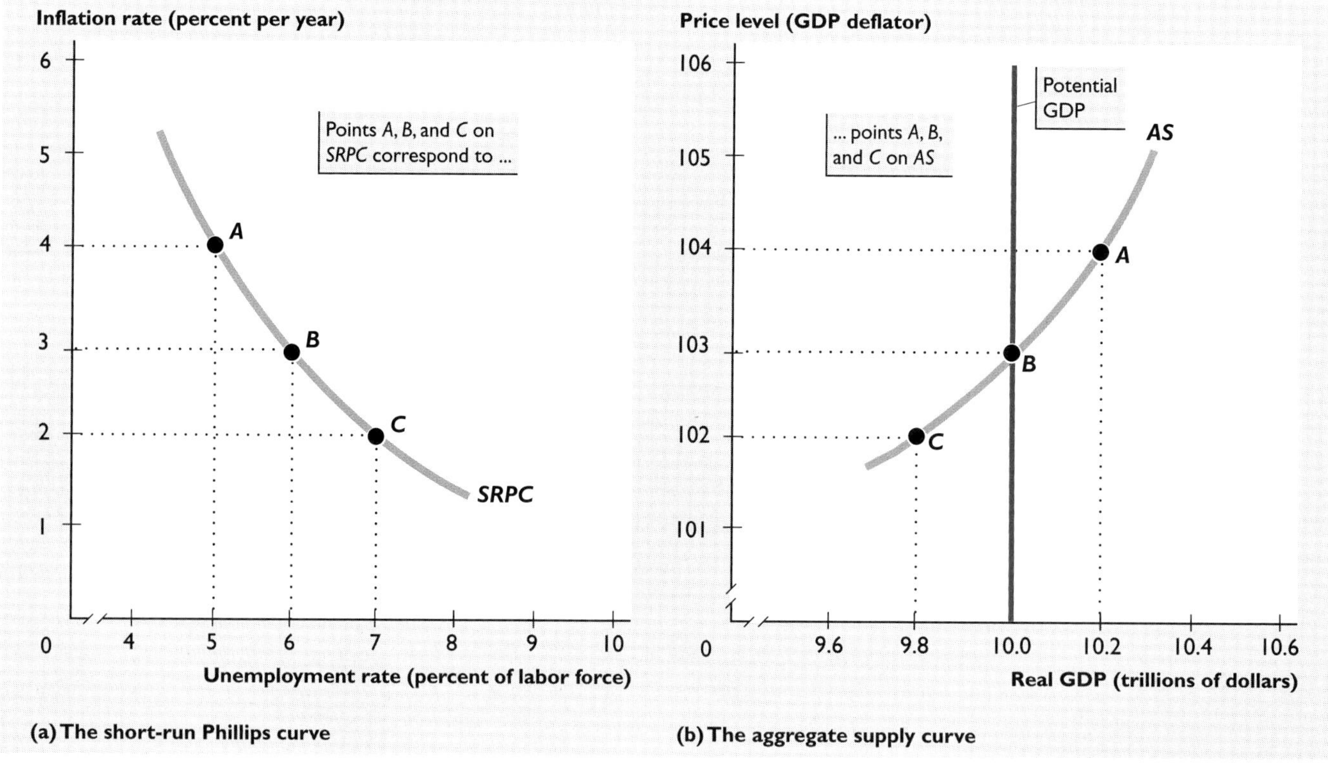

Point *A* on the Phillips curve corresponds to point *A* on the aggregate supply curve: The unemployment rate is 5 percent and the inflation rate is 4 percent a year (in part a), and real GDP is $10.2 trillion and the price level is 104 (in part b).

Point *B* on the Phillips curve corresponds to point *B* on the aggregate supply curve: The unemployment rate is 6 percent and the inflation rate is 3 percent a year (in part a), and real GDP is $10 trillion and the price level is 103 (in part b).

Point *C* on the Phillips curve corresponds to point *C* on the aggregate supply curve: The unemployment rate is 7 percent and the inflation rate is 2 percent a year (in part a), and real GDP is $9.8 trillion and the price level is 102 (in part b).

Aggregate Demand Fluctuations

Aggregate demand fluctuations bring movements along the aggregate supply curve and equivalent movements along the short-run Phillips curve. A decrease in aggregate demand that brings a movement along the aggregate supply curve from point *B* to point *C* lowers the price level and decreases real GDP relative to what they would have been. That same decrease in aggregate demand brings a movement along the Phillips curve from point *B* to point *C*. The inflation rate falls, and the unemployment rate increases.

Similarly, an increase in aggregate demand that brings a movement along the aggregate supply curve from point *B* to point *A* raises the price level and increases real GDP relative to what they would have been. That same increase in aggregate demand brings a movement along the Phillips curve from point *B* to point *A*. The inflation rate rises, and the unemployment rate decreases.

The U.S. Phillips Curve

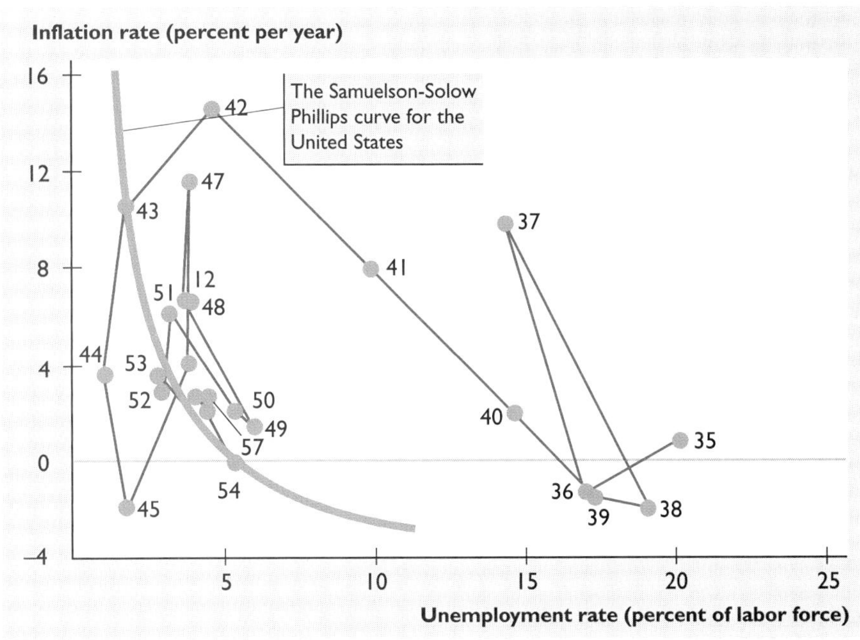

SOURCE: Samuelson, Paul A. and Robert M. Solow, "Problem of Achieving and Maintaining a Stable Price Level, Analytical Aspects of Anti-Inflation Policy." *American Economic Review*, 50(2). May 1960.

The Phillips curve is so named because New Zealand economist A.W. (Bill) Phillips discovered the relationship in about 100 years of unemployment and wage inflation data for the United Kingdom.

Phillips made his discovery in 1958, two years before the election of John F. Kennedy as President of the United States. Very soon thereafter, two young American economists, Paul A. Samuelson and Robert M. Solow, both at MIT and eager to help the new Kennedy administration to pursue a low-unemployment strategy, looked for a Phillips curve in the U.S. data. The figure shows what they found: no recognizable relationship between inflation and unemployment for the 20 or so years that they studied.

Giving more weight to the 1950s experience, and viewing the 1930s and 1940s as special because of the Great Depression and World War II, Samuelson and Solow proposed the U.S. Phillips curve shown in the figure. They believed that the U.S. Phillips curve provided support for the then growing view that the new Kennedy administration could pursue a low unemployment policy with only a moderate rise in the inflation rate.

As the 1960s unfolded, the Samuelson-Solow Phillips curve began to look like a permanent tradeoff between inflation and unemployment. But in the late 1960s and early 1970s, the relationship disappeared in the face of rising inflation expectations.

Eye on the Global Economy

Inflation and Unemployment

The figures show data on inflation and unemployment in the United Kingdom and the United States over most of the twentieth century. Like the U.S. data that Samuelson and Solow used, the data for each country reveal no neat, tight tradeoff. The short-run tradeoff shifts around a great deal.

The highest inflation rates have not occurred at the lowest unemployment rates. And the highest unemployment rates during the Great Depression of the 1930s did not bring the lowest inflation rates, although the price level did fall rapidly in the United States during the recession years of 1931 and 1932.

A. W. Phillips

(a) United States 1900–1997

(b) United Kingdom 1900–1997

SOURCE: Michael Parkin, "Unemployment, Inflation, and Monetary Policy," *Canadian Journal of Economics*, November 1998.

Why Bother with the Phillips Curve?

You've seen that the short-run Phillips curve is another way of looking at the aggregate supply curve. And you might be wondering, why bother with the short-run Phillips curve? Isn't the aggregate supply curve adequate for describing the short-run tradeoff?

There are two reasons for using the Phillips curve. First, it focuses directly on two policy targets: the inflation rate and the unemployment rate. Second, the aggregate supply curve shifts whenever the money wage rate or potential GDP changes. Such changes occur every day. So the aggregate supply curve is not a stable tradeoff. The short-run Phillips curve isn't a stable tradeoff either, but it is more stable than the aggregate supply curve. It shifts only when the natural unemployment rate changes or when the expected inflation rate changes.

CHECKPOINT 17.1

1 Describe the short-run tradeoff between inflation and unemployment.

Study Guide pp. 244–248

Practice Online 17.1

Practice Problem 17.1

Table 1 describes five possible situations that might arise in 2003, depending on the level of aggregate demand in that year. Potential GDP is \$7 trillion, and the natural unemployment rate is 5 percent.

a. Calculate the inflation rate for each possible outcome.
b. Use Okun's Law to find the real GDP associated with each unemployment rate in Table 1.
c. What is the expected inflation rate in 2003?
d. What is the expected price level in 2003?
e. Plot the short-run Phillips curve for 2003.
f. Plot the aggregate supply curve for 2003.
g. Mark the points *A*, *B*, *C*, *D*, and *E* on each curve that correspond to the data provided in Table 1 and the data that you have calculated.

TABLE 1

	Price level (2002 = 100)	Unemployment rate (percentage)
A	102.5	9
B	105.0	6
C	106.0	5
D	107.5	4
E	110.0	3

TABLE 2

	Price level (2002 = 100)	Unemployment rate (percentage)
A	108	9
B	113	6
C	115	5
D	118	4
E	123	3

Exercises 17.1

1. In the economy in the practice problem, the outcome in 2003 turned out to be row B of Table 1. Table 2 shows five possible outcomes for 2004 depending on the level of aggregate demand in that year. Potential GDP has grown to \$7.35 trillion, but the natural unemployment rate has remained at 5 percent.
   a. Plot the short-run Phillips curve for 2004.
   b. Use Okun's Law to find the real GDP associated with each unemployment rate in Table 2.
   c. What is the expected inflation rate in 2004?
   d. What is the expected price level in 2004?
   e. Plot the aggregate supply curve for 2004.
   f. Mark the points *A*, *B*, *C*, *D*, and *E* on each curve that correspond to the data provided in Table 2 and the data you have calculated.

2. Compare the short-run Phillips curves and aggregate supply curves of 2004 with those of 2003. Thinking about the definitions of the short-run Phillips curve and the aggregate supply curve, what might have changed between the two years to make the curves shift?

FIGURE 1

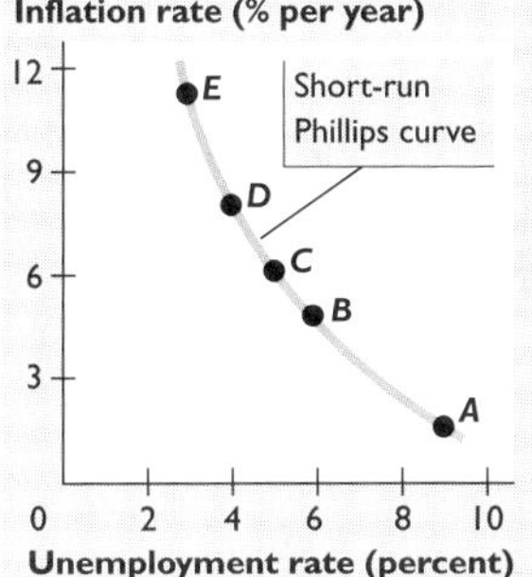

FIGURE 2

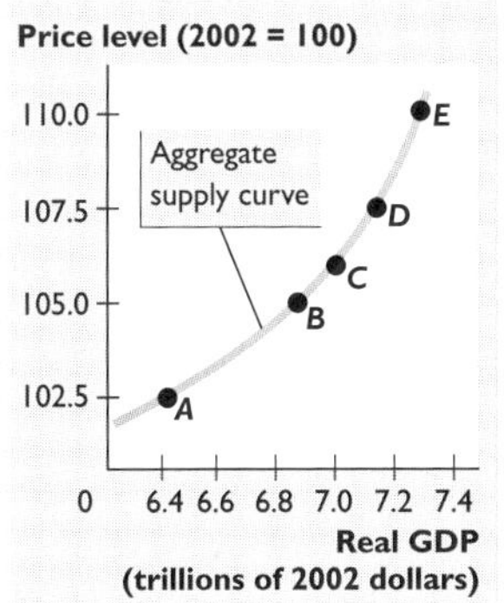

Solution to Practice Problem 17.1

a. and **b.** The inflation rate equals the price level minus 100; real GDP equals potential GDP minus x percent of potential GDP, where $x = 2 \times$ (unemployment rate – natural unemployment rate)—Okun's Law.
c. The expected inflation rate in 2003 is 6 percent a year.
d. The expected price level in 2003 is 106.
e. Figure 1 shows the short-run Phillips curve for 2003.
f. Figure 2 shows the aggregate supply curve for 2003.
g. The points are *A*, *B*, *C*, *D*, and *E* on each curve in Figures 1 and 2.

17.2 SHORT-RUN AND LONG-RUN PHILLIPS CURVES

The short-run Phillips curve is the *short-run tradeoff* between inflation and unemployment when aggregate demand changes and the natural unemployment rate and expected inflation rate remain the same. Over time, these two factors do not remain the same. And you've seen in the data that the actual fluctuations in inflation and unemployment do not fall along a neat Phillips curve.

Changes in the expected inflation rate influence the short-run tradeoff most. And changes in expected inflation create a long-run Phillips curve. Let's look at the properties of the long-run Phillips curve.

The Long-Run Phillips Curve

Long-run Phillips curve
The vertical line that shows the relationship between inflation and unemployment when the economy is at full employment.

The **long-run Phillips curve** shows the relationship between inflation and unemployment when the economy is at full employment. You learned in Chapter 8 that at full employment, the unemployment rate is the *natural unemployment rate*. So on the long-run Phillips curve, there is only one possible unemployment rate: the natural unemployment rate.

In contrast, the inflation rate can take on any value at full employment. You learned in Chapter 13 (pp. 327–330) that at full employment, for a given real GDP growth rate, the greater the money growth rate, the greater is the inflation rate.

This description of the economy in the long run tells us the properties of the long-run Phillips curve. The long-run Phillips curve is a vertical line located at the natural unemployment rate. In Figure 17.3, it is the vertical line *LRPC*. The long-run Phillips curve tells us that any inflation rate is possible at the natural unemployment rate.

FIGURE 17.3
The Long-Run Phillips Curve

Practice Online

The long-run Phillips curve is a vertical line at the natural unemployment rate. In the long run, there is no unemployment-inflation tradeoff.

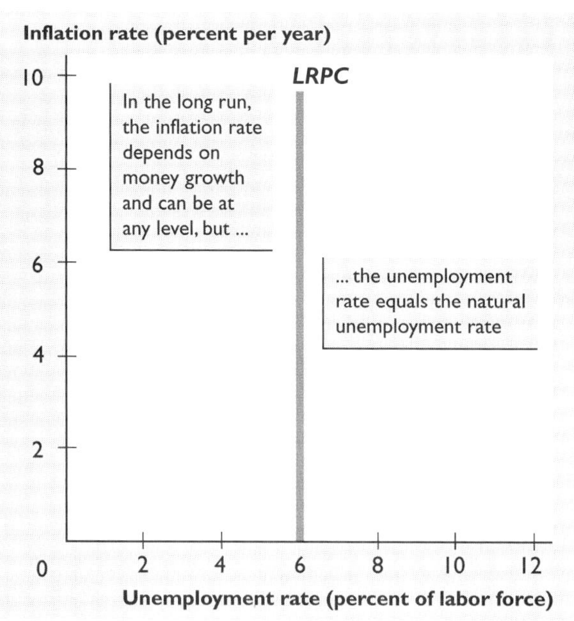

No Long-Run Tradeoff

Because the long-run Phillips curve is vertical, there is no long-run tradeoff between unemployment and inflation. In the long run, the only unemployment rate available is the natural unemployment rate, but any inflation rate can occur.

You can think of the long-run Phillips curve as another way of looking at the potential GDP line in the *AS-AD* model. Let's examine this parallel.

Long-Run Adjustment in the *AS-AD* Model

The *AS-AD* model explains both the short-run and long-run effects of a change in aggregate demand. Figure 17.4 shows the long-run effect. Last year, aggregate demand was AD_0 and aggregate supply was AS_0. The price level was 100, and real GDP was $10 trillion—potential GDP. (To simplify the story, suppose there is no economic growth, so potential GDP remains at $10 trillion.)

Case 1: In the current year, aggregate demand increases from AD_0 to AD_1. The money wage rate rises to keep the real wage rate at its full-employment level. So the aggregate supply shifts to AS_1. The price level rises to 103—the inflation rate is 3 percent—and real GDP remains at potential GDP.

Case 2: In the current year, aggregate demand increases from AD_0 to AD_2. The money wage rate rises to keep the real wage rate at its full-employment level. So the aggregate supply shifts to AS_2. The price level rises to 107—the inflation rate is 7 percent—and real GDP remains at potential GDP.

In the *AS-AD* model, any price level is possible in the long run, but only one level of real GDP can occur—potential GDP. Aggregate demand and aggregate supply determine the price level.

FIGURE 17.4

Long-Run Adjustment in the *AS-AD* Model

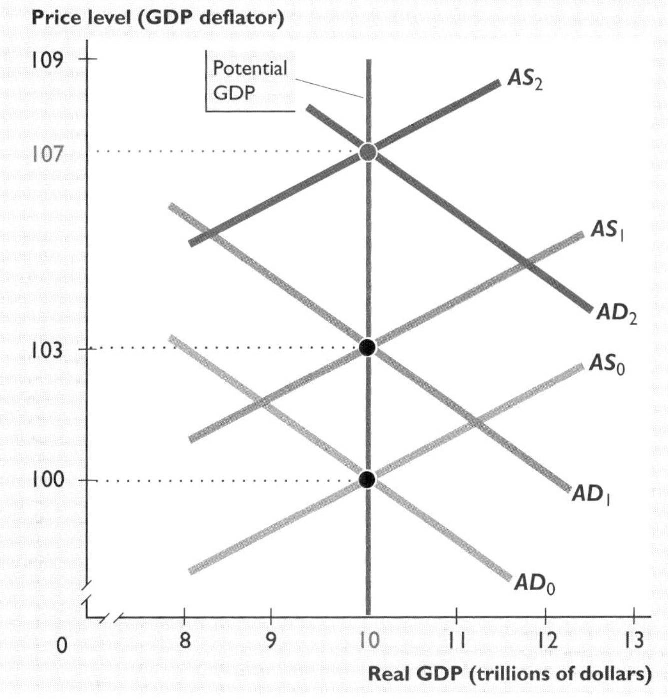

Last year, aggregate demand was AD_0, aggregate supply was AS_0, the price level was 100, and real GDP was $10 trillion (at full employment).

If aggregate demand increases to AD_1 and aggregate supply changes to AS_1, the price level rises by 3 percent to 103.

But if aggregate demand increases to AD_2 and aggregate supply changes to AS_2, the price level rises by 7 percent to 107.

In both cases, real GDP remains at $10 trillion, and because the economy is at full employment, unemployment remains at the natural unemployment rate.

Expected Inflation

Expected inflation rate
The inflation rate that people forecast and use to set the money wage rate and other money prices.

Full employment occurs when the *AD* and *AS* curves intersect at potential GDP. We're going to see that at full employment, the inflation rate equals the expected inflation rate. The **expected inflation rate** is the inflation rate that people forecast and use to set the money wage rate and other money prices.

Suppose there is full employment and McDonald's servers earn $7 an hour. With no inflation, a money wage rate of $7 an hour keeps the market for servers in equilibrium. But with 10 percent inflation, a constant money wage rate means a falling real wage rate and a shortage of servers. Now, a 10 percent rise in the money wage rate to $7.70 is needed to keep the market for servers in equilibrium. If McDonald's and everyone else expect 10 percent inflation, the money wage rate will rise by 10 percent to prevent a labor shortage from arising.

If expectations about the inflation rate turn out to be correct, the price level rises by the 10 percent expected and the real wage rate remains constant at its full employment equilibrium level. Real GDP remains at potential GDP and unemployment remains at the natural unemployment rate.

Because the actual inflation rate equals the expected inflation rate at full employment, we can interpret the long-run Phillips curve as the relationship between inflation and unemployment when the inflation rate equals the expected inflation rate.

Figure 17.5 shows short-run Phillips curves for two expected inflation rates. A short-run Phillips curve shows the tradeoff between inflation and unemployment at *a particular expected inflation rate*. When the expected inflation rate changes, the

FIGURE 17.5
Short-Run and Long-Run Phillips Curves

Practice Online

If the natural unemployment rate is 6 percent, the long-run Phillips curve is *LRPC*. ❶ If the expected inflation rate is 3 percent a year, the short-run Phillips curve is $SRPC_0$. ❷ If the expected inflation rate is 7 percent a year, the short-run Phillips curve is $SRPC_1$.

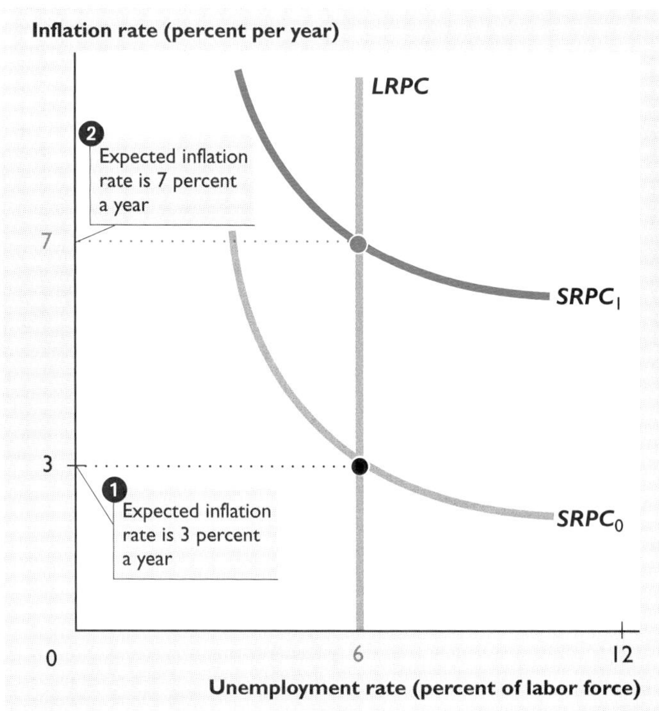

short-run Phillips curve shifts to intersect the long-run Phillips curve at the new expected inflation rate.

In Figure 17.5, when the expected inflation rate is 3 percent a year, the short-run Phillips curve is $SRPC_0$, and when the expected inflation rate is 7 percent a year, the short-run Phillips curve is $SRPC_1$.

The Natural Rate Hypothesis

The **natural rate hypothesis** is the proposition that when the money growth rate changes (and the aggregate demand growth rate changes), the unemployment rate changes *temporarily* and eventually returns to the natural unemployment rate.

Natural rate hypothesis
The proposition that when the money growth rate changes, the unemployment rate changes temporarily and eventually returns to the natural unemployment rate.

Figure 17.6 illustrates the natural rate hypothesis. Initially, aggregate demand growth generates inflation at 3 percent a year and the economy is at full employment, at point *A*. Then aggregate demand grows more rapidly, at a rate that will eventually generate inflation at 7 percent a year. But in the short run, with a sticky money wage rate, the increase in aggregate demand brings an increase in real GDP and a decrease in the unemployment rate. The inflation rate increases to 5 percent a year, and the economy moves from point *A* to point *B*. Eventually, the higher inflation rate is expected and the money wage rate increases. As the expected inflation rate increases from 3 percent to 7 percent a year, the short-run Phillips curve shifts upward from $SRPC_0$ to $SRPC_1$. Inflation speeds up, real GDP moves back to its full-employment level, and the unemployment rate returns to the natural unemployment rate. In Figure 17.6, the economy moves from point *B* to point *C*.

FIGURE 17.6
The Natural Rate Hypothesis

Practice Online

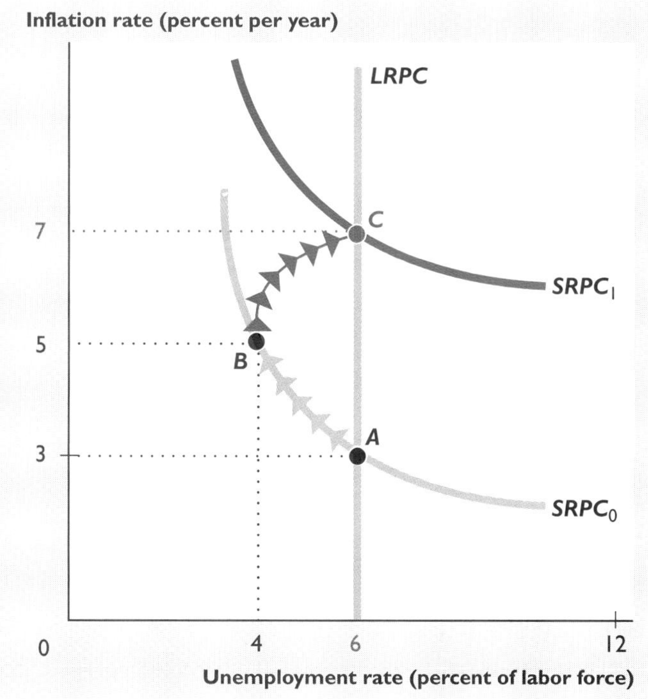

The inflation rate is 3 percent a year and the economy is at full employment, at point *A*. Then the inflation rate increases. In the short run, the increase in inflation brings a decrease in the unemployment rate—a movement along $SRPC_0$ to point *B*. Eventually, the higher inflation rate is expected and the short-run Phillips curve shifts upward to $SRPC_1$. At the higher expected inflation rate, unemployment returns to the natural unemployment rate—the natural rate hypothesis.

Eye on the Past

A Live Test of the Natural Rate Hypothesis

The figure describes the U.S. economy during the 11 years from 1960 to 1971 and shows that the natural rate hypothesis provides a good description of reality during these years.

The natural unemployment rate was around 6 percent, so the long-run Phillips curve, *LRPC*, was located at that unemployment rate.

At the beginning of the period, the inflation rate and the expected inflation rate were around 1 percent a year. So the short-run Phillips curve was $SRPC_0$.

Through 1966, the expected inflation rate remained at 1 percent a year but the actual inflation rate edged upward and the unemployment rate decreased below the natural unemployment rate. The economy moved up along $SRPC_0$ from point *A* to point *B*.

Then, from 1967 through 1969, the inflation rate increased and so did the expected inflation rate. By 1969, the economy had moved to point *C*. By 1970, the expected inflation rate was around 5 percent a year and the short-run Phillips curve had shifted upward to $SRPC_1$. As the higher inflation rate came to be expected, the unemployment rate increased; by 1971, it had returned to the natural unemployment rate and the economy had moved to point *D*.

Notice the similarity between the actual events of this period and the natural rate hypotheses in Figure 17.6.

Interestingly, Edmund S. Phelps of Columbia University and Milton Friedman of the University of Chicago suggested the natural rate hypothesis, which is an implication of the classical dichotomy that you learned about in Chapter 8, *before* these events occurred.

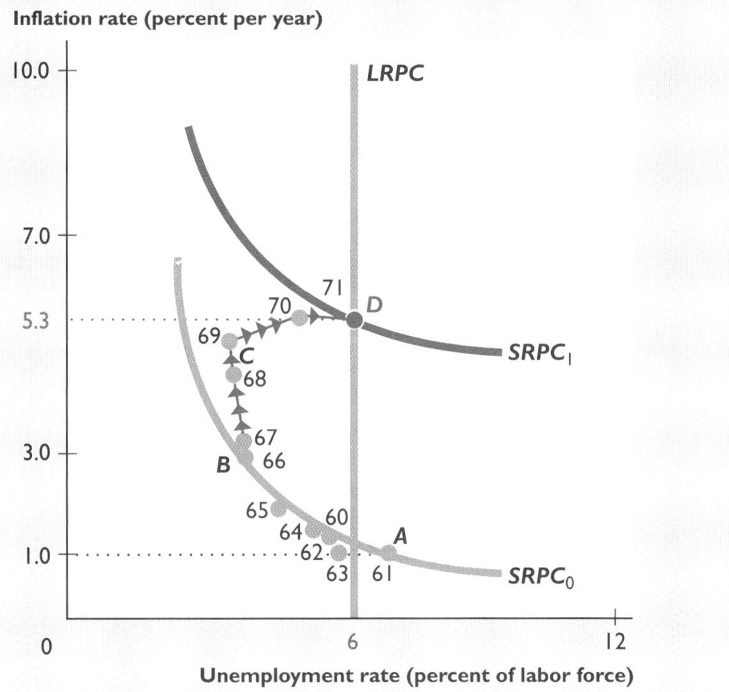

SOURCE: Bureau of Labor Statistics and Bureau of Economic Analysis.

Changes in the Natural Unemployment Rate

If the natural unemployment rate changes, both the long-run Phillips curve and the short-run Phillips curve shift. When the natural unemployment rate increases, both the long-run Phillips curve and the short-run Phillips curve shift rightward; and when the natural unemployment rate decreases, both the long-run Phillips curve and the short-run Phillips curve shift leftward.

Figure 17.7 illustrates these changes. When the natural unemployment rate is 6 percent, the long-run Phillips curve is $LRPC_0$. If the expected inflation rate is 3 percent a year, the short-run Phillips curve is $SRPC_0$. An increase in the natural unemployment rate, with no change in the expected inflation rate, shifts the two Phillips curves rightward to $LRPC_1$ and $SRPC_1$. And a decrease in the natural unemployment rate, with no change in the expected inflation rate, shifts the two Phillips curves leftward to $LRPC_2$ and $SRPC_2$.

FIGURE 17.7
Changes in the Natural Unemployment Rate

Practice Online

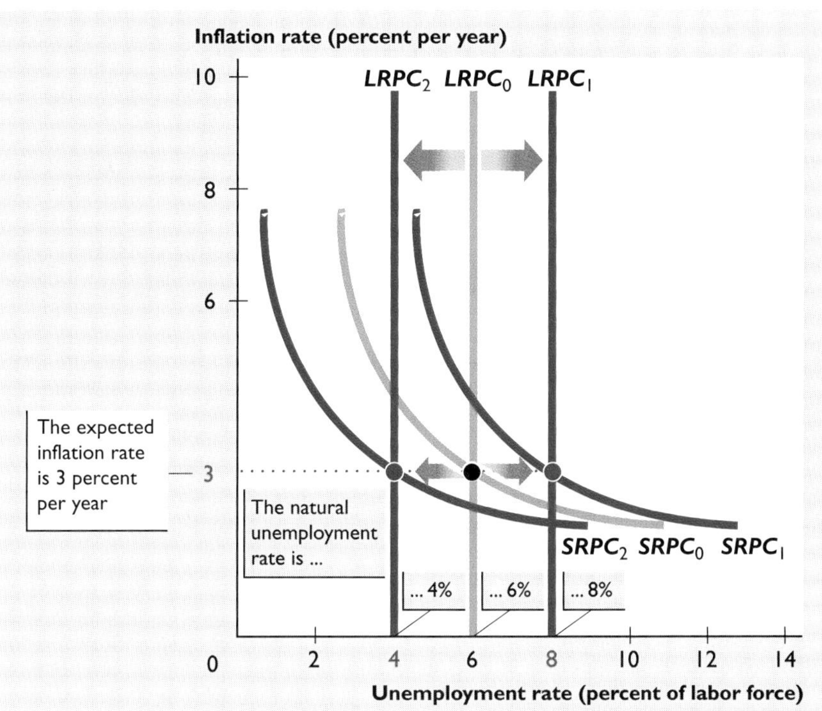

The natural unemployment rate is 6 percent, and the long-run Phillips curve is $LRPC_0$. The expected inflation rate is 3 percent a year, and the short-run Phillips curve is $SRPC_0$. An increase in the natural unemployment rate shifts the two Phillips curves rightward to $LRPC_1$ and $SRPC_1$. And a decrease in the natural unemployment rate shifts them leftward to $LRPC_2$ and $SRPC_2$.

Does the Natural Unemployment Rate Change?

You learned in Chapter 6 (p. 152) that economists don't agree about the size of the natural unemployment rate or the extent to which it fluctuates. The majority view is that the natural unemployment rate changes slowly or barely at all and is around 6 percent, the actual average unemployment rate since 1960.

An increasing number of economists question the constant natural rate view and believe that changes in frictional and structural unemployment bring changes in the natural rate of unemployment. It seems likely that the natural unemployment rate fell to perhaps as low as 4 percent in 2000 and then increased to perhaps 5 or 6 percent in 2002. But economists do not yet have a definite way of measuring the natural unemployment rate, so estimating it remains tricky and controversial.

You learned about the factors that determine the natural unemployment rate in Chapter 8 (pp. 198–203). Those factors divide into two groups: influences on job search and influences on job rationing. Job search is influenced by demographic change, unemployment compensation, and structural change. And job rationing arises from efficiency wages, the minimum wage, and union wages.

No one is sure how important these factors are in changing the natural unemployment rate. But to the extent that they do have an influence, they probably increased the natural unemployment rate during the 1970s. A bulge in the birth rate (known as the "baby boom") that occurred after World War II in the late 1940s and early 1950s brought a bulge in the number of young people entering the labor force during the late 1960s and early 1970s. This bulge in the number of new entrants increased the amount of job search and probably increased the natural unemployment rate.

Structural change during the 1970s and 1980s, much of it a response to massive hikes in the world price of oil, probably increased the natural unemployment rate further during the later 1970s and early 1980s.

Eye on the U.S. Economy

The Shifting Short-Run Tradeoff

The short-run tradeoff between inflation and unemployment becomes less favorable—more inflation and more unemployment—if either the expected inflation rate or the natural unemployment rate increases.

The short-run tradeoff becomes more favorable—less inflation and less unemployment—if either the expected inflation rate or the natural unemployment rate decreases.

When the tradeoff becomes less favorable, the short-run Phillips curve shifts rightward and upward. When the tradeoff becomes more favorable, the short-run Phillips curve shifts leftward and downward.

The short-run tradeoff is fixed when the natural unemployment rate and the expected inflation rate don't change.

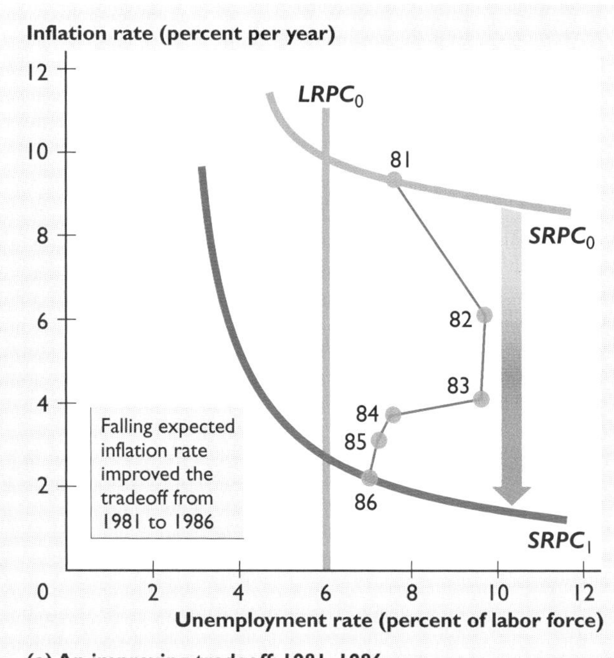

(a) An improving tradeoff: 1981–1986

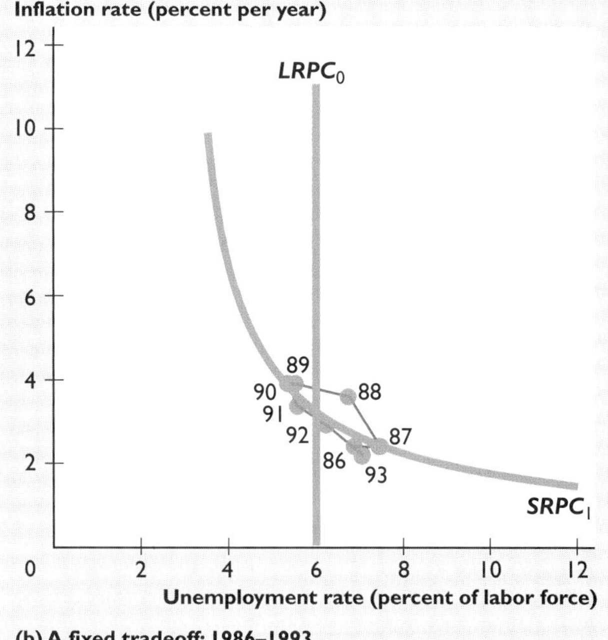

(b) A fixed tradeoff: 1986–1993

As the baby boom generation approached middle age, during the 1980s and 1990s, the number of new labor market entrants decreased and the natural unemployment rate probably decreased too.

Also, during the 1990s, rapid technological change brought an increase in productivity and an increase in the demand for labor that made job search faster and lowered the natural unemployment rate yet further.

The description of the changing natural rate that we've just provided is consistent with the data and consistent with the shifting short-run tradeoff between inflation and unemployment. But it remains speculation rather than solid knowledge.

The figures describe the shifting tradeoff in the United States.

Between 1981 and 1986, the natural unemployment rate was around 6 percent and the expected inflation rate decreased. The long-run Phillips curve was $LRPC_0$, and the short-run Phillips curve shifted downward from $SRPC_0$ to $SRPC_1$. The tradeoff improved.

Between 1986 and 1993, the expected inflation rate was constant at 3 percent a year and the natural unemployment rate was constant at 6 percent. The Phillips curves remained at $LRPC_0$ and $SRPC_1$. The tradeoff was constant.

Between 1993 and 2000, the expected inflation rate was constant but the natural unemployment rate decreased from 6 percent to around 5 percent. The Phillips curves shifted from $LRPC_0$ and $SRPC_1$ to $LRPC_1$ and $SRPC_2$. The tradeoff improved again.

Finally, between 2000 and 2002, the natural unemployment rate was constant at 5 percent and the expected inflation rate remained constant. The Phillips curves remained at $LRPC_1$ and $SRPC_2$. The tradeoff was constant.

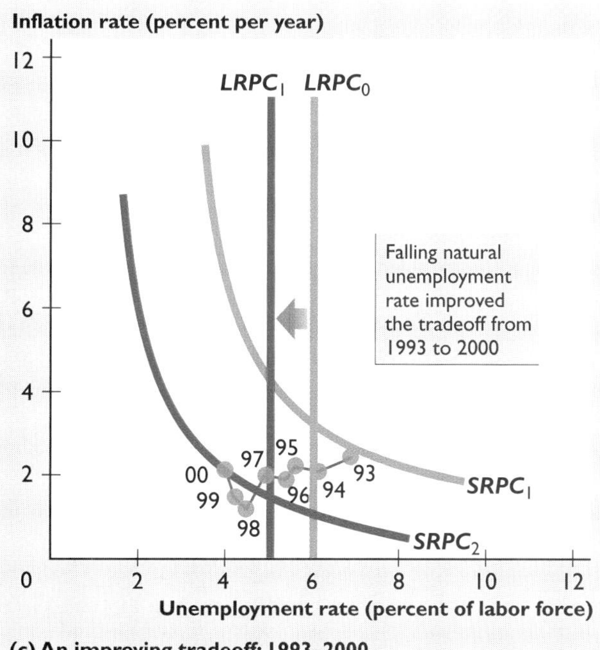

(c) An improving tradeoff: 1993–2000

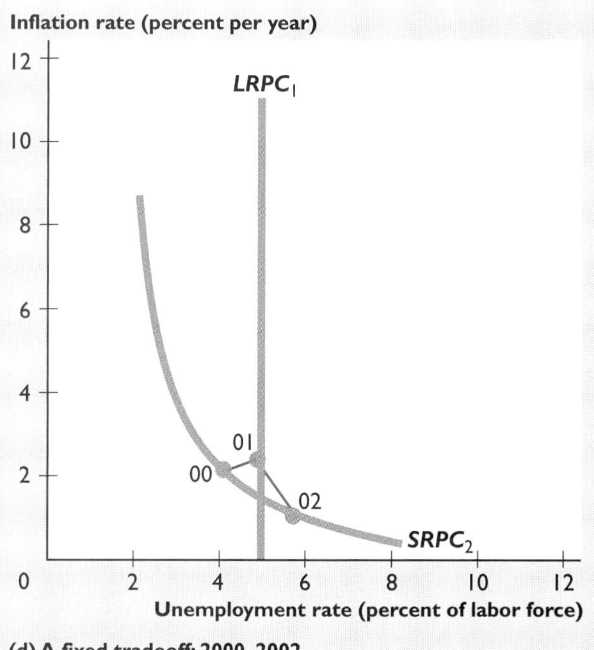

(d) A fixed tradeoff: 2000–2002

CHECKPOINT 17.2

Study Guide pp. 248–251

Practice Online 17.2

2 **Distinguish between the short-run and the long-run Phillips curves and describe the shifting tradeoff between inflation and unemployment.**

FIGURE 1

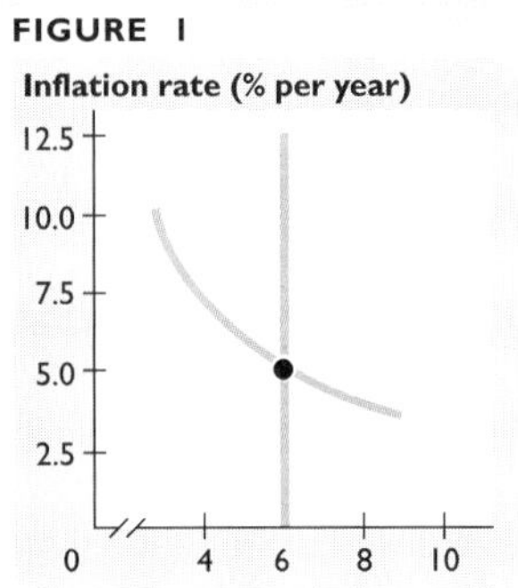

FIGURE 2

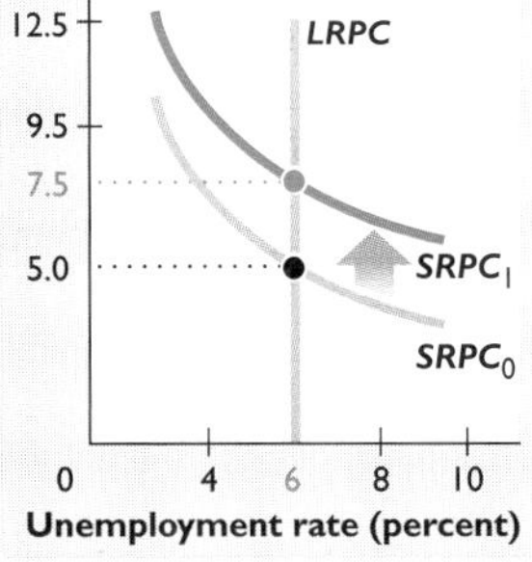

FIGURE 3

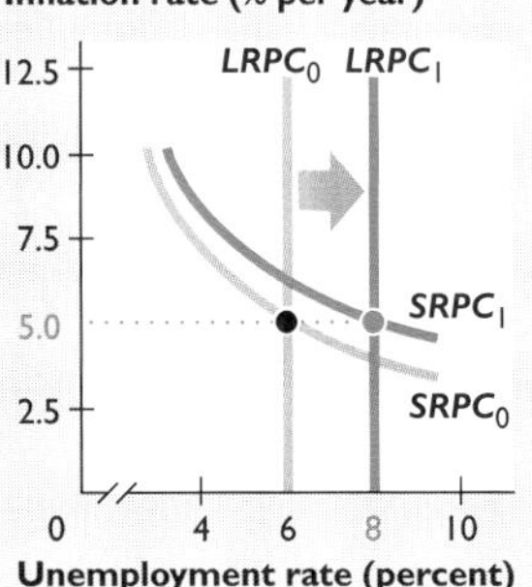

FIGURE 4

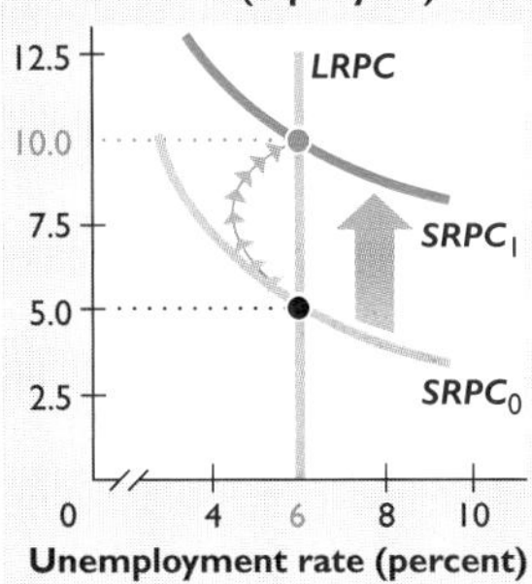

Practice Problems 17.2

1. Figure 1 shows a short-run Phillips curve and a long-run Phillips curve.
   - **a.** Label the two curves to identify which is the long-run curve and which is the short-run curve.
   - **b.** What is the expected inflation rate?
   - **c.** What is the natural unemployment rate?
   - **d.** If the expected inflation rate increases to 7.5 percent a year, show the new short-run and long-run Phillips curves.
   - **e.** If the natural unemployment rate increases to 8 percent, show the new short-run and long-run Phillips curves.
2. In the economy illustrated in Figure 1, aggregate demand starts to grow more rapidly, and eventually, the inflation rate rises to 10 percent a year. Explain the course of unemployment and inflation in this economy.

Exercises 17.2

1a. Draw a graph to show the short-run Phillips curve and long-run Phillips curve in an economy in which the natural unemployment rate is 7 percent and the expected inflation rate is 4 percent a year.

1b. If the expected inflation rate changes to 3 percent a year, show the new short-run and long-run Phillips curves.

1c. If the natural unemployment rate becomes 6 percent, show the new short-run and long-run Phillips curves.

2. In exercise 1, aggregate demand starts to grow more slowly, and eventually, the inflation rate will fall to 2 percent a year. Explain the course of unemployment and inflation in this economy.

Solutions to Practice Problems 17.2

1a. The long-run Phillips curve is the vertical curve, *LRPC*, and the short-run Phillips curve is the downward-sloping curve, $SRPC_0$ (Figure 2).

1b. The expected inflation rate is 5 percent a year. The expected inflation rate is the inflation rate at which *LRPC* and $SRPC_0$ intersect.

1c. The natural rate of unemployment is 6 percent. The *LRPC* is vertical at the natural rate of unemployment.

1d. The short-run Phillips curve shifts upward, but the long-run Phillips curve does not change (Figure 2).

1e. Both the short-run and long-run Phillips curves shift rightward (Figure 3).

2. Figure 4 shows the course of unemployment and inflation. As expectations change, the inflation rate rises to 10 percent a year and unemployment returns to the natural unemployment rate.

17.3 EXPECTED INFLATION

You've seen that expected inflation plays a big role in determining the position of the short-run tradeoff. When the expected inflation rate is low, as it was in 2000, the tradeoff is more favorable than when the expected inflation rate is high, as it was in 1980. The effect of expected inflation on the short-run tradeoff raises three questions:

- What determines the expected inflation rate?
- How responsive is the short-run tradeoff to a change in expected inflation?
- What can policy do to lower expected inflation?

What Determines the Expected Inflation Rate?

The *expected inflation rate* is the inflation rate that people forecast and use to set the money wage rate and other money prices. To forecast the inflation rate, people use the same basic method that they use to forecast other variables that affect their lives.

Data make up the first ingredient in forecasting—data about the past behavior of the phenomenon that we want to forecast. When people laid heavy bets that Tiger Woods would win the British Open in 2000, they based their forecast on the performance of Tiger and the other golfers in the months leading up to that event.

Science is the second ingredient in forecasting—the specific science that seeks to understand the phenomenon that we wish to forecast. If we want to know whether it is likely to rain tomorrow, we turn to the science of meteorology. Science is not a substitute for data. It is knowledge that tells people how to interpret data.

So to forecast inflation, people use data about past inflation and other relevant variables and the science of economics, which seeks to understand the forces that cause inflation.

You already know the relevant economics: the *AS-AD* model. You know that the money growth rate determines the growth of aggregate demand in the long run. And you know that the trend growth rate of real GDP is the growth rate of aggregate supply in the long run. So the trend money growth rate minus the trend real GDP growth rate determines the trend inflation rate.

The inflation rate fluctuates around its trend as the state of the economy changes over the business cycle. In an expansion, the inflation rate rises above trend, and in a recession, the inflation rate falls below trend as aggregate demand fluctuates to bring movements along the aggregate supply curve. And you know that the money growth rate is one of the influences on these aggregate demand fluctuations.

The Fed determines the money growth rate, so the major ingredient in a forecast of inflation is a forecast of the Fed's actions. Professional Fed watchers and economic forecasters use these ideas along with a lot of data and elaborate statistical models of the economy to forecast the inflation rate.

When all the relevant data and economic science are used to forecast inflation, the resulting forecast is called a **rational expectation**. The rational expectation of the inflation rate is a forecast based on the Fed's forecasted monetary policy along with forecasts of the other forces that influence aggregate demand and aggregate supply. But the dominant factor is the Fed's monetary policy.

Rational expectation
The inflation forecast resulting from use of all the relevant data and economic science.

How Responsive Is the Tradeoff to a Change in Expected Inflation?

A change in the expected inflation rate shifts the short-run tradeoff gradually. The reason is that the tradeoff depends on the rate of increase in the money wage rate. The tradeoff changes only when the rate of increase in the money wage rate changes in response to a change in the expected inflation rate.

Some money wage rates respond quickly to a changed expectation about inflation. But most money wage rates are determined on long-term contracts. Contracts that are in place in the current year were agreed upon one, two, or perhaps three years ago. And the inflation forecasts that were used to set those wage rates were the rational expectations of the past, not the present. So even if people now change their forecast of future inflation, many of them can't use their new forecast right away. They must wait until they negotiate a new long-term contract.

The presence of long-term labor contracts means that the short-run tradeoff responds gradually to a change in the expected inflation rate. If the Fed increases the trend inflation rate, it will take several years before the tradeoff shifts upward to reflect that change.

The gradual response of the tradeoff to a change in the expected inflation rate leads to fluctuations around full employment. For example, during the 1970s when inflation increased, the tradeoff shifted upward and became less favorable, but the actual inflation rate exceeded the expected inflation rate for several years and the unemployment rate was below the natural unemployment rate. Similarly, during the 1980s when inflation decreased, the tradeoff shifted downward and became more favorable, but the actual inflation rate decreased below the expected inflation rate for several years and the unemployment rate was above the natural unemployment rate.

What Can Policy Do to Lower Expected Inflation?

If the Fed wants to lower the inflation rate, it can pursue two alternative lines of attack:

- A surprise inflation reduction
- A credible announced inflation reduction

A Surprise Inflation Reduction

In Figure 17.8, the economy is at full employment with inflation raging and expected to rage at 10 percent a year. Unemployment is at its natural rate, which is 6 percent. The economy is on its long-run Phillips curve, *LRPC*, and its short-run Phillips curve, $SRPC_0$ at point *A*.

No one is expecting the Fed to change its policy but the Fed does change its policy and starts to slow inflation to a target rate of 3 percent a year. The Fed raises interest rates and slows money growth. With no change in the expected inflation rate, wage rates continue to rise by the same amount as before but aggregate demand growth slows. The unemployment rate rises and the inflation rate falls along $SRPC_0$. Gradually, the expected inflation rate falls and the short-run Phillips curve shifts downward toward $SRPC_1$. The Fed slows inflation but at the cost of recession. The economy follows the path of the red arrows—and unemployment remains above its natural rate until, eventually, the economy arrives at point *B*.

FIGURE 17.8
Slowing Inflation

Practice Online

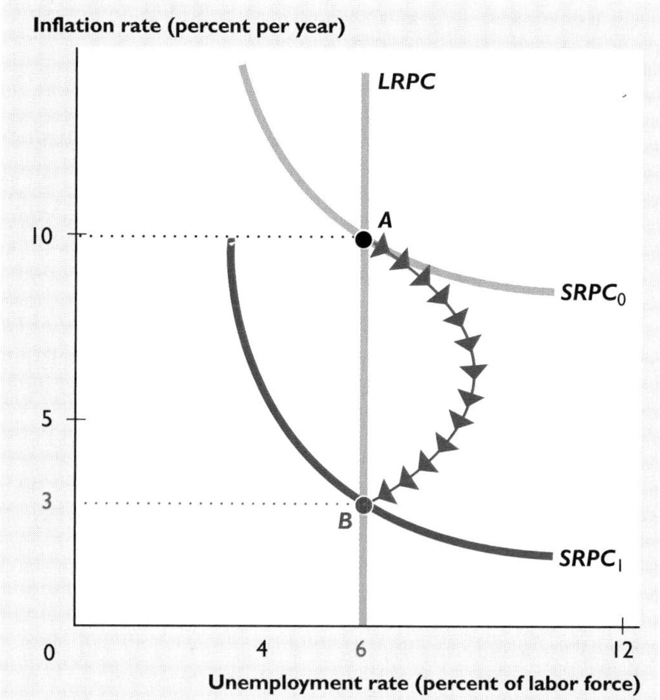

The economy is at point *A* on the short-run Phillips curve $SRPC_0$ and on the long-run Phillips curve *LRPC*. The natural unemployment rate is 6 percent, and inflation is 10 percent a year.

An unexpected slowdown in aggregate demand growth slows inflation and increases the unemployment rate as the economy slides down along $SRPC_0$. Eventually, the expected inflation rate falls and the short-run Phillips curve shifts to $SRPC_1$. The unemployment rate remains above 6 percent through the adjustment to point *B*.

Alternatively, a credible, announced slowdown in aggregate demand growth lowers the expected inflation rate and shifts the short-run Phillips curve downward to $SRPC_1$. Inflation slows to 3 percent a year and unemployment remains 6 percent as the economy moves along the *LRPC* curve to point *B*.

A Credible Announced Inflation Reduction

Suppose that instead of unexpectedly slowing inflation, the Fed announces its intention to bring the inflation rate down. Ahead of its action, the Fed convinces everyone that it has a credible plan, so its announcement is believed.

Because people believe the Fed will lower the inflation rate, the expected inflation rate falls. And because the expected inflation rate falls, the rate of increase in the money wage rate slows.

The lower expected inflation rate shifts the short-run Phillips curve downward to $SRPC_1$, and the inflation rate falls to 3 percent a year, while the unemployment rate remains at the natural rate of 6 percent.

This announced inflation reduction lowers the inflation rate but with no accompanying loss of output or increase in unemployment. The economy moves directly from *A* to *B* in Figure 17.8.

Inflation Reduction in Practice

When the Fed slowed inflation in 1981, we paid a high price. The Fed's policy action was unexpected. It occurred in the face of money wage rates that had been set at too high a level to be consistent with the growth of aggregate demand that the Fed subsequently allowed. The consequence was recession—a decrease in real GDP and increased unemployment. We followed a path like the red arrows in Figure 17.8. Whether policy can lower inflation without a deep recession is a controversial question. We'll return to it in the next chapter, where we review policy debates.

CHECKPOINT 17.3

Study Guide pp. 251–254

Practice Online 17.3

3 **Explain how the Fed can influence the expected inflation rate and how expected inflation influences the short-run tradeoff.**

FIGURE 1

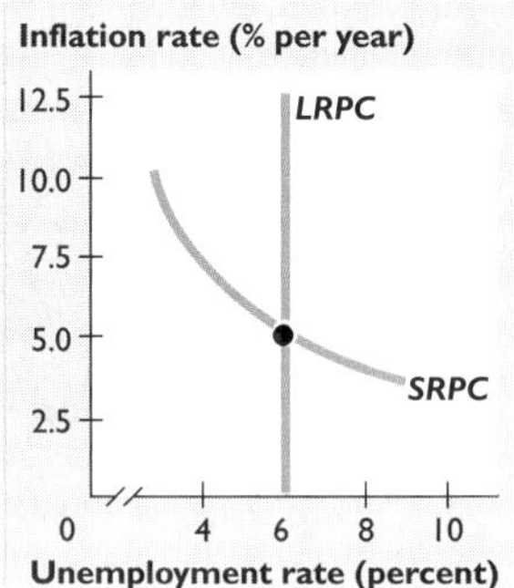

FIGURE 2

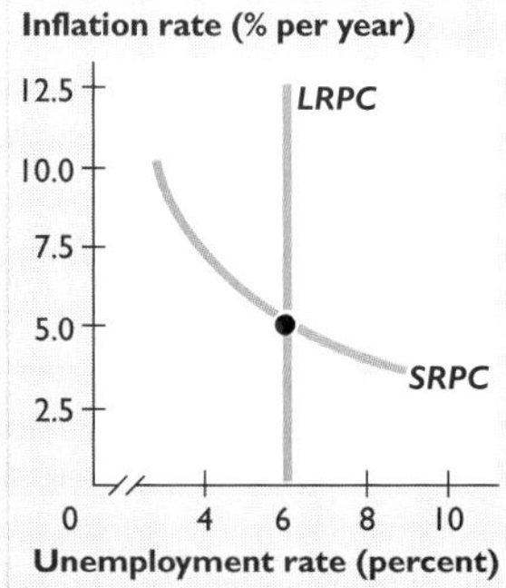

FIGURE 3

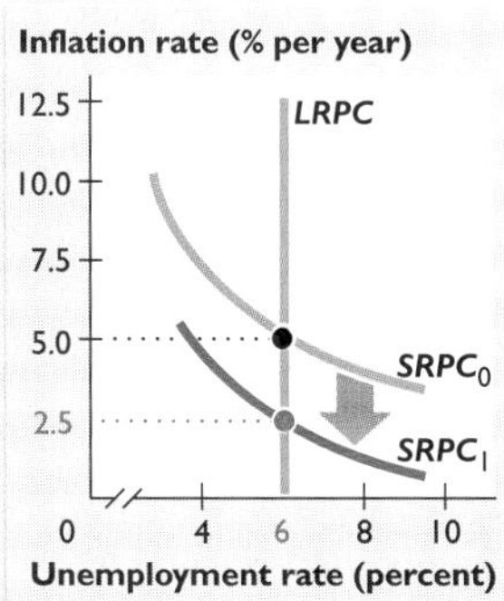

FIGURE 4

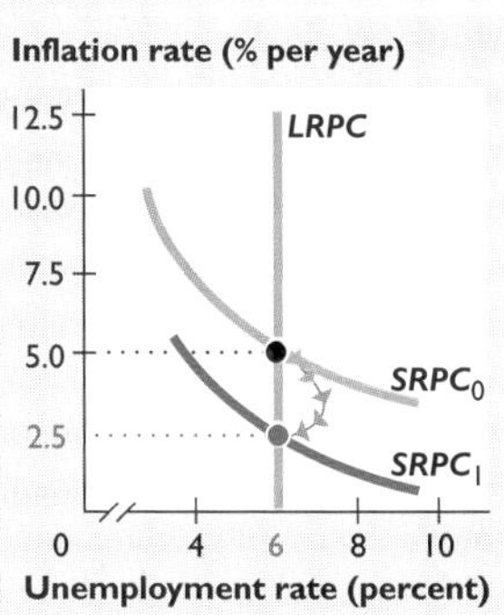

Practice Problem 17.3

Figure 1 shows the short-run and long-run Phillips curves. The current inflation rate is 5 percent a year.

a. Inflation is expected to remain at 5 percent next year. If the Fed slows the money growth rate, explain the effect of the Fed's action on inflation and unemployment next year.

b. If the Fed announces that it will slow the money growth rate such that inflation will fall to 2.5 percent a year and everyone believes the Fed, explain the effect of the Fed's action on inflation and unemployment next year.

c. Inflation is expected to remain at 5 percent next year. If the Fed slows the money growth rate such that inflation will fall to 2.5 percent a year and keeps it there for many years, explain the effect of the Fed's action on inflation and unemployment.

Exercise 17.3

In Figure 1, the current inflation rate is 5 percent a year.

a. If the Fed announces that it will increase the money growth rate such that the inflation rate will rise to 6 percent a year and everyone believes the Fed, explain the effect of the Fed's action on inflation and unemployment next year.

b. Inflation is expected to remain at 5 percent next year. If the Fed speeds up the money growth rate, explain the effect of the Fed's action on inflation and unemployment next year.

c. In part **b**, if the Fed keeps the money growth rate constant for many years, explain the effect of the Fed's action on inflation and unemployment.

Solution to Practice Problem 17.3

a. The inflation rate will fall below 5 percent a year and the unemployment rate will rise above 6 percent as the economy moves down along its short-run Phillips curve (see Figure 2).

b. The inflation rate falls to 2.5 percent a year, and unemployment remains at 6 percent. If people believe the Fed's policy announcement, the expected inflation rate will fall to 2.5 percent a year. The short-run Phillips curve will shift downward from $SRPC_0$ to $SRPC_1$ (Figure 3).

c. Initially, inflation falls below 5 percent a year and unemployment rises above 6 percent. The longer the Fed maintains the slower money growth rate, the more people will start to expect lower inflation and the short-run Phillips curve will start to shift downward. As the short-run Phillips curve shifts downward, the unemployment rate will start to decrease. Eventually, inflation falls to 2.5 percent a year and the unemployment rate returns to 6 percent (Figure 4).

CHAPTER CHECKPOINT

Key Points

1 Describe the short-run tradeoff between inflation and unemployment.

- The short-run Phillips curve is the downward-sloping relationship between the inflation rate and the unemployment rate when all other influences on these two variables remain the same.
- The short-run Phillips curve presents a *tradeoff* between inflation and unemployment.
- The short-run Phillips curve is another way of looking at the aggregate supply curve.

2 Distinguish between the short-run and long-run Phillips curves and describe the shifting tradeoff between inflation and unemployment.

- The long-run Phillips curve shows the relationship between inflation and unemployment when the unemployment rate equals the natural unemployment rate and the inflation rate equals the expected inflation rate.
- The long-run Phillips curve is vertical at the *natural unemployment rate*, and there is no long-run tradeoff between unemployment and inflation.
- When the expected inflation rate changes, the short-run Phillips curve shifts to intersect the long-run Phillips curve at the new expected inflation rate.
- When the money growth rate changes, the unemployment rate changes temporarily and eventually returns to the natural unemployment rate—the natural rate hypothesis.
- Changes in the natural unemployment rate shift both the *SRPC* and the *LRPC*.

3 Explain how the Fed can influence the expected inflation rate and how expected inflation influences the short-run tradeoff.

- The rational expectation of the inflation rate is based on the forecasted actions of the Fed's monetary policy and the other forces that influence aggregate demand and aggregate supply.
- A change in the expected inflation rate changes the short-run tradeoff gradually because the money wage rate responds only gradually to a change in the expected inflation rate.
- To lower the expected inflation rate, the Fed must take actions that will slow the actual inflation rate.

Key Terms

Expected inflation rate, 432
Long-run Phillips curve, 430
Natural rate hypothesis, 433
Okun's Law, 425
Rational expectation, 439
Short-run Phillips curve, 424

Exercises

1. Table 1 describes four possible situations that might arise in 2004, depending on the level of aggregate demand in that year.

TABLE 1

	Price level (2003 = 100)	Real GDP (trillions of 2003 dollars)	Unemployment rate (percent of labor force)
A	102	8.0	9
B	104	8.1	7
C	106	8.2	5
D	108	8.3	4
E	110	8.4	3

   a. Plot the Phillips curve and the aggregate supply curve for 2004.
   b. Mark the points *A*, *B*, *C*, *D*, and *E* on each curve that correspond to the data provided in the table.

2. In the economy in exercise 1, the outcome in 2004 turned out to be row *C* of Table 1. Four possible outcomes for 2005 are shown in Table 2.

TABLE 2

	Price level (2003 = 100)	Real GDP (trillions of 2003 dollars)	Unemployment rate (percent of labor force)
A	108	8.1	9
B	110	8.2	7
C	112	8.3	5
D	114	8.4	4
E	116	8.5	3

   a. Plot the Phillips curve and the aggregate supply curve for 2005.
   b. Mark the points *A*, *B*, *C*, *D*, and *E* on each curve that correspond to the data provided in the table.
   c. Compare the Phillips curves and aggregate supply curves of 2005 with those of 2004.

3. Refer to the data in exercise 1.
   a. The natural rate of unemployment is 6 percent in 2003. What is the expected inflation rate?
   b. If the natural rate of unemployment increases to 7 percent in 2004, explain how the short-run and long-run tradeoffs change.
   c. If the natural rate of unemployment remains at 6 percent in 2004 but the expected inflation rate is 4 percent a year, explain how the short-run and long-run tradeoffs change.

4. What is Okun's Law and does the economy described in Tables 1 and 2 above behave in accordance with Okun's Law?

5. What is the relationship between the long-run Phillips curve and potential GDP and the short-run Phillips curve and the aggregate supply curve?

6. The inflation rate is 5 percent a year and the quantity of money is growing at a pace that will maintain that inflation rate. The natural unemployment rate is 6 percent and the current unemployment rate is 4 percent.
   a. In what direction will the unemployment rate change?

b. How will the short-run Phillips curve shift?
c. How will the long-run Phillips curve shift?
d. How will the *AS* and *AD* curves shift as the events you've described in parts **a**, **b**, and **c** unfold?

7. The inflation rate is 5 percent a year and the quantity of money is growing at a pace that will maintain that inflation rate. The natural unemployment rate is 6 percent and the current unemployment rate is 8 percent.
   a. In what direction will the unemployment rate change?
   b. How will the short-run Phillips curve shift?
   c. How will the long-run Phillips curve shift?
   d. How will the *AS* and *AD* curves shift as the events you've described in parts **a**, **b**, and **c** unfold?

8. The inflation rate is 6 percent a year, the unemployment rate is 4 percent, and the economy is at full employment. The Fed declares that it wants to slow the inflation rate to 3 percent a year and that it intends to slow the money growth rate to keep the inflation rate at 3 percent a year for the foreseeable future. People believe the Fed.
   a. Explain how unemployment and inflation change in the short run, and use the short-run Phillips curve and *AS* curve to illustrate your explanation.
   b. Explain how unemployment and inflation change in the long run, and use the short-run and long-run Phillips curves and the *AS* curve to illustrate your explanation.

9. The inflation rate is 6 percent a year, the unemployment rate is 4 percent, and the economy is at full employment. Without warning and to everyone's astonishment, the Fed slows the money growth rate to keep inflation at 3 percent a year.
   a. Explain how unemployment and inflation change in the short run, and use the short-run Phillips curve and *AS* curve to illustrate your explanation.
   b. Compare and contrast the situation in exercise 9 with that in exercise 8.

10. The Reserve Bank of New Zealand signed an agreement with the New Zealand government in which the Bank agreed to maintain inflation inside a low target range. Failure to achieve the target would result in the governor of the Bank (the equivalent of Chairman Greenspan at the Fed) losing his job.
    a. Explain how this arrangement might have influenced New Zealand's short-run Phillips curve.
    b. Explain how this arrangement might have influenced New Zealand's long-run Phillips curve.

11. Brazil, Chile, Bolivia, and Uruguay have repeatedly permitted inflation to rise to levels unheard of in the United States.
    a. Explain how a history of rapid inflation might influence the short-run Phillips curves in these countries.
    b. Explain how a history of rapid inflation might influence the long-run Phillips curves in these countries.

Critical Thinking

12. In light of the fact that whenever the inflation rate is lowered, the unemployment rate increases, do you think it is ever worth lowering inflation? Would it be better to simply live with the inflation rate we've currently got?

13. In light of the fact that whenever the inflation rate is lowered, the unemployment rate increases, do you think we should ever permit the inflation rate to rise to an unacceptable level? Would it be better to nip an increase in inflation in the bud even if it meant a small and brief recession?

14. Looking at the data on inflation and unemployment, it is very difficult to see any sign of a short-run tradeoff.
    a. Explain why it is difficult to see the short-run tradeoff.
    b. Does the fact that the short-run tradeoff is hard to see in the data mean that we can ignore it? Why or why not?

15. "The Phillips curve adds nothing to the *AS-AD* model." Argue against this proposition.

Practice Online

Web Exercises

Use the links on your Foundations Web site to work the following exercises.

16. Visit the Web site of the Bureau of Labor Statistics and obtain data on the unemployment rate and the inflation rate for the past 20 years.
    a. In a spreadsheet, make a scatter diagram of the two variables, placing the unemployment rate on the *x*-axis.
    b. Interpret the data in terms of shifting short-run and long-run Phillips curves.
    c. In any periods in which you think the natural unemployment rate was falling, can you think of some of the reasons for the fall?
    d. In any periods in which you think the natural unemployment rate was rising, can you think of some of the reasons for the rise?
    e. In any periods in which you think the expected inflation rate was falling, can you think of some of the reasons for the fall?
    f. In any periods in which you think the expected inflation rate was rising, can you think of some of the reasons for the rise?

17. Visit the Web site of the *Economic Report of the President* and obtain data on the unemployment rate and the inflation rate for the major industrial countries for the past 20 years.
    a. In a spreadsheet, make scatter diagrams of the two variables for each country, placing the unemployment rate on the *x*-axis.
    b. Interpret the data in terms of short-run and long-run Phillips curves.
    c. In which of the countries for which you have data do you think the natural unemployment rate is highest? Can you explain why?
    d. In which of the countries for which you have data do you think the natural unemployment rate is lowest? Can you explain why?
    e. In which of the countries for which you have data do you think the expected inflation rate is highest? Can you explain why?
    f. In which of the countries for which you have data do you think the expected inflation rate is lowest? Can you explain why?

CHAPTER 18

Fiscal and Monetary Policy Debates

CHAPTER CHECKLIST

When you have completed your study of this chapter, you will be able to

1. **Discuss whether fiscal policy or monetary policy is the better stabilization tool.**
2. **Explain the rules-versus-discretion debate and compare Keynesian and monetarist policy rules.**
3. **Assess whether policy should target the price level rather than real GDP.**

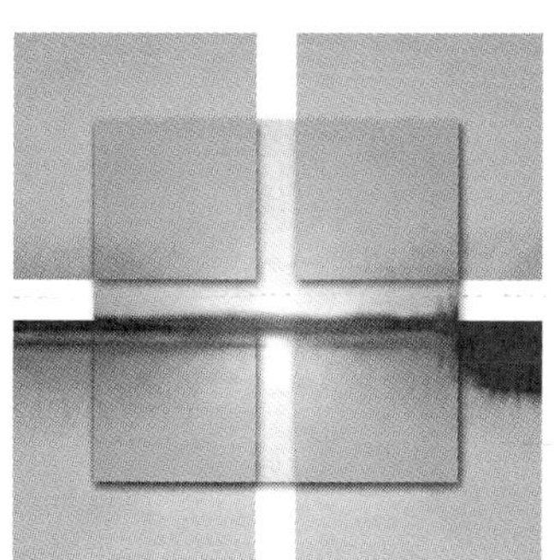

Should macroeconomic stability be left to the Fed and monetary policy, or should the government use fiscal policy to maintain stability? Should stabilization be left to the discretion of experts or should the government lay down rules for policy makers to follow? If rules should be laid down, what rules? Should we try to keep the economy at full employment and not worry about the price level? Or should we target the price level rather than output and employment?

You've seen the *effects* of monetary and fiscal policy, and you've seen the *short-run tradeoff* that stabilization policy faces. These aspects of stabilization policy define the constraints. They tell us "what if," but they don't tell us "what" monetary or fiscal policy to pursue.

This chapter studies some hard "should" questions about fiscal and monetary policy. How should stabilization policy be conducted? Surprisingly, economists are agreed on most of the answers. But some disputes remain, as you're about to discover.

18.1 FISCAL POLICY VERSUS MONETARY POLICY

Should short-run economic fluctuations be stabilized with fiscal policy or monetary policy? Which policy tool does the better job? These questions have been debated for many decades and were at the core of a controversy that raged during the 1960s. That old debate has been settled, but the lessons that we learn from it are important and remain relevant today. We will examine the fiscal policy versus monetary policy debate by considering its three aspects:

- Policy effects
- Goal conflicts
- Timing and flexibility

Policy Effects

Which policy action has the larger and more predictable effect on aggregate demand: a change in government purchases or a change in the supply of money? The answer to this question was once controversial, and the question lay at the heart of the original 1960s debate.

Investment demand (Chapter 9, pp. 215–217) and the demand for money Chapter 13, pp. 315–318) determine the effects of monetary policy and fiscal policy. Let's look first at the effects of monetary policy.

The Effects of Monetary Policy

The two steps in the transmission of monetary policy are

Step 1 A change in the supply of money influences the interest rate, and

Step 2 A change in the interest rate influences investment and other interest-sensitive components of aggregate expenditure.

The demand for money and investment demand determine whether monetary policy has a powerful or a weak effect. Look first at Step 1.

Step 1 Whether a given increase in the supply of money lowers the interest rate by a lot or a little depends on the sensitivity of the demand for money to the interest rate. Suppose that the quantity of money demanded is relatively insensitive to the interest rate, so a change in the interest rate brings a small change in the quantity of money demanded. Then, when the supply of money increases by a given amount, the decrease in the interest rate is large. In contrast, suppose that the quantity of money demanded is highly sensitive to the interest rate, so even a small change in the interest rate brings a large change in the quantity of money demanded. Then, when the supply of money increases by a given amount, the decrease in the interest rate is small.

Look next at step 2.

Step 2 Whether a given decrease in the interest rate increases aggregate expenditure by a lot or a little depends on the sensitivity of investment and other components of aggregate expenditure to the interest rate. If aggregate expenditure is highly sensitive to the interest rate, then a given change in the interest rate brings a large change in aggregate expenditure. If aggregate expenditure is insensitive to the interest rate, then a given change in the interest rate brings a small change in aggregate expenditure.

Figure 18.1 illustrates the two cases. In part (a), when the supply of money curve shifts from MS_0 to MS_1, the interest rate falls from 6 percent to 4 percent a year and investment increases from $2 trillion to $4 trillion. In contrast, in part (b), the same change in the supply of money lowers the interest rate from 6 percent to 5 percent a year, and investment increases from $2 trillion to $2.25 trillion. In part (a), the monetary policy is powerful; in part (b) it is weak.

FIGURE 18.1
The Effectiveness of Monetary Policy

Practice Online

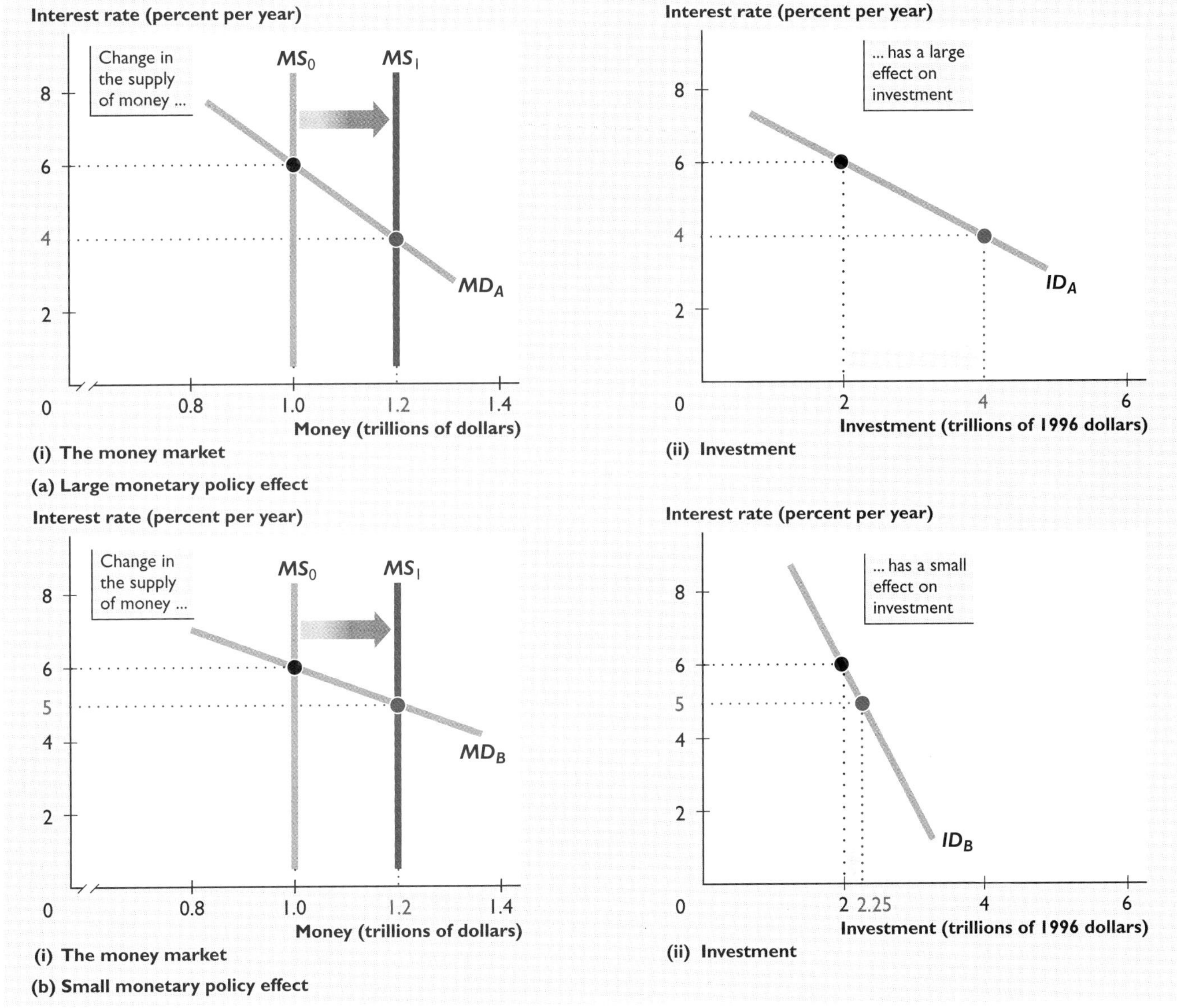

In part (a), when the supply of money increases and the supply of money curve shifts from MS_0 to MS_1, the interest rate falls from 6 percent to 4 percent a year and investment increases from $2 trillion to $4 trillion.

In part (b), the same change in the supply of money lowers the interest rate from 6 percent to 5 percent a year and increases investment from $2 trillion to $2.25 trillion. Monetary policy is more powerful in the conditions shown in part (a).

The Predictability of Monetary Policy The two steps in the transmission of monetary policy determine the predictability of monetary policy.

At step 1, for a given change in the supply of money to have a predictable effect on the interest rate, the demand for money must be predictable.

At step 2, for a given change in the interest rate to have a predictable effect on investment and aggregate expenditure, the investment demand must be predictable.

So the more predictable the demand for money and investment demand, the more predictable is the effect of monetary policy.

Let's now look at the effects of fiscal policy.

The Effects of Fiscal Policy

The three steps in the transmission of fiscal policy are

Step 1 An increase in government purchases or a tax cut increases aggregate expenditure and increases aggregate demand with a multiplier.

Step 2 A change in real GDP changes the demand for money, which changes the interest rate.

Step 3 A change in the interest rate changes investment and other interest-sensitive components of aggregate expenditure, which counteract the effects of the initial increase in aggregate expenditure—a crowding-out effect.

If a given change in the demand for money has a large effect on the interest rate and if a given change in the interest rate has a large effect on aggregate expenditure, then the crowding-out effect is large and fiscal policy has a weak effect on aggregate demand.

The conditions that we've just described that make fiscal policy weak are the ones that make monetary policy powerful.

If a given change in the demand for money has a small effect on the interest rate and if a given change in the interest rate has a small effect on aggregate expenditure, then the crowding-out effect is small and fiscal policy has a powerful effect on aggregate demand.

These conditions that make fiscal policy powerful are the ones that make monetary policy weak.

Extreme Conditions

At one extreme, monetary policy is all-powerful and fiscal policy is completely ineffective. This extreme occurs if the quantity of money demanded is independent of the interest rate. The demand for money curve is vertical. In such a situation, the amount of money that people want to hold depends only on their expenditure. For a given supply of money, there is only one equilibrium level of aggregate expenditure. So a change in the supply of money changes aggregate expenditure. But a change in government purchases changes the interest rate, which in turn changes expenditure and completely crowds out the increase in government purchases. So aggregate expenditure is unchanged.

At the other extreme, monetary policy is completely ineffective and fiscal policy is all-powerful. This extreme occurs if the quantity of money demanded is infinitely sensitive to the interest rate. The demand for money curve is horizontal at a particular interest rate. At that interest rate, people are willing to hold any quantity of money. This situation is called a **liquidity trap**. In a liquidity trap, a change in the supply of money changes the quantity of money held but has no effect on the interest rate and so it has no effect on aggregate expenditure. But a change in government purchases leaves the interest rate unchanged, so there is no crowding out and fiscal policy has a large multiplier effect on aggregate expenditure.

Liquidity trap
An interest rate at which people are willing to hold any quantity of money.

Reality

The extreme conditions were once thought to apply to real economies. Keynesian economists believed that a liquidity trap rendered monetary policy useless and fiscal policy all-powerful. Monetarist economists believed the opposite. We now know, as a result of an enormous amount of research using data for all the major economies, that neither extreme occurs in real economies. Some people have suggested that Japan was in a liquidity trap in the late 1990s and early 2000s. But this suggestion is not supported by evidence. Either fiscal policy or monetary policy can be used to manipulate aggregate demand.

Goal Conflicts

You've seen that both fiscal policy and monetary policy influence aggregate demand, so either policy can be used in the attempt to stabilize aggregate demand, real GDP, and the price level.

But stabilization policy actions have side effects—effects on factors other than the stabilization goals. These side effects can create a conflict between stabilization and some other goals. It turns out that goal conflict is more serious for fiscal policy than for monetary policy.

Fiscal Policy Goal Conflicts

Fiscal policy has three goals: to provide public goods and services, to redistribute income, and to stabilize aggregate demand. These goals can come into conflict.

One aspect of the government's budget that does not create conflict is its *automatic stabilizer* effect. We described these features in Chapter 16 (p. 408). The income tax and needs-tested spending programs, such as unemployment benefits, that automatically adjust expenditure and tax receipts in response to the state of the economy help to achieve the government's goals of redistributing income and improving economic stability.

In contrast, *discretionary* fiscal actions—actions that require changes in spending or taxes to be legislated—create goal conflicts. The main source of conflict is the very large number of spending programs and tax arrangements in place and the difficulty (impossibility perhaps) of changing all of them to balance the costs and benefits of one against the cost and benefits of others.

For example, suppose that fiscal stimulation is called for in a recession. Should the government spend more on the space program, national defense, the environment, or education? Or should it cut the income tax? And whose income tax should it cut? Or should it cut the excise tax on alcohol, tobacco, or gasoline? The government must make a very large number of detailed decisions about what to produce more of, whom to benefit, which industries to benefit, and which regions to benefit.

If the government wants to meet its goals in the provision of public goods and services and achieve its income redistribution goals, fiscal policy must be freed up from the additional task of helping to stabilize the economy.

Monetary Policy Goal Conflicts

Monetary policy has three main goals: price level stability, real GDP stability, and stability of the financial system. There is less conflict among these goals than among those of fiscal policy.

First, stability of the financial system and aggregate demand stability go together. Each contributes to the other. So there is no conflict here.

Second, stability of real GDP and stability of the price level are both served by stabilizing aggregate demand. There is a conflict about how much weight to place on price level stability versus real GDP stability. But this conflict is also present for fiscal policy. So fiscal policy does not outperform monetary policy in this area.

Timing and Flexibility

The ability to forecast the near future state of the economy and act at the appropriate time to counteract any unwanted recession or inflation is a crucial part of a successful stabilization policy. The timing of policy actions is vitally important. How do fiscal policy and monetary policy stack up on this dimension?

Inflexible Fiscal Policy

Fiscal policy is political. Lawmakers must debate and make deals for months before they are ready to vote on and change a spending program or a tax code. And the issues that matter most in this process do not include the forecast of aggregate demand over the next 18 months.

Worse, the election cycle dominates fiscal policy making, and only by coincidence are the business cycle and the election cycle aligned. So fiscal policy is inflexible and incapable of the rapid-fire response that is often called for to keep aggregate demand growing smoothly.

Flexible Monetary Policy

In contrast, stabilization is the purpose of monetary policy. The Fed and its policy committee, the FOMC, were created to enable policy actions to be taken quickly and on the basis of a careful, professional evaluation of the current and likely future state of the economy. And every day, the financial markets are watched for signs that policy needs to be tweaked to keep the economy on track.

Monetary policy *effects* are long and drawn out, but actions can be taken quickly.

And the Winner Is?

There is no clear winner. Automatic fiscal stabilizers do an important part of the job of maintaining macroeconomic stability. Discretionary fiscal policy is sometimes a vital part of the policy mix, especially if the economy is in a deep recession or in a seriously overheated condition. But for dealing with normal fluctuations, monetary policy is the preferred stabilization tool because it is more flexible in its timing.

What should monetary policy try to achieve? Should it try to maintain full employment? Or should it try to stabilize the inflation rate (or price level) rather than real GDP and employment? We study these questions in the next section.

CHECKPOINT 18.1

1 Discuss whether fiscal policy or monetary policy is the better stabilization tool.

Study Guide pp. 260–263

Practice Online 18.1

Practice Problems 18.1

1. The Fed decreases the quantity of money.
   a. Use a graph like Figure 18.1 to work out the effects of the Fed's policy on the interest rate, the quantity of money demanded, and investment.
   b. Explain the effects of the Fed's policy on aggregate expenditure and aggregate demand.
   c. Explain the conditions that make the Fed's policy more effective.
2. If a change in the supply of money leads to a large change in the interest rate and investment is very sensitive to the interest rate, would a decrease in government purchases be an effective fiscal policy? Explain why or why not.

Exercises 18.1

1. If the government decreases its purchases of goods and services, explain
   a. The effects of the government's policy on the interest rate, the quantity of money demanded, and investment.
   b. The effects of the government's policy on aggregate expenditure and aggregate demand.
   c. The conditions that make the government's policy more effective.
2. If a change in the supply of money leads to a small change in the interest rate and investment is not very sensitive to the interest rate, would an increase in government purchases be an effective fiscal policy? Explain why or why not.
3. Explain why monetary policy is a better tool than fiscal policy for stabilizing aggregate demand.

FIGURE 1

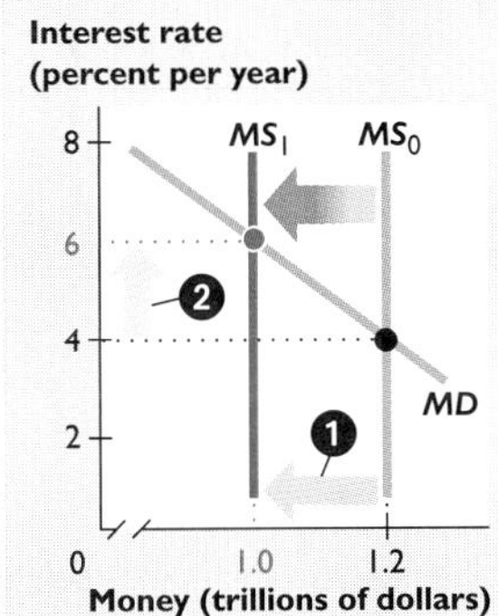

(a) Money market

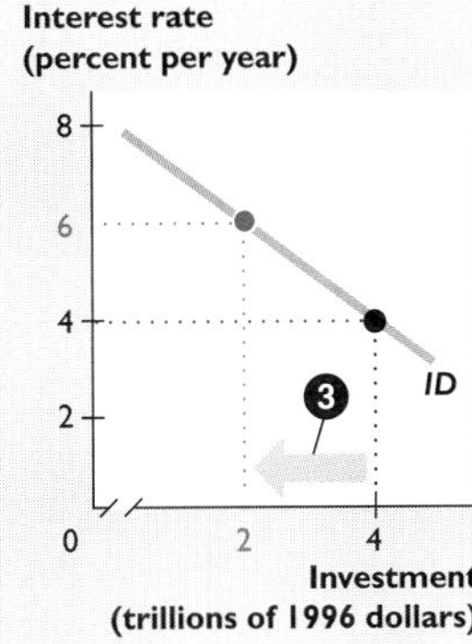

(b) Investment

Solutions to Practice Problems 18.1

1a. When the Fed decreases the quantity of money, ❶ the supply of money decreases and ❷ the interest rate rises. The quantity of money demanded decreases and ❸ investment decreases (Figure 1).

1b. The decrease in investment decreases aggregate expenditure. Aggregate demand decreases.

1c. The Fed's policy is more effective when the change in aggregate demand is larger. The change in aggregate demand will be larger, the bigger is the change in investment resulting from a given change in the interest rate. And the change in the interest rate will be larger, the less sensitive is the demand for money to the interest rate. Figure 18.1(a) illustrates these conditions.

2. A decrease in government purchases decreases aggregate demand and decreases real GDP. The decrease in real GDP decreases the demand for money, and the interest rate falls by a large amount. With investment highly sensitive to the interest rate, investment increases by a large amount. The increase in investment works against the decrease in government purchases, and limits the effectiveness of the fiscal policy action.

18.2 RULES VERSUS DISCRETION

We've seen that monetary policy is more suited to macroeconomic stabilization than is fiscal policy. But *how* should the Fed conduct its monetary policy? Should the Fed be free to use its own discretion, or should it be constrained to follow rules? And if it should follow rules, what kind of rules?

There is little disagreement with the view that Congress should formulate the broad goals for the Fed to pursue. But there is debate about how closely the Fed should be directed in the detailed policy objectives and the means of achieving them. Three broad approaches to the Fed's monetary policy are

- Discretionary policy
- Fixed-rule policy
- Feedback-rule policy

Discretionary Policy

Discretionary monetary policy
Monetary policy that is based on the judgments of policy makers about the current needs of the economy.

Discretionary monetary policy is monetary policy that is based on the judgments of the policy makers about the current needs of the economy. Discretionary monetary policy is setting the discount rate and determining open market operations by the Fed on the basis of the expert opinion of the members of the FOMC and their advisors.

Examples of discretionary policy occur every minute on our highways. Each driver uses discretionary policy in deciding how fast to go and how close to other vehicles to travel.

An example of discretionary monetary policy occurred during 1998 in the face of a sagging Asian economy. During this "Asia Crisis," the Fed cut interest rates several times to maintain economic growth. The Fed might have delayed cutting interest rates until it was sure that lower interest rates were needed and then cut them in larger increments. The Fed used discretion based on lessons it had learned from earlier expansions.

Fixed-Rule Policies

Fixed-rule policy
A policy that is pursued independently of the state of the economy.

A **fixed-rule policy** specifies an action to be pursued independently of the state of the economy. A stop sign is an everyday-life example of a fixed rule. It says, "Stop regardless of the state of the road ahead, even if no other vehicle is trying to use the road." One fixed-rule policy, proposed by Nobel Prize–winning economist Milton Friedman, is to keep the quantity of money growing at a constant rate year in and year out, regardless of the state of the economy, to make the average inflation rate zero. Fixed rules are rarely followed in practice, but they have some merits in principle. Later in this chapter, we will study how they would work if they were pursued.

Feedback-Rule Policies

Feedback-rule policy
A policy that specifies how policy actions respond to changes in the state of the economy.

A **feedback-rule policy** specifies how policy actions respond to changes in the state of the economy. A yield sign is an everyday feedback rule. It says, "Stop if another vehicle is attempting to use the road ahead, but otherwise, proceed." A feedback-rule for monetary policy is one that changes the quantity of money or the interest rate in response to the state of the economy. Some feedback-rules guide the actions of policy makers. For example, the Fed's FOMC used a feedback rule when it kept pushing interest rates ever higher through 1999 and 2000 in response to persistently falling unemployment and strong real GDP growth. And it continued to use the same feedback rule but in the reverse direction when it lowered interest rates during 2002.

We'll study the effects of stabilization policy rules by comparing the performance of real GDP and the price level under a fixed rule and a feedback rule. Because fluctuations can result from demand shocks or supply shocks, we need to consider these two cases. We'll begin by studying demand shocks.

Stabilizing Aggregate Demand Shocks

We'll study an economy that starts out at full employment and has no inflation. Figure 18.2 illustrates this situation. The economy is on aggregate demand curve AD_0 and aggregate supply curve *AS*. The price level is 110, and real GDP is $10 trillion, which is also potential GDP.

Investment decreases because of a wave of pessimism about future profits, and aggregate demand decreases. The aggregate demand curve shifts leftward, to AD_1 in Figure 18.2. Aggregate demand curve AD_1 intersects the aggregate supply curve, *AS*, at a price level of 107 and real GDP of $9.8 trillion. The economy is in a recession. Real GDP is less than potential GDP, and unemployment is above the natural unemployment rate.

At some later time, when profit prospects improve and firms increase investment, the aggregate demand curve will return from AD_1 to AD_0. In the meantime, while aggregate demand is depressed at AD_1, the course of real GDP and the price level depend on the stabilization policy that is pursued. We'll work out how the economy responds under a fixed rule and under a feedback rule.

FIGURE 18.2

A Decrease in Aggregate Demand Brings Recession

Practice Online

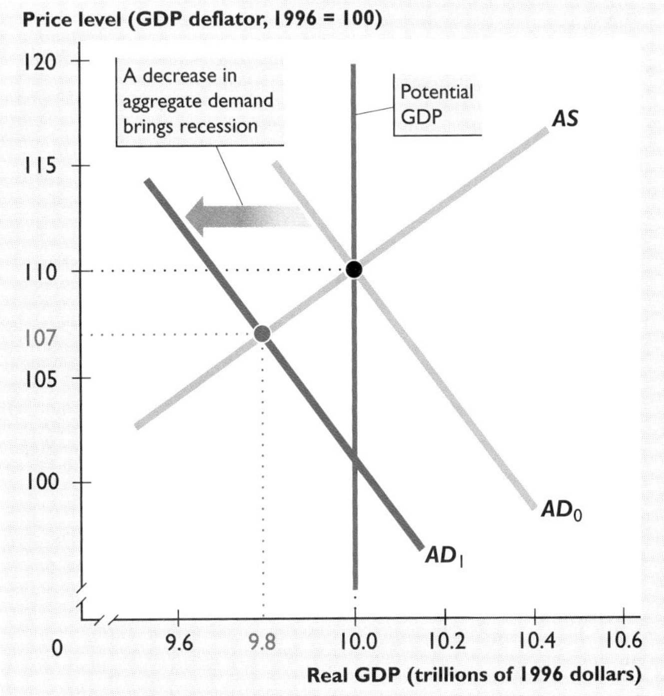

Aggregate demand decreases and the aggregate demand curve shifts from AD_0 to AD_1. The economy goes into recession. Real GDP decreases to $9.8 trillion, and the price level falls to 107.

Fixed Rule: Monetarism

Monetarist
An economist who believes that fluctuations in the quantity of money are the main source of economic fluctuations, and who advocates that the quantity of money grow at a constant rate.

A **monetarist** is an economist who believes that fluctuations in the quantity of money are the main source of economic fluctuations, and who advocates that the quantity of money grow at a constant rate. The fixed rule that we'll study here is one in which the quantity of money remains constant.

Figure 18.3(a) illustrates the response of the economy under this rule. A decrease in aggregate demand brings recession as the economy moves from *A* to *B*. With a deflationary gap and unemployment above the natural unemployment rate, the money wage rate gradually falls. Aggregate supply increases toward AS_1 to take the economy from *B* to *C* and back to full employment.

Eventually, aggregate demand returns to its original level, and the aggregate demand curve shifts rightward to AD_0. Real GDP now expands in a move from *C* to *D*. With an inflationary gap and unemployment below the natural unemployment rate, the money wage rate gradually rises. Aggregate supply decreases toward AS_0 to take the economy from *D* to *A* and to full employment once more.

With a fixed-rule monetary policy, fluctuations in aggregate demand bring fluctuations in real GDP around potential GDP. Let's contrast the performance of the economy under a fixed rule with that under a feedback rule.

FIGURE 18.3
Stabilization Policies: Aggregate Demand Shocks

Practice Online

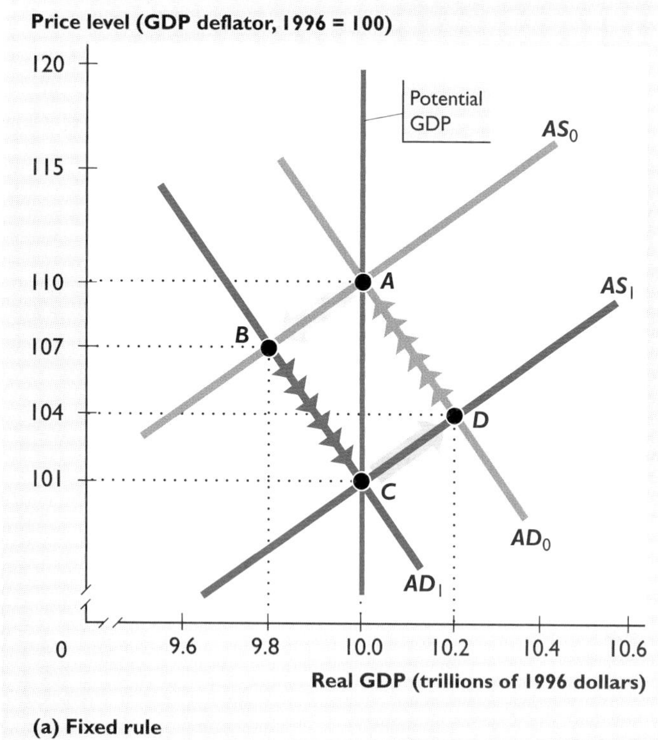

(a) Fixed rule

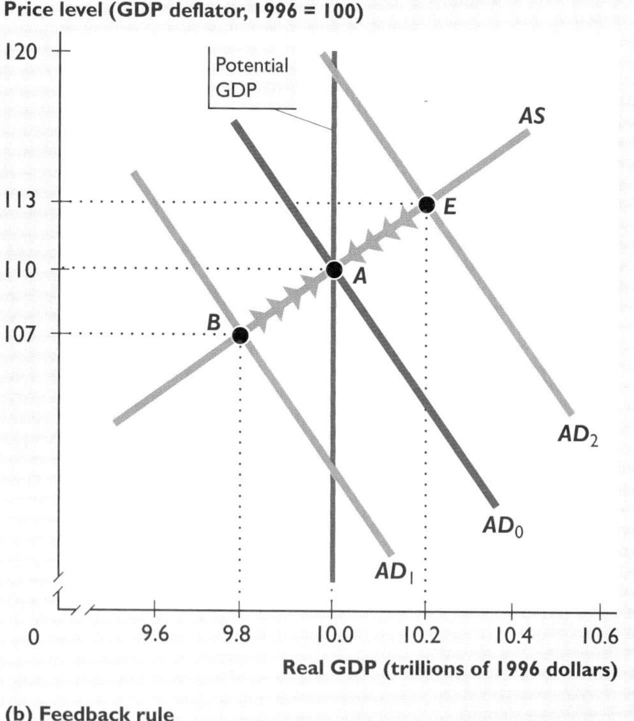

(b) Feedback rule

A fixed-rule policy leaves real GDP and the price level to fluctuate from *A* to *B*, to *C*, to *D* and back to *A* in part (a).

A feedback-rule policy tries to restores full employment as quickly as possible (in part b).

Feedback Rule: Keynesian Activism

A **Keynesian activist** is an economist who believes that fluctuations in investment are the main source of economic fluctuations, and who advocates interest rate cuts when real GDP falls below potential GDP and interest rate hikes when real GDP exceeds potential GDP.

Keynesian activist
An economist who believes that fluctuations in investment are the main source of economic fluctuations, and who advocates interest rate cuts when real GDP falls below potential GDP and interest rate hikes when real GDP exceeds potential GDP.

Figure 18.3(b) illustrates the response of the economy under this feedback-rule policy. When aggregate demand decreases to AD_1, the economy is at point *B*. There is a deflationary gap to which the Fed reacts by increasing the quantity of money and cutting the interest rate. This policy action increases aggregate demand, but only gradually. So the aggregate demand curve moves toward AD_0. As it does so, real GDP increases and the price level rises. Eventually, the economy is back at point *A*, its starting point before the recession.

When profit prospects improve and firms increase investment, aggregate demand increases from AD_0 to AD_2, and the economy moves to point *E*. This expansion brings an inflationary gap to which the Fed reacts. The Fed now decreases the quantity of money and raises the interest rate. This policy action gradually decreases aggregate demand, and the aggregate demand curve moves leftward toward AD_0. As it does so, real GDP decreases and the price level falls. Again, the economy returns to point *A*, its starting point before the expansion.

The Two Rules Compared

Under a fixed-rule policy, a decrease in aggregate demand puts real GDP below potential GDP, where it remains until either a fall in the money wage rate or a subsequent increase in aggregate demand restores full employment. Similarly, an increase in aggregate demand puts real GDP above potential GDP, where it remains until either a rise in the money wage rate or a subsequent decrease in aggregate demand restores full employment.

Under a feedback-rule policy, the economy is pulled out of a deflationary gap or an inflationary gap by a policy action. There is no need to wait for an adjustment in the money wage rate—which everyone agrees takes a long time—for full employment to be restored.

Real GDP decreases and increases by the same amounts under the two policies, but real GDP stays below potential GDP and above potential GDP for longer with a fixed rule than it does with the feedback rule.

Are Feedback Rules Better?

Isn't it obvious that a feedback rule is better than a fixed rule? Can't the Fed use feedback rules to keep the economy close to full employment with a stable price level? Of course, unforecasted events—such as a collapse in business confidence—will hit the economy from time to time. But by responding with a change in the quantity of money and the interest rate, can't the Fed minimize the damage from such a shock?

Despite the apparent superiority of a feedback rule, many economists remain convinced that a fixed rule stabilizes aggregate demand more effectively than does a feedback rule. These economists assert that fixed rules are better than feedback rules because

- Potential GDP is not known.
- Policy lags are longer than the forecast horizon.
- Feedback-rule policies are less predictable than fixed-rule policies.

Let's look at these assertions.

Knowledge of Potential GDP To decide whether a feedback-rule policy needs to stimulate or retard aggregate demand, it is necessary to determine whether real GDP is currently above or below potential GDP. But potential GDP is not known with certainty. It depends on a large number of factors, one of which is the level of employment when unemployment is at the natural unemployment rate. But with uncertainty and disagreement about how the labor market works, we can only estimate the natural unemployment rate. As a result, there is often uncertainty about the direction in which a feedback policy should be pushing the level of aggregate demand.

Policy Lags and the Forecast Horizon The effects of policy actions taken today are spread out over the following two years or even more. But no one is able to forecast accurately that far ahead. The forecast horizon—the distance into the future that forecasters can see—is less than a year. Further, the Fed can't predict the precise timing and magnitude of the effects of its policy actions. So feedback-rule policies that react to today's economy might be inappropriate for the state of the economy at that uncertain future date when the policy's effects are felt.

Predictability of Policies To make decisions about long-term contracts for employment (wage contracts) and for borrowing and lending, people must anticipate the future course of the price level—the future inflation rate. To forecast the inflation rate, it is necessary to forecast aggregate demand. And to forecast aggregate demand, it is necessary to forecast the Fed's policy actions.

If the Fed sticks to a rock-steady, fixed rule for money growth rate, then policy is predictable and it does not contribute to unexpected fluctuations in aggregate demand.

In contrast, if the Fed pursues a feedback rule, there is more scope for the policy actions to be unpredictable. The main reason is that feedback rules are not written down for all to see. Rather, they have to be inferred from the Fed's behavior. So with a feedback-rule policy, it is necessary to predict the variables to which the Fed reacts and the extent to which it reacts. Consequently, a feedback rule for monetary policy can create more unpredictable fluctuations in aggregate demand than a fixed rule can.

We reviewed three reasons why feedback-rule policies might not be more effective than fixed-rule policies in controlling aggregate demand. But there is a fourth reason why some economists prefer fixed rules: Not all shocks to the economy are on the demand side. Advocates of feedback rules generally believe that most fluctuations do come from aggregate demand. Some advocates of fixed rules believe that aggregate supply fluctuations are the dominant ones. Let's now see how aggregate supply fluctuations affect the economy under a fixed rule and under a feedback rule. We will also see why those economists who believe that aggregate supply fluctuations are the dominant ones also favor a fixed rule rather than a feedback rule.

Stabilizing Aggregate Supply Shocks

Everyone agrees that the economy is sometimes hit by an aggregate supply shock. There is disagreement about how frequent and important these supply shocks are. But there is no disagreement about the effect on aggregate supply of a change in the world oil price. In 1974, when the world oil price increased from $2 a barrel to

$10 a barrel, the global economy was delivered a severe negative supply shock. A further negative supply shock occurred in 1980 and 1981 when the world oil price jumped first to $26 and then to $32 a barrel. Positive supply shocks occurred during the 1980s as the world oil price fell back to around $13 a barrel. A price hike to $24 in 1991 delivered another negative shock, and price cuts through 1994 brought a further positive supply shock.

To see the effects of supply shocks and the policy to stabilize them, we'll again start out at full employment with no inflation. Figure 18.4 illustrates an economy with aggregate demand curve *AD* and aggregate supply curve AS_0. The price level is 110, and real GDP is $10 trillion, which is also potential GDP.

The world oil price jumps and aggregate supply decreases. The aggregate supply curve shifts leftward, to AS_1 in Figure 18.4. Aggregate supply curve, AS_1, intersects the aggregate demand curve, *AD*, at a price level of 113 and real GDP of $9.9 trillion. The economy is in a recession. Real GDP is less than potential GDP, and unemployment is above the natural unemployment rate.

At some later time, when world oil production increases, the world price of oil will fall to its original level and aggregate supply will return from AS_1 to AS_0. In the meantime, while aggregate supply is at AS_1, the course of real GDP and the price level depend on the stabilization policy that is pursued. We'll again work out how the economy responds under a fixed rule and under a feedback rule.

FIGURE 18.4

A Decrease in Aggregate Supply Brings Recession

Practice Online

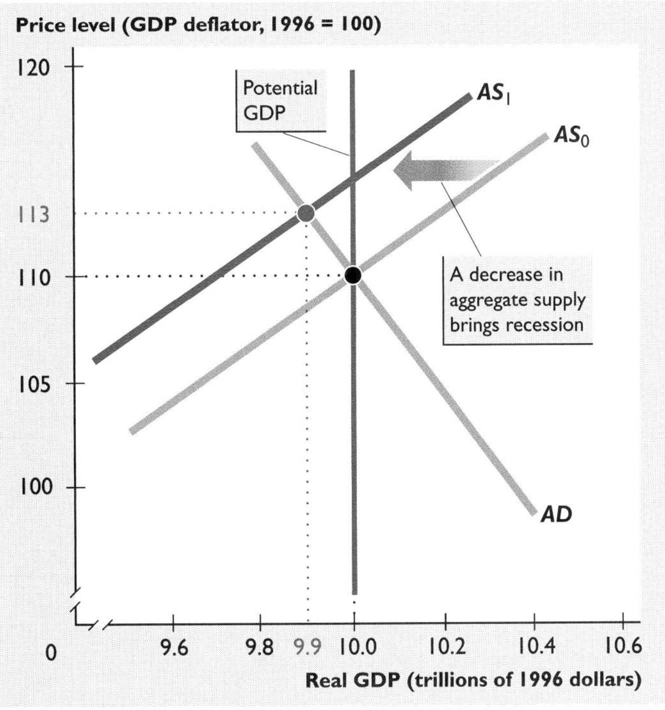

Aggregate supply decreases and the aggregate supply curve shifts from AS_0 to AS_1. The economy goes into recession. Real GDP decreases to $9.9 trillion, and the price level rises to 113.

Fixed Rule

Under a fixed-rule policy, the decrease in aggregate supply has no effect on aggregate demand. Real GDP decreases in a recession as the economy moves from point *A* to point *B* in Figure 18.5(a). With a deflationary gap and unemployment above the natural unemployment rate, the money wage rate gradually falls. The falling money wage rate increases aggregate supply and shifts the aggregate supply curve from AS_1 toward AS_0. Real GDP gradually returns to potential GDP as the economy moves from point *B* back to point *A*.

Feedback Rule

Under a Keynesian activist feedback rule, when the economy is at point *B* in Figure 18.5(b), the Fed reacts to the deflationary gap by increasing the quantity of money and cutting the interest rate. This policy action gradually increases aggregate demand and shifts the aggregate demand curve from AD_0 toward AD_1. Real GDP increases toward potential GDP but at a higher price level, as the economy moves from point *B* to point *C*. What happens next depends on the interaction between the policy rule and the shock to aggregate supply. We'll examine this topic in the next section.

FIGURE 18.5

Stabilization Policies: Aggregate Supply Shocks

Practice Online

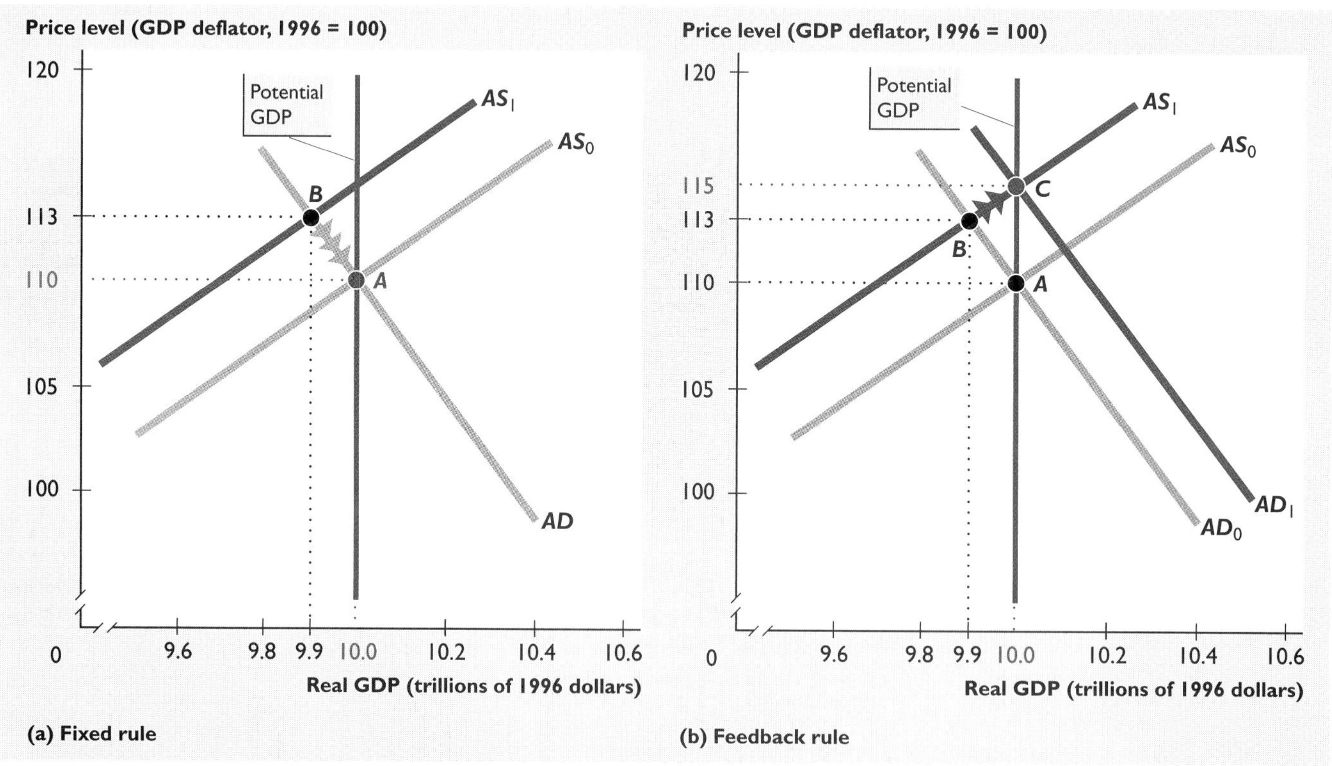

A fixed-rule policy leaves real GDP and the price level to gradually return from *B* to *A* as the money wage rate falls in part (a).

A feedback-rule policy tries to restores full employment as quickly as possible, moving from *B* to *C* (in part b).

CHECKPOINT 18.2

2 Explain the rules-versus-discretion debate and compare Keynesian and monetarist policy rules.

Study Guide pp. 264–267

Practice Online 18.2

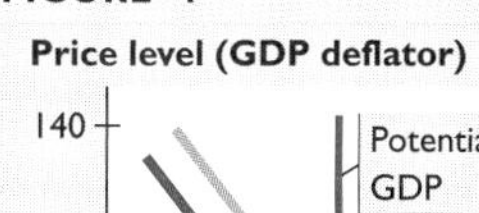

Practice Problem 18.2

The economy shown in Figure 1 is initially on aggregate demand curve AD_0 and aggregate supply curve AS. Then aggregate demand decreases, and the aggregate demand curve shifts leftward to AD_1.

a. What are the initial equilibrium real GDP and price level?

b. If the decrease in aggregate demand is temporary and the Fed adopts a fixed-rule policy, what happens to real GDP and the price level?

c. If the decrease in aggregate demand is temporary and the Fed adopts a feedback-rule policy, what happens to real GDP and the price level?

d. If the decrease in aggregate demand is permanent and the Fed adopts a fixed-rule policy, what happens to real GDP and the price level?

e. If the decrease in aggregate demand is permanent and the Fed adopts a feedback-rule policy, what happens to real GDP and the price level?

FIGURE 1

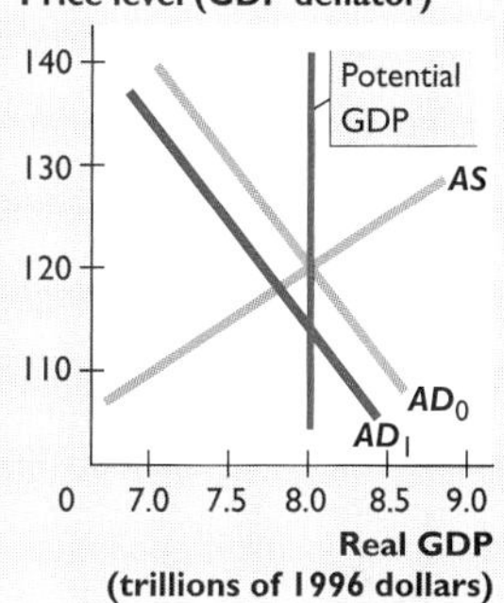

Exercises 18.2

1. The economy shown in Figure 2 is initially on aggregate demand curve AD_0 and aggregate supply curve AS. Then aggregate demand increases, and the aggregate demand curve shifts rightward to AD_2. What happens to real GDP and the price level if the increase in aggregate demand is
   a. Temporary and the Fed adopts a fixed-rule policy?
   b. Temporary and the Fed adopts a feedback-rule policy?
   c. Permanent and the Fed adopts a fixed-rule policy?
   d. Permanent and the Fed adopts a feedback-rule policy?

2. Compare the fluctuations in the price level if the Fed adopts a feedback-rule policy or a fixed-rule policy in response to a positive aggregate supply shock.

FIGURE 2

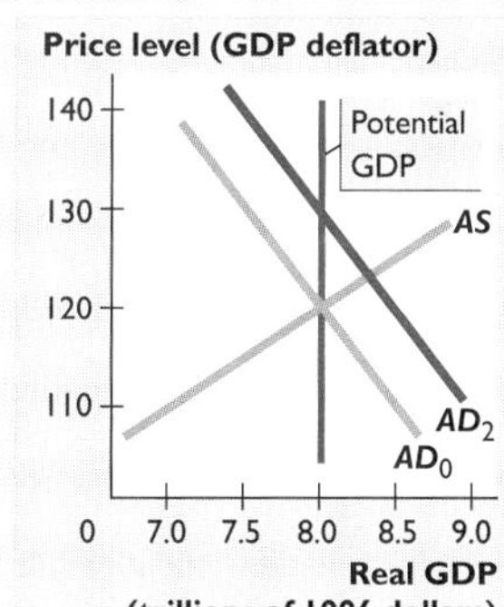

Solution to Practice Problem 18.2

a. Initially, ❶ real GDP is \$8 trillion, and the price level is 120 (Figure 3).

b. ❷ Real GDP decreases to \$7.8 trillion, and the price level falls to 118. If the shock is temporary, then the aggregate demand curve will shift rightward to AD_0, real GDP will return to \$8 trillion, and the price level will rise to 120 (Figure 3).

c. ❶ Real GDP remains at \$8 trillion, and the price level remains at 120. The Fed will increase the quantity of money to keep the aggregate demand curve at AD_0. As the shock goes away, the Fed will decrease the quantity of money to keep the aggregate demand curve at AD_0 (Figure 3).

d. ❶ Real GDP decreases to \$7.8 trillion, and the price level falls to 118 (Figure 4). Unemployment exceeds the natural unemployment rate, so after some time, the money wage rate will start to fall. ❷ Real GDP will increase to \$8 trillion, and the price level will fall to 115 (Figure 4).

e. Real GDP remains at \$8 trillion, and the price level remains at 120. The Fed will increase the quantity of money to keep the aggregate demand curve at AD_0.

FIGURE 3

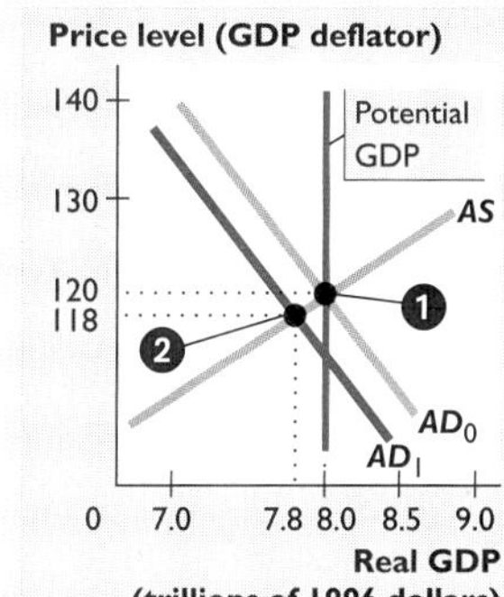

FIGURE 4

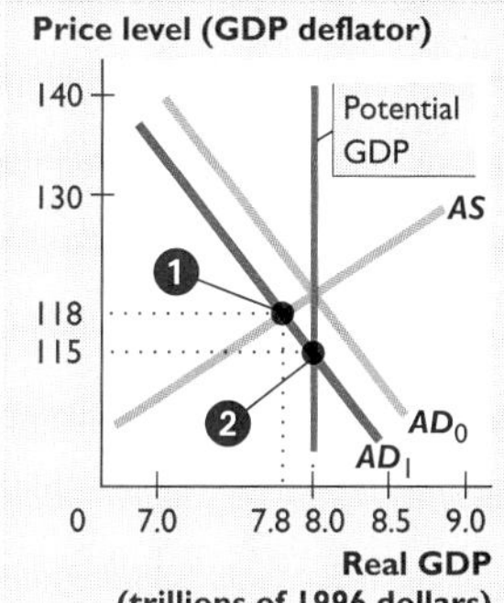

18.3 TARGETING INFLATION

Shocks to aggregate demand and aggregate supply bring fluctuations in real GDP and the price level. We've just examined stabilization policies that target real GDP and aim to keep it as close as possible to potential GDP. But

- Should policy target real GDP or the price level?
- Should the target inflation rate be zero or positive?

Real GDP Versus the Price Level

When real GDP fluctuates around potential GDP, the unemployment rate also fluctuates around its natural rate. So targeting real GDP is equivalent to targeting the unemployment rate. Aiming to keep real GDP equal to potential GDP is the same as aiming to keep the unemployment rate equal to the natural unemployment rate.

When real GDP is below potential GDP, the economy is in a deflationary gap, output is lost and jobs are hard to find. So if monetary policy can close a deflationary gap, people become better off.

When real GDP is above potential GDP, the economy is in an inflationary gap, resources are overworked, and inefficient plant breakdowns and bottlenecks arise. Also, inflation increases, which brings its own costs. So if monetary policy can close an inflationary gap, people become better off.

If aggregate demand shocks were the only source of economic fluctuations, the choice of a target for monetary policy would be easy: Stabilize aggregate demand. By doing so, real GDP would remain close to potential GDP, and the price level and the inflation rate would be as stable as possible.

But aggregate supply shocks also bring economic fluctuations. And this fact poses a problem for monetary policy. How should monetary policy try to influence aggregate demand when aggregate supply changes?

Two possible targets for monetary policy are

- Real GDP
- The price level

Real GDP Target

If monetary policy targets real GDP, it seeks to neutralize the effects of aggregate supply shocks on real GDP. That is, an increase in aggregate supply is met by a decrease in aggregate demand; and a decrease in aggregate supply is countered by an increase in aggregate demand.

Figure 18.6(a) illustrates real GDP targeting. The blue band is the real GDP target. If aggregate supply is AS_0, monetary policy aims to place the aggregate demand curve (not shown) through point *A*. Here, real GDP is on target at $10 trillion and the price level is 110. If aggregate supply increases to AS_1, monetary policy aims to *decrease* aggregate demand and place the aggregate demand curve through point *B*. Here, real GDP remains on target at $10 trillion but the price level falls to 107. If aggregate supply decreases to AS_2, monetary policy aims to *increase* aggregate demand and place the aggregate demand curve through point *C*. Again, real GDP remains on target at $10 trillion, but the price level now rises to 113.

You can see that in the face of shocks to aggregate supply, stabilizing real GDP means destabilizing the price level.

FIGURE 18.6
Alternative Monetary Policy Targets

Practice Online

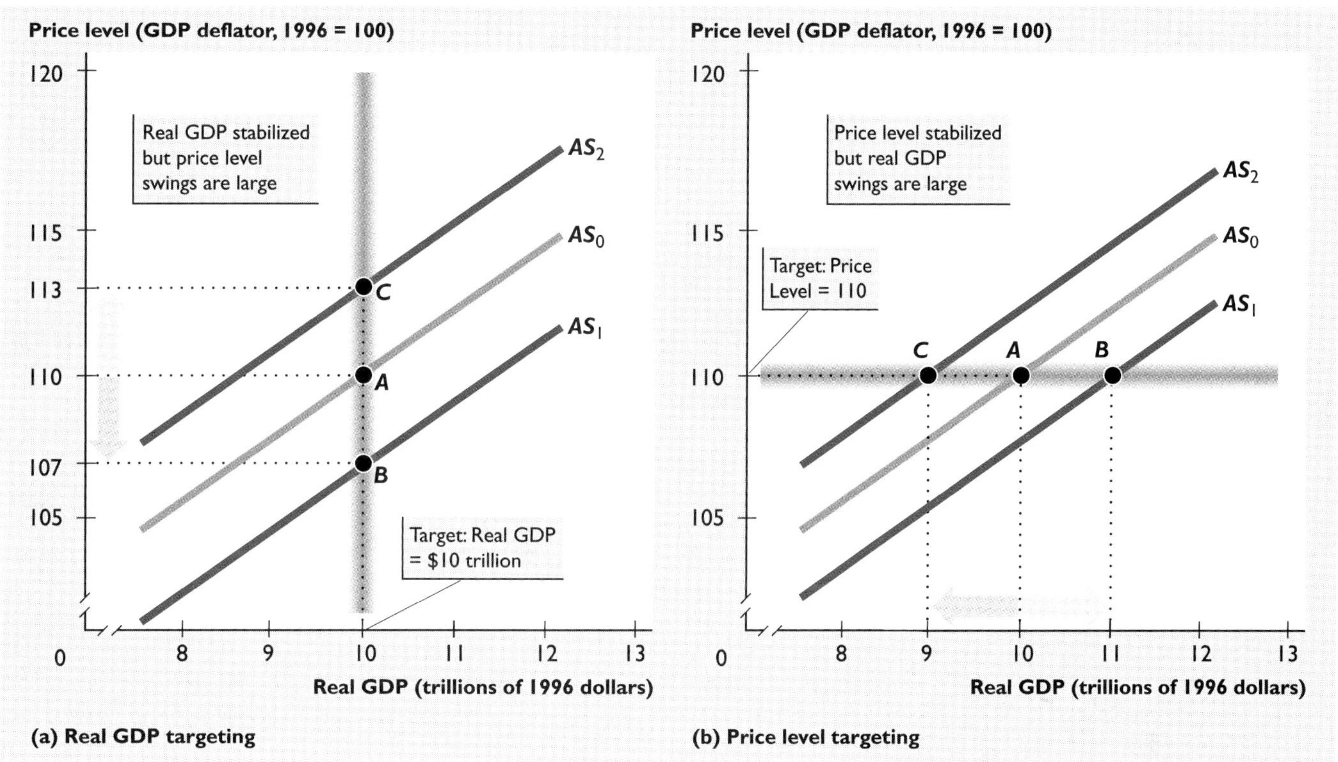

The blue band is the real GDP target. When aggregate supply increases from AS_0 to AS_1 or decreases from AS_0 to AS_2, monetary policy aims to change aggregate demand to keep real GDP on target at $10 trillion.

The blue band is the price level target. When aggregate supply increases from AS_0 to AS_1 or decreases from AS_0 to AS_2, monetary policy aims to change aggregate demand to keep the price level on target at 110.

Price Level Target

If monetary policy targets the price level, it seeks to neutralize the effects of aggregate supply shocks on the price level. That is, an increase in aggregate supply is met by an *increase* in aggregate demand; a decrease in aggregate supply is countered by a *decrease* in aggregate demand.

Figure 18.6(b) shows the outcome if monetary policy targets the price level. The blue band is now the price level target. If aggregate supply is AS_0, monetary policy aims to place the aggregate demand curve (not shown) through point A. Here, the price level is on target at 110 and real GDP is $10 trillion.

If aggregate supply increases to AS_1, monetary policy aims to *increase* aggregate demand and place the aggregate demand curve through point B. Here, the price level remains on target at 110 but real GDP increases to $11 trillion.

If aggregate supply decreases to AS_2, monetary policy aims to *decrease* aggregate demand and place the aggregate demand curve through point C. Again, the price level remains on target at 110 but real GDP decreases to $9 trillion.

You can see that in the face of shocks to aggregate supply, stabilizing the price level means destabilizing real GDP.

More General Targets

Monetary policy might target something less extreme than either real GDP or the price level. It might place some weight on fluctuations in both real GDP and the price level.

You can think of the macroeconomic stabilization target as the target in a shooting contest. Figure 18.7 illustrates this idea. In this figure, we represent fluctuations in real GDP as the output gap—the percentage difference between real GDP and potential GDP. And we represent fluctuations in the price level as the inflation rate—the percentage change in the price level in a given period.

The *x*-axis measures the output gap, and the *y*-axis measures the inflation rate centered on zero. Here, the bull's-eye is an output gap and an inflation rate of zero. Let's suppose the score for hitting the bull's-eye is 100. Missing the bull's-eye by 1 percent scores 75; missing by 2 percent scores 50; and missing by 3 percent scores 25. A bigger miss is completely off target!

If the macroeconomic stabilization target was like Figure 18.7(a), equal weight would be placed on the output gap and the inflation rate. Policy would try to get as close to the bull's-eye as possible and would not worry about real GDP or the price level independently of each other. For example, hitting the target at a 2 percent inflation rate and a zero output gap is just as good as hitting it at zero inflation and a 2 percent output gap or at any other point on the circle on which those two points lie. Unlike the target at a shooting competition, the macroeconomic stabilization target need not be round. It might be elliptical, like the targets in Figure 18.7(b) and 18.7(c). In part (b), an output-gap miss is penalized more heavily than an inflation miss. And in part (c), the penalty is reversed—an inflation miss is penalized more heavily than an output-gap miss.

Real GDP targeting is an extreme case of Figure 18.7(b) in which the target is a vertical line running along the *y*-axis. Any inflation rate is acceptable, but only one output gap is acceptable: a zero gap. Price level targeting is an extreme case of Figure 18.7(c) in which the target is a horizontal line running along the *x*-axis. Any output gap is acceptable, but only one inflation rate is acceptable: zero inflation.

FIGURE 18.7
The Shape of the Target

Practice Online

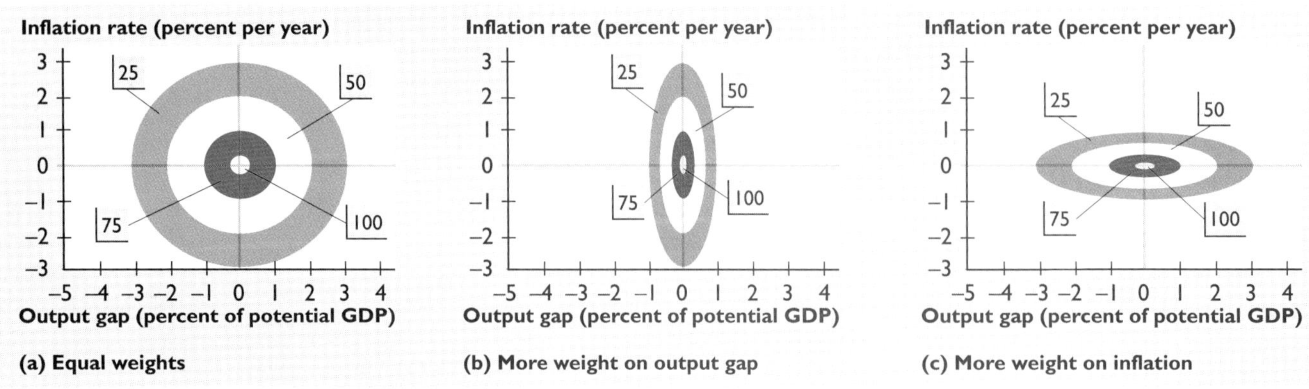

The "bull's-eye" is an output gap and an inflation rate of zero. The bigger the miss, the lower is the score. In part (a), equal weight is placed on fluctuations in real GDP and the inflation rate. In part (b), an output-gap miss is penalized more heavily than an inflation miss, and in part (c), an inflation miss is penalized more heavily than an output-gap miss.

A Tradeoff or a Free Lunch?

You've seen that in the face of shocks to aggregate supply, stabilizing real GDP means destabilizing the price level; and stabilizing the price level means destabilizing real GDP. It appears that there is a tradeoff between real GDP stability and price level stability. To make real GDP more stable, we must bear the cost of a more unstable price level. Or to make the price level more stable, we must bear the cost of a more unstable real GDP.

Lars Svensson, a prominent Swedish economist who divides his time between Princeton University and the University of Stockholm and who is a member of the committee that awards the annual Nobel Prize for Economic Sciences, says there is no tradeoff and that stabilizing the price level brings a "free lunch" of more stable real GDP. (See Chapter 3, pp. 63–64, for a reminder of the distinction between a tradeoff and a free lunch.)

The "free lunch" arises because stabilizing the price level helps to stabilize aggregate supply. You've seen that stabilizing real GDP means destabilizing the price level. But if the price level fluctuates more, the *expected* price level also fluctuates more. And fluctuations in the expected price level bring fluctuations in the money wage rate and aggregate supply. So, stabilizing real GDP means destabilizing aggregate supply.

But if the price level targeting brings smaller fluctuates in the *expected* price level, it also brings smaller fluctuations in the money wage rate and aggregate supply. So, stabilizing the price level means stabilizing aggregate supply, which brings more stable real GDP—a free lunch. Sweden's experience with price level targeting (see below) suggests that Lars Svensson might be correct.

Eye on the Past

Price Level Targeting

In September 1931, the Swedish central bank, the Riksbank, began targeting the CPI (reset at 100). The experiment ran until April 1937.

The figure shows what happened during the 67 months of CPI targeting.

The Great Depression was raging through this period and Sweden had a much less severe recession than most countries did. This outcome has been attributed to Sweden's decision to target the price level. Sweden eventually abandoned this policy because of concerns (probably misplaced) about the foreign exchange rate.

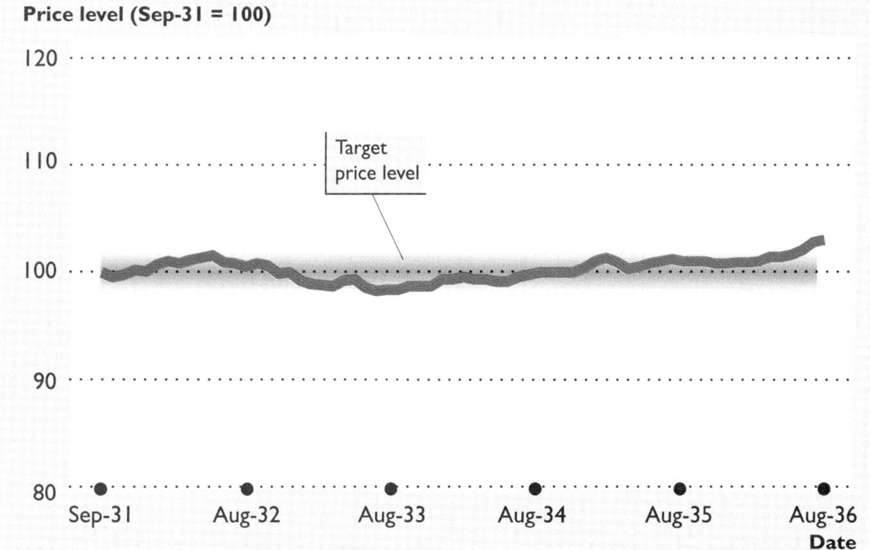

SOURCE: Federal Reserve Bank of St. Louis.

Zero Versus Positive Inflation

Inflation is costly. It slows economic growth and wastes leisure time (see Chapter 13, pp. 333–336). To avoid these costs, some economists advocate a zero inflation target. But other economists say that low inflation is better than zero inflation. Two reasons why low inflation might be preferred to zero inflation are that

- Inflation lubricates the labor market.
- The nominal interest rate cannot fall below zero.

Labor Market Lubricant

The labor market lubricant view is based on the belief that the natural rate hypothesis is incorrect and that a long-run tradeoff between inflation and unemployment exists—the long-run Phillips curve (see Chapter 17, p. 430) is not vertical. That is, the lower the inflation rate, the higher is the unemployment rate on the average in the long run.

The claim is that to maintain full employment, some real wage rates need to fall. But money wage rates don't fall, so a little bit of inflation is needed to make real wage rates fall. For example, advances in ATM technology decreased the demand for bank tellers, and the equilibrium real wage rate of tellers fell. The lower real wage rate encouraged some tellers to quit and to look for new types of work. The money wage rate of tellers didn't fall, but inflation lowered their real wage rate.

If we had no inflation, it is argued, the real wage of bank tellers would not have fallen and many people would be spending time looking for impossible-to-find jobs as tellers, so the unemployment rate would increase.

This labor market lubricant justification for inflation appears to be incorrect. While there is plenty of evidence that money wage rates are sticky, there is no evidence that they are stickier downward than upward. So while there is plenty of evidence that a short-run tradeoff exists, there is no evidence that a long-run tradeoff exists. The natural rate hypothesis appears to be correct, and in the long run the unemployment rate is not higher at a zero inflation rate than it is at a low positive inflation rate.

The Zero Lower Bound

Lawrence Summers, former U.S. Secretary of the Treasury, suggested some years ago when he was a professor at Harvard that there is a long-run tradeoff between inflation and unemployment that arises from the fact that the nominal interest rate cannot fall below zero. The claim is that expansionary monetary policy cannot be used to get the economy out of recession if the nominal interest rate is zero, so in such a situation, recession will last longer. Because the nominal interest rate will be zero more frequently the lower the inflation rate, the economy will spend longer in recession, on the average, the lower the inflation rate. The experience of Japan during recent years is often cited as an example of an economy that has hit the zero lower bound.

This argument is an old one and has, for many years, been known to be incorrect. And it was a subject of much debate before and during the Great Depression. The Fed can always inject more money into the economy. And even if the nominal interest rate does not fall, more money brings more spending by way of an exchange rate effect and a buying power of money effect.

Eye on the U.S. Economy

The Fed's Targeting and the Taylor and McCallum Rules

The Fed's monetary policy objective is to maintain low inflation because that is the best contribution that it can make to achieving sustained long-term growth of real GDP. But the Fed also pays attention to deviations of real GDP from potential GDP.

John Taylor, formerly an economics professor at Stanford University and now Undersecretary of the Treasury for International Affairs in the Bush administration, has suggested a feedback-rule policy that he believes is a reasonable description of what the Fed does but that would actually deliver a better performance than what the Fed has achieved.

The Taylor rule adjusts the federal funds rate according to whether the inflation rate exceeds its target and whether real GDP exceeds potential GDP. The Taylor rule places equal weights on inflation and real GDP (like the circular target in Figure 18.7).

Part (a) of the figure shows that the Fed's actual policy makes the federal funds rate fluctuate more than it would if the Taylor rule were followed.

Bennett McCallum, a leading monetary economist and a professor at Carnegie Mellon University, believes that the Fed should target the growth rate of the monetary base, not the federal funds rate.

If the Fed followed the McCallum rule, the monetary base would grow at a rate equal to the target inflation rate plus the growth rate of real GDP over the preceding decade minus the growth rate of the velocity of circulation of the monetary base over the preceding four years.

Part (b) of the figure shows that the Fed makes the monetary base growth rate more unstable than it would be if the McCallum rule were followed.

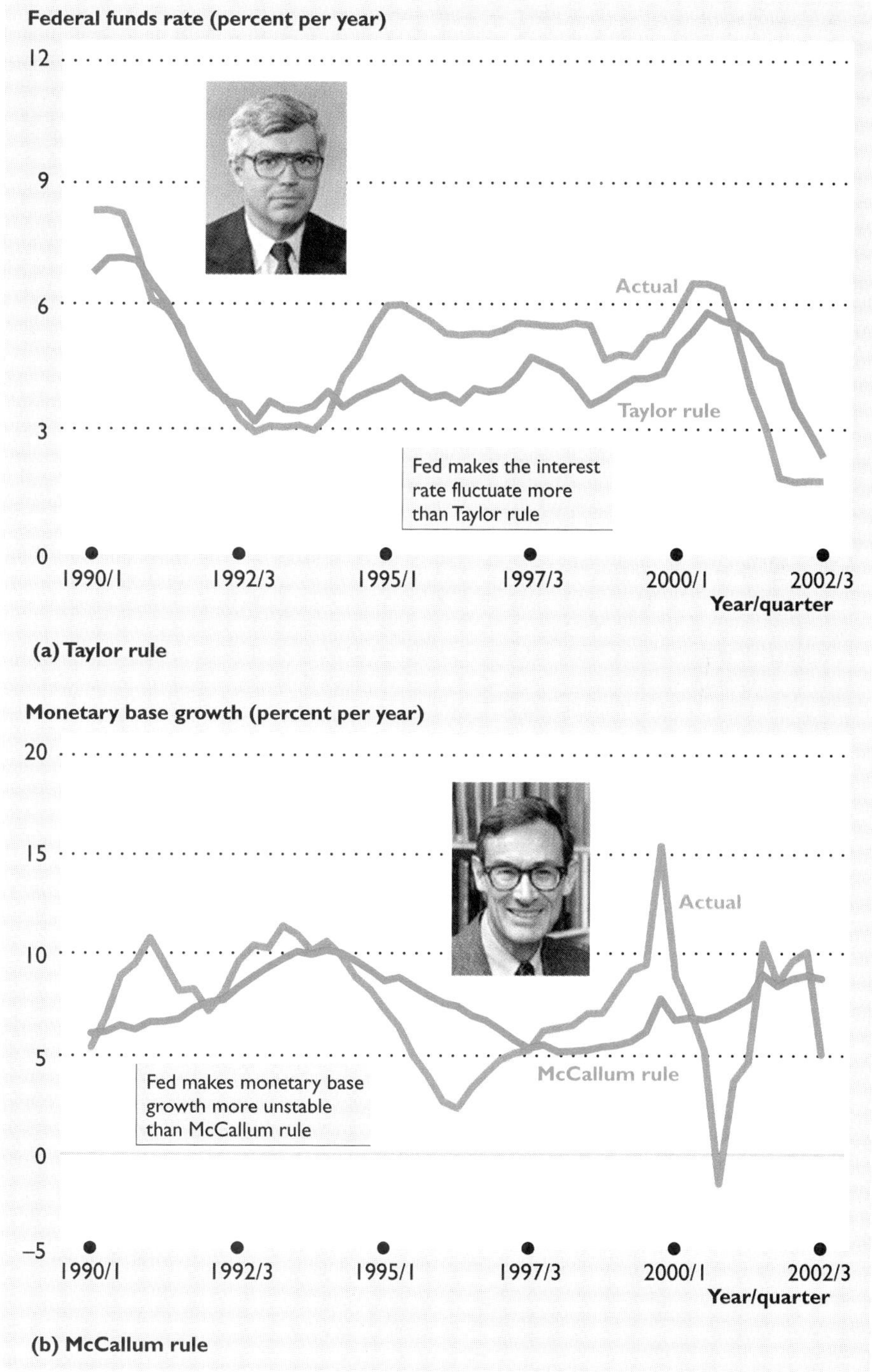

Federal funds rate (percent per year)

12, 9, 6, 3, 0

Actual

Taylor rule

Fed makes the interest rate fluctuate more than Taylor rule

1990/1 1992/3 1995/1 1997/3 2000/1 2002/3

Year/quarter

(a) Taylor rule

Monetary base growth (percent per year)

20, 15, 10, 5, 0, –5

Actual

McCallum rule

Fed makes monetary base growth more unstable than McCallum rule

1990/1 1992/3 1995/1 1997/3 2000/1 2002/3

Year/quarter

(b) McCallum rule

SOURCE: Federal Reserve Board.

CHECKPOINT 18.3

Study Guide pp. 267–269

Practice Online 18.3

3 **Assess whether policy should target the price level rather than real GDP.**

Practice Problems 18.3

1. Suppose that the economy experiences a positive aggregate supply shock and the Fed reacts to this shock by adjusting its monetary policy. Explain the effect of the Fed's action on real GDP and the price level if the Fed places
   a. No weight on real GDP fluctuations.
   b. No weight on inflation.
   c. Equal weight on inflation and real GDP fluctuations.
2. Suppose that in 2005, the inflation rate is 3 percent a year and potential GDP is $12 trillion. Faced with a decrease in aggregate supply, the Fed decides that it wants to keep the inflation rate between 1 percent and 5 percent a year and to keep real GDP within the range $11.9 trillion to $12.1 trillion.
   a. Is the Fed placing more weight on inflation or on real GDP?
   b. What actions will the Fed take?

Exercises 18.3

1. Suppose that the economy experiences a negative aggregate supply shock and the Fed reacts to this shock by adjusting its monetary policy. Explain the effect of the Fed's action on real GDP and the price level if the Fed
   a. Places more weight on real GDP fluctuations than on inflation.
   b. Places more weight on inflation than on real GDP fluctuations.
   c. Targets the price level.
2. Suppose that in 2004, the inflation rate is 4 percent a year and potential GDP is $11 trillion. Faced with a world recession, the Fed decides it wants to keep the inflation rate between 4 percent and 5 percent a year and to keep real GDP at $11 trillion.
   a. Is the Fed placing more weight on inflation or on real GDP?
   b. What actions will the Fed take?

Solutions to Practice Problems 18.3

1a. If the Fed places no weight on real GDP fluctuations, then it targets the price level. The price level will remain steady, and real GDP will increase.

1b. If the Fed places no weight on inflation, then it targets real GDP and adjusts the quantity of money to remove any output gap. Real GDP remains at potential GDP, and the price level falls.

1c. If the Fed places equal weight on inflation and real GDP fluctuations, then it targets a combination of the price level and real GDP. The outcome would be somewhere between the outcomes in **a** and **b**.

2a. The Fed is placing more weight on real GDP. A deviation from potential GDP of $12 trillion by $0.1 trillion is less than a 1 percent deviation. The Fed is willing to tolerate a much larger spread in inflation.

2b. When aggregate supply decreases, the Fed will cut the interest rate and increase the quantity of money to increase aggregate demand and keep real GDP inside its target range.

Key Points

1 Discuss whether fiscal policy or monetary policy is the better stabilization tool.

- The demand for money and investment demand determine the effects of monetary policy and fiscal policy on aggregate demand. Both policy tools affect aggregate demand.
- Monetary policy has less conflict among its goals than does fiscal policy and is the more flexible.
- Monetary policy and automatic fiscal policy are the preferred tools for stabilizing aggregate demand in normal times.

2 Explain the rules-versus-discretion debate and compare Keynesian and monetarist policy rules.

- In the face of a shock to aggregate demand or aggregate supply, a fixed-rule policy takes no action. Real GDP and the price level fluctuate.
- In the face of a shock to aggregate demand or aggregate supply, a feedback-rule policy takes offsetting action. An ideal feedback rule keeps the economy at full employment, with a stable price level.
- Some economists say that a feedback rule creates fluctuations because it requires greater knowledge of the economy than we have, operates with time lags that extend beyond the forecast horizon, and introduces unpredictability about policy reactions.

3 Assess whether policy should target the price level rather than real GDP.

- If monetary policy targets real GDP, aggregate demand and aggregate supply change in opposite directions, and price level fluctuations increase.
- If monetary policy targets the price level, aggregate supply and aggregate demand change in the same direction.
- Stabilizing real GDP destabilizes the price level and destabilizes the expected price level, so it makes aggregate supply *less* stable. So price level targeting might deliver more stable real GDP than real GDP targeting.
- The case for positive inflation is weak.

Key Terms

Discretionary monetary policy, 454
Feedback-rule policy, 454
Fixed-rule policy, 454
Keynesian activist, 457
Liquidity trap, 451
Monetarist, 456

Exercises

1. Describe the steps in the transmission of monetary policy and fiscal policy and explain why the conditions that make monetary policy highly effective make fiscal policy ineffective and the conditions that make fiscal policy highly effective make monetary policy ineffective.
2. Draw graphs to illustrate the conditions under which
   - **a.** Fiscal policy is highly effective and monetary policy is ineffective.
   - **b.** Monetary policy is highly effective and fiscal policy is ineffective.
   - **c.** Monetary policy and fiscal policy are equally effective.
3. For the Fed to stabilize aggregate demand, what does the Fed have to be able to accurately predict?
4. What are the goals of discretionary fiscal policy? Why does discretionary fiscal policy create goal conflicts? Why does monetary policy not have the goal conflicts of discretionary fiscal policy?
5. Why is monetary policy more flexible than fiscal policy?
6. Define and distinguish among discretionary monetary policy, a fixed-rule policy, and a feedback-rule policy. Provide examples of each type of policy.
7. As the U.S. economy went into recession in 2001, the Fed repeatedly lowered the federal funds interest rate.
   - **a.** Would you describe the Fed's actions as a feedback-rule policy or a fixed-rule policy?
   - **b.** What do you predict the effects of the Fed's policies would be on real GDP and the price level?
8. Coinciding with the U.S. economy entering recession in 2001, Congress passed some tax cuts and voted to increase expenditure on homeland security.
   - **a.** Would you describe the Congress's actions as a feedback-rule policy, a fixed-rule policy, or neither?
   - **b.** What do you predict the effects of Congress's actions would be on real GDP and the price level?
9. Explain why a Keynesian activist feedback-rule for monetary policy could create more fluctuations in aggregate demand than a monetarist fixed-rule policy creates.
10. Which type of monetary or fiscal stabilization policy requires accurate knowledge of the value of potential GDP? Explain why.
    - **a.** A feedback-rule policy that targets real GDP
    - **b.** A fixed-rule policy that targets real GDP
    - **c.** A feedback-rule policy that targets the price level
    - **d.** A fixed-rule policy that targets the price level
11. The U.S. economy in 2004 is at full employment when it is hit by a positive aggregate supply shock. Explain how the U.S. price level and real GDP will change in the short run and the long run if the Fed adopts
    - **a.** A feedback-rule policy that targets real GDP.
    - **b.** A feedback-rule policy that targets the price level.
    - **c.** A fixed-rule policy.

12. The U.S. economy in 2004 is at full employment when it is hit by a negative aggregate supply shock. Explain how the U.S. price level and real GDP will change in the short run and the long run if the Fed adopts
a. A feedback-rule policy that targets real GDP.
b. A feedback-rule policy that targets the price level.
c. A fixed-rule policy.

13. The U.S. economy in 2004 is at full employment when it is hit by a positive aggregate demand shock. Explain how the U.S. price level and real GDP will change in the short run and the long run if the Fed adopts
a. A feedback-rule policy that targets real GDP.
b. A feedback-rule policy that targets the price level.
c. A fixed-rule policy.

14. The U.S. economy in 2004 is at full employment when it is hit by a negative aggregate demand shock. Explain how the U.S. price level and real GDP will change in the short run and the long run if the Fed adopts
a. A feedback-rule policy that targets real GDP.
b. A feedback-rule policy that targets the price level.
c. A fixed-rule policy.

15. In a deep recession, the Fed, Congress, and the White House are discussing ways of restoring full employment. The President wants to stimulate aggregate demand but to do so in a way that will give the best chance of boosting investment and long-term economic growth. Explain which of the following actions would best meet the President's objectives and which would present the greatest obstacles to those objectives.
a. A tax cut
b. An increase in government purchases
c. An increase in the quantity of money and cut in the federal funds rate

16. What are the arguments for and against attempting to achieve zero inflation?

17. Inflation is rising toward 5 percent a year, and the Fed, Congress, and the White House are discussing ways of containing inflation without damaging employment and output. The President wants to cut aggregate demand but to do so in a way that will give the best chance of keeping investment high to encourage long-term economic growth. Explain which of the following actions would best meet the President's objectives and which would present the greatest obstacles to those objectives.
a. A tax rise
b. A decrease in government purchases
c. A decrease in the quantity of money and a rise in the federal funds rate

Critical Thinking

18. All things considered, do you think the Fed should stabilize the economy with no help from fiscal policy or do you think fiscal policy should seek to stabilize the economy and the Fed should concentrate on keeping inflation low?

19. Do you think it likely that a Keynesian activist feedback rule for monetary policy would create more fluctuations in aggregate demand than a monetarist fixed rule would? Why or why not?

20. Compare and contrast the Taylor rule and the McCallum rule for monetary policy.
    a. Why do you think the Fed doesn't follow one of these rules?
    b. Why do you think the Fed makes the federal funds rate fluctuate by more than it would if the Taylor rule were followed?
    c. Why do you think the Fed makes the monetary base growth rate fluctuate more than it would if the McCallum rule were followed?

Practice Online

Web Exercises

Use the links on your Foundations Web site to work the following exercises.

21. Visit the Web sites of the Bank of Canada and Statistics Canada. Find the Canadian price level, inflation rate, and target inflation rate for the current year.
    a. What is the Bank of Canada's target for the inflation rate?
    b. If the Bank of Canada achieves its target, show on a graph the path of the Canadian price level.
    c. What events might force the Bank of Canada to abandon its inflation target?

22. Visit the Web site of the International Monetary Fund (IMF). When the economies of Indonesia, Korea, Thailand, Malaya, and the Philippines entered into recession in 1997, the IMF made loans but only on condition that the recipients of the loans increase interest rates, raise taxes, and cut government expenditures.
    a. Would you describe the IMF prescription as a feedback-rule policy or a fixed-rule policy?
    b. What do you predict the immediate effects of the IMF policies would be on real GDP and the price level?

23. Visit the Web site of the Bureau of Economic Analysis and obtain data on real GDP since 1990. Then visit the Web site of the Federal Reserve Bank of St Louis and obtain data on the Congressional Budget Office's estimates of potential GDP.
    a. Use a spreadsheet program to calculate the size of the deflationary and inflationary gap each quarter since 1990.
    b. In which periods do you think policy was seeking to stimulate aggregate demand and in which periods was policy seeking to restrain aggregate demand?

24. Visit the Web site of the Federal Reserve and obtain data on the federal funds rate since 1990. Compare and comment on the movements in the federal funds rate in relation to the predictions you made in part **b** of exercise 23.

CHAPTER 19

International Trade

CHAPTER CHECKLIST

When you have completed your study of this chapter, you will be able to

1. **Describe the patterns and trends in international trade.**
2. **Explain why nations engage in international trade and why trade benefits all nations.**
3. **Explain how trade barriers reduce international trade.**
4. **Explain the arguments used to justify trade barriers and show why they are incorrect but also why some barriers are hard to remove.**

We live in a global economy, and macroeconomic disturbances in one part of the world quickly transmit to other parts. Also, wages in most nations are lower than wages in the United States. How can we compete with countries that pay their workers a fraction of U.S. wages?

Would it be better if we isolated our economy from the rest of the world? Or are there some gains from trading with other nations that are worth the macroeconomic disturbances and international competition they bring?

In this chapter, you are going to learn about international trade. You will discover how all nations can gain by specializing in producing the goods and services in which they have a comparative advantage and trading with other countries. You will discover that all countries can compete, no matter how high their wages. And you'll learn why, despite the fact that international trade brings benefits to all countries, they nevertheless restrict trade.

19.1 TRADE PATTERNS AND TRENDS

The goods and services that we buy from people in other countries are called *imports*. The goods and services that we sell to people in other countries are called *exports*. What are the most important things that we import and export? Most people would probably guess that a rich nation such as the United States imports raw materials and exports manufactured goods. Although that is one feature of U.S. international trade, it is not its most important feature. The vast bulk of U.S. exports and imports are manufactured goods. We sell foreigners earth-moving equipment, airplanes, supercomputers, scientific equipment, movies, and magazines, and we buy televisions, VCRs, blue jeans, and T-shirts from them. Also, we are a major exporter of agricultural products and raw materials. We also import and export a huge volume of services.

Trade in Goods

In 2002, manufactured goods accounted for 47 percent of U.S. exports and for 58 percent of U.S. imports. Raw materials and semimanufactured items accounted for 16 percent of U.S. exports and for 20 percent of U.S. imports, and agricultural products accounted for only 5 percent of U.S. exports and 3 percent of U.S. imports. The largest U.S. export and import item in 2002 was autos and auto parts.

But goods accounted for only 72 percent of U.S. exports and 84 percent of U.S. imports in 2002. The rest of U.S. international trade in 2002 was in services.

Trade in Services

You might be wondering how a country can export and import services. Here are some examples.

If you take a vacation in France and travel there on an Air France flight from New York, the United States imports transportation services from France. The money you spend in France on hotel bills and restaurant meals is also classified as a U.S. import of services. Similarly, the vacation taken by a French student in the United States counts as a U.S. export of services to France.

When we import TV sets from South Korea, the owner of the ship that transports them might be Greek and the company that insures them might be British. The payments that we make for the transportation and insurance are U.S. imports of services. Similarly, when a U.S. shipping company transports California wine to Tokyo, the transportation cost is a U.S. export of a service to Japan. U.S. international trade in these types of services is large and growing.

Trends in the Volume of Trade

In 1960, we exported 5 percent of total output and imported 4 percent of the goods and services that we bought. In 2002, we exported 10 percent of total output and imported 14 percent of the goods and services that we bought.

On the export side, automobiles, aircraft, food, and raw materials have remained large items and have held a roughly constant share of total exports. But the composition of imports has changed. Food and raw material imports have fallen steadily. Imports of fuel increased dramatically during the 1970s, fell during the 1980s, and increased again during the 1990s. Imports of machinery have grown and today approach 50 percent of total imports.

Eye on the Global Economy

The Major Items That We Trade with Other Nations

The figure shows the U.S. volume of trade and balance of trade for the 20 largest items traded in 2002. If a bar has more red (imports) than blue (exports), the United States has a trade deficit in that item.

Automobiles and parts is the largest item traded. Fuels, travel, computers, and aircraft and parts are also large items. Notice that travel is a larger item than most goods.

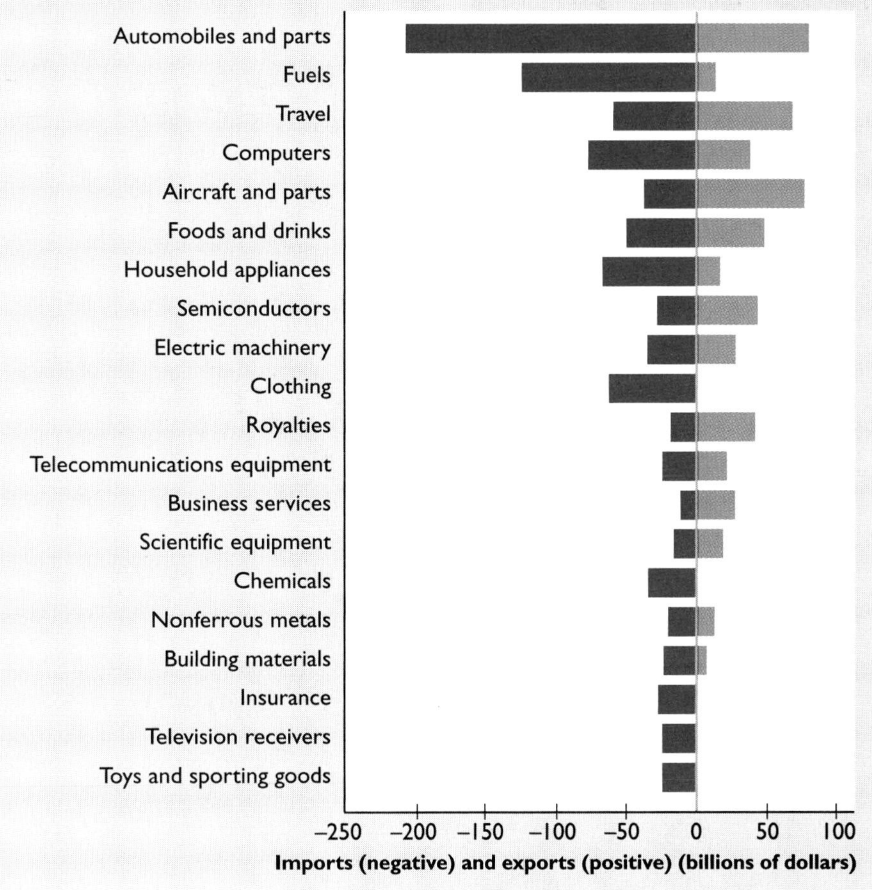

SOURCE: Bureau of Economic Analysis.

Trading Partners and Trading Blocs

The United States has trading links with every part of the world and is a member of several international organizations that seek to promote international trade and regional trade.

U.S. Trading Partners

Canada is the United States' biggest trading partner. Mexico and Japan are the second biggest and almost equal. Our other large trading partners are China, Germany, and the United Kingdom. But we also have significant volumes of trade with the other rapidly expanding Asian economies such as South Korea, Taiwan, Singapore, and Hong Kong. Eye on the Global Economy on p. 476 shows the data for our 17 largest trading partners.

Trading Blocs

Trading blocs are groupings of nations in an international organization. The world today divides into three major geographical blocs, and the United States is a member of two of them. The two blocs of which the United States is a member are the North American Free Trade Agreement and the Asia-Pacific Economic Cooperation. The other large bloc is the European Union. We'll provide a brief description of each of these groupings.

Eye on the Global Economy

The Major U.S. Trading Partners and Volumes of Trade

The figure shows the U.S. volume of trade and balance of trade with its 17 largest trading partners in 2002. If a bar has more red (imports) than blue (exports), the United States has a trade deficit with that country.

Canada is the major trading partner of the United States by a big margin. Mexico and Japan come next, followed by China, Germany, and the United Kingdom. Trade with the newly industrialized countries of Asia (South Korea, Taiwan, Singapore, and Hong Kong) is also large.

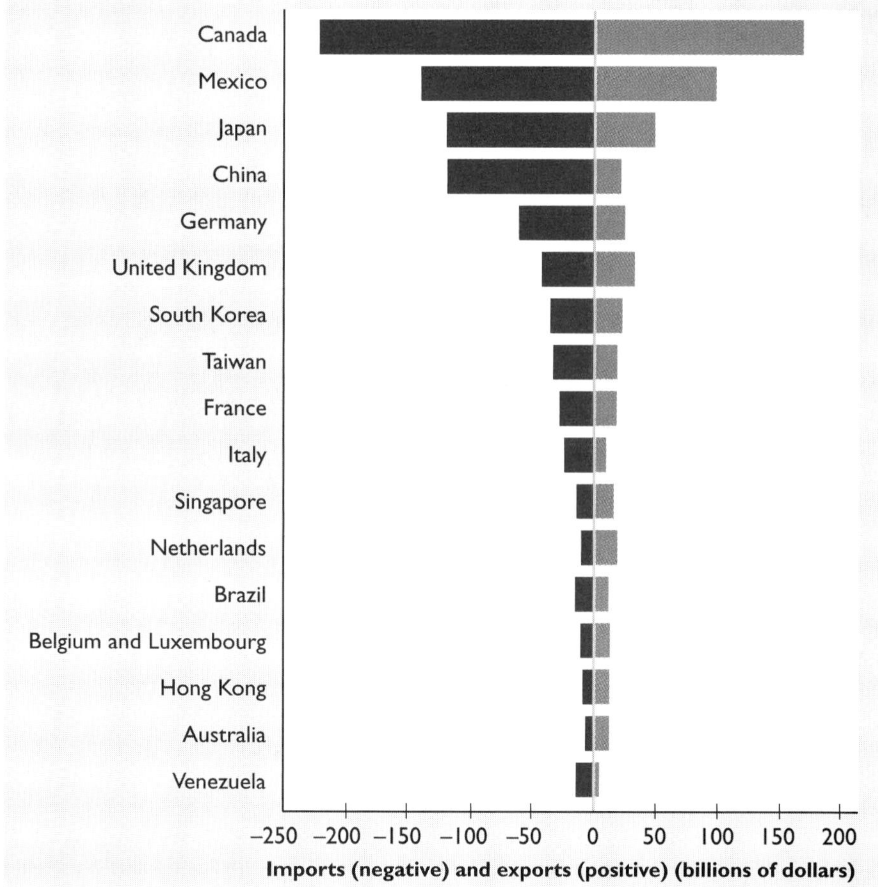

SOURCE: Bureau of Economic Analysis.

North American Free Trade Agreement The North American Free Trade Agreement, or NAFTA, is an agreement among the United States, Canada, and Mexico, to make trade among the three countries easier and freer. The Agreement came into effect in 1994. During the years since then, trade among the three nations has expanded rapidly.

The American continents consist of 35 nations and the governments of the 34 democracies (which excludes Cuba) have entered into a Free Trade of the Americas process. The objective of this process is to achieve free international trade among all the nations of the Americas by 2005.

Asia-Pacific Economic Cooperation Asia-Pacific Economic Cooperation, or APEC, is a group of 21 nations that border the Pacific Ocean. The largest of these are the United States, China, Japan, and Canada, but other significant members are Australia, Indonesia, and the dynamic new industrial Asian economies. In 2002, APEC nations conducted 47 percent of the world's international trade.

APEC was established in 1989 as an informal discussion group, but it has developed into an organization that promotes freer trade and cooperation among its member nations.

European Union The European Union, or EU, is a group of 15 nations of Western Europe. The EU began as the European Common Market when six countries (Belgium, Germany, France, Italy, Luxembourg, and the Netherlands) embarked on a process of economic integration in 1951. The EU has developed its own money, the euro, and institutions of government that are more like those of a federal state than a group of independent states.

Balance of Trade and International Borrowing

The value of exports minus the value of imports is called the **balance of trade**. In 2002, the United States imported more than it exported. When a country imports more than it exports, it has a trade deficit and pays by borrowing from foreigners or selling some of its assets. When a country exports more than it imports, it has a trade surplus and lends to other countries or buys more foreign assets to enable the rest of the world to pay its deficit.

Balance of trade
The value of exports minus the value of imports.

CHECKPOINT 19.1

1 Describe the patterns and trends in international trade.

Study Guide pp. 276–278

Practice Online 19.1

Practice Problem 19.1

Use the link on your Foundations Web site to answer the following questions:

a. In 1990, what percentage of Canadian production was exported to the United States and what percentage of total goods and services bought by Canadians was imported from the United States?

b. In 2000, what percentage of Canadian production was exported to the United States and what percentage of total goods and services bought by Canadians was imported from the United States?

Exercise 19.1

Use the link on your Foundations Web site to answer the following questions:

a. In 1990, what percentage of Mexican production was exported to the United States and what percentage of total goods and services bought by Mexicans was imported from the United States?

b. In 1998, what percentage of Mexican production was exported to the United States and what percentage of total goods and services bought by Mexicans was imported from the United States?

Solution to Practice Problem 19.1

a. In 1990, Canada exported 16.5 percent of total production to the United States and imported 14.4 percent of total goods and services purchased from the United States.

b. In 2000, Canada exported 34.6 percent of total production to the United States and imported 27 percent of goods and services purchased from the United States.

19.2 THE GAINS FROM INTERNATIONAL TRADE

Comparative advantage is the fundamental force that generates international trade. And comparative advantage arises from differences in opportunity costs. You met this idea in Chapter 3 (pp. 70–72), but we're now going to put some flesh on the bones of the basic idea. We'll begin by looking at an item that we export.

Why the United States Exports Airplanes

Boeing produces many more airplanes each year than airlines in the United States buy. Most of Boeing's production goes to airlines in other parts of the world. The United States is an exporter of airplanes. Why?

The answer is that the United States has a comparative advantage in the production of airplanes. The opportunity cost of producing an airplane is lower in the United States than in most other countries. So buyers can obtain airplanes from Boeing for a lower price than the price at which they could buy them from other potential suppliers. And Boeing can sell airplanes to foreigners for a higher price than it could obtain from an additional U.S. buyer.

So both countries gain. The foreign buyer gains from lower-priced airplanes. And Boeing's stockholders, managers, and workers gain from higher-priced airplanes. A win-win situation!

Figure 19.1 illustrates the effects of international trade in airplanes. The demand curve *D* shows the demand for airplanes in the United States. This curve tells us the quantity of airplanes that U.S. airlines are willing to buy at various prices. The demand curve also tells us the most that an additional airplane is worth to a U.S. airline at each quantity.

The supply curve *S* shows the supply of airplanes in the United States. This curve tells us the quantity of airplanes that U.S. aircraft makers are willing to sell at various prices. The supply curve also tells us the opportunity cost of producing an additional airplane at each quantity.

No Trade

First, let's see what happens in the market for airplanes if there is no international trade. Figure 19.1(a) shows the situation. The airplane market is in equilibrium when 400 airplanes are produced by U.S. aircraft makers and bought by U.S. airlines. The price is $80 million an airplane.

Trade

Second, let's see what happens in the market for airplanes if international trade takes place. Figure 19.1(b) shows the situation. The price of an airplane is determined in the world market, not the U.S. domestic market. Suppose that world demand and world supply determine a world equilibrium price of $100 million per airplane. In Figure 19.1(b), the world price line shows this price.

The U.S. demand curve, *D*, tells us that at $100 million an airplane, U.S. airlines buy 300 airplanes a year. The U.S. supply curve, *S*, tells us that at $100 million per airplane, U.S. aircraft makers produce 800 airplanes a year. So domestic production at 800 a year exceeds domestic purchases of 300 a year.

The quantity produced in the United States minus the quantity purchased by U.S. airlines is the quantity of U.S. exports, which is 500 airplanes a year.

FIGURE 19.1
An Export

Practice Online

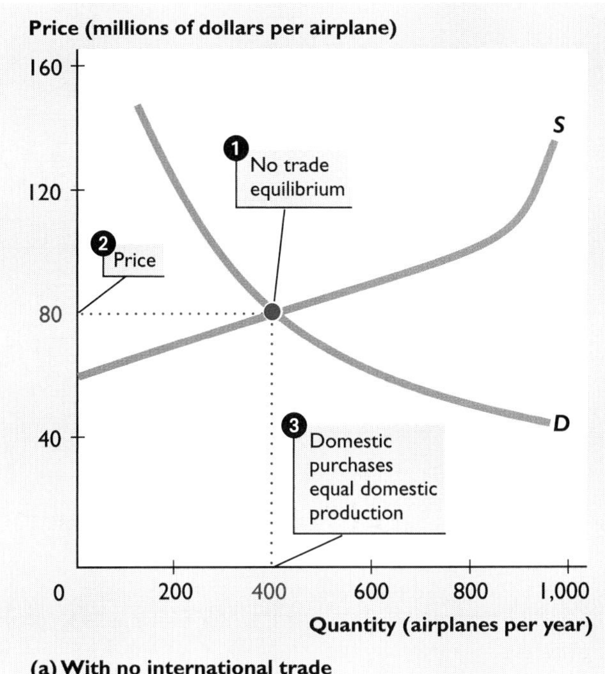

(a) With no international trade

With no international trade in airplanes, 1 equilibrium at the intersection of the domestic demand and supply curves determines 2 the price at $80 million an airplane and 3 the quantity at 400 airplanes a year.

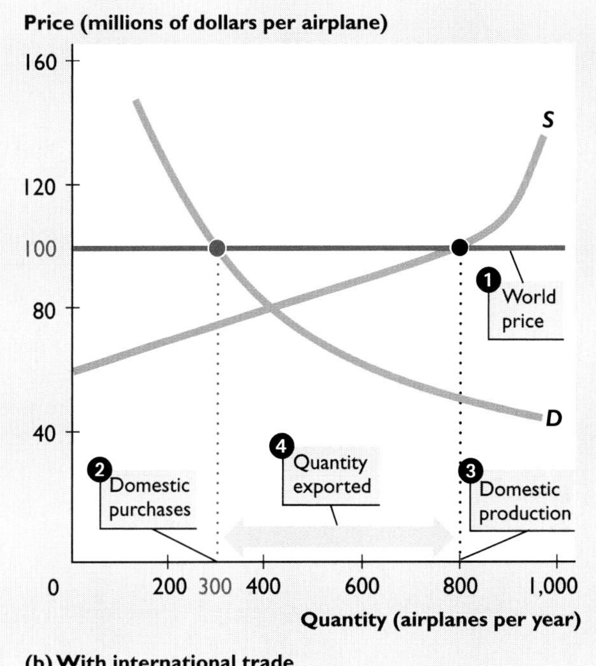

(b) With international trade

With international trade, world demand and supply determine 1 the world price, which is $100 million an airplane. 2 Domestic purchases decrease to 300 a year, and 3 domestic production increases to 800 a year; 4 500 airplanes a year are exported.

Comparative Advantage

You can see that U.S. aircraft makers have a comparative advantage in producing airplanes by comparing the U.S. supply curve and the world price line. At the equilibrium quantity of 800 airplanes a year, the world opportunity cost of producing an airplane is $100 million. But the U.S. supply curve tells us that only the 800th airplane has an opportunity cost of $100 million. Each of the other 799 airplanes has an opportunity cost of less than $100 million.

Why the United States Imports T-Shirts

Americans spend more than twice as much on clothing as the value of U.S. apparel production. That is, more than half of the clothing that we buy is manufactured in other countries and imported into the United States. Why?

The answer is that the rest of the world (mainly Asia) has a comparative advantage in the production of clothes. The opportunity cost of producing a T-shirt is lower in Asia than in the United States. So buyers can obtain T-shirts from Asia for a lower price than the price at which they could buy them from U.S. garment makers. And Asian garment makers can sell T-shirts to Americans for a higher price than they could obtain from an additional Asian buyer.

So again, both countries gain. The U.S. buyer gains from lower-priced T-shirts, and Asian garment makers gain from higher-priced T-shirts. Another win-win situation!

Figure 19.2 illustrates the effects of international trade in T-shirts. Again, the demand curve *D* and the supply curve *S* show the demand and supply in the U.S. domestic market only.

The demand curve tells us the quantity of T-shirts that Americans are willing to buy at various prices. The demand curve also tells us the most that an additional T-shirt is worth to an American at each quantity.

The supply curve tells us the quantity of T-shirts that U.S. garment makers are willing to sell at various prices. The supply curve also tells us the opportunity cost of producing an additional T-shirt in the United States at each quantity.

No Trade

Again, we'll first look at a market with no international trade, shown in Figure 19.2(a). The T-shirt market is in equilibrium when 20 million shirts are produced by U.S. garment makers and bought by Americans. The price is $8 a shirt.

FIGURE 19.2
An Import

Practice Online

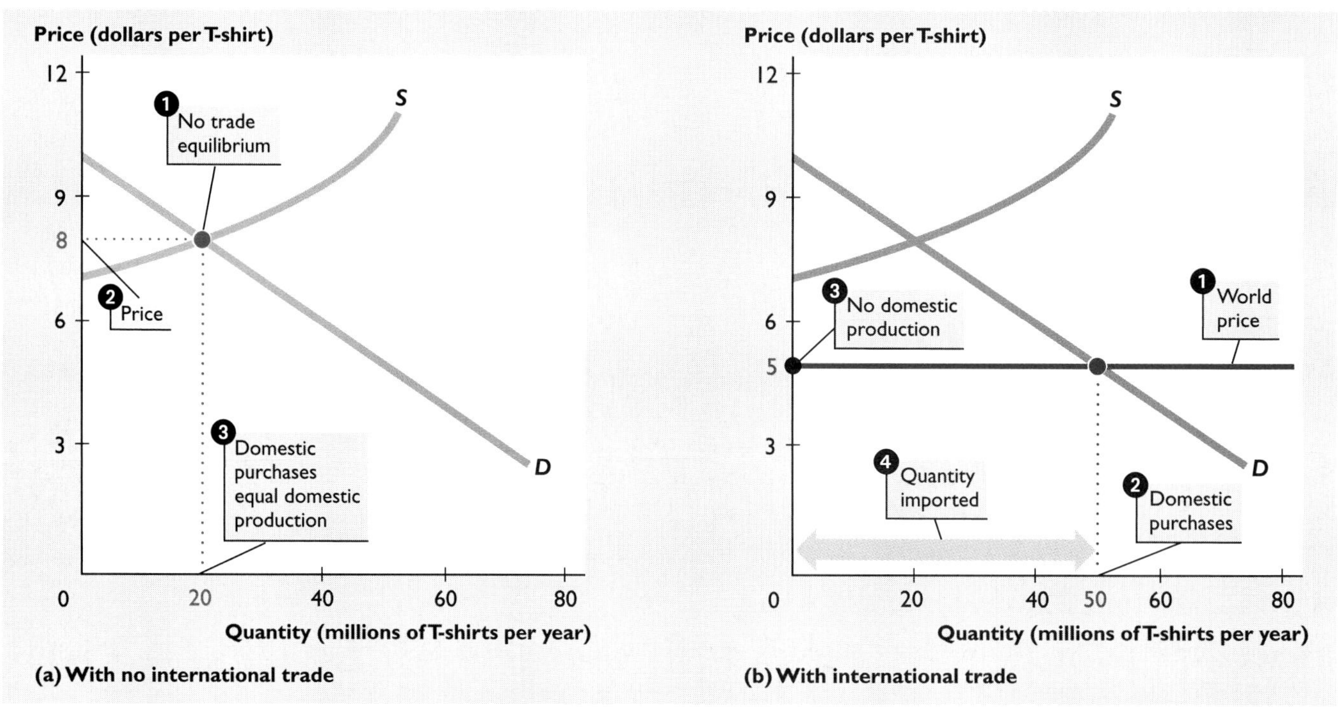

With no international trade in T-shirts, ❶ equilibrium at the intersection of the domestic demand and supply curves determines ❷ the price at $8 a shirt and ❸ the quantity at 20 million shirts a year.

With international trade, world demand and supply determine the ❶ world price, which is $5 a shirt. ❷ Domestic purchases increase to 50 million shirts a year, and ❸ domestic production decreases to zero. ❹ The entire 50 million shirts a year are imported.

Trade

Figure 19.2(b) shows what happens in the market for T-shirts if international trade takes place. Now the price of a T-shirt is determined in the world market, not the U.S. domestic market. Suppose that world demand and world supply determine a world equilibrium price of $5 a shirt. In Figure 19.2(b), the world price line shows this price.

The U.S demand curve, *D*, tells us that at $5 a shirt, Americans buy 50 million shirts a year. The U.S. supply curve, *S*, tells us that at $5 a shirt, U.S. garment makers produce no T-shirts. So there is no domestic production, and domestic purchases are 50 million T-shirts a year. The entire quantity of T-shirts purchased in the United States is the quantity imported.

Comparative Advantage

Now you can see that Asian garment makers have a comparative advantage in producing T-shirts by comparing the U.S. supply curve and the world price line. At the equilibrium quantity of 50 million T-shirts a year, the world opportunity cost of producing a T-shirt is $5. But the U.S. supply curve tells us that no U.S. garment maker has such a low opportunity cost, not even at smaller outputs. So Asian garment makers have a comparative advantage in producing T-shirts.

Gains from Trade and the *PPF*

The demand and supply model that you've just studied makes it clear why we export some goods and import others. But it doesn't show directly the gains from international trade. Another way of looking at comparative advantage uses the production possibilities frontier (*PPF*) that you learned about in Chapter 3. This approach shows the gains from trade in a powerful way, as you're about to discover.

Let's explore comparative advantage by looking at production possibilities in the United States and China.

Production Possibilities in the United States and China

To focus on the essential idea, suppose that the United States can produce only two goods: communications satellites and sports shoes. China can also produce only these same two goods. But production possibilities are different in the two countries.

If the United States uses all of its resources to produce satellites, its output is 10 satellites per year and no sports shoes. If it uses all of its resources to produce sports shoes, its output is 100 million pairs of shoes a year and no satellites. We'll assume that the U.S. opportunity cost of producing a satellite is constant. To produce 10 satellites, the United States must forgo 100 million pairs of shoes, which means that to produce 1 satellite, the United States must forgo 10 million pairs of shoes. That is,

The U.S. opportunity cost of producing 1 satellite is 10 million pairs of shoes.

In contrast, if China uses all of its resources to make satellites, it can produce 2 satellites a year and no sports shoes. And if it uses all of its resources to make sports shoes, it can produce 100 million pairs of shoes a year and no satellites. We'll assume that China's opportunity cost of producing a satellite is constant. To produce 2 satellites, China must forgo 100 million pairs of shoes, which means that to produce 1 satellite, China must forgo 50 million pairs of shoes. That is,

China's opportunity cost of producing 1 satellite is 50 million pairs of shoes.

The assumption that the opportunity costs of producing a satellite in the United States and in China are constant makes the point that we're illustrating in the simplest and cleanest way. We could assume increasing opportunity cost. We would reach the same conclusion that we'll reach here, but the story would be a bit more complicated and the point wouldn't jump out as clearly as it does by making the assumption of constant opportunity costs.

Figure 19.3(a) shows the production possibilities for the United States, and Figure 19.3(b) shows the production possibilities for China. The assumption that the opportunity costs are constant means that the two *PPF*s are linear. Along the U.S. *PPF*, 1 satellite costs 10 million pairs of shoes. And along China's *PPF*, 1 satellite costs 50 million pairs of shoes.

FIGURE 19.3
Production Possibilities in the United States and China

Practice Online

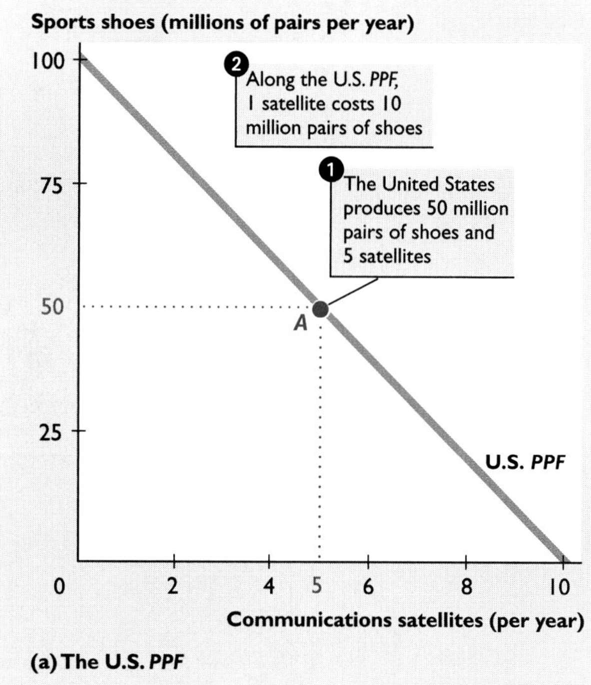

(a) The U.S. *PPF*

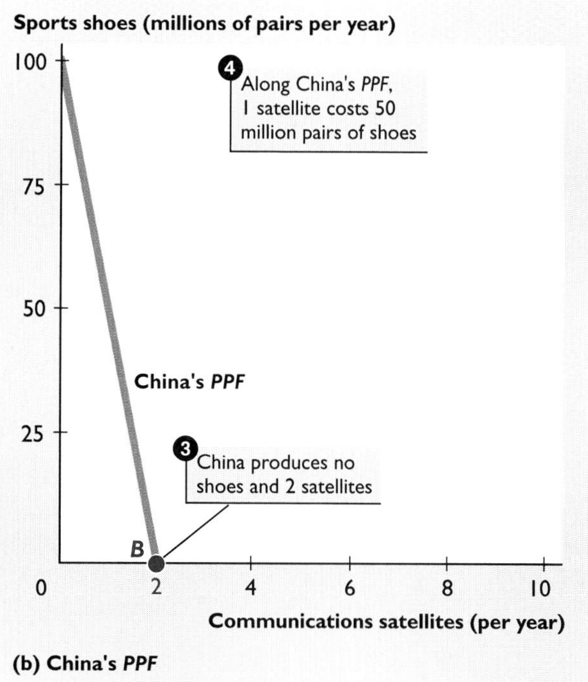

(b) China's *PPF*

❶ The United States produces at point *A* on its *PPF* (part a). ❷ The opportunity cost of a satellite is 10 million pairs of shoes. ❸ China produces at point *B* on its *PPF* (part b). ❹ The opportunity cost of a satellite is 50 million pairs of shoes.

The opportunity cost of a satellite is lower in the United States than in China, so the United States has a comparative advantage in producing satellites. The opportunity cost of a pair of shoes is lower in China than in the United States, so China has a comparative advantage in producing shoes.

No Trade

With no international trade, we'll suppose that the United States produces 5 satellites and 50 million pairs of shoes at point *A* on its *PPF*. And we'll suppose that China produces 2 satellites and no shoes at point *B* on its *PPF*.

Comparative Advantage

In which of the two goods does China have a comparative advantage? Recall that comparative advantage is a situation in which one nation's opportunity cost of producing a good is lower than another nation's opportunity cost of producing that same good. China has a comparative advantage in producing shoes. The opportunity cost of a pair of shoes is 1/50,000,000 of a satellite in China and 1/10,000,000 of a satellite in the United States.

You can see China's comparative advantage by looking at the *PPF*s for China and the United States in Figure 19.3. China's *PPF* is steeper than the U.S. *PPF*. To produce an additional 1 million pairs of shoes, China must give up fewer satellites than does the United States. So China's opportunity cost of shoes is less than the U.S. opportunity cost of shoes. This means that China has a comparative advantage in producing shoes.

The United States has a comparative advantage in producing satellites. In Figure 19.3, the U.S. *PPF* is less steep than China's *PPF*. This means that the United States must give up fewer shoes to produce an additional satellite than does China. The U.S. opportunity cost of producing a satellite is 10 million pairs of shoes, which is less than China's 50 million pairs. So the United States has a comparative advantage in producing satellites.

Because China has a comparative advantage in producing shoes and the United States has a comparative advantage in producing satellites, both China and the United States can gain from specialization and trade. China specializes in shoes, and the United States specializes in satellites.

Achieving the Gains from Trade

If the United States, which has a comparative advantage in producing satellites, allocates all of its resources to that activity, it can produce 10 satellites a year. If China, which has a comparative advantage in producing shoes, allocates all of its resources to that activity, it can produce 100 million pairs a year. By specializing, the United States and China together can produce 100 million pairs of shoes and 10 satellites. With no trade, their total production had been 7 satellites (5 from the United States and 2 from China) and 50 million pairs of shoes (all produced by the United States).

So with specialization and trade, the United States and China can consume outside their production possibilities frontiers.

To achieve the gains from specialization, the United States and China must trade with each other. Suppose they agree to the following deal: China agrees to pay the United States 30 million pairs of shoes per satellite; the United States agrees to sell China 3 satellites a year at this price.

With this deal in place, the United States has 90 million pairs of shoes and 7 satellites—a gain of 40 million pairs of shoes and 2 satellites. China now has 10 million pairs of shoes and 3 satellites—a gain of 10 million pairs of shoes and one satellite.

Figure 19.4 shows these gains from trade. The United States originally produced and consumed at point *A*. It now produces at point *P* and consumes at point *A*'. China originally produced and consumed at point *B*. It now produces at point *Q* and consumes at point *B*'. As a result of specialization and trade, both countries can consume outside their production possibilities frontiers. Both countries gain from trade.

In this example, the United States can out-produce China and has an *absolute advantage* (see Chapter 3, p. 72), but it can get shoes at a lower cost by trading satellites for shoes with China. Gains from specialization and trade are always available when opportunity costs diverge.

Dynamic Comparative Advantage

Learning-by-doing
Repeatedly performing the same task and becoming more productive at producing a particular good or service.

Dynamic comparative advantage
A comparative advantage that a person (or country) obtains by specializing in an activity, resulting from learning-by-doing.

Resources and technology determine comparative advantage. But just by repeatedly producing a particular good or service, people become more productive in that activity, a phenomenon called **learning-by-doing**. **Dynamic comparative advantage**, a comparative advantage that a person (or country) obtains by specializing in an activity, results from learning-by-doing.

Hong Kong, South Korea, and Taiwan are examples of countries that have pursued dynamic comparative advantage vigorously. They have developed electronics and biotechnology industries in which initially they did not have a comparative advantage, but through learning-by-doing, they have become low opportunity cost producers in those industries.

FIGURE 19.4
The Gains from Trade

Practice Online

1. If the United States specializes in satellites, it produces 10 a year at point *P*.
2. If China specializes in shoes, it produces 100 million pairs a year at point *Q*.
3. If shoes and satellites are traded at 30 million pairs of shoes per satellite, both countries can increase their consumption of both goods and consume at points *A*' and *B*'. The gains from trade are the increases in consumption of the two countries.

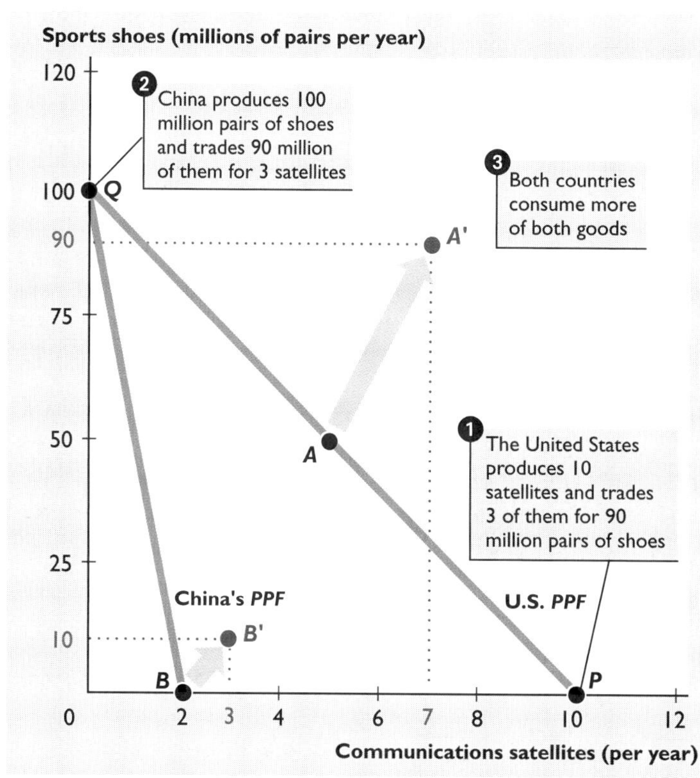

CHECKPOINT 19.2

2 **Explain why nations engage in international trade and why trade benefits all nations.**

Study Guide pp. 278–281

Practice Online 19.2

Practice Problem 19.2

During most of the Cold War, the United States and Russia did not trade with each other. The United States produced manufactured goods and farm produce. Russia produced manufactured goods and farm produce. Suppose that in the last year of the Cold War, the United States could produce 100 million units of manufactured goods or 50 million units of farm produce and Russia could produce 30 million units of manufactured goods or 10 million units of farm produce.

a. What was the opportunity cost of 1 unit of farm produce in the United States?
b. What was the opportunity cost of 1 unit of farm produce in Russia?
c. Which country had a comparative advantage in producing farm produce?
d. With the end of the Cold War and the opening up of trade between Russia and the United States, which good did the United States import from Russia?
e. Did the United States gain from this trade? Explain why or why not.
f. Did Russia gain from this trade? Explain why or why not.

Exercise 19.2

In 2003, the United States does not trade with Cuba. Suppose that the United States can produce 1,000 million units of manufactured goods or 500 million units of food. Suppose that Cuba can produce 2 million units of manufactured goods or 5 million units of food.

a. What was the opportunity cost of 1 unit of food in the United States?
b. What was the opportunity cost of 1 unit of food in Cuba?
c. Which country had a comparative advantage in producing food?
d. Suppose that the United States opens up trade with Cuba. Which good will the United States import from Cuba?
e. Will the United States gain from this trade? Explain why or why not.
f. Will Cuba gain from this trade? Explain why or why not.

Solution to Practice Problem 19.2

a. The U.S. opportunity cost of 1 unit of farm produce was 2 units of manufactured goods.
b. The Russian opportunity cost of 1 unit of farm produce was 3 units of manufactured goods.
c. The United States had a comparative advantage in producing farm produce because the U.S. opportunity cost of a unit of farm produce was less than the Russian opportunity cost of a unit of farm produce.
d. The United States imported from Russia the good in which Russia had a comparative advantage. The United States imported manufactured goods.
e. and f. Both the United States and Russia gained because each country ended up with more of both goods. When countries specialize in producing the good in which they have a comparative advantage and then trade with each other, both countries gain.

19.3 INTERNATIONAL TRADE RESTRICTIONS

Governments use two main tools to restrict international trade and protect domestic industries from foreign competition. They are

- Tariffs
- Nontariff barriers

Tariff
A tax on a good that is imposed by the importing country when an imported good crosses its international boundary.

Nontariff barrier
Any action other than a tariff that restricts international trade.

A **tariff** is a tax on a good that is imposed by the importing country when an imported good crosses its international boundary. A **nontariff barrier** is any action other than a tariff that restricts international trade. Examples of nontariff barriers are quantitative restrictions and health and safety standards.

Tariffs

The temptation for governments to impose tariffs is a strong one. First, tariffs provide revenue to the government. Second, they enable the government to satisfy special interest groups in import-competing industries. But as we will see, free international trade brings enormous benefits that are reduced when tariffs are imposed. Let's see how.

The History of the U.S. Tariff

U.S. tariffs today are modest in comparison with their historical levels. The figure shows the average tariff rate—total tariffs as a percentage of total imports. Tariffs peaked during the 1930s when Congress passed a law known as the Smoot-Hawley Act. The General Agreement on Tariffs and Trade (GATT), an international agreement to eliminate trade restrictions that was signed in 1947, resulted in a series of rounds of negotiations that have brought widespread tariff cuts. Today, the World Trade Organization (WTO) continues the work of GATT.

The United States is a party to the North American Free Trade Agreement (NAFTA), which became effective on January 1, 1994, and under which barriers to international trade between the United States, Canada, and Mexico will be virtually eliminated after a 15-year phasing-in period.

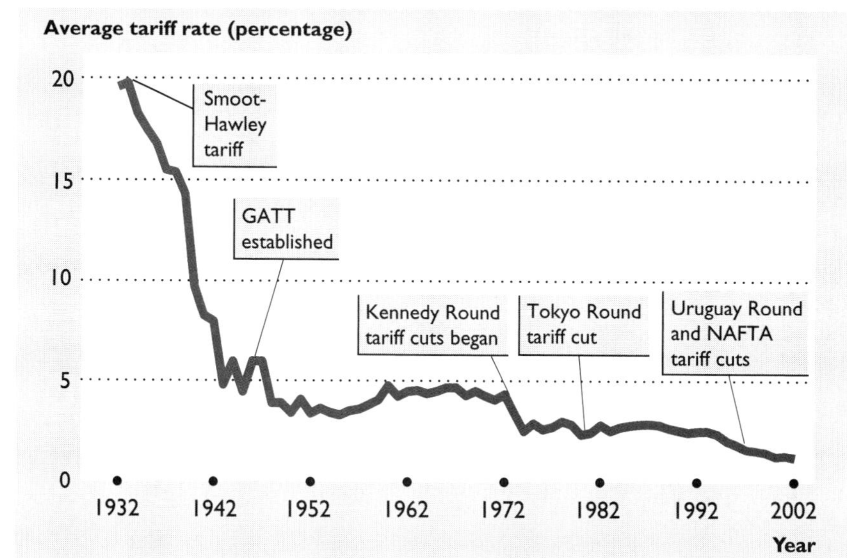

SOURCES: The Budget for Fiscal Year 2003, Historical Tables, Table 2.5 and Bureau of Economic Analysis, National Income and Product Accounts

To analyze how tariffs work, let's return to the example of U.S. T-shirt imports. Figure 19.5 shows the market for T-shirts in the United States. Part (a) is the same as Figure 19.2(b) and shows the situation with free international trade. The United States produces no T-shirts and imports 50 million shirts a year at the world market price of $5 a shirt.

Now suppose that under pressure from U.S. garment makers, the U.S. government imposes a tariff on imported T-shirts. In particular, suppose that a tariff of 50 percent is imposed. What happens?

- The price of a T-shirt in the United States rises.
- The quantity of T-shirts bought in the United States decreases.
- The quantity of T-shirts produced in the United States increases.
- The quantity of T-shirts imported by the United States decreases.
- The U.S. government collects the tariff revenue.
- U.S. consumers lose.

FIGURE 19.5
The Effects of a Tariff

Practice Online

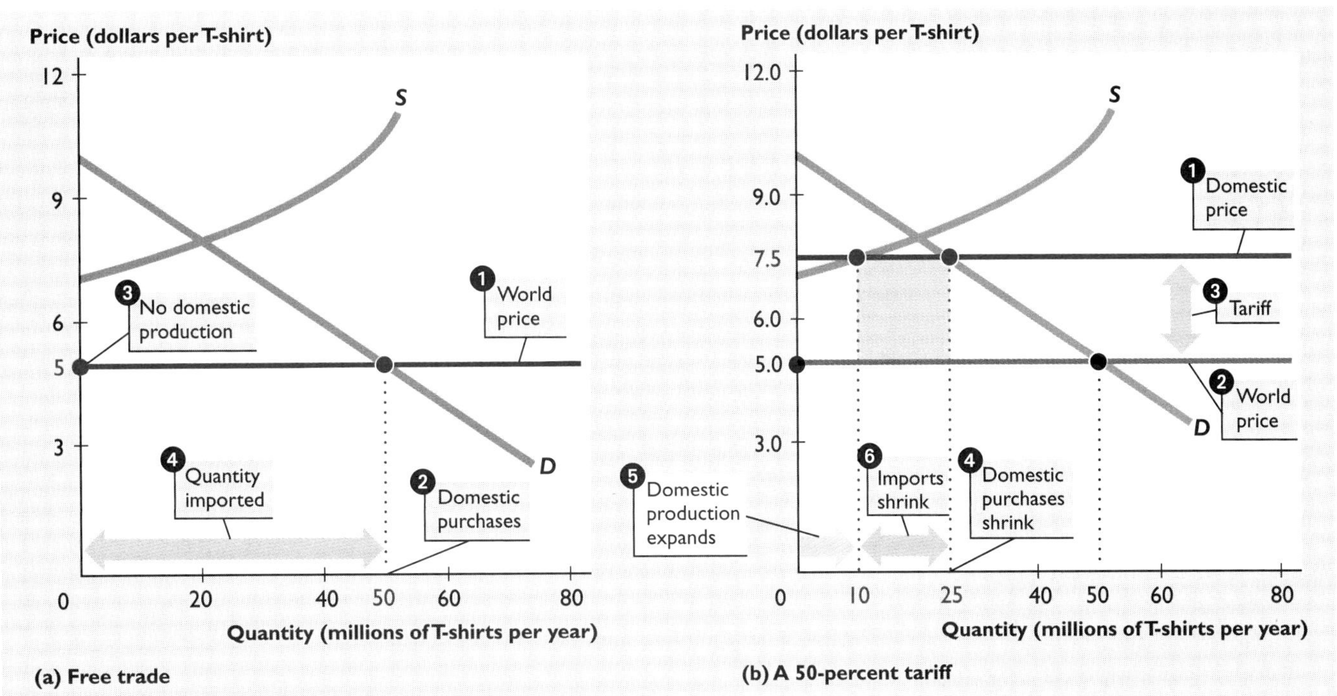

With free trade (part a), ❶ the world price is $5 a T-shirt and ❷ the United States buys 50 million T-shirts. ❸ The United States produces no T-shirts and ❹ imports 50 million T-shirts.

In part (b), the United States imposes a tariff on imports of T-shirts. ❶ The domestic price equals ❷ the world price plus ❸ the tariff, so the tariff raises the price that Americans pay for a T-shirt.

❹ The quantity of T-shirts purchased decreases, ❺ the quantity produced in the United States increases, and ❻ the quantity imported decreases. The U.S. government collects tariff revenue shown by the purple rectangle.

Rise in Price of a T-Shirt

To buy a T-shirt, Americans must pay the world market price plus the tariff. So the price of a T-shirt rises by 50 percent to $7.50. Figure 19.5(b) shows the domestic price line, which lies 50 percent (or $2.50) above the world price line.

Decrease in Purchases

The higher price of a T-shirt brings a decrease in the quantity demanded, which Figure 19.5(b) shows as a movement along the demand curve for T-shirts from 50 million a year at $5 a shirt to 25 million a year at $7.50 a shirt.

Increase in Domestic Production

The higher price of a T-shirt stimulates domestic production, which increases from zero to 10 million shirts a year—a movement along the supply curve in Figure 19.5(b).

Decrease in Imports

T-shirt imports decrease by 35 million from 50 million to 15 million a year. Both the decrease in purchases and the increase in domestic production contribute to this decrease in imports.

Tariff Revenue

The government collects tariff revenue of $2.50 per shirt on the 15 million shirts imported each year, a total of $37.5 million, as shown by the purple rectangle.

U.S. Consumers Lose

A T-shirt costs only $5 to produce—the opportunity cost of that shirt is $5. But the American consumer pays $7.50 for a T-shirt. So the consumer pays $2.50 a shirt more than its opportunity cost. Consumers are willing to buy up to 50 million T-shirts a year at a price that equals the opportunity cost of a shirt. The tariff makes people pay more than the opportunity cost and deprives them of items they are willing to buy at a price that exceeds the opportunity cost.

Let's now look at the other tools for restricting trade: nontariff barriers.

Nontariff Barriers

Quota
A specified maximum amount of a good that may be imported in a given period of time.

A **quota**, which is a quantitative restriction on the import of a good that specifies the maximum amount of the good that may be imported in a given period, is a widely used nontariff barrier. The United States imposes quotas on many items, including sugar, tomatoes, bananas, and textiles.

How a Quota Works

Figure 19.6 shows how a quota works. Begin by identifying the situation with free international trade. The United States produces no T-shirts and imports 50 million shirts a year at the world market price of $5 a shirt.

Now suppose that the United States imposes a quota that restricts imports to 15 million T-shirts a year. The imports permitted under the quota plus the quantity produced in the United States is the market supply in the United States. This market supply curve is the one labeled $S + quota$ in Figure 19.6.

FIGURE 19.6
The Effects of a Quota

Practice Online

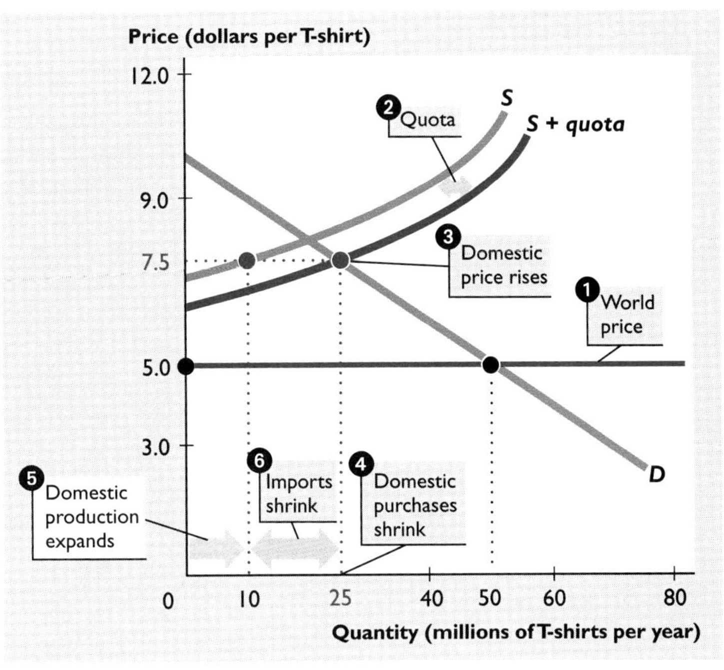

❶ The world price is $5 a T-shirt. ❷ A quota of 15 million shirts a year is added to the U.S. supply to give the market supply curve, *S* + *quota*. ❸ The equilibrium domestic price rises to $7.50 a shirt, and ❹ domestic purchases decrease. ❺ The United States produces 10 million shirts a year, and ❻ U.S. imports equal the quota of 15 million a year.

With this new supply curve, the U.S. price of a T-shirt is $7.50, the price that makes the quantity demanded by Americans equal the quantity supplied by U.S. producers plus imports. This quantity is 25 million shirts a year.

At a price of $7.50, U.S. garment makers produce 10 million shirts a year and U.S. imports equal the quota of 15 million a year.

We've made the outcome with a quota in Figure 19.6 the same as that with a tariff in Figure 19.5(b). But there is a difference between a tariff and a quota. In the case of a tariff, the U.S. government collects tariff revenue. In the case of a quota, there is no tariff revenue and the difference between the world price and the U.S. price goes to the person who has the right to import T-shirts under the import quota regulations.

Health, Safety, and Other Nontariff Barriers

Thousands of detailed health, safety, and other regulations restrict international trade. Here are just a few examples. All U.S. imports of food products are examined by the Food and Drug Administration to determine if the imported food is "pure, wholesome, safe to eat, and produced under sanitary conditions." In 2001, the scare of foot and mouth disease virtually closed down international trade in live cattle and beef. The European Union has banned imports of most genetically modified foods, such as U.S.-produced soybeans and Canadian granola. Australia has banned the import of U.S. grapes to protect its domestic grapes from a virus that is present in California. Restrictions also apply to many nonfood items. Although regulations of the type we've just described are not designed to limit international trade, they have that effect.

CHECKPOINT 19.3

Study Guide pp. 281–284

Practice Online 19.3

3 **Explain how trade barriers reduce international trade.**

Practice Problems 19.3

1. Before 1995, the United States imposed tariffs on goods imported from Mexico and Mexico imposed tariffs on goods imported from the United States. In 1995, Mexico joined NAFTA. U.S. tariffs on imports from Mexico and Mexican tariffs on imports from the United States are gradually being removed. Explain how the removal of tariffs will change
   - **a.** The price that U.S. consumers pay for goods imported from Mexico.
   - **b.** The quantity of U.S. imports from Mexico.
   - **c.** The quantity of U.S. exports to Mexico.
   - **d.** The U.S. government's tariff revenue from trade with Mexico.
2. In 2000, the U.S. government placed a ban on potato imports from Canada. Explain how this ban influences
   - **a.** The price that U.S. consumers pay for potatoes.
   - **b.** The quantity of potatoes consumed in the United States.
   - **c.** The price received by Canadian potato growers.
   - **d.** The U.S. and Canadian gains from trade.

Exercises 19.3

1. In 2000, the U.S. Congress and Senate extended an arrangement that limits the tariffs on imports from China. If the United States imposed higher tariffs on imports from China, explain how a higher tariff on toys will change
   - **a.** The price that U.S. consumers pay for toys imported from China.
   - **b.** The quantity of U.S. imports of toys from China.
   - **c.** The quantity of toys produced in the United States.
   - **d.** The U.S. government's tariff revenue from trade in toys with China.
   - **e.** The U.S. and Chinese gains from trade.
2. Australia has a comparative advantage in producing beef, but the United States sets a quota on beef imports from Australia. Explain how the quota influences
   - **a.** The price that U.S. consumers pay for beef.
   - **b.** The quantity of beef produced in the United States.
   - **c.** The U.S. and Australian gains from trade.

Solutions to Practice Problems 19.3

1a. The price that U.S. consumers pay for goods imported from Mexico will fall.
1b. The quantity of U.S. imports from Mexico will increase.
1c. The quantity of U.S. exports to Mexico will increase.
1d. The U.S. government's tariff revenue from trade with Mexico will fall to zero.

2a. The price that U.S. consumers pay for potatoes will rise.
2b. The quantity of potatoes consumed in the United States will fall.
2c. The price received by Canadian potato growers will fall.
2d. Both the U.S. and Canadian gains from trade will decrease.

19.4 THE CASE AGAINST PROTECTION

For as long as nations and international trade have existed, people have debated whether a country is better off with free international trade or with protection from foreign competition. The debate continues, but for most economists, a verdict has been delivered and it is the one you have just seen. Free trade promotes prosperity for all countries: Protection reduces the potential gains from trade. We've seen the most powerful case for free trade: All countries benefit from their comparative advantage. But there is a broader range of issues in the free trade versus protection debate. Let's review these issues.

Three Arguments for Protection

The three main arguments for protection and restricting international trade are

- The national security argument
- The infant-industry argument
- The dumping argument

Let's look at each in turn.

The National Security Argument

The national security argument for protection is that a country must protect industries that produce defense equipment and armaments and those on which the defense industries rely for their raw materials and other intermediate inputs. This argument for protection does not withstand close scrutiny.

First, it is an argument for international isolation, for in a time of war, there is no industry that does not contribute to national defense. Second, if the case is made for boosting the output of a strategic industry, it is more efficient to achieve this outcome with a subsidy to the firms in the industry, which is financed out of taxes, than with a tariff or quota. A subsidy would keep the industry operating at the scale judged appropriate, and free international trade would keep the prices faced by consumers at their world market levels.

The Infant-Industry Argument

The **infant-industry argument** for protection is that it is necessary to protect a new industry to enable it to grow into a mature industry that can compete in world markets. The argument is based on the idea of dynamic comparative advantage, which can arise from learning-by-doing.

Infant-industry argument
The argument that it is necessary to protect a new industry to enable it to grow into a mature industry that can compete in world markets.

Learning-by-doing is a powerful engine of productivity growth, and comparative advantage evolves and changes because of on-the-job experience. But these facts do not justify protection.

The infant-industry argument is valid only if the benefits of learning-by-doing not only accrue to the owners and workers of the firms in the infant industry, but also spill over to other industries and parts of the economy. For example, there are huge productivity gains from learning-by-doing in the manufacture of aircraft. But almost all of these gains benefit the stockholders and workers of aircraft producers such as Boeing. Because the people making the decisions, bearing the risk, and doing the work are the ones who benefit, they take the dynamic gains into account when they decide on the scale of their activities. In this case, almost no benefits spill over to other parts of the economy, so there is no need for government assistance to achieve an efficient outcome.

The Dumping Argument

Dumping
When a foreign firm sells its exports at a lower price than its cost of production.

Dumping occurs when a foreign firm sells its exports at a lower price than its cost of production. A firm that wants to gain a global monopoly might use dumping. In this case, the foreign firm sells its output at a price below its cost to drive domestic firms out of business. When the domestic firms have gone, the foreign firm takes advantage of its monopoly position and charges a higher price for its product. Dumping is usually regarded as a justification for temporary countervailing tariffs.

But there are powerful reasons to resist the dumping argument for protection. First, it is virtually impossible to detect dumping because it is hard to determine a firm's costs. As a result, the test for dumping is whether a firm's export price is below its domestic price. But this test is a weak one because it can be rational for a firm to charge a lower price in markets in which the quantity demanded is highly sensitive to price and a higher price in a market in which demand is less price-sensitive.

Second, it is hard to think of a good that is produced by a natural global monopoly. So even if all the domestic firms were driven out of business in some industry, it would always be possible to find several and usually many alternative foreign sources of supply and to buy at prices determined in competitive markets.

Third, if a good or service were a truly global natural monopoly, the best way to deal with it would be by regulation—just as in the case of domestic monopolies. Such regulation would require international cooperation.

The three arguments for protection that we've just examined have an element of credibility. The counterarguments are in general stronger, so these arguments do not make the case for protection. But they are not the only arguments that you might encounter. The many other arguments that are commonly heard are quite simply wrong. They are fatally flawed.

Fatally Flawed Arguments for Protection

Six commonly made but flawed arguments for restricting international trade are that protection

- Saves jobs
- Allows us to compete with cheap foreign labor
- Brings diversity and stability
- Penalizes lax environmental standards
- Protects national culture
- Prevents rich countries from exploiting developing countries

Saves Jobs

The argument is: When we buy shoes from Brazil or shirts from Taiwan, U.S. workers lose their jobs. With no earnings and poor prospects, these workers become a drain on welfare and spend less, causing a ripple effect of further job losses. The proposed solution to this problem is to ban imports of cheap foreign goods and to protect U.S. jobs. The proposal is flawed for the following reasons.

First, free trade does cost some jobs, but it also creates other jobs. It brings about a global rationalization of labor and allocates labor resources to their highest-valued activities. Because of international trade in textiles, tens of thousands of workers in the United States have lost jobs because textile mills and other factories have closed. But tens of thousands of workers in other countries now have jobs because textile mills have opened there. And tens of thousands of U.S. workers now have better-paying jobs than textile workers because other export industries have expanded and created more jobs than have been destroyed.

Second, imports create jobs. They create jobs for retailers that sell imported goods and for firms that service those goods. They also create jobs by creating incomes in the rest of the world, some of which are spent on imports of U.S.-made goods and services.

Although protection does save some particular jobs, it does so at an inordinate cost. For example, textile jobs are protected in the United States by quotas imposed under an international agreement called the Multifiber Arrangement. The U.S. International Trade Commission (ITC) has estimated that because of quotas, 72,000 jobs exist in textiles that would otherwise disappear and annual clothing expenditure in the United States is $15.9 billion, or $160 per family, higher than it would be with free trade. In other words, the ITC estimates that each textile job saved costs consumers $221,000 a year.

Allows Us to Compete with Cheap Foreign Labor

With the removal of protective tariffs in U.S. trade with Mexico, prominent Texan Ross Perot said that jobs rushing to Mexico would make a "giant sucking sound" (see the cartoon). Let's see what's wrong with this view.

The labor cost of a unit of output equals the wage rate divided by labor productivity. For example, if a U.S. autoworker earns $30 an hour and produces 15 units of output an hour, the average labor cost of a unit of output is $2. If a Mexican auto assembly worker earns $3 an hour and produces 1 unit of output an hour, the average labor cost of a unit of output is $3. Other things remaining the same, the higher a worker's productivity, the higher is the worker's wage rate. High-wage workers have high productivity. Low-wage workers have low productivity.

"I don't know what the hell happened—one minute I'm at work in Flint, Michigan, then there's a giant sucking sound and suddenly here I am in Mexico."

SOURCE: © The New Yorker Collection 1993 Mick Stevens from cartoonbank.com. All rights reserved.

Although high-wage U.S. workers are more productive, on the average, than lower-wage Mexican workers, there are differences across industries. U.S. labor is relatively more productive in some activities than in others. For example, the productivity of U.S. workers in producing movies, financial services, and customized computer chips is relatively higher than their productivity in the production of metals and some standardized machine parts. The activities in which U.S. workers are relatively more productive than their Mexican counterparts are those in which the United States has a comparative advantage. By engaging in free trade, increasing our production and exports of the goods and services in which we have a comparative advantage, and decreasing our production and increasing our imports of the goods and services in which our trading partners have a comparative advantage, we can make ourselves and the citizens of other countries better off.

Brings Diversity and Stability

A diversified investment portfolio is less risky than one that has all of its eggs in one basket. The same is true for an economy's production. A diversified economy fluctuates less than an economy that produces only one or two goods.

But big, rich, diversified economies like those of the United States, Japan, and Europe do not have this type of stability problem. Even a country such as Saudi Arabia that produces almost only one good (in this case, oil) can benefit from specializing in the activity at which it has a comparative advantage and then investing in a wide range of other countries to bring greater stability to its income and consumption.

Penalizes Lax Environmental Standards

A new argument for protection is that many poorer countries, such as Mexico, do not have the same environmental standards that we have, and because they are willing to pollute and we are not, we cannot compete with them without tariffs. So if they want free trade with the richer and "greener" countries, they must clean up their environments to our standards.

This argument for trade restrictions is weak. While everyone wants a clean environment, a poor country is less able than a rich one to devote resources to achieving this goal. The best hope for a better environment in the developing countries is rapid income growth through free trade. As their incomes grow, developing countries will have the means to match their desires to improve their environment. Also, because poor countries are willing to accept "dirty" activities (such as iron ore smelting and chemical production), it is easier for rich countries to achieve the high environmental standards that they seek.

Protects National Culture

The national culture argument for protection is not heard much in the United States, but it is a commonly heard argument in Canada and Europe.

The expressed fear is that free trade in books, magazines, movies, and television programs means U.S. domination and the end of local culture. So, the reasoning continues, it is necessary to protect domestic "culture" industries from free international trade to ensure the survival of a national cultural identity.

Protection of these industries is common and takes the form of nontariff barriers. For example, regulations often require local content on radio and television broadcasting and in magazines.

The cultural identity argument for protection has no merit. Writers, publishers, and broadcasters want to limit foreign competition so that they can earn larger economic profits. There is no actual danger to national culture. In fact, many of the creators of so-called American cultural products are not Americans, but the talented citizens of other countries, ensuring the survival of their national cultural identities in Hollywood! Also, if national culture is in danger, there is no surer way of helping it on its way out than by impoverishing the nation whose culture it is. And protection is an effective way of doing just that.

Prevents Rich Countries from Exploiting Developing Countries

Another new argument for protection is that international trade must be restricted to prevent the people of the rich industrial world from exploiting the poorer people of the developing countries, forcing them to work for slave wages.

Wage rates in some developing countries are indeed very low. But by trading with developing countries, we increase the demand for the goods that these countries produce, and, more significantly, we increase the demand for their labor. When the demand for labor in developing countries increases, the wage rate also increases. So, far from exploiting people in developing countries, trade improves their opportunities and increases their incomes.

We have reviewed the arguments that are commonly heard in favor of protection and the counterarguments against them. There is one counterargument to protection that is general and quite overwhelming. Protection invites retaliation and can trigger a trade war. The best example of a trade war occurred during the Great Depression of the 1930s when the Smoot-Hawley Tariff was introduced. Country after country retaliated with its own tariff, and in a short period, world trade had almost disappeared. The costs to all countries were large and led to a renewed international resolve to avoid such self-defeating moves in the future. They also led to the creation of GATT and are the impetus behind NAFTA, APEC, and the European Union.

Why Is International Trade Restricted?

Why, despite all the arguments against protection, is trade restricted? There are two key reasons:

- Tariff revenue
- Rent seeking

Tariff Revenue

Government revenue is costly to collect. In developed countries, such as the United States, well-organized tax collection systems exist that can generate billions of dollars of income tax and sales tax revenues. These tax collection systems are made possible by the fact that firms that must keep properly audited financial records do most economic transactions. Without such records, the revenue collection agencies (such as the Internal Revenue Service in the United States) would be severely hampered in their work. Even with audited financial accounts, some proportion of potential tax revenue is lost. Nonetheless, for industrialized countries, the income tax and sales taxes are the major sources of revenue and the tariff plays a very small role.

But governments in developing countries have a difficult time collecting taxes from their citizens. Much economic activity takes place in an informal economy with few financial records. So these countries collect only a small amount of revenue from income taxes and sales taxes. The one area in which economic transactions are well recorded and audited is international trade. So this activity is an attractive base for tax collection in these countries and is used much more extensively than in the developed countries.

Rent Seeking

Rent seeking
Lobbying and other political activity that seeks to capture the gains from trade.

The major reason why international trade is restricted is because of rent seeking. **Rent seeking** is lobbying and other political activity that seeks to capture the gains from trade. Free trade increases consumption possibilities on the average, but not everyone shares in the gain and some people even lose. Free trade brings benefits to some and imposes costs on others, with total benefits exceeding total costs. It is the uneven distribution of costs and benefits that is the principal source of impediment to achieving more liberal international trade.

Suppose that we had a tariff on T-shirts, as in the example that you studied earlier in this chapter. A few thousand (perhaps a few hundred) garment makers and their employees who must switch to some other activity would bear the cost of the United States moving to free trade. The millions of T-shirt buyers would reap the benefits of moving to free trade. The number of people who gain will, in general, be enormous in comparison with the number who lose. The gain per person will therefore be small. The loss per person to those who bear the loss will be large. Because the loss that falls on those who bear it is large, it will pay those people to incur considerable expense to lobby against free trade. On the other hand, it will not pay those who gain to organize to achieve free trade. The gain from trade for any one individual is too small for that individual to spend much time or money on a political organization to lobby for free trade. The loss from free trade will be seen as being so great by those bearing that loss that they will find it profitable to join a political organization to prevent free trade. Each group is weighing benefits against costs and choosing the best action for themselves. But the anti-free-trade group will undertake a larger quantity of political lobbying than the pro-free-trade group.

Compensating Losers

If, in total, the gains from free international trade exceed the losses, why don't those who gain compensate those who lose so that everyone is in favor of free trade? To some degree, such compensation does take place. When Congress approved the NAFTA deal with Canada and Mexico, it set up a $56 million fund to support and retrain workers who lost their jobs because of the new trade agreement. During the first six months of the operation of NAFTA, only 5,000 workers applied for benefits under this scheme.

The losers from freer international trade are also compensated indirectly through the normal unemployment compensation arrangements. But only limited attempts are made to compensate those who lose from free international trade. The main reason why full compensation is not attempted is that the costs of identifying all the losers and estimating the value of their losses would be enormous. Also, it would never be clear whether a person who has fallen on hard times is suffering because of free trade or for other reasons, perhaps reasons that are largely under the control of the individual. Furthermore, some people who look like losers at one point in time may, in fact, end up gaining. The young autoworker who loses his job in Michigan and becomes a computer assembly worker in Minneapolis resents the loss of work and the need to move. But a year or two later, looking back on events, he counts himself fortunate. He has made a move that has increased his income and given him greater job security.

It is because we do not, in general, compensate the losers from free international trade that protectionism is such a popular and permanent feature of our national economic and political life.

Competing with Low-Wage Nations

New Balance athletic shoes are made in two ways:

At a New Balance factory in Norridgewock, Maine, skilled workers who earn $14 an hour operate "see-and-sew" machines—$100,000 automated sewing machines guided by cameras. It costs $4 to make a pair of shoes in Maine.

At a subcontractor's factory in China, low-skilled women in their teens and early twenties who earn 40 cents an hour operate ordinary sewing machines. It costs $1.30 to make a pair of shoes in China.

New Balance is willing to pay the additional $2.70, which is about 4 percent of the retail price of a shoe, to produce shoes in the United States.

New Balance produces 25 percent of its output in the United States and the rest in Asia.

Nike, Reebok, and all the other makers of athletic shoes produce their entire output in Asia.

The Asian economies have a comparative advantage in making athletic shoes. Even when New Balance has invested heavily in equipment to make its U.S. work force much more productive than the Chinese work force, the labor cost alone of a pair of shoes is more than three times the cost in China. Add the capital cost to the equation, and New Balance pays much more for its shoes than do its competitors.

You would predict, and you'd be correct, that New Balance is not the most profitable shoemaker.

CHECKPOINT 19.4

Study Guide pp. 284–286

Practice Online 19.4

4 **Explain the arguments used to justify trade barriers and show why they are incorrect but also why some barriers are hard to remove.**

Practice Problems 19.4

1. Japan sets quotas on imports of rice. California rice growers would like to export more rice to Japan. What are Japan's arguments for restricting imports of Californian rice? Are these arguments correct? Who loses from this restriction in trade?
2. The United States has, from time to time, limited imports of steel from Europe. What is the argument that the United States has used to justify this quota? Who wins from this restriction? Who loses?
3. The United States maintains a quota on imports of textiles. What is the argument for this quota? Is this argument flawed? If so, explain why.

Exercises 19.4

1. Texan Ross Perot has argued against NAFTA. What is his argument against a free trade zone in North America? What was wrong with Perot's argument? Whom did Perot see as the loser from NAFTA?
2. The Summit of the Americas in April 2001 decided to extend NAFTA to cover all of the Americas. What was President George W. Bush's argument for this extension? Who will be the winners? Who will be the losers?
3. Hong Kong has never restricted trade. What gains has Hong Kong reaped by unilaterally adopting free trade with all nations? Is there any argument for restricted trade that might have benefited Hong Kong?

Solutions to Practice Problems 19.4

1. Japan has used a number of arguments for low quotas on rice imports. Some of these are that Japanese consumers can get a better quality of rice from Japanese producers and that the quota limits competition faced by Japanese producers. The arguments are not correct. If Japanese consumers do not like the quality of Californian rice, they will not buy it. The quota does limit competition, but the Japanese quota allows Japanese farmers to use their land less efficiently. The big losers are the Japanese consumers because the price of rice in Japan is about three times the price paid by U.S. consumers.
2. The U.S. argument for a quota on imports of European steel is that European producers dump steel on the U.S. market. With a quota, U.S. producers will face less competition in the market for steel and U.S. jobs will be saved. Workers in the steel industry and owners of steel companies will win at the expense of U.S. buyers of steel.
3. The argument for a quota on U.S. imports of textiles is that textiles are produced in developing countries where labor is cheap. That is, the quota protects the jobs of U.S. workers. The argument is flawed because the United States does not have a comparative advantage in the manufacture of textiles and so a quota allows the U.S. textile industry to be inefficient. With free trade in textiles, the U.S. textile industry would exit but it would be smaller and more efficient.

CHAPTER CHECKPOINT

Key Points

1 Describe the patterns and trends in international trade.

- Large flows of trade take place between countries; most trade is in manufactured goods exchanged among rich industrialized countries.
- Since 1960, the volume of U.S. trade has more than doubled.

2 Explain why nations engage in international trade and why trade benefits all nations.

- When opportunity costs between countries diverge, comparative advantage enables countries to gain from international trade.
- By increasing production of goods in which it has a comparative advantage and then trading some of the increased output, a country can consume at points outside its production possibilities frontier.

3 Explain how trade barriers reduce international trade.

- Countries restrict international trade by imposing tariffs and quotas.
- Trade restrictions raise the domestic price of imported goods, lower the volume of imports, and reduce the total value of imports.

4 Explain the arguments used to justify trade barriers and show why they are incorrect but also why some barriers are hard to remove.

- The arguments that protection is necessary for national security, for infant industries, and to prevent dumping are weak.
- Arguments that protection saves jobs, allows us to compete with cheap foreign labor, makes the economy diversified and stable, protects national culture, prevents rich countries from exploiting developing countries, and is needed to offset the costs of environmental policies are fatally flawed.
- Trade is restricted because tariffs raise government revenue and because protection brings a small loss to a large number of people and a large gain per person to a small number of people.

Key Terms

Balance of trade, 477
Dumping, 492
Dynamic comparative advantage, 484
Infant-industry argument, 491
Learning-by-doing, 484
Nontariff barrier, 486
Quota, 488
Rent seeking, 496
Tariff, 486

Exercises

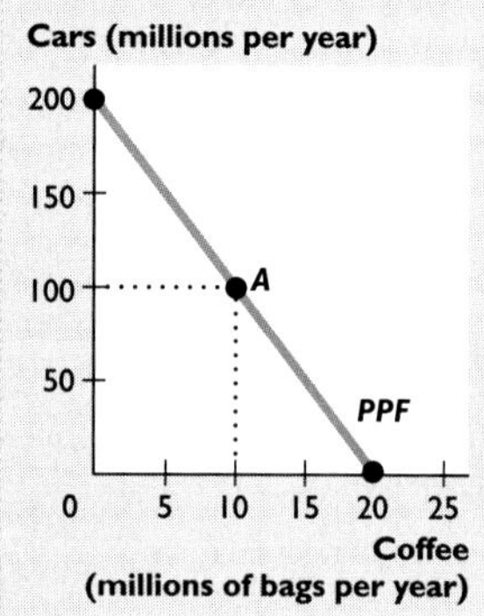

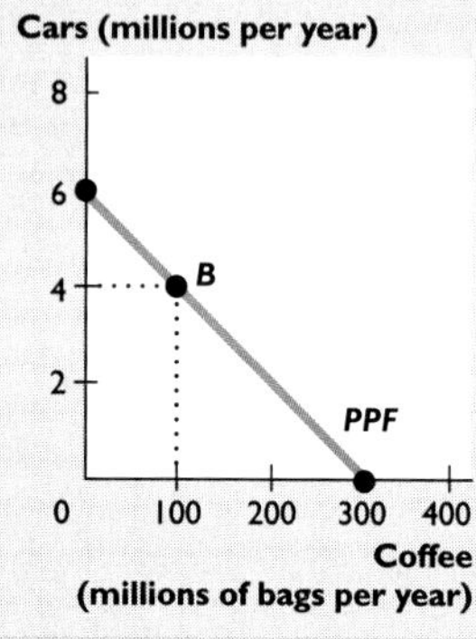

1. Suppose that with no international trade between the United States and Brazil, Figure 1 shows the U.S. production possibilities and the quantities of coffee and cars produced (point *A*). Figure 2 shows Brazil's production possibilities and the quantities of coffee and cars produced (point *B*).
   a. What is the opportunity cost of a bag of coffee in the United States?
   b. What is the opportunity cost of a bag of coffee in Brazil?
   c. Which country has a comparative advantage in producing coffee?
   d. Which country has a comparative advantage in producing cars?
   e. With free trade between Brazil and the United States, what does the United States import from Brazil and what does it export to Brazil? Explain your answer.
   f. Does Brazil gain from trade with the United States? Why or why not?
2. When free trade occurs in exercise 1, the world price of a bag of coffee is 1/25th of a car. If Brazil completely specializes in coffee and exports half of it to the United States,
   a. Show on Figure 2 the quantities of the two goods that Brazil consumes.
   b. Show on Figure 1 the quantities of the two goods that the United States consumes.
3. The table provides information about production possibilities in Kenya and Morocco.

	Kenya's production possibilities			
Item	***A***	***B***	***C***	***D***
Coffee (millions of bags per year)	0	2	4	6
Oranges (millions per year)	3	2	1	0

	Morocco's production possibilities			
Item	***A***	***B***	***C***	***D***
Coffee (millions of bags per year)	0	1	2	3
Oranges (millions per year)	6	4	2	0

   a. What is the opportunity cost of producing a bag of coffee in Kenya?
   b. What is the opportunity cost of producing a bag of coffee in Morocco?
   c. What is the opportunity cost of producing an orange in Kenya?
   d. What is the opportunity cost of producing an orange in Morocco?
   e. Suppose that there is no trade between Kenya and Morocco and that in each country, production and consumption are 2 million bags of coffee and 2 million oranges. Make a graph of the two *PPF*s and mark on them the point at which each country produces and consumes.
   f. Now suppose that trade opens up between the two countries and that each specializes in producing the item at which it has a comparative advantage. What now is the total quantity produced of coffee and oranges?

g. If one bag of coffee exchanges for one orange on the world market, what are the volumes of exports and imports of Kenya and Morocco?
h. What are the consumption levels of coffee and oranges in Kenya and Morocco?

4. Look at the information provided in the figure in Eye on the Global Economy on p. 475.
   a. Select an item from the figure in which the United States has a comparative advantage.
   b. Select an item from the figure in which the rest of the world has a comparative advantage.
   c. Make some assumptions about prices and quantities and draw your own figures similar to Figure 19.1 and 19.2 to illustrate the situation in the markets for the two items you chose in parts **a** and **b**.
   d. Make some assumptions about opportunity costs and draw your own figures similar to the two parts of Figure 19.3 to illustrate the U.S. *PPF* and the rest-of-the-world *PPF* for the two items you chose in parts **a** and **b**.

5. Figure 3 shows the car market in Brazil when Brazil places no restriction on imports of cars. The world price of a car is $10,000. If the government of Brazil introduces a 20 percent tariff on car imports, what will be
   a. The price of a car in Brazil?
   b. The quantity of cars imported into Brazil?
   c. The quantity of cars produced in Brazil?
   d. The government's tariff revenue?

FIGURE 3

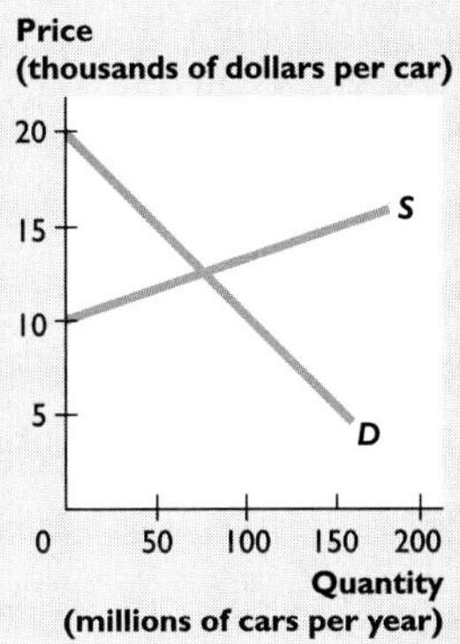

6. Suppose that in exercise 5, the Brazilian government introduces a quota of 50 million cars a year. Show on the figure
   a. The price of a car in Brazil.
   b. The quantity of cars imported into Brazil.
   c. The quantity of cars produced in Brazil.

7. If the tariff described in exercise 5 was imposed,
   a. Who would gain and who would lose?
   b. Why might a tariff be imposed?

8. If the quota described in exercise 6 was imposed,
   a. Who would gain and who would lose?
   b. Why might a quota be imposed?

Critical Thinking

9. In the 1950s, Ford and General Motors established a small car-producing industry in Australia and argued for a high tariff on car imports. The tariff has remained through the years. In 2000, the tariff was cut from 22.5 percent to 15 percent. What might have been the argument for the high tariff? Is the tariff the best way to achieve the goals of the argument?

10. The Canadian government argues against free trade in magazines and movies. Why is the Canadian government concerned about the quantity of U.S. magazines and movies that Canadians see? What is wrong with the Canadian government's argument? Who in Canada gains from the government's argument?

11. The U.S. government imposes a quota on lamb imports from New Zealand and Australia. New Zealand and Australia have lobbied the U.S. government for an increase in the quota. What is the argument put forward by the New Zealand and Australian governments? What is the counterargument put forward by the U.S. government? Which argument is really an example of rent seeking?

12. In 1845, French economist Frédéric Bastiat wrote a satirical "petition of the candlemakers" in which he argued that competition from the sun was unfair to the makers of artificial lighting. He suggested that to level the playing field, boost the production of artificial light, and create much employment and economic activity, the government should pass a law ordering the shutting up of all windows, openings, and chinks through which sunlight may enter buildings.
    a. Explain why passing the law called for in Bastiat's petition would create inefficiency.
    b. Explain why the argument presented in Bastiat's petition is similar to that of people who argue for protection from foreign competition.

Practice Online

Web Exercises

Use the links on your Foundations Web site to work the following exercises.

13. Visit the Web site of the World Trade Organization (WTO).
    a. What is the WTO?
    b. Review the ten benefits of the WTO trading system listed on the Web site. Do you agree that these are benefits? Who benefits?
    c. Review the ten common misunderstandings about the WTO listed on the Web site. Do you agree that these are misunderstandings? Explain why or why not.

14. Visit the Agriculture Negotiations page of the WTO Web site.
    a. What are the problems facing international trade in agricultural products?
    b. What is the WTO plan for dealing with these problems?
    c. If international trade in agricultural products becomes freer, do you expect U.S. farms to expand or contract? Why?

15. Visit the Global Trade Watch page on the Web site of the Public Citizen.
    a. What are the views expressed by Global Trade Watch?
    b. Are these views among the ten common misunderstandings about the WTO?
    c. Are the views of Global Trade Watch consistent with the ideas about the gains from international trade that you've studied in this chapter?
    d. Explain why you agree or disagree with the views of Global Trade Watch.

16. Visit the Web site of the U.S. International Trade Commission (USITC).
    a. What are the main functions and responsibilities of the USITC?
    b. How does the role of the USITC differ from that of the WTO?
    c. Review the page on effects of the proposed Free Trade Agreement between the United States and the Southern Africa Customs Union. Whom do you think would gain from such an agreement and why?

CHAPTER 20

International Finance

CHAPTER CHECKLIST

When you have completed your study of this chapter, you will be able to

1. **Describe a country's balance of payments accounts and explain what determines the amount of international borrowing and lending.**
2. **Explain how the exchange rate is determined and why it fluctuates.**

Every single year since 1982, the United States has spent more on imports than it has earned on exports. During these years, imports exceeded exports by a total of $3 trillion! How can a nation spend more than it earns? What determines the balance of international payments?

The world's three big currencies are the dollar, the yen, and the euro. The dollar (the currency of the United States) and the yen (the currency of Japan) have been around for a long time. The euro is new. It was launched on January 1, 1999, as the fledgling currency of 11 members of the European Union. Most of the world's international trade and finance is conducted using these three currencies. Currencies fluctuate in value. In 1971, one U.S. dollar bought 360 Japanese yen. In 1995, one dollar bought only 94 yen, and in 2002, it bought 122 yen. Why does our dollar fluctuate against other currencies? Is there anything we can do or should do to stabilize the value of the dollar?

In this chapter, you are going to learn about international finance. You will discover how nations keep their international accounts, what determines the balance of payments, and how the value of the dollar is determined in the foreign exchange market.

20.1 FINANCING INTERNATIONAL TRADE

When Sony Stores in the United States imports CD players from Japan, it does not pay for them with U.S. dollars—it uses Japanese yen. When a French construction company buys an earthmover from Caterpillar, Inc., it uses U.S. dollars. Whenever we buy things from another country, we use the currency of that country to make the transaction. It doesn't make any difference what the item being traded is; it might be a consumption good or a capital good, a building, or even a firm.

We're going to study the markets in which money—different types of currency—is bought and sold. But first we're going to look at the scale of international trading and borrowing and lending and at the way in which we keep our records of these transactions. Such records are called the balance of payments accounts.

Balance of Payments Accounts

Balance of payments accounts
The accounts in which a nation records its international trading, borrowing, and lending.

A country's **balance of payments accounts** record its international trading, borrowing, and lending. There are in fact three balance of payments accounts:

- Current account
- Capital account
- Official settlements account

Current account
Record of international receipts and payments—current account balance equals exports minus imports, plus net interest and transfers received from abroad.

Capital account
Record of foreign investment in the United States minus U.S. investment abroad.

Official settlements account
Record of the change in U.S. official reserves.

U.S. official reserves
The government's holdings of foreign currency.

The **current account** records receipts from the sale of goods and services to other countries (exports), minus payments for goods and services bought from other countries (imports), plus the net amount of interest and transfers (such as foreign aid payments) received from and paid to other countries. The **capital account** records foreign investment in the United States minus U.S. investment abroad. The **official settlements account** records the change in official U.S. reserves. **U.S. official reserves** are the government's holdings of foreign currency. If U.S. official reserves increase, the official settlements account balance is negative. The reason is that holding foreign money is like investing abroad. U.S. investment abroad is a minus item in the capital account and in the official settlements account. (By the same reasoning, if official reserves decrease, the official settlements account balance is positive.)

The sum of the balances on the three accounts always equals zero. That is, to pay for our current account deficit, we must either borrow more from abroad than we lend abroad or use our official reserves to cover the shortfall.

Table 20.1 shows the U.S. balance of payments accounts in 2002. Items in the current account and capital account that provide foreign currency to the United States have a plus sign; items that cost the United States foreign currency have a minus sign. The table shows that in 2002, U.S. imports exceeded U.S. exports and the current account deficit was $520 billion. We paid for imports that exceeded the value of our exports by borrowing from the rest of the world. The capital account tells us by how much. We borrowed $885 billion (foreign investment in the United States) but made loans of $556 billion (U.S. investment abroad). Our measured net foreign borrowing was $329 billion. Measurement error (recorded in the balance of payments accounts as a statistical discrepancy) was $198 billion. Our official reserves increased by $7 billion and are shown in Table 20.1 as an increase of $7 billion, a convention that makes the three accounts sum to zero.

You might better understand the balance of payments accounts and the way in which they are linked together if you think about the income and expenditure, borrowing and lending, and bank account of an individual.

Eye on the Past

The U.S. Balance of Payments

The numbers in Table 20.1 provide a snapshot of the U.S balance of payments in 2002. The figure puts this snapshot into perspective by showing how the balance of payments evolved from 1982 to 2002.

(Because the economy grows and the price level rises, changes in the dollar value of the balance of payments do not convey much information. To remove the influences of growth and inflation, the figure shows the balance of payments as a percentage of GDP.)

The capital account balance is almost a mirror image of the current account balance because the official settlements balance is very small in comparison with the balances on these other two accounts. A large current account deficit (and capital account surplus) emerged during the 1980s but declined from 1987 to 1991. Throughout the 1990s and 2000s, the current account deficit increased.

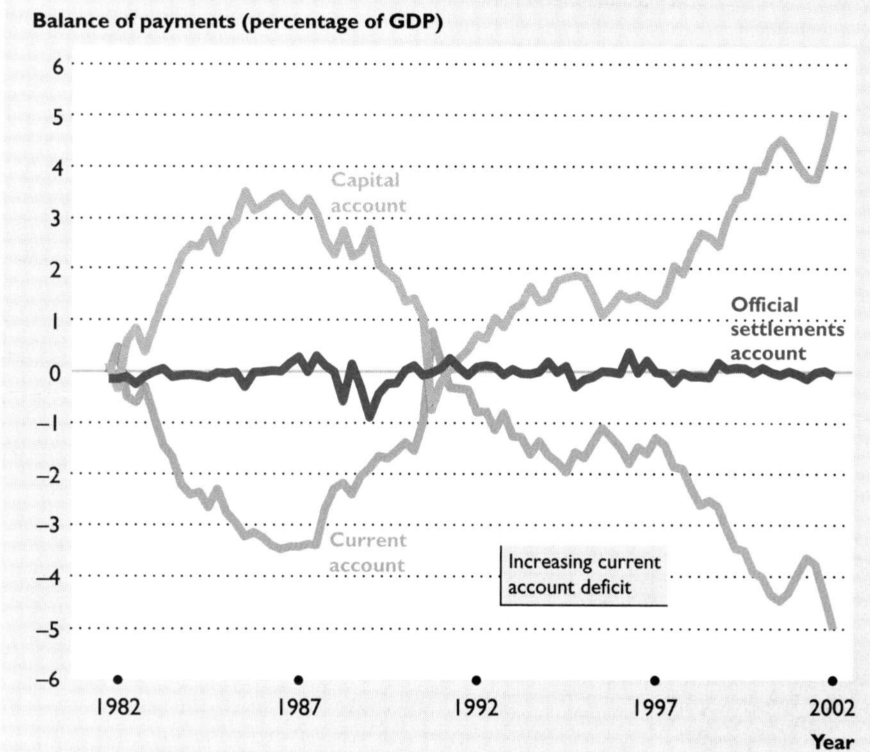

SOURCE: Bureau of Economic Analysis.

TABLE 20.1

The U.S. Balance of Payments Accounts in 2002

Current account	**(billions of dollars)**
Exports of goods and services	+975
Imports of goods and services	–1,418
Net interest	–25
Net transfers	–52
Current account balance	–520
Capital account	
Foreign investment in the United States	+885
U.S. investment abroad	–556
Statistical discrepancy	198
Capital account balance	+527
Official settlements account	
Official settlements account balance	–7

SOURCE: Bureau of Economic Analysis.

Individual Analogy

An individual's current account records the income from supplying the services of factors of production and the expenditure on goods and services. Consider, for example, Joanne. She worked in 2002 and earned an income of $25,000. Joanne has $10,000 worth of investments that earned her an interest of $1,000. Joanne's current account shows an income of $26,000. Joanne spent $18,000 buying goods and services for consumption. She also bought a new house, which cost her $60,000. So Joanne's total expenditure was $78,000. The difference between her expenditure and income is $52,000 ($78,000 minus $26,000). This amount is Joanne's current account deficit.

To pay for expenditure of $52,000 in excess of her income, Joanne has to use the money that she has in the bank or she has to take out a loan. In fact, Joanne took out a mortgage of $50,000 to help buy her house. This mortgage was the only borrowing that Joanne did, so her capital account surplus was $50,000. With a current account deficit of $52,000 and a capital account surplus of $50,000, Joanne is still $2,000 short. She got that $2,000 from her own bank account. Her cash holdings decreased by $2,000.

Joanne's income from her work is analogous to a country's income from its exports. Her income from her investments is analogous to a country's interest from foreigners. Her purchases of goods and services, including her purchase of an apartment, are analogous to a country's imports. Joanne's mortgage—borrowing from someone else—is analogous to a country's borrowing from the rest of the world. The change in her bank account is analogous to the change in the country's official reserves.

Borrowers and Lenders, Debtors and Creditors

Net borrower
A country that is borrowing more from the rest of the world than it is lending to the rest of the world.

Net lender
A country that is lending more to the rest of the world than it is borrowing from the rest of the world.

A country that is borrowing more from the rest of the world than it is lending to it is called a **net borrower**. Similarly, a **net lender** is a country that is lending more to the rest of the world than it is borrowing from it.

The United States is a net borrower, but it is a relative newcomer to the ranks of net borrower nations. Throughout the 1960s and most of the 1970s, the United States was a net lender to the rest of the world. It had a surplus on its current account and a deficit on its capital account. It was not until 1983 that the United States became a significant net borrower from the rest of the world. Between 1983 and 1987, U.S. borrowing increased each year. Then it decreased and was briefly zero in 1991. After 1991, it started to increase again. The average net foreign borrowing by the United States between 1983 and 2002 was $146 billion a year.

Most countries are net borrowers like the United States. But a small number of countries, including Japan and oil-rich Saudi Arabia, are net lenders.

Debtor nation
A country that during its entire history has borrowed more from the rest of the world than it has lent to it.

Creditor nation
A country that during its entire history has invested more in the rest of the world than other countries have invested in it.

A net borrower might be reducing its net assets held in the rest of the world, or it might be going deeper into debt. A nation's total stock of foreign investment determines whether the nation is a debtor or creditor. A **debtor nation** is a country that during its entire history has borrowed more from the rest of the world than it has lent to it. It has a stock of outstanding debt to the rest of the world that exceeds the stock of its own claims on the rest of the world. A **creditor nation** is a country that during its entire history has invested more in the rest of the world than other countries have invested in it.

Flows and Stocks

At the heart of the distinction between a net borrower and a net lender on the one hand and between a debtor nation and a creditor nation on the other hand is the distinction between flows and stocks, which you have encountered many times in your study of macroeconomics. Borrowing and lending are flows—amounts borrowed or lent per unit of time. Debts are stocks—amounts owed at a point in time. The flow of borrowing and lending changes the stock of debt.

The United States was a debtor nation through the nineteenth century as we borrowed from Europe to finance our westward expansion, railroads, and industrialization. We paid off our debt and became a creditor nation for most of the twentieth century. But following a string of current account deficits, we became a debtor nation again in 1989.

Since 1989, the total stock of U.S. borrowing from the rest of the world has exceeded U.S. lending to the rest of the world. The largest debtor nations are the capital-hungry developing countries (as the United States was during the nineteenth century). The international debt of these countries grew from less than a third to more than a half of their gross domestic product during the 1980s and created what was called the "Third World debt crisis."

Should we be concerned that the United States is a net borrower? The answer to this question depends mainly on what the net borrower is doing with the borrowed money. If borrowing is financing investment that in turn is generating economic growth and higher income, borrowing is not a problem. If the borrowed money is being used to finance consumption, then higher interest payments are being incurred, and consequently, consumption will eventually have to be reduced. In this case, the more the borrowing and the longer it goes on, the greater is the reduction in consumption that will eventually be necessary. We'll see below whether the United States is borrowing for investment or for consumption.

Current Account Balance

What determines a country's current account balance and net foreign borrowing? You've seen that net exports (*NX*) is the main item in the current account. We can define the current account balance (*CAB*) as

$$CAB = NX + \text{Net interest and transfers from abroad.}$$

Fluctuations in net exports are the main source of fluctuations in the current account balance. Net interest and transfers from abroad are small and have trends but do not fluctuate much. So we can study the current account balance by looking at what determines net exports.

Net Exports

The government budget and private saving and investment determine net exports. To see how they determine net exports, we need to recall some of the things that we learned about the National Income Accounts in Chapter 5. Table 20.2 will refresh your memory and summarize some calculations.

TABLE 20.2

Net Exports, the Government Budget, Saving, and Investment

	Symbols and equations	United States in 2002 (billions of dollars)
(a) Variables		
Exports	X	1,021
Imports	M	1,436
Investment	I	1,586
Saving	S	1,587
Government purchases	G	1,971
Net taxes	NT	1,555
(b) Balances		
Net exports	$X - M$	1,021 – 1,436 = –415
Private sector balance	$S - I$	1,587 – 1,586 = 1
Government sector balance	$NT - G$	1,555 – 1,971 = –416
(c) Relation among balances		
National accounts	$Y = C + I + G + X - M = C + S + NT$	
Rearranging:	$X - M = S - I + NT - G$	
Net exports	$X - M$	–415
Equals:		
Private sector balance	$S - I$	1
Plus		
Government sector balance	$NT - G$	–416

SOURCE: Bureau of Economic Analysis, 2002. (The National Income and Product Accounts measures of exports and imports are slightly different from the Balance of Payments Accounts measures in Table 20.1 on p. 505. The government sector includes state and local governments.)

Part (a) of Table 20.2 lists the national income variables that are needed, with their symbols. Part (b) defines three balances. *Net exports* are exports of goods and services minus imports of goods and services.

Private sector balance
Saving minus investment.

The **private sector balance** is saving minus investment. If saving exceeds investment, a private sector surplus is lent to other sectors. If investment exceeds saving, borrowing from other sectors finances a private sector deficit.

Government sector balance
Net taxes minus government purchases of goods and services.

The **government sector balance** is equal to net taxes minus government purchases of goods and services. If that number is positive, a government sector surplus is lent to other sectors; if that number is negative, borrowing from other sectors must finance a government deficit. The government sector is the sum of the federal, state, and local governments.

Part (b) also shows the values of these balances for the United States in 2002. As you can see, net exports were –$415 billion, a deficit of $415 billion. The private sector saved $1,587 billion and invested $1,586 billion, so it had a balance of $1 billion, a surplus of $1 billion. The government sector's revenue from net taxes was $1,555 billion, and it purchased $1,971 billion worth of goods and services. The government sector balance was –$416 billion, a deficit of $416 billion.

Part (c) of Table 20.2 shows the relationship among the three balances. From the national income accounts, we know that real GDP, Y, is the sum of consumption expenditure, C; investment, I; government purchases, G; and net exports, $X - M$. Real GDP also equals the sum of consumption expenditure; saving, S, and net taxes, NT. Rearranging these equations tells us that net exports equals $(S - I)$, the private sector balance, plus $(NT - G)$, the government sector balance. That is,

$$\text{Net exports} = (S - I) + (NT - G).$$

Should we be concerned that the United States is a net borrower? The answer is probably not. Our international borrowing finances the purchase of new capital goods. In 2002, businesses spent $1,586 billion on new buildings, plant, and equipment. Government spent $353 billion on defense equipment and public structures such as highways and dams. All these purchases added to the nation's capital, and much of it increased productivity. Governments also purchased education and health care services, which increased human capital.

Our international borrowing is financing private and public investment, not consumption.

Current Account Balances Around the World

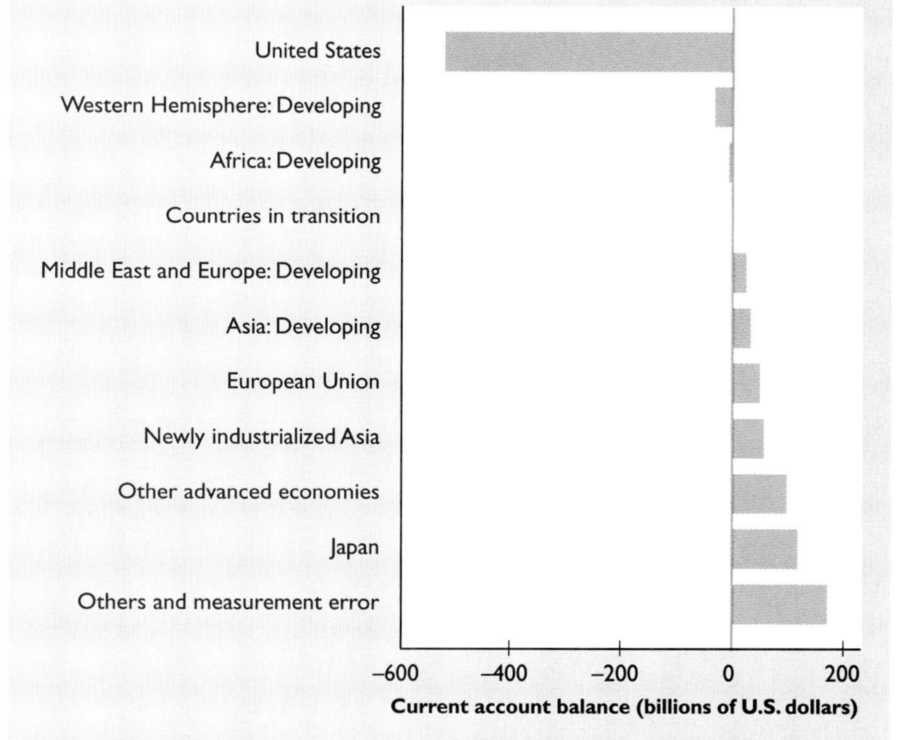

SOURCE: International Monetary Fund, *World Economic Outlook*, September 2002.

The U.S. current account deficit in 2002 is the major international payments deficit. No other country has a deficit remotely similar to that of the United States.

The next largest deficits are those of the developing countries in the Western Hemisphere—the nations of Latin America.

Japan and the newly industrialized Asian economies have current account surpluses, as do most of the other groups of countries.

In 2002, there was a large (positive) measurement error in the international payments data. This error reflects a few missing countries and poor record keeping because of underground economic activity.

CHECKPOINT 20.1

Study Guide pp. 292–296

Practice Online 20.1

1 Describe a country's balance of payments accounts and explain what determines the amount of international borrowing and lending.

Practice Problem 20.1

It is 2004 and the U.S. economy records the following transactions:

Imports of goods and services, $2,000 billion; interest paid to the rest of the world, $500 billion; interest received from the rest of the world, $400 billion; decrease in U.S. official reserves, $10 billion; government sector balance, $200 billion; saving, $1,800 billion; investment, $2,000 billion; net transfers, zero.

a. Calculate the current account balance, the capital account balance, the official settlements account balance, and exports of goods and services.

b. Is the United States a debtor or a creditor nation in 2004?

c. If government purchases increase by $100 billion, what happens to the current account balance?

Exercise 20.1

It is 2005 and the U.S. economy records the following transactions:

Exports of goods and services, $1,800 billion; interest payments to the rest of the world, $550 billion; interest received from the rest of the world, $350 billion; decrease in U.S. official reserves, $10 billion; government sector balance, $200 billion; saving, $1,800 billion; investment, $2,000 billion; net transfers are zero.

a. Calculate the current account balance, the capital account balance, the official settlements account balance, and imports of goods and services.

b. Has the United States become a larger or smaller debtor or creditor nation in 2005 than it was in 2004 (practice problem 20.1)?

c. If net taxes increase by $100 billion, what happens to the capital account balance?

Solution to Practice Problem 20.1

a. The current account balance equals net exports plus net interest from abroad (–$100 billion) plus net transfers (zero). Net exports equal the government sector balance ($200 billion) plus the private sector balance. The private sector balance equals saving ($1,800 billion) minus investment ($2,000 billion), which is –$200 billion. So net exports are zero, and the current account balance is –$100 billion. The capital account balance is the negative of the sum of the current account and official settlements account balances, which is $90 billion. The official settlements account balance is a *surplus* of $10 billion. Exports of goods and services equal net exports (zero) plus imports ($2,000 billion), which equals $2,000 billion.

b. The United States is a debtor nation in 2004. You can determine this fact because it pays more in interest to the rest of the world than it receives from the rest of the world.

c. If government purchases increase by $100 billion, the government sector balance decreases. Net exports decrease and the current account deficit increases.

20.2 THE EXCHANGE RATE

When we buy foreign goods or invest in another country, we have to obtain some of that country's currency to make the transaction. When foreigners buy U.S.-made goods or invest in the United States, they have to obtain some U.S. dollars. We get foreign currency, and foreigners get U.S. dollars in the foreign exchange market. The **foreign exchange market** is the market in which the currency of one country is exchanged for the currency of another. The foreign exchange market is not a place like a downtown flea market or produce market. The market is made up of thousands of people: importers and exporters, banks, and specialists in the buying and selling of foreign exchange, called foreign exchange brokers. The foreign exchange market opens on Monday morning in Hong Kong, which is still Sunday evening in New York. As the day advances, markets open in Singapore, Tokyo, Bahrain, Frankfurt, London, New York, Chicago, and San Francisco. As the West Coast markets close, Hong Kong is only an hour away from opening for the next business day. Dealers around the world are in continual contact, and on a typical day in 2002, $1.5 trillion changed hands.

Foreign exchange market
The market in which the currency of one country is exchanged for the currency of another.

The price at which one currency exchanges for another is called a **foreign exchange rate**. For example, in November 2002, one U.S. dollar bought 122 Japanese yen. The exchange rate was 122 yen per dollar. We can also express the exchange rate in terms of dollars (or cents) per yen, which in November 2002 was a bit less than 1 cent per yen.

Foreign exchange rate
The price at which one currency exchanges for another.

Currency depreciation is the fall in the value of one currency in terms of another currency. For example, if the dollar falls from 100 yen to 80 yen, the dollar depreciates by 20 percent.

Currency depreciation
The fall in the value of one currency in terms of another currency.

The Dollar and the Yen Since 1982

The figure shows the exchange rate of the U.S. dollar in terms of the Japanese yen between 1982 and 2002.

From 1982 to 1995 and again in 1999 and 2000, the value of the dollar fell against the yen—the dollar depreciated.

From 1995 to 1998 and again in 2001 and 2002, the value of the dollar rose against the yen—the dollar appreciated.

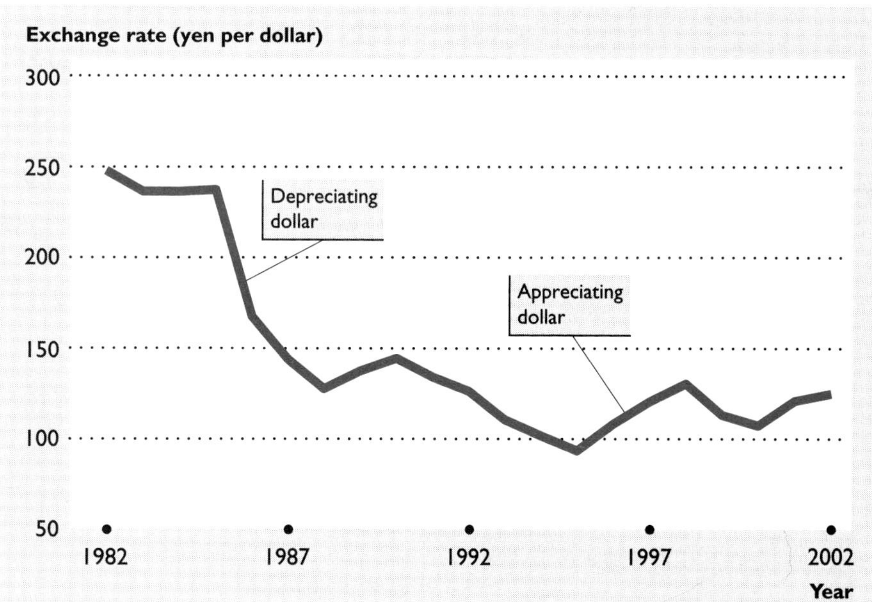

SOURCE: PACIFIC FX Service, University of British Columbia.

Currency appreciation
The rise in the value of one currency in terms of another currency.

Currency appreciation is the rise in the value of one currency in terms of another currency. For example, if the dollar rises from 100 yen to 120 yen, the dollar appreciates by 20 percent. When the U.S. dollar appreciates against the yen, the yen depreciates against the dollar.

Why does the U.S. dollar fluctuate in value? Why does it sometimes depreciate and sometimes appreciate? To answer these questions, we need to understand the forces that determine the exchange rate.

The exchange rate is a price—the price of one country's money in terms of another country's money. And like all prices, demand and supply determine the exchange rate. So to understand the forces that determine the exchange rate, we need to study demand and supply in the foreign exchange market. We'll begin by looking at the demand side of the market.

Demand in the Foreign Exchange Market

The quantity of U.S. dollars demanded in the foreign exchange market is the amount that traders plan to buy during a given time period at a given exchange rate. This quantity depends on many factors but the main ones are

- The exchange rate
- Interest rates in the United States and other countries
- The expected future exchange rate

Let's look first at the relationship between the quantity of dollars demanded in the foreign exchange market and the exchange rate.

The Law of Demand for Foreign Exchange

People do not buy dollars because they enjoy them. The demand for dollars is a *derived demand*. People demand dollars so that they can buy U.S.-made goods and services (U.S. exports). They also demand dollars so that they can buy U.S. assets such as bank accounts, bonds, stocks, businesses, and real estate. Nevertheless, the law of demand applies to dollars just as it does to anything else that people value.

Other things remaining the same, the higher the exchange rate, the smaller is the quantity of dollars demanded. For example, if the price of the U.S. dollar rises from 100 yen to 120 yen but nothing else changes, the quantity of U.S. dollars that people plan to buy decreases. Why does the exchange rate influence the quantity of dollars demanded? There are two separate reasons, and they are related to the two sources of the derived demand for dollars. They are

- Exports effect
- Expected profit effect

Exports Effect

The larger the value of U.S. exports, the larger is the quantity of dollars demanded. But the value of U.S. exports depends on the exchange rate. The lower the exchange rate, other things remaining the same, the cheaper are U.S.-made goods and services to people in the rest of the world, the more the United States exports, and the greater is the quantity of U.S. dollars demanded to pay for them.

Expected Profit Effect

The larger the expected profit from holding dollars, the greater is the quantity of dollars demanded in the foreign exchange market. But expected profit depends on the exchange rate. The lower the exchange rate, other things remaining the same,

FIGURE 20.1
The Demand for Dollars

Practice Online

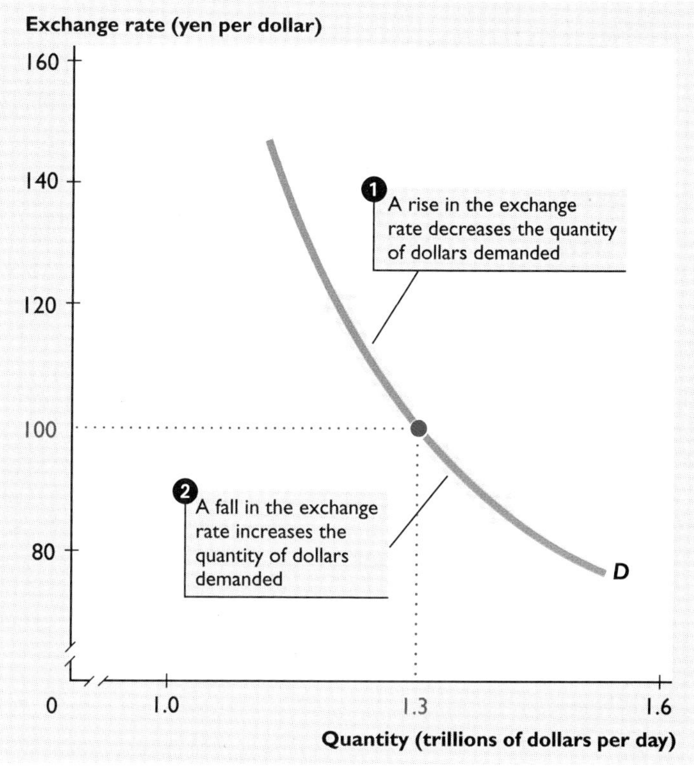

Other things remaining the same, the quantity of dollars that people plan to buy depends on the exchange rate.

1. If the exchange rate rises, the quantity of dollars demanded decreases and there is a movement up along the demand curve for dollars.
2. If the exchange rate falls, the quantity of dollars demanded increases and there is a movement down along the demand curve for dollars.

the larger is the expected profit from holding dollars and the greater is the quantity of dollars demanded on the foreign exchange market.

To understand this effect, suppose you think the dollar will be worth 120 yen by the end of the month. If a dollar costs 115 yen today, you buy dollars. But a person who thinks that the dollar will be worth 115 yen at the end of the month does not buy dollars. Now suppose the exchange rate falls to 110 yen per dollar. More people think that they can profit from buying dollars, so the quantity of dollars demanded increases.

Figure 20.1 shows the demand curve for U.S. dollars in the foreign exchange market. For the two reasons we've just reviewed, when the foreign exchange rate rises, other things remaining the same, the quantity of dollars demanded decreases and there is a movement up along the demand curve, as shown by the arrow. When the exchange rate falls, other things remaining the same, the quantity of dollars demanded increases and there is a movement down along the demand curve, as shown by the arrow.

Changes in the Demand for Dollars

A change in any other influence on the quantity of U.S. dollars that people plan to buy in the foreign exchange market brings a change in the demand for dollars and the demand curve for dollars shifts. These other influences are

- Interest rates in the United States and other countries
- The expected future exchange rate

Interest Rates in the United States and Other Countries

U.S. interest rate differential
The U.S. interest rate minus the foreign interest rate.

People and businesses buy financial assets to make a return. The higher the interest rate on U.S. assets compared with foreign assets, the more U.S. assets they buy. What matters is not the level of U.S. interest rates, but the U.S. interest rate minus the foreign interest rate, a gap called the **U.S. interest rate differential**. If the U.S. interest rate rises and the foreign interest rate remains constant, the U.S. interest rate differential increases. The larger the U.S. interest rate differential, the greater is the demand for U.S. assets and the greater is the demand for dollars.

The Expected Future Exchange Rate

Other things remaining the same, the higher the expected future exchange rate, the greater is the demand for dollars. To see why, suppose you are Toyota's finance manager. The exchange rate is 100 yen per dollar, and you think that by the end of the month, it will be 120 yen per dollar. You spend 100,000 yen today and buy $1,000. At the end of the month, the dollar equals 120 yen, as you predicted, and you sell the $1,000. You get 120,000 yen. You've made a profit of 20,000 yen. The higher the expected future exchange rate, other things remaining the same, the greater is the expected profit and the greater is the demand for dollars.

Figure 20.2 summarizes the influences on the demand for dollars. A rise in the U.S. interest rate differential or the expected future exchange rate increases the demand for dollars and shifts the demand curve rightward from D_0 to D_1. A fall

FIGURE 20.2
Changes in the Demand for Dollars

Practice Online

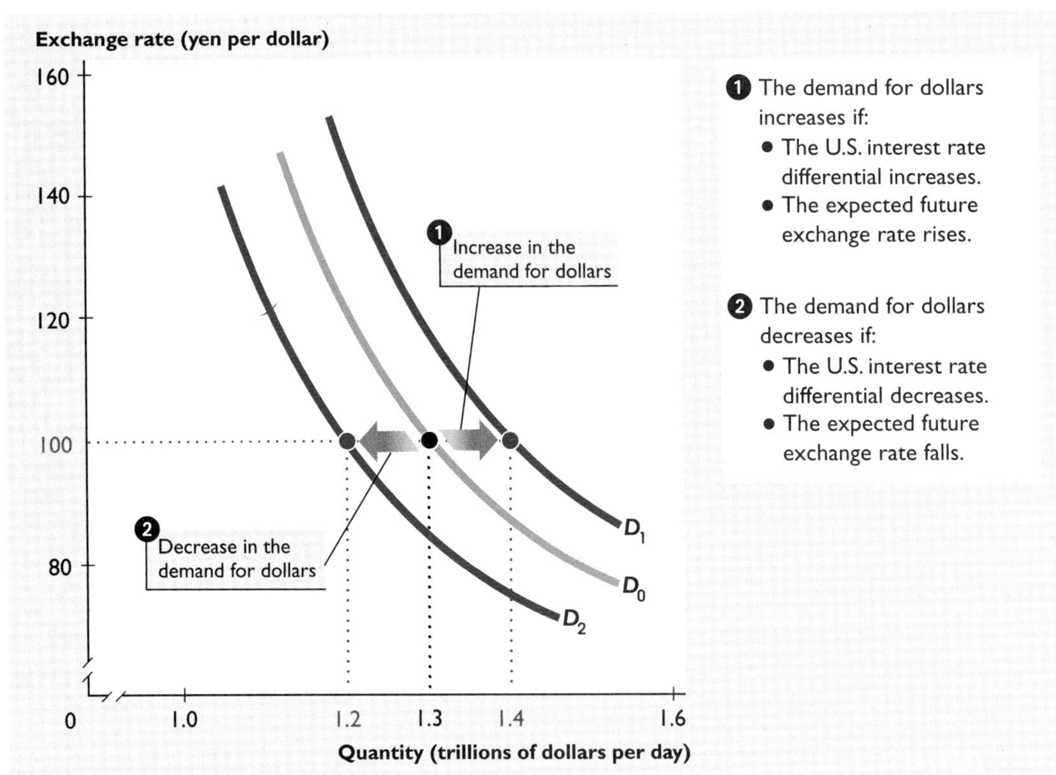

❶ The demand for dollars increases if:

- The U.S. interest rate differential increases.
- The expected future exchange rate rises.

❷ The demand for dollars decreases if:

- The U.S. interest rate differential decreases.
- The expected future exchange rate falls.

in the U.S. interest rate differential or the expected future exchange rate decreases the demand for dollars and shifts the demand curve leftward from D_0 to D_2.

Supply in the Foreign Exchange Market

The quantity of U.S. dollars supplied in the foreign exchange market is the amount that traders plan to sell during a given time period at a given exchange rate. This quantity depends on many factors, but the main ones are

- The exchange rate
- Interest rates in the United States and other countries
- The expected future exchange rate

Let's look first at the relationship between the quantity of dollars supplied in the foreign exchange market and the exchange rate.

The Law of Supply of Foreign Exchange

Traders supply U.S. dollars in the foreign exchange market when people and businesses buy other currencies. And they buy other currencies so that they can buy foreign-made goods and services (U.S. imports). They also supply dollars and buy foreign currencies so that they can buy foreign assets such as bank accounts, bonds, stocks, businesses, and real estate. The law of supply applies to dollars just as it does to anything else that people plan to sell.

Other things remaining the same, the higher the exchange rate, the greater is the quantity of dollars supplied in the foreign exchange market. For example, if the price of the U.S. dollar rises from 100 yen to 120 yen but nothing else changes, the quantity of U.S. dollars that people plan to sell in the foreign exchange market increases. Why does the exchange rate influence the quantity of dollars supplied?

There are two reasons, and they parallel the two reasons on the demand side of the market. They are

- Imports effect
- Expected profit effect

Imports Effect

The larger the value of U.S. imports, the larger is the quantity of foreign currency demanded to pay for these imports. And when people buy foreign currency, they supply dollars. So the larger the value of U.S. imports, the greater is the quantity of dollars supplied on the foreign exchange market. But the value of U.S. imports depends on the exchange rate. The higher the exchange rate, other things remaining the same, the cheaper are foreign-made goods and services to Americans. So the more the United States imports, the greater is the quantity of U.S. dollars supplied on the foreign exchange market to pay for these imports.

Expected Profit Effect

The larger the expected profit from holding a foreign currency, the greater is the quantity of that currency demanded and the greater is the quantity of dollars supplied in the foreign exchange market. But the expected profit from holding a foreign currency depends on the exchange rate. The higher the exchange rate, other things remaining the same, the larger is the expected profit from selling dollars and the greater is the quantity of dollars supplied on the foreign exchange market.

FIGURE 20.3
The Supply of Dollars

Practice Online

Other things remaining the same, the quantity of dollars that people plan to sell depends on the exchange rate.

1. If the exchange rate rises, the quantity of dollars supplied increases and there is a movement up along the supply curve of dollars.
2. If the exchange rate falls, the quantity of dollars supplied decreases and there is a movement down along the supply curve of dollars.

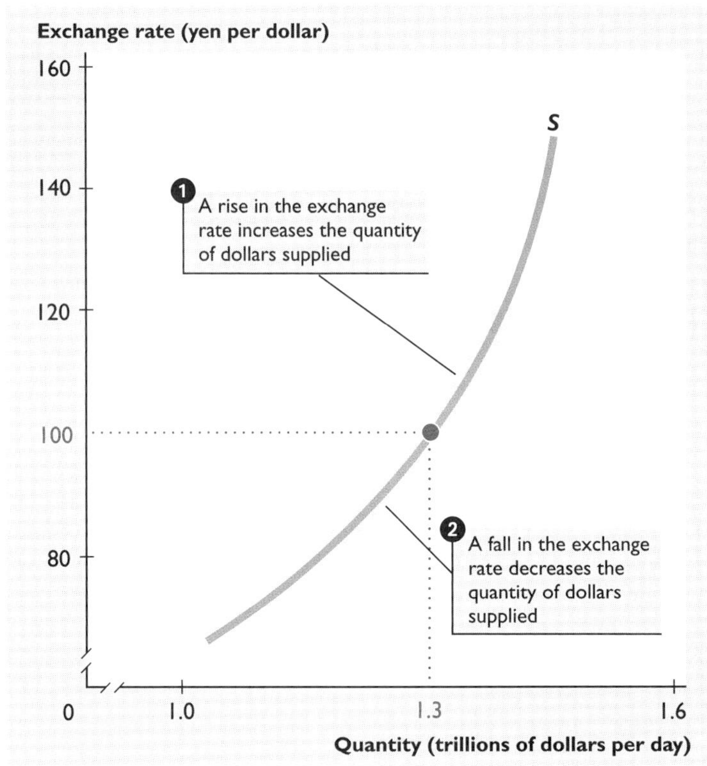

For the two reasons we've just reviewed, other things remaining the same, when the foreign exchange rate rises, the quantity of dollars supplied increases, and when the foreign exchange rate falls, the quantity of dollars supplied decreases. Figure 20.3 shows the supply curve of U.S. dollars in the foreign exchange market. In this figure, when the foreign exchange rate rises, other things remaining the same, there is an increase in the quantity of dollars supplied and a movement up along the supply curve, as shown by the arrow. When the exchange rate falls, other things remaining the same, there is a decrease in the quantity of dollars supplied and a movement down along the supply curve, as shown by the arrow.

Changes in the Supply of Dollars

A change in any other influence on the quantity of U.S. dollars that people plan to sell in the foreign exchange market brings a change in the supply of dollars and the supply curve of dollars shifts. Supply either increases or decreases. These other influences on supply parallel the other influences on demand but have exactly the opposite effects. These influences are

- Interest rates in the United States and other countries
- The expected future exchange rate

Interest Rates in the United States and Other Countries

The larger the U.S. interest rate differential, the smaller is the demand for foreign assets and the smaller is the supply of dollars on the foreign exchange market.

The Expected Future Exchange Rate

Other things remaining the same, the higher the expected future exchange rate, the smaller is the supply of dollars. To see why, suppose that the dollar is trading at 100 yen per dollar today and you think that by the end of the month, the dollar will trade at 120 yen per dollar. You were planning on selling dollars today, but you decide to hold off and wait until the end of the month. If you supply dollars today, you get only 100 yen per dollar. But at the end of the month, if the dollar is worth 120 yen as you predict, you'll get 120 yen for each dollar you supply. You'll make a profit of 20 percent. So the higher the expected future exchange rate, other things remaining the same, the smaller is the expected profit from selling U.S. dollars today and the smaller is the supply of dollars today.

Figure 20.4 summarizes the above discussion of the influences on the supply of dollars. A rise in the U.S. interest rate differential or a rise in the expected future exchange rate decreases the supply of dollars and shifts the supply curve leftward from S_0 to S_1. A fall in the U.S. interest rate differential or a fall in the expected future exchange rate increases the supply of dollars and shifts the supply curve rightward from S_0 to S_2.

FIGURE 20.4

Changes in the Supply of Dollars

Practice Online

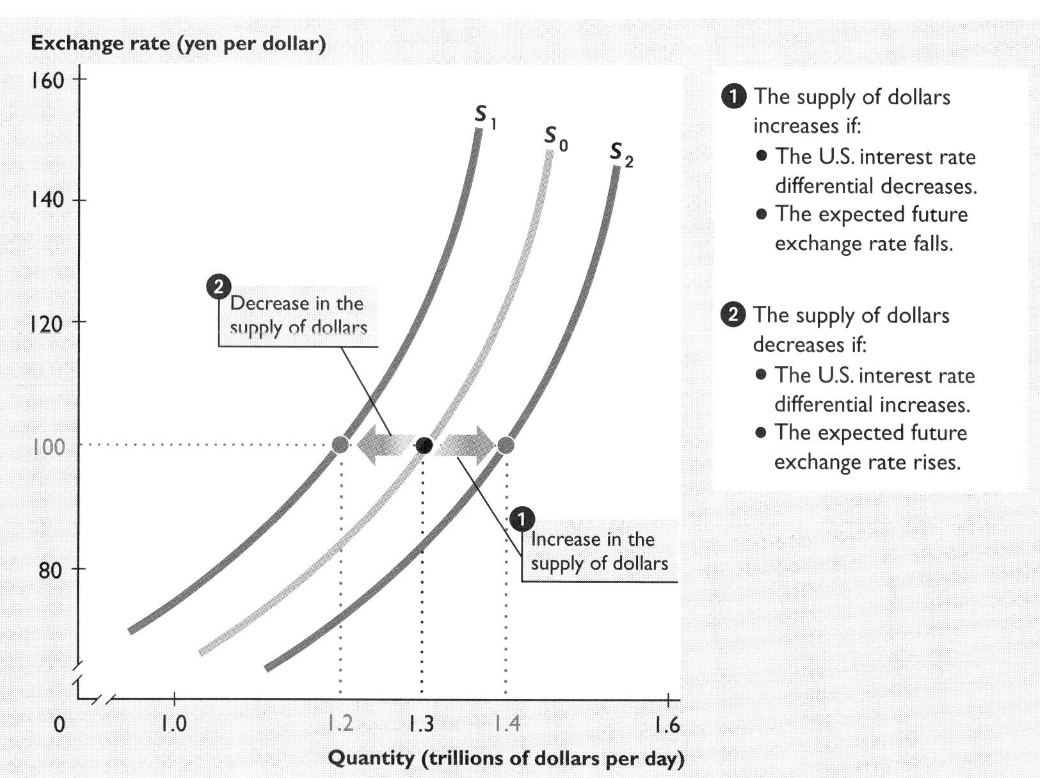

1. The supply of dollars increases if:
   - The U.S. interest rate differential decreases.
   - The expected future exchange rate falls.

2. The supply of dollars decreases if:
   - The U.S. interest rate differential increases.
   - The expected future exchange rate rises.

Market Equilibrium

Figure 20.5 shows how demand and supply in the foreign exchange market determine the exchange rate. The demand curve is *D*, and the supply curve is *S*. Just like all the other markets you've studied, the price (the exchange rate) acts as a regulator. If the exchange rate is too high, there is a surplus—the quantity supplied exceeds the quantity demanded. For example, in Figure 20.5, if the exchange rate is 120 yen per dollar, there is a surplus of dollars.

If the exchange rate is too low, there is a shortage—the quantity supplied is less than the quantity demanded. For example, in Figure 20.5, if the exchange rate is 80 yen per dollar, there is a shortage of dollars.

At the equilibrium exchange rate, there is neither a shortage nor a surplus. The quantity supplied equals the quantity demanded. In Figure 20.5, the equilibrium exchange rate is 100 yen per dollar. At this exchange rate, the quantity demanded equals the quantity supplied and is $1.3 trillion a day.

The foreign exchange market is constantly pulled to its equilibrium by the forces of supply and demand. Foreign exchange dealers are constantly looking for the best price they can get. If they are selling, they want the highest price available. If they are buying, they want the lowest price available. Information flows from dealer to dealer through the worldwide computer network, and the price adjusts second by second to keep buying plans and selling plans in balance. That is, price adjusts second by second to keep the market at its equilibrium.

FIGURE 20.5

Equilibrium Exchange Rate

Practice Online

The demand curve for dollars is *D*, and the supply curve is *S*.

1. If the exchange rate is 120 yen per dollar, there is a surplus of dollars and the exchange rate falls.
2. If the exchange rate is 80 yen per dollar, there is a shortage of dollars and the exchange rate rises.
3. If the exchange rate is 100 yen per dollar, there is neither a shortage nor a surplus of dollars and the exchange rate remains constant. The market is in equilibrium.

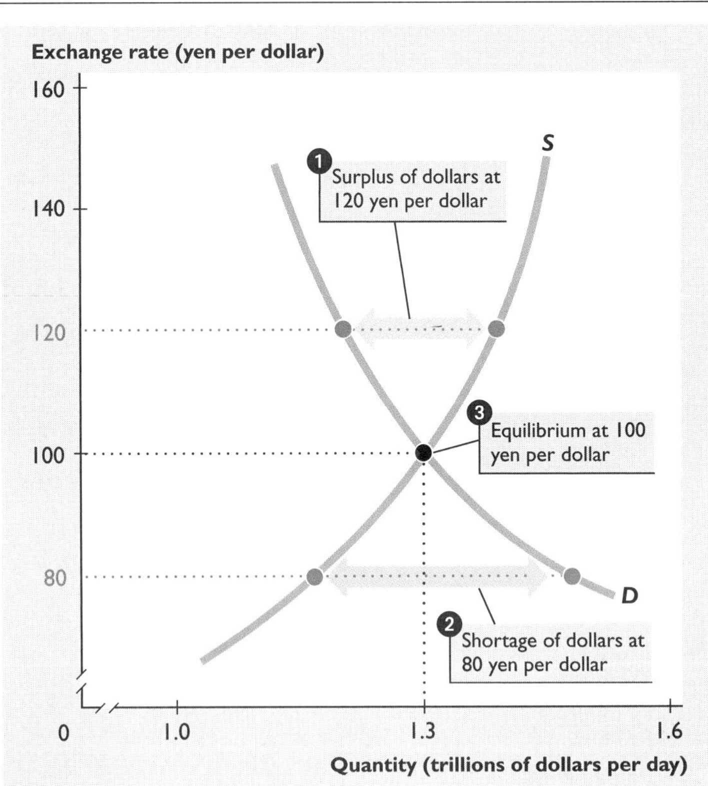

Changes in the Exchange Rate

If the demand for dollars increases and the supply of dollars does not change, the exchange rate rises. If the demand for dollars decreases and the supply of dollars does not change, the exchange rate falls. Similarly, if the supply of dollars decreases and the demand for dollars does not change, the exchange rate rises. If the supply of dollars increases and the demand for dollars does not change, the exchange rate falls.

These predictions about the effects of changes in demand and supply are exactly the same as for any other market.

Why the Exchange Rate Is Volatile

Sometimes the dollar depreciates and at other times it appreciates, but the quantity of dollars traded each day barely changes. Why? The main reason is that supply and demand are not independent of each other in the foreign exchange market.

When we studied the demand for dollars and the supply of dollars, we saw that unlike other markets, the demand side and the supply side of the market have some common influences. A change in the expected future exchange rate or a change in the U.S. interest rate differential changes both demand and supply, and they change in opposite directions. These common influences on both demand and supply explain why the exchange rate can be volatile at times, even though the quantity of dollars traded does not change.

Everyone in the market is potentially either a demander or a supplier. Each has a price above which he or she will sell and below which he or she will buy. Let's see how these common supply and demand effects work by looking at two episodes: one in which the dollar appreciated and one in which it depreciated.

A Depreciating Dollar: 1994–1995

Between 1994 and the summer of 1995, the exchange rate fell from 100 yen to a low of 84 yen per dollar. Figure 20.6(a) explains this fall. In 1994, the demand and supply curves were those labeled D_{94} and S_{94}. The exchange rate was 100 yen per dollar. During 1994, traders expected the U.S. dollar to depreciate. They expected a lower exchange rate. As a result, the demand for dollars decreased and the supply of dollars increased. The demand curve shifted leftward to D_{95}, and the supply curve shifted rightward to S_{95}. The exchange rate fell to 84 yen per dollar.

An Appreciating Dollar: 1995–1998

Between 1995 and 1998, the dollar appreciated against the yen. It rose from 84 yen to 130 yen per dollar. Figure 20.6(b) explains why this happened. In 1995, the demand and supply curves were those labeled D_{95} and S_{95}. The exchange rate was 84 yen per dollar—where the supply and demand curves intersect. During the next two years, Japan was in recession and the U.S. economy was expanding. Interest rates in Japan fell, and the yen was expected to depreciate. The demand for yen decreased, and the demand for dollars increased. The demand curve shifted from D_{95} to D_{98}. The supply of dollars decreased, and the supply curve shifted from S_{95} to S_{98}. These two shifts reinforced each other, and the exchange rate increased to 130 yen per dollar.

FIGURE 20.6
Exchange Rate Fluctuations

Practice Online

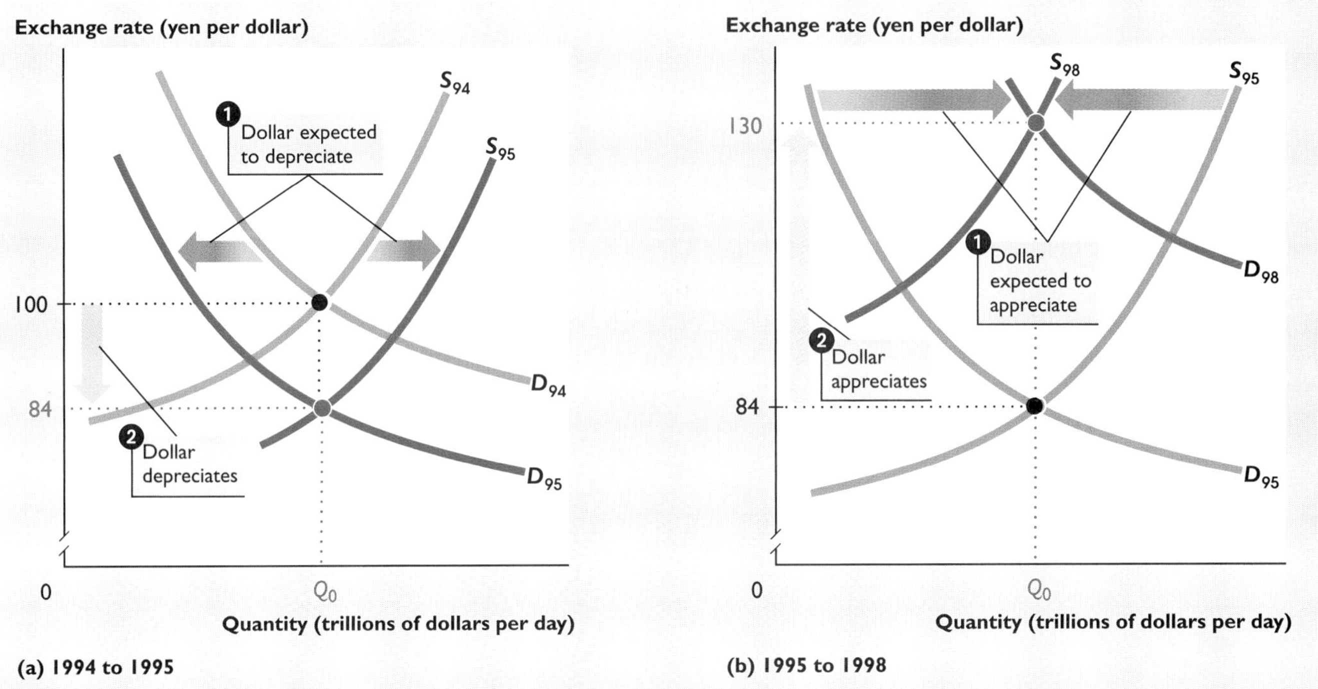

(a) 1994 to 1995

(b) 1995 to 1998

Exchange Rate Expectations

The changes in the exchange rate that we've just examined occurred in part because the exchange rate was expected to change. This explanation sounds a bit like a self-fulfilling forecast. But what makes expectations change? The answer is new information about the deeper forces that influence the value of money. There are two such forces:

- Purchasing power parity
- Interest rate parity

Purchasing Power Parity

Money is worth what it will buy. But two kinds of money, U.S. dollars and Canadian dollars, for example, might buy different amounts of goods and services. Suppose a Big Mac costs $4 (Canadian) in Toronto and $3 (U.S.) in New York. If the Canadian dollar exchange rate is $1.33 Canadian per U.S. dollar, the two monies have the same value. You can buy a Big Mac in either Toronto or New York for either $4 Canadian or $3 U.S.

Purchasing power parity
Equal value of money—a situation in which money buys the same amount of goods and services in different currencies.

The situation we've just described is called **purchasing power parity**, which means equal value of money. If purchasing power parity does not prevail, some powerful forces go to work. To understand these forces, let's suppose that the price of a Big Mac in New York rises to $4 U.S., but in Toronto it remains at $4 Canadian. Suppose the exchange rate remains at $1.33 Canadian per U.S. dollar. In this case, a Big Mac in Toronto still costs $4 Canadian or $3 U.S. But in New York, it costs $4 U.S. or $5.32 Canadian. Money buys more in Canada than in the United States. Money is not of equal value in both countries.

If all (or most) prices have increased in the United States and not increased in Canada, then people will generally expect that the U.S. dollar exchange rate is to fall. The demand for U.S. dollars decreases, and the supply of U.S. dollars increases. The U.S. dollar exchange rate falls, as expected. If the U.S. dollar falls to $1.00 Canadian and there are no further price changes, purchasing power parity is restored. A Big Mac now costs $4 in either U.S. dollars or Canadian dollars in both New York and Toronto.

If prices increase in Canada and other countries but remain constant in the United States, then people will generally expect that the value of the U.S. dollar on the foreign exchange market is too low and that the U.S. dollar exchange rate will rise. The demand for U.S. dollars increases, and the supply of U.S. dollars decreases. The U.S. dollar exchange rate rises, as expected.

Ultimately, the value of money is determined by prices. So the deeper forces that influence the exchange rate have tentacles that spread throughout the economy. If prices in the United States rise faster than those in other countries, the exchange rate falls. And if prices in the United States rise more slowly than those in other countries, the exchange rate rises.

Purchasing Power Parity

Purchasing power parity (PPP) is a long-run phenomenon. In the short run, deviations from PPP can be large.

The figure shows the range of deviations from PPP in November 2002.

At that time, the Norwegian krone was overvalued by 45 percent and the Japanese yen was overvalued by 22 percent. The yen has been overvalued for most of the past 10 years. An overvalued currency is one that, according to PPP, will depreciate at some point in the future.

The most undervalued currency in November 2002 was the Czech koruna. An undervalued currency is one that, according to PPP, will appreciate at some time in the future. But PPP does not predict *when* a currency will depreciate or appreciate.

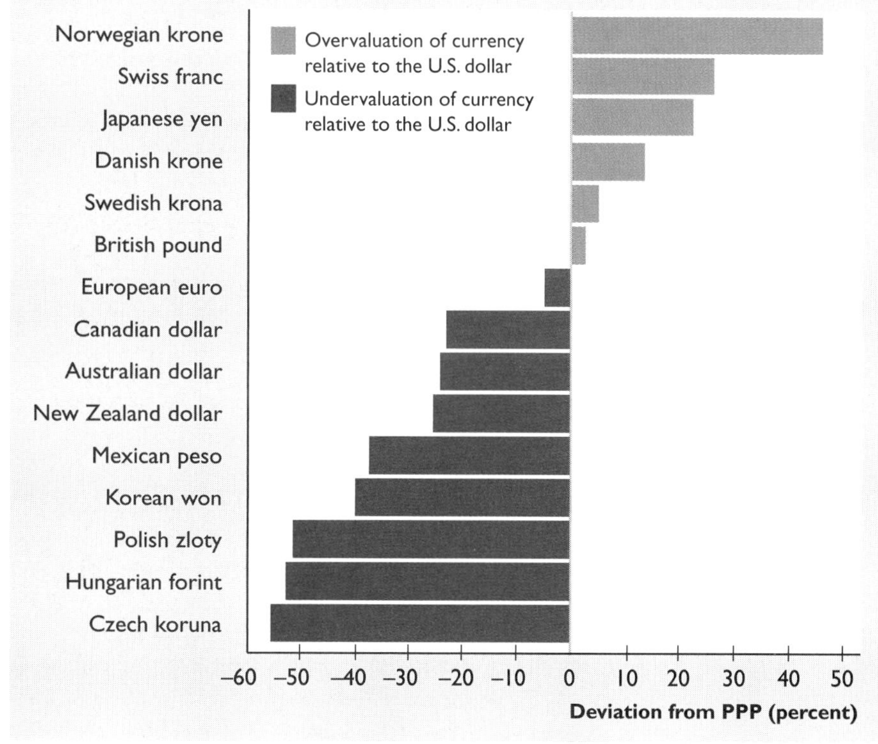

SOURCE: PACIFIC FX Service, University of British Columbia, November 22, 2002.

Interest Rate Parity

Suppose a Canadian dollar deposit in a Toronto bank earns 5 percent a year and a U.S. dollar deposit in a New York bank earns 3 percent a year. Why does anyone deposit money in New York? Why doesn't all the money flow to Toronto? The answer is: because of exchange rate expectations. Suppose people expect the Canadian dollar to depreciate by 2 percent a year. This 2 percent depreciation must be subtracted from the 5 percent interest to obtain the net return of 3 percent a year that an American can earn by depositing funds in a Toronto bank. The two returns are equal. This situation is one of **interest rate parity**—equal interest rates when exchange rate changes are taken into account.

Interest rate parity
Equal interest rates—a situation in which the interest rate in one currency equals the interest rate in another currency when exchange rate changes are taken into account.

Adjusted for risk, interest rate parity always prevails. Funds move to get the highest return available. If for a few seconds a higher return is available in New York than in Toronto, the demand for U.S. dollars increases, the supply of U.S. dollars decreases, and the exchange rate rises until expected interest rates are equal.

The Fed in the Foreign Exchange Market

The Fed's monetary policy influences the U.S. interest rate (see Chapter 13, pp. 319–321). So the Fed's monetary policy influences the exchange rate. When the U.S. interest rate rises relative to those in other countries, the demand for U.S. dollars increases, the supply decreases, and the U.S. dollar exchange rate rises. (Similarly, when the U.S. interest rate falls relative to those in other countries, the demand for U.S. dollars decreases, the supply increases, and the U.S. dollar exchange rate falls.)

But the Fed can intervene directly in the foreign exchange market. It can buy or sell dollars and try to smooth out fluctuations in the exchange rate. Let's look at the foreign exchange interventions the Fed can make.

Suppose the Fed wants the exchange rate to be steady at 100 yen per dollar. If the exchange rate rises above 100 yen, the Fed sells dollars. If the exchange rate falls below 100 yen, the Fed buys dollars. By these actions, the Fed changes the supply of dollars and keeps the exchange rate close to its target rate of 100 yen.

Figure 20.7 shows this Fed intervention in the foreign exchange market. The supply of dollars is S, and initially, the demand for dollars is D_0. The equilibrium exchange rate is 100 yen per dollar. This exchange rate is the Fed's target—the horizontal red line.

When the demand for dollars increases and the demand curve shifts rightward to D_1, the Fed sells \$0.1 trillion. This action increases the supply of dollars by \$0.1 trillion and prevents the exchange rate from rising. When the demand for dollars decreases and the demand curve shifts leftward to D_2, the Fed buys \$0.1 trillion. This action decreases the supply of dollars by \$0.1 trillion and prevents the exchange rate from falling. If the demand for dollars fluctuates between D_1 and D_2, and on the average is D_0, the Fed sometimes buys and sometimes sells but, on the average, it neither buys nor sells.

But suppose the demand for dollars increases permanently from D_0 to D_1. To maintain the exchange rate at 100 yen per dollar indefinitely, the Fed would have to sell dollars every day and buy foreign currency. The Fed would be piling up foreign currency and increasing U.S. official reserves.

Now suppose the demand for dollars decreases permanently from D_0 to D_2. To maintain the exchange rate at 100 yen per dollar indefinitely, the Fed would have to sell U.S. official reserves to buy dollars every day. Eventually, it would run out of reserves and have to abandon its attempt to fix the exchange rate.

Eye on the Global Economy

The Bouncing Euro

The European Central Bank, the ECB, based in Frankfurt, Germany, sometimes intervenes to support the value of its currency, the euro.

Launched in January 1999 at 1 euro equal to 1.16 U.S. dollars, the euro fell to 85 U.S. cents in October 2000. The ECB increased interest rates and intervened in the foreign exchange market, and after fluctuating for a bit more than a year, the euro began to rise in value. At the end of 2002, the euro was close to equality with the U.S. dollar.

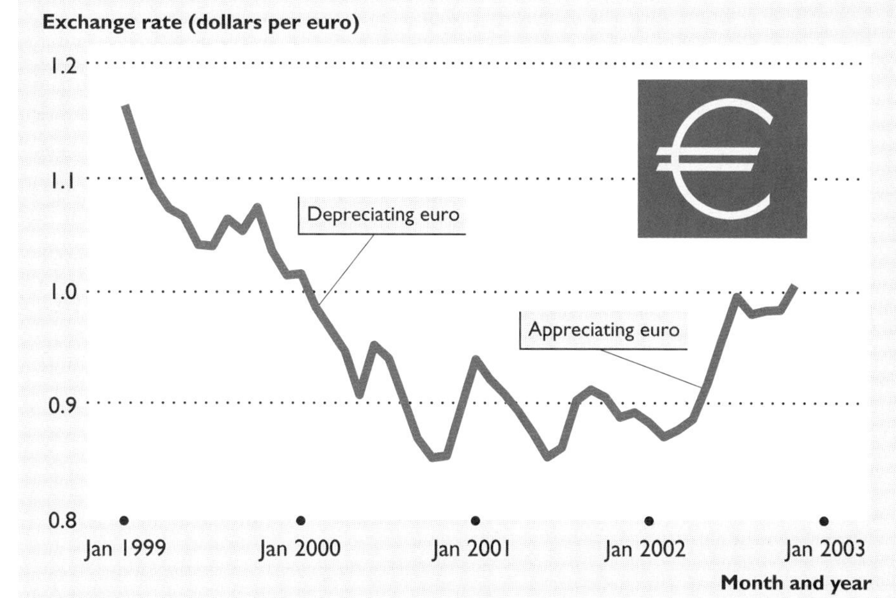

SOURCE: PACIFIC FX Service, University of British Columbia.

FIGURE 20.7

Foreign Exchange Market Intervention

Practice Online

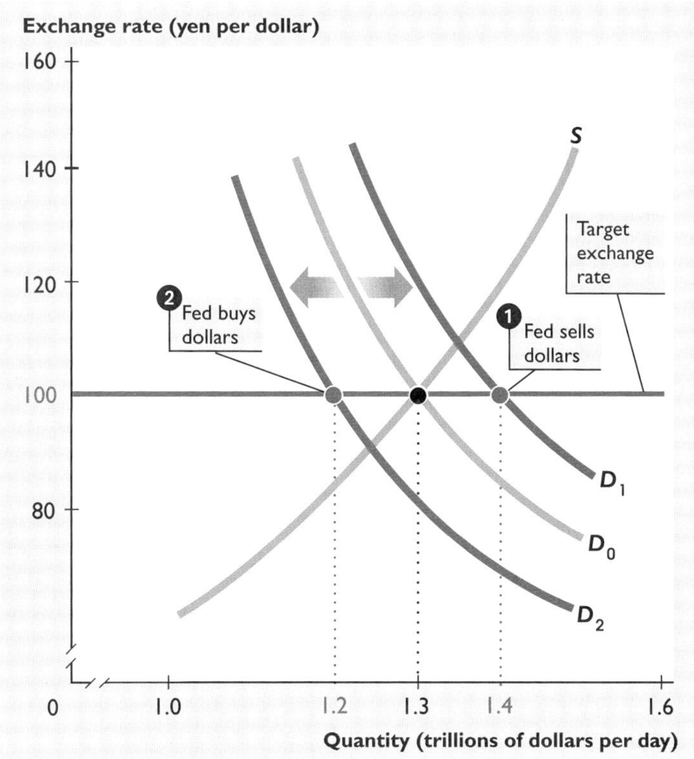

Initially, the demand for dollars is D_0, the supply of dollars is S, and the exchange rate is 100 yen per dollar. The Fed can intervene in the foreign exchange market to keep the exchange rate close to its target rate (100 yen in this example).

1. If demand increases from D_0 to D_1, the Fed sells dollars to increase supply.
2. If demand decreases from D_0 to D_2, the Fed buys dollars to decrease supply.

Persistent intervention on one side of the market cannot be sustained.

CHECKPOINT 20.2

Study Guide pp. 296–299

Practice Online 20.2

2 **Explain how the exchange rate is determined and why it fluctuates.**

Practice Problem 20.2

Suppose that yesterday, the U.S. dollar was trading on the foreign exchange market at 100 yen per dollar. Today, the U.S. dollar is trading at 105 yen per dollar.

a. Which of the two currencies (the dollar or the yen) has appreciated and which has depreciated today?

b. List the events that could have caused today's change in the value of the U.S. dollar on the foreign exchange market.

c. Did the events that you listed in part **b** change the demand for U.S. dollars, the supply of U.S. dollars, or both the demand for and supply of U.S. dollars?

d. If the Fed had tried to stabilize the value of the U.S. dollar at 100 yen per dollar, what action would it have taken?

e. In part **d**, what effect would the Fed's actions have had on U.S. official reserves?

Exercise 20.2

Suppose that yesterday, the Canadian dollar ($C) was trading on the foreign exchange market at $0.75 U.S. per $C. Today, the Canadian dollar is trading at $0.70 U.S. per $C.

a. Which of the two currencies (the Canadian dollar or the U.S. dollar) has appreciated and which has depreciated today?

b. List the events that could have caused today's change in the value of the Canadian dollar on the foreign exchange market.

c. Did the events that you listed in part **b** increase or decrease the demand for Canadian dollars, the supply of Canadian dollars, or both the demand for and supply of Canadian dollars?

d. If the Bank of Canada had tried to stabilize the value of the Canadian dollar at $0.75 U.S., what action would it have taken?

e. In part **d**, what effect would the Bank of Canada's actions have had on Canadian official reserves?

Solution to Practice Problem 20.2

a. Because the U.S. dollar costs a larger number of yen, the U.S. dollar has appreciated. The yen has depreciated because it buys fewer dollars.

b. The main events might be an increase in the U.S. interest rate, a decrease in the Japanese interest rate, or a rise in the expected future exchange rate of the U.S. dollar.

c. The events that you listed in part **b** change both the demand for and supply of dollars. They increase demand and decrease supply.

d. To stabilize the value of the U.S. dollar at 100 yen per dollar, the Fed would have increased the supply of U.S. dollars in the foreign exchange market. The Fed would have sold U.S. dollars.

e. When the Fed sells U.S. dollars, it buys foreign currency. U.S. official reserves would have increased.

CHAPTER CHECKPOINT

Key Points

1 Describe a country's balance of payments accounts and explain what determines the amount of international borrowing and lending.

- Foreign currency is used to finance international trade.
- A country's balance of payments accounts record its international transactions.
- Historically, the United States has been a net lender to the rest of the world, but in 1983, that situation changed and the United States became a net borrower and in 1989 the United States became a debtor nation.
- Net exports are equal to the private sector balance plus the government sector balance.

2 Explain how the exchange rate is determined and why it fluctuates.

- Foreign currency is obtained in exchange for domestic currency in the foreign exchange market.
- The exchange rate is determined by demand and supply in the foreign exchange market.
- The lower the exchange rate, the greater is the quantity of dollars demanded. A change in the exchange rate brings a movement along the demand curve for dollars.
- Changes in the expected future exchange rate and the U.S. interest rate differential change the demand for dollars and shift the demand curve.
- The lower the exchange rate, the smaller is the quantity of dollars supplied. A change in the exchange rate brings a movement along the supply curve of dollars.
- Changes in the expected future exchange rate and the U.S. interest rate differential change the supply of dollars and shift the supply curve.
- Fluctuations in the exchange rate occur because fluctuations in the demand for and supply of dollars are not independent.
- The Fed can intervene in the foreign exchange market to smooth fluctuations in the dollar.

Key Terms

Exercises

1. The following data describes the economy of Antarctica in 2050:

Item	(billions of Antarctica dollars)
Imports of goods and services	150
Exports of goods and services	50
Net interest	−10
Net transfers	35
Foreign investment in Antarctica	125
Antarctica's investment abroad	55

   a. Calculate Antarctica's current account balance.
   b. Calculate Antarctica's capital account balance.
   c. Calculate the increase in Antarctica's official reserves.

2. In Antarctica in exercise 1,
   a. Is Antarctica a debtor nation or a creditor nation?
   b. Are Antarctica's international assets increasing or decreasing?
   c. Can you determine whether Antarctica is borrowing to finance investment or consumption? Why or why not?

3. The U.S. dollar appreciates, and the nation's official holdings of foreign currency increase. State which of the following events could have caused these changes to occur and why.
   a. The Fed intervened in the foreign exchange market and sold dollars.
   b. The Fed conducted an open market operation and sold bonds.
   c. People began to expect the dollar to appreciate.
   d. The U.S. interest rate differential narrowed.
   e. The U.S. current account went into deficit.

4. The U.S. dollar depreciates. State which of the following events could have caused the depreciation and why.
   a. The Fed intervened in the foreign exchange market and sold dollars.
   b. The Fed intervened in the foreign exchange market and bought dollars.
   c. People began to expect the dollar to depreciate.
   d. The U.S. interest rate differential increased.
   e. Foreign investment in the United States increased.

5. The euro appreciates. State which of the following events could have caused the appreciation and why.
   a. The ECB intervened in the foreign exchange market and sold euros.
   b. The Fed intervened in the foreign exchange market and bought dollars.
   c. People began to expect the euro to depreciate.
   d. The EU interest rate differential increased.
   e. The EU interest rate differential decreased.
   f. Profits increased in Europe, and foreign investment in European companies surged.

6. If Japan has a lower inflation rate than the United States and the difference in inflation rates persists for some years, will
   a. The dollar appreciate or depreciate against the yen?

b. The yen appreciate or depreciate against the dollar?
c. Purchasing power parity be violated? Why or why not?
d. Interest rate parity hold? Why or why not?
e. U.S. interest rates be higher or lower than Japanese interest rates? Why or why not?
f. The inflation difference influence the expected future exchange rate? Why or why not?
g. The inflation difference influence the U.S. current account balance? Why or why not?

7. Suppose that the euro keeps rising and hits $2 U.S. At this point, the Fed decides to stop the euro from rising (stop the dollar from falling) by intervening in the foreign exchange market.
   a. What actions might the Fed take in the foreign exchange market?
   b. Could the Fed take the actions you described in part **a** forever if necessary?
   c. Would the Fed's actions prevent interest rate parity from being achieved? Why or why not?
   d. Are there any other actions that the Fed could take to raise the foreign exchange value of the dollar? Explain your answer.

Critical Thinking

8. Many people think that a current account deficit is a sign that a nation is not able to compete in international markets. Explain why this view is incorrect and describe the factors that create a current account deficit.

9. For most of the 1990s, Argentina pegged the value of its currency, the peso, to the U.S. dollar. 1 peso equaled 1 U.S. dollar. Then, at the end of 2001, the peso was allowed to find its own value on the foreign exchange market and it fell dramatically.
   a. Why might it be difficult for Argentina to peg the value of its currency to the U.S. dollar?
   b. Why, nonetheless, might it be a good idea for Argentina to peg the value of its currency to the U.S. dollar? What are the potential benefits to Argentina?
   c. On balance, do you think a country like Argentina should peg its currency to the U.S. dollar?

10. With Europe having replaced its national currencies (such as the French franc, German mark, and Italian lira) with a new single currency, the euro, some people say that North America should do the same. The suggestion is that the Mexican peso and Canadian dollar should be scrapped and that the entire NAFTA area should use the U.S. dollar for all domestic and international transactions.
    a. What are some of the differences between the European and North American situations that might mean that the European solution would not work in North America?
    b. What are some of the similarities between the European and North American situations that might mean that the European solution *would* work in North America?

Practice Online

Web Exercises

Use the links on your Foundations Web site to work the following exercises.

11. Visit the FRED, the Federal Reserve Economic Database, and find data on the exchange rate and international trade.
    - **a.** When did the United States last have a current account surplus?
    - **b.** Does the United States have a surplus or a deficit in trade in goods?
    - **c.** Does the United States have a surplus or a deficit in trade in services?
    - **d.** What has happened to foreign investment in the United States during the past 10 years?
    - **e.** Do you think the U.S. balance of payments record is a matter for concern? Why or why not?
12. Visit the PACIFIC Exchange Rate Service and obtain data on the exchange rate of the U.S. dollar against two other currencies.
    - **a.** Use the demand and supply model to explain the changes (or absence of changes) in the exchange rates.
    - **b.** What specific events might have changed exchange rate expectations?
    - **c.** What forces might have prevented the exchange rate from changing?
    - **d.** What information would you need to determine whether the central bank intervened in the foreign exchange market to limit the change in the exchange rate?

Glossary

Above full-employment equilibrium When equilibrium real GDP exceeds potential GDP. (p. 187)

Absolute advantage When one person is more productive than another person in several or even all activities. (p. 72)

Aggregate demand The relationship between the quantity of real GDP demanded and the price level when all other influences on expenditure plans remain the same. (p. 185)

Aggregate hours The total number of hours worked by all the people employed, both full time and part time, during a year. (p. 139)

Aggregate planned expenditure Planned consumption expenditure plus planned investment plus planned government purchases plus planned exports minus planned imports. (p. 371)

Aggregate supply The relationship between the quantity of real GDP supplied and the price level when all other influences on production plans remain the same. (p. 183)

Automatic fiscal policy A fiscal policy action that is triggered by the state of the economy such as an increase in payments to the unemployed and a decrease in tax receipts triggered by recession. (p. 400)

Automatic stabilizers Features of fiscal policy that stabilize real GDP without explicit action by the government. (p. 408)

Autonomous expenditure The components of aggregate expenditure that do not change when real GDP changes. (p. 372)

Balance of payments accounts The accounts in which a nation records its international trading, borrowing, and lending. (p. 504)

Balance of trade The value of exports minus the value of imports. (p. 477)

Balance sheet A statement that summarizes assets (amounts owned) and liabilities (amounts owed). (p. 290)

Balanced budget The budget balance when tax receipts equal expenditures. (p. 398)

Balanced budget multiplier The magnification effect on aggregate demand of a *simultaneous* change in government purchases and taxes that leaves the budget balanced unchanged. (p. 401)

Barter The direct exchange of goods and services for other goods and services, which requires a double coincidence of wants. (p. 265)

Beige Book A report that summarizes current economic conditions in each Federal Reserve district and each sector of the economy. (p. 410)

Below full-employment equilibrium When potential GDP exceeds equilibrium real GDP. (p. 187)

Benefit The benefit of something is the gain or pleasure that it brings. (p. 13)

Bond A promise to pay specified sums of money on specified dates; it is a debt for the issuer. (p. 213)

Bond market A financial market in which bonds issued by firms and governments are traded. (p. 213)

Budget deficit The budget balance when expenditures exceed tax receipts. (p. 398)

Budget surplus The budget balance when tax receipts exceed expenditures. (p. 398)

Business cycle A periodic but irregular up-and-down movement in production and jobs. (p. 5)

Capital Tools, instruments, machines, buildings, and other constructions that have been produced in the past and that businesses now use to produce goods and services. (p. 38)

Capital account Record of foreign investment in the United States minus U.S. investment abroad. (p. 504)

Central bank A public authority that provides banking services to banks and regulates financial institutions and markets. (p. 279)

Ceteris paribus Other things remaining the same (often abbreviated as *cet. par.*). (p. 10)

Change in demand A change in the quantity that people plan to buy when any influence on buying plans other than the price of the good changes. (p. 85)

Change in supply A change in the quantity that suppliers plan to sell when any influence on selling plans other than the price of the good changes. (p. 90)

Change in the quantity demanded A change in the

quantity of a good that people plan to buy that results from a change in the price of the good. (p. 85)

Change in the quantity supplied A change in the quantity of a good that suppliers plan to sell that results from a change in the price of the good. (p. 90)

Circular flow model A model of the economy that shows the circular flow of expenditures and incomes that result from decision makers' choices and the way those choices interact to determine what, how, and for whom goods and services are produced. (p. 42)

Classical dichotomy When the economy is operating at full employment, the forces that determine the real variables are independent of those that determine the nominal variables. (p. 182)

Classical growth theory The theory that the clash between an exploding population and limited resources will eventually bring economic growth to an end. (p. 245)

Commercial bank A firm that is chartered by the Comptroller of the Currency in the U.S. Treasury (or by a state agency) to accept deposits and make loans. (p. 272)

Comparative advantage The ability of a person to perform an activity or produce a good or service at a lower opportunity cost than someone else. (p. 70)

Complement A good that is consumed with another good. (p. 85)

Complement in production A good that is produced along with another good. (p. 90)

Consumer Price Index A measure of the average of the prices paid by urban consumers for a fixed market basket of consumer goods and services. (p. 160)

Consumption expenditure The expenditure by households on consumption goods and services. (p. 113)

Consumption function The relationship between consumption expenditure and disposable income, other things remaining the same. (p. 372)

Consumption goods and services Goods and services that are bought by individuals and used to provide personal enjoyment and contribute to a person's standard of living. (p. 36)

Correlation The tendency for the values of two variables to move in a predictable and related way. (p. 11)

Cost of living The number of dollars it takes to buy the goods and services that achieve a given standard of living. (p. 5)

Cost of living index A measure of changes in the amount of money that people would need to spend to achieve a given standard of living. (p. 166)

Credit union A financial institution owned by a social or economic group such as a firm's employees, that accepts savings deposits and makes mostly consumer loans. (p. 274)

Creditor nation A country that during its entire history has invested more in the rest of the world than other countries have invested in it. (p. 506)

Cross-section graph A graph that shows the values of an economic variable for different groups in a population at a point in time. (p. 26)

Crowding-out effect The tendency for a government budget deficit to decrease investment. (p. 227)

Currency Notes (dollar bills) and coins. (p. 266)

Currency appreciation The rise in the value of one currency in terms of another currency. (p. 512)

Currency depreciation The fall in the value of one currency in terms of another currency. (p. 511)

Currency drain An increase in currency held outside the banks. (p. 304)

Current account Record of international receipts and payments—current account balance equals exports minus imports, plus net interest and transfers received from abroad. (p. 504)

Cyclical unemployment The fluctuating unemployment over the business cycle that increases during a recession and decreases during an expansion. (p. 150)

Debtor nation A country that during its entire history h as borrowed more from the rest of the world than it has lent to it. (p. 506)

Deflation A situation in which the cost of living is falling and the value of money is rising. (p. 5)

Deflationary gap A gap that exists when potential GDP exceeds real GDP and that brings a falling price level. (p. 362)

Demand The relationship between the quantity demanded and the price of a good when all other influences on buying plans remain the same. (p. 83)

Demand curve A graph of the relationship between the quantity demanded of a good and its price when all the other influences on buying plans remain the same. (p. 84)

Demand for labor The relationship between the quantity of labor demanded and real wage rate when all other influences on firms' hiring plans remain the same. (p. 191)

Demand for money The relationship between the quantity of money demanded and the nominal interest rate, when all other influences on the amount of money that people wish to hold remain the same. (p. 316)

Demand schedule A list of the quantities demanded at each different price when all the other influences on buying plans remain the same. (p. 84)

Deposit multiplier The number by which an increase in bank reserves is multiplied to find the resulting increase in bank deposits. (p. 298)

Depreciation The decrease in the value of capital that results from its use and from obsolescence—also called capital consumption. (p. 120)

Diminishing returns The tendency for each additional hour of labor employed to produce a successively smaller additional amount of real GDP. (p. 190)

Direct relationship A relationship between two variables that move in the same direction. (p. 28)

Discount rate The interest rate at which the Fed stands ready to lend reserves to commercial banks. (p. 282)

Discouraged worker A person who is available and willing to work but has not made specific efforts to find a job within the previous four weeks. (p. 138)

Discretionary fiscal policy A fiscal policy action that is initiated by an act of Congress. (p. 400)

Discretionary monetary policy Monetary policy that is based on the judgments of policy makers about the current needs of the economy. (p. 454)

Disposable income Income earned minus net taxes. (p. 218)

Dumping When a foreign firm sells its exports at a lower price than its cost of production. (p. 492)

Dynamic comparative advantage A comparative advantage that a person (or country) obtains by specializing in an activity, resulting from learning-by-doing. (p. 484)

Economic freedom A condition in which people are able to make personal choices, their private property is protected, and they are free to buy and sell in markets. (p. 255)

Economic growth The sustained expansion of production possibilities. (p. 74)

Economic growth rate The annual percentage change of real GDP. (p. 234)

Economic model A description of some aspect of the economic world that includes only those features of the world that are needed for the purpose at hand. (p. 9)

Economic theory A generalization that summarizes what we understand about the economic choices that people make and the economic performance of industries and nations based on models that have repeatedly passed the test of corresponding well with real-world data. (p. 9)

Economics The social science that studies the choices that we make as we cope with *scarcity* and the *incentives* that influence and reconcile our choices. (p. 3)

Efficiency wage A real wage rate that is set above the full-employment equilibrium wage rate to induce greater work effort. (p. 201)

Electronic cash (or **e-cash**) An electronic equivalent of paper notes and coins. (p. 268)

Electronic check (or **e-check**) An electronic equivalent of a paper check. (p. 268)

Entrepreneurship The human resource that organizes labor, land, and capital. (p. 39)

Equation of exchange An equation that states that the quantity of money multiplied by the velocity of circulation equals the price level multiplied by real GDP. (p. 327)

Equilibrium expenditure The level of aggregate expenditure that occurs when aggregate planned expenditure equals real GDP. (p. 380)

Equilibrium price The price at which the quantity demanded equals the quantity supplied. (p. 93)

Equilibrium quantity The quantity bought and sold at the equilibrium price. (p. 93)

Excess demand A situation in which the quantity demanded exceeds the quantity supplied. (p. 94)

Excess reserves Bank reserves that exceed those needed to meet the required reserve ratio. (p. 273)

Excess supply A situation in which the quantity supplied exceeds the quantity demanded. (p. 94)

Expected inflation rate The inflation rate that people forecast and use to set the money wage rate and other money prices. (p. 432)

Export goods and services Goods and services produced in one country and sold in other countries. (p. 36)

Exports of goods and services Items that firms in the United States produce and sell to the rest of the world. (p. 114)

Factor markets Markets in which factors of production are bought and sold. (p. 42)

Factors of production The productive resources used to produce goods and services—land, labor, capital, and entrepreneurship. (p. 37)

Federal budget An annual statement of the expenditures, tax receipts, and surplus or deficit of the government of the United States. (p. 398)

Federal funds rate The interest rate on interbank loans (loans made in the federal funds market). (p. 273)

Federal Open Market Committee The Fed's main policy-making committee. (p. 280)

Federal Reserve System The central bank of the United States. (p. 279)

Feedback-rule policy A policy that specifies how policy actions respond to changes in the state of the economy. (p. 454)

Fiat money Objects that are money because the law decrees or orders them to be money. (p. 266)

Final good or service A good or service that is produced for its final user and not as a component of another good or service. (p. 112)

Financial capital The funds that firms use to buy and operate physical capital. (p. 210)

Financial markets The collection of households, firms, governments, banks, and other financial institutions that lend and borrow. (p. 212)

Firms The institutions that organize the production of goods and services. (p. 42)

Fiscal policy The use of the federal budget to smooth the business cycle and encourage economic growth. (p. 398)

Fixed-rule policy A policy that is pursued independently of the state of the economy. (p. 454)

Foreign exchange market The market in which the currency of one country is exchanged for the currency of another. (p. 511)

Foreign exchange rate The price at which one currency exchanges for another. (p. 511)

Frictional unemployment The unemployment that arises from normal labor turnover—from people entering and leaving the labor force and from the ongoing creation and destruction of jobs. (p. 149)

Full employment When there is no cyclical unemployment or, equivalently, when all the unemployment is frictional, structural, and seasonal. (p. 152)

Full-employment equilibrium When equilibrium real GDP equals potential GDP. (p. 187)

Full-time workers People who usually work 35 hours or more a week. (p. 138)

Functional distribution of income The distribution of income among the factors of production. (p. 39)

GDP deflator An average of current prices expressed as a percentage of base-year prices. (p. 125)

Goods and services The objects that people value and produce to satisfy human wants. Goods are physical objects, and services are tasks performed for people. (p. 4)

Goods markets Markets in which goods and services are bought and sold. (p. 42)

Government goods and services Goods and services that are bought by governments. (p. 36)

Government purchases multiplier The magnification effect of a change in government purchases of goods and services on aggregate demand. (p. 401)

Government purchases of goods and services The purchases by all levels of government of goods and services. (p. 114)

Government sector balance Net taxes minus government purchases of goods and services. (p. 508)

Great Depression A period during the 1930s in which the economy experienced its worst-ever recession. (p. 6)

Gross domestic product (GDP) The market value of all the final goods and services produced within a country in a given time period. (p. 112)

Gross investment The total amount spent on new capital goods. (p. 210)

Households Individuals or groups of people living together. (p. 42)

Human capital The knowledge and skill that people obtain from education, on-the-job training, and work experience. (p. 38)

Hyperinflation Inflation at a rate that exceeds 50 percent a month. (p. 331)

Imports of goods and services Items that households, firms, and governments in the United States buy from the rest of the world. (p. 114)

Incentive A reward or a penalty—a "carrot" or a "stick"—that encourages or discourages an action. (p. 2)

Induced expenditure The components of aggregate expenditure that change when real GDP changes. (p. 372)

Induced taxes Taxes that vary with real GDP. (p. 408)

Infant-industry argument The argument that it is necessary to protect a new industry to enable it to grow into a mature industry that can compete in world markets. (p. 491)

Inferior good A good for which demand decreases when income increases. (p. 85)

Inflation A situation in which the cost of living is rising and the value of money is shrinking. (p. 5)

Inflation rate The percentage change in the price level from one year to the next. (p. 163)

Inflationary gap A gap that exists when real GDP exceeds potential GDP and that brings a rising price level. (p. 362)

Interest Income paid for the use of capital. (p. 39)

Interest rate parity Equal interest rates—a situation in which the interest rate in one currency equals the interest rate in another currency when exchange rate changes are taken into account. (p. 522)

Intermediate good or service A good or service that is produced by one firm, bought by another firm, and used as a component of a final good or service. (p. 112)

Inverse relationship A relationship between two variables that move in opposite directions. (p. 29)

Investment The purchase of new *capital goods* (tools, instruments, machines, buildings, and other constructions) and additions to inventories. (p. 113)

Investment demand The relationship between the quantity of investment demanded and the real interest rate, other things remaining the same. (p. 215)

Investment goods Goods that are bought by businesses to increase their productive resources. (p. 36)

Involuntary part-time workers People who work 1 to 34 hours a week but who are looking for full-time work. (p. 138)

Job rationing A situation that arises when the real wage rate is above the equilibrium level. (p. 200)

Job search The activity of looking for an acceptable vacant job. (p. 199)

Keynesian activist An economist who believes that fluctuations in investment are the main source of economic fluctuations, and who advocates interest rate cuts when real GDP falls below potential GDP and interest rate hikes when real GDP exceeds potential GDP. (p. 457)

Labor The work time and work effort that people devote to producing goods and services. (p. 37)

Labor force The number of people employed plus the number unemployed. (p. 136)

Labor force participation rate The percentage of the working-age population who are members of the labor force. (p. 138)

Labor productivity The quantity of real GDP produced by one hour of labor. (p. 238)

Land The "gifts of nature," or natural resources, that we use to produce goods and services. (p. 37)

Law of demand Other things remaining the same, if the price of a good rises, the quantity demanded of that good decreases; and if the price of a good falls, the quantity demanded of that good increases. (p. 83)

Law of market forces When there is a shortage, the price rises; when there is a surplus, the price falls. (p. 94)

Law of supply Other things remaining the same, if the price of a good rises, the quantity supplied of that good increases; and if the price of a good falls, the quantity supplied that good decreases. (p. 88)

Learning-by-doing Repeatedly performing the same task and becoming more productive at producing a particular good or service. (p. 484)

Linear relationship A relationship that graphs as a straight line. (p. 28)

Liquid asset An asset that can be easily, and with certainty, converted into money. (p. 276)

Liquidity trap An interest rate at which people are willing to hold any quantity of money. (p. 451)

Long-run Phillips curve The vertical line that shows the relationship between inflation and unemployment when the economy is at full employment. (p. 430)

Loss Income earned by an entrepreneur for running a business when that income is negative. (p. 39)

M1 Currency held outside banks and traveler's checks plus checkable deposits owned by individuals and businesses. (p. 269)

M2 M1 plus savings deposits and small time deposits, money market funds, and other deposits. (p. 269)

Macroeconomic equilibrium When the quantity of real GDP demanded equals the quantity of real GDP supplied at the point of intersection of the *AD* curve and the *AS* curve. (p. 186)

Macroeconomics The study of the aggregate (or total) effects on the national economy and the global economy of the choices that individuals, businesses, and governments make. (p. 3)

Malthusian theory Another name for classical growth theory—named for Thomas Robert Malthus. (p. 245)

Margin A choice on the margin is a choice that is made by comparing *all* the relevant alternatives systematically and incrementally. (p. 14)

Marginal benefit The benefit that arises from a one-unit increase in an activity. The marginal benefit of something is measured by what you *are willing to* give up to get one more unit of it. (p. 14)

Marginal cost The cost that arises from a one-unit increase in an activity. The marginal cost of something is what you *must* give up to get one more unit of it. (p. 14)

Marginal propensity to consume The fraction of a change in disposable income that is spent on consumption—the change in consumption expenditure divided by the change in disposable income that brought it about. (p. 374)

Marginal propensity to import The fraction of an increase in real GDP that is spent on imports—the change in imports divided by the change in real GDP. (p. 376)

Marginal tax rate The fraction of a change in real GDP that is paid in income taxes—the change in tax payments divided by the change in real GDP. (p. 387)

Market Any arrangement that brings buyers and sellers together and enables them to get information and do business with each other. (p. 42)

Market equilibrium When the quantity demanded equals the quantity supplied—when buyers' and sellers' plans are consistent. (p. 93)

Means of payment A method of settling a debt. (p. 264)

Medium of exchange An object that is generally accepted in return for goods and services. (p. 265)

Microeconomics The study of the choices that individuals and businesses make and the way these choices respond to incentives, interact, and are influenced by governments. (p. 3)

Minimum wage law A government regulation that makes hiring labor for less than a specified wage illegal—an example of a price floor. (p. 103)

Monetarist An economist who believes that fluctuations in the quantity of money are the main source of economic fluctuations, and who advocates that the quantity of money grow at a constant rate. (p. 456)

Monetary base The sum of coins, Federal Reserve notes, and banks' reserves at the Fed. (p. 282)

Monetary policy Adjusting the quantity of money in the economy. (p. 279)

Monetary system The Federal Reserve and the banks and other institutions that accept deposits and provide the services that enable people and businesses to make and receive payments. (p. 272)

Money Any commodity or token that is generally accepted as a means of payment. (p. 264)

Money market fund A financial institution that obtains funds by selling shares and uses these funds to buy assets such as U.S. Treasury bills. (p. 274)

Money multiplier The number by which a change in the monetary base is multiplied to find the resulting change in the quantity of money. (p. 306)

Multiplier The amount by which a change in any component of autonomous expenditure is magnified or multiplied to determine the change that it generates in equilibrium expenditure and real GDP. (p. 384)

National debt The total amount that the federal government has borrowed to make expenditures that exceed tax revenue—to run a government budget deficit. (p. 46)

Natural rate hypothesis The proposition that when the money growth rate changes, the unemployment rate changes temporarily and eventually returns to the natural unemployment rate. (p. 433)

Natural unemployment rate The unemployment rate at full employment. (p. 152)

Needs-tested spending Spending on programs that entitle suitably qualified people and businesses to receive benefits—benefits that vary with need and with the state of the economy. (p. 408)

Negative relationship A relationship between two variables that move in opposite directions. (p. 29)

Neoclassical growth theory The theory that real GDP per person will increase as long as technology keeps advancing. (p. 247)

Net borrower A country that is borrowing more from the rest of the world than it is lending to the rest of the world. (p. 506)

Net domestic product at factor cost The sum of the five components of incomes—compensation of employees, net interest, rental income of persons, corporate profits, and proprietors' income. (p. 120)

Net exports of goods and services The value of exports of goods and services minus the value of imports of goods and services. (p. 114)

Net investment The change in the quantity of capital—equals gross investment minus depreciation. (p. 210)

Net lender A country that is lending more to the rest of the world than it is borrowing from the rest of the world. (p. 506)

New growth theory The theory that our unlimited productivity will lead us to ever greater productivity and perpetual economic growth. (p. 249)

Nominal GDP The value of the final goods and services produced in a given year valued at the prices that prevailed in that same year. (p. 123)

Nominal interest rate The percentage return on a loan expressed in dollars. (p. 175)

Nominal wage rate The average hourly wage rate measured in *current* dollars. (p. 172)

Normal good A good for which demand increases when income increases. (p. 85)

Nontariff barrier Any action other than a tariff that restricts international trade. (p. 486)

Official settlements account Record of the change in U.S. official reserves. (p. 504)

Okun's Law For each percentage point that the unemployment rate is above the natural unemployment rate, there is a 2 percent gap between real GDP and potential GDP. (p. 425)

One third rule The observation that on the average, with no change in human capital and technology, a *one percent* increase in capital per hour of labor brings a *one third percent* increase in labor productivity. (p. 243)

Open market operation The purchase or sale of government securities—U.S. Treasury bills and bonds—by the Federal Reserve in the open market. (p. 282)

Opportunity cost The opportunity cost of something is the best thing you *must* give up to get it. (p. 13)

Part-time workers People who usually work less than 35 hours a week. (p. 138)

Personal distribution of income The distribution of income among households. (p. 40)

Physical capital The tools, instruments, machines, buildings, and other constructions that have been produced in the past and that are used to produce goods and services. (p. 210)

Positive relationship A relationship between two variables that move in the same direction. (p. 28)

***Post hoc* fallacy** The error of reasoning that a first event *causes* a second event because the first occurred *before* the second. (p. 11)

Potential GDP The level of real GDP that the economy would produce if it were at full employment. (pp. 152, 183)

Price ceiling The highest price at which it is legal to trade a particular good, service, or factor of production. (p. 101)

Price floor The lowest price at which it is legal to trade a particular good, service, or factor of production. (p. 103)

Private sector balance Saving minus investment. (p. 508)

Production function A relationship that shows the maximum quantity of real GDP that can be produced as the quantity of labor employed changes and all other influences on production remain the same. (p. 190)

Production possibilities frontier The boundary between the combinations of goods and services that can be produced and the combinations that cannot be produced, given the available factors of production and the state of technology. (p. 60)

Productivity Total production per person employed. (p. 15)

Productivity curve The relationship between real GDP per hour of labor and the quantity of capital per hour of labor with a given state of technology. (p. 241)

Profit Income earned by an entrepreneur for running a business. (p. 39)

Property rights The social arrangements that govern the protection of private property. (p. 255)

Purchasing power parity Equal value of money—a situation in which money buys the same amount of goods and service sin different currencies. (p. 520)

Quantity demanded The amount of any good, service, or resource that people are willing and able to buy during a specified period at a specified price. (p. 83)

Quantity of labor demanded The total labor hours that all the firms in the economy plan to hire during a given time period at a given real wage rate. (p. 191)

Quantity of labor supplied The number of labor hours that all the households in the economy plan to work during a given time period and at a given real wage rate. (p. 193)

Quantity of money demanded The amount of money that households and firms choose to hold. (p. 315)

Quantity supplied The amount of any good, service, or resource that people are willing and able to sell during a specified period at a specified price. (p. 88)

Quantity theory of money The proposition that when real GDP equals potential GDP, an increase in the quantity of money brings an equal percentage increase in the price level. (p. 327)

Quota A specified maximum amount of a good that may be imported in a given period of time. (p. 488)

Rational choice A choice that uses the available resources to most effectively satisfy the wants of the person making the choice. (p. 13)

Rational expectation The inflation forecast resulting from use of all the relevant data and economic science. (p. 439)

Real GDP The value of the final goods and services produced in a given year when valued at constant prices. (p. 123)

Real GDP per person Real GDP divided by the population. (p. 234)

Real interest rate The percentage return on a loan expressed in purchasing power—the nominal interest rate adjusted for the effects of inflation. (p. 175)

Real wage rate The average hourly wage rate measured in the dollars of a given reference base year. (p. 172)

Recession A decrease in real GDP that lasts for at least two quarters (six months) or a period of significant decline in total output, income, employment, and trade, usually lasting from six months to a year, and marked by widespread contractions in many sectors of the economy. (p. 342)

Reference base period A period for which the CPI is defined to equal 100. Currently, the reference base period is 1982–1984. (p. 160)

Rent Income paid for the use of land. (p. 39)

Rent ceiling A law that makes it illegal for landlords to charge a rent that exceeds a set limit—an example of a price ceiling. (p. 101)

Rent seeking Lobbying and other political activity that seeks to capture the gains from trade. (p. 496)

Required reserve ratio The minimum percentage of deposits that banks and other financial institutions must hold in reserves. (p. 273)

Reserves The currency in the bank's vaults plus the balance on its reserve account at a Federal Reserve Bank. (p. 273)

Rule of 70 The number of years it takes for the level of any variable to double is approximately 70 divided by the annual percentage growth rate of the variable. (p. 235)

Saving The amount of income that is not paid in taxes or spent on consumption goods and services—adds to wealth. (p. 212)

Savings and loan association A financial institution that accepts checkable deposits and savings deposits and that makes personal, commercial, and home-purchase loans. (p. 274)

Savings bank A financial institution that accepts savings deposits and makes mostly consumer and home-purchase loans. (p. 274)

Saving supply The relationship between the quantity of saving supplied and the real interest rate, other things remaining the same. (p. 218)

Scarcity The condition that arises because the available resources are insufficient to satisfy wants. (p. 2)

Scatter diagram A graph of the value of one variable against the value of another variable. (p. 26)

Seasonal unemployment The unemployment that arises because of seasonal weather patterns. (p. 150)

Shortage A situation in which the quantity demanded exceeds the quantity supplied. (p. 94)

Short-run Phillips curve A curve that shows the relationship between the inflation rate and the unemployment rate when the natural unemployment rate and the expected inflation rate remain constant. (p. 424)

Slope The change in the value of the variable measured on the y-axis divided by the change in the value of the variable measured on the x-axis. (p. 31)

Stagflation A combination of recession (falling real GDP) and inflation (rising price level). (p. 360)

Standard of living The level of consumption of goods and services that people enjoy, on the average; it is measured by average income per person. (p. 4)

Stock A certificate of ownership and claim to the profits that a firm makes. (p. 212)

Stock market A financial market in which shares of companies' stocks are traded. (p. 213)

Store of value Any commodity or token that can be held and exchanged later for goods and services. (p. 265)

Structural unemployment The unemployment that arises when changes in technology or international competition change the skills needed to perform jobs or change the locations of jobs. (p. 150)

Substitute A good that can be consumed in place of another good. (p. 85)

Substitute in production A good that can be produced in place of another good. (p. 90)

Supply The relationship between the quantity supplied and the price of a good when all other influences on selling plans remain the same. (p. 88)

Supply curve A graph of the relationship between the quantity supplied of a good and its price when all the other influences on selling plans remain the same. (p. 89)

Supply of labor The relationship between the quantity of labor supplied and the real wage rate when all other influences on work plans remain the same. (p. 193)

Supply of money The relationship between the quantity of money supplied and the nominal interest rate. (p. 319)

Supply schedule A list of the quantities supplied at each different price when all the other influences on selling plans remain the same. (p. 89)

Surplus A situation in which the quantity supplied exceeds the quantity demanded. (p. 94)

Tariff A tax on a good that is imposed by the importing country when an imported good crosses its international boundary. (p. 486)

Tax multiplier The magnification effect of a change in taxes on aggregate demand. (p. 401)

Time-series graph A graph that measures time on the x-axis and the variable or variables in which we are interested on the y-axis. (p. 26)

Tradeoff A constraint or limit to what is possible that forces an exchange or a substitution of one thing for something else. (p. 63)

Trend A general tendency for the value of a variable to rise or fall. (p. 26)

U.S. interest rate differential The U.S. interest rate minus the foreign interest rate. (p. 514)

Unemployment The state of being available and willing to work but unable to find an acceptable job. (p. 4)

Unemployment rate The percentage of the people in the labor force who are unemployed. (p. 137)

Union wage A wage rate that results from collective bargaining between a labor union and a firm. (p. 201)

Unit of account An agreed-upon measure for stating the prices of goods and services. (p. 265)

U.S. official reserves The government's holdings of foreign currency. (p. 504)

Value added The value of a firm's production minus the value of the intermediate goods it buys from other firms. (p. 121)

Velocity of circulation The number of times in a year that the average dollar of money gets used to buy final goods and services. (p. 327)

Wages Income paid for the services of labor. (p. 39)

Wealth The value of all the things that a person owns (p. 212)

Working-age population The total number of people aged 16 years and over who are not in jail, hospital, or some other form of institutional care. (p. 136)

Index

Key terms and pages where they are defined appear in **boldface**.

Credits

(continuation from page iv)

Cover Image © 2003 D. Wiggett/First Light/Panoramic Images.

Chapter 1: p. 3 left and right: Scott Foresman/Addison Wesley Longman, Focus on Sports; p. 4 left: © CORBIS; p. 4 right: Digital Image © 2001/PhotoDisc, Inc.; p. 6 left: AP/Wide World Photos; p. 6 right: © Bettmann/CORBIS; p. 9: National Museum of Photography, Film, & Television/ Science & Society Picture Library; p. 10: Bettmann/CORBIS; p. 14 left: Digital Image © 2001/ PhotoDisc, Inc.; p. 14 right: Copyright © David Young-Wolff/PhotoEdit; p. 16 left: © Charles E. Rotkin/CORBIS; p. 16 right: Digital Image © 2001/PhotoDisc, Inc.

Chapter 3: p. 76: Steve Vidler/SuperStock.

Chapter 4: p. 82 left: Roderick Chen/SuperStock; p. 82 center: AP/Wide World Photos; p. 82 right: © Steven Rubin/The Image Works; p. 97 top: Digital Image © 2001/PhotoDisc, Inc.; p. 97 bottom: photo courtesy of Washington State University.

Chapter 5: p. 118: © Reuters NewMedia Inc./CORBIS.

Chaper 6: p. 139: Courtesy of U.S. Census Bureau; p. 142: © CORBIS; p. 149: Copyright © David Young-Wolff/PhotoEdit; p. 150: © Jim Sugar Photography/ CORBIS.

Chapter 8: p. 203: Digital Image © 2001/PhotoDisc, Inc.

Chapter 10: p. 240 top: © Minnesota Historical Society/CORBIS; p. 240 bottom: © Bob Rowan, Progressive Image/CORBIS.

Chapter 11: p. 281: Copyright © John Neubauer/PhotoEdit.

Chapter 12: p. 291: Scala/Art Resource, NY.

Chapter 13: p. 331: © Bettmann/CORBIS.

Chapter 14: p. 263: Photo courtesy of Stanford University.

Chapter 15: p. 382 top: Private Collection/Roger Viollet, Paris/Bridgeman Art Library; p. 382 bottom: © Bettmann/ CORBIS.

Chapter 16: p. 400 top and bottom: AP/Wide World Photos.

Chapter 17: p. 428: © MIT Museum.

Chapter 18: p. 467 top: photo courtesy of Stanford University; p. 467 bottom: photo courtesy of Carnegie Mellon.

Chapter 19: p. 497 left: Jason Grow/SABA; p. 497 right: David G. McIntyre/BLACK STAR.